SAP PRESS e-books

Print or e-book, Kindle or iPad, workplace or airplane: Choose where and how to read your SAP PRESS books! You can now get all our titles as e-books, too:

- By download and online access
- For all popular devices
- And, of course, DRM-free

Convinced? Then go to www.sap-press.com and get your e-book today.

Integrating Sales and Distribution in SAP S/4HANA®

SAP PRESS is a joint initiative of SAP and Rheinwerk Publishing. The know-how offered by SAP specialists combined with the expertise of Rheinwerk Publishing offers the reader expert books in the field. SAP PRESS features first-hand information and expert advice, and provides useful skills for professional decision-making.

SAP PRESS offers a variety of books on technical and business-related topics for the SAP user. For further information, please visit our website: *www.sap-press.com*.

Christian van Helfteren
Configuring Sales in SAP S/4HANA (2nd Edition)
2022, 905 pages, hardcover and e-book
www.sap-press.com/5401

James Olcott, Jon Simmonds
Sales and Distribution with SAP S/4HANA: Business User Guide
2021, 434 pages, hardcover and e-book
www.sap-press.com/5263

Jawad Akhtar, Martin Murray
Materials Management with SAP S/4HANA:
Business Processes and Configuration (2nd Edition)
2020, 939 pages, hardcover and e-book
www.sap-press.com/5132

Jawad Akhtar
Production Planning with SAP S/4HANA (2nd Edition)
2021, 1092 pages, hardcover and e-book
www.sap-press.com/5373

Stoil Jotev
Configuring SAP S/4HANA Finance (2nd Edition)
2021, 738 pages, hardcover and e-book
www.sap-press.com/5361

Ankita Ghodmare, Saurabh Bobade, Kartik Dua

Integrating Sales and Distribution in SAP S/4HANA®

Editor Megan Fuerst
Acquisitions Editor Emily Nicholls
Copyeditor Julie McNamee
Cover Design Graham Geary
Photo Credit Shutterstock: 1996234196/© Mila_22 79
Layout Design Vera Brauner
Production Hannah Lane
Typesetting SatzPro, Germany
Printed and bound in Canada, on paper from sustainable sources

ISBN 978-1-4932-2329-9

1st edition 2023

Library of Congress Cataloging-in-Publication Data
Names: Ghodmare, Ankita, author. | Bobade, Saurabh, author. | Dua, Kartik, author.
Title: Integrating sales and distribution in SAP S/4HANA / by Ankita Ghodmare, Saurabh Bobade, Kartik Dua.
Description: Boston : Rheinwerk Publishing, [2022] | Includes index.
Identifiers: LCCN 2022046056 | ISBN 9781493223299 (hardcover) | ISBN 9781493223299 (ebook)
Subjects: LCSH: Selling--Data processing. | Management--Data processing. | SAP HANA (Electronic resource)
Classification: LCC HF5438.35 .G476 2022 | DDC 658.810028553--dc23/eng/20220922
LC record available at https://lccn.loc.gov/2022046056

Contents at a Glance

Dear Reader,

The cover of this book reminds me of something I'd long forgotten: the knitting needles in my desk drawer.

A few years ago, a friend gifted me a handknit scarf. The woolen thread was an interwoven pattern of greens, blues, and purples, and, most important for Boston's winter weather, very warm. The thought struck me—I should learn to knit!

Twenty dollars and two days later, I had in my possession yarn and a pair of bamboo knitting needles. I pulled up YouTube to find a video tutorial, awkwardly clasped the needles, and attempted a long tail cast-on to create my first row of stitches. As I proceeded with the basic knit technique, it quickly became apparent that something was wrong—no stitch should look quite that lumpy—and it was time to try again. And again. And another dozen times.

After a few hours, I concluded that I wasn't very good at knitting. Beyond lacking the hand-eye coordination for even the simplest stitch, I was missing the patience for knitting with even a single skein of yarn—let alone integrating several colors and types of yarn into a cohesive, functional piece. Hope springs eternal, but I may need to try my hand at different needle crafts (cross-stitch?) to find success.

If the knitting project you're undertaking involves software systems and interconnected business processes, you've come to the right place. These pages offer the expert guidance you need to configure the sales and distribution integration points across your SAP S/4HANA system, from materials management to finance and beyond. Get ready to weave together your core cross-functional processes—you're on your way to fully integrated SD!

What did you think about *Integrating Sales and Distribution in SAP S/4HANA*? Your comments and suggestions are the most useful tools to help us make our books the best they can be. Please feel free to contact me and share any praise or criticism you may have.

Thank you for purchasing a book from SAP PRESS!

Megan Fuerst
Editor, SAP PRESS

meganf@rheinwerk-publishing.com
www.sap-press.com
Rheinwerk Publishing · Boston, MA

Contents

Appendices 547

Preface

Welcome to our book on integrating sales and distribution in SAP S/4HANA. SAP S/4HANA is the present and immediate future for SAP, so having a good understanding of sales and distribution integration is a great value add for you, our fellow SAPers, who are taking time out to read this book.

Objective of This Book

Integrating Sales and Distribution in SAP S/4HANA is all about getting the basics right. It will take you on a journey to discover and revive your core foundational knowledge about sales and distribution and its integrated modules. The book talks about fundamental elements of how the sales and distribution functionality integrates with other functionalities in SAP S/4HANA. It is a one-stop shop for all key sales and distribution integration components. Based on SAP best practices and with accompanying screenshots, we'll walk you through the steps to configure the integration components. We're confident that when you apply the concepts of the book to your day-to-day project activities, you'll feel confident in your knowledge so you can graduate from your SAP S/4HANA journey as a successful champion.

Our book talks about integration points of sales and distribution with the following functionalities:

- Materials management
- Finance
- Revenue recognition
- Resource-related billing (RRB)
- Production planning

The book provides you with a thorough understanding of each functionality's integration points and explains every configuration in detail with case studies and use cases. As functional consultants, we've seen our share of challenges in cross-functional projects when the lack of integration knowledge leads to project delays or failures. Those challenges have motivated us to write this book with the hope that after reading it, you'll gain the education required to overcome similar hurdles, thus making you self-sufficient and bankable SAP consultants.

Target Audience

This book benefits all SAP functional consultants with a special value add for sales and distribution and integration consultants. If you are a consultant of a specific functionality, you can refer to your specific sections in the book to learn and understand how your functionality integrates with sales and distribution. If you like, you can even broaden your horizon and learn about integrations for other functionalities.

Our book caters to all functional integration consultants and solution architects whose day-to-day job involves looking at various modules to find the right solution for their business stakeholders. If you're a quality analyst, you'll also see a lot of benefit in this book from the testing and validation standpoint. In addition, if you are a manager, SAP leader, or business IT stakeholder, you'll get a holistic picture of the entire SAP S/4HANA landscape from the sales and distribution integration standpoint by reading this book. This book will also help you in your digital transformation journey, as various chapters showcase how you can leverage standard SAP solution capabilities to integrate sales and distribution to different functionalities in SAP S/4HANA.

How to Read This Book

We've given deep thought to the structure of our book and shaped the chapters in a way that will benefit you to the fullest. You can either directly jump into the integration chapter of your interest, for example, materials management in Chapter 4 or finance in Chapter 5, or follow the sequence where we start with introductory chapters and then venture into individual integration functionalities. We intentionally started with the primary integration functionalities, materials management and finance, and then moved on to other dependent functionalities, as materials management and finance provide a good segway for you to better understand revenue recognition, RRB, and production planning.

Let's walk through the chapters in this book:

- **Chapter 1: Integrated Sales**
  Chapter 1 talks about sales as a process within an enterprise resource planning (ERP) system and highlights sales and distribution as a functionality in SAP S/4HANA. This chapter gives an overview of what the finance and supply chain management (SCM) processes look like in SAP S/4HANA and how they closely integrate with the sales process. This chapter is a great starting point because you'll get a good teaser on what to expect in the chapters to follow. Key highlights of this chapter are the examples we used to conceptually explain each integration subprocess.

- **Chapter 2: The SAP Organizational Structure**
  Chapter 2 highlights different organizational components of sales and distribution, materials management, finance, Project System, SAP Revenue Accounting and Reporting, and SAP Concur. This chapter lays down the core foundation for you to build on as you continue reading other integration chapters in the book.
- **Chapter 3: Master Data**
  Chapter 3 is focused on master data configurations shared between sales and distribution and its integrated functionalities. This chapter touches on two key topics:
  - Business partner master data, which covers topics such as business partner general role, customer role, company code role, and credit management role
  - Material master data, which covers views for basic data, sales organization data, sales general/plant data, material requirements planning (MRP), and accounting
- **Chapter 4: Materials Management**
  Chapter 4 dives into key integration points between the sales and distribution functionality and materials management by focusing your attention on key configuration components such as availability check, stock transport orders (STO), general ledger account determination, third-party processing, and inventory management. In this chapter, you'll get a great understanding of how materials management integrates with sales and distribution in the most seamless manner within the SAP S/4HANA system.
- **Chapter 5: Finance**
  Chapter 5 gives a deep understanding of finance in SAP S/4HANA and walks you through how finance integrates with sales and distribution using the following key touch points: pricing and taxation, account determination, credit management, profitability analysis, and intercompany billing. Each integration point is explained in detail with configuration steps and supporting screenshots.
- **Chapter 6: Revenue Recognition**
  Chapter 6 explains how revenue recognition and sales and distribution shake hands in SAP S/4HANA. The chapter also talks about the International Financial Reporting Standards (IFRS) 15 compliance regulations and how SAP S/4HANA addresses these regulations with a standard out-of-the-box solution called SAP Revenue Accounting and Reporting. In this chapter, you'll be exposed to a wealth of knowledge around price allocation, BRFplus rules, and optimized contract management (OCM) concepts.
- **Chapter 7: Resource-Related Billing**
  Chapter 7 ventures into a key integration point between the sales and distribution functionality and Project System: RRB. In this chapter, you'll have the opportunity to learn about different concepts of the sales and distribution RRB process such as cross-application time sheets (CATS) and dynamic item processor (DIP) profiles.

You'll also get to see how expense reports flow from SAP Concur to SAP S/4HANA. All the knowledge in this chapter is represented by configuration steps, transaction codes, examples, screenshots, and a case study.

- **Chapter 8: Production Planning**
  Chapter 8 dives into important integration points between the sales and distribution functionality and production planning. The chapter talks about the make-to-order (MTO) process, MRP, variant configuration, and transfer of requirements.

We end the book with Appendix A, which teaches you about Electronic Data Interchange (EDI). EDI is a vital integration process by which systems electronically transfer data between each other. Each EDI communication, at minimum, involves two systems: a sender system and a receiver system. The sender and receiver systems can belong to the same company or different companies. Appendix A focuses most of its time on intermediate documents (IDocs). IDocs are the most-used SAP documents for connecting external systems to SAP S/4HANA or for connecting one SAP functionality to another.

Acknowledgments

This book has been a great learning experience for all three of us. It feels like we are a parenting team raising our first child. As they say, it takes a village to raise a child, and that is exactly what has happened with us. We would like to take this opportunity to acknowledge and thank the entire tribe who helped us bring our first book to success. First, a huge thank you to Emily Nicholls, Megan Fuerst, and the entire Rheinwerk Publishing team. Our dream project would have continued to be a dream if it wasn't for you guys. We appreciate the guidance, the mentorship, the kind and encouraging words, and the trust you guys have shown in us to write this book for Rheinwerk Publishing. We strongly believe this is just the first step of our journey together, and we're looking forward to collaborating with you all on future projects. Thank you, Emily, Megan, and the team!

Now, we'll move on to individual acknowledgements.

First and foremost: I would like to acknowledge and extend my heartful gratitude to my wonderful husband, friend, and coauthor Saurabh Bobade. You have always been the primary mover and source of my strength. I'm overwhelmed when I think back to the times when we spent countless weekends and evenings researching the use cases, brainstorming the flow, supporting each other in tough times, and juggling multiple responsibilities while writing the book. Without you, none of this would have been possible. My thoughts of gratitude and appreciation for you are as numerous as the stars in the sky.

A special thanks to my parents for being a great role models and providing an exceptional upbringing. I am grateful for your blessings and unwavering support throughout. I'd like to express my appreciation to my parents-in-law and brother-in-law for providing me with so much inspiration and encouragement. I am grateful for all of your support.

Thank you to all of my colleagues, clients, and friends who have influenced my career in one way or another. I've learned a lot from you all. I want to thank *everyone* who ever said anything positive to me or taught me something. I heard it all, and it meant something.

Last but not the least, a big thank you goes to my coauthor Kartik Dua for sharing this opportunity with me and for being part of this journey. Your support and guidance were cornerstones in completing the book on time. It was a pleasure working with you.

—**Ankita Ghodmare**

I would like to start by thanking my beautiful wife, friend, and coauthor Ankita for her encouragement and support in keeping the book on schedule. I'm moved just thinking about how many weekends and late nights we've sacrificed to finish the book on time. For my burden-bearing, laughter-sharing, forever-caring friend, a very happy, hug-filled, heartfelt thanks. You are the best thing that has ever happened to me, and I am grateful for all your love and support.

Next, I'd like to thank my parents Kalidas Bobade and Meena Bobade and my brother Sarang Bobade, a cabal of supremely positive individuals who encouraged, pushed, and supported us through the long months of this project. I am eternally grateful for your love and blessings. I wish to express my gratitude to my longtime friends Adwait Rode and Digvijay Singh for their unwavering support and courage while writing the book.

I'd also like to thank all of the customers and clients I've had the privilege of working with in my career span. I'd like to express my gratitude to my current and former coworkers. I have learned so much from you guys. Thank you to my current manager, Rahul Goyal, and my colleagues, Mathan and Kuldeep, for always assisting and supporting me while I worked on the book. It's been an honor to work with you all.

Finally, I'd like to express my appreciation and gratitude to Kartik Dua, my colleague, friend, and coauthor, who offered me the honor of participating in the project and making our dream a reality. You are the best coauthor I could have asked for. Thank you for everything.

—**Saurabh Bobade**

I would like to thank my wife Tripti Upadhyay and my baby boy Ayaansh Dua for being patient with me and holding me tight throughout this incredible journey. Super appreciate those hugs, the motivational words, and those selfless days where you all had to play, cook, and do the household chores without me. I cannot thank you enough. You guys are the heroes of all my success stories!

Next, I would like to appreciate my work colleagues Rahul Goyal, Mathanagopalan Ravichandran, and Kuldeep Mahalatkar. Rahul has always been an inspirational boss and an excellent leader. He made sure I did justice to my work commitments and at the same time gave my wholehearted attention to the book. Thank you, Rahul! Mathan, on the other hand, is that silent work colleague who you know is always there when you need him. He had his own life going (congratulations on being a first-time dad!), but he still found time to help me with the EDI content. Thank you, Mathan! Kuldeep is an awesome colleague and a super awesome friend. He helped me a lot with the accounting and finance topics in this book for which I am very grateful. Thank you, Kuldeep!

Next, a huge round of applause for my coauthoring team—Ankita Ghodmare and Saurabh Bobade. You guys are just super awesome and the best team I have worked with so far. Together we have conquered this milestone that had days full of surprises, laughter, personal commitments, sick days, follow-ups and "don't worry, we will get this done" conversations. The glue that bonded us together in this journey is trust and faith. Thank you both, and let's write another book together soon!

—**Kartik Dua**

Chapter 1
Integrated Sales

Welcome to this first chapter on integrated sales, where we'll walk you through the concepts of sales and distribution first as a general business scenario and then as a functionality in SAP S/4HANA.

In this chapter, we'll share our knowledge about sales and distribution in an enterprise resource planning (ERP) system (with special emphasis on SAP S/4HANA), and we'll also focus our attention on how and why the sales and distribution functionality integrates with the finance and supply chain management (SCM) functionalities. This chapter will provide a high-level introduction to the concepts of sales and its integrated components. We'll define key integrated sales processes and provide examples.

By the end of this chapter, you'll have a good understanding of what our book is all about and what the flow of information will look like. While this chapter is an excellent appetizer, we're confident you'll enjoy the entire meal along with the dessert (that is, Appendix A). Let's jump right in!

1.1 Sales in an Enterprise Resource Planning System

Sales is a process by which businesses sell goods or services to their customers based on a signed contract, for a price agreed upon by the business and customer, and with predetermined payment terms. Goods/services are provisioned to customers on the promised date, and revenue is recognized per the revenue schedule.

In this section, we'll explain the general sales process, and explain the differences between product sales and professional services.

1.1.1 Sales Process Overview

A typical sales process for any business involves five stages: presales, sales order, delivery, invoice, and revenue. Figure 1.1 shows a sales process in an SAP S/4HANA system.

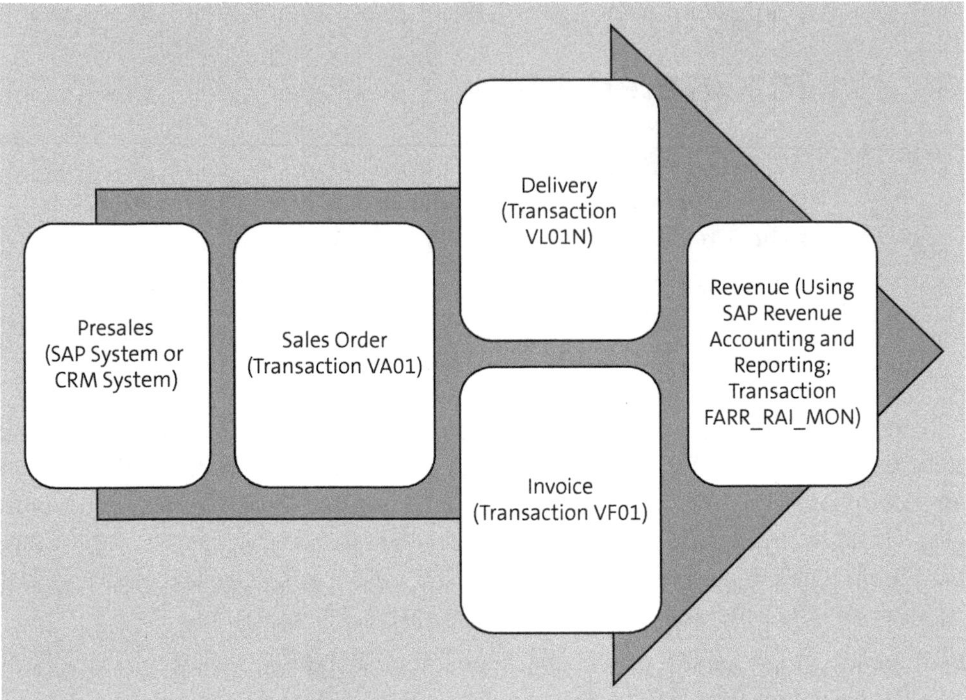

Figure 1.1 Sales Process in SAP S/4HANA

The *presales* process includes subprocesses such as inquiry, quotation, and contract. In our experience, we've seen these processes being housed in an SAP system or a customer relationship management (CRM) system depending on business preferences. Within SAP S/4HANA, these processes are controlled by standard transactions. The underlying configuration to build and customize the subprocesses is also native in SAP S/4HANA. Table 1.1 shows the list of transactions you can use to run the presales processes.

Process	SAP Transaction
Inquiry	Transaction VA11
Quotation	Transaction VA21
Contract	Transaction VA41

Table 1.1 Presales Processes and Transaction Codes

The *inquiry* process is used by customers to send an inquiry for the products/services they are looking to purchase. Customers can inquire about the availability of the products and prices, as well as request an estimated delivery time. Typically, an inquiry also has validity dates. Following up on the inquiry, the business issues a *quotation* to the customer that addresses all inquired data. Finally, when the quotation is accepted and approved, an official *contract* is created that seals the sales deal between the business and the customer.

Referring to Figure 1.1, presales is followed by the *sales order* process. Once the presales activities are completed and the contract is created in the system, a sales order get created against the contract that kick-starts the sales and distribution process. Transaction VA01 is used to create a sales order in SAP S/4HANA.

Two processes that are usually used in conjunction with the sales process are returns and credit management. *Returns* is a process by which a customer uses their right-to-return privilege to return goods purchased per clauses agreed upon in the return policy. *Credit management* is a process by which businesses determine credit limit and payment terms for their customers. Credit management can do various other things, but the most common are handling credit limits and payment terms. While we're introducing credit management as part of our discussion of sales, it's important to note that it also has a major footprint in finance.

The sales order process is followed by either the *delivery* or *invoicing* process. Once a sales order is created in the system, you either deliver the materials on the sales order or bill them directly. Transaction VL01N is used to create a delivery document in SAP S/4HANA. Following the delivery process is the *billing* (also a part of invoicing) process. As mentioned, sales order items can be invoiced directly, or they can be billed after delivery, depending on the type of product sold or service rendered. Transaction VF01 is used for invoicing. Typically, we've seen clients do mass billing as a month-end process, which can be executed via Transaction VF04. The transaction to do one-off billing is Transaction VF01. A few other processes that are commonly used along with the invoicing process are pro forma invoicing process, debit and credit memo process, payment process, and collections process.

After delivery and billing, businesses run their *revenue recognition* process to record and report revenue. The legacy way of recognizing revenue in SAP was through Transaction VF44. Depending on item category configuration, whether delivery-based or time-based, revenue was recognized on sales orders. A more modernized way of performing revenue recognition and reporting is via SAP Revenue Accounting and Reporting. We'll discuss revenue accounting and reporting in detail in Chapter 6.

1.1.2 Product Sales

Let's look at a basic end-to-end sales scenario within an SAP S/4HANA system. We'll assume presales activities were performed in a CRM system and an intermediate document (IDoc) interfaced all the details from CRM to SAP S/4HANA to create a sales order. Figure 1.2 shows the sales order from the SAP S/4HANA system.

Figure 1.2 Sales Order

Sales order **64691** has a delivery-based item, so the next step is to perform delivery via Transaction VL01N. Figure 1.3 shows the delivery document.

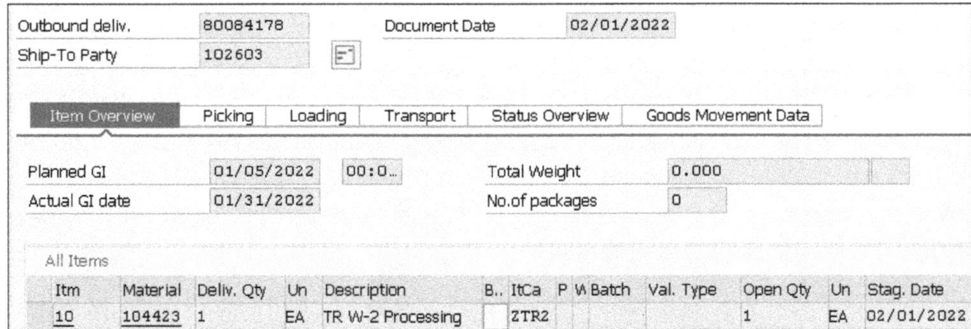

Figure 1.3 Delivery Document

Now that the delivery is done, we invoice the sales order via Transaction VF04, as shown in Figure 1.4.

Invoice 90358858 Net Value 240.00 USD
Payer 102603
Billing Date 01/31/2022

Item	Description	Billed Quantity	SU	Net value	Material	Cost	Tax amount	amount
10	TR W-2 Processing	1	EA	240.00	104423	0.00	0.00	0

Figure 1.4 Invoice Document

Next, all revenue-related information is moved to SAP Revenue Accounting and Reporting where the revenue accounting and reporting (RAR) configuration kicks in and revenue recognition is performed. Figure 1.5 shows what the RAR contract for sales order 64691 looks like in the SAP S/4HANA RAR functionality.

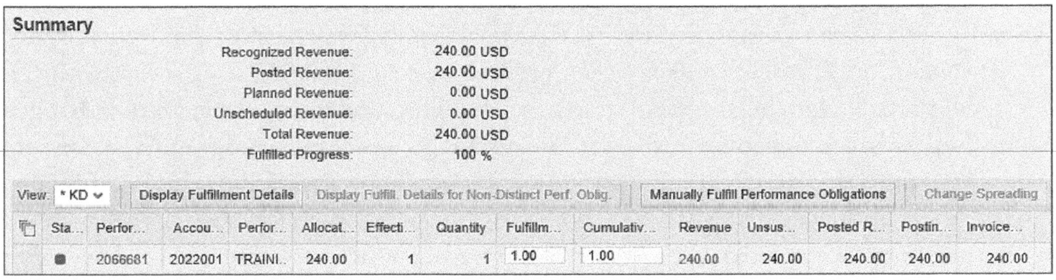

Figure 1.5 RAR Contract

1.1.3 Professional Services

The example in the previous section was of a sales process that involves products either delivered or provisioned and that have an underlying delivery document. There is one more bifurcation of the sales process, which is referred to as *services* or *professional services*. Within this type of a sales process, businesses don't physically delivery inventory but rather offer professional services to their customers. These services can be in the form of consulting services, support, or maintenance. There is a standard functionality in SAP S/4HANA that helps you configure professional services, which you can then connect to sales and distribution to form an end-to-end sales cycle. The functionality is called Project System. Let's look at a simple professional services sales example to better understand this process.

Let's consider an example company, S4 Technologies, that has signed a professional services contract with SAP for one year of consulting services. S4 Technologies starts work on a data migration project for which they need SAP's help. SAP sends two of its A team members to work on the project. Both consultants travel from Philadelphia to Indiana to be on-site for the project and are lodged in a hotel for two weeks until they wrap up their commitments. Following is what the end-to-end professional services sales scenario would look like for S4 Technologies in their SAP S/4HANA system:

- Creation of presales documents for the contract signed between S4 Technologies and SAP (inquiry, quotation, contract)
- Creation of sales order stating the total number of hours contracted
- Maintenance of hourly rates using condition records
- Time sheet entry for the two weeks SAP consultants were on-site

- Expenses incurred by the consultants, including airfare, hotels, and meals
- RRB document (sales and distribution to Project Systems integration) for the hours and expenses
- Billing document for the hours and expenses
- Revenue postings for the hours and expenses

One of the key differences between product sales and services sales is that with services, all underlying transactions (e.g., sales, billing, and revenue recognition) happen on an as-incurred basis, whereas the values to generate billing and revenue are dynamic. Said differently, with product sales, you know the products and their selling prices at the beginning of the sales process, versus with services sales, in which you'll get to know about the type and rate of service when the consultant is ready to work on the project. If the consultant is on-site, then the service provided will be on-site consulting with X rate; if the consultant is off-site, then the service provided will be off-site consulting with Y rate. Even the expense portion is only known when the expenses occur. More details about the Project System functionality and resource-related billing (RRB) will be provided in Chapter 7.

With this, we conclude the sales discussion. Next, we'll look at how sales and finance complement and supplement each other in a strong end-to-end order-to-cash scenario.

1.2 Sales and Finance

If we could choose a best friend for the sales process, it would be finance. They work as a team and often complement each other. Sales has a finance impact at almost every subprocess it encompasses, whether it's sales order, delivery, billing, or revenue. Almost no sales process is complete without an underlying finance transaction. *Finance* is a process by which businesses manage and monitor their general ledger numbers. The numbers could be in the form of accounts receivable (sales) or accounts payable (procurement). Sales and finance have many integration points, but the most common ones are pricing and taxation, account determination, credit management, profitability analysis, and intercompany billing.

Figure 1.6 shows the key touch points between a standard sales and finance process. We'll walk through them in the following sections.

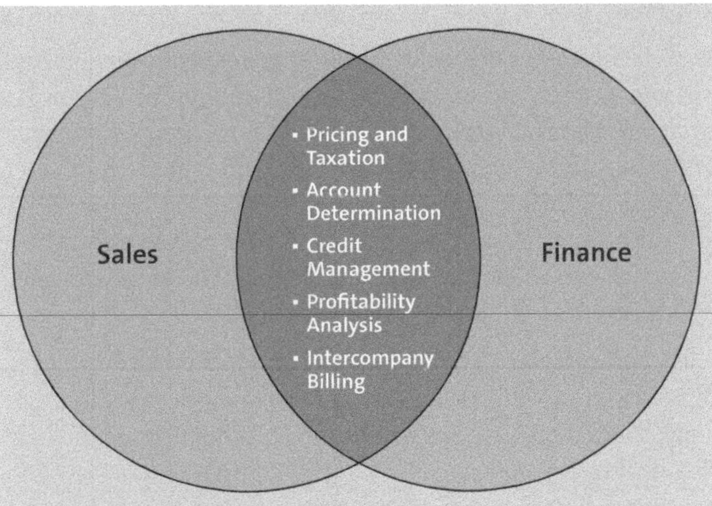

Figure 1.6 Sales and Finance

1.2.1 Pricing and Taxation

Pricing and taxation are two of the core processes within a sales–finance integration. *Pricing* is a process by which a business determines prices for the various products and services it offers. Pricing can be determined either in a CRM system or in SAP S/4HANA using condition records. Let's consider an example of pricing in which you ordered a laptop bundle from an online retailer. The invoice shows the bundle was priced at USD 500. But internally for the online retailer, the bundle had individual prices attached to each component. The laptop was priced at USD 300, software at USD 100, and peripherals at USD 100. At a very high-level, the price offered by a business to a customer includes cost of the product plus a profit percentage. In the same example, the USD 500 price of the bundle cost the online retailer USD 450, and USD 50 was the profit they made when they sold the bundle to their customer.

Tax, on the other hand, is a process by which businesses charge tax to their customers based on location and type of product/service sold. Tax rates are dependent on federal and/or geographic tax rules. Within SAP S/4HANA, pricing and taxation are configured using a pricing procedure, condition technique, access sequence, and condition tables. Tax processes can be sourced externally too using third-party tax engines that integrate with SAP naturally using standard tax determination configurations. Following are a few key transactions for pricing and taxation used in SAP S/4HANA:

- Transaction VOKO: SD Pricing Configuration
- Transaction VK11: Condition Record Creation
- Transaction OVK1: Tax Category Determination by Country
- Transaction FTXP: Tax Code Configuration

1.2.2 Account Determination

The *account determination* process in SAP S/4HANA is used to determine general ledger accounts for various sales and finance transactions. Account determination is a standard SAP process that can be achieved in various ways depending on business requirements. Different functionalities in SAP S/4HANA have different account determination transactions. For a sales–finance account determination, a key transaction is Transaction VKOA. Within Transaction VKOA, depending on how the access sequence is configured, you can set up general ledger account determination for revenue, unbilled, deferred, and trade accounts receivable processes.

Pricing procedures are another important component in the account determination process. Pricing procedures are used within sales orders to trigger pricing conditions. Each pricing condition has an account key attached to it, which helps integrate sales and distribution with finance. Conditions available in SAP S/4HANA include price conditions, discount or surcharge conditions, expense reimbursements, tax conditions, extra pay conditions, fees or differential conditions, tax classification, sales deal determination conditions, compare price protection conditions, totals record for fees conditions, and wage withholding tax conditions.

Using the same example from the previous section, let's say there was a sale, and the online retailer offered a 10% discount on the laptop bundle. The internal sales order created within their SAP system will have three conditions: prices condition with net value USD 500, discount condition with net value 10% or USD 50, and tax condition for USD 25 (assuming tax charged by the online retailer is 5%).

Following are a few other key transactions for account determination used in SAP S/4HANA:

- Transaction OB40: Accounting Maintain Configuration
- Transaction FS00: General Ledger Master Configuration

1.2.3 Credit Management

Credit management is a process by which businesses offer credit limit and payment terms to their customers depending on a company's predefined credit policy. Credit management is seen more commonly in the business-to-business (B2B) industry. Many factors go into determining credit limit and payments terms, and a few of the key ones are risk assessment and risk category, risk class, risk score, credit evaluation, and payment history. Credit management configuration in SAP S/4HANA involves setting up credit control area and credit segment; configuring risk score rules, risk class, and risk category; and defining credit limits.

Let's consider an example of credit management. S4 Technology partnered with SAP to offer ERP solutions to their customers. SAP has a credit management process configured for S4 Technology. SAP has looked at S4 Technology's payment history and performed a credit evaluation on them, based on which, they have assigned a risk score to S4 Technology. They also assigned a risk class, risk category, credit segment, and credit control area to S4 Technology's customer account within their cloud system. Based on all these configurations, whenever a sale is made to S4 Technology, they automatically get assigned payment terms. The credit limit is fixed for S4 technology and is dynamically evaluated and updated based on the payments made to SAP. So, let's say they are making their payments on time, their credit limit is automatically increased (based on system configuration), and/or their payment terms are extended.

Following are some key transactions for credit management used in SAP S/4HANA:

- Transaction OB45: Credit Control Area definition
- Transaction OVA8: Automatic Credit Control definition
- Transaction OVAK: Sales Document Types: Credit Limit Check
- Transaction OVAD: Delivery Types: Credit Limit Check

1.2.4 Profitability Analysis

Profitability analysis is a process by which businesses evaluate and measure profits. This is a key process because every business, at the end of the day, wants to grow profits. One of the best ways to grow profits is to evaluate the trends and strategies that contribute to profit growth, and then expand those trends and strategies with a proper profitability analysis plan. Two key factors driving profits are earnings and revenue. Factors that contribute to earnings and revenue are customers, vendors, and products, and with the right combination of these three factors, businesses can be very profitable.

Within SAP S/4HANA, profitability is determined based on characteristics. Characteristics can be in any form ranging from sales groups to customer groups, materials to material groups, countries, regions, and states. At an organizational level, a profit and loss (P&L) report can be run for a company code (finance functionality). But businesses also measure P&L for their organizational units such as countries, regions, product lines, customers, and so on, and, for that, profitability analysis is a very powerful tool. The simple definition of P&L is *Profit & loss = Revenue – Expenses – Taxes*.

If we use the same online retailer example from previous sections and apply it to this formula, we'll have something like this: *P&L for laptop bundle = 525 – 450 – 25 = 50*.

Following are the key transactions for profitability analysis used in SAP S/4HANA:

- Transaction KEA0: Maintain Operating Concern
- Transaction KEA0: Maintain Characteristics

1.2.5 Intercompany Billing

Intercompany billing is a process by which different company codes, under the same company, perform business transactions with each other.

Let's consider an example: S4 Technology has two company codes, S4 Tech India and S4 Tech USA. S4 Technology has physical inventory under both company codes and does business under both legal entities. S4 Tech India does business with customers in the Asia-Pacific region, and S4 Tech USA does business with North America and South America regions. Let's say S4 Tech India receives an order from a client in the United Arab Emirates. The S4 Tech India company doesn't have the physical stock available, but S4 Tech USA does. Rather than sourcing the products from an outside vendor, S4 Tech India buys the products from S4 Tech USA and ships the products directly to their United Arab Emirates customer. Because S4 Tech India and S4 Tech USA are two separate legal entities, there will be an intercompany sales and billing transaction performed between them; however, at the parent S4 Technology general ledger level, both transactions will balance each other out. This would help S4 Tech India and S4 Tech USA record their own P&L while S4 Technology will have zero net effect within their accounting books.

Following are key transactions for intercompany billing used in SAP S/4HANA:

- Transaction VF01: Create Billing Document
- Transaction VFX3: Release Billing Document to Accounting
- Transaction VF21: Invoice List
- Transaction VTFL: Copy Control Delivery to Billing

1.3 Sales and Supply Chain Management

SCM comes in many flavors depending on the source defining it. From the standpoint of this book, we'll look at the SCM process as a combination of two subprocesses: materials management and production planning.

As the name suggests, SCM deals with anything and everything to do with managing the supply chain for any large-, medium-, or small-sized company. Management of the supply chain can be in the form of an availability check or stock transport order (STO). It could also be in the form of general ledger account determination, third-party processing, or inventory management. From the production planning standpoint, SCM encompasses subprocess such as make to order (MTO), material requirements planning (MRP), variant configuration, and transfer of requirements.

Figure 1.7 shows how materials management and production planning come together to form a strong SCM process. We'll discuss both sides of SCM in the following sections.

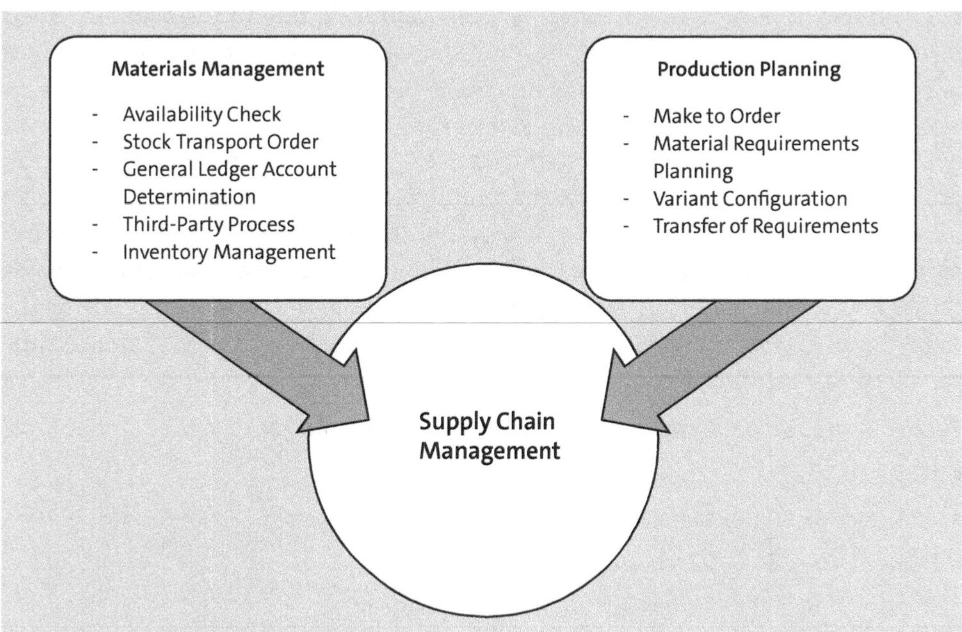

Figure 1.7 Sales and Supply Chain Management

1.3.1 Materials Management

The materials management bucket of SCM includes the following components, which we'll discuss in the following sections:

- Availability check
- STO
- General ledger account determination
- Third-party process
- Inventory management

Availability Check

Availability check is used synonymously with the term *available-to-promise (ATP)*. SAP S/4HANA has enhanced availability checks to the next level and is now called SAP S/4HANA for advanced ATP. It's a process by which businesses manage their stocks to make sure they are storing only the needed inventory and not overburdening themselves with excessive storage. Businesses consider numbers for demand, supply, and available stock while calculating an advanced ATP quantity. The formula to calculate ATP quantity is *ATP quantity = Quantity in hand + Supply – Demand.*

For example, let's say S4 Technology has 500 laptops sitting in their warehouse as ready stock. This is quantity in hand per our formula. They expect to manufacture and/or receive 200 laptops in the coming month. A customer of theirs places an order for 800 laptops with a requested delivery date of next month. Based on the formula, ATP quantity for S4 Technology is *500 + 200 – 800 = –100*. This means S4 Technology can promise the customer to delivery 700 laptops by the end of the month and place an order with their vendor for the deficit 100 laptops. They could even do a STO or a third-party order for the 100 laptops based on their business situation and/or commitments. This is how the advanced ATP process helps businesses ensure they are promising the right things to their customer and acting on the proper to-do tasks, based on the advanced ATP quantity, to satisfy the customer order.

Following are the key transactions for ATP used in SAP S/4HANA:

- Transaction OVZ9: Scope of Availability Check
- Transaction OVZ2: Availability Check Group Configuration
- Transaction OPPQ: Purchasing Processing Time
- Transaction OVLK: Storage Location Determination

Stock Transport Order

Stock transport order (STO) is a process of moving inventory from one location to another. In SAP S/4HANA, stocks are moved between plants. Plants can belong to the same company code or different company codes. The process of moving stock between plants within the same company code is called intracompany STO, while the process of moving stock between plants from different company codes is called intercompany STO.

As an example of STO, let's say you order a laptop from HP India and want to ship it to a Bangalore location. HP India doesn't have the laptop stocked at their Bangalore plant but have it in stock at their Mumbai plant. HP will make an STO and move the laptop from Mumbai to Bangalore and then ship it to you.

Following are key transactions for STO used in SAP S/4HANA:

- Transaction VL10B: Purchase Orders for Execution of Replenishment Delivery
- Transaction OVKK: Pricing Procedure Determination
- Transaction MIGO: Good Receipt
- Transaction MIRO: Accounts Payable Invoice

General Ledger Account Determination

General ledger account determination is used to determine general ledger accounts for various sales and materials management transactions that have a finance impact. General ledger account determination is a standard process in SAP S/4HANA and can be achieved in various ways depending on business requirements. Different functionalities in SAP have different account determination transactions. One of the key components of general ledger account determination in SCM is the transaction key. This key helps an account determination rule connect directly to a general ledger.

As an example of general ledger account determination, let's say a customer orders 10 laptops from S4 Technology. S4 Technology has laptops in stock and immediately creates a sales order and delivery document for the customer in their SAP S/4HANA system. As soon as the laptops are shipped, a PGI document is created against the delivery. The post goods issue (PGI) document has two line items, one for the laptops and one for the freight. Based on the account determination configuration in Transaction OBYC, the laptops line item gets determined to an inventory general ledger, and the freight line item gets determined to a freight general ledger. This way, at the end of the month, S4 Technology can clearly differentiate what really went into laptop deliveries versus the cost incurred for freight.

Following are a few other important transactions for material master general ledger account determination used in SAP S/4HANA:

- Transaction MR21: Material Price Update
- Transaction OB62: Company Code to Chart of Accounts Assignment
- Transaction OMSK: Account Category Reference and Valuation Class
- Transaction OMWN: Account Grouping Configuration

Third-Party Processing

Third-party processing, also known as drop shipping, is when businesses don't directly sell products to their customers but instead sources them from external vendors or third-party providers. In a third-party process, the seller business doesn't store physical inventory nor does the shipment of goods happen from their warehouse. The customer places an order with the seller business, and the seller business internally creates another order with their vendor to source and ship products directly to the customer. There is a price difference between what the vendor offers to the seller and what the seller offers to the customer, and that difference is revenue for the seller.

Let's consider an example: S4 Technology Services offers SAP and CRM products to its customers. The customer places an order for an SAP license (USD 2,000) with S4 Technology. S4 Technology places an internal order with SAP to provision the license directly to their customer. The price negotiated between S4 Technology and SAP for the license product is USD 1,600. SAP with bill S4 Technology for USD 1,600 and S4 Technology will bill its customer USD 2,000. The difference of USD 400 is S4 Technology's profit.

Following are key transactions for third-party process used in SAP S/4HANA:

- Transaction VL10: Delivery Due List
- Transaction ME21N: Purchase Order Creation
- Transaction MIGO: Good Receipt
- Transaction MIRO: Vendor Invoice

Inventory Management

Inventory management is a process by which businesses manage inventory through their warehouse. Inventory can be sourced, stored, or sold, and each movement of inventory has an underlying movement type. Inventory management movements in SAP S/4HANA go through either one or all these stages depending on stock type:

- Document concept
- Goods receipt
- Goods issue
- Stock transfer

Let's consider an example of inventory management using the same scenario as in the previous sections, where customer orders goods from S4 Technology, and S4 Technology either purchases those goods from an external vendor or does an intercompany transaction or STO. If S4 Technology buys the goods from a vendor, it will be a like a third party or ATP kind of inventory management, or if S4 Technology uses its internal plants and company codes to ship the goods, then it would be an STO kind of inventory management.

Following are the key transactions for inventory management used in SAP S/4HANA:

- Transaction MMBE: Stock Overview
- Transaction MD04: Stocks/Requirements List
- Transaction MB11: Goods Movement
- Transaction OBYC: General Ledger Account Determination for Inventory Management

1.3.2 Production Planning

The production planning bucket of SCM includes the following components, which we'll discuss in upcoming sections:

- MTO
- MRP
- Variant configuration
- Transfer of requirements

Make to Order

MTO is a process by which businesses manufacture goods only when they receive a customer order and don't build products ahead of time. Two main advantages of following this process are as follows:

- Excess inventory is never sitting in the warehouse as limbo stock.
- Businesses can design products based on customers' unique requirements as the manufacturing will only happen after the fact.

The starting point of the MTO process is the sales order. If raw materials are available in stock, then the manufacturing happens right away, and the sales order is fulfilled promptly. If the business needs to source raw materials, then a purchase order is created with the vendor, raw materials are procured, and then the final product is built to fulfill the sales order. The final step of the MTO process is billing.

For example, say a customer places an order for an assembled desktop from S4 Technology. The assembled desktop contains the following components: Windows 10 Pro, Intel Core I7, 16 GB RAM, 1 TB HDD, a 24-inch HD monitor, and a wireless keyboard/mouse. S4 Technology has the hard drive, monitor, and wireless keyboard/mouse available in stock, but needs to order the Windows license, Intel board, and RAM. As soon as the sales order is created in S4 Technologies' SAP S/4HANA system, they will create a production order and release the order and confirmation for the hard drive, monitor, and wireless keyboard/mouse. They will also create a purchase order for the Windows license, Intel board, and RAM with their vendor. Once they receive the inventory from their vendor, they will create the goods receipt and finally assemble the desktop with all components from the customer sales order. Once everything is assembled, S4 Technology will create the delivery document, ship the desktop to their customer, and bill them.

Here are the key transactions for make to order used in SAP S/4HANA:

- Transaction MD11: Planned Order
- Transaction CO05N: Release Production Order
- Transaction VA01: Customer Sales Order
- Transaction VF01: Invoicing

Material Requirements Planning

MRP is a popular production planning tool within the SCM space. It's widely used by manufacturing companies who produce their own inventory. More than a process, MRP is a strategy that companies use to make sure their SCM process is efficient. MRP uses budgeting and forecasting data to estimate inventory production (time and quantity) to avoid overstocking or shipment delays. MRP, for the most part, is an automated process that helps companies avoid manual errors, which in turn adds great productivity to their production planning process.

In SAP S/4HANA, the MRP process is controlled by two things: master data settings within the material master and configuration of different nodes within the material master from Transaction SPRO.

Let's consider an example of MRP where a customer places an order for 500 laptops with S4 Technology at the start of the year with a requested delivery date of June 1st. S4 Technology runs their MRP process on this request and finds out that by June, they will have 100 laptops sitting in their warehouse as ready stock and will receive 200 laptops from Dell in May as a part of their ongoing contract with them. This basically leaves S4 Technology with 200 more laptops that they have to either manufacture themselves or place an order for with their vendor. This is the core of the MRP process: all data pertaining to inventory is stored in the system for analysis, the system does the analysis for you, and the system specifies the exact next step to meet customer requirements. Thus, the MRP process helps companies with optimal production planning.

A key formula used by most companies for their MRP process is as follows:

Available stock = Plant stock – Safety stock + Receipt (purchase order, firmed purchase order) – Requirement quantity (forecast requirements)

Here are some key transactions for MRP used in SAP S/4HANA:

- Transaction MD61: Create Planned Independent Requirements
- Transaction MD02: MRP Single-Item, Multi-Level
- Transaction MP30: Execute Forecast Run
- Transaction MD04: Stocks/Requirements List

Variant Configuration

Variant configuration is a process by which materials are configured to be dynamic or variable and are determined on the sales order based on ad hoc customer requirements. Material variants can be of any kind: type, dimension, quantity, and so on. Depending on the kind of material variant the customer orders, sales and distribution sends a query to the material master to bring in only that specific portion of the product on the sales order (and not the whole product data) along with the associated characteristics and fields.

For example, say a customer orders an assembled desktop from S4 Technology. While placing the order, the customer selects the following components: Windows 10 Pro, Intel Core I7, 16 GB RAM, 1 TB HDD, a 24-inch HD monitor, and a wireless keyboard/mouse. In S4 Technologies' SAP S/4HANA system, a sales order is created for an assembled desktop material, and based on the variant configuration setup and the pricing of the individual components, a final order of the desktop is prepared for the customer. In this example, "components" is set up as a variable for the assembled desktop material, so they follow the variant configuration process.

Following are some key components of variant configuration that need to be set up properly for the process to work seamlessly:

- Material type
- Material characteristics
- Material class
- Configuration profile of the material
- Variant condition type on the pricing procedure
- Pricing condition records

Here are a few key transactions for variant configuration used in SAP S/4HANA:

- Transaction CT04: Creation of Characteristics
- Transaction CL01: Creation of Class
- Transaction CU41: Creation of Configuration Profile

Transfer of Requirements

Transfer of requirements is a process by which sales and distribution transfers requirements to MRP when a sales order is created. Requirements are details about the material (quantity and delivery date), which the sales order passes to MRP. Based on the information received, MRP makes sure those materials are available on the given date for a sales and distribution process to complete smoothly. The following are key components of transfer of requirements:

- Requirement class
- Requirement type
- Schedule line category

For example, say a customer places an order for 100 laptops with S4 Technology with a requested delivery date of August 22nd. A sales order for 100 laptops is created in S4 Technologies' SAP S/4HANA system. As soon as the sales order is saved, based on the transfer of requirements configuration, a transfer of requirements happens from the sales order to MRP. Two key data sets sent to MRP are the quantity of 100 laptops and the delivery date of August 22nd. Once the request is sent to MRP, the system validates if all the laptops are available; if so, the system will place a hold on those laptops and make sure they are ready to be delivered on the requested delivery date. If S4 Technology doesn't have 100 laptops in stock, it will send a request to order more laptops from a vendor to ensure that all 100 are available to be shipped to the customer on the requested delivery date.

Following are a few key transactions for transfer of requirements used in SAP S/4HANA:

- Transaction MD01: MRP Run
- Transaction OVZH: Requirement Type
- Transaction OVZG: Requirement Class

1.4 Summary

In this chapter, we covered three vital areas that are a good introduction for all forthcoming chapters in the book. If you've liked what you read in this chapter, you'll most definitely love the entire book.

In Section 1.1, we first talked about sales as a general business process, and then we talked about how the parent sales process comprises different children subprocesses in a typical sales and distribution setup in SAP S/4HANA. We focused our discussion on these five subprocesses: presales, sales order, delivery, invoice, and revenue.

In Section 1.2, we touched briefly on the topic of two best friends: sales and finance. We walked you through examples and transaction codes of the important touch points between a sales and finance integration. The touch points are pricing and taxation, account determination, credit management, profitability analysis, and intercompany billing.

And, finally, in Section 1.3, we walked you through the sales and SCM process. We defined SCM as a combination of materials management and production planning processes. We discussed materials management components (availability check, STOs, general ledger account determination, third-party processing, and inventory management) and production planning components (MTO, MRP, variant configuration, and transfer of requirements), as well as how they all come together to construct an extremely powerful SCM process.

In the following chapters, we'll dive into all the concepts you read in this chapter pertaining to the sales and distribution functionality and its organizational structure in SAP S/4HANA. We'll explain the integration configurations within sales and distribution and all the other mentioned functionalities, which will make you a confident SAP integration champion. So, without further ado, let's continue on to the next chapter on organizational structures.

Chapter 2
The SAP Organizational Structure

Now that we've covered the basics of integrated sales, it's time to dive into the SAP S/4HANA system. This chapter will help you understand how different organizations are structured in SAP S/4HANA to provide a foundation for the rest of this book.

Understanding the organizational structure is critical to learning about integration. Knowing the structure and key components within the structure will make subsequent integration chapters easy to comprehend and master. In this chapter, we'll share our knowledge about the following organizational structures: sales and distribution, materials management, finance, Project System, SAP Revenue Accounting and Reporting, and SAP Concur.

Note

This chapter will only focus on components relevant for sales and distribution integration. To get more insight that's outside the scope of this book, we recommend referring to the SAP Help Portal (*https://help.sap.com*) or checking out other books by SAP PRESS.

You most likely have seen many flavors of SAP S/4HANA organizational structures on the web or by reading various books. To set the stage for this chapter, Figure 2.1 shows the organizational structure of SAP S/4HANA, specifically developed with sales and distribution at the center, integrating with other functionalities scoped in this book.

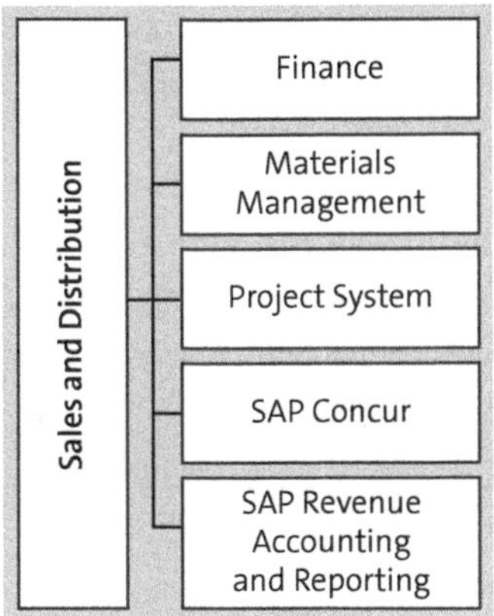

Figure 2.1 SAP Organizational Structure (Sales and Distribution)

2.1 Sales and Distribution

The sales and distribution organizational structure in SAP S/4HANA comprises three key components: sales organization, distribution channel, and division. In this section, we'll look at how these components are configured at a high level from the integration standpoint.

Let's first look at how these three components connect with each other, and then we'll deep dive into each one of them individually. We'll use an example of a food company called S4 Inc. to explain all the components and connections:

- S4 Inc. has three sales organizations: S4 Food, S4 Beverages, and S4 Water.
- S4 Food has three distribution channels: S4 Distributor, S4 Reseller, and S4 Consumer.
- S4 Distributor has two divisions: Produce and Meat.
- S4 Reseller has one division: Meat.
- S4 Consumer has one division: Deli.

Figure 2.2 shows how the three components integrate with each other in a typical sales and distribution organizational structure in SAP S/4HANA.

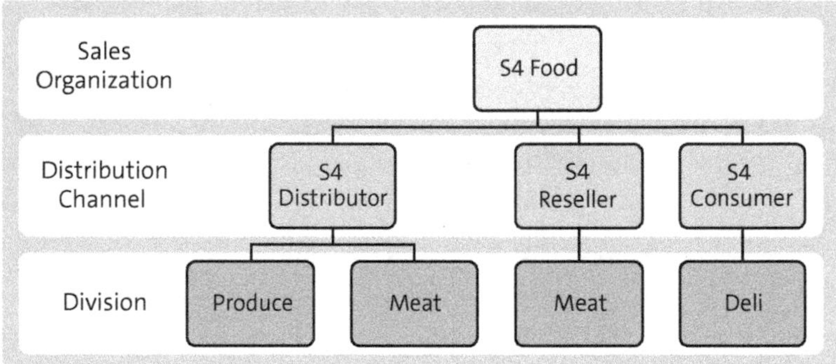

Figure 2.2 Sales and Distribution Organizational Structure

Now, let's jump into each component individually, starting with sales organization.

2.1.1 Sales Organization

Sales organization is an entity from which the actual sales originate. All sales-related activities are driven by the sales organization. On one side, the sales organization is connected to a company code (part of the finance functionality); on the other side, the sales organization is connected to the distribution channel (explained in Section 2.1.2).

Note

One company code can have many sales organizations, but one sales organization can have only one parent company code. This means that S4 Inc. can have many sales organizations (S4 Food, S4 Beverages, and S4 Water), but S4 Food can only have one parent company code (S4 Inc.).

One sales organization can have many distribution channels. This means that S4 Food can have multiple distribution channels (S4 Distributor, S4 Reseller, and S4 Consumer).

To set up the sales organization, you can execute Transaction OVX5. Alternatively, you can execute Transaction SPRO and follow IMG menu path **Enterprise Structure • Definition • Sales and Distribution • Define, Copy, Delete, Check Sales Organization.**

Tip

It's good practice to copy existing entities while creating new ones. By doing so, in the backend, SAP copies all dependent configurations from the source entity to the target entity and sets them up automatically. You'll see how we use this tip in all the configurations in this book and how it saves time in the long term.

On the page that opens, click on the **Copy org.object** button or press F6, and enter values into the **From Sales Org.** and **To Sales Org.** fields. Follow the system prompts until you see the **Information** screen shown in Figure 2.3. In our example, we've copied sales organization **001** to a new sales organization, **SGIN**.

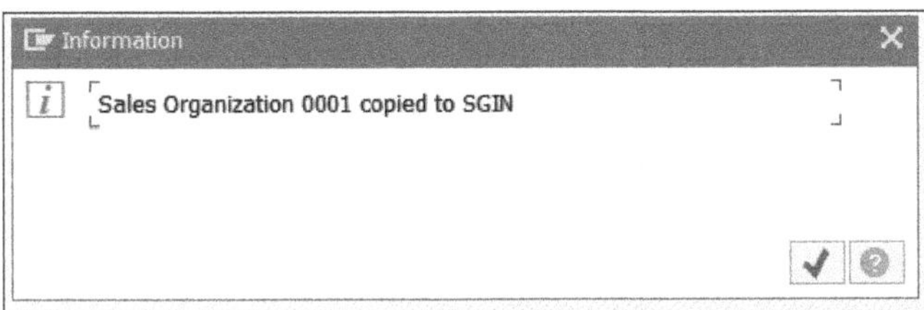

Figure 2.3 Sales Organization Information

Note

Each time you click **Save** during configuration, the system will ask you to save changes to a transport. Try to save one logical entity configuration to one transport. For example, save all sales organizational structure configuration to one transport, all materials management organizational structure configuration to another transport, and so on.

From Figure 2.3, click the green checkmark, and then click the green back arrow. Next, double-click on **Define Sales Organization**. Scroll down to the sales organization you created (**SGIN**, in our example), and update the **Name** (**S4 Food**), as shown in Figure 2.4. Click **Save** at the top of the screen.

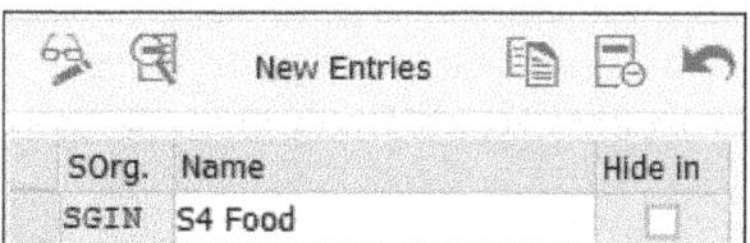

Figure 2.4 SGIN Sales Organization

The SGIN sales organization is now created successfully! That was easy, wasn't it?

The sales organization detail view shown in Figure 2.5 comprises two main sections: **Detailed Information** and **ALE: Data for purchase order**. From these two sections, **ALE: Data for purchase order** is important for sales and distribution integration with material masters.

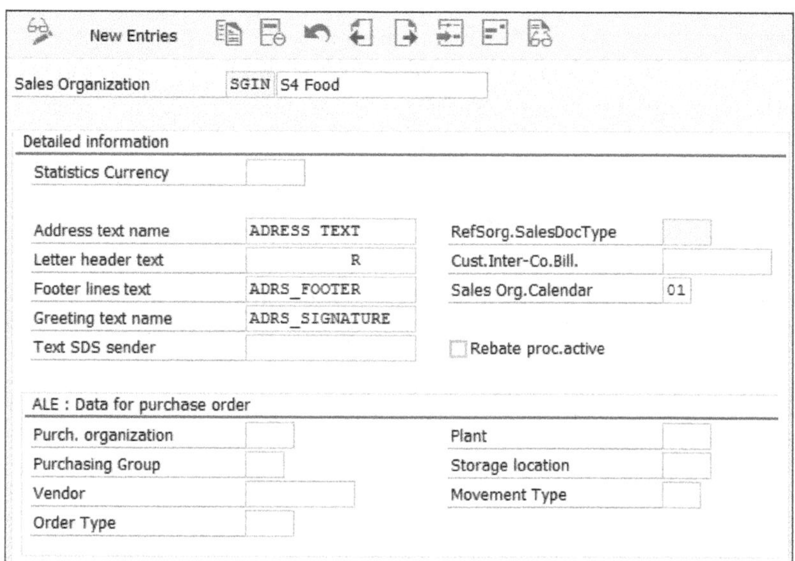

Figure 2.5 SGIN: S4 Food Details

Let's quickly touch on some of the key fields shown here:

- **Purch. organization**, **Purchasing Group**, **Plant**, and **Storage location**
  These fields are explained in detail in Section 2.2, Chapter 3, and Chapter 4. There, you'll see how these fields come together to form a strong alliance to connect various materials management and sales and distribution processes.
- **Movement Type**
  This field is very important for general ledger account determination for deliveries explained in Chapter 4, Section 4.3.

- **Vendor**
  This field is used to identify the supplier.
- **Order Type**
  This field is used to identify which type of purchase order is allowed for a sales organization. If left blank, as shown in Figure 2.5, then all order types are allowed for that sales organization.

2.1.2 Distribution Channel

The *distribution channel* is the medium through which products are distributed to end users. In our example, as shown earlier in Figure 2.2, S4 Food distributes its products (produce, meat, deli, etc.) through S4 Distributor, S4 Reseller, and S4 Consumer.

You can configure distribution channels by executing Transaction OVXI or following IMG menu path **Enterprise Structure • Definition • Sales and Distribution • Define, Copy, Delete, Check Distribution Channel.**

On the page that opens, click on the **Copy org.object** button or press F6, and enter values in **From Distr. Channel** and **To Distr. Channel**. Follow the system prompts until you see the **Information** window shown in Figure 2.6. In our example, we've copied distribution channel **00** to a new distribution channel **41**.

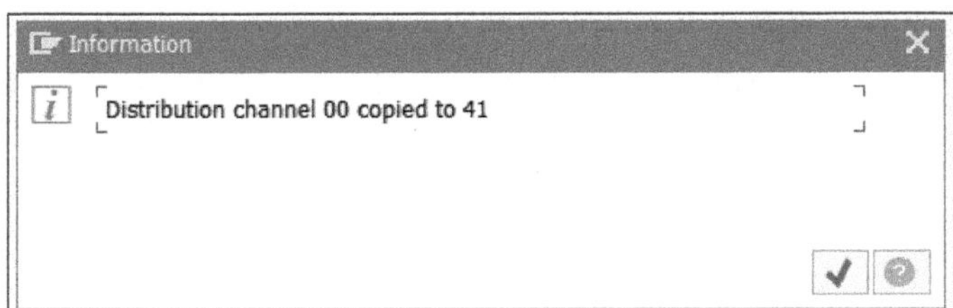

Figure 2.6 Distribution Channel Information

From the screen shown in Figure 2.6, click the green checkmark, and then click the green back arrow. Next double-click on **Define distribution channel**. Scroll down to the distribution channel (**Distr. Channel**) you created (**41**, in our example, as shown in Figure 2.7), change the **Name** to "S4 Distributor", and click **Save**. Follow the same process to create other distribution channels: S4 Reseller and S4 Consumer.

Distr. Channel	Name	Hide in
41	S4 Distributor	☐
42	S4 Reseller	☐
43	S4 Consumer	☐

Figure 2.7 Distribution Channel 41, 42, 43 Overview

Note

If you want to hide a distribution channel from showing up in a sales transaction, check the **Hide in** field in the distribution channel configuration (the rightmost field in Figure 2.7).

2.1.3 Division

Division is where the actual production of goods happens for a company. In a service-based company, division is the entity from which services are built and rendered. Each product/service should technically have its own division. In our example, as shown previously in Figure 2.2, S4 Distributor has two divisions (Produce and Meat), which means that S4 Distributor distributes its products via divisions Produce and Meat.

To configure divisions, execute Transaction OVXB or follow IMG menu path **Enterprise Structure • Definition • Logistics – General • Define Copy, Delete, Check Division.**

Next, double-click on **Copy, delete, check division.** On the page that opens, click on the **Copy org.object** button or press F6, and enter values into **From Division** and **To Division.** Follow system prompts until you see the box shown in Figure 2.8. In our example, we've copied division **00** to a new division, **51.**

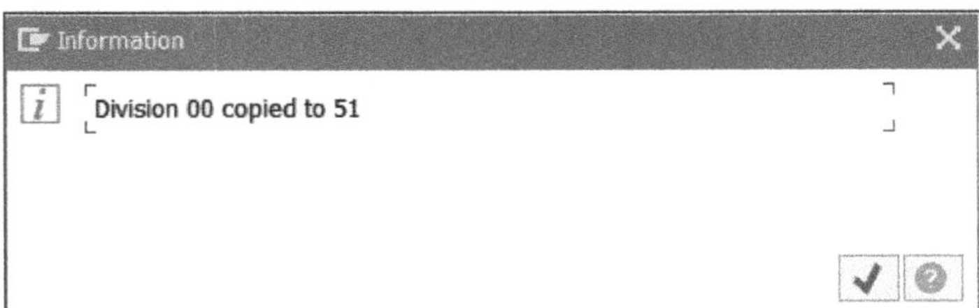

Figure 2.8 Division Information

From this dialog box, click the green checkmark and then click the green back arrow. Next, double-click on **Define division.**

Scroll down to the **Division** you created (**51**, in our example, as shown in Figure 2.9), change the **Name** ("Produce"), and click **Save.** Follow the same process to create **Division 52** for **Meat.**

Division	Name	Hide in
51	Produce	☐
52	Meat	☐

Figure 2.9 Division 51 and 52 Overview

Divisions 51 and 52 are now created successfully.

Note

If you want to hide a division from showing up in a sales transaction, check the **Hide in** field in the division configuration (the rightmost field in Figure 2.9).

2.1.4 Sales Area Determination

Now that all three components are created, you must connect them so they can talk to each other, as shown in Figure 2.10. This process is called *assignment* or *sales area determination* in SAP S/4HANA and is typically a three-step process:

1. Assign the distribution channel to the sales organization.
2. Assign the division to the sales organization.
3. Set up the sales area.

The good news is that SAP does this assignment automatically.

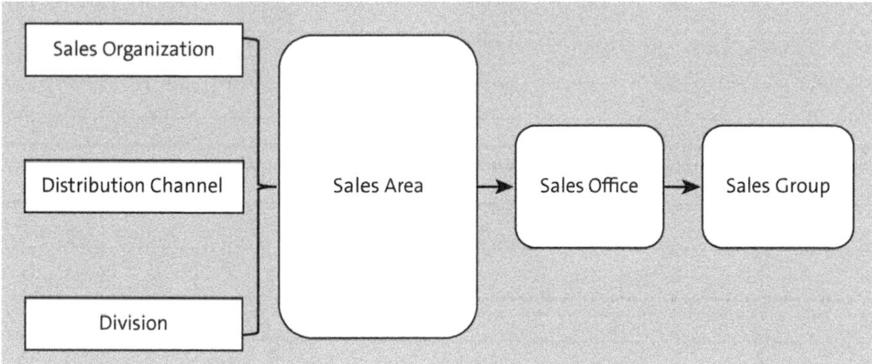

Figure 2.10 Sales Area Determination

Tip

Do you remember the tip in Section 2.1.1 about using the **Copy** feature in place of the **Create** feature to configure each of the three components? That tip will save you valuable minutes in your day that you can use to call a friend and recommend this book!

To validate if the assignments are correct in the system, go through the following IMG menu paths:

- **Distribution channel to sales organization assignment**
  Follow menu path **Enterprise Structure • Assignment • Sales and Distribution • Assign Distribution Channel to Sales Organization**. You'll arrive at the screen shown in Figure 2.11, where sales organization **SGIN** needs to be assigned to distribution channels **41**, **42**, and **43** correctly. This means that whenever a sales order is created

for **SGIN**, you can use any of the three distribution channels to distribute the products depending on the type of sale. If the sales order is for a distributor, then **41** should be used; if for a reseller, then **42** should be used; and if for a consumer, then **43** should be used.

Assignment Sales Organization - Distribution Channel

SOrg.	Name	DChl	Name	Status	Hide in
SGIN	S4 Food	41	S4 Distributor		☐
SGIN	S4 Food	42	S4 Reseller		☐
SGIN	S4 Food	43	S4 Consumer		☐

Figure 2.11 Distribution to Sales Organization Assignment

- **Division to sales organization assignment**
  Follow menu path **Enterprise Structure • Assignment • Sales and Distribution • Assign Division to Sales Organization**. You'll arrive at the screen shown in Figure 2.12, where sales organization **SGIN** is correctly assigned to division **51** and **52** per our configuration. This means that whenever a sales order is created for **SGIN**, you can use either of two divisions depending on the type of product sold. If **SGIN** is selling produce, then division **51** should be used; if **SGIN** is selling meat, then division **52** should be used.

Assignment Sales Organization - Division

SOrg.	Name	Dv	Name	Status	Hid...
SGIN	S4 Food	51	Produce		☐
SGIN	S4 Food	52	Meat		☐

Figure 2.12 Division to Sales Organization Assignment

- **Sales area**
  Sales area determination in the SAP S/4HANA system involves connecting the three core components of the sales and distribution organization together. In this configuration step, you validate if the three components are connected correctly with all permutations and combinations. If you want to delete a combination that doesn't fit into your business requirement, then this configuration is where that can be done.

  Follow menu path **Enterprise Structure • Assignment • Sales and Distribution • Set Up Sales Area.** You'll arrive at the screen shown in Figure 2.13, where standard SAP created all possible determinations between the sales organization, distribution channels, and divisions based on your configuration. When creating a sales order in the system, any of the combinations of sales organization, distribution channel, and division can be used depending on the type of sales made and the channel used for distribution. For example, say S4 Foods confirms a sale of produce through a reseller. The sales order that gets created because of this sale in S4 Food's SAP S/4HANA system will have **SGIN** as the sales organization, **42** as the distribution channel, and **51** as the division.

Assignment Sales Org. - Distribution Channel - Division								
SOrg.	Name	DChl	Name	Dv	Name	Status	Hide in	Hide in
SGIN	S4 Food	41	S4 Distributor	51	Produce		☐	☐
SGIN	S4 Food	41	S4 Distributor	52	Meat		☐	☐
SGIN	S4 Food	42	S4 Reseller	51	Produce		☐	☐
SGIN	S4 Food	42	S4 Reseller	52	Meat		☐	☐
SGIN	S4 Food	43	S4 Consumer	51	Produce		☐	☐
SGIN	S4 Food	43	S4 Consumer	52	Meat		☐	☐

Figure 2.13 Assignment Sales Org. – Distribution Channel – Division Screen

- **Sales area is connected to sales office**
  An optional further drilldown on the sales area is the sales office. Follow menu path **Enterprise Structure • Assignment • Sales and Distribution • Assign Sales Office to Sales Areas**. You'll arrive at the screen shown in Figure 2.14.

  In our example, let's say S4 Food wants to sell meat to a distributor, and they can either do that through their India sales office or their Germany sales office. Logically, if their distributor is in a country in Asia, then they will use the India sales office, and if their distributor is in Europe, then they should use their German sales office to complete the sales.

Assignment Sales Office - Sales Area									
SOrg.	Name	DChl	Name	Dv	Name	SOff.	Description	Status	Hid...
SGIN	S4 Food	41	S4 Distributor	51	Produce	1418	India		☐
SGIN	S4 Food	41	S4 Distributor	51	Produce	ZDE1	Germany 1		☐
SGIN	S4 Food	41	S4 Distributor	52	Meat	1418	India		☐
SGIN	S4 Food	41	S4 Distributor	52	Meat	ZDE1	Germany 1		☐

Figure 2.14 Sales Area to Sales Office Determination

- **Sales office is connected to sales group**
  An optional further drilldown on the sales office is sales groups. Follow menu path **Enterprise Structure • Assignment • Sales and Distribution • Assign Sales Group to Sales Office**. You'll arrive at the screen shown in Figure 2.15.

  In our example, if S4 Food wants to sell chicken through their India sales office, they should use their Chicken sales group to complete the sales; similarly, if they want to sell fish to their customer, then they should use the Fish sales group.

Assignment Sales Office - Sales Groups					
SOff.	Description	SGrp	Description	Status	Hid...
1418	India	101	Chicken		☐
1418	India	102	Fish		☐

Figure 2.15 Sales Office: Sales Groups Determination

2.2 Materials Management

In this section, we'll focus on materials management organizational structure components useful for sales and distribution integration in SAP S/4HANA. At the end of this section, you'll have a good understanding of components such as plants, storage locations, purchasing organizations, and purchasing groups. You'll learn how these components communicate with each other to form a strong organization structure, which integrates with sales and distribution seamlessly.

Figure 2.16 shows the materials management organizational structure for company S4 Inc. We'll refer to this organizational structure as an example throughout this section.

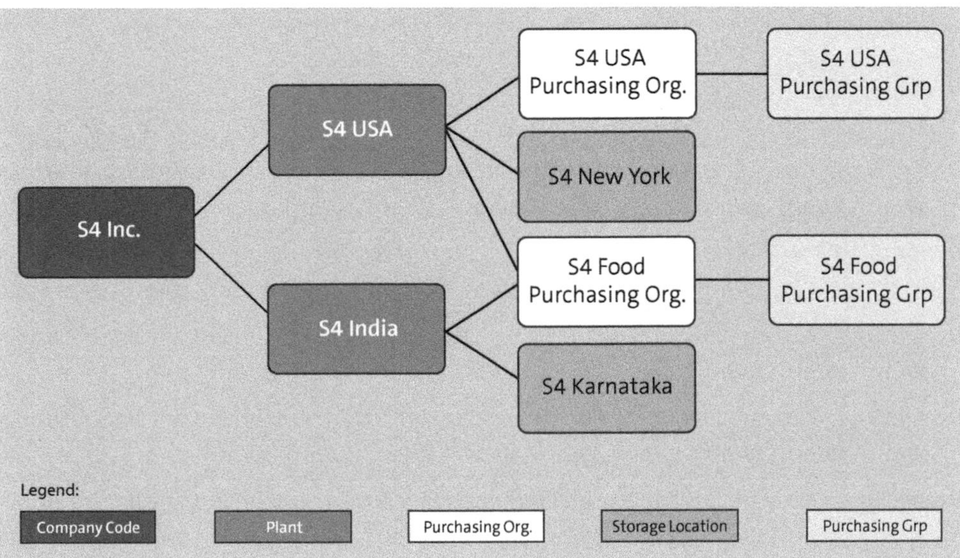

Figure 2.16 Material Management Organizational Structure

2.2.1 Plant

Within materials management in SAP S/4HANA, the *plant* is defined as an entity that holds material stock until it's ready to be dispatched or consumed. Plants can be location-specific, product-specific, or any other way you want, depending on your business processes. In our example in Figure 2.16, plants for S4 Inc. are driven off locations in the United States and India.

> **Note**
>
> One company code can have many plants, but usually one plant is associated with only one parent company code.

Plant is a key integration field between the sales and distribution functionality and materials management functionality. When you create a sales order and enter a material, the plant you see on the sales order comes from the material master. Technically, plant is the first entry point of materials management into sales and distribution.

To set up a plant, execute Transaction OX10 or follow IMG menu path **Enterprise Structure • Definition • Logistics – General • Define Copy, Delete, Check Plant • Define Plant**. Then click on **New Entries** on the top of the screen so you can enter the details pertaining to your plant definition, as shown in Figure 2.17.

New Entries

Plant	1712	
Name 1	US Plant 1901	
Name 2		

Detailed Information

Language Key	EN	English
Street and House No.		
PO Box		
Postal Code	88456	
City		
Country Key	US	USA
Region		
County Code		
City code		
Tax Jurisdiction		
Factory Calendar	US	USA

Note: The address fields Name1 and Name2 are not copied from the address screen and you must maintain them separately.
All other addr. data can only be maintained in addr. screen.
The changes can only be seen in the overview and detail view after they have been saved.

Figure 2.17 Plant Details

From here, you can see plant has two sections: the header and **Detailed information**. We'll walk through the fields to fill out in both sections next.

The header section has three fields:

- **Plant**
  This field is a unique alphanumeric key used to represent a plant.
- **Name 1**
  This field is used to represent the name of a plant.
- **Name 2**
  This field is used to represent an alternate name or an extension to the **Name 1** field for a plant.

Next, the **Detailed information** section has the following fields:

- **Language Key**
  This field is used to represent the system language of a plant.
- **Street and House No.**
  This field is used to represent the street details and house number of the plant address.
- **PO Box**
  This field is used to represent the post office box of the plant address.
- **Postal Code**
  This field is used to represent the postal code of the plant address.
- **City**
  This field is used to represent the city of the plant address.
- **Country Key**
  This field is used to represent the country key of the plant address.
- **Region**
  This field is used to represent the region of the plant address.
- **County Code**
  This field is used to represent the county code of the plant address.
- **City code**
  This field is used to represent the city code of the plant address.
- **Tax Jurisdiction**
  This field represents a unique code used to determine taxes within the United States.
- **Factory Calendar**
  This field is used to represent the factory calendar code valid for a plant.

After filling in the relevant fields, click the **Save** button or press Ctrl+S to finish setting up the plant.

2.2.2 Storage Location

The *storage location* is a subsection under a plant where physical stock or goods are stored. Movement of goods to customers originates from the storage location. One plant can have many storage locations. In our example, S4 USA plant has storage locations S4 New York and S4 Los Angeles, and S4 India plant has storage locations S4 Maharashtra and S4 Karnataka.

Storage locations are crucial for creating delivery documents within a sales order process, thus making it another key field within the sales and distribution-materials management integration. In our example, let's say we created a sales order for a US-based customer with Meat Poultry as a material. When we deliver this line item, based on our configuration, S4 New York is picked as the storage location because delivery of the poultry is to a US-based customer via the S4 USA plant.

To set up a storage location, execute Transaction OX09 or follow IMG menu path **Enterprise Structure • Definition • Material Management • Maintain Storage Location**. You'll arrive at the screen shown in Figure 2.18.

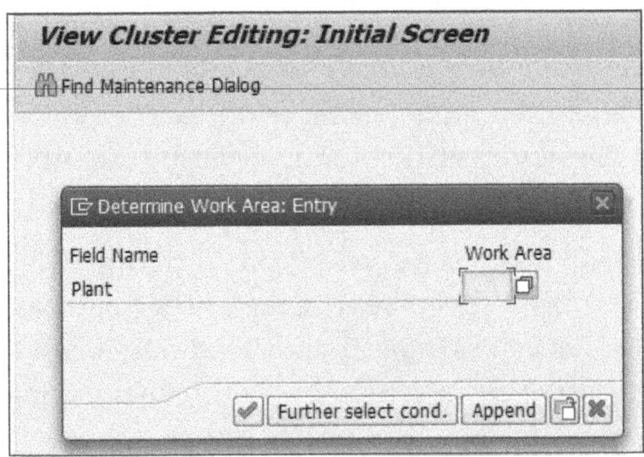

Figure 2.18 Enter Plant for Storage Location

Enter the plant for which you want to set up storage location, and click the green checkmark. You'll arrive at the screen shown in Figure 2.19.

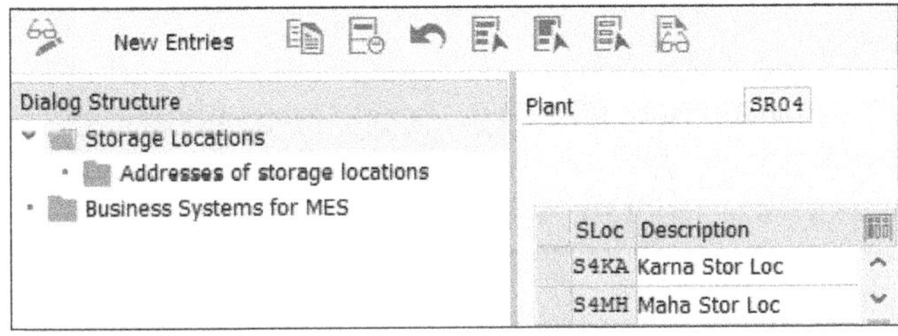

Figure 2.19 Storage Locations

Next, click on the **New Entries** button, and enter the two fields for setting up a plant:

- **SLoc**
  This field is a unique alphanumeric key used to represent a storage location. We've added storage locations **S4KA** and **S4MH**, per our example.
- **Description**
  This field is used to describe a storage location. We've added **Karna Stor Loc** and **Maha Stor Loc**.

Click **Save** or press Ctrl+S to finish setting up the storage locations.

2.2.3 Purchasing Organizations and Purchasing Groups

Purchasing organizations are responsible for procurement functions in an organization. Procuring can happen through external vendors or through internal plants.

> **Note**
>
> One purchasing organization can be associated with many plants, and one plant can have multiple purchasing organizations.

Purchasing groups and purchasing organizations are tag team partners. For all purchasing that is done by a purchasing organization, there is an entity or group of entities called *purchasing groups*, which help implement purchasing activities.

Figure 2.16 shows two purchasing orgs: **S4 US Purch Org** and **S4 Food Purch Org**. While the S4 USA purchasing organization is only tied to plant S4 USA, the S4 Food purchasing organization is tied to both plants, S4 USA and S4 India. For any food-related product purchases made by the S4 Food purchasing organization, the S4 Food purchasing group will take care of buying, shelving, and other purchase-related activities.

For example, say you create info records, condition types, and a purchase order for an India-based customer using purchasing organization S4 Food and purchasing group S4 Food. When the purchase order is converted to a sales order, all relevant data—purchase order number, material, quantity, customer material number, conditions, and purchase order data—flows over to the sales order based on the sales and distribution–materials management integration.

We'll dive deeper into sales and distribution–materials management integration in Chapter 4, where you'll see how data from these objects flows from materials management to sales and distribution and learn about the different integration points.

For the purposes of this chapter, we'll discuss the basic setup. Purchasing organization and purchasing group are vital for the sales and distribution–materials management integration. To set up a purchasing organization, execute Transaction OX08 or follow IMG menu path **Enterprise Structure • Definition • Material Management • Maintain Purchasing Organization**. You'll arrive at the screen shown in Figure 2.20, where you can either view existing purchasing organizations or create new ones by clicking the **New Entries** button.

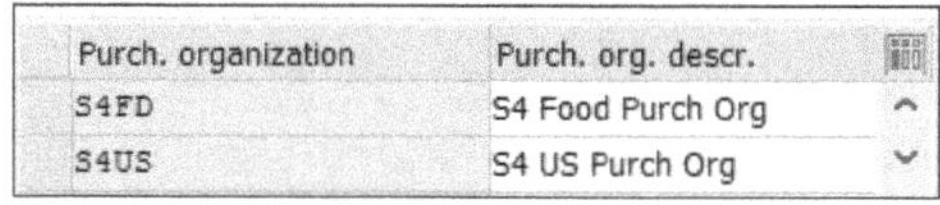

Purch. organization	Purch. org. descr.
S4FD	S4 Food Purch Org
S4US	S4 US Purch Org

Figure 2.20 Purchasing Organizations

As shown in Figure 2.20, the purchasing organization has two key fields:

- **Purch. organization**
  This field is a unique alphanumeric key used to represent a purchasing organization. We've set up two purchasing organizations, **S4FD** and **S4US**, per our example.
- **Purch. org. descr.**
  This field is used to describe a purchasing organization. We've added **S4 Food Purch Org** and **S4 US Purch Org**.

After filling in the relevant fields, click the **Save** button or press Ctrl+S to finish setting up the purchasing organizations.

Next, to set up purchasing groups in SAP S/4HANA, execute Transaction OME4 or follow IMG menu path **Material Management • Purchasing • Create Purchasing Groups**. You'll arrive at the screen shown in Figure 2.21, where you can either view existing purchasing groups or create new ones by clicking on the **New Entries** button.

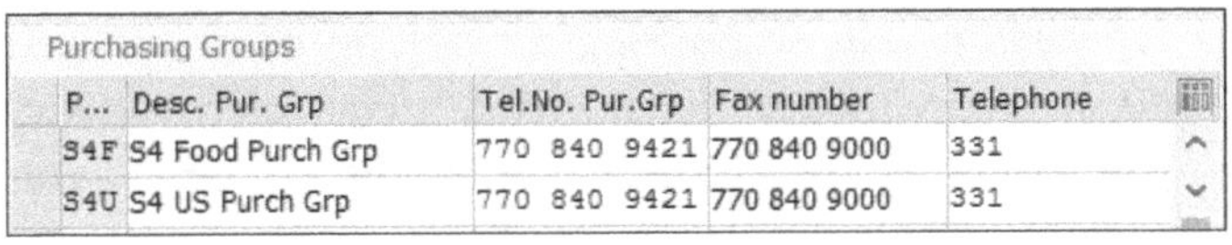

Purchasing Groups

P...	Desc. Pur. Grp	Tel.No. Pur.Grp	Fax number	Telephone
S4F	S4 Food Purch Grp	770 840 9421	770 840 9000	331
S4U	S4 US Purch Grp	770 840 9421	770 840 9000	331

Figure 2.21 Purchasing Groups

As shown in Figure 2.21, the purchasing group has the following key fields:

- **P...**
  This field is a unique alphanumeric key used to represent a purchasing group. We've set up two purchasing groups, **S4F** and **S4U**, per our example.
- **Desc. Pur. Grp**
  This field is used to describe a purchasing group. We've added **S4 Food Purch Grp** and **S4 US Purch Grp**.
- **Tel.No. Pur.Grp**
  This field is used to represent the telephone number of a purchasing group.
- **Fax number**
  This field is used to represent the fax number of a purchasing group.
- **Telephone**
  This field is used to represent an alternate telephone number of a purchasing group.
- **Extension**
  This field (not shown) is used to represent the extension of a telephone number for a purchasing group.
- **E-mail Address**
  This field (not shown) is used to represent the email address of a purchasing group.

After filling in the relevant fields, click the **Save** button or press Ctrl+S to finish setting up the purchasing groups.

2.3 Finance

In SAP S/4HANA, finance is often used in conjunction with controlling. In this section, we'll look at various key components of a finance organizational structure relevant to sales and distribution integration. We'll also touch on a few supplemental controlling components, as together with finance components, they will help you understand sales and distribution to financial accounting/controlling integration better. By the end of this section, you'll have a good fundamental knowledge of the following financial accounting/controlling components: client, operating concern, credit controlling area, controlling area, company, company code, business area, functional area, cost center, profit center, and segment.

Figure 2.22 depicts what a typical financial accounting/controlling organizational structure looks like in SAP S/4HANA, starting with the highest-level object (client) and expanding to the more granular objects. We'll set up each of these objects throughout this section.

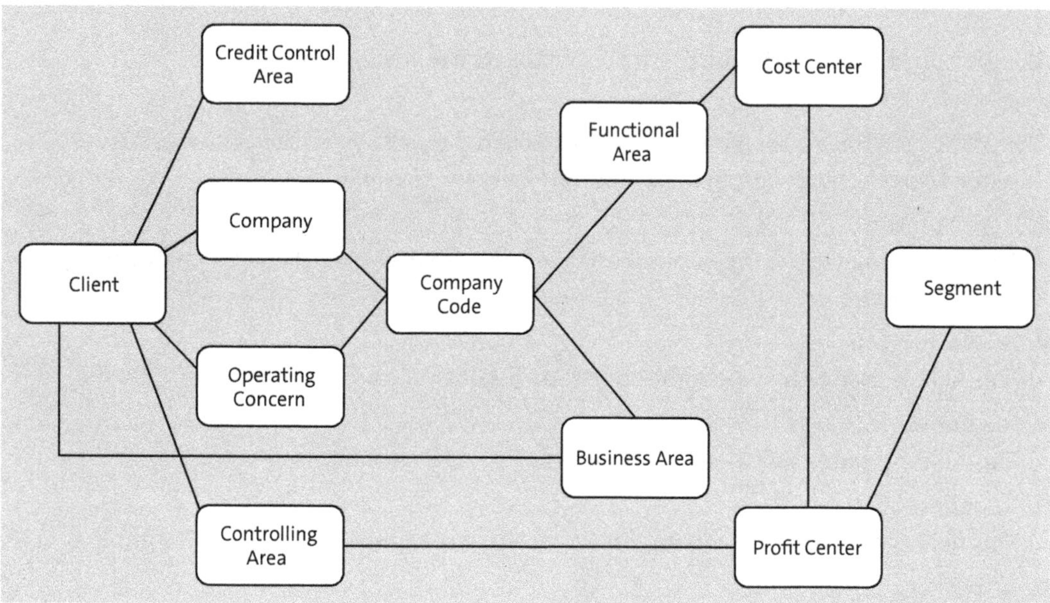

Figure 2.22 Finance Organizational Structure

2.3.1 Client

Client is the top-most component of an organizational structure in an SAP S/4HANA system. We typically show client in a finance structure, but it's truly a part of any organization structure. While client isn't an integration field, having knowledge about it is beneficial to understanding many SAP S/4HANA concepts.

Note

One SAP system can have many clients, but generally we see three to four clients for a standard SAP landscape: development, sandbox, quality and production.

The following types of clients are available in SAP S/4HANA:

- **Development client**
  This is where configuration, development, and unit testing happen. At our example company, we have two separate development clients, 001 and 201. We do configurations in 001 and then move transports to 201 for unit testing. This is a good practice as it keeps the 001 client clean from any test data.
- **Sandbox client**
  This is used when you want to try out a solution before implementing it as a part of your change process. There is only one sandbox client where you do configuration and unit testing.
- **Quality client**
  This is where business stakeholders perform user acceptance testing (UAT).
- **Production client**
  This is the live system where daily business transactions are performed.

To set up clients, execute Transaction SCC4 or follow SAP menu path **Tools • Administration • Administration • Client Administration • SCC4 – Client Maintenance**. Click on **New Entries**, and enter the details per your system landscape requirements. Details entered in Figure 2.23 are based on the example client's requirements.

After filling in the relevant fields, click the **Save** button or press Ctrl+S to finish setting up the client.

Note

You should work with an SAP admin or a Basis expert on your team to set up clients. They are the experts at doing this and will know what information needs to be filled in on the screen shown in Figure 2.23 to set up an error-free client.

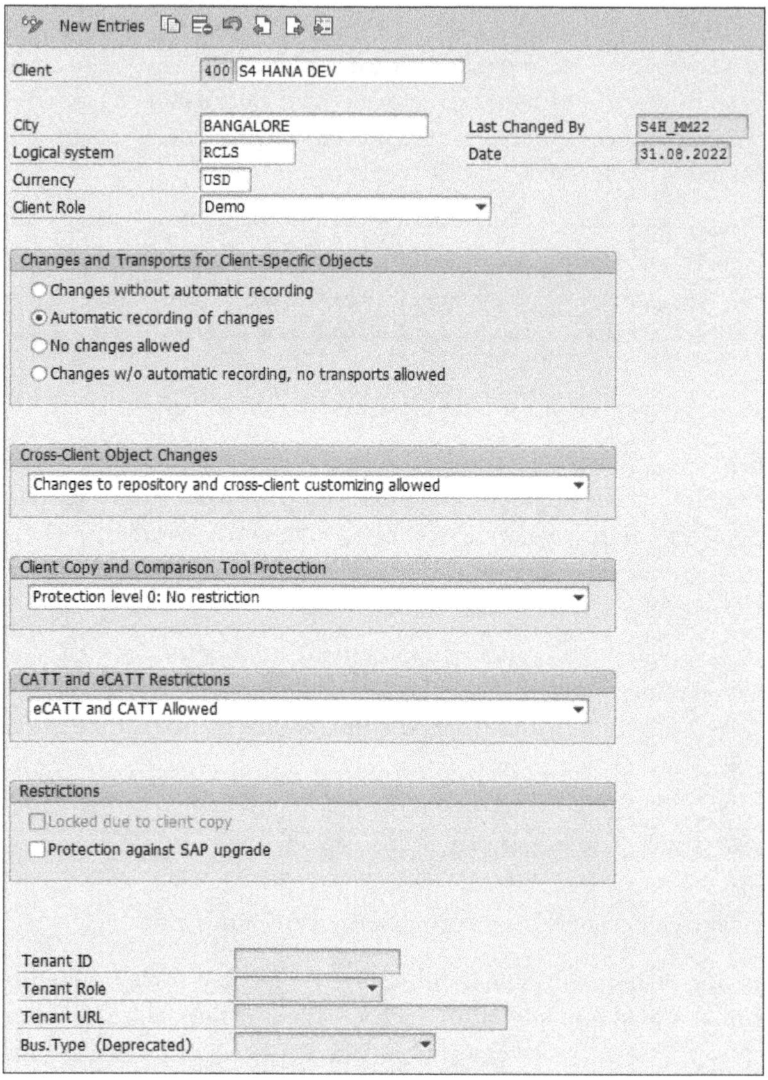

Figure 2.23 Client Configuration

2.3.2 Operating Concern

Operating concern is the most important organizational component of profitability analysis and finance in SAP S/4HANA. It forms the base for analysis and reporting by gathering data from various sources within SAP, depending on characteristics and values configured within it. SAP provides a standard list of characteristics and values in an operating concern, but you can add more if needed.

Characteristics can be thought of as high-level buckets holding different value fields. For example, sales organization is a characteristic, while revenue and costs are *value fields* that help a company analyze sales profits.

To maintain operating concerns, execute Transaction KEA0 or follow IMG menu path **Controlling • Profitability Analysis • Structures • Define Operating Concern • Maintain Operating Concern**. Enter the operating concern you want to create, and press Enter. You'll arrive at the screen shown in Figure 2.24.

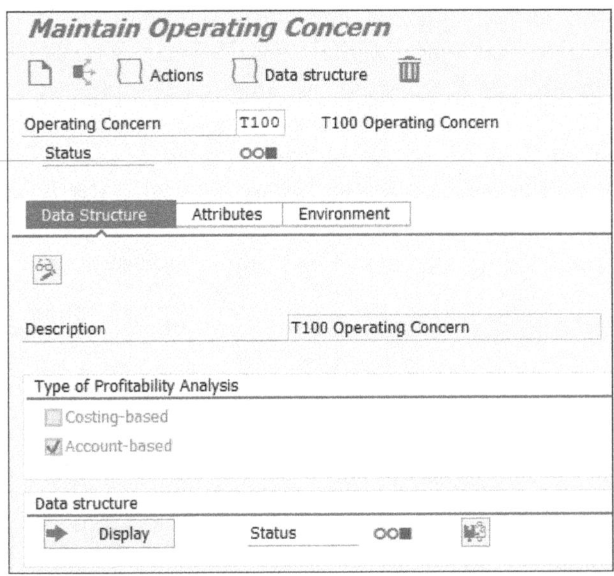

Figure 2.24 Operating Concern Header and Data Structure

The **Maintain Operating Concern** screen has four sections: header area, **Data Structure**, **Attributes**, and **Environment**.

As shown in Figure 2.24, the header section has two fields:

- **Operating Concern**
  This field is a unique four-character alphanumeric key used to represent an operating concern (**T100**, in our example).
- **Status**
  This indicator represents whether the operating concern is ready to be used. A green light means the operating concern is active.

Next, the **Data Structure** section has three key fields:

- **Description**
  This field is used to describe the operating concern.
- **Type of Profitability Analysis**
  This is an indicator field that helps you control how you want to use an operating concern by choosing from the following options:
  - **Costing-based**: Select this checkbox if you want the operating concern to be used for costing-based profitability analysis.

- **Account-based**: Select this checkbox if you want the operating concern to be used for account-based profitability analysis.

Note

The concept of account-based profitability analysis has been replaced by *margin analysis* in SAP S/4HANA. Margin analysis includes almost all the account-based profitability analysis features and a few of the costing-based profitability analysis features. Costing-based profitability analysis features, which are closely dependent on account-based features, are consolidated in margin analysis, while the independent features continue to remain in their dedicated costing-based profitability analysis bucket. In SAP S/4HANA, in the frontend SAP Fiori interface, this process is referred to as margin analysis, but in the backend (within the configuration SAP GUI that we use in this book), this check is still called **Account-based**.

If you want the operating concern to be used for both costing-based and account-based profitability analysis, then select both checkboxes.

For more information on costing-based versus account-based profitability analysis, see Chapter 5, Section 5.4.

- **Status**
  This indicator represents whether the data structure in an operating concern is ready to be used. A green light means the data structure is active.

Next, as shown in Figure 2.25, the **Attributes** section has the following key fields:

- **Operating concern currency**
  This field is used to specify the default currency code for an operating concern.
- **Fiscal year variant**
  This field represents the fiscal year variant for an operating concern.
- **Currency types for costing-based Profitability Analysis**
  This field is used to control currency types that can be used for profitability analysis within an operating concern. There are three options available:
  - **Company Code Currency**: Select this checkbox if you want profitability analysis data to be stored in company code currency.
  - **OpConcern crcy,PrCtr valuation**: Select this checkbox if you want profitability analysis data to be stored in operating concern currency along with profit center valuation.
  - **Comp.Code crcy,PrCtr valuation**: Select this checkbox if you want profitability analysis data to be stored in company code currency along with profit center valuation.
  - **2nd period type – weeks**
    This indicator is set if you want profitability analysis data to be stored in weeks. There are two options to choose from:

- **Act. 2nd per. type**: Select this checkbox if you want to save actual data in weeks for costing-based profitability analysis.
- **Plan 2nd per. type**: Select this checkbox if you want to save planned data in weeks for costing-based profitability analysis.

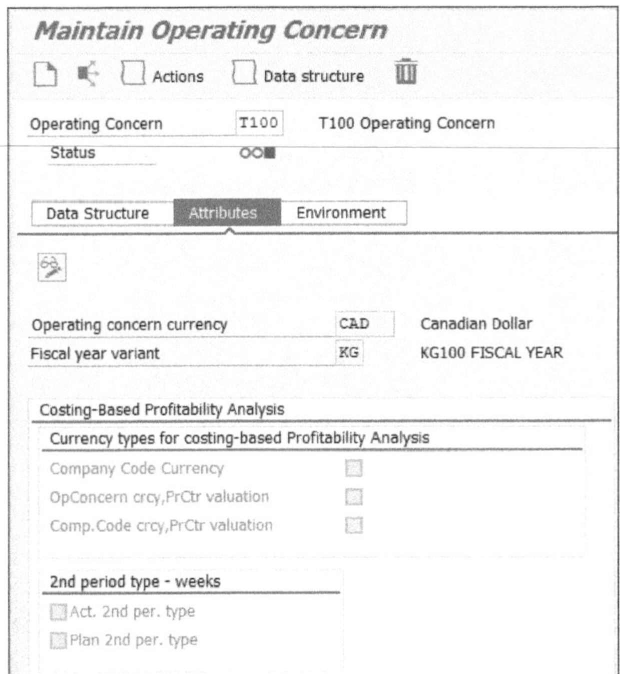

Figure 2.25 Operating Concern Attributes

Finally, as shown in Figure 2.26, the **Environment** section has two key fields:

- **Cross-client part Status**
  This indicator represents whether the cross-client part of the operating concern is ready to be used. The cross-client part includes components such as programs and screens that aren't dependent on the SAP client, meaning that if you make a change to these components in one client, those changes will reflect in other clients too. For example, say you make a screen enhancement in your development client dev001. If you log in to your dev002 client, you'll see the same changes in there too. A green light for **Cross-client part Status** means all the cross-client components are active and can be used for development right away.
- **Client-specific part Status**
  This indicator represents whether the client-specific part of the operating concern is ready to be used. The client-specific part includes components such as number ranges, condition records, and z tables, which are confined to only one client and don't impact other clients in any way. For example, say you update condition records in dev0001 and want the same condition records to show up in dev002.

You'll have to add them manually in dev002 too. A green light for **Client-specific part Status** means all the client-specific components are active and can be used or configured right away.

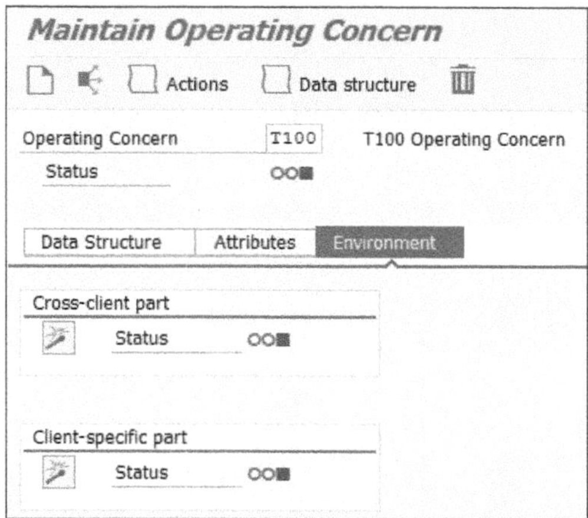

Figure 2.26 Operating Concern Environment

After filling in the relevant fields, click the **Save** button or press [Ctrl]+[S] to finish setting up the operating concern.

After you've set up the overarching operating concern, you can configure the characteristics and value fields. To maintain characteristics, execute Transaction KEA5 or follow IMG menu path **Controlling • Profitability Analysis • Structures • Define Operating Concern • Maintain Characteristics**. Enter a specific characteristic you want to create/change or select the **All Characteristics** radio button, and click **Display** under the **Choose Characteristics** section. You'll arrive at the screen shown in Figure 2.27.

Char.	Description	Short text	DTyp	Lgth.	Origin Table	Origin field d
ARTNRG	Generic Article	GenArticle	CHAR	40	MARA	SATNR
BONUS	Vol. Rebate Grp	Rebate Grp	CHAR	2	MVKE	BONUS
BRSCH	Industry	Industry	CHAR	4	KNA1	BRSCH
BZIRK	Sales District	District	CHAR	6	KNVV	BZIRK
COLLE	Collection	Collection	CHAR	10	VBAP	FSH_COLLECTION

Figure 2.27 Characteristics

The following characteristics fields are shown in Figure 2.27:

- **Char.**
  This field represents the actual characteristic configured or present within an operating concern.
- **Description**
  This field represents the description of the characteristic fields.

- **Short text**
  This field represents the short text of the characteristic fields.
- **DTyp**
  This field represents the built-in data type for the characteristic in an operating concern. As a default, there are two data types available for these characteristics in SAP S/4HANA: **CHAR** for alphanumeric data types and **NUMC** for numerical data types.
- **Lgth.**
  This field represents the allowed length of the characteristic field in an operating concern. For both CHAR and NUMC data types, the minimum length is 1, and the maximum length is 18.
- **Origin Table**
  This field represents the table name from which the characteristic field is picked.
- **Origin field d**
  This field represents the name of the characteristic field picked from the origin table.

Note

For the most part, you'll almost always find the characteristic you're looking for in the **Display Characteristics** list provided by standard SAP. If you don't, you can reach out to a finance consultant on your team to create one for you. Because they are experts at doing this and understand the implications of the configuration change, it's a best practice to reach out to them.

To maintain value fields, execute Transaction KEA6 or follow IMG menu path **Controlling • Profitability Analysis • Structures • Define Operating Concern • Maintain Value Fields**. Enter a specific value you want to create/change, or select the **All value fields** radio button, and click **Display** under the **Choose value fields** section. You'll arrive at the screen shown in Figure 2.28.

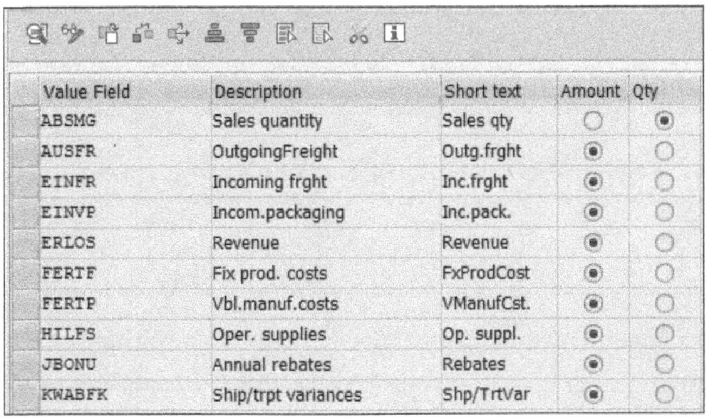

Value Field	Description	Short text	Amount	Qty
ABSMG	Sales quantity	Sales qty	○	◉
AUSFR	OutgoingFreight	Outg.frght	◉	○
EINFR	Incoming frght	Inc.frght	◉	○
EINVP	Incom.packaging	Inc.pack.	◉	○
ERLOS	Revenue	Revenue	◉	○
FERTF	Fix prod. costs	FxProdCost	◉	○
FERTP	Vbl.manuf.costs	VManufCst.	◉	○
HILFS	Oper. supplies	Op. suppl.	◉	○
JBONU	Annual rebates	Rebates	◉	○
KWABFK	Ship/trpt variances	Shp/TrtVar	◉	○

Figure 2.28 Value Fields

As shown in Figure 2.28, value fields have the following key fields:

- **Value Field**
  This field represents the actual value field configured or present within an operating concern.
- **Description**
  This field represents the description of the **Value Field** field.
- **Short text**
  This field represents the short text of the **Value Field** field.
- **Amount**
  This field is used to indicate if the value field is amount based.
- **Qty**
  This field is used to indicate if the value field is quantity based.

Note

For the most part, you'll usually always find the value field you're looking for in the **Display Value Fields** list provided by standard SAP. If you don't, you can reach out to a finance consultant on your team to create one for you. Again, because they are experts at doing this and understand the implications of making the configuration change, it's best practice to reach out to them.

2.3.3 Credit Control Area

Credit control area is a key organizational component that helps finance connect with sales and distribution at different stages in a sales and distribution–finance integration. Credit control area primarily helps you with two things:

- Defining credit limits for customers
- Applying credit checks at various stages for a sales cycle: sales order creation, delivery, or billing

Note

Setting up credit control area is mandatory and important in a finance organizational structure. One credit control area can be assigned to multiple company codes if needed.

To define credit control areas, execute Transaction OB45 or follow IMG menu path **Enterprise Structure • Definition • Financial Accounting • Define Credit Control Area**. Next click on **New Entries**, and you'll arrive at the screen shown in Figure 2.29.

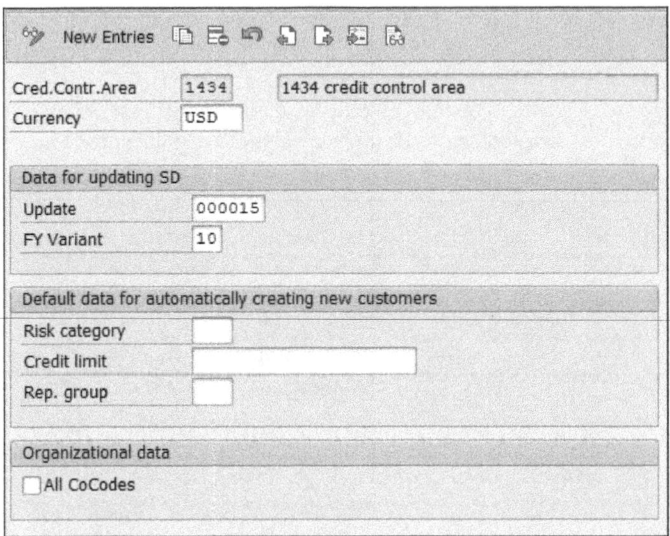

Figure 2.29 Credit Control Area

As shown in Figure 2.29, the credit control area screen is made of four sections: header, **Data for updating SD**, **Default data for automatically creating new customers**, and **Organizational data**.

The header section contains three fields, the **Cred.Contr.Area** code (**1434**, in our example), description box (**1434 credit control area**, in our example), and **Currency** (**USD**, in our example).

Next, the **Data for updating SD** section has two fields:

- **Update**
  This field is used for the credit update on open order, delivery, or billing document values. The default value for this field is blank, which means no updates from sales and distribution documents. But if the business requirement is to make updates, then you must select an option, as shown in Figure 2.30.

Update	Short Descript.
	No update from SD documents
000012	Open order value on time axis, delivery and bill.doct value
000015	Open delivery and billing document value
000018	Open delivery value for sales order, open billing doct value

Figure 2.30 Update List

Table 2.1 depicts how credit statistics are updated when you choose from the **Update** grouping options.

Update Group	Sales Order	Delivery	Billing Document	Financial Journal Entry
000012	Increases open order value	Reduces open order value, increases open delivery value	Reduces open delivery value, increases open billing document value	Reduces open billing document value, increases open items
000015	N/A	Increases open delivery value	Reduces open delivery value, increases open billing document value	Reduces open billing document value, increases open items
000018	Increases open delivery value	N/A	Reduces open delivery value, increases open billing document value	Reduces open billing document value, increases open items

Table 2.1 Update Group Options

- **FY Variant**
  This field will help you determine the fiscal year variant for a credit control area. Fiscal year variant is crucial in situations when a single credit control area is used across multiple company codes that belong to different countries. Based on the country's fiscal year, the posting period and posting entries are adjusted. For example, **10** in our SAP S/4HANA system means the fiscal year is from April through March with four special periods.

Next, the **Default data for automatically creating new customers** section has three fields:

- **Risk category**
  This flag helps you set up different risk categories for a customer. Risk categories help businesses tag their customer as high risk or low risk by assigning a category to them in the credit master record. Based on the category, the business determines the credit limit and credit terms for its customer.

> **Note**
>
> Risk categories can be added in SAP S/4HANA via IMG menu path **Financial Supply Chain Management • Credit Management • Integration with Accounts Receivable Account and Sales and Distribution • Integrating with Sales and Distribution • Define Risk Categories**. For more information about risk categories and credit management, see Chapter 5, Section 5.3.

- **Credit limit**
  This flag is used to set a credit limit for a control area, and all customers belonging to that control area will have the same set credit limit.
- **Rep. group**
  Credit management representative group is a user-defined representative group configured in the credit management functionality. It's assigned to employees who are responsible for credit management and is used to run reports for credit evaluation and release functions periodically.

Note

To configure **Rep. group**, use IMG menu path **Conversion of Accounting to SAP S/4HANA • Preparation and Migration of Customizing • Preparatory Activities and Migration of Customizing for Credit Management • Assign Credit Representative Group to Customer Credit Group**. Further detail is beyond the scope of this book.

Finally, the **Organizational data** section has one field, **All CoCodes**. This checkbox helps you control if posting is allowed for a credit control area across all company codes.

After filling in the relevant fields, click the **Save** button or press Ctrl+S to finish setting up the credit control area.

2.3.4 Controlling Area

Controlling area is a core organizational component of the controlling functionality used to perform cost accounting. It combines with finance organization to manage costs and profits that have a direct or indirect impact on the sales and distribution functionality. You can associate one controlling area to many company codes.

To set up a controlling area in SAP S/4HANA, execute Transaction OKKP or follow IMG menu path **Enterprise Structure • Definition • Controlling • Maintain Controlling Area • Maintain Controlling Area**. Next, click on **New Entries**, and you'll arrive at the screen shown in Figure 2.31.

As shown in Figure 2.31, the controlling area screen has six sections: header, **Assignment Control**, **Currency Setting**, **Other Settings**, **Reconciliation Ledger**, **Setting for Authorization Hierarchies for Cost Centers**, and **Setting for Authorization Hierarchies for Profit Centers**. Let's walk through the relevant settings for each of them.

The header section has three fields: **Controlling Area (0003**, in our example), **Name (SAP US (is-ht-sw)**, in our example), and **Person Responsible**. The **Person Responsible** field is used to specify the name of the user responsible for creating the controlling area.

Controlling Area	0003		
Name	SAP US (is-ht-sw)		
Person Responsible			

Assignment Control

CoCd->CO Area	1 Controlling area same as company code

Currency Setting

Currency Type	10	Company code currency	
Currency	USD	United States Dollar	☐ Diff. CCode Currency
Curr/Val. Prof.			☐ Active

Other Settings

Chart of Accts	INT	TAATA INFO CHART OF ACCOUNTS
Fiscal Year Variant	K4	Cal. Year, 4 Special Periods
CCtr Std. Hierarchy	0003	
Leading FS Version		

☐ Hide Controlling Area in F4

Reconciliation Ledger

☐ Recon.Ledger Active

Setting for Authorization Hierarchies for Cost Centers

Do Not Use Std Hier.	☐	Alternative Hierarchy1	☐
		Alternative Hierarchy2	☐

Setting for Authorization Hierarchies for Profit Centers

Do Not Use Std Hier.	☐	Alternative Hierarchy1	☐
		Alternative Hierarchy2	☐

Figure 2.31 Controlling Area

The **Assignment Control** section has one field, **CoCd->CO Area**. This is an indicator used to control the controlling area assignment to company code. SAP provides two standard options: **1 Controlling area same as company code** and **2 Cross-company-code cost accounting**. If you choose the first option, there is a one-to-one mapping between the controlling area and company code. If you choose the second option, then one controlling area can be assigned to multiple company codes.

Next, the **Currency Setting** section has the following fields:

- **Currency Type**
  This field helps you indicate which currency is permitted for a controlling area and if the currency should be company code currency or some other currency.
- **Currency**
  This field is used to specify currency for a controlling area.

- **Diff. CCode Currency**
  In conjunction with the **Currency Type** field, this checkbox helps you define if a different company code currency is allowed for a controlling area.
- **Curr/Val. Prof.**
  This field is used to assign the currency and valuation profile to a controlling area. Currency and valuation profiles are useful in determining currency valuation views for a controlling area. You only fill in this field when you have more than one valuation view in your system.

Note

To maintain the currency and valuation profile, use the following IMG menu path **Controlling • General Controlling • Maintain Valuation Approaches/Transfer Prices • Maintain Currency and Valuation Profile**. Further detail is beyond the scope of this book.

- **Active**
  This indicator tells you if the currency and valuation profile is active for a controlling area.

Next, the **Other Settings** section has the following fields:

- **Chart of Accts**
  This field is used to assign a chart of accounts to a controlling area.
- **Fiscal Year Variant**
  This field is used to determine the fiscal year variant for a controlling area.
- **Leading FS Version**
  This field is used to assign a leading financial statement version to a controlling area. Financial statement version is used for budget reporting and controlling reporting. For example, you can have one financial statement version BAL for balance sheets and another financial statement version PNL for profit and loss (P&L) statements.
- **Hide Controlling Area in F4**
  This is an indicator used to hide a controlling area in the F4 value help.

Then, the **Setting for Authorization Hierarchies for Cost Centers** section has three checkboxes:

- **Do Not Use Std Hier.**
  You can check this checkbox if you don't want to use standard hierarchy groups for authorization checks within overhead cost controlling, as it relates to cost centers.
- **Alternative Hierarchy1**
  If you've defined an alternative hierarchy (**Hierarchy1**) based on fiscal year and want to use it for authorization checks, then you must check this box.

- **Alternative Hierarchy2**
  If you've defined an alternative hierarchy (**Hierarchy2**) based on fiscal year and want to use it for authorization checks, then you must check this box.

Note

A *standard hierarchy* is a group of cost centers and profit centers, structurally combined in a controlling area, to form the base for statutory reporting and authorization checks.

An *alternative hierarchy* is like an add-on to the standard hierarchy that may contain the same cost center and profit center structure. It's not mandatory for the alternative hierarchy to have cost centers and profit centers though. Alternative hierarchies, as the name suggests, are optional alternates to the standard hierarchy that can used to perform the same reporting and authorization check functions as the standard hierarchy.

Finally, the **Setting for Authorization Hierarchies for Profit Centers** section has three checkboxes:

- **Do Not Use Std Hier.**
  You can check this checkbox if you don't want to use standard hierarchy groups for authorization checks within overhead cost controlling, as it relates to profit centers. This option is seldom used because, in most cases, you'll always use the standard hierarchy. However, if you've built an alternate hierarchy based on your business requirements and that hierarchy is stronger and more efficient than the standard hierarchy, check this checkbox.
- **Alternative Hierarchy1**
  If you've defined an alternative hierarchy (**Hierarchy1**) based on fiscal year and want to use it for authorization checks, then you must check this box.
- **Alternative Hierarchy2**
  If you've defined an alternative hierarchy (**Hierarchy2**) based on fiscal year and want to use it for authorization checks, then you must check this box.

After filling in the relevant fields, click the **Save** button or press Ctrl+S to finish setting up the controlling area.

2.3.5 Company

Company is the smallest organizational unit of a finance organizational structure in SAP S/4HANA. It's an optional component and is often used to consolidate multiple company codes together. If your company is operating with different names in different parts of the businesses or geographies, then setting up one company to consolidate all those company codes makes sense.

For example, say that at our company we have 14 company codes, one for each geographic location we operate in. We combine information from all 14 company codes into one company to finalize our financial statements and to do our year-end reporting.

To set up a company in SAP S/4HANA, execute Transaction OX15 or follow IMG menu path **Enterprise Structure • Definition • Financial Accounting • Define Company**. Next click on **New Entries** to arrive at the screen shown in Figure 2.32.

New Entries

Company	S4SD
Company name	S4 Company for SD
Name of company 2	

Detailed information

Street	
PO Box	
Postal code	
City	
Country	US
Language Key	EN
Currency	USD

Figure 2.32 Company

As shown in Figure 2.32, company has two sections: header and **Detailed information**.

The header section has three fields:

- **Company**
  This field is a unique alphanumeric key used to represent the company. We've defined company **S4SD**, per our example.
- **Company name**
  This field is used to represent the name of a company. We've added **S4 Company for SD**.
- **Name of company 2**
  This field is used to represent an alternate name or an extension to the **Company name** field.

Next, the **Detailed information** section has the following fields:

- **Street**
  This field is used to represent street details of the registered company address.
- **PO Box**
  This field is used to represent the post office box of the registered company address.

- **Postal code**
  This field is used to represent the postal code of the registered company address.
- **City**
  This field is used to represent the city name of the registered company address.
- **Country**
  This field is used to represent the country name of the registered company address.
- **Language Key**
  This field is used to represent the system language of the company.
- **Currency**
  This field is used to represent the local currency of the company.

After filling in the relevant fields, click the **Save** button or press Ctrl+S to finish setting up the company.

2.3.6 Company Code

Company code is the most important component of a financial organizational structure. All financial transactions related to sales or purchases are posted at the company code level. Company code is also crucial from the sales and distribution–finance integration standpoint as it has direct or indirect impact on all integration components (explained in Chapter 5), including pricing procedure, account determination, credit management, profitability analysis, and intercompany billing.

Note

One company can have many company codes tied to it as long as the company codes have the same chart of accounts and fiscal year.

To set up a company code in SAP S/4HANA, execute Transaction OX02 or follow IMG menu path **Enterprise Structure • Definition • Financial Accounting • Edit, Copy, Delete Check Company Code • Edit Company Code Data**. Next, click on **New Entries** to arrive at the screen shown in Figure 2.33.

Company Code	0808
Company Name	Company Code 0808
Additional data	
City	Pune
Country	IN
Currency	INR
Language	EN

Figure 2.33 Company Code

As shown in Figure 2.33, the company code screen has three sections: header, **Additional data**, and **Address** (not shown).

The header section has two fields:

- **Company Code**
  This field is a unique alphanumeric key used to represent the company code. In our example, we've entered company code **0808**.
- **Company Name**
  This field is used to represent name of the company code (**Company Code 0808**, in our example).

The **Additional data** section has four fields:

- **City**
  This field is used to represent the city name of the registered company code address.
- **Country**
  This field is used to represent the country name of the registered company code address.
- **Currency**
  This field is used to represent the local currency of the company code.
- **Language**
  This field is used to represent the system language of the company code.

The **Address** section stores information such as **Name**, **Search Terms**, **Street Address**, **PO Box Address**, **Communication**, and **Comments**.

After filling in the relevant fields, click the **Save** button or press Ctrl+S to finish setting up the company code.

2.3.7 Business Area

Business area is an optional finance organizational component in SAP S/4HANA used to generate balance sheets and P&L reports for a company. While they aren't required for sales and distribution–finance integration, having knowledge about them is essential because P&L is driven by sales.

> **Note**
> A one-to-many relationship exists between the business and company codes.

To set up a business area, execute Transaction OX03 or follow IMG menu path **Enterprise Structure • Definition • Financial Accounting • Define Business Area**. You'll arrive at the screen shown in Figure 2.34, where you can either view existing business areas or create new ones by clicking on the **New Entries** button.

New Entries: Overview of Added Entries

Business Area	Description
01PR	Produce Bus. Area
02MT	Meat Bus. Area
03DL	Deli Bus, Area

Figure 2.34 Business Area

From Figure 2.34, you can see how straightforward it is to set up a business area with just two fields:

- **Business Area**
  This field is a unique four-character alphanumeric key used to represent a business area.
- **Description**
  This field is used to describe the **Business Area** field.

After filling in the relevant fields, click the **Save** button or press [Ctrl]+[S] to finish setting up the business area.

2.3.8 Functional Area

Functional area is a finance organizational component used for classifying expenses incurred in various business functions, for example, legal, marketing, sales, subscriptions, and so on.

> **Note**
> A one-to-many relationship exists between the functional area and company codes as well.

To set up a functional area in SAP S/4HANA, execute Transaction OKBD or follow IMG menu path **Enterprise Structure • Definition • Financial Accounting • Define Functional Area**. You'll arrive at the screen shown in Figure 2.35, where you can either view existing functional areas or create new ones by clicking on the **New Entries** button.

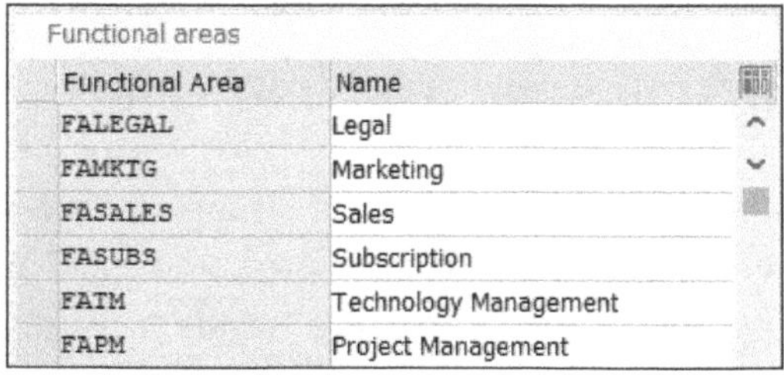

Functional areas

Functional Area	Name
FALEGAL	Legal
FAMKTG	Marketing
FASALES	Sales
FASUBS	Subscription
FATM	Technology Management
FAPM	Project Management

Figure 2.35 Functional Area

From Figure 2.35, you can see setting up functional area is also a straightforward process with just two fields:

- **Functional Area**
  This field is a unique alphanumeric key used to represent a functional area.
- **Name**
  This field is used to describe the **Functional Area** field.

After filling in the relevant fields, click the **Save** button or press Ctrl+S to finish setting up the functional area.

2.3.9 Cost Center

Cost center is a controlling organizational component in SAP S/4HANA used to capture and track costs. Costs can be tracked based on business areas, geographies, vendors and so on, depending on how your company wants to analyze, capture, and report costs. Cost centers are associated with functional areas and profit centers.

Note

One cost center is generally assigned to only one profit center, but one profit center can be tied to multiple cost centers.

One cost center is often linked to one functional area, but one functional area can be linked to many cost centers.

To set up a cost center in SAP S/4HANA, execute Transaction KS01 or follow SAP menu path **Accounting • Controlling • Cost Center Accounting • Master Data • Cost Center • Individual Processing • KS01 – Create**. You'll be prompted to enter the controlling area under which you want to create a cost center. Enter the controlling area ("A000", in our example), and click the green checkmark. Next, enter the cost center number you want to create, enter a **Valid From** and **Valid To** date, and press Enter. You'll arrive at the screen shown in Figure 2.36.

As shown in Figure 2.36, cost center configuration has seven sections: header, **Basic data**, **Control**, **Templates**, **Address**, **Communication**, and **History**. Keeping the scope of this book in mind, we'll deep dive into header and **Basic data** sections only as they are important from sales and distributions integrations standpoint.

The header section has three fields:

- **Cost Center**
  This field represents the cost center number.
- **Controlling Area**
  This field represents the controlling area to which the cost center belongs.

- **Valid From/to**
  This field is used to indicate the validity dates of a cost center.

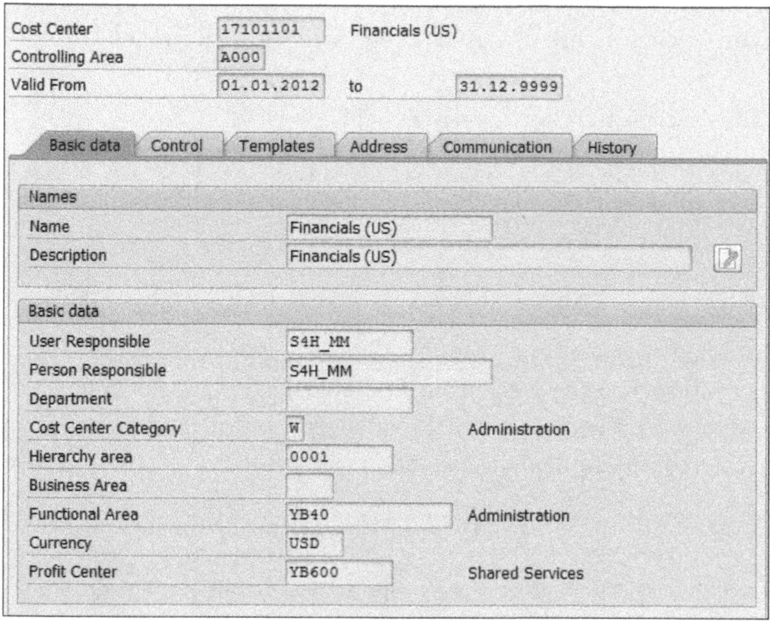

Figure 2.36 Cost Center

Next, the **Basic data** tab page is further divided into two subsections:

- **Names**, which has two fields:
  - **Name**: This field represents the name of the cost center.
  - **Description**: This field describes the cost center name.
- **Basic data**, which has the following fields:
  - **User Responsible**: This field represents the user ID of the person responsible for the cost center.
  - **Person Responsible**: This field displays the person's name who is responsible for the cost center.
  - **Department**: This field represents the department to which the cost center belongs.
  - **Cost Center Category**: This field represents the category to which the cost center belongs.

Note

You can configure cost center categories using IMG menu path **Controlling • Cost Center Accounting • Master Data • Cost Centers • Define Cost Center Categories**. Further detail is beyond the scope of this book.

- **Hierarchy area**: This field represents the hierarchy area to which the cost center belongs.
- **Business Area**: This field represents the business area to which the cost center belongs.
- **Functional Area**: This field represents the functional area to which the cost center belongs.
- **Currency**: This field represents the cost center currency.
- **Profit Center**: This fields represents the profit center to which the cost center is associated.

After filling in the relevant fields, click the **Save** button or press Ctrl+S to finish setting up the cost center.

2.3.10 Profit Center

Profit center is a financial accounting/controlling organizational component in SAP S/4HANA used for tracking profits based on areas of responsibility. Profit centers are used for profitability reporting and segment reporting. Profit centers are tied to profit center hierarchies and controlling areas.

Note

You can link one profit center to many controlling areas.

To set up a profit center in SAP S/4HANA, execute Transaction KE51 or follow SAP menu path **Accounting • Controlling • Profit Center Accounting • Master Data • Profit Center • Individual Processing • KE51 – Create**. When prompted, enter the controlling area under which you want to create the profit center, and click the green checkmark. Next, enter the profit center number you want to create and press Enter. You'll arrive at the screen shown in Figure 2.37.

The profit center configuration screen has seven sections: **General Data**, **Basic Data**, **Indicators**, **Company Codes**, **Address**, **Communication**, and **History**. For profit centers, we'll deep dive into the **General Data**, **Basic Data**, **Indicators**, and **Company Codes** sections only as they hold more weightage from a sales and distribution integration standpoint.

As shown in Figure 2.37, the **General Data** section has three fields:

- **Profit Center**
  This field represents the profit center number.
- **Controlling Area**
  This field represents the controlling area to which the profit center belongs.

- **Validity Period**
  This field is used to indicate the validity period of a profit center.

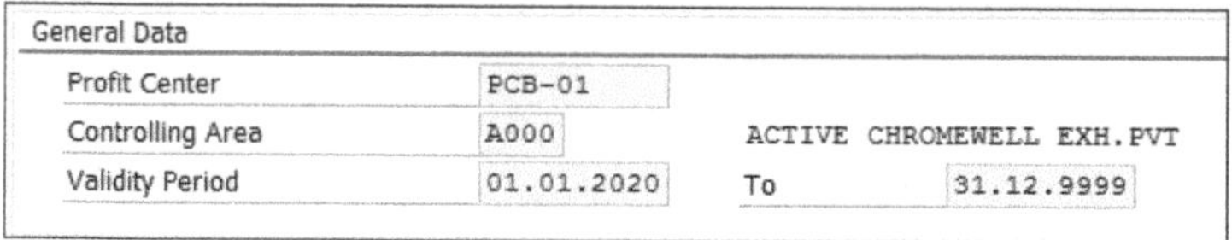

Figure 2.37 Profit Center: General Data

As shown in Figure 2.38, the **Basic Data** section is further divided into two subsections:

- **Descriptions**, which has the following fields:
  - **Profit Center**: This field represents the profit center number.
  - **Status**: This field represents the profit center status. Profit center can have either of these four statuses: **Inactive: Create**, **Inactive: Change**, **Inactive: Delete**, or **Active**.
  - **Analysis Period**: This field is used to indicate the analysis period of a profit center. The analysis period is a subset of the validity period. If within a validity period, you want more than one analysis period based on profit center master data, you can do so using this field. For example, say the validity period for profit center PCB-01 is **01.01.2020** to **31.12.9999**, and, within that, there are multiple five-year analysis periods such as 01/01/2020 to 31/12/2025, 01/01/2026 to 31/12/2030, and so on.
  - **Name**: This field represents the name of the profit center.
  - **Long Text**: This field represents the long text used to describe a profit center.

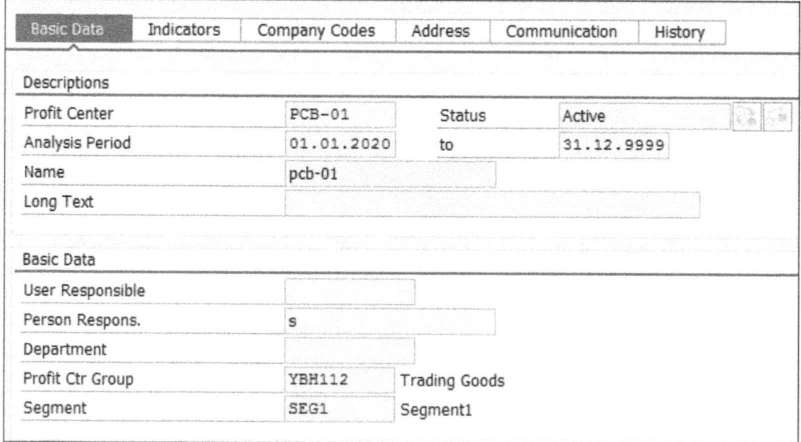

Figure 2.38 Profit Center Basic Data

- **Basic Data**, which has the following fields:
  - **User Responsible**: This field represents the user ID of the person responsible for the profit center.
  - **Person Respons.**: This field displays the person's name responsible for the profit center.
  - **Department**: This field represents the department to which the profit center belongs.
  - **Profit Ctr Group**: This field represents category group to which the profit center belongs. A collection of profit centers logically grouped together based on business requirements is known as a profit center group. For example, all profit centers belonging to the human resources team can be grouped under the HRPC group (human resource profit center group) or all trading goods for a company can be grouped together under a **Trading Goods** profit center group called **YBH112**, as shown in Figure 2.38.
  - **Segment**: This field represents the segment to which the profit center is tied. We'll discuss segments further in the next section.

As shown in Figure 2.39, the **Indicators** section has two subsections:

- **Indicator**, which has two fields:
  - **Dummy Profit Ctr**: This checkbox indicates if a profit center is a dummy profit center for a controlling area. As the same suggests, a dummy profit center is a pseudo profit center and not a real profit center. The numbers that don't qualify to be posted to a real profit center can be posted to a dummy profit center. Dummy profit center numbers can later be evaluated by a finance user and moved to a real profit center depending on business needs.
  - **Lock indicator**: This field indicates if a profit center is locked for postings. As a best practice, you should not delete profit centers from the system but rather lock them when they are no longer needed. By selecting this checkbox, a profit center is locked for postings.
- **Formula Planning**, which has one field, **Form. Planning Temp.**, which represents the template for formula planning in a profit center. A formula is a group of user-defined logical rules used for planning costs, revenue, balance sheet, and other statistical requirements. Formulas are independent and can be used for various profit centers depending on financial organizational needs.

Finally, as shown in Figure 2.40, the **Company Codes** tab is used to assign/unassign company codes to a profit center. To do so, you must first assign a company code to a controlling area using Transaction OX19. Then, in Transaction KE56, you must assign a company code to a profit center. Once you've done this, you'll see the company code entity under the **Company Codes** section, as shown in Figure 2.40. You can then use the checkbox to check or uncheck assignments based on your requirements. If you want the company code to be assigned the profit center, you can check the checkbox, or if you want to remove the link between company code and profit center, you simply uncheck the checkbox.

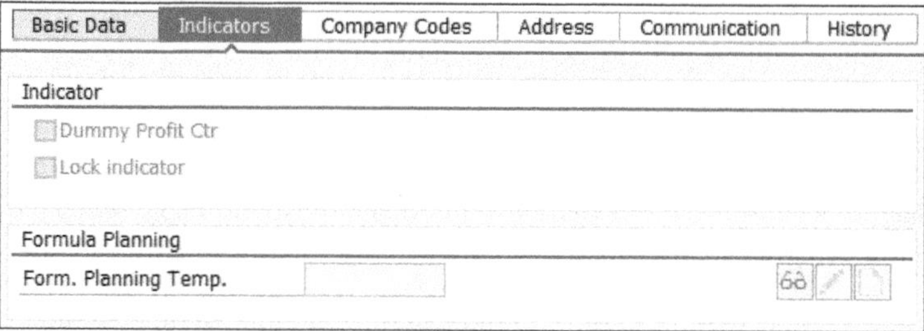

Figure 2.39 Profit Center Indicators

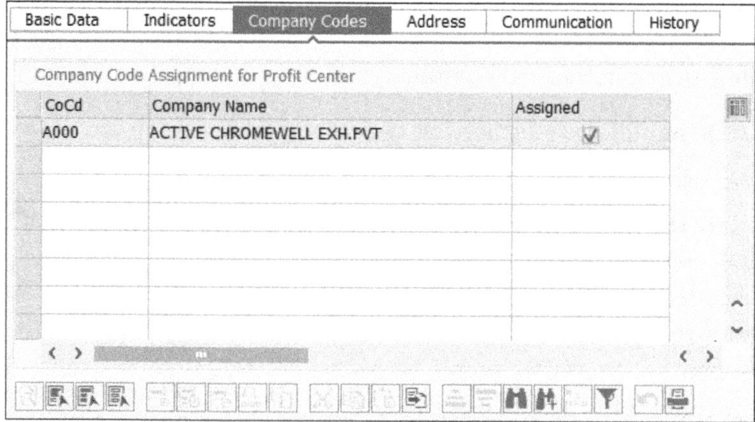

Figure 2.40 Profit Center Company Codes

> **Note**
>
> One profit center can be assigned to multiple company codes.

After filling in the relevant fields, click the **Save** button or press [Ctrl]+[S] to finish setting up the profit center.

2.3.11 Segment

Segment is a finance organizational component in SAP S/4HANA and is used for generating reports based on various segments configured within the system. Depending on your business processes, segments can be department specific (e.g., sales, marketing, IT), product specific (e.g., license, subscription), and/or location specific (e.g., India, United States).

To set up a segment in SAP S/4HANA, follow IMG menu path **Enterprise Structure • Definition • Financial Accounting • Define Segment**. You'll arrive at the screen shown in Figure 2.41, where you can either view existing segments or create new ones by clicking on the **New Entries** button.

Segment	Description
S4SALES	Sales Segment
S4MARKET	Marketing Segment
S4IT	IT Segment
S4LIC	License Segment
S4SUBS	Subscription Segment
S4IND	India Segment
S4USA	United States Segment

Figure 2.41 Segment

As shown in Figure 2.41, segment configuration is very straightforward and has only two fields:

- **Segment**
  This field represents the unique alphanumeric code used for the segment.
- **Description**
  This field describes the segment.

After filling in the relevant fields, click the **Save** button or press Ctrl+S to finish setting up the segment.

2.4 Project System

In this section, we'll focus on Project System's organizational structure components that are useful for sales and distribution integration in SAP S/4HANA. The Project System functionality involves planning and organizing various tasks in a project wheel of life. Resource-related billing (RRB) is one of the prime integration points between sales and distribution and Project System. While we'll deep dive into RRB in Chapter 7, in this section, you'll get insights into Project System components needed for RRB to function successfully.

Note

Project System doesn't have an organizational structure; it uses components from other organization structures, such as sales and distribution, finance, and materials management, to derive its data.

In an RRB process, for Project System components to work seamlessly, you must first make sure sales and distribution components are configured correctly.

Let's look at the following Project System components now: projects, work breakdown structure (WBS), networks, and activities.

2.4.1 Projects

Projects can be defined as a collection of tasks, planned and organized in a strategic manner and targeted to meet end goals of business requirements. Projects are time, resource, and cost sensitive, meaning that a successful project should be completed within committed deadlines, shouldn't exceed allocated resources, and should be within an estimated budget.

To create a project in SAP S/4HANA, execute Transaction CJ20N or follow SAP menu path **Logistics • Project System • Project • CJ20N – Project Builder**. From the Project Builder screen, as shown in Figure 2.42, navigate to **Project • New • Project.**

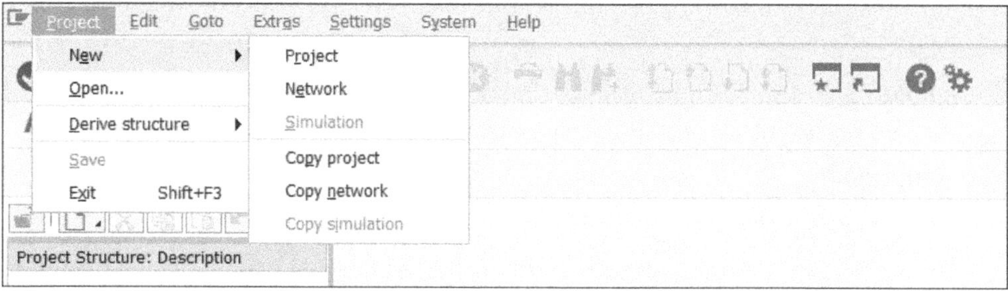

Figure 2.42 Creating a Project

In Chapter 7, Section 7.1.2, we'll deep dive into integration-relevant fields within a project.

2.4.2 Work Breakdown Structure

The tasks that define a project are logically grouped together into structures, called *work breakdown structures (WBSs)*. A project is a group of WBSs, which help break a huge project into smaller deliverables where each deliverable is denoted by a WBS. A WBS is normally represented by a hierarchy of elements called *WBS elements*.

To create a WBS element in SAP S/4HANA, execute Transaction CJ20N or follow SAP menu path **Logistics • Project System • Project • CJ20N – Project Builder**. From the Project Builder screen, after creating or searching for your project, navigate to **Create • WBS element**, as shown in Figure 2.43.

In Chapter 7, Section 7.1.3, we'll deep dive into integration-relevant fields within a WBS.

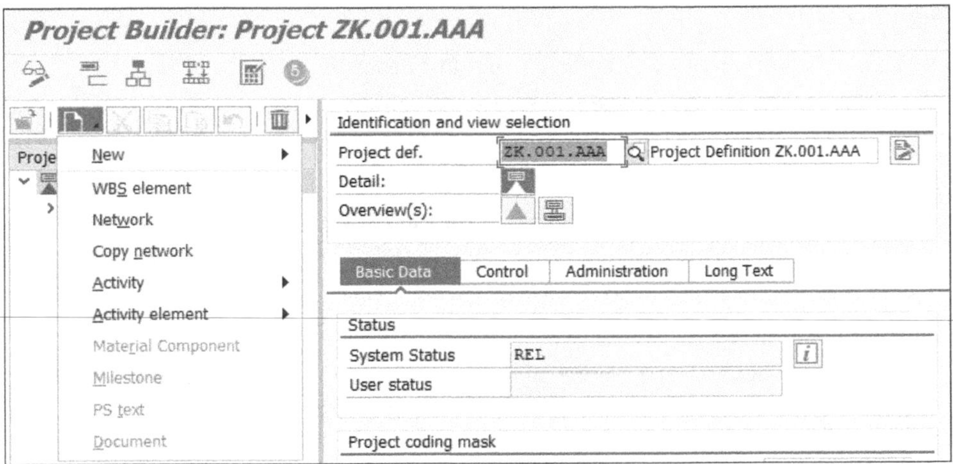

Figure 2.43 Creating a WBS

2.4.3 Networks

Networks can be defined as a group of activities used to track time, resources, and costs associated with a project. Networks are components of WBSs within which activities are sequenced in a logical manner and have a time quotient associated to them.

To create a network in SAP S/4HANA, execute Transaction CJ20N, or follow SAP menu path **Logistics • Project System • Project • CJ20N – Project Builder**. From the Project Builder screen, as shown in Figure 2.44, navigate to **Project • New • Network**.

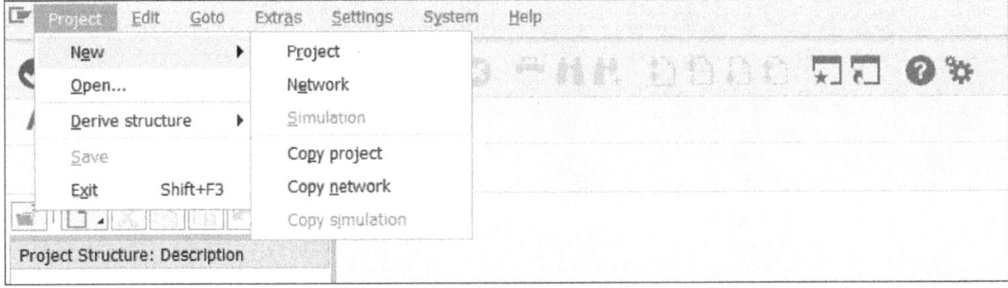

Figure 2.44 Creating a Network

> **Note**
>
> Networks don't play any role in sales and distribution–Project System integration using RRB, which is why they are outside the scope of this book.

2.4.4 Activities

Activities are components of a network that are basically time-based tasks (i.e., tasks with start and end dates) completed by using project resources at a certain estimated cost. There are three types of activities available in Project System:

- **Internal activities**
  Internal activities are tasks performed internally within an organizational component, for example, work center and/or plant. Activities include planning actual work commitments, internal dates, and so on.
- **External activities**
  External activities are tasks performed from outside an organizational component, for example, purchasing organization and/or purchasing group. Activities include planning of services, external dates, and so on.
- **Cost activities**
  General cost activities are tasks performed for planning costs for a network or a project. Cost activities include both internal and external costs. Cost activities are generally associated or tied to a plant, for example, labor cost, logistics cost, and so on.

To create activities in SAP S/4HANA, execute Transaction CJ20N or follow SAP menu path **Logistics • Project System • Project • CJ20N – Project Builder**. Create a new WBS (as shown in Section 2.4.2) or find an existing one. Then right-click on the WBS in the **Project Structure: Description** column on the left-hand side, go to **Create**, and select the type of activity you want to add (see Figure 2.45).

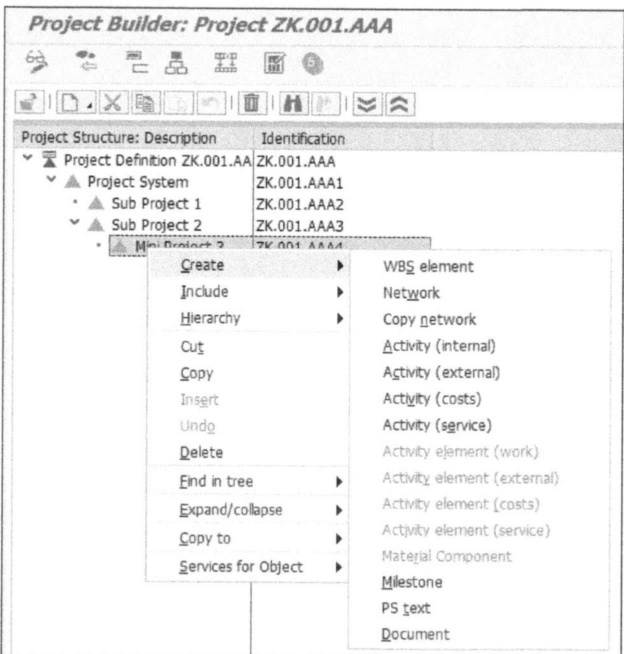

Figure 2.45 Creating an Activity

2.5 Peripheral Systems

In this section, we'll talk about structural components of SAP Revenue Accounting and Reporting and SAP Concur that are relevant for sales and distribution integration. Because SAP Revenue Accounting and Reporting and SAP Concur aren't organizational entities in SAP S/4HANA, they don't have an organizational structure. They do have a modular structure though, using which they derive intermodular and intramodular data. By the end of this section, you'll have a good understanding of the following:

- Modular components of SAP Revenue Accounting and Reporting used in sales and distribution–SAP Revenue Accounting and Reporting integrations to record and report revenues
- Modular components of SAP Concur used in sales and distribution–SAP Concur integrations to derive expense data into the RRB process

2.5.1 SAP Revenue Accounting and Reporting

SAP Revenue Accounting and Reporting is SAP's response to the Generally Accepted Accounting Principles (GAAP) and International Financial Reporting Standards (IFRS) 15 regulations made mandatory in January 2018. SAP Revenue Accounting and Reporting follows the five-step model of IFRS 15 and is structurally made of two key components: contracts and performance obligations (POBs). We'll discuss both in the following sections.

Contracts

Contracts are the highest level of structural components within the revenue account and reporting (RAR) functionality. Data arriving from various source systems into RAR is logically combined to create a RAR contract. Contracts are made up of POBs. Contract and POBs together help determine transactional price, standalone selling price (SSP), and allocation.

To configure revenue accounting contracts in SAP S/4HANA, execute Transaction FARR_IMG, and then set up nodes under the **Revenue Accounting Contracts** section, as shown in Figure 2.46.

We'll look at revenue account contracts in detail in Chapter 6, Section 6.2 and Section 6.3.

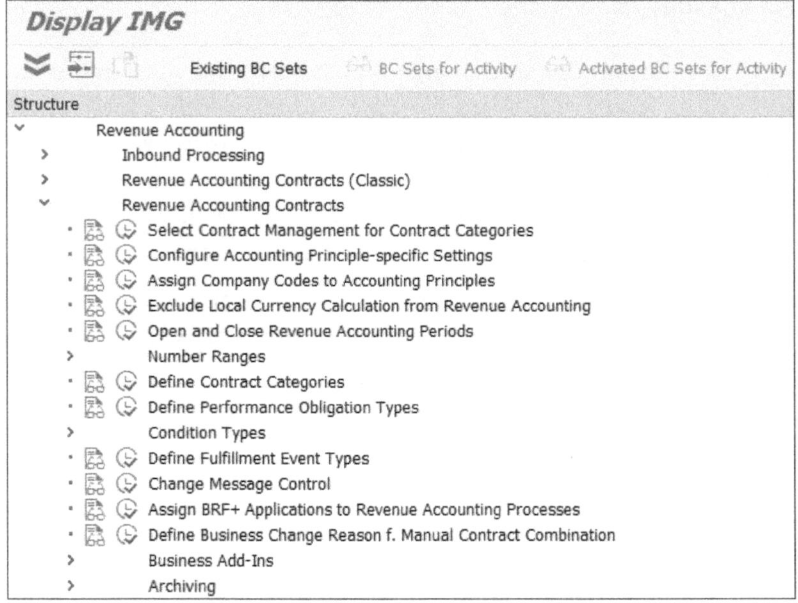

Figure 2.46 Revenue Accounting Contracts

Performance Obligations

POBs are second-level structural components within a RAR functionality. POBs represent line-item data of the source document or the source contract. For example, a sales order from sales and distribution = a revenue contract in RAR, and sales order line items from sales and distribution = POBs in RAR. The trigger for revenue recognition is fulfillment, which happens at the POB level.

We'll look at POB types in detail in Chapter 6, Section 6.2 and Section 6.3.

2.5.2 SAP Concur

SAP Concur is SAP's travel and expense cloud solution. SAP Concur offers three key solutions: Concur Expense, Concur Invoice, and Concur Travel. In this book, we'll touch on Concur Expense frequently, especially when we look at RRB in Chapter 7. For this section, we'll look at two structural components for Concur Expense that will help you understand RRB and other sales and distribution–SAP Concur integration topics better: expenses and employee.

Expenses

In a corporate setup, when we make transactions that involve the use of funds, we normally charge those transactions to our company's cost center or WBS. These transactions are called *expenses*. For example, say you purchased an SAP PRESS book on sales and distribution integrations in SAP S/4HANA using your corporate card. The purchase transaction created an expense record that moved from the bank to SAP Concur using credit card integration.

You submit expenses for reimbursements through expense reports. Each expense has a unique expense type. Typically, for every expense type, there is an equivalent material record in SAP S/4HANA. Figure 2.47 shows what a standard expense type looks like in SAP Concur.

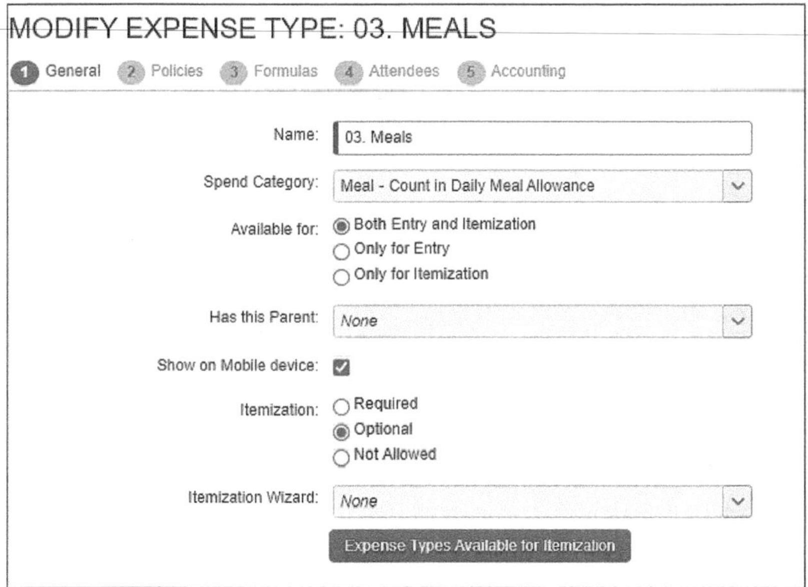

Figure 2.47 Expense Type

You'll learn more about expense types, expense reports, SAP material records, and how data maps from SAP Concur to sales and distribution in Chapter 7, Section 7.4.

Employees

Employees are people submitting expense reports. SAP Concur just hosts employee data coming in from the SAP S/4HANA system; it doesn't create employee records of its own. It uses employee data to drive user details and accounting information, which are key integration points from sales and distribution to SAP Concur in the RRB process. Figure 2.48 shows what a standard employee record looks like in SAP Concur.

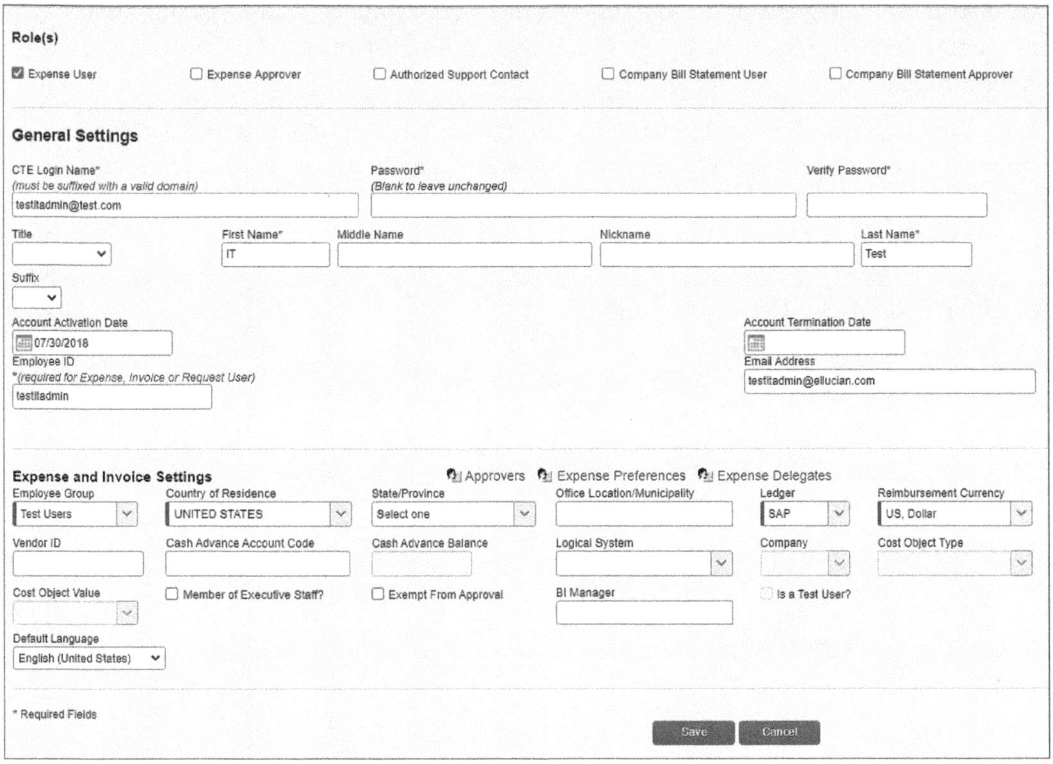

Figure 2.48 Employee Record

There are many fields on the employee record screen that are important for SAP Concur expense processes, but from the sales and distribution–Project System integration standpoint, they don't contribute a lot. Having said that, a few key fields under the **Expense and Invoice Settings** section are vital for the sales and distribution–Project System integration, which is what we'll focus on:

- **Ledger**
  If your company has multiple ledgers, and only one of them must be linked to expense reports and travel, then you should maintain that ledger in this field so any transactions posted by the employee in SAP Concur will automatically hit that ledger in SAP S/4HANA system. For example, say a company has different ledgers defined in SAP and Oracle systems, but SAP Concur-related postings must only happen in SAP. In this case, the ledger field should have the value **SAP** for all employee records in SAP Concur.

- **Reimbursement Currency**
  This field represents the currency type in which the employee expects reimbursements to be processed. Generally, reimbursement currency matches the country or the company code the employee belongs to. For example, an employee belonging to an India company code will have reimbursement currency INR, whereas an employee belonging to a US company code will have reimbursement currency USD.

- **Company**
  This field is generally mapped to a company code field in SAP. Like reimbursement currency, if an employee belongs to an India company code, their company will be listed as India in the employee record versus the employee who lives in the US, who will have USA listed as the company.
- **Cost Object Type**
  This field maps to different cost object types available in SAP S/4HANA. For most SAP Concur projects we've worked on, we've mainly seen two cost object types: cost center and WBS. If an employee submits an expense report that is project driven, then it will have WBS as the cost object type; if the employee is submitting a general expense report (let's say for a conference), then it will have cost center as the cost object type.
- **Cost Object Value**
  This field represents the value of the cost object type. If the cost object type is a cost center, then the value will be the cost center number; if the cost object type is a WBS, then the value will be the WBS code.

2.6 Summary

After reading this chapter, you're now well equipped with structural components of various organizations and functionalities in SAP S/4HANA. Having this knowledge adds tremendous value to your resume, but we won't stop here. Let's hold on to this foundation as we progress through our journey of becoming integration champions of the sales and distribution functionality in SAP S/4HANA.

Here is a summary of what we covered in this chapter:

- In Section 2.1, you learned about sales organization, distribution channel, and division, plus how these three components come together to form the sales area, which is the core of the sales and distribution organizational structure. A very important tip handed out in this section was to always copy an entity while configuring a new one rather than starting from scratch. It saves valuable time and resources.
- In Section 2.2, you learned about plant, storage location, purchasing organization and purchasing group, and why they are key components of the materials management organizational structure. The plant from the material master flows over to the sales order in sales and distribution. The storage location from the mater master controls sales delivery in sales and distribution. For any purchasing done by a purchasing organization, purchasing groups help implement purchasing activities.
- In Section 2.3, you learned that finance and controlling functionalities in SAP S/4HANA are often used in conjunction. While this section was primarily focused on the finance organizational structure components, we also ventured into a few controlling components. We looked at financial accounting/controlling components

such as client, operating concern, credit controlling area, controlling area, company, company code, business area, functional area, cost center, profit center, and segment.

- In Section 2.4, you learned about projects, WBSs, networks, and activities, and why they are integral components of the Project System organizational structure. They are important for the RRB process, which is one of the main integration points between sales and distribution and Project System.
- In Section 2.5, you learned about two peripheral functionalities in SAP S/4HANA that integrate with sales and distribution very closely: SAP Revenue Accounting and Reporting and SAP Concur. We looked at key structural components of RAR: contracts and POBs, as well as key structural components of Concur Expense: expense type and employees.

Next, we'll cover more fundamental knowledge for sales and distribution integration: the key master data.

Chapter 3
Master Data

Master data acts as a cornerstone for a successful SAP S/4HANA implementation. From the perspective of integration, a thorough understanding of master data is essential. This knowledge is vital in understanding the intra-ERP integrations that we'll cover in this book.

The three types of data you'll see in SAP S/4HANA are master data, transactional data, and configuration data. Master data, which we'll discuss in this chapter, is stored centrally and used in day-to-day transactions. It's also used to derive further configuration elements in various business processes.

This chapter will explore the various master data elements related to business partners and the material master. In Section 3.1, we'll explore the configuration elements required to set up a business partner, and then we'll deep dive into each role of the business partner in detail. In Section 3.2, we'll study essential views in material master, such as the **Basic data** view, **Sales: sales org.** data views, **MRP** views, and **Accounting** views.

> **Note**
>
> Throughout this chapter, there are many adjacent configuration activities that are beyond the scope of our focus on the key integration points with sales and distribution. We've provided configuration text boxes to give some information on these activities to get you started.

Let's start with the business partner master data.

3.1 Business Partner

A *business partner* is a central object in SAP S/4HANA for storing the data related to master data objects of the various business processes. The same customer can also act as a vendor in business scenarios. Business partners provide the advantage to create a synergy between the master data objects and reduce the data redundancy or duplicity by storing the data in a single transaction. Due to the integrated nature of the business process, understanding various business partner roles is key to understanding the integration points of sales and distribution with other functionalities.

We'll discuss business partner master data in two parts in the following sections. In Section 3.1.1, we'll briefly discuss the configuration elements of the business partner, and in the subsequent sections, we'll explore the different views of the business partner.

3.1.1 Business Partner Configuration

Let's explore the various configuration parameters for a business partner, including the business partner role, business partner role category, field attributes for the business partner role category, number ranges, and business partner types.

Business Partner Role and Role Categories

The *business partner role* defines the function of the business partner and business transactions in which it can be involved. The business partner role controls the field status, that is, **Optional** or **Mandatory**, within the business partner. SAP has provided the standard business partner roles, which, in most cases, are sufficient to meet all requirements. If a custom business partner role is required, you can create it by copying an existing role.

To define business partner roles, execute Transaction SPRO and follow the menu path **Cross-Application Components • SAP Business Partner • Business Partner • Basic Settings • Business Partner Roles • Define BP Roles**. You'll arrive at the list of business partner customer roles. Select the desired role from the list, and click on the **Details** icon to arrive at the screen in Figure 3.1, which shows the standard customer role **FLCU01** for our example.

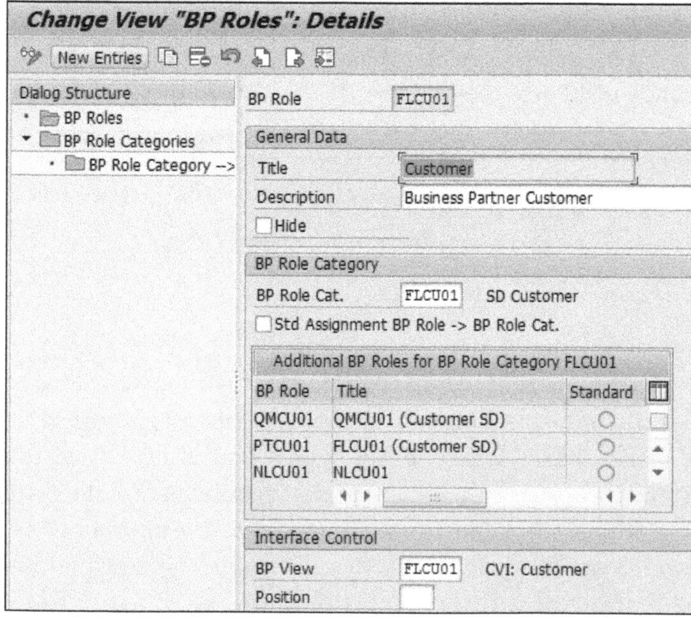

Figure 3.1 Business Partner Roles

On this screen, fill in the following fields to define your business partner role:

- **Title**
  If you're creating a custom role, include the name and title of the business partner role in this field. In our example, we're creating a **Customer** role.
- **Hide**
  This field allows you to hide the irrelevant business partner roles that aren't required in the business partner setup.
- **BP Role Category**
  The business partner role category is assigned in the business partner role. It controls the field's status of the business partner role. The relationship between the business partner role categories and business partner role is 1: N, which means the same business partner role category can be assigned to multiple business partner roles.
- **Additional BP Roles for BP Role Category**
  You can assign additional roles for which the same business partner role category is used. We'll discuss the business partner role category in detail in the next section.
- **Interface Control**
  This section controls the screen elements in dialog mode during creation of the business partner. The recommended approach is to maintain the default business partner view, which is given by standard SAP.

The next step in the business partner setup configuration is to define the business partner role category, which you assign back into the desired business partner role. To create the business partner role category, follow the menu path **Cross-Application Components • SAP Business Partners • Business Partner • Basic Settings • Define BP Roles • BP Role Categories**. You'll arrive at the screen shown in Figure 3.2.

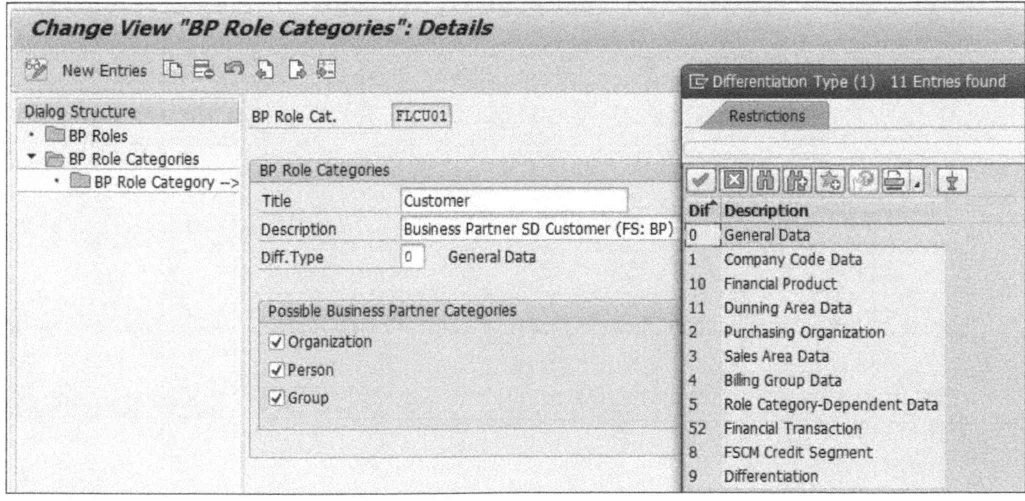

Figure 3.2 Business Partner Role Categories

You'll need to fill in the following fields for the business partner role category:

- **Title**
  Here, you maintain the title of the business partner role category.
- **Description**
  You can keep the same description as the title here, but if you want a more detailed description, use this field.
- **Diff. Type**
  The differentiation type controls the data or the screens available while creating the business partner. SAP has provided various differentiation types based on the role of the business partner. When you click on this field, it opens the options shown on the right side of Figure 3.2. Use type **3** (**Sales Area Data**) for sales-specific maintenance.
- **Possible Business Partner Categories**
  The business partner role category also controls the possible business partner category, such as which category should be populated in the initial screen of business partner creation. You can choose from the following options:
  - **Organization**: If the business partner is an organization, such as XYZ Inc., select **Organization** as a business partner category when creating the business partner.
  - **Person**: When creating a business partner for an individual person, such as a contact person, select the **Person** business partner category.
  - **Group**: When creating a business partner for a group of people, such as the sales department of XYZ Inc., select **Group** as a business partner category while creating the business partner.

  As shown at the top of Figure 3.3, business partner categories **Organization**, **Person**, and **Group** are populated in the screen, as we've checked all business partner categories.

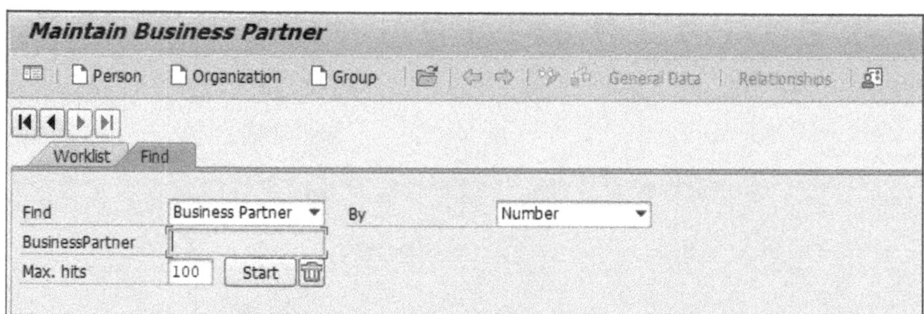

Figure 3.3 Maintain Business Partner: Initial Screen

Click on the **Save** icon from the SAP menu bar or press [Ctrl]+[S] to save the configuration.

Number Ranges in Business Partners

In SAP S/4HANA, every master data object is identified with a unique number. You can configure the number ranges related to the object and then assign the created number range to the master data object. You'll follow the same modus operandi for the business partner as well.

In business partner configuration, you need to set up a business partner number range and customer account group number range, as follows:

- **Customer account number range**

  First, create customer number ranges in the menu path **Financial Accounting • Account Receivable and Accounts Payable • Customer Accounts • Master Data • Preparation for Creating Customer Master Data • Create Number Ranges for Customer Accounts**. You'll arrive at the screen shown in Figure 3.4, where you'll select the **Intervals** button (with the pencil).

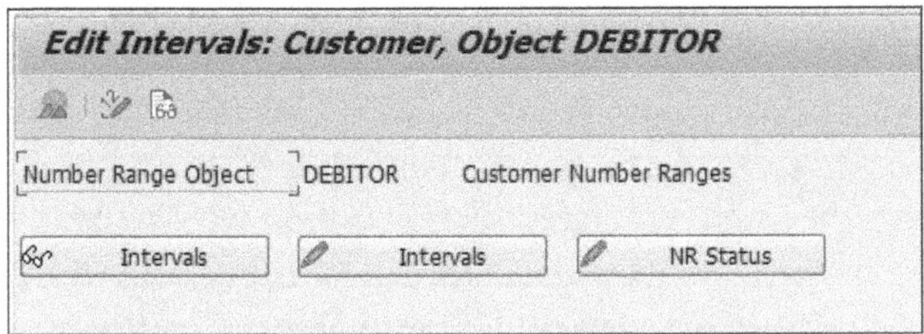

Figure 3.4 Customer Number Range: Initial Screen

  In the resulting screen shown in Figure 3.5, you can create a new number range by clicking on the **Insert Line** icon.

Edit Intervals: Customer, Object DEBITOR

N..	From No.	To Number	NR Status	Ext
01	0000000001	0000099999	10	☐

Figure 3.5 Customer Number Range

  In our example, we've created number range **01**, from **0000000001** to **0000099999**. The **NR Status** field displays the number of business partners that were created using the number range. When the **Ext** (external) checkbox is checked, the system considers the number range to be external. In this case, when creating a business partner, you must enter an available number from the number range. If you leave this checkbox unchecked, the system will select the next available number automatically from the number range for the business partner.

  After creating the number range, assign it to the customer account group in menu path **Financial Accounting • Account Receivable and Accounts Payable • Customer Accounts • Master Data • Preparation for Creating Customer Master Data • Assign**

Number Ranges to Customer Account Groups. Here, assign the **Number Range** to the customer **Group**, and click on **Save** or press Ctrl+S.

As shown in Figure 3.6, we've assigned number range **01** to customer account groups **0001**, **0002**, **0003**, and **0004**.

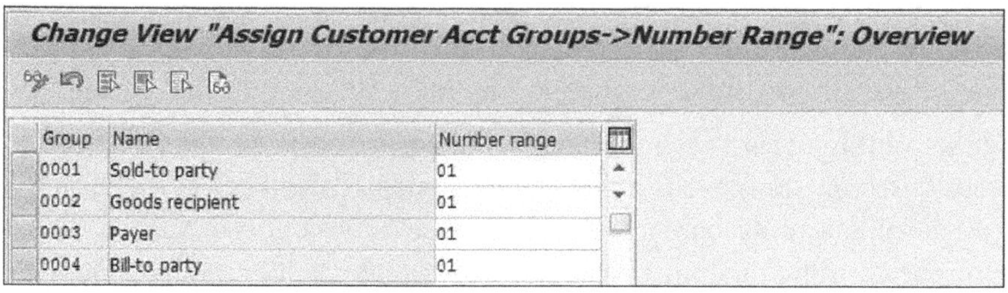

Change View "Assign Customer Acct Groups->Number Range": Overview

Group	Name	Number range
0001	Sold-to party	01
0002	Goods recipient	01
0003	Payer	01
0004	Bill-to party	01

Figure 3.6 Assign Number Range to Customer Account Group

Note

Numerous customer account groups can be assigned to one number range. Prior to SAP S/4HANA, in SAP ERP, we used to create the number ranges only for the customer account group while configuring the number ranges for the customer. In the SAP S/4HANA world, you have to configure the number ranges for both the customer account group and business partner. Usually, the process follows that for each account group, you need to create a similar business partner group as well.

- **Business partner number range**

  Define the business partner number range in menu path **Cross-Application Components • SAP Business Partner • Business Partner • Basic Settings • Number Ranges and Groupings • Define Number Ranges**. Follow similar steps that you followed for the customer account number range as explained earlier.

  In our example, we've defined business partner number range **01** from **0000001000** to **0000001999**, as shown in Figure 3.7.

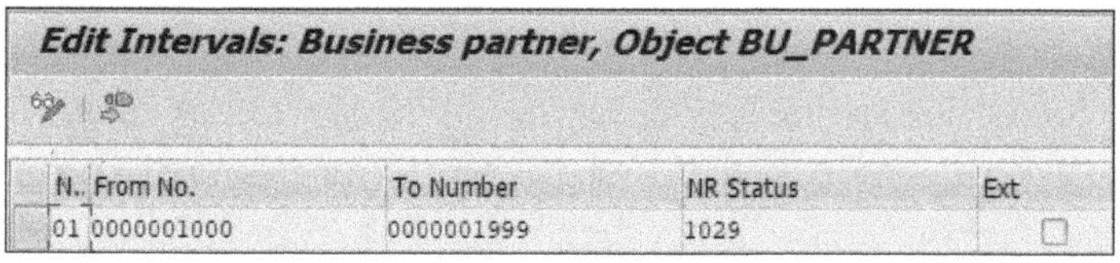

Edit Intervals: Business partner, Object BU_PARTNER

N..	From No.	To Number	NR Status	Ext
01	0000001000	0000001999	1029	☐

Figure 3.7 Business Partner Number Range: Define

Once the business partner number range is defined, assign it to business partner groupings in the menu path **Cross-Application Components • SAP Business Partner • Business Partner • Basic Settings • Number Ranges and Groupings • Define Groupings and Assign Number Ranges**. Here, assign the number range (**Number ra...**) with the business partner **Grouping**.

The business partner number range is now assigned to business partner grouping **0001**, as shown in Figure 3.8.

Display View "BP groupings": Overview

Grouping	Short name	Description	Number ra...	External	Int.Std.Grpi...	Ext.Std Grp
0001	Int.no.assgnmt	Internal number assignment	01	☐	○	

Figure 3.8 Assign Business Partner Number Range to Business Partner Groupings

> **Note**
> When creating a business partner with Transaction BP, you should first select the grouping and then the business partner role. This will help adopt the number range we've assigned with the business partner grouping while creating a business partner for a particular role.

Exploring Various Business Partner Roles

In the previous section, we've explored the configuration that needs to be set up to create a business partner. Now we'll go through each business partner role in detail. We'll explore the general data role, customer sales role, financial accounting customer role, and credit management role. These roles are essential for understanding the sales and distribution integration points with other functionalities, which we'll talk about in subsequent chapters.

Transaction BP is used to create/display the business partner in SAP S/4HANA. As illustrated in Figure 3.9, in the **Find** tab, first select **Business Partner** in the **Find** field, and then choose **Number** in the **By** field. You can then enter the business partner number in the **BusinessPartner** field and press Enter to display the business partner.

To create a business partner with a **Person**, **Organization**, or **Group**, click the respective buttons, and the creation screen will be populated, as shown in Figure 3.10.

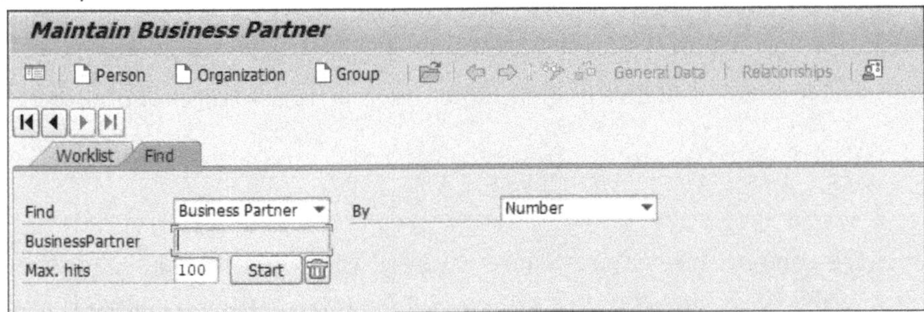

Figure 3.9 Business Partner: Initial Screen

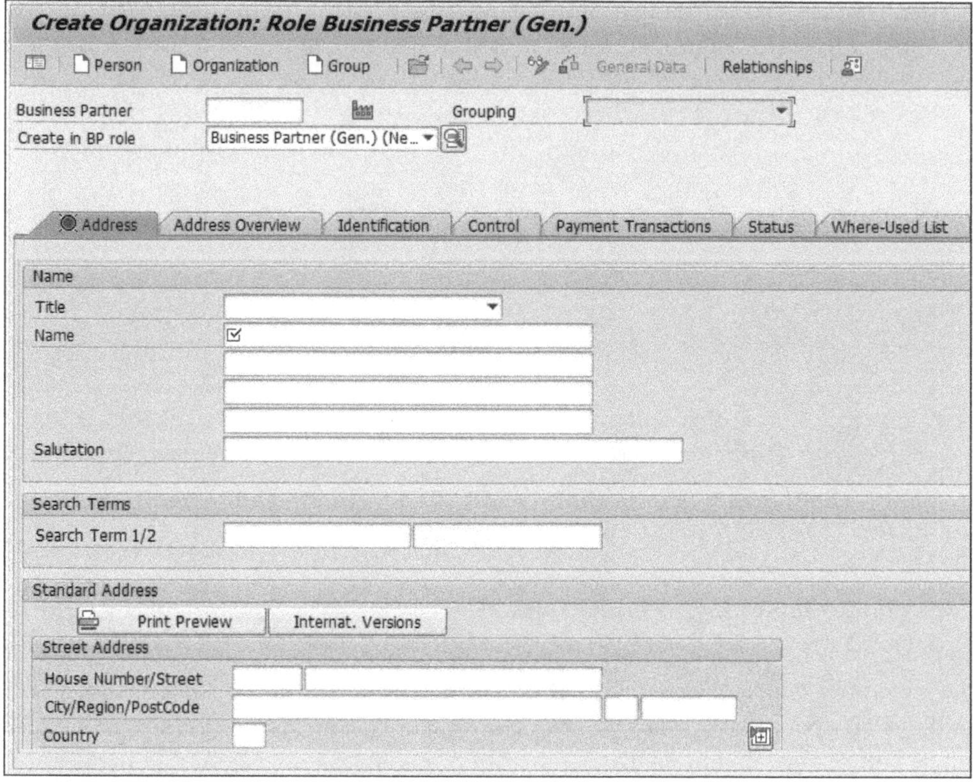

Figure 3.10 Business Partner: Create

Let's look at the significance of each role and field in the business partner master data in the following sections.

3.1.2 General Data Role

The *general data role* is common for all the views of the business partner. You can select it in the **Create in BP role** field (**Business Partner (Gen.)**, as shown previously in Figure 3.10. We'll briefly discuss the necessary fields related to the business processes that we'll cover in the book. All the data associated with the business partner roles are segregated into various tabs. We'll dive into each tab that is an important part of integration.

Address

The **Address** tab contains the relevant data associated with the title, name, address, search term, postal codes, and communication of a business partner. Figure 3.11 and Figure 3.12 show the **Address** view of a business partner in the general data role.

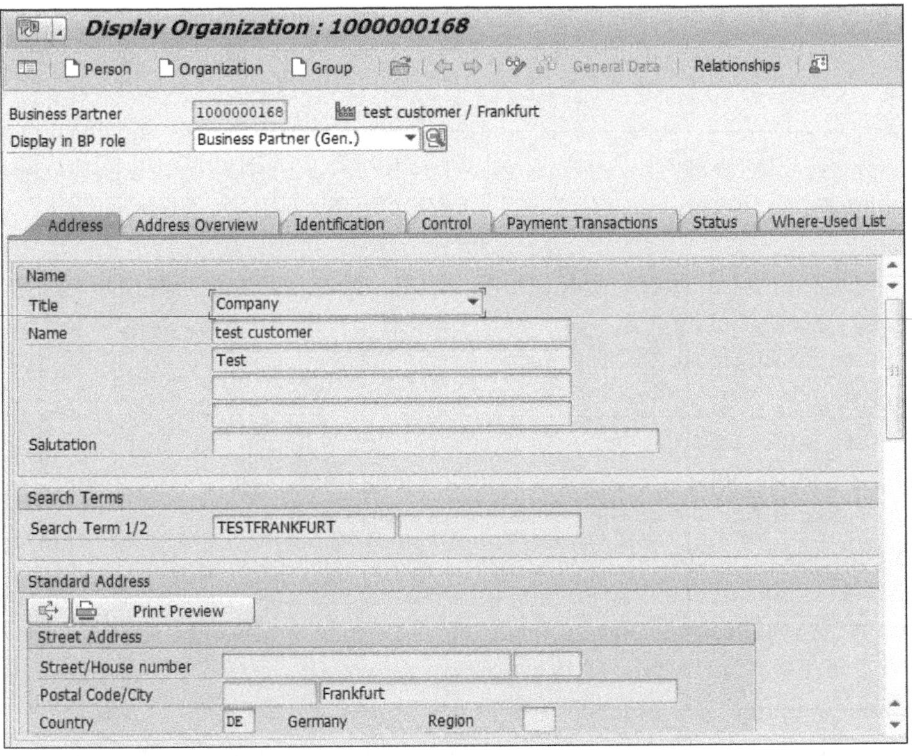

Figure 3.11 Business Partner General Data Role: Address (1 of 2)

Figure 3.12 Business Partner General Data Role: Address (2 of 2)

Fill in the following fields to set up the address data for business partner:

- **Title**
  This field states whether the business partner is a company or any group. You can maintain the titles in the check tables (this table checks if the data is available in the foreign key table field). The titles associated with the business partner are language dependent. You can choose the title that is appropriate for the business partner.
- **Name**
  The field corresponds to the name of the business partner. SAP has provided four fields to give the name of the customer/business partner. Organizations follow the set nomenclature for the naming purpose.
- **Salutation**
  This field can be used to greet the business partner while sending the printouts of any operational documents such as order confirmation, quotation, or billing. The salutation mentioned here will be used in print forms.
- **Search Terms**
  This field is used for a quick search of the business partners. For example, you can concatenate the customer's name and geography, such as APMollerDelhi or, in our case, **TESTFRANKFURT**, as shown in Figure 3.11.
- **Standard Address**
  This section comprises the business partner's address information, such as street address, city/region, postal code, country, and so on. The country key along with jurisdiction code helps in determining the taxes for the business partner in operational documents such as sales orders and invoices.
- **Transportation Zone**
  This is one of the parameters used to determine the route in the sales order. You can expand the standard address block to view the transportation zone of the business partner.
- **Communication**
  Here, you can maintain the communication mediums by which you can communicate with the business partner such as telephone number, mobile phone number, fax address, and email address.
- **External Address No.**
  If the address stored in the business partner is different from the address stored in the external system or the legacy system, then you can use this field (not shown) to save the address number of the external system for information purposes.
- **Address Valid From**
  You can maintain validity to the business partner address in this field.

Address Overview

You can maintain multiple addresses for one business partner in the **Address Overview** tab, which is shown in Figure 3.13.

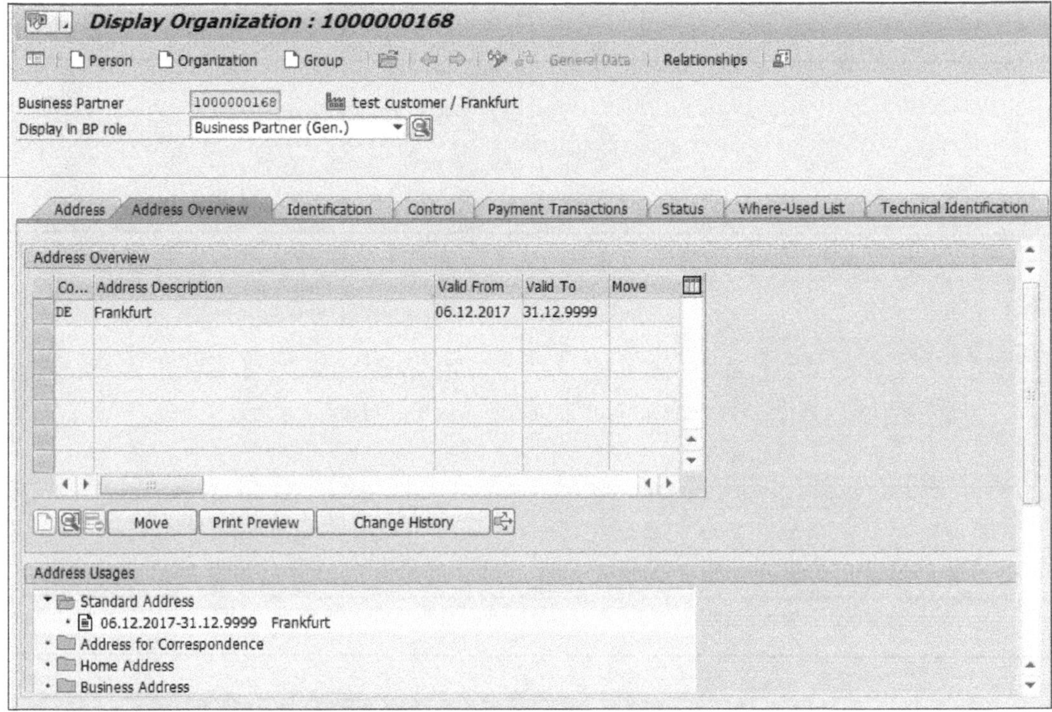

Figure 3.13 Business Partner General Data Role: Address Overview

To maintain other addresses, go to change mode of the business partner by clicking the **Change** icon in the **Address Overview** tab. Click the **Create** icon located at bottom of the **Address Overview** section to open the popup shown on the right side of Figure 3.14, where you can add the address details. Click the green checkmark when you're done. The new address will be displayed in the **Address Overview** section.

Now, assign this new address to the address type from the **Address Usages** section. Select the address type (**Business Address**, in our example), click on the **Create** icon to open the popup on the right side of Figure 3.15, and assign the new address by clicking the green checkmark.

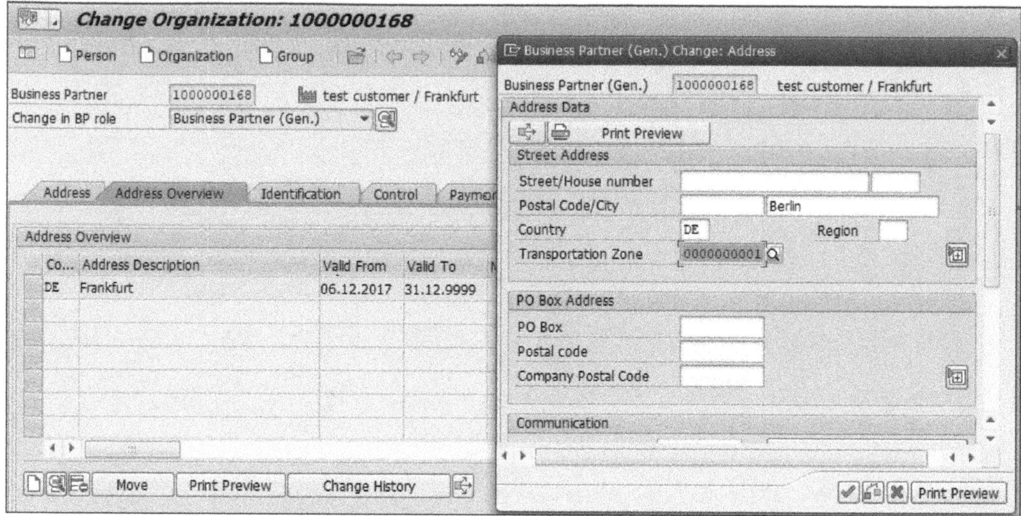

Figure 3.14 Business Partner General Data Role: Maintain New Address

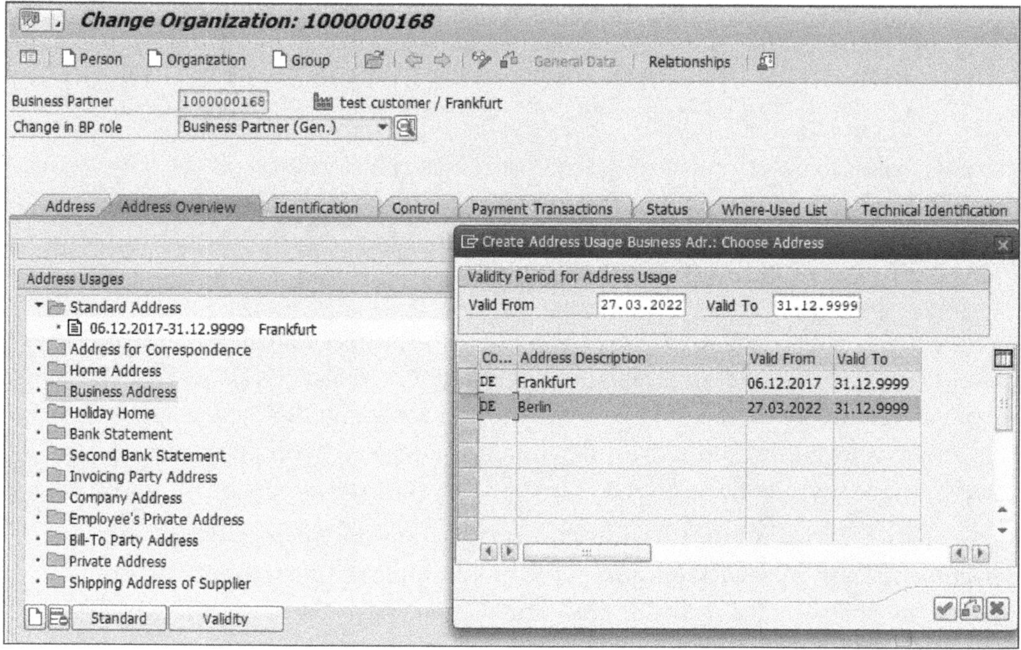

Figure 3.15 Business Partner General Data Role: Assign New Address

You can see the new address is assigned with **Business Address** in Figure 3.16.

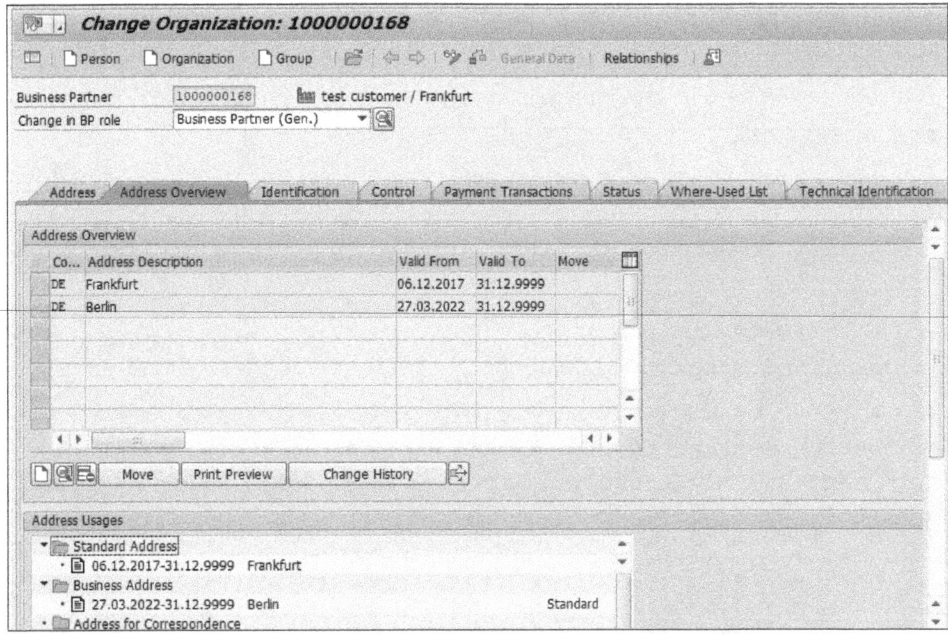

Figure 3.16 Business Partner General Data Role: Display Multiple Addresses

Control Tab

The **Control** tab, as shown in Figure 3.17, contains the general data associated with the business partner type, authorization group, and print format.

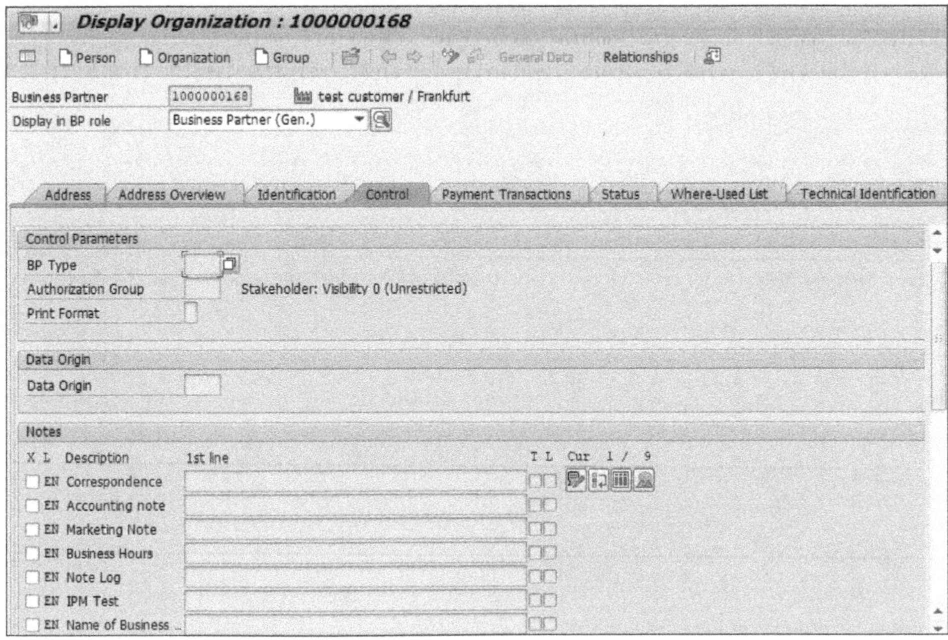

Figure 3.17 Business Partner General Data Role: Control

Fill in the following fields to set up the control data for the business partner:

- **BP Type**
  You can use this field to group business partners according to the client's needs.
- **Authorization Group**
  This field is used to restrict the users or person from accessing the business partner. You can assign the authorization group to any of the objects in SAP S/4HANA, such as table, program, and master data, and then drive the authorization objectives from it.

Configuration: Business Partner Type

The configuration of business partner type can be done by executing Transaction SPRO and following menu path **Cross Application Components • SAP Business Partners • Business Partner • Basic Settings • Business Partner Types • Define Business Partner Types**.

Figure 3.18 shows the standard business partner types.

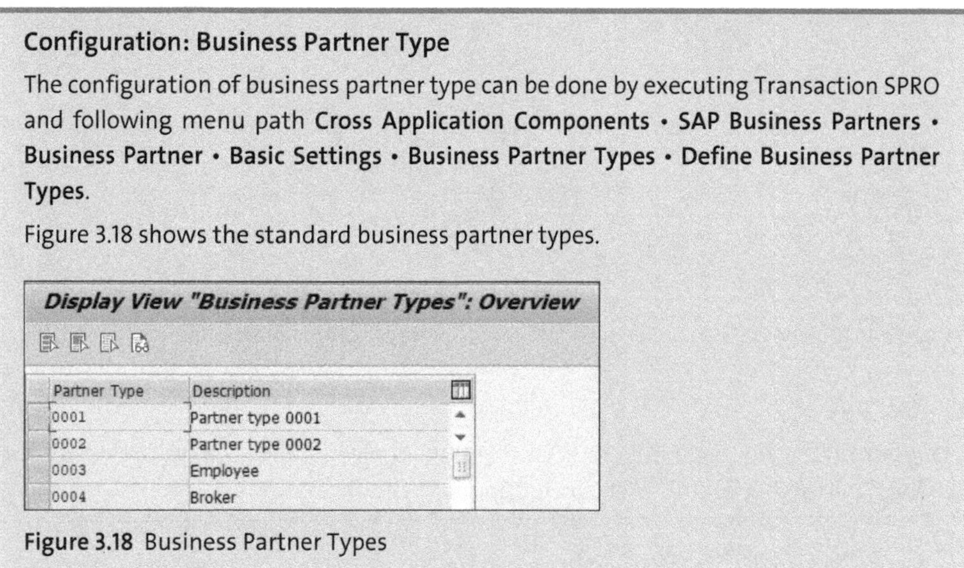

Display View "Business Partner Types": Overview

Partner Type	Description
0001	Partner type 0001
0002	Partner type 0002
0003	Employee
0004	Broker

Figure 3.18 Business Partner Types

3.1.3 Customer Role

In change mode, you can extend the business partner to the sales role FLCU01. After extending the business partner to the *customer role* by selecting **Customer** in the **Change in BP role** field, the **Sales Area** data view will get added to the screen. By clicking on the **Sales Area** data, you can fill in the appropriate sales-related data in the fields.

Note

You can extend the business partner to additional sales areas in the **Sales Area** data view. Similarly, you can use the **Switch Area** button to switch to the other sales area to view the sales-specific data of the business partner.

We'll now look at the fields in the **Sales Area** data view in detail. The sales area data is segregated based on the tabs, which we'll explore along with their relevant fields in the following subsections.

Orders

The **Orders** tab, as shown in Figure 3.19 and again later in Figure 3.22, plays an important role in the order-to-cash cycle. Fields such as **Item proposal** need an extra configuration layer, which is explained in this section.

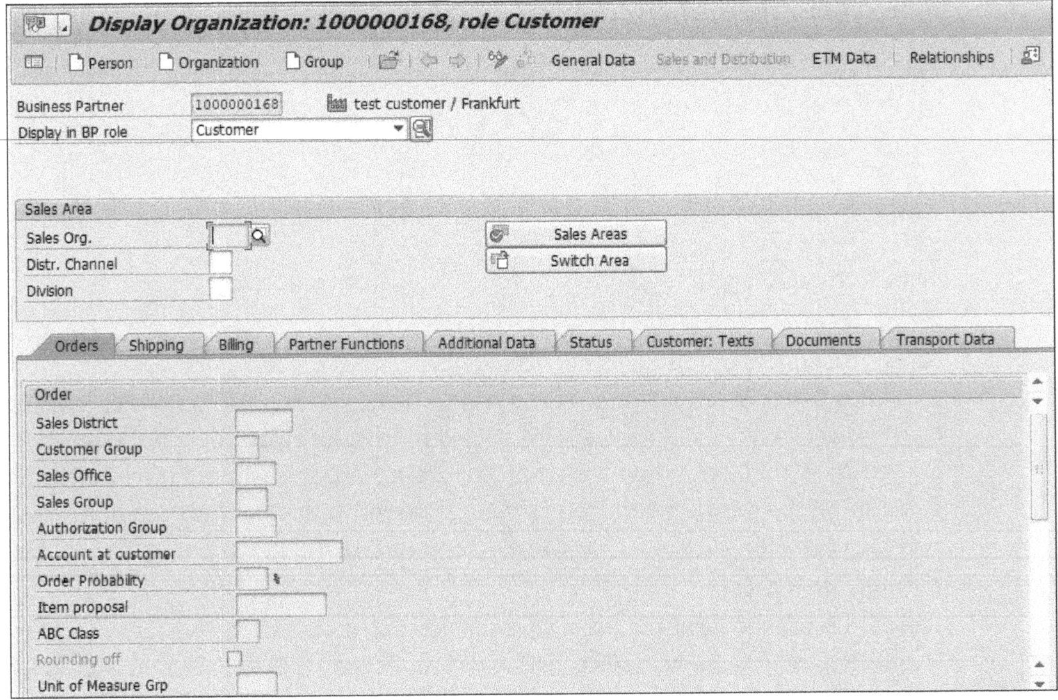

Figure 3.19 Business Partner Customer Role: Orders (1 of 2)

Fill in the following fields to setup the order data for the business partner customer role:

- **Sales District**
  This represents the sales region to which the customer belongs. The **Sales District** field is further used for setting up the prices maintained in the condition records as well as for reporting purposes. You can create your own sales district based on the market that you're serving. The created sales district is assigned in this field.

- **Customer Group**
  This two-digit alpha numeric character field is used to group customers based on specific attributes, such as their sales channel (e.g., dealer, distributor, institution, etc.).

Configuration: Customer Groups

You can create your own customer group using Transaction OVS9 by clicking on the **New Entries** button and giving the appropriate **Name**, as shown in Figure 3.20.

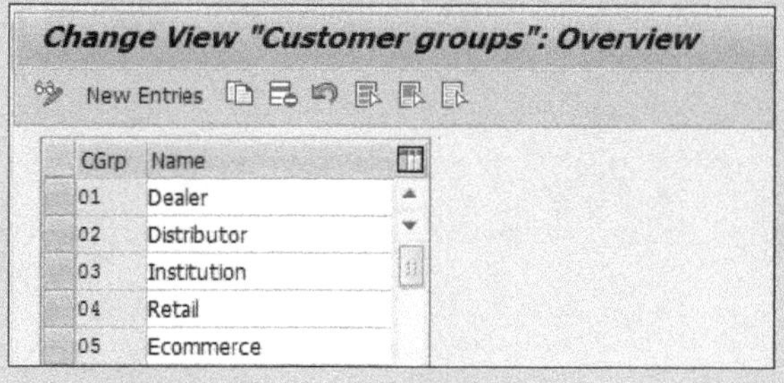

Change View "Customer groups": Overview

New Entries

CGrp	Name
01	Dealer
02	Distributor
03	Institution
04	Retail
05	Ecommerce

Figure 3.20 Customer Groups

- **Sales Office/Sales Group**
  The **Sales Office** is defined in the enterprise structure configurations and serves as the physical location of the sales team. One or more sales areas might be assigned to a sales office. The **Sales Group** represents the group of people who are responsible for performing the sales activity in that region. Based on the business requirements, you can create the sales offices and sales group and then assign them in these fields.
- **Authorization Group**
  The field is used to limit the users who can access the data in the business partner. It's created by an SAP governance, risk, and compliance (GRC) or Basis consultant. By assigning the authorization group in this field, you can restrain the users from viewing the data related to the **Sales Area** tab.
- **Account at customer**
  The field is used to store the company's number in the customer's system. This is for the reconciliation of the data that has been exchanged between the customer and the company.
- **Order Probability**
  This field is used to indicate the possibility of the business partner turning an inquiry or quotation into an order. It's mostly used for reporting purposes. This field can also be used for demand planning or capacity planning in material requirements planning (MRP). Based on the historical data associated with the business partner, you can update the order probability percentage in the field.
- **Item proposal**
  This field is used for the item proposal concept in sales and distribution. If a customer places orders for similar items on a regular basis, then rather than entering the items manually into the sales document each time, you create an item list and refer to it when creating a sales order. End users can save time by selecting goods from the list and copying them into the sales orders.

Configuration: Item Proposals

You can use Transaction VA51 to create an item proposal list. Create the item proposal document by entering the relevant data such as **Item Proposal Type, Sales Organization, Distribution Channel, Division, Sales office**, and **Sales group**, as shown in Figure 3.21.

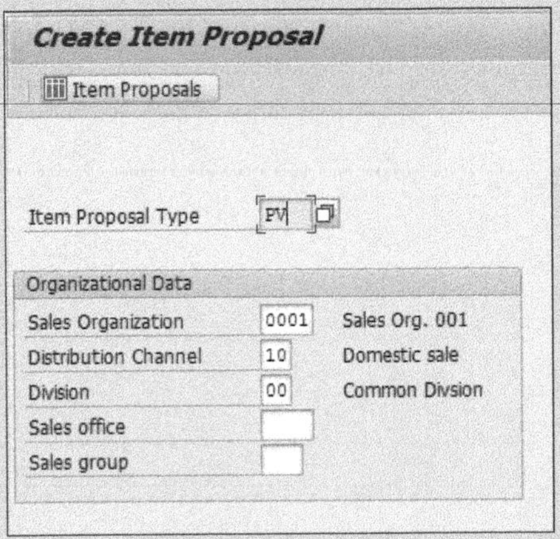

Create Item Proposal
Item Proposals
Item Proposal Type FV
Organizational Data
Sales Organization 0001 Sales Org. 001
Distribution Channel 10 Domestic sale
Division 00 Common Divsion
Sales office
Sales group

Figure 3.21 Create Item Proposal

Next, you must assign the created proposal number to the **Item proposal** field in the business partner.

- **ABC Class**
  This field is used for the classification of customers based on any set parameter given by the business. This field is used to generate the customer classification-based reports.
- **Currency**
  You must maintain the business partner currency in this field that will be used to create sales orders in SAP S/4HANA. If the customer currency varies from the company code currency, then, while performing a sales transaction, the values in the sales order will be in the customer currency but the accounting document generated post billing will use the company code currency. (This field and the following fields can be seen in Figure 3.22).

Configuration: Exchange Rates

To have the transactions in currency other than the company code currency, you have to maintain the exchange rates. SAP S/4HANA uses table TCURR to maintain this rate. The exchange rates need to be updated daily. In usual scenarios, an exchange rate file is received daily by the business from the bank at a specified time to update the exchange rates.

You can use Transaction OC41 to maintain the currency exchange rate. The exchange rates are maintained manually by finance experts.

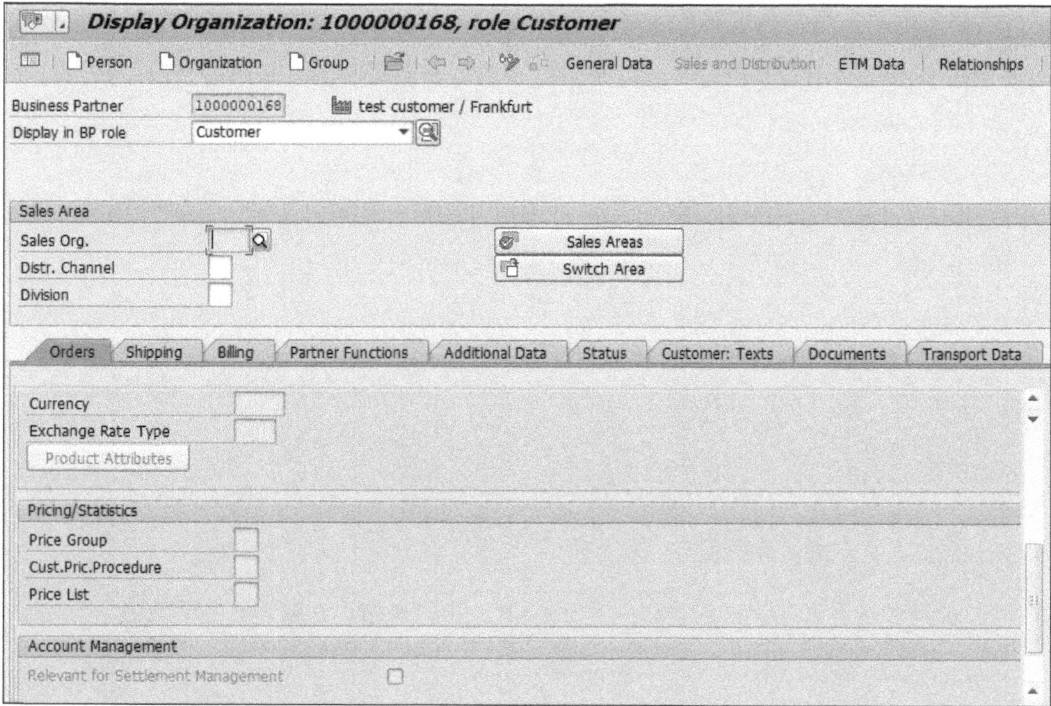

Figure 3.22 Business Partner Customer Role: Orders (2 of 2)

- **Exchange Rate Type**
  You can maintain the exchange rate type that has been agreed on with the customer in this field. You use the exchange rate to store the currency conversion rates. If the field is left blank, the exchange rate type **M** (standard translation at average rate) is used by default.
- **Price Group**
  This field is used to provide discounts and to set up the pricing condition records. If two or more customers have the same pricing features, they will be assigned to the same pricing group. In general, this will help to simplify the maintenance of the prices.
- **Cust.Pric.Procedure**
  Customer pricing procedure is one of the parameters used to determine the pricing procedure in sales documents.

Configuration: Pricing Procedure

Pricing procedure is determined in the sales order based on three parameters: sales area, customer pricing procedure, and document pricing procedure. To define the customer pricing procedure, execute Transaction OVKK. Refer to Chapter 5, Section 5.1, for more information on pricing.

- **Price List**
  This is used to group customers based on the same pricing attribute and segregate them in the form of a price list, such as wholesaler, dealer, or distributor.

Configuration: Price List

You can configure the price list with Transaction OVSI or by following menu path **Sales and Distribution • Basic Functions • Pricing • Maintain Price Relevant Master Data • Define Price List for Customer**. You can create your own price list by clicking on the **New Entries** button, as shown in Figure 3.23.

Change View "Conditions: Price List Types": Overview

New Entries

Price List Type	Description
01	Wholesale
02	Retail

Figure 3.23 Price List Types

- **Relevant for Settlement Management**
  This field indicates whether the business partner is relevant for settlement management. In SAP S/4HANA, settlement management has taken the place of the previous rebate management functionality.

Shipping

The delivery and shipment fields are derived from the **Shipping** tab of the business partner customer role, as shown in Figure 3.24.

Fill in the following fields to set up the shipping data for the business partner customer role:

- **Delivery Priority**
  This field is used to classify the customers based on the goods or services delivery priority such as high delivery priority (**01**), medium delivery priority (**02**), or low delivery priority (**03**). The goods will be delivered to the customer with the highest delivery priority first, followed by the medium, and so on. The value in the field is also used to drive the other processes such as backorder processing and rescheduling.

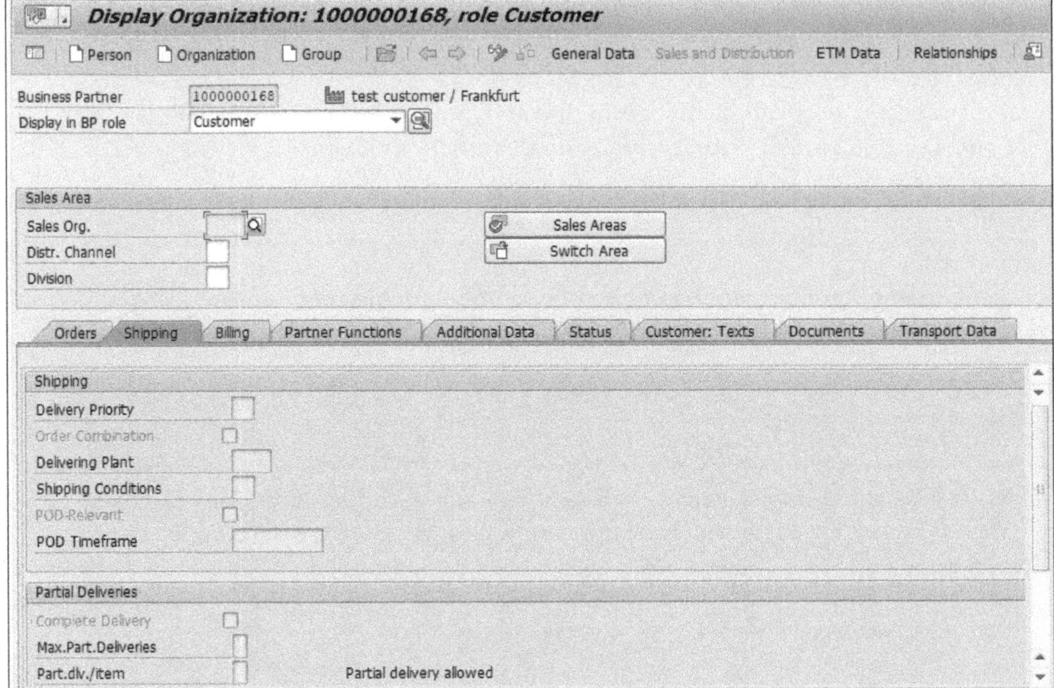

Figure 3.24 Business Partner Customer Role: Shipping

- **Order Combination**
  Order combination is the process of consolidating many sales orders into a single delivery document. If you check this checkbox, the system will allow the orders generated for the several business partners to be combined into a single delivery document. However, the system follows the standard delivery split criteria before combining the deliveries of sales orders. If any or all the criteria (e.g., ship-to party, Incoterms, delivery priority, shipping point, shipping condition, confirmed quantity date, and route associated with the sales orders) are different, then there will be a default delivery split for the sales documents.
- **Delivering Plant**
  This is a four-character alphanumeric field that you create as a part of the enterprise structure. It's used to determine the delivering plant in the sales order. The plant is also maintained in the material master and customer material info record. When determining the plant in the sales document, the system prioritizes the plant maintained in the customer material data record, followed by the customer master, and finally the material master.
- **Shipping Conditions**
  This field is used to determine the characteristics of the shipping condition such as if a business partner demands immediate delivery (**10**) or standard delivery (**01**). It's one of the parameters used to determine the shipping point in the sales order. The

shipping point is determined in the sales order with the combination of three parameters: shipping condition, loading group maintained in the material master, and plant.

Configuration: Shipping Conditions

Shipping conditions can be maintained in the document type (Transaction VOV8) control as well. While determining the shipping condition in the sales order, the first preference is given to the document type, followed by the customer master.

- **POD-Relevant**
  The procedure of ensuring the receipt of goods from the customer after doing the delivery is known as proof of delivery (POD). In the service-level agreement (SLA) with the customer, customers can explicitly demand that the invoices must be sent to them only after the delivery has been acknowledged. SAP provides POD as a standard feature that can be configured to meet the requirement. The **POD-Relevant** flag in a business partner is a prerequisite for the process. The item category is the other criteria.

Configuration: POD Relevancy

You can maintain the POD relevancy for item category via menu path **Logistics Execution • Shipping • Deliveries • Proof of Delivery • Set POD-Relevance Depending on Delivery Item Category**. After navigating through the menu path, you can select the **POD-Relevant** option for the item category.

Transaction VLPOD is used to complete the POD process, which follows the creation of the sales order (Transaction VA01) → creation of delivery (Transaction VL01N) → POD (Transaction VLPOD) → confirmation of POD (Transaction VLPODQ) → billing (Transaction VF01).

- **POD Timeframe**
  In the POD process, if the customer fails to provide you with the POD in the time frame mentioned in the given field, the business can create and send the invoices for the total delivered quantity. You can maintain the time frame in the field after the agreement with the business partner.
- **Complete Delivery**
  This field determines whether or not the customer can accept partial delivery. If you check this box, the system won't let you make partial deliveries to the business partner.
- **Part.dlv./item**
  If you enable partial deliveries for the business partner, you may limit how many partial deliveries are allowed for the same via this field. If partial deliveries aren't

permitted, you must enter **C**. If partial deliveries are permitted, you must keep **D** or blank in this field.

- **Unlimited Tolerance**
  This field (not shown) allows the increment and decrement of the delivery quantities in the delivery document.
- **Underdel. Tolerance**
  You can maintain the percentage of delivery quantities that fall within the permissible underdelivery tolerance (not shown). It mentions specifically how much quantity can be reduced in the delivery document, which will be accepted by the customer.
- **Overdeliv. Tolerance**
  You can maintain the percentage of delivery quantities that are within the acceptable overdelivery tolerance (not shown), that is, how much quantity can be increased in the delivery document.

Billing

The **Billing** tab, as shown in Figure 3.25, consists of fields relevant for the invoicing of the operational document such as sales order and delivery. The system uses these fields to derive further configurations for invoice-related processes downstream.

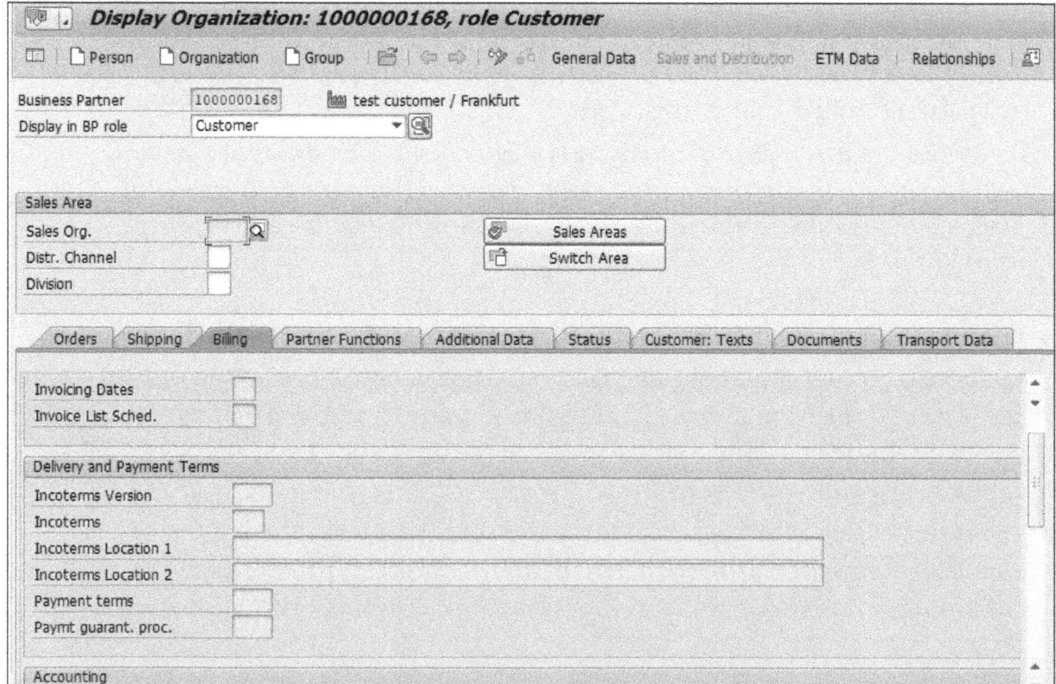

Figure 3.25 Business Partner Customer Role: Billing

Fill in the following fields to set up the billing-specific data for the business partner customer role:

- **Invoicing Dates**
  The field is used to determine the billing schedule dates for the customer. The system automatically derives the billing date from the calendar ID during billing. Based on the agreement signed with the customers, you set up the invoicing date calendar and assign it here. The system proposes the billing dates from the payer partner function. However, you can change the billing date manually while creating the invoice.
- **Invoice List Sched.**
  An invoicing list is a feature that allows you to consolidate all invoices for a specific period or month and send them to the payer in a single invoice list document. To run the invoice list, you can use Transaction VF21 for individual invoice list creation and Transaction VF24 for mass worklist creation.
- **Incoterms**
  Incoterms (short for international commercial terms) are the trading terms that adhere to the International Chamber of Commerce (ICC) guidelines. It's essentially a contract between the customer and the service/goods provider for the successful fulfillment of the deliveries. This field identifies the responsible party for loading charges, insurance charges, and freight charges, and indicates whether the charges are the responsibility of the service provider or the customer consuming the service or items. This is one of the parameters of the delivery split. Figure 3.26 shows a visualization of incoterms from the seller to the buyer.

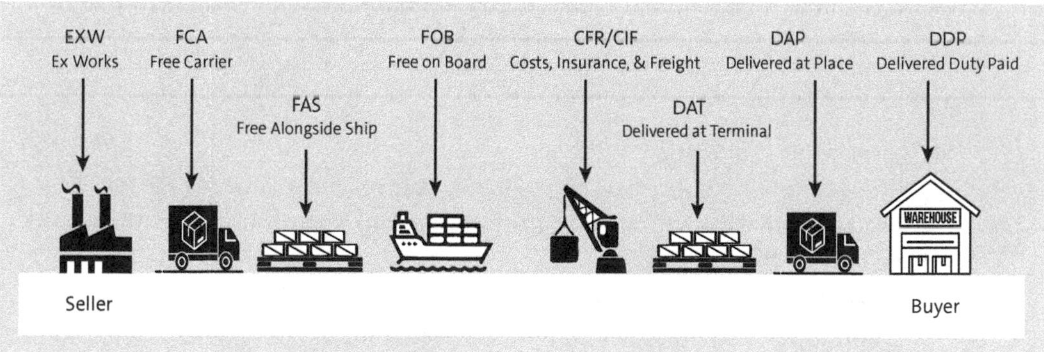

Figure 3.26 Incoterms Involved in Order to Cash

- **Incoterms Version**
  You can add the new version details of Incoterms in this field. With this feature, you can use the 2010 version published by the ICC associated with international commercial law.

- **Payment terms**
  This refers to an agreement between the business and the customer regarding the number of days permitted to make the payment. It's also known as the credit period.

Configuration: Payment Terms

The menu path for configuring the payment terms is **Sales and Distribution • Master Data • Business Partner • Customer Billing Document • Define Terms of Payment**. You'll see the screen shown in Figure 3.27, with the following key fields:

- **Account type**
  The payment terms created here can be explicitly allocated to the customer, vendor, or both by checking the **Customer** and **Vendor** checkboxes, as shown in Figure 3.27.

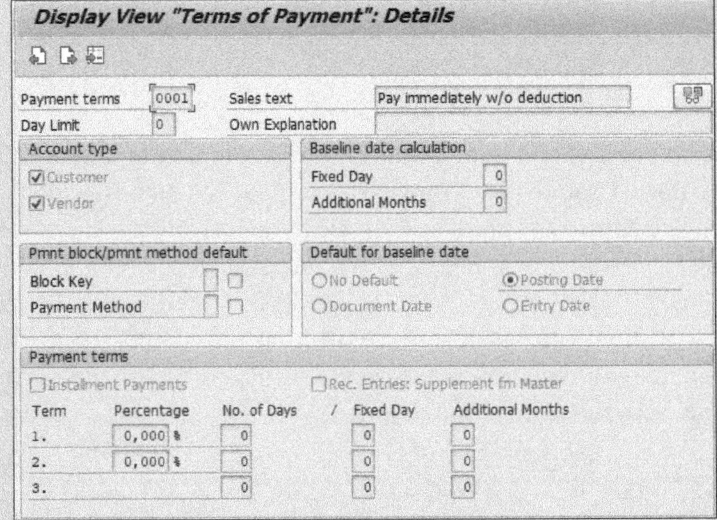

Figure 3.27 Define Terms of Payment

- **Baseline date calculation**
  The date on which the system begins to calculate payment terms is called the baseline date. In the majority of cases, the baseline date is the invoice date. The following options are available here:
  - **Fixed Day**: You can provide the number of fixed days in this field, and the system will calculate the payment term from that point on, regardless of the invoice date.
  - **Additional Months**: If you provide a number of months here, the system will wait up to that number of months before computing payment terms.
- **Default for baseline date**
  You have four options to choose from to determine the baseline date: **Posting Date** (the date on which the accounting document is posted), **Document Date** (the date on which the billing document is created), **Entry Date** (for the users who have to enter the baseline date while posting the document), and **No Default**.

- **Cash discount**
  This is the discount that you provide to customers who pay on or before the due date. The cash discount percentage that you maintain here will be calculated in the sales document using the SKTO condition type.

Configuring payment terms is usually done by the financial accounting consultant, so we've only explained the fields from the sales and distribution billing document type perspective.

- **Payment guarant. proc.**
  In business scenarios, there is always an invoice payment risk associated with the newly onboarded customer who resides in a foreign country. Usually, a business needs some sort of guarantee of payments from this customer. This can be achieved with the help of payment guarantee procedures in SAP S/4HANA. The system won't allow deliveries to be created for the customer unless you have payment guarantee documentation. The payment guarantee documentation includes a letter of credit or a bank guarantee. The financial accounting consultant is responsible for the payment guarantee procedure configuration and setup.
- **Account Assignment Group**
  This field is one of the parameters you can use to determine the revenue account during billing document creation. We'll cover this topic in detail in Chapter 5, Section 5.2.1.
- **Output tax**
  This field determines whether or not the customer is liable for taxes.

Configuration: Account Assignment Groups

You can create a new material account assignment group using configuration path **Sales and Distribution • Basic Functions • Account Assignment/Costing • Revenue Account Determination • Check Master Data Relevant for Account Assignment**. After executing the path, click on the **New Entries** button to create your own account assignment group of customers.

A few standard account assignment groups are shown in Figure 3.28.

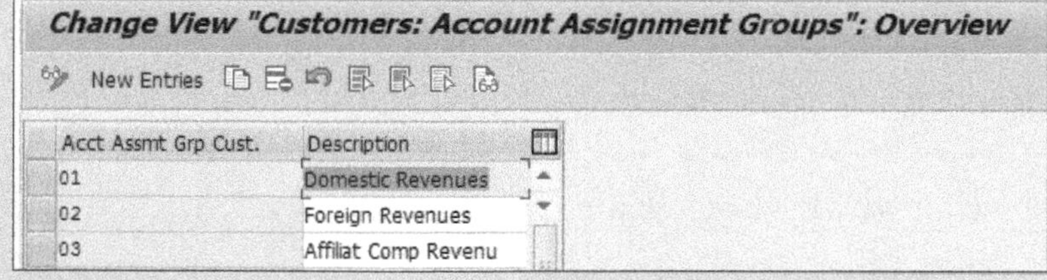

Figure 3.28 Customers: Account Assignment Groups

Partner Functions

A partner function represents a function that the customer carries out. SAP S/4HANA comprises commonly used partner functions; however, you can define your own partner functions per the business requirement.

Figure 3.29 shows the **Partner Functions** tab in the business partner customer role.

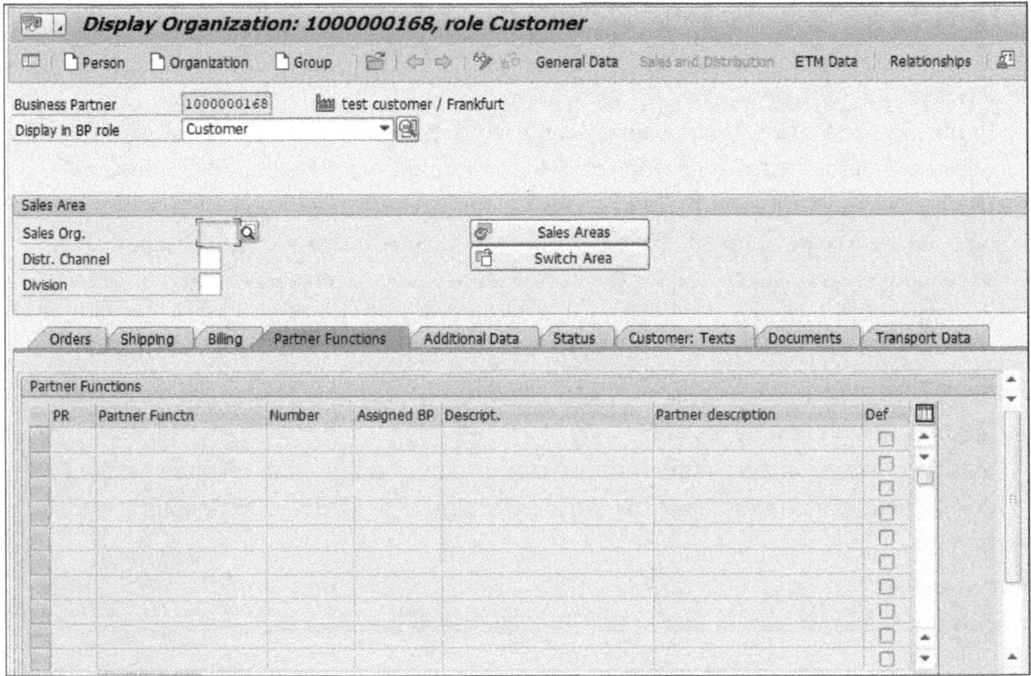

Figure 3.29 Business Partner Customer Role: Partner Functions

The system automatically generates the following four partner functions while creating a new business partner with a customer role:

- **Sold-to party**
  This partner function places the sales order for materials or services.
- **Bill-to party**
  This is the partner function to whom the goods are delivered.
- **Payer**
  This partner function will receive the invoice.
- **Ship-to party**
  This partner function pays the invoice raised.

The system will determine these four functions, respectively, in the sales order. When you create an outbound delivery, the partner function ship-to party will get determined in the outbound delivery. In invoicing, the bill-to party and payer partner functions are determined.

Configuration: Partner Functions

You can configure the partner function in Transaction VOPAN or by navigating to menu path **Sales and Distribution • Basic Functions • Partner Determination • Set Up Partner Determination • Set Up Partner Determination for Customer Master.**

3.1.4 Financial Accounting Customer Role

The business partner *financial accounting customer role* is used for standalone finance-related activities, which are handled by the financial accounting consultants. This role consists of details that will also be used in sales and distribution-related processes for general ledger account determination in invoicing.

To choose the financial accounting customer role, choose **FI Customer** in the **Display in BP role** field. We'll walk through setting up the different tabs in the following sections.

Customer: Account Management

Let's explore the fields associated with the **Customer: Account Management** tab, as shown in Figure 3.30.

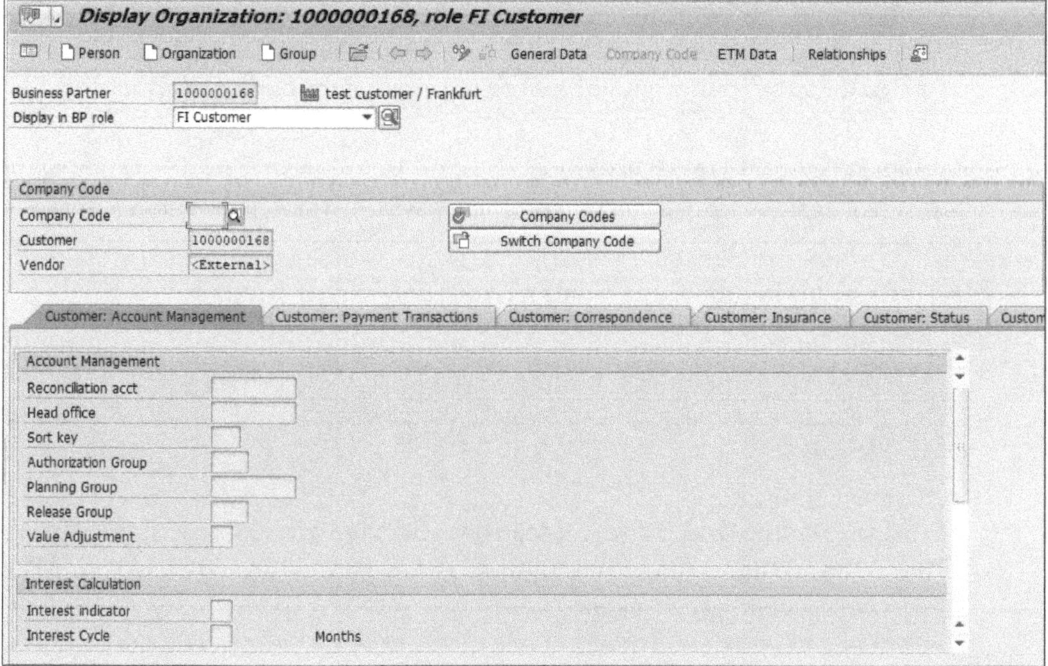

Figure 3.30 Business Partner FI Customer Role: Account Management

Fill in the following fields to set up the customer account management data for the business partner financial accounting customer role:

- **Reconciliation acct**
  You can maintain the reconciliation general ledger account in the field to accumulate the total outstanding for the business partner. The accounting document created post invoicing will have an accounting entry as customer account debit and revenue account credit. The customer general ledger account will be picked from the **Reconciliation acct** field. The financial accounting consultant will create the reconciliation general ledger account in Transaction FS00 with the account type set as a balance sheet.

  The customer and vendors are called subledger accounts. The postings in the subledgers (customer accounts) are automatically posted to the assigned reconciliation account by which the general ledger will be updated. The reconciliation account ensures that the total general ledger balance is always zero. Thus, it fulfills the prerequisite for the balance sheet accounts, and it's not needed to transfer account balances from subledger to general ledger accounts because the balances are updated automatically in the general ledger.
- **Authorization Group**
  The authorization group is a method of increasing object security. Entering an authorization group in this field restricts object access to users who have this authorization group in their SAP profiles. Like the other business partner objects, you can assign the authorization group based on the views of the business partner.

Customer: Payment Transactions

Next, we'll explore the fields in the **Customer: Payment Transactions** tab, as shown in Figure 3.31.

Fill in the following important payment transaction-related fields:

- **Payment terms**
  This field represents an agreement between the company and the customer regarding the number of days allowed to make the payment. It's also referred to as the credit period.
- **Payment Methods**
  The payment method is the procedure by which the vendors or customers make incoming or outgoing payments. The payment method configuration is done by the financial accounting consultant.

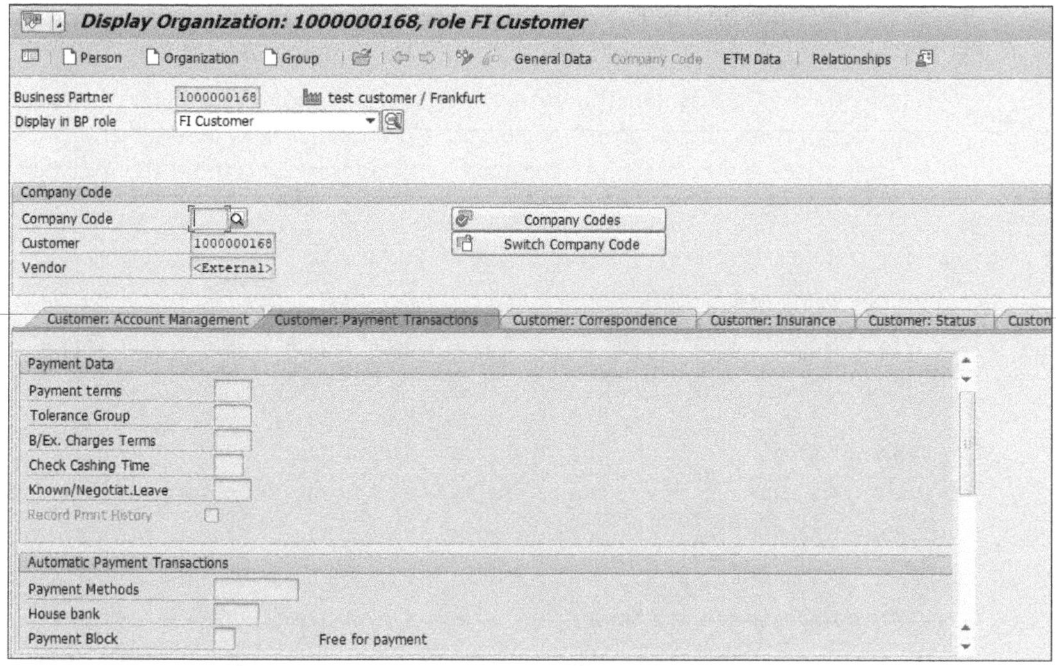

Figure 3.31 Business Partner FI Customer Role: Payment Transactions

Customer: Correspondence

The **Customer: Correspondence** tab, as shown in Figure 3.32, contains the fields that are used for the customer payment reminder process (dunning process).

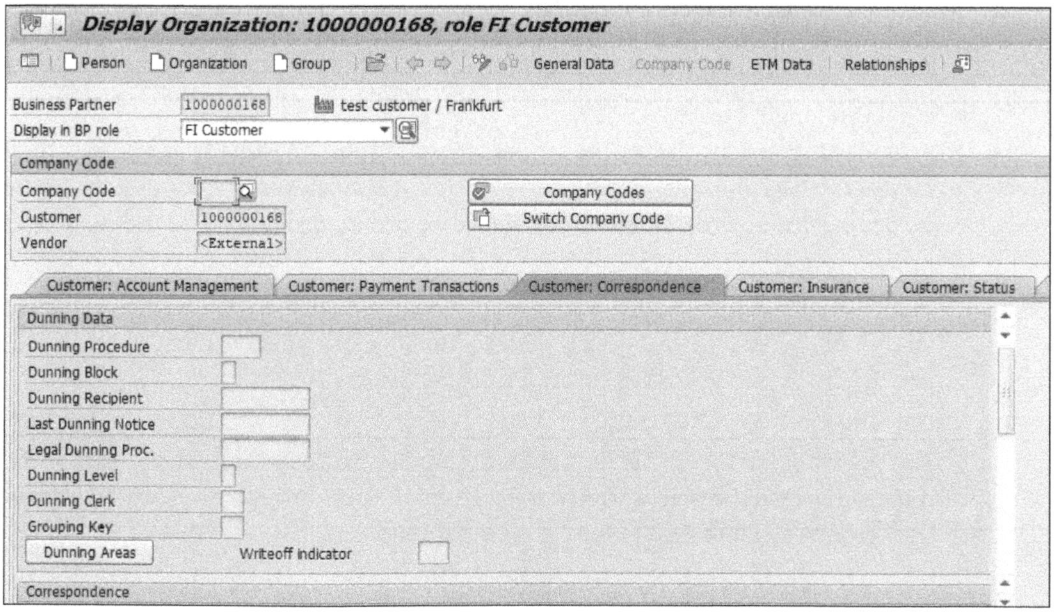

Figure 3.32 Business Partner FI Customer Role: Correspondence

Fill in the following important dunning-related fields:

- **Dunning Procedure**
  This field is used to maintain the dunning procedure. When a customer fails to make a payment for an outstanding invoice by the due date, the system generates the dunning letter and delivers it to the customer's address to remind them of their overdue payment.

Configuration: Dunning Procedures

Transaction FBMP is used to configure the dunning procedure. The dunning procedure configuration is typically handled by the financial accounting consultant.

- **Dunning Block**
  You can use this field if you want to bypass the dunning procedure run. You can maintain the dunning block reason here.

Configuration: Dunning Blocks

You can do the configuration for the dunning block in the menu path **Financial Accounting (New) • Account Receivable and Account Payable • Business Transactions • Dunning • Basic Setting for Dunning • Define Dunning Block Reasons.**

- **Dunning Recipient**
  In some cases, you must send the dunning notice to another partner function associated with the business partner. It can be configured as a separate partner function, and the customer can be assigned to the field. Typically, the customer is related to the business partner's main or head office.
- **Legal Dunning Proc.**
  If the customer fails to pay the amount despite receiving several warnings, then there's the legal dunning procedure to go through. A lawyer or a counselor usually carries out the process, and the documents are generated and sent to the customer.
- **Dunning Level**
  When a customer or vendor receives a dunning notice, the dunning run program automatically sets the dunning level. The **Dunning Level** field can be used to calculate the credit ratings for the customer.
- **Dunning Clerk**
  The person in charge of sending dunning notices to customers or vendors is the dunning clerk. If the field is blank, the values of the dunning clerk are retrieved from the **Accounting Clerk** field in the customer or vendor master.

3.1.5 Credit Management Role

The master data associated with the credit management process is stored in the SAP Credit Management (UKM000) role. You must extend the business partner to the UKM000 role by choosing **SAP Credit Management** in the **Change in BP role** field to set up the credit management process for the business partner. Let's explore each tab in the following sections.

> **Note**
>
> Credit management can be implemented in two ways in the SAP S/4HANA world: the first approach is to use the functionalities of sales and distribution-based credit management and keep the credit limit and risk categories static. The second approach is to leverage the capabilities of financial supply chain management (FSCM) credit management and make the credit limit and credit risk categories dynamic based on formulas.
>
> We'll discuss sales and distribution-based credit management and FSCM credit management in detail in Chapter 5, Section 5.3.

Credit Profile Data

This data in the **Credit Profile** tab, as shown in Figure 3.33, is applicable throughout the business partner for all the credit segments. We'll explore credit segments in detail in the next section.

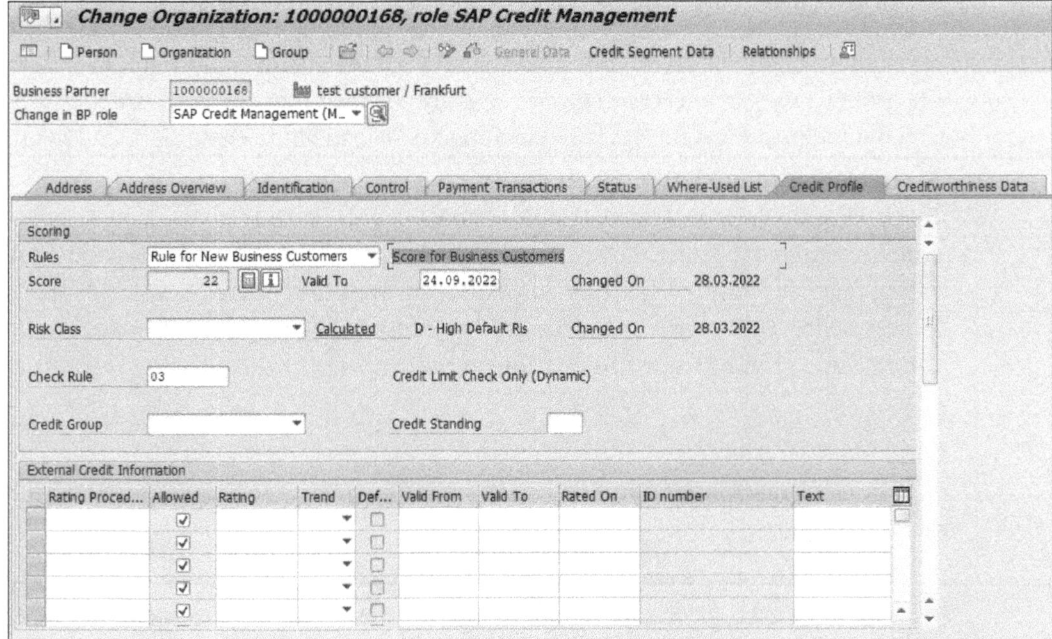

Figure 3.33 Business Partner Credit Management Role: Credit Profile

Note

All the configuration objects from credit management are covered in Chapter 5, Section 5.3.

Fill in the important credit profile related fields as follows:

- **Rules**
  The scoring rules engine enables the creation of customer scores based on custom rules. These scores can also be combined with those from third-party credit agencies. For example, you can determine the score based on the ratings from the third-party credit agencies such as Coface, Creditsafe, and so on.
- **Risk Class**
  The risk class can be determined automatically or entered manually based on the credit score value. By default, SAP has provided the history log for the risk class because of the dynamic nature of the risk class. You must keep in mind that the risk category configured in sales and distribution-based credit management and the risk class configured in the FSCM component must be the same. We'll cover the risk class creation in detail in Chapter 5, Section 5.3.
- **Check Rule**
  This specifies which credit check steps should be used for a customer when an external system requests a credit check, such as dynamic credit limit check, static credit limit check, and oldest open item.
- **Credit Group**
  You can maintain the credit group associated with the business partner. Customers are grouped into various credit groups relevant to credit management. SAP has provided standard groups such as large customers, small/medium customers, and so on.
- **External Credit Information**
  By clicking the **Import Data** button (not shown), you can directly update the data from the external rating agency into this tab. You could only connect to an external rating agency through partner products in traditional credit management. However, in FSCM credit management, you can configure an XML-based credit information service by creating a rating procedure.

Configuration: Rules

You can use Transaction UKM_LIMIT_RULE to create a rule. We'll cover rule creation in Chapter 5, Section 5.3.

It's possible to monitor a customer across multiple credit segments using proprietary rules. Credit segments can represent different business areas, organizations, and branches. The primary credit segment assigned in the general data consolidates credit exposure into a single unit.

Credit Segment Data

The data in the **Credit Limit and Control** tab, as shown in Figure 3.34, is only applicable to the particular credit segment. You can maintain data for each credit segment associated with the business partner individually.

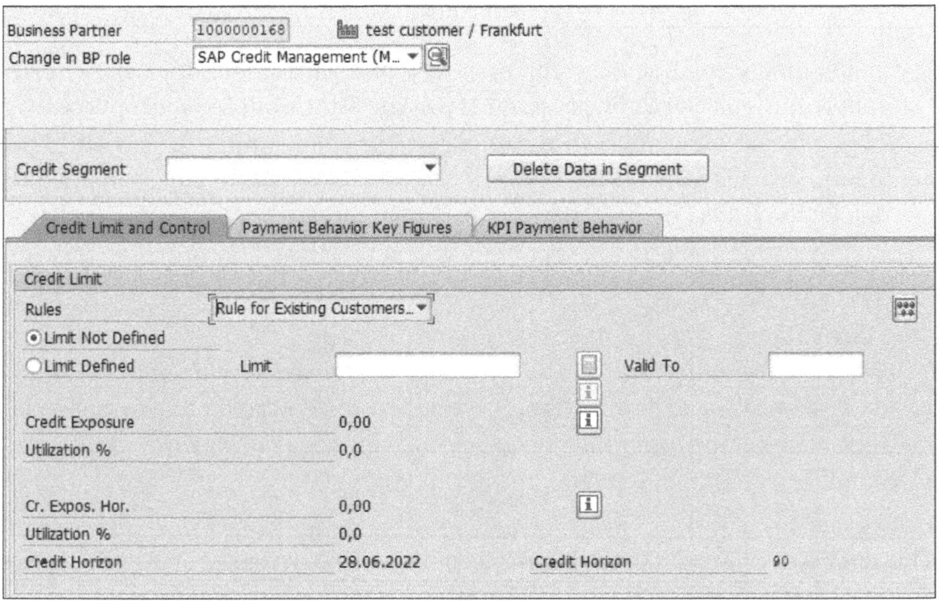

Figure 3.34 Business Partner Credit Management Role: Credit Segment

Fill in the credit limit and control transaction-related fields as follows:

- **Credit Segment**
  When creating an order in the organizational area, the credit check uses the credit segment data associated with the business partner. Credit segments can be created separately for sales organization, company code, or any of the functional geographical areas within the operating business. They manage credit limits and provide information about the customer's payment behavior (payment behavior summary). While configuring the credit segment, SAP by default creates two credit segments: a primary credit segment with characters **000000** and a secondary segment. The primary credit segment consolidates credit exposure into a single unit. A customer can be assigned a different credit limit for each credit segment. Additional functions for the credit segment maintenance are available, such as validity period, history, and change display for the credit segment.

- **Rules**
  You have the option of selecting which credit checks are performed on the order. Checks, such as the maximum age of the oldest open item or the maximum number of dunning transactions by the business partner, might be used in addition to the credit limit utilization check. The score is calculated using parameters related to a

business partner's master data element, number of dunning notices sent to the customer, and the customer's payment history. The rule assigned to the general **Credit Profile** tab applies to the entire business partner, whereas the rule specified in the segment only applies to the specific credit segment. In addition to the **Rules** dropdown, a **Simulation** icon to the right allows you to conduct credit checks.

- **Limit**
  If you don't want to define the credit limit for a particular premium customer, you can choose the **Limit Not Defined** option. If you check the **Limit Defined** option, then credit management logic kicks in and calculates the credit limit with the help of the credit limit formula assigned in the credit rule for that specific credit segment. You can default the validity of the limit through configurations, or you can manually add the validity period in the business partner. You can review the information on a formula used to calculate via the **Information** icon in the tab.
- **Credit Exposure**
  You calculate the credit exposure at the credit control area level in credit management based on sales and distribution. However, in the FSCM credit management, it's been estimated at the credit segment level, and you can aggregate the credit exposure at the main segment level in a business partner.
- **Utilization %**
  This represents the credit limit that the business partner has used up to this point.
- **Control Block**
  In the control block (not shown), you can block the specific business partner for the credit management by specifying the blocking reason or without specifying the blocking reason.

Payment Behavior Key Figures

The *payment behavior* summarizes the business partner's payment behavior, including the highest dunning level, the oldest open item, the most recent payment, and key figures such as the average period outstanding or the average customer sales.

Figure 3.35 shows the **Payment Behavior Key Figures** tab in the business partner.

Fill in the important payment behavior-related fields as follows:

- **Oldest Open Item**
  If the customer hasn't yet paid the previous invoice, and the due date associated with the invoice has passed, that item is called the oldest open item. You can mention the specific number of days in the business partner, and if the due date has passed, the system can block the operational document of the customer.
- **Last Payment**
  By analyzing the last payment date, the credit analyst can better judge the creditworthiness of the business partner of the blocked sales order.

- **Days Sales Outstanding (DSO)**
  Days sales outstanding (DSO) (not shown) measures the average number of days a company takes to collect payment after a sale. You can use the DSO as one of the parameters in a credit check and in a formula to calculate the credit score and credit limit.

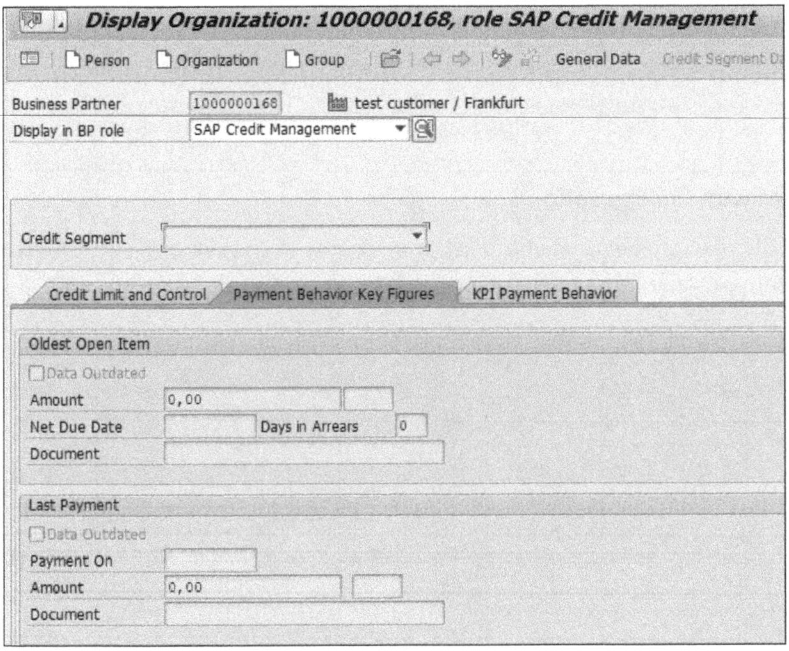

Figure 3.35 Business Partner Credit Management Role: Payment Behavior Key Figures

3.2 Material Master

The material-specific data of a company is stored in the *material master* data record. This data is stored centrally and is used in all logistics modules for the smooth processing of transactions and processes. The material master data is used in various activities and processes such as sales, purchasing, inventory management, planning, and so on. You can maintain the material master data across several organizational levels such as sales organization, plant, storage location, and so on.

Note

A few important tables from material master data are as follows:

- Table MARA: General Material Data
- Table MVKE: Sales Data for Material
- Table MAKT: Material Descriptions
- Table MARC: Plant Data for Material

- Table MARD: Storage Location Data for Material
- Table MARM: Unit of Measure for Material
- Table MLAN: Tax Classification for Material
- Table MBEW: Material Valuation

In this section, first we'll discuss the creation of the material master record and then explore various material master views. This section will only focus on the views and fields that are relevant from the perspective of sales and distribution integration.

3.2.1 Material Master Configuration

Transaction MM01 is used to create material master records in the system. You'll arrive at the initial screen for material master creation, as shown in Figure 3.36.

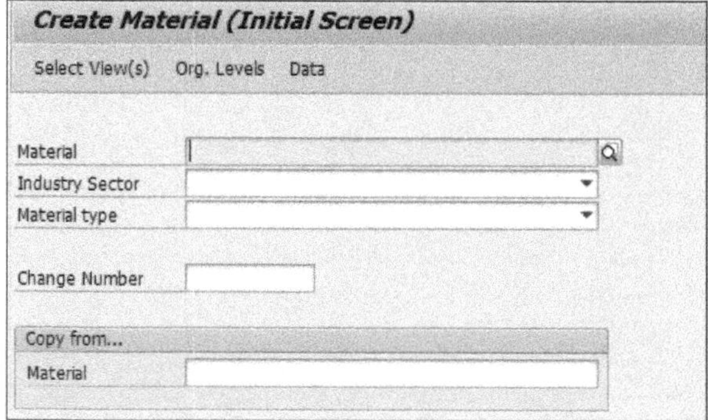

Figure 3.36 Material Master: Create

Specify the **Industry Sector** and **Material type** while creating a material master record by filling in the following fields:

- **Industry Sector**
  This indicates to which industry the material belongs. It controls the screens and order in which they can be accessed or displayed.

Configuration: Industry Sectors

You can configure the industry sector types per the business requirement with Transaction OMS3 or by navigating to menu path **Logistics-General • Material Master • Field Selection • Define Industry Sectors and Industry-Sector-Specific Field Selection**. This is usually handled by materials management consultants.

- **Material type**
  This is used to groups the materials with shared attributes and features together. It's further used to default many important fields in the material master such as

valuation category, MRP group, and so on. The standard material type typically used in sales and distribution processes are in Table 3.1.

Material Type	Description
FERT	Finished goods
HALB	Semifinished products
ROH	Raw materials
HAWA	Third-party materials

Table 3.1 Standard Material Types

Configuration: Material Types

You must configure the material type in the system before creating a material master record because you need to select a specific material type while creating the material master record.

You can configure a custom material type with Transaction OMS2 or by navigating to menu path **Logistics-General • Material Master • Basic Settings • Material Type • Define Attributes of Material Type**.

After selecting **Industry Sector** and **Material type** in the initial screen, press Enter. The dialog box will appear to choose the views, as shown in Figure 3.37.

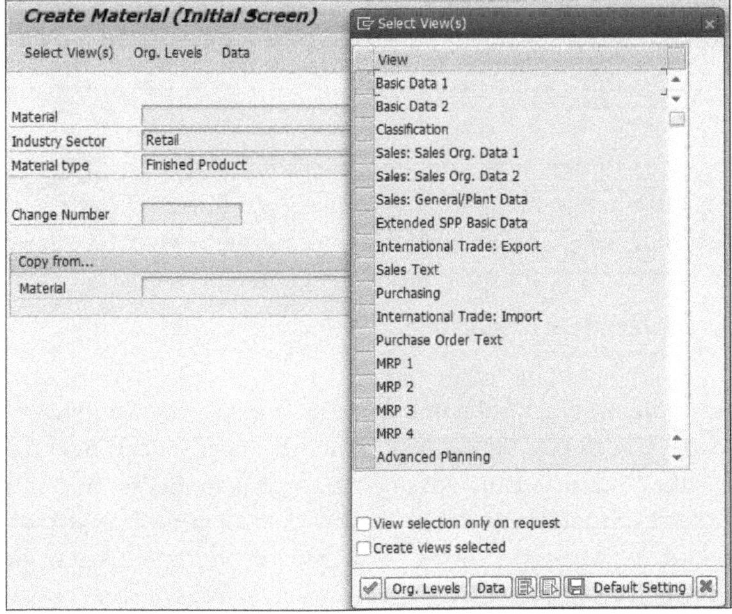

Figure 3.37 Material Master: Selection of Views

Once you select the required views and press [Enter], another dialog box will appear, as shown in Figure 3.38, where you can enter relevant organizational data such as plant, sales organization, distribution channel, storage location, and so on.

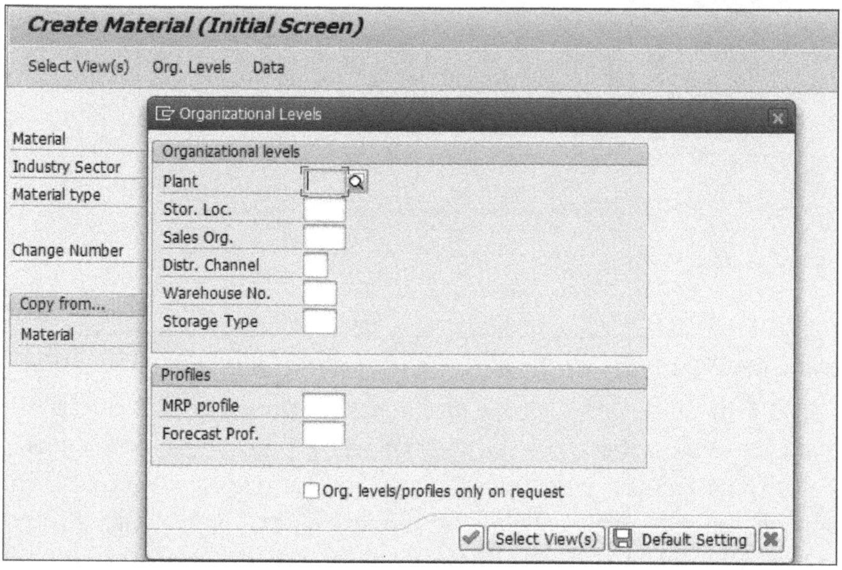

Figure 3.38 Material Master: Selection of Organizational Elements

After entering the relevant details, press [Enter] to go to the selected views.

Several views (tabs) are available in the material master to define data to perform further processes and activities. We'll explore the various views and the relevance of fields in the material master data in detail in the following sections.

3.2.2 Basic Data 1 View

The basic data views are used to store the information related to the general attributes about the material. This data is applicable across all the sales organizations, plants, and storage locations in the business. Figure 3.39 illustrates the **Basic data 1** view. (The **Basic data 2** view isn't relevant from a sales and distribution integration perspective.)

Let's explore the fields available in the basic data:

- **Material** and **Descr.**
  The material number uniquely denotes the number associated with the material or stock keeping unit (SKU). Use the configuration of number ranges for this material number assignment. Like other master data elements, you can configure the number ranges as internal or external. The material number field length was 18 characters in SAP ERP; however, in SAP S/4HANA, the `MATNR` field length is increased to 40 characters. You can integrate SAP S/4HANA with the downstream or upstream systems seamlessly because of this field extension.

You can add the material description in various languages. The material description should usa a standard naming convention as devised by the business.

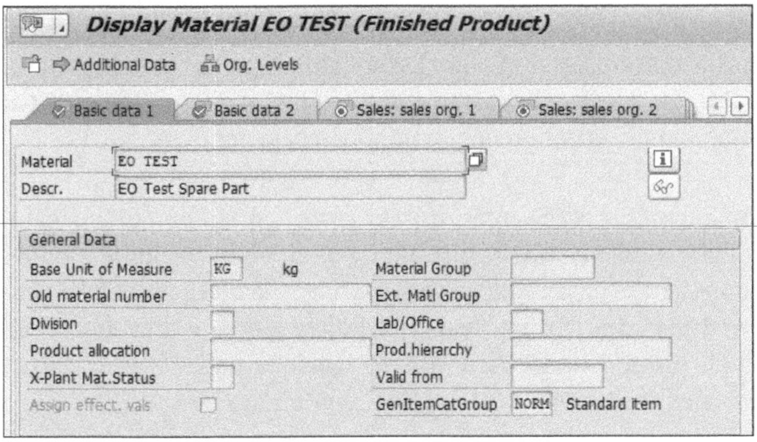

Figure 3.39 Material Master: Basic Data 1

- **Base Unit of Measure**
  This is the unit of measure (UoM) you use to manufacture, procure, store, or service tangible goods and services. The base UoM varies based on the industry you're serving. If you're in the professional service industry, then the UoM will be hours; if it's consumer packaged goods (CPG), it will be boxes or cartons. Inventory management will manage the inventory of the products based on the base UoM maintained in the field.
- **Material Group**
  When you group the material with similar attributes to drive reporting as well as other downstream processes, this is called material grouping. The material group is a nine-character field. You can use material groups in reporting and pricing condition record maintenance. In some cases, the requirement can be to set up the prices based on the combination of material group and customers.

Configuration: Material Groups

Materials management consultants are responsible for the configuration of the material group by navigating to menu path **Logistics-General • Material Master • Settings for Key Fields • Define Material Groups**. Figure 3.40 shows the standard material groups.

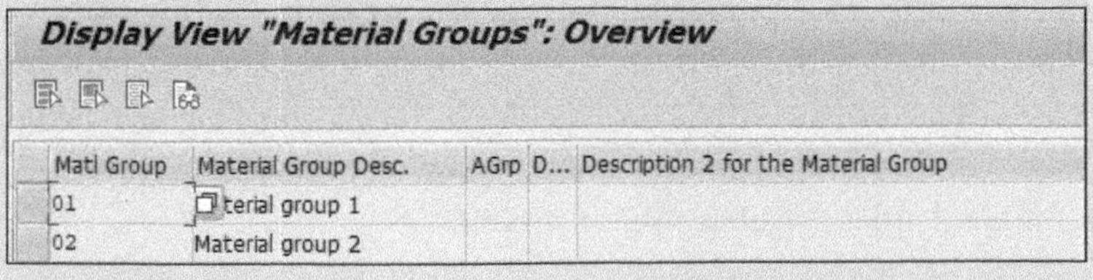

Figure 3.40 Material Groups

- **Old material number**
  You can use this field in two ways. For example, in a greenfield implementation, if the legacy system uses a different material number, you can maintain the old material number in this field, which can later be used for reconciliation. The other use of the field is if the organization uses third-party logistics for deliveries and shipments, then you can use this field to map the material number maintained in the external system. Note that the old material number is still an 18-character field.
- **Division**
  You create the division as part of the enterprise structure and assign it to the material. The **Division** field is used to distinguish between different business product offerings. For example, if the organization is selling tires, the divisions can be two-wheeler tire, three-wheeler tire, bus tire, heavy machinery specialty tires, and so on. There can be multiple materials associated with the same division. We've discussed the configuration of divisions in detail in Chapter 2, Section 2.1.3.
- **X-Plant Mat.Status**
  You'll use this field to block the material from operational activities such as sales, manufacturing, or procurement across all plants. You can define the material status with a warning or error message in Transaction OMS4.
- **Prod.hierarchy**
  You can configure this alphanumeric field in Transaction V/76. The nomenclature of the hierarchy is segregated into three levels. Levels **1** and **2** consist of five characters each, and level **3** consists of eight characters. If you take the example of a tire industry, level **1** will determine the tire type for the car; the next level determines the plant in which its produced, and level **3** determines the granular specification of the tire, whether it's a nonskid tire, puncture-proof tire, and so on.

  You can use this field for profitability analysis; also, it has the use cases for setting up the condition records for the pricing.
- **GenItemCatGroup**
  The general item category group is one of the parameters to determine the item category in the sales document. The item category governs the behavior of the item in the sales document and is determined based on four parameters: sales document type, item category group, higher-level item category, and usage.

Configuration: Item Category Groups

You can configure the general item category group by navigating to menu path **Sales and Distribution • Sales • Sales Documents • Sales Documents Item • Define Item Category Groups**. You can create your own item category group by clicking on the **New Entries** button.

Figure 3.41 shows the standard item category group **NORM**.

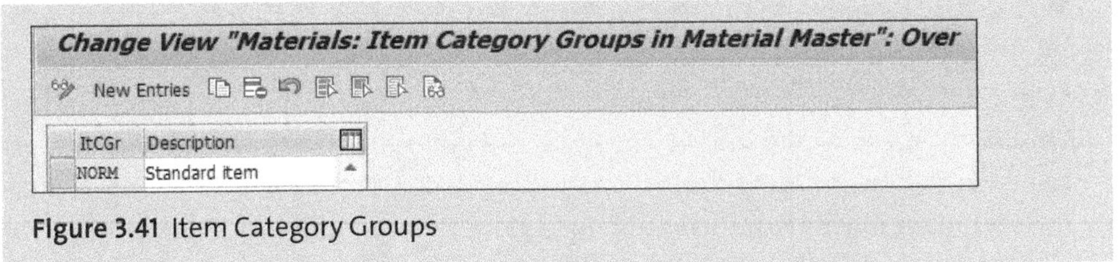

Figure 3.41 Item Category Groups

3.2.3 Sales: Sales Org. 1 View

The **Sales: sales org. 1** view, as shown in Figure 3.42, plays an important role in the order-to-cash process. You maintain the data in the **Sales: sales org. 1** view by providing the appropriate sales organization and distribution channel. To summarize, the data present in the view is specific to the sales organization and distribution channel. Let's explore the fields next.

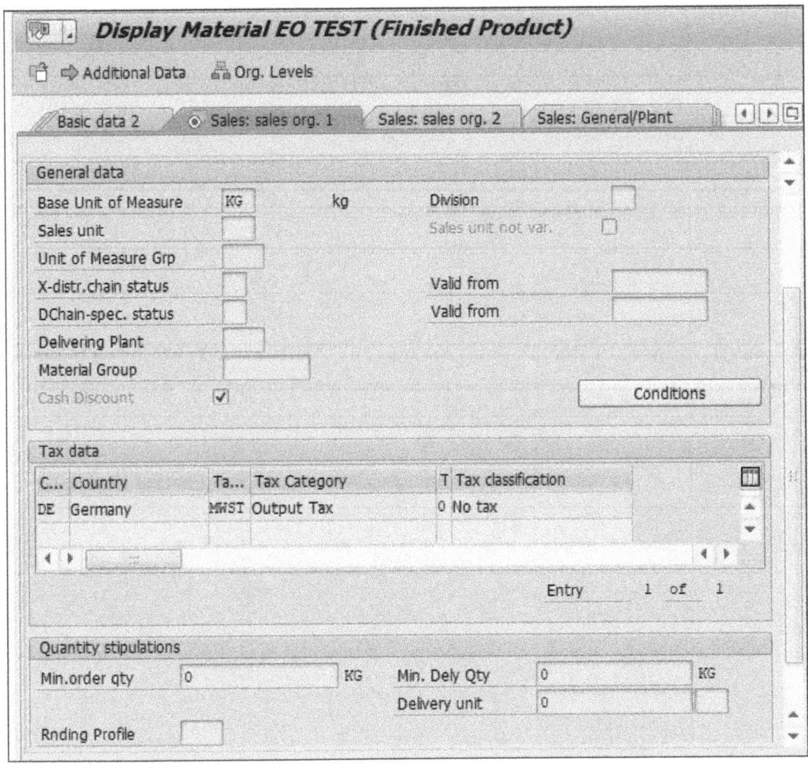

Figure 3.42 Material Master: Sales Org. 1

To set up the **Sales: sales org. 1** data of the material master, fill in the following fields:

- **Base Unit of Measure**
  This is the unit you use to manufacture, procure, store, or service tangible goods and services. The field is the same as described in the **Basic data 1** view. The **Base Unit of**

Measure that you maintain here will be applicable only to the specific sales organization.

- **Sales unit**
  This field represents the unit in which you sell goods or provide services to the customer. While determining the unit in the sales order, the system will first prioritize the unit maintained in the **Sales unit** field. If the **Sales unit** field is blank, the system will use the base UoM.

  The use case of the field is that you can keep a separate sales unit for each sales organization or geography that you serve. For example, the product sold in India can be maintained in cartons compared to products sold in Sri Lanka as boxes.

Configuration: Conversion Factors

If the base and sales units are different, the system will prompt the conversion. You can maintain the conversion factor of the base UoM to the sales unit by clicking the **Additional Data** button and navigating to the **Units of measure** tab, as shown in Figure 3.43 and Figure 3.44. After navigating to the **Units of measure** tab, you can add the conversion factor, for example, 1 carton (**CAR**) is equal to 10 **PCs**, which means if you enter 10 PCs in the sales order for a material, it will get converted to 1 carton in the **Quantity** field.

Change Material 2296 (FINISHED MATERIAL)

Additional Data | Org. Levels | Check Screen Data

Classification | Sales: sales org. 1 | Sales: sales org. 2 | Sales: General/...

Figure 3.43 Additional Data Button

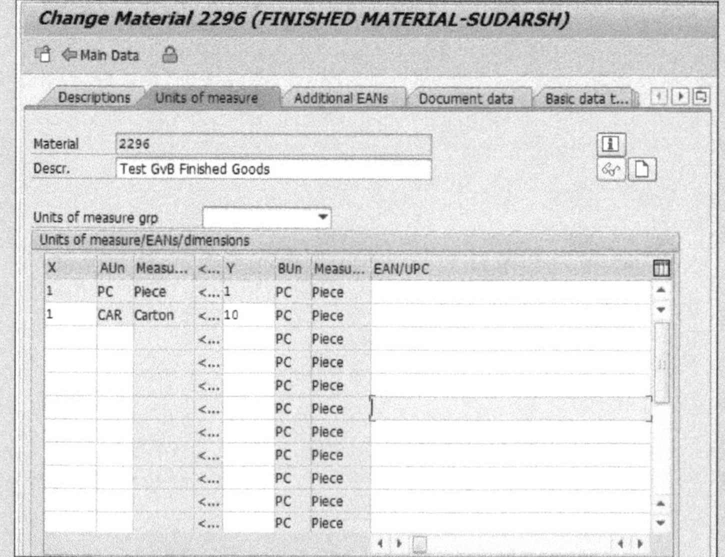

Figure 3.44 Conversion Factor

- **Sales unit not var.**
  This indicator controls whether you can change the UoM in the sales order. If you check this, then the user isn't allowed to change the UoM in the operational document.
- **X-distr.chain status**
  You can use **X-distr.chain status** to block the material for all distribution channels.
- **Dchain-spec status**
  If the user wants to block the material for a specific sales organization, then they can use the **Dchain-spec status** field.
- **Delivering Plant**
  The plant determined in the sales order can be picked from the material master. You can maintain the plant in the customer material info record, customer master, and material master. The priority for determining the plant in a sales order is given first to the customer material info record, then to the customer master, and last to the material master.
- **Cash Discount**
  The checkbox is marked by default. The checkbox is one of the prerequisites to determine the cash discount during the payments for the invoice. Condition type SKTO determines this discount in the pricing procedure.
- **Tax data**
  The tax calculation in SAP S/4HANA is driven by Transaction FTXP. You assign the tax procedure to the country based on the country key. However, if the taxes don't apply to specific materials, SAP has provided the **Tax data** fields in the material master to achieve this requirement.

  You can make the material relevant for tax or not applicable for tax through the tax classification of the material, along with the combination of country key and tax condition type.
- **Min. order qty**
  This field controls the minimum quantity the customer should order. If the order quantity is less than the minimum quantity maintained in this field, the system can give a warning or error message based on this field's configuration settings.
- **Min. Dely Qty**
  This field controls the minimum delivery quantity that can be delivered to the customer. The field is used for partial deliveries where you need to configure the minimum delivery quantity. If the delivery quantity in the sales document is less than the minimum quantity in this field, the system can give a warning or error message based on the field's configuration settings.
- **Delivery unit**
  If you maintain any numeric value in the field, the delivery quantity should be a multiple of that quantity; otherwise, the system will give an error or warning message.

- **Rounding Profile**
  You use this field to round the quantity of the material in the delivery or sales order based on the settings maintained in the rounding profile. For example, when the customer has ordered 14 quantities, and you've maintained that 10 to 15 quantities are rounded to 15 in the rounding profile, then, automatically, the order and delivery quantity will round the quantities to 15 instead of 14 quantities.

3.2.4 Sales: Sales Org. 2 View

This view is an extension of the **Sales: sales org. 1** view. The implication of the first view holds true for the second view as well. Let's dive into the fields associated with the view.

Figure 3.45 shows the fields in **Sales: sales org. 2** view of the material master.

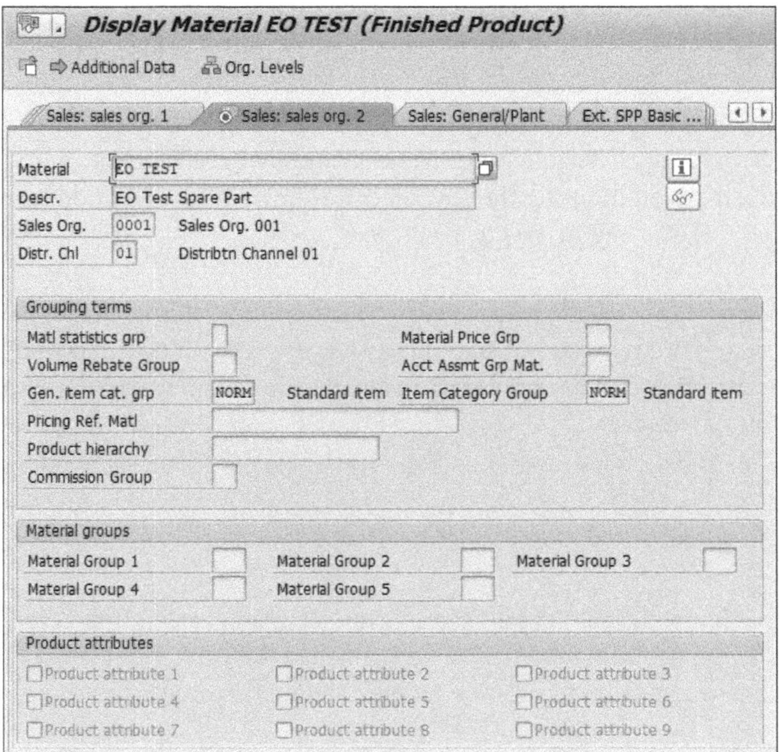

Figure 3.45 Material Master: Sales Org. 2 View

Fill in the following fields to set up the material master **Sales: sales org. 2** view:

- **Matl statistics grp**
  The Logistics Information System (LIS) will fetch the values from this field for reporting purposes.
- **Volume Rebate Group**
  Rebate is the process of giving an extra discount that is paid retroactively to the

customer. This field can group several materials and maintain the records for these groups. If the customer purchases any of the material from this group, then the discount is provided to the customer and paid retroactively to the customer via credit memo.

Configuration: Rebate Groups

You can configure your own rebate groups by navigating to menu path **Sales and Distribution • Billing • Rebate Processing • Define Material Rebate Groups**. Click on the **New Entries** button to create new rebate groups in the system.

Standard material rebate groups **01** (**Maximum Rebate**) and **02** (**Minor Rebate**) are illustrated in Figure 3.46.

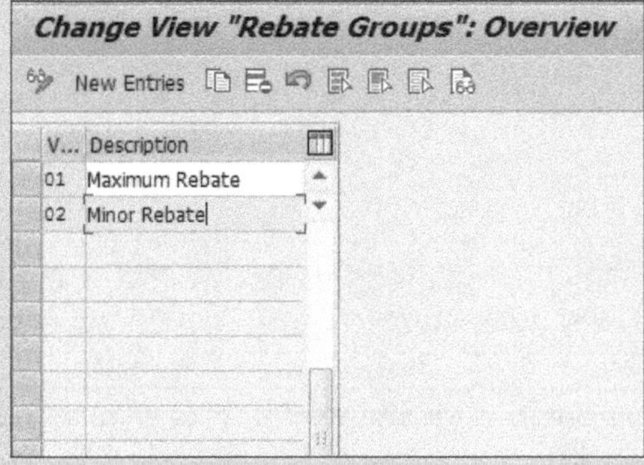

Figure 3.46 Material Rebate Groups

- **Pricing Ref. Matl**
  In the scenario where the prices associated with the materials are the same, then to optimize the condition record maintenance, you can maintain the price of a single material and use that material number as a reference to pricing of other materials that share the same price attributes. You have to enter the reference material number in this field.
- **Commission Group**
  In sales, commissions may be provided to sales representatives based on the targets or deals they achieve. The process incentivizes them with extra cash bonus. You can use the field to group the material to offer similar commissions.

Configuration: Commission Groups

You can define commission groups by navigating to menu path **Logistics – General • Material Master • Settings for Key Fields • Data Relevant to Sales and Distribution • Define Commission Groups**. You can create the new commission group by clicking on the **New Entries** button.

Figure 3.47 shows the standard commission groups defined: **01** and **02**.

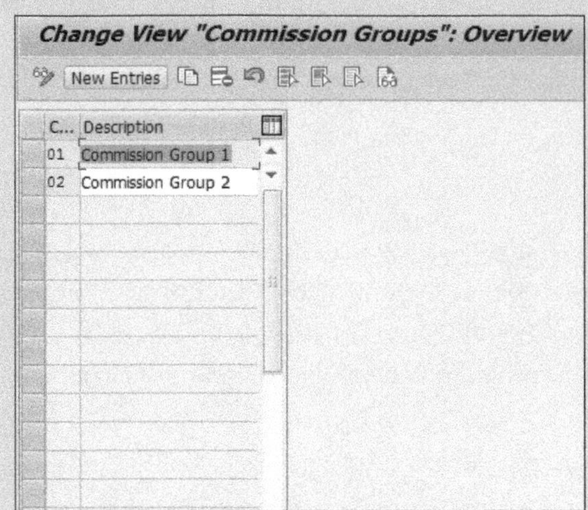

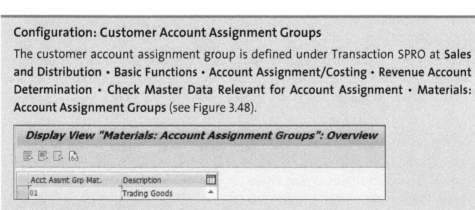

Figure 3.47 Commission Groups

- **Material Price Grp**
  This field is used to sort various materials into a single group to provide the group condition pricing. For example, say the requirement is to consider the total document value or group of material values to propose the discount in the sales order. Here, you can group the material under one specific material pricing group. Then the condition discount amount will be distributed among all the line items in proportion to the value of the line items.
- **Acct Assmt Grp Mat.**
  You can use this field to determine the revenue accounts in the sales process. You can group materials with the same accounting requirements, create the account assignment group for those materials, and assign the same account assignment group of the materials to this field.

Configuration: Customer Account Assignment Groups

The customer account assignment group is defined under Transaction SPRO at **Sales and Distribution • Basic Functions • Account Assignment/Costing • Revenue Account Determination • Check Master Data Relevant for Account Assignment • Materials: Account Assignment Groups** (see Figure 3.48).

Display View "Materials: Account Assignment Groups": Overview

Acct Assmt Grp Mat.	Description
01	Trading Goods

Figure 3.48 Materials: Account Assignment Group

- **Gen. item cat. grp**
  This field is one of the prerequisites for determining the item category in the sales order. SAP has provided standard item category groups, as shown in Table 3.2, that you can use by default for the underlying business process.

Item Category Group	Description
NORM	Standard item category group
BANC	IPO item category group
BANS	Third-party item category group
0001	Make to order
ERLA	Bill of materials (BOM) header pricing
LUMF	BOM item pricing

Table 3.2 Standard Item Category Groups

- **Material groups** and **Product attributes**
  You can use these fields to further break down the material for reporting purposes. These fields can also be used for setting up the condition records and discount records in pricing.

3.2.5 Sales: General/Plant View

The data in the **Sales: General/Plant** view is used for the various downstream processes such as availability check, delivery scheduling, and serial number maintenance. The view can be maintained separately for each sales organization, plant, and distribution channel. Let's explore the important fields associated with the view in detail, as shown in Figure 3.49.

Fill in the following fields to set up the material master sales general/plant data:

- **Availability check**
  The process of checking the availability of stock or material and creating requirements for material planning while creating a sales order is called an availability check. This field drives the availability check functionality, which we'll discuss in detail in Chapter 4, Section 4.1.

  The options that you can maintain in the field are as follows:

  - **01** (daily requirement): The system combines all the sales order quantities on a specific day and updates them in a single line in the stock/requirement list. The stock/requirement list can be viewed in Transaction MD04.

- **02** (individual requirement): The system will update the stock/requirement list with each sales order quantity into separate lines along with the sales order number.
- **KP** (no requirement): If, for certain materials, the business doesn't want to perform the availability check, then you can maintain the parameter as **KP**, which will bypass the availability check settings made in the system.

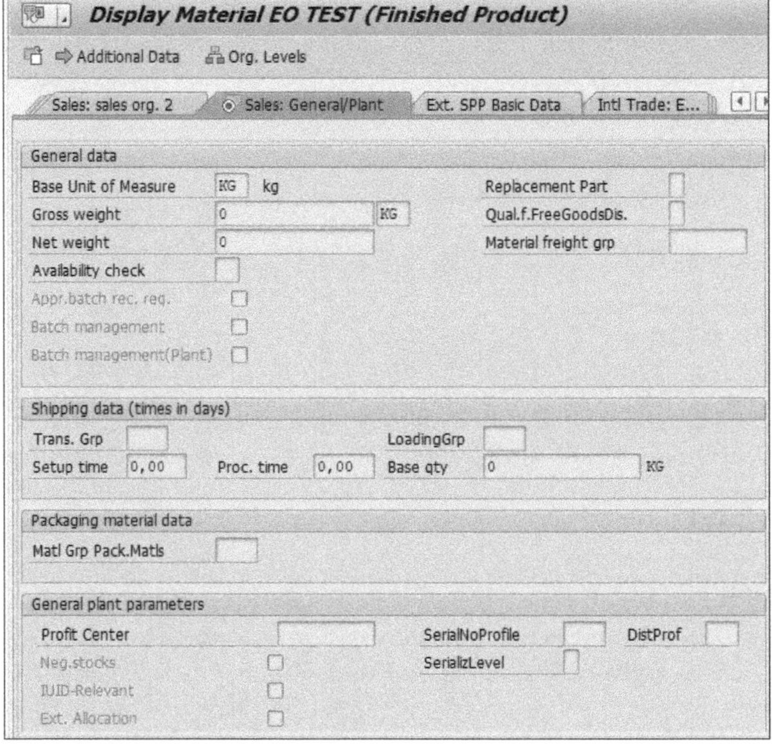

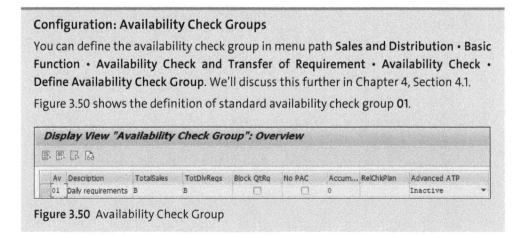

Figure 3.49 Material Master: Sales General/Plant View

Configuration: Availability Check Groups

You can define the availability check group in menu path **Sales and Distribution • Basic Function • Availability Check and Transfer of Requirement • Availability Check • Define Availability Check Group**. We'll discuss this further in Chapter 4, Section 4.1.

Figure 3.50 shows the definition of standard availability check group **01**.

Display View "Availability Check Group": Overview

Av	Description	TotalSales	TotDlvReqs	Block QtRq	No PAC	Accum...	RelChkPlan	Advanced ATP
01	Daily requirements	B	B	☐	☐	0		Inactive

Figure 3.50 Availability Check Group

- **Batch management**
  To track the expiry date of the defective goods, you can assign a unique number to a specific lot of products manufactured on the premises or procured from outside. This lot is called a batch, and the given number is called the batch number.

  A batch can contain multiple units of the same product. One prerequisite for batch functionality is checking the material master field. Usually, materials management consultants are responsible for creating the batch management process.

- **Replacement Part**
  The field specifies whether the material can be a replacement part or not. The further use of the field is to calculate value-added tax (VAT) on the material.

- **Material freight grp**
  You can group several materials based on the freight requirement and assign the group in this field. Material freight group is used to maintain the freight cost for the shipment document in logistics execution and SAP Transportation Management (SAP TM).

- **Trans. Grp**
  Transportation group is one of the parameters to determine the route in sales orders. In logistics, you need to group the materials with similar transportation attributes. For example, liquefied materials can only be transported through special containers, and certain food items will need refrigeration during transportation. You can create the associated transportation groups and assign them to the material.

Configuration: Transportation Groups

The menu path for transportation group definition is **Sales and Distribution • Basic Functions • Routes • Route Determination • Define Transportation Groups**, which lands you at the screen shown in Figure 3.51. You can click on the **New Entries** button to create your own transport groups.

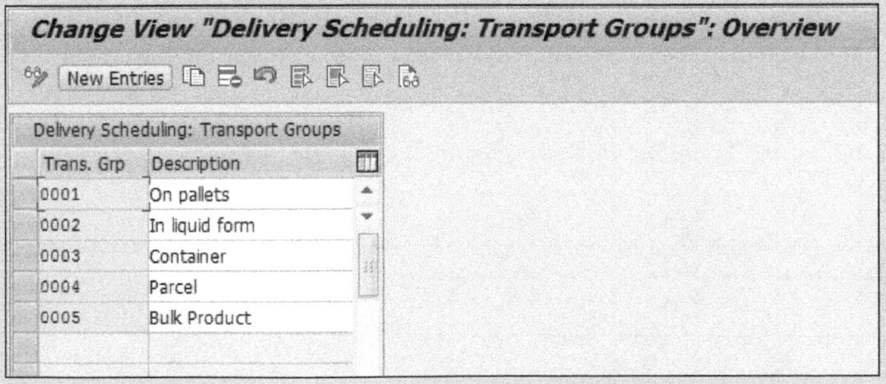

Change View "Delivery Scheduling: Transport Groups": Overview

New Entries

Delivery Scheduling: Transport Groups

Trans. Grp	Description
0001	On pallets
0002	In liquid form
0003	Container
0004	Parcel
0005	Bulk Product

Figure 3.51 Transportation Groups

- **LoadingGrp**
  Grouping the material with the loading attributes is called the loading group. The loading requirement of the material varies with the product type. For example, you need lifts and cranes for heavy machinery, you need specialized lifting trucks for cement bags, and you need to load crockery items manually by human intervention. Specifying the loading group in the material master helps in setting the transportation processes for the material.

Configuration: Loading Groups and Shipping Points

You can define loading groups based on your requirements through menu path **Logistics Execution • Shipping • Basic Shipping Functions • Shipping Point and Goods Receiving Point Determination • Define Loading Groups**. You can create your own loading group by clicking on the **New Entries** button, as shown in Figure 3.52.

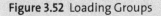

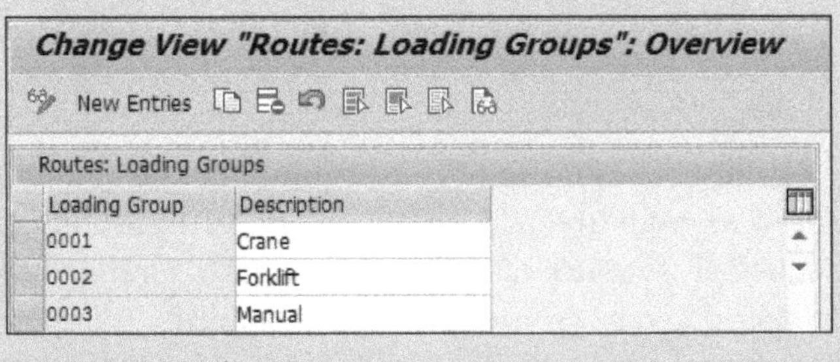

Change View "Routes: Loading Groups": Overview

New Entries

Routes: Loading Groups

Loading Group	Description
0001	Crane
0002	Forklift
0003	Manual

Figure 3.52 Loading Groups

The loading group is one of the parameters to determine the shipping point in sales documents. The system determines the shipping point in the sales order with three parameters: shipping condition, loading group, and plant.

The system picks the shipping condition from a business partner or sales document type, loading group from the material master, and plant from the customer material info record, customer master, or material master.

You can configure shipping point determination by executing Transaction SPRO and navigating to menu path **Logistics Execution • Shipping • Basic Shipping Functions • Shipping Point and Goods Receiving Point Determination • Assign Shipping Points**. Figure 3.53 shows the shipping point determination.

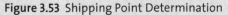

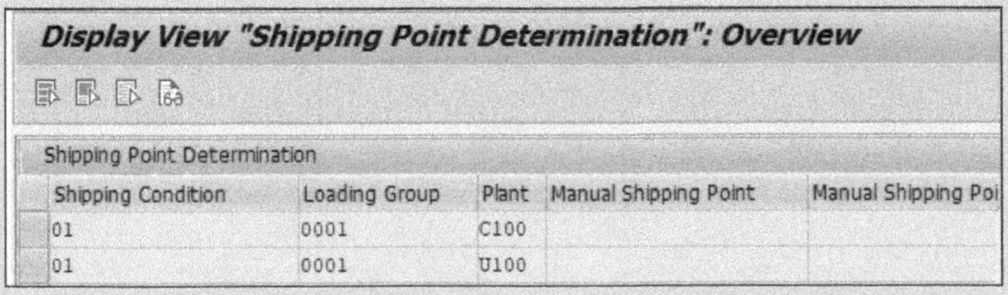

Display View "Shipping Point Determination": Overview

Shipping Point Determination

Shipping Condition	Loading Group	Plant	Manual Shipping Point	Manual Shipping Poi
01	0001	C100		
01	0001	U100		

Figure 3.53 Shipping Point Determination

- **Setup time**
  The time required to set up the instrument or machines for loading the material in trucks and vehicles is called the setup time. This field is used for capacity planning for shipments.
- **Proc. time**
  The time required to load the materials or products into transportation means such as truck, train, or plane is called processing time.
- **Base qty**
  The setup time and processing time maintained in the preceding fields refer to the quantity mentioned in the **Base qty** field. It's measured in the base UoM.
- **Packing material data**
  Grouping of materials based on the packaging requirement is called a packing material group. You can create your own packing material group and assign it in this field. You can also create condition records for the shipment cost using this field.
- **Ref material for packing**
  This field is used to save the packing instruction for the material. For example, suppose two materials, A and B, can be packed similarly. In that case, you can create a packing reference material C and assign the reference material C in both A and B. While performing the packing activities in the delivery document, the packing material instruction will be used to pack both materials A and B.
- **Neg.stocks**
  This indicator is on if you want to allow negative stocks in your inventory management. This is specifically used in the cases where the goods receipt for the stock hasn't yet been done, but the business wants to use the stock. By default, the negative stocks are activated for special stocks such as sales from stock and consignment stock at the customer and vendor.

Note

The activation for negative stock functionality is done in the following areas:

- **Valuation area level**
  This level is used to activate the negative stock at the plant or company code.
- **Storage location level**
  This can limit the further activation of negative stock at a specific storage location of a plant.
- **Material master level**
  This is maintained in the plant data.

- **Profit Center**
  This is an organizational unit in the controlling functionality configured for internal management reporting. It evaluates the personal profit or loss for the specific

entities. After creating the invoice and releasing the invoice to accounting, a profit center document gets generated along with the other accounting documents. It's one of the mandatory fields while creating the material master.

- **SerialNoProfile**
  You can manage the stock in SAP S/4HANA at the batch level and at the serialized stock level. You need to serialize the stocks to manage the stock at a serial number, and this is achieved with the help of a serial number profile. The serial number profile is usually maintained for equipment such as heavy machinery, truck tires, motors, and so on.

  While doing the outbound deliveries, you can assign the serial numbers automatically to the line items of deliveries. This serial number can be used as tracking for warranty and claims processes. In a third-party scenario where the automatic purchase requisition is created, the serial number assigned to the sales item will be transferred to the purchase requisition and the purchase order by default.

Configuration: Serial Number Profiles and Serializing Procedures

Serial number profiles can be configured in menu path **Plant Maintenance and Customer Service • Master Data in Plant Maintenance and Customer Service • Technical Objects • Serial Number Management • Define Serial Number Profiles.** The serial number configuration falls under the purview of the quality management consultant or materials management consultant. Figure 3.54 shows an example serial number profile definition. Consider the following key fields:

- **ExistReq**
  This field controls whether you need to create the serial number entered for the operational documents first as a master record, through Transactions IQ01 or IQ04, and then assign it to the document. If the indicator isn't set, then the serial numbers will be automatically created during the business transaction execution.
- **StkCk**
  While serializing the material, the system can perform the stock check, or you can default the system to avoid the stock check with the help of the stock check indicator.

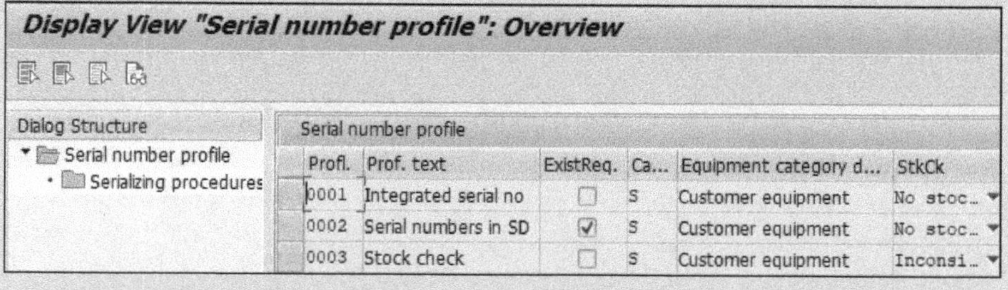

Display View "Serial number profile": Overview

Dialog Structure
- Serial number profile
  - Serializing procedures

Serial number profile

Profl.	Prof. text	ExistReq.	Ca...	Equipment category d...	StkCk
0001	Integrated serial no	☐	S	Customer equipment	No stoc...
0002	Serial numbers in SD	☑	S	Customer equipment	No stoc...
0003	Stock check	☐	S	Customer equipment	Inconsi...

Figure 3.54 Serial Number Profiles

After configuring the serial number profile, you need to select and activate the profile for the business transactions associated with production processing, sales order, or planned order. Based on your requirements for serialization, you can choose the related **Serializing procedures** provided by SAP as a standard (as shown in Figure 3.55). You can't create your own serializing procedure.

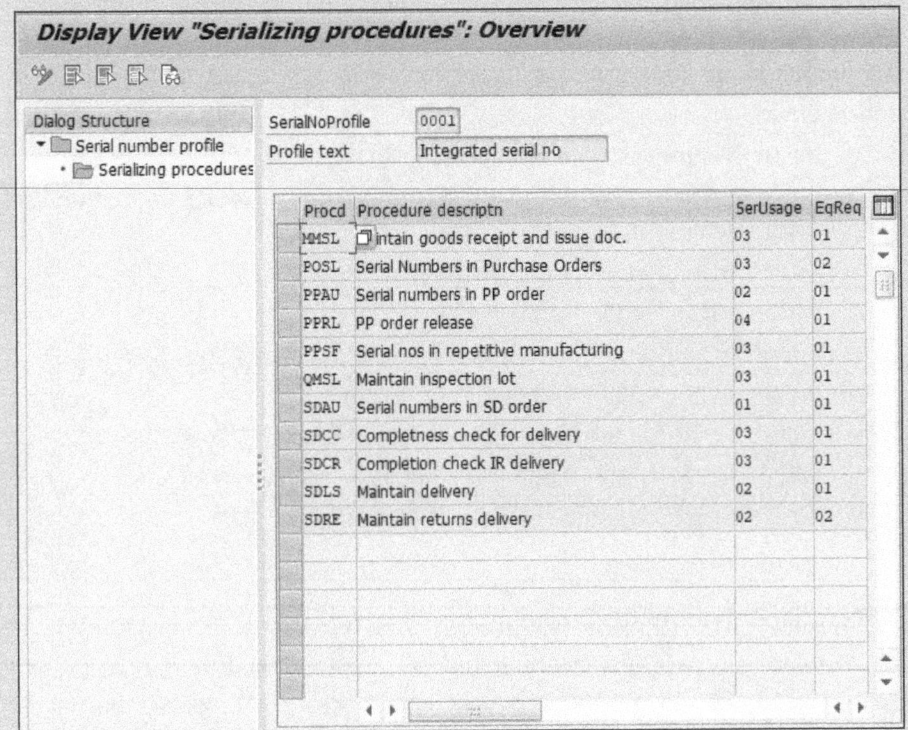

Procd	Procedure descriptn	SerUsage	EqReq
MMSL	Maintain goods receipt and issue doc.	03	01
POSL	Serial Numbers in Purchase Orders	03	02
PPAU	Serial numbers in PP order	02	01
PPRL	PP order release	04	01
PPSF	Serial nos in repetitive manufacturing	03	01
QMSL	Maintain inspection lot	03	01
SDAU	Serial numbers in SD order	01	01
SDCC	Completness check for delivery	03	01
SDCR	Completion check IR delivery	03	01
SDLS	Maintain delivery	02	01
SDRE	Maintain returns delivery	02	02

Figure 3.55 Serializing Procedure

For assigning the serial number to a sales order, you have to use the **SDAU** serializing procedure. Note the following key fields:

- **SerUsage**
  This field governs the logic where you need to create the serial numbers first before assigning them to the business transaction, or you can post them during the business transaction.
- **EqReq**
  This field governs whether the equipment master is mandatory or not for serializing.
- **Serial Number Status**
  The status of the serial number plays an important role while assigning the serial number to sales order or deliveries. A few serial number statuses are listed here:
  - **EDEL**: Assigned in delivery note
  - **ESTO**: At customer site
  - **ECUS**: In the warehouse

Note

The following are the process steps for executing the sales cycle with serial number integration:

1. Create the serial number profile.
2. Assign the serializing order procedure (**SDAU**) and delivery procedure (**SDLS**) to the serial number.
3. Assign the serial number profile in the material master.
4. Say there is a stock of 50 quantities without a serial number. Create a serial number for all 50 stock items with Transaction IQ01.
5. Create a sales order for one quantity with Transaction VA01.
6. Assign one serial number for this material.
7. The sales order is saved, and delivery and post goods issue (PGI) is performed for the same serial number and material.
8. Stock is reduced with one quantity in stock overview (Transaction MMBE).
9. In the material document list (Transaction MB51), you can see a message that **The material is managed in serial numbers** in the **Serial Number** field.

3.2.6 Material Requirements Planning

Material requirements planning (MRP) is the planning tool used by organizations to plan materials required for production or sales purposes. SAP S/4HANA has its own functionality related to MRP. The prerequisite for the MRP process is the filled material master data relevant to the MRP process.

As shown in Figure 3.56, the process starts with the forecasting data preparation. The required materials and quantities are forecasted based on past historical sales and consumption data. These requirements are called planned independent requirements. The planned independent requirements are fed into the demand program. The customer requirement generated on the sales order is also fed into the demand program.

Based on the data provided to the demand program, the system creates the procurement proposal after running the MRP. The procurement proposal consists of either a purchase requisition, which will be turned into a purchase order (and a subsequent procure-to-pay cycle will follow), or it will create a planned order, which will be turned into a production order (and a plan-to-produce cycle will follow).

Now, let's explore relevant MRP views and their fields in detail.

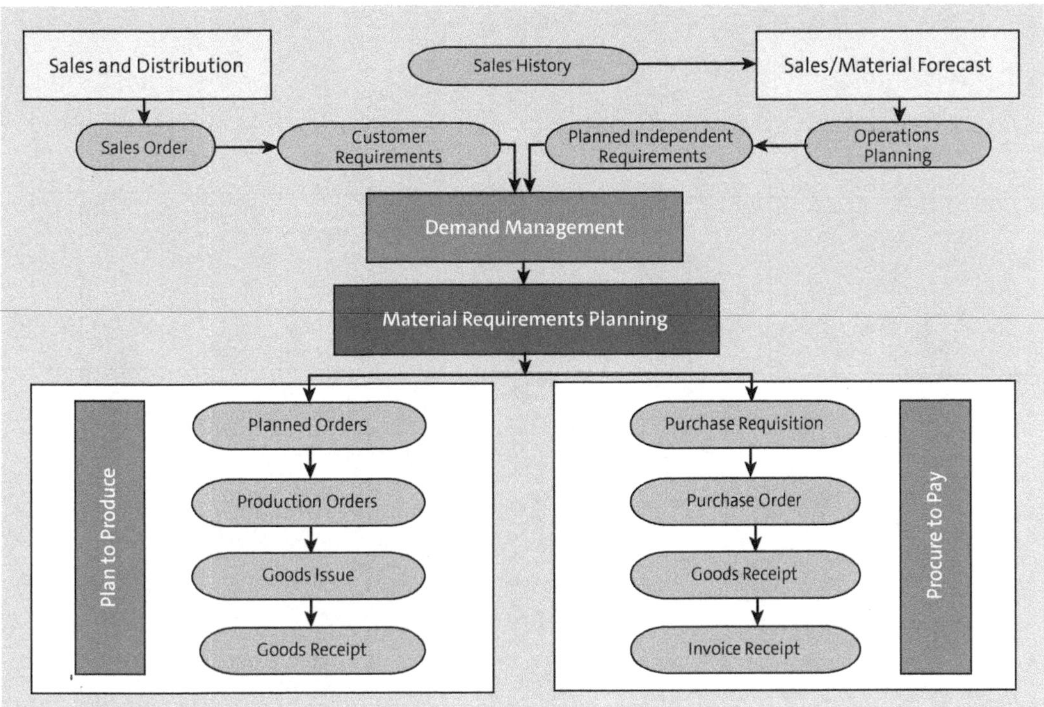

Figure 3.56 MRP Process

MRP 1 View

The **MRP 1** tab, as shown in Figure 3.57, contains important fields that will be used to run the MRP process. In this section, we'll discuss the important fields that will be used for sales and distribution–production planning integration. (Note that not all fields are explained as it will deviate from the scope of the book.)

Fill in the following fields to set up the material master **MRP 1** tab:

- **MRP Group**
  This is an organizational element that you create in conjunction with a plant. You run the MRP process through Transaction MD01, and the primary parameter while running the transaction is a plant. As plant-level controls aren't enough for complex processes, you need to configure an extra component that will store the MRP-relevant controls, and this extra component is the MRP group.

  You'll create MRP groups based on the planning requirement of varied materials produced or procured in the organization and then assign those defined MRP groups to the desired material. From a sales and distribution perspective, this field can determine the requirement type in the sales order. If you don't maintain the MRP group in the material, the system uses plant parameters to run the MRP process.

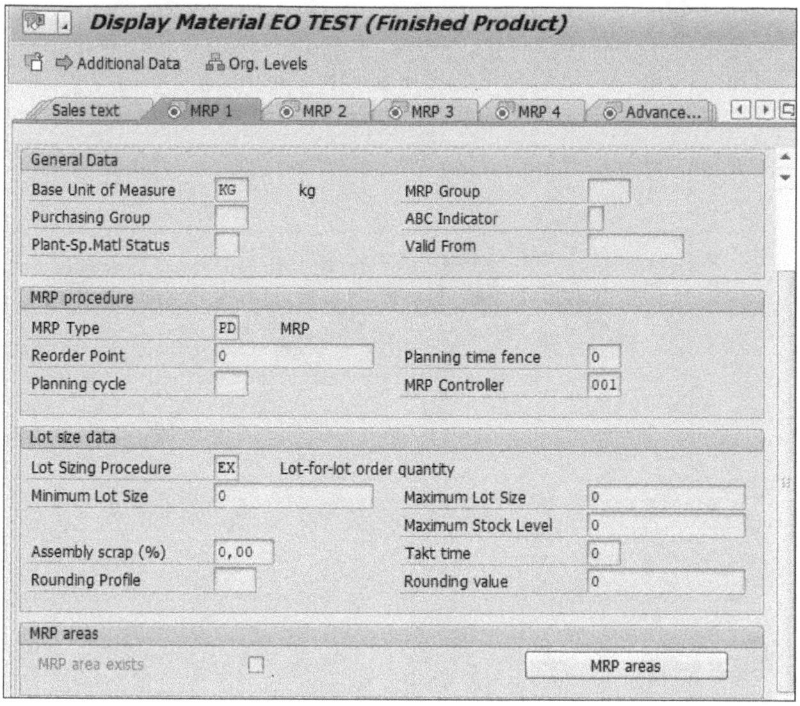

Figure 3.57 MRP 1 View

Configuration: MRP Groups

You can configure the MRP groups through Transaction OPPR or by navigating menu path **Production • Materials Requirements Planning • MRP Groups • Carry Out Overall Maintenance of MRP Groups**. This configuration is typically handled by the production planning consultant.

- **MRP Type**

  This field determines the process of planning the material for procurement and production. While configuring the material type, production planning consultants must select the MRP procedure relevant to the MRP type. The MRP procedure governs the further logic and the field's availability in the MRP type configuration.

  Basically, this field controls whether or not a particular material is relevant for planning. SAP has provided out-of-the-box standard MRP types. You can choose the MRP type based on your requirements while setting up the master data.

  Following are a few standard MRP types:

  - **PD**: Planning (standard MRP type used for make to order [MTO] and make to stock [MTS] scenarios)
  - **ND**: No planning

- **VM**: Automatic reorder planning
- **VV**: Forecast-based planning

From a sales and distribution perspective, the **MRP Type** field is used for following determinations:

- Requirement type determination in sales orders.
- Schedule line category determination in the schedule line of sales orders. Schedule lines are determined in the sales order based on item category and MRP type.

- **MRP Controller**
  The person responsible for running the MRP runs and monitoring the material availability in the production system is called an MRP controller. You can configure the MRP controller based on the production or procurement plants.

MRP 2 View

The **MRP 2** tab, as shown in Figure 3.58, includes information such as procurement type, planned delivery time, goods receipt delivery time, and safety stock. These fields are also used for the downstream processes such as delivery scheduling. In this section, we'll discuss the important fields that will be used for sales and distribution integration with production planning.

Fill in the following fields to set up the material master **MRP 2** tab:

- **Procurement type**
  The procurement type is one of the parameters used while executing the MRP run to create the procurement proposals. The field can default in the material master when assigning the material type with the procurement type in configuration.

  You can maintain three options in the **Procurement type** field as follows:

  - **E** (in-house production): This option specifies that the material is manufactured in house, which creates the production order.
  - **F** (external procurement): This option represents that the material is procured externally, for example, raw materials, specialized third-party components, and so on.
  - **X** (both procurement types): If you maintain both in this field, then the material can either be manufactured in-house or can be procured externally, for example, semifinished goods.

- **In-house production**
  This is the time taken to manufacture the material in-house. To determine the planned dates for planned orders in materials planning, the system requires an in-house production time. This field is also used for delivery scheduling in sales and distribution.

- **Planned Deliv. Time**
  The time required to procure material from the vendor is called planned delivery

time. You maintain the time require to procure material from the vendor in this field.

- **GR processing time**
  This is the time required to process the goods receipt, that is, inspecting the quality of the material before entering it into the system. This field is also used to calculate the delivery date to the customer for backward scheduling.

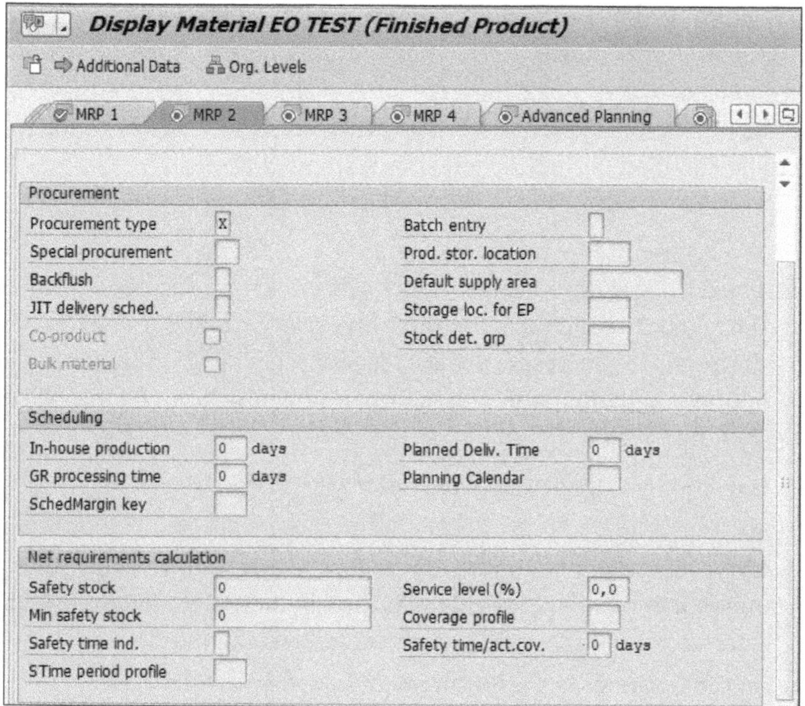

Figure 3.58 MRP 2 View

- **Safety stock**
  If the business is experiencing any unforeseen conditions, they should not impact the day-to-day production operations. Organizations maintain this stock as a safety net for such situations. Thus, the organization maintains a minimum inventory in this field to meet unforeseen future requirements.

MRP 3 View

The **MRP 3** tab, as shown in Figure 3.59, contains important fields that will be used to run the MRP process. We'll briefly discuss the strategy group, total replenishment lead time, and availability check. From an integration standpoint, these are important fields that will be used for sales and distribution–production planning integration.

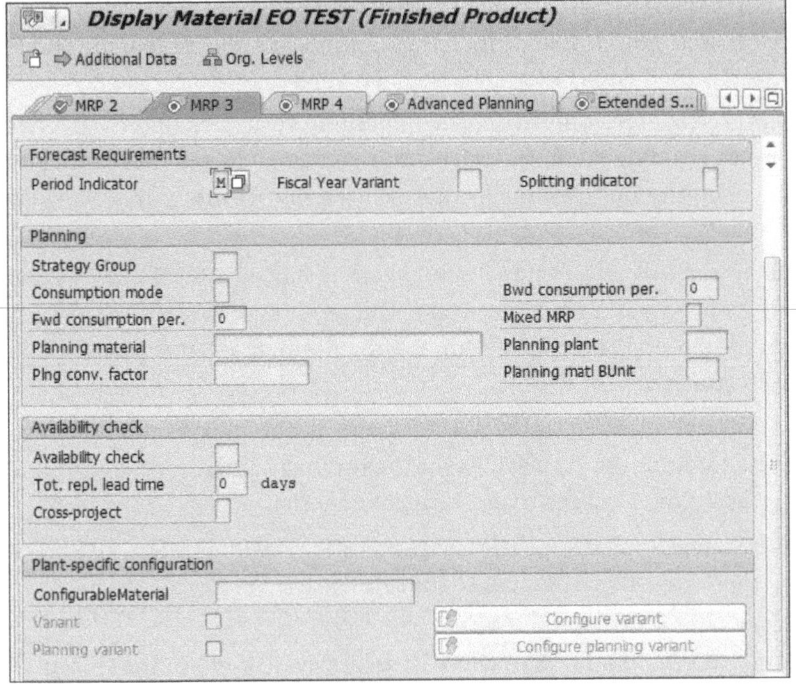

Figure 3.59 MRP 3 View

Fill in the following fields to set up the material master **MRP 3** tab:

- **Strategy Group**
  This field specifies how planned independent requirements (forecasts) from demand management and customer requirements from sales orders should communicate during the planning (MRP) run. It's a plant-specific field, which means that the same material present in different plants may have a different strategy group. The strategy group's configuration also controls the system's availability check controls. The strategy group is one of the parameters to determine the requirement type in sales orders.

> **Note**
> The requirement type is determined in the sales order based on four parameters: **Strategy Group**, **MRP Group**, **MRP Type**, and **Item Category**.

The strategy groups that are relevant from a sales standpoint are listed here:

- **10** (MTS): This strategy is used when materials are manufactured regardless of customer requirements. In this strategy, material production planning is dependent on independent planning derived from demand management. Individual customer requirements from sales orders have no significance in this strategy, so sales orders don't affect production. The product is stocked and then delivered to the customer as needed. This strategy is straightforward to implement and is appropriate for finished goods where the finished good can be forecasted.

SAP defines MTS production in two distinct planning strategies, 10 and 11. They differ in how they handle available stock. Planning strategy 10 will take stock into account (net requirements planning), whereas planning strategy 11 won't take stock into account (gross requirements planning).

- **20** (MTO): In this strategy, the material production is started after the sales order requirement has been passed to the system. The production orders are directly linked to the sales order. Planned independent requirement or forecast data isn't required in this strategy.

  Usually, the material involved in the MTO strategy is complex to manufacture, and an accurate forecast isn't achievable for the products. Customers are willing to wait for the lead time required to produce the material.

  The common strategies used for the MTO process are 20 and 21. The difference between the two is the cost settlement to the sales order.

- **Availability check**
  This field indicates whether and how to check the stock availability in the system. It also generates the requirement for material planning. We'll discuss availability check in detail in Chapter 4, Section 4.1.

  You can do availability checks at various stages in the business:

  - Sales order processing: The system does the availability check while creating a sales order to know if the materials can be delivered at the requested date.
  - Planned order processing: When converting a planned order into a production order, the availability check is carried out to know the material availability to fulfill the production order.
  - Production order processing: The system checks the availability during production order processing to know the available stock of the material.
  - Inventory management: An availability check can be done when changing reservations or during goods issue to know if it can fulfill the requirement and affect the availability of other elements.

- **Tot. repl. lead time**
  This is the total time required to manufacture the products and take the finished product to the storage location. This involves the time needed for both in-house production time and planned delivery time.

  This field is also crucial for the delivery scheduling in the availability check. Delivery scheduling is the technique of determining the delivery dates in the sales document. While determining the delivery dates in the sales order, the system will consider the total replenishment lead time if stock isn't available.

3.2.7 Accounting View

The fields in the **Accounting 1** tab, as shown in Figure 3.60, are used for account determination in deliveries. You can configure various valuation subprocesses, such as split valuation, by using the fields in the tab.

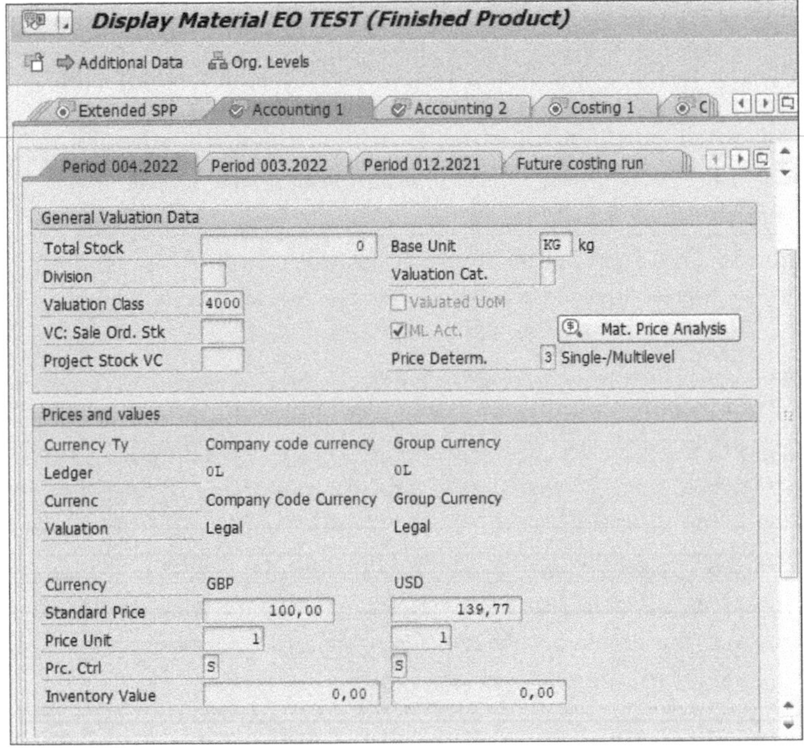

Figure 3.60 Accounting View

Fill in the following fields to set up the material master **Accounting 1** tab:

- **Valuation Cat.**
  To distinguish between material stocks, a valuation category and a valuation type must be defined. The valuation type describes the potential characteristics of partial stocks. The valuation category is used during split valuation to determine on what basis your stocks are valued together. For example, stocks can be valuated separately based on quality or source of supply. You use the valuation category also to determine the general ledger account in the inventory accounting document during goods receipt and goods issue.

> **Note**
>
> *Split valuation* permits you to valuate a material's substocks (part of the total stock) in various ways. The reason for valuating substocks separately are as follows:

- Based on the country or geographical region the material is procured.
- Based on whether the product is internally manufactured or externally procured.
- Based on valuating the scrap or damaged products seprately in the returns process if the damaged products enter the plant.

Valuation area is an organizational unit on which the material valuation is carried out. SAP has provided two levels at which you can set the valuation area:

- Plant level (recommended by SAP)
- Company code level

Valuation type is a key that determines split-valued stocks of material and denotes a partial stock's characteristics.

The *valuation category* is assigned in the material master record, and the valuation type is chosen during material transactions such as goods issues and goods receipts.

- **Valuation Class**
  This helps to determine the inventory accounting document. It's the key to categorizing materials with the same account determination. Suppose a different general ledger account is to be posted to the valuation class in a transaction. In that case, the account determination for this transaction must depend on the valuation class in the automatic account determination configuration (Transaction OBYC settings).

  The valuation class can default based on the material type while setting up the material master. However, you should note that different materials with the same material type can be assigned to different valuation classes.

3.3 Summary

This chapter briefly discussed the master data elements related to business partners and the material master. We've covered business partner configurations and the necessary settings involved in business partner setup in Section 3.1. Then we delved into various business partner roles such as general role, sales role, company code role, and credit management role. This will lay the groundwork for understanding intra-ERP integrations, which we'll go over in more detail in subsequent chapters.

In Section 3.2 on the material master, we studied various views such as **Basic data** views, **Sales: sales org.** data views, **MRP** views, and **Accounting** views. Understanding these views plays a vital role in solidifying the intra-ERP integrations that we'll discuss in further chapters.

In the next chapter, we'll move on to the specific integration configurations, starting with materials management.

Chapter 4
Materials Management

Materials management is a core component that every organization includes in the scope of their enterprise resource planning (ERP) implementation. It's nearly impossible to set up sales, production, and revenue reporting in an SAP landscape without first establishing materials management. Materials management seamlessly integrates with all the other peripheral functionalities.

Sales and procurement are two sides of the same coin. Business processes by nature tend to get complex due to the flow of data points from one module to another module and intra-ERP integrations with different modules. The sales and distribution functionality integrates tightly with materials management in various ways.

In this chapter, we'll deep dive into some of the major integration points between sales and distribution and materials management functionalities. We'll start the discussion by covering the available-to-promise (ATP) functionality in the SAP S/4HANA system along with configuration settings. After ATP, we cover the stock transport order (STO) and relevant configurations followed by the STO accounting entries. We'll next discuss the general ledger account determination on deliveries topic and its associated configuration. Then we'll dive into the third-party process and the relevant configurations. The chapter will conclude with the inventory management functionality integration points.

4.1 Available-to-Promise

ATP is a critical component of inventory management that helps organizations manage their supply chain. With ATP, firms can store the smallest amount of a specific product in their warehouses to maximize inventory space. ATP leverages data to match supply to demand as closely as possible, ensuring that customers never face issues with the nonavailability of stocks.

Let's dive into the ATP functionality in SAP S/4HANA in detail.

4.1.1 What Is Available-to-Promise?

ATP, in a business context, allows companies to store only the bare minimum of products to better manage inventory levels. This helps businesses minimize the risks of overstocking products while also allowing for timely replacement of any low-selling items. It allows businesses to maintain a healthy balance of client satisfaction and profitability.

The quantity of inventory that a company can commit to selling in the near future is referred to as ATP quantities. The formula for calculating the ATP quantities is as follows:

ATP quantity = Quantity in hand + Supply – Demand

Let's break down the different variables of this formula:

- **Quantity in hand**
  Total quantity that is available in the stock in the organization.
- **Supply**
  Planned orders, scheduled receipts such as purchase orders, and purchase requisitions.
- **Demand**
  The number of products customers are ready to purchase or for which the production orders are created, for example, sales order created for customers and component demands for the production orders.

If the ATP quantities aren't available for the customer, then the following remediation steps apply:

- If ATP quantities aren't available and the customer needs the order on priority, then you can check the ATP quantities on another plant and replenish the stock with the help of STOs.
- If backorder processing is active for the customers and materials, then you can allocate the stock allocated to other customers and redirect the stock to the existing customer with higher priority.
- If the customer agrees, you can replace the material with similar material in stock.
- The system considers backward scheduling and creates the schedule line for the future date based on the available parameters. We'll explore this functionality in Section 4.1.3.

Now that you have a general idea of what the availability check is, we'll walk through the key capabilities of ATP and provide a process overview of the availability check, specifically, in the following sections.

Solution Capabilities

The ATP functionality is enhanced in the SAP S/4HANA core, known as SAP S/4HANA for advanced ATP. However, the license for enhanced functionality needs to be purchased separately from your regular SAP S/4HANA license.

Advanced ATP comes with the functionalities shown in Figure 4.1. Due to our focus on sales and distribution integration, we'll be focusing on the product availability check, which is used extensively across industries.

First, let's discuss the business benefits of SAP S/4HANA for advanced ATP:

- Consists of the functionalities associated with the release for delivery, product allocation check, and alternative-based confirmations (ABC)
- Plans and manages allocations in case of material shortage situations
- Makes informed decisions to change confirmations
- Allows substitution of the delivering plant from the sales item by another plant, which can be achieved with the help of ABC

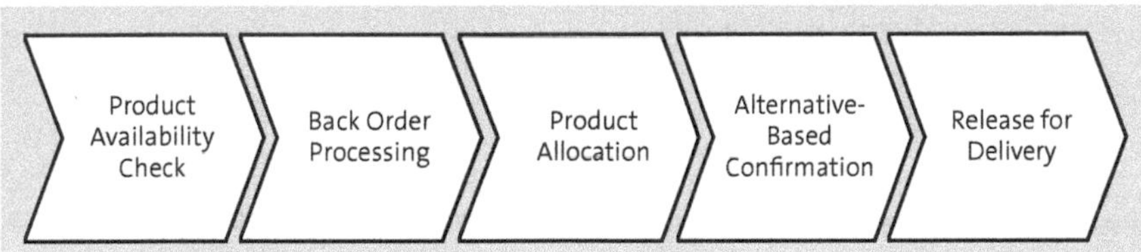

Figure 4.1 Advanced ATP Functionalities

Now, let's briefly discuss the capabilities of each functionality:

- **Product availability check**
  This is the key ATP functionality from a sales and distribution perspective. As part of the SAP S/4HANA changes, you can now perform availability checks for STOs. It supports special stocks such as consignment, along with batch management integrations, which are commonly used in the consumer packaged goods (CPG) and pharma industries. The response time for the availability check has been reduced due to the underlying SAP HANA database.
- **Backorder processing**
  Backorder processing is an SAP feature that allows you to adjust commitments and override stock blockages associated with sales documents and deliveries. For example, suppose you receive an order for material "X" from a highly significant client, but the full quantity of A has already been committed to another customer "Y" via prior sales orders. Backorder processing can assist you to modify the commitment and shifting stock due from Y to X. You can achieve backorder processing by configuring the SAP Fiori app called Backorder Processing via win, gain, redistribute, fill,

and lose strategies. Supply assignment run, which was part of SAP Apparel and Footwear, has now been integrated with the backorder processing functionality so that other industries can leverage the solution capabilities. Since the 1909 release, you can use the ABC functionality as part of backorder processing.

- **Product allocations**
  This function in SAP S/4HANA for advanced ATP is designed to help businesses avoid critical requirements and procurement scenarios by implementing certain control choices. This allows companies to limit production to a bare minimum while also reacting swiftly to bottlenecks and changing market conditions. If demand exceeds supply, the product allocation capability allows companies to distribute supplies fairly to clients while staying within their manufacturing capacity. You can allocate quantities for individual materials in various hierarchical combinations and then reserve these amounts for these characteristics in production allocation. These qualities or hierarchical combinations can range from sales area data to customer groups or individual customers. You must define the product allocation procedure and assign it to products and plants.
- **Alternative-based confirmation (ABC)**
  ABC assists organizations in increasing order fulfillment rates by automatically selecting alternative locations or items based on current demand and supply. This enables organizations to efficiently confirm orders, lowering inventory carrying costs and reducing the number of back orders. Furthermore, supply chain issues, such as late deliveries, can be addressed dynamically by confirming orders from multiple locations or using alternate items. If a material is unavailable in the plant where the sales order is being processed, location substitution is used to ensure that it's available in another plant. For example, if a material sales order is generated in Mumbai, but the material isn't available, the system can look for availability in a different plant, such as Pune, and confirm the sales order. This location replacement is handled by global ATP's rule-based ATP functionality in SAP Advanced Planning and Optimization (SAP APO) based on business rules stored in master data.
- **Release for delivery**
  Manual backorder processing capabilities are provided through the release to delivery functionality. SAP has provided this functionality to alter the delivery quantities post-execution of backorder processing via the Release for Delivery app. After the app is configured, you can perform multiple operations. For example, if material redistribution doesn't occur on time, the app displays the confirmation, delivery status, and potential financial impact of the business situation; prevents quantities of sales order items from being processed further; postpones further sales order processing; allows the materials to be delivered; and triggers subsequent logistics processes such as picking and packing.

Process Overview

Now that you've established the key capabilities of SAP S/4HANA for advanced ATP, let's focus on the availability check process. As shown in Figure 4.2, the process gets initiated when the sales order is entered into the system manually via a front-office representative or by Electronic Data Interchange (EDI) and intermediate documents (IDocs). The product availability check or any availability check is always carried out with the combination of the plant and the material. The plant will get determined in the sales order via the customer material info record, customer master, or material master.

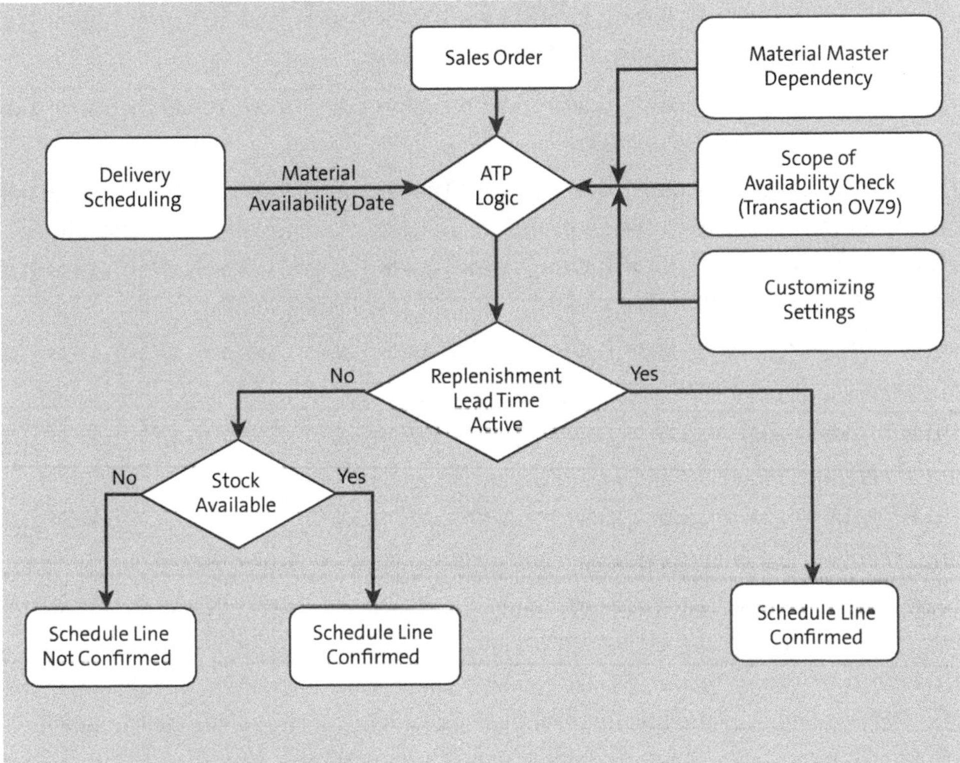

Figure 4.2 Process Overview of Availability Check

The checking group maintained in the material master and Customizing helps to determine whether the system needs to perform the availability check or not. You can carry out the product availability check with Transaction CO09 as well.

The delivery scheduling process will be initiated, and the material availability date will be calculated using the requested delivery date provided by the customer. The material availability date is calculated as follows:

Material availability date= Requested delivery date – Transportation time – Loading time – Pick/pack time

The following variables are included in this formula:

- **Requested delivery date**
  This is the customer-requested delivery date.
- **Transportation time**
  This consists of both transportation lead time and transit time.
- **Loading time**
  This is the time needed to load the products in the transportation mode for dispatch.
- **Pick/pack time**
  This is the number of days it takes to allocate products to delivery as well as the number of days it takes to pick and pack them.

We'll discuss briefly the configuration and determination of the dates mentioned in the formula in subsequent sections.

The material availability date is fed into the ATP logic, and then the ATP quantities get calculated with the help of the Customizing settings made for the ATP logic. The formula by which the system calculates the ATP quantity in SAP S/4HANA is as follows (generalized formula for ATP):

ATP quantity = Quantity in hand + Supply – Demand

In addition, consider SAP's elaborated formula:

ATP quantity = Quantity in hand for the plant + Supply (Purchase requisition + Purchase order + Planned order) – Demand (Sales order + Delivery + Reservations)

The logic for the calculation can be set in the scope of the availability check in Transaction OVZ9. We'll discuss the related configuration elements extensively in Section 4.1.4.

Orders will be confirmed if the ATP quantity is greater than the requested delivery quantity. If the calculated material availability date or transportation scheduling date is in the past, the system must use forward scheduling. Forward scheduling has the effect of creating two schedule lines for the sales order line item. If the customer allows for partial quantities, then partial delivery is possible in the sales order. As illustrated previously in Figure 4.2, the activation of replenishment lead time (RLT) in the scope of availability check leads to confirmation of the quantities in the sales order in the event of nonavailability of stock.

4.1.2 Prerequisites for the Availability Check

To perform the availability check, there are configuration elements that need to be set up in the system. Let's explore each of the configuration elements in the following sections.

Schedule Line Category Changes

A sales order is divided into three parts: sales order header data, which corresponds to header relevant information; sales order line-item data, which covers line item details; and schedule line data, which contains the delivery date and exact quantity needed to be delivered to the customer for each line item. The data in the schedule line can be controlled using the schedule line category configuration, which we'll discuss further in Section 4.4.4.

To perform schedule line category changes, execute Transaction SPRO and navigate to menu path **Sales and Distribution • Basic Functions • Availability Check and Transfer of Requirements • Availability Check with ATP Logic or Against Planning • Define Availability Check Procedure for Each Schedule Line Category**.

You'll arrive at the screen shown in Figure 4.3. For the availability check, you must enable the **AvC** checkboxes. If you want to transfer the requirements to material requirements planning (MRP), you must also activate the **Rq** checkbox. The third checkbox, **All.**, enables the scheduling line's product allocation capability.

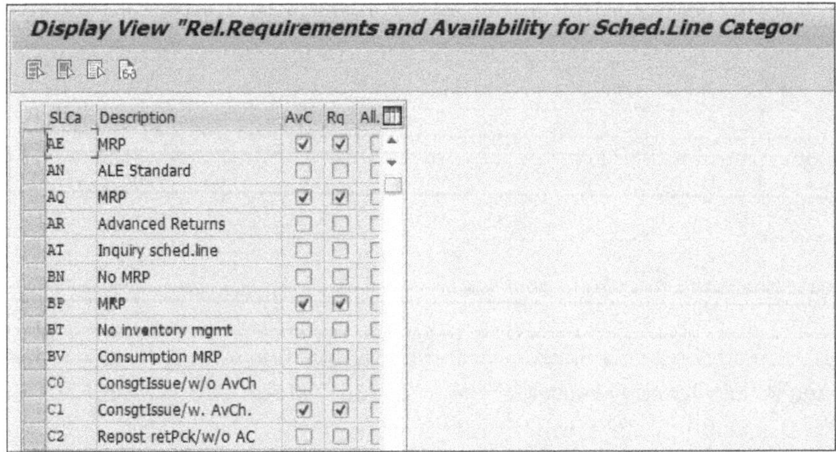

SLCa	Description	AvC	Rq	All.
AE	MRP	☑	☑	☐
AN	ALE Standard	☐	☐	☐
AQ	MRP	☑	☑	☐
AR	Advanced Returns	☐	☐	☐
AT	Inquiry sched.line	☐	☐	☐
BN	No MRP	☐	☐	☐
BP	MRP	☑	☑	☐
BT	No inventory mgmt	☐	☐	☐
BV	Consumption MRP	☐	☐	☐
C0	ConsgtIssue/w/o AvCh	☐	☐	☐
C1	ConsgtIssue/w. AvCh.	☑	☑	☐
C2	Repost retPck/w/o AC	☐	☐	☐

Figure 4.3 Defining the Availability Check Procedure for Each Schedule Line Category

Click the **Save** button or press Ctrl+S once the required checkboxes are selected.

Requirement Class Changes

The *requirement class* is used to pass the requirements from the sales order to the material planning functionality. In Chapter 8, Section 8.2, we'll discuss the transfer of requirements. The requirement class governs how ATP configuration behaves.

To perform requirement class changes, execute Transaction SPRO and follow menu path **Sales and Distribution • Basic Functions • Availability Check and Transfer of Requirements • Availability Check with ATP Logic or Against Planning • Define Procedure by Requirement Class**.

You'll arrive at the screen shown in Figure 4.4. For the availability check, you must enable the **AvC** checkboxes, and if you want to transfer the requirements to MRP, you must also activate the **Rq** checkbox. The third checkbox, **All.**, enables the scheduling line's product allocation capability. We'll explore the requirement type and requirement class in detail in Chapter 8, Section 8.2.

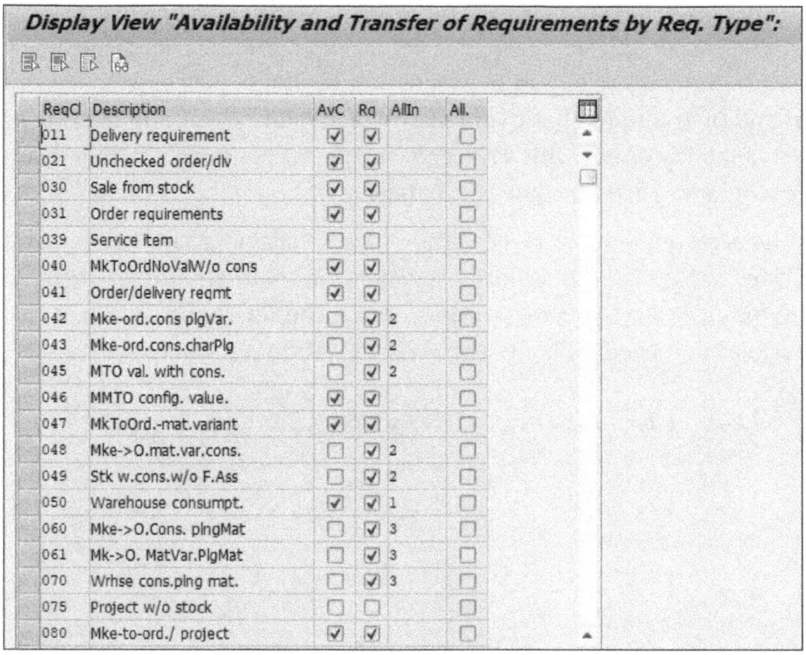

Display View "Availability and Transfer of Requirements by Req. Type":

ReqCl	Description	AvC	Rq	AllIn	All.
011	Delivery requirement	☑	☑		☐
021	Unchecked order/dlv	☑	☑		☐
030	Sale from stock	☑	☑		☐
031	Order requirements	☑	☑		☐
039	Service item	☐	☐		☐
040	MkToOrdNoValW/o cons	☑	☑		☐
041	Order/delivery reqmt	☑	☑		☐
042	Mke-ord.cons plgVar.	☐	☑	2	☐
043	Mke-ord.cons.charPlg	☐	☑	2	☐
045	MTO val. with cons.	☐	☑	2	☐
046	MMTO config. value.	☑	☑		☐
047	MkToOrd.-mat.variant	☑	☑		☐
048	Mke->O.mat.var.cons.	☐	☑	2	☐
049	Stk w.cons.w/o F.Ass	☐	☑	2	☐
050	Warehouse consumpt.	☑	☑	1	☐
060	Mke->O.Cons. plngMat	☐	☑	3	☐
061	Mk->O. MatVar.PlgMat	☐	☑	3	☐
070	Wrhse cons.plng mat.	☐	☑	3	☐
075	Project w/o stock	☐	☐		☐
080	Mke-to-ord./ project	☑	☑		☐

Figure 4.4 Define Procedure by Requirement Class

It's possible to turn off the availability check at the schedule line level if it's enabled at the requirements class level. However, if the availability check is turned off at the requirements class level, you can't turn it on at the schedule line level. If you disable the availability check at the schedule line level, then the system ignores it, and the setting from the requirement type takes precedence.

Note

The material master should be populated with the availability check group, which we'll configure in the following sections.

Fixed Date and Quantity

The **Fixed date and qty** checkbox can be defaulted by executing Transaction SPRO and following menu path **Sales and Distribution • Basic Functions • Availability Check and Transfer of Requirements • Availability Check • Availability Check with ATP Logic or Against Planning • Define Default Settings by Sales Organization**.

You'll arrive at the screen in Figure 4.25. The **Fixed date and qty** checkbox is one of the parameters that can be set by default (in the customization of the availability check rule) for sales area documents or manually only for products that you choose to set with this checkbox.

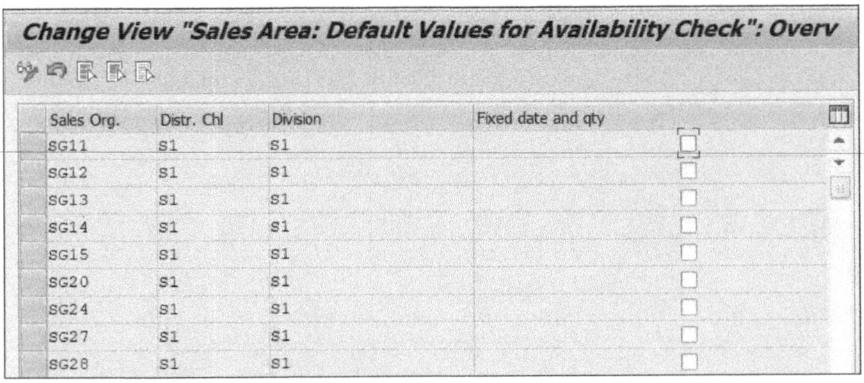

Change View "Sales Area: Default Values for Availability Check": Overv

Sales Org.	Distr. Chl	Division	Fixed date and qty
SG11	S1	S1	☐
SG12	S1	S1	☐
SG13	S1	S1	☐
SG14	S1	S1	☐
SG15	S1	S1	☐
SG20	S1	S1	☐
SG24	S1	S1	☐
SG27	S1	S1	☐
SG28	S1	S1	☐

Figure 4.5 Default Setting by Sales Organization

If you opt to set this checkbox, the following are the main cons:

- In Transaction MD04, you only see needs for data that has been confirmed, not for data that the customer has requested.
- When using a program such as rescheduling, fixed items aren't taken into account when confirming amounts.
- If you have an availability rule that doesn't validate the item amount for a date in some situations, you risk "fixing" some things without confirmation, which prevents you from creating a delivery.

4.1.3 Delivery Scheduling

Delivery scheduling is the functionality used in SAP S/4HANA to arrive at the material availability date. To arrive at the material availability date, the system considers various parameters such as transit time, loading time, pick/pack time, and transportation lead time. This is the date when the stocks are available. On this material availability date, you perform the product availability check and allocate the stock to the operational documents such as sales orders and delivery.

We'll explain how to configure delivery scheduling in the following sections, and we'll explore considerations for backward versus forward scheduling.

Configure Delivery Scheduling

You can configure delivery scheduling by navigating to menu path **Sales and Distribution • Basic Functions • Delivery Scheduling and Transportation Scheduling • Delivery Scheduling by Shipping Point** in Transaction SPRO.

You'll arrive at the screen in Figure 4.6, which shows the configuration of loading time and pick/pack time at the shipping point.

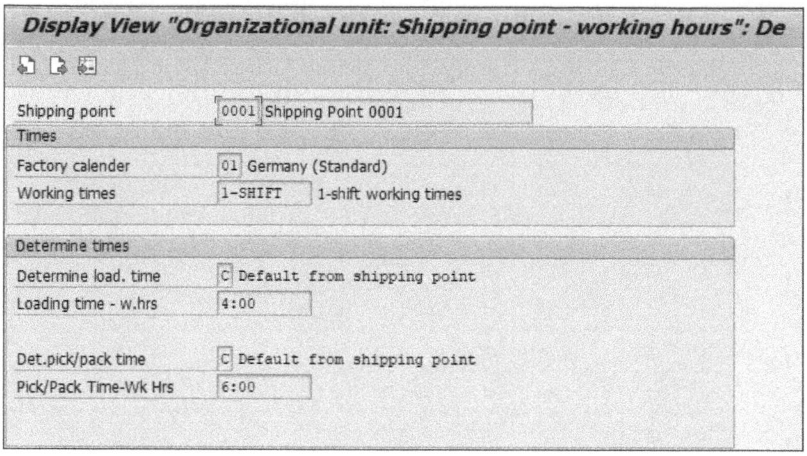

Display View "Organizational unit: Shipping point - working hours": De

Shipping point 0001 Shipping Point 0001

Times

Factory calender 01 Germany (Standard)

Working times 1-SHIFT 1-shift working times

Determine times

Determine load. time C Default from shipping point

Loading time - w.hrs 4:00

Det.pick/pack time C Default from shipping point

Pick/Pack Time-Wk Hrs 6:00

Figure 4.6 Loading Time and Pick/Pack Time

Let's explore the fields that are important with respect to delivery scheduling:

- **Factory calendar**

  A sequentially numbered working days calendar is called a *factory calendar*. A public holiday calendar serves as the foundation for the factory calendar. A factory calendar's validity period must coincide with the validity period of the public holiday calendar. It's the foundation of most of the activities in SAP. You can configure the factory calendar using Transaction SCAL. It's mostly configured by the materials management team.

  When it comes to the finance functionality, the factory calendar is used to calculate the payment due dates, which in turn will be used by sales and distribution during billing document creation. The system will do the scheduling and creation of procurement proposals based on the factory calendar in production planning. Materials management will use the factory calendar for procurement activities in purchase order dates calculation and goods receipts dates.

- **Determine load. time**

  Loading time is the time needed to load the products in the transportation modes for dispatch. You can determine loading time from the shipping point, loading group, and route. This field determines how the loading time should get calculated in the operational document. SAP has provided four options to choose from for the loading time determination:

  - Blank: No loading point determination.
  - **A (Route dependent)**: The loading time maintained in the route is used to determine the loading time during the delivery schedule. Because the route is necessary for defining the mode of transportation, a processing delay or faster

processing can be considered. The loading group from the material master record can be used to determine pick/pack time, and the weight can be used to determine loading time.

  - **C (Default from shipping point)**: The loading time is determined from the shipping point.

- **Loading time – w.hrs.**
  You have to maintain the total loading time in working hours in this field.
- **Det.pick/pack time**
  The pick/pack time is the number of days it takes to allocate products to delivery as well as the number of days it takes to pick and pack them. It's determined using the order item's shipping point, route, and weight group. SAP has provided two options to choose from to determine the pick/pack time:
  - Blank: No pick/pack time is determined.
  - **C (Default from shipping point)**: The pick/pack time is determined from the shipping point.
  - **A (Route independent)**: If the route isn't taken into consideration when establishing the pick/pack time or loading time, the shipping point and weight become the only criteria for determining the pick/pack time. The loading time is determined using the shipping location and the loading group as criteria.
- **Pick/Pack Time-Wk Hrs**
  You have to maintain the total pick/pack time in working hours in this field.

Click the **Save** button or press [Ctrl]+[S] once the required fields are filled in.

There are two other parameters that are used for delivery scheduling:

- **Transportation lead time**
  This is the time it takes to arrange for the means of transportation (e.g., truck) and container to deliver the product to the end customer. The transportation planning date is calculated by the system based on the transportation lead time. The system determines the dates by which the items must be ready for picking, packaging, and loading. You maintain transportation lead time while defining the route.
- **Transit time**
  This is the time required to deliver the goods from the plant to the end customer. The system uses the transit time from delivery schedules as well as other time estimates, such as loading time, to determine the dates by which the goods must be available for picking, packing, and loading.

The path to maintain the times for the delivery scheduling is **Sales and Distribution • Basic Functions • Delivery Scheduling and Transportation Scheduling • Maintain Duration**. You'll arrive at the screen shown in Figure 4.7, where you can choose the **Routes** folder to arrive at the screen shown in Figure 4.8.

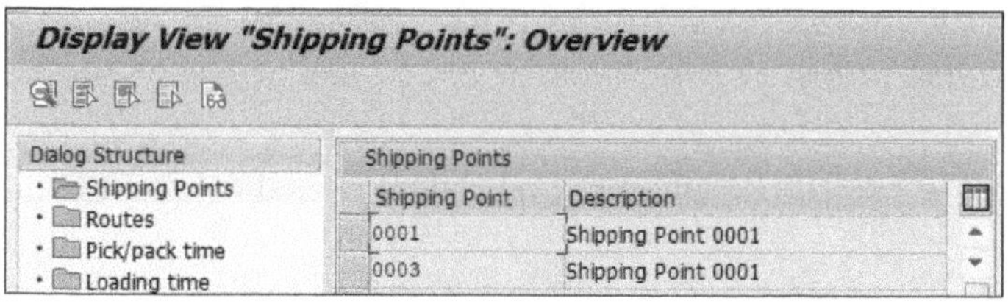

Display View "Shipping Points": Overview

Dialog Structure
- Shipping Points
- Routes
- Pick/pack time
- Loading time

Shipping Points

Shipping Point	Description
0001	Shipping Point 0001
0003	Shipping Point 0001

Figure 4.7 Transportation Lead Time and Transit Time

Display View "Routes": Overview

Display BC Set

Dialog Structure
- Shipping Points
- Routes
- Pick/pack time
- Loading time

Routes

Route	Description	ST	PL	Un	ServcAgent	TransitDur	Trav. Dur.	TransLdTm.	Tr.Lead Ti...	Cal	Distance	Unit	MoT	D..	T..
											0,000			☐	☑
000001	Northern Route										0,000			☐	☑
000002	Southern Route										0,000			☐	☑

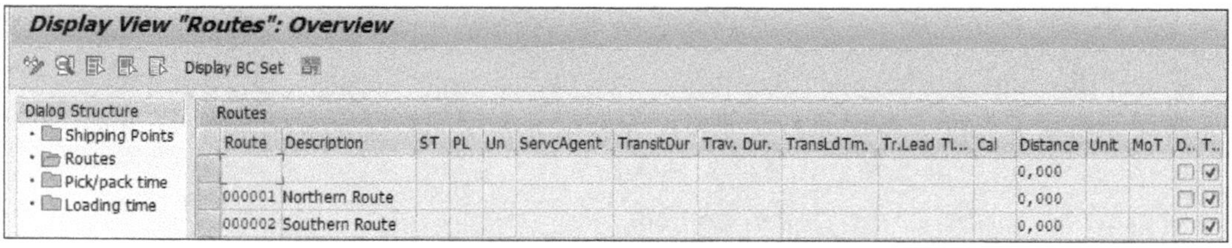

Figure 4.8 Transportation Lead Time and Transit Time

Here, maintain the transportation lead time (**TransLdTm.**) and transit time (**TransitDur**).

You can define the delivery scheduling with respect to the sales document type by executing Transaction SPRO and navigating to menu path **Sales and Distribution • Basic Functions • Delivery Scheduling and Transportation Scheduling • Define Scheduling by Sales Document Type**. You'll arrive at Figure 4.9, which shows the sales document types for scheduling.

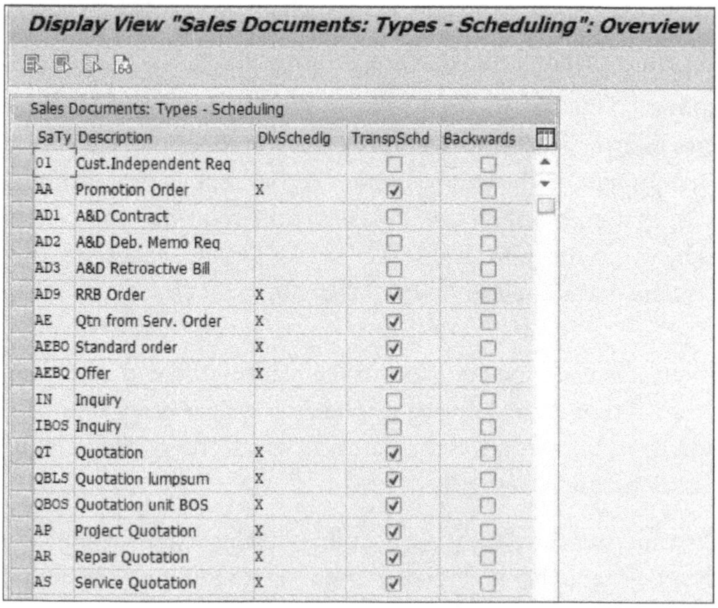

Display View "Sales Documents: Types - Scheduling": Overview

Sales Documents: Types - Scheduling

SaTy	Description	DlvSchedlg	TranspSchd	Backwards
01	Cust.Independent Req		☐	☐
AA	Promotion Order	X	☑	☐
AD1	A&D Contract		☐	☐
AD2	A&D Deb. Memo Req		☐	☐
AD3	A&D Retroactive Bill		☐	☐
AD9	RRB Order	X	☑	☐
AE	Qtn from Serv. Order	X	☑	☐
AEBO	Standard order	X	☑	☐
AEBQ	Offer	X	☑	☐
IN	Inquiry		☐	☐
IBOS	Inquiry		☐	☐
QT	Quotation	X	☑	☐
QBLS	Quotation lumpsum	X	☑	☐
QBOS	Quotation unit BOS	X	☑	☐
AP	Project Quotation	X	☑	☐
AR	Repair Quotation	X	☑	☐
AS	Service Quotation	X	☑	☐

Figure 4.9 Define Scheduling by Sales Document Type

Let's explore each field in the configuration:

- **SaTy**
  This is the sales order document type that you configure in Transaction VOV8 and use while creating the sales order.
- **DlvSchedlg**
  The system automatically determines the pick/pack time and loading time for each schedule line based on the shipping location from which an item is shipped when you choose the delivery scheduling. The pick/pack time and loading time are used by the system to compute the material availability date and loading date, respectively. SAP has provided three options to choose from while configuring it:
  - **X**: Shipping scheduling on
  - Blank: Shipping scheduling off
  - **A**: Shipping scheduling delivery order
- **TranspSchd**
  When you activate this checkbox, the system automatically carries out the transportation scheduling. After activating the transport scheduling, each schedule line in the sales order will be populated with the transportation lead time and transit time. These parameters are used to determine the transportation planning date and the goods issue date, respectively.
- **Backwards**
  This indicates that the sales order document type should only have backward scheduling activated for all schedule lines in the sales document. When you make a change to a sales document, such as adding or deleting schedule lines, the system automatically schedules delivery for all lines. The system may execute forward scheduling in some instances, which may have the unintended consequence of rescheduling lines that have already been confirmed. To avoid such circumstances, you can activate the checkbox for some document types. You'll learn about backward scheduling in the next section.

Backward and Forward Scheduling

Delivery scheduling can be done in two ways: forward scheduling and backward scheduling. By default, the system first performs backward scheduling, and if backward scheduling fails, the system performs forward scheduling. The end objective of both processes is to determine the material availability date.

Let's explore in detail the backward scheduling process first, and then forward scheduling.

Backward scheduling is always performed on the customer's requested delivery date. In this process, the system calculates the material availability date by subtracting the dates backward. In Figure 4.10, the system subtracts the transit time, loading time, lead time from transportation planning, and pick/pack time to arrive at the material availability date. This date will be used for the availability check.

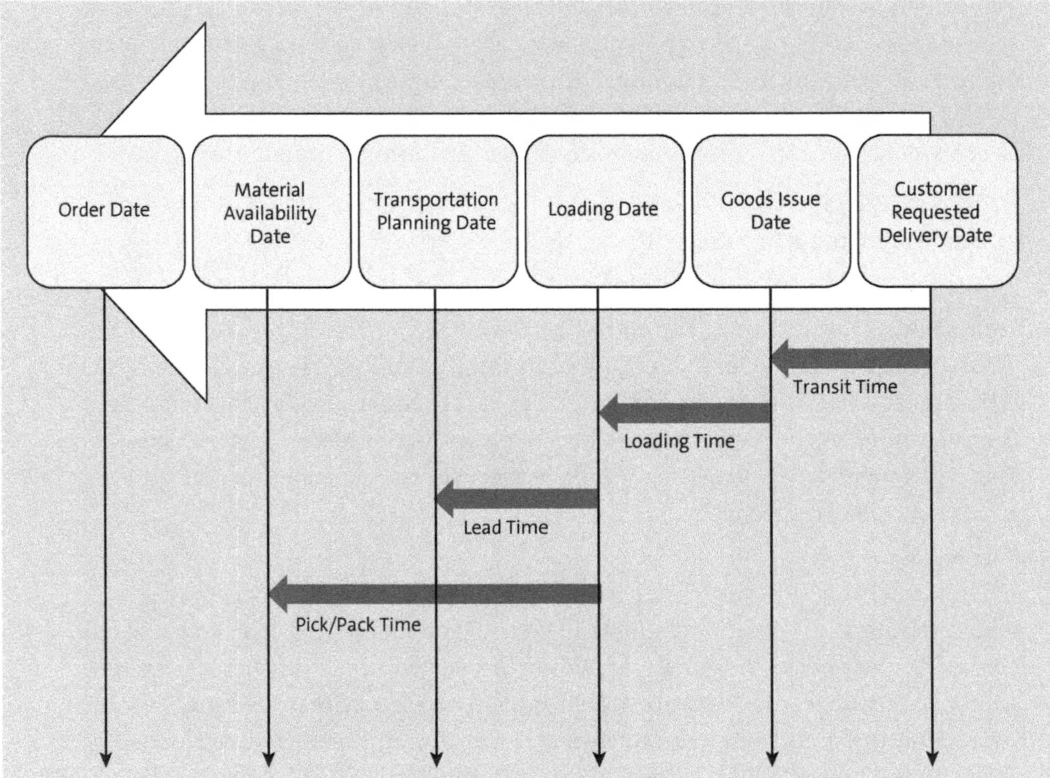

Figure 4.10 Backward Scheduling

If the material availability date lies in the past compared to the present date, backward scheduling fails because you can't deliver the goods in the past. The system then performs *forward scheduling*, as shown in Figure 4.11, and tries to determine the nearest date on which the product will be available. The new material date that you get via forwarding scheduling will be used to calculate the date on which the goods will be delivered to the customer. When the system calculates forward scheduling, two schedule lines will be created in the schedule data. The first schedule line will be because of the failed backward scheduling, and the second schedule line will be of the forward scheduling data.

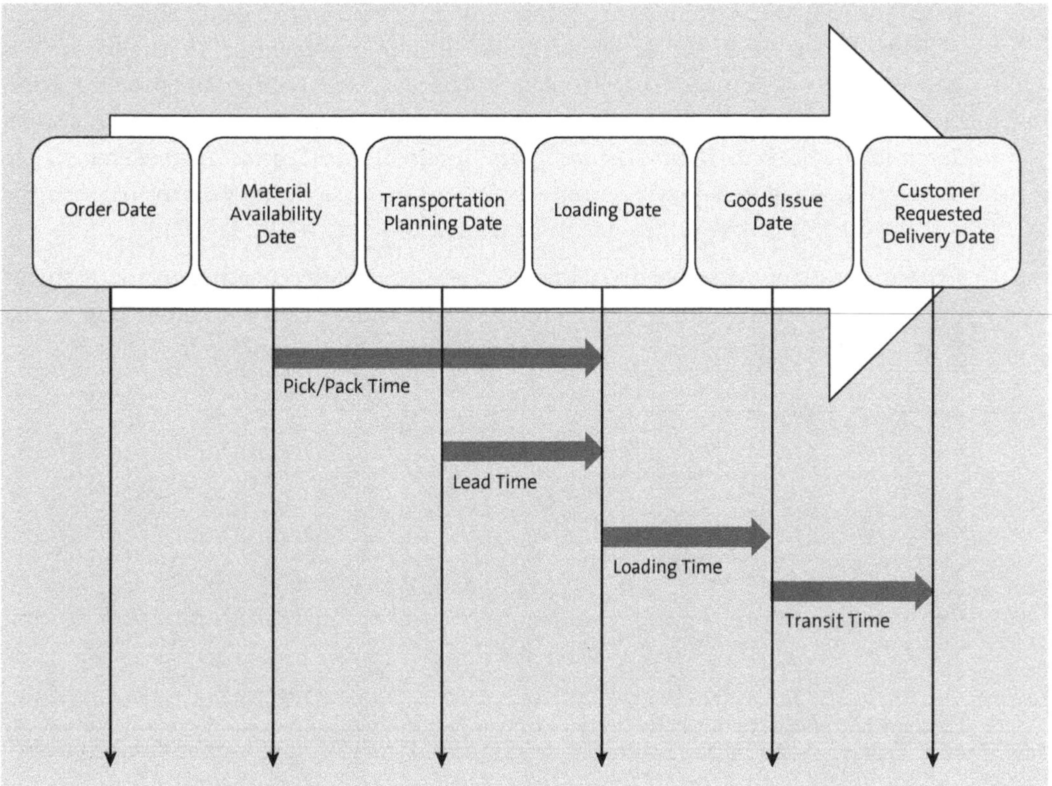

Figure 4.11 Forward Scheduling

Now let's look at examples of forward and backward scheduling. In our first example, we'll use the details shown in Table 4.1 for successful backward scheduling.

Parameter	Value
Order date	20-12-2021
Order quantity	90 quantities
Customer-requested delivery date	03-01-2022
Material stock	100 quantities
Pick/pack time	3 days
Transportation lead time	0 day
Loading time	0 day
RLT	10 days
Transit time	4 days

Table 4.1 Example 1: Details

When the system performs backward scheduling, it considers the customer-requested delivery date as the base date, which is 03.01.2022 in this example. The transit time is four days; therefore, the goods issue date will be 27.12.2021. Loading time and transportation lead time are both zero days, so the loading date and transportation planning date will be 27.12.2021. Next is the pick/pack time, which is three days, which means the material availability date will become 24.12.2021; because the stock is available in the system, the RLT isn't considered in this case. The order date is 20.12.2021.

The various dates are shown in Figure 4.12. Here, backward scheduling is successful as the delivery date isn't going beyond today's date. Therefore, the schedule line is confirmed on the requested delivery date, which is 03.01.2022, as shown in Figure 4.13.

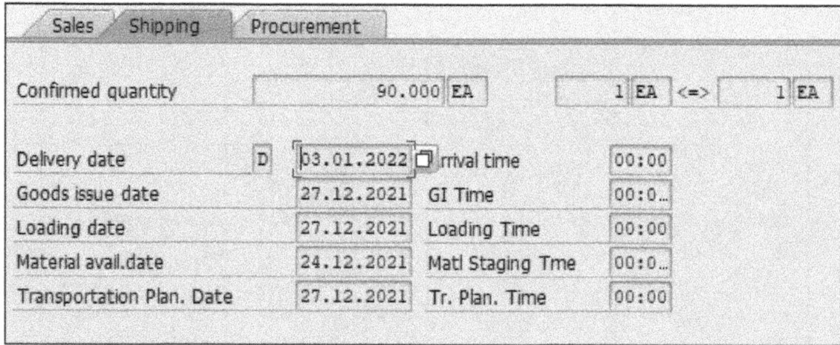

Figure 4.12 Schedule Line Dates

Figure 4.13 Schedule Lines Tab from Sales Order

Now let's move on to a second example, as shown in Table 4.2, where forward scheduling is required.

Parameter	Value
Order date	11-10-2021
Order quantity	6 EA
Customer-requested delivery date	15-10-2021
Material stock	0
Pick/pack time	1 day
Transportation lead time	0 day

Table 4.2 Example 2: Details

Parameter	Value
Loading time	0 day
RLT	35 days
Transit time	2 days

Table 4.2 Example 2: Details (Cont.)

First, the system performs backward scheduling by considering the customer-requested delivery date as the baseline date, which is 15.10.2021 in this case. Transit time is two days, so the goods issue date will be 13.10.2021. Loading and lead time are zero-days, meaning the loading date and transportation lead date will be the same as the goods issue date, i.e., 13.10.2021. The material availability date should be 12.10.2021 because the pick/pack time is one day. However, in this case, the stock isn't available in the warehouse; therefore, the RLT maintained in the material master will come into the picture. The RLT is maintained as 35 days for this material. Hence, the material will be available on 07.09.2021. This date is going beyond the order/line-item creation date, that is, 11.10.2021. Therefore, backward scheduling fails here, and the **Confirmed quantity** on schedule line 1 is **0**, as shown in Figure 4.14. You can see that the dates correspond to the actual confirmed quantity dates; SAP S/4HANA doesn't display the unconfirmed dates.

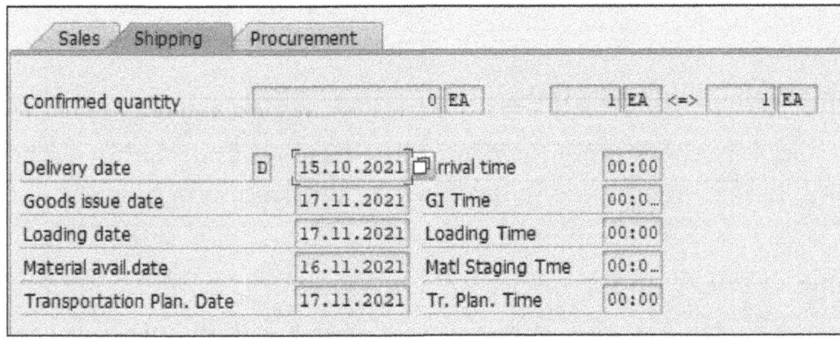

Figure 4.14 Schedule Line 1 Dates

If backward scheduling fails, the system will go for forward scheduling. The baseline date here is the order date, which is 11.10.2021; from here, the RLT is 35 days, which makes the material availability date 16.11.2021. The pick/pack time is 1 day, and both lead time and transit time are 0, so the transportation planning date, loading date, and goods issue date become 17.11.2021. Because the transit time is 2 days, the delivery date will be 19.11.2021. Figure 4.15 shows the dates of forward scheduling where the **Confirmed quantity** is **6 EA**.

Sales | Shipping | Procurement

Confirmed quantity	6.000 EA	1 EA <=> 1 EA	
Delivery date	D 19.11.2021	rrival time	00:00
Goods issue date	17.11.2021	GI Time	00:0...
Loading date	17.11.2021	Loading Time	00:00
Material avail.date	16.11.2021	Matl Staging Tme	00:0...
Transportation Plan. Date	17.11.2021	Tr. Plan. Time	00:00

Figure 4.15 Schedule Line 2 Dates

Whenever backward scheduling fails, the system determines two schedule lines in the **Schedule lines** tab, as shown in Figure 4.16, where the second schedule line has confirmed quantities.

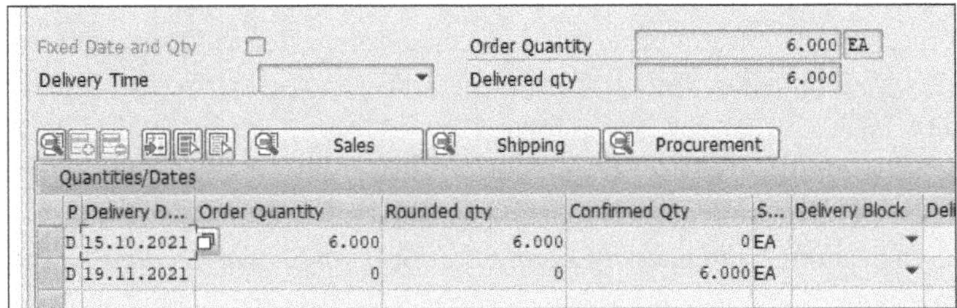

Fixed Date and Qty ☐ Order Quantity 6.000 EA

Delivery Time Delivered qty 6.000

Sales | Shipping | Procurement

Quantities/Dates

P	Delivery D...	Order Quantity	Rounded qty	Confirmed Qty	S...	Delivery Block	Deli
D	15.10.2021	6.000	6.000	0	EA		
D	19.11.2021	0	0	6.000	EA		

Figure 4.16 Schedule Lines Tab from the Sales Order

4.1.4 Configuration of Available-to-Promise

We've covered the availability check prerequisites in the previous section. Now, let's explore the availability check configuration in detail in the subsequent sections.

Define Availability Check Groups

Availability check groups control whether the system can create individual requirements or collective requirements to pass it to MRP. To configure the availability check group, execute Transaction OVZ2 or use menu path **Sales and Distribution • Basic Functions • Availability Check and Transfer of Requirements • Availability Check with ATP Logic or Against Planning • Define Availability Check Group**. You'll arrive at the screen in Figure 4.17, which shows the availability check groups and the relevant fields.

Display View "Availability Check Group": Overview

Av	Description	TotalSales	TotDlvReqs	Block QtRq	No PAC	Accum...	RelChkPlan	Advanced ATP
01	Daily requirements	B	B	☐	☐	0		Inactive
02	Individ.requiremen...	A	A	☐	☐	0		Inactive

Figure 4.17 Availability Check Groups

Let's explore each field in detail:

- **Av**
  You can configure your own two-character checking group for the availability check based on customer requirements. You have to assign the configured checking group in the material master at the plant organization level in the **MRP 3** view (see Chapter 3, Section 3.2.6). It basically controls whether the system can create individual requirements or collective requirements to pass it to MRP.
- **TotalSales**
  This field determines how you can transfer the data from sales orders to MRP for planning. You can set an individual requirement or summarized requirement. If you set it as **A**, the system will generate a single requirement for the sales document, and, in the background, table VBBE will be populated along with the sales document and item number. If you select a value other than **A**, then the system will generate collective requirements, and, in the background, table VBBS will be populated with material and plant details. You won't be able to see the sales order and line-item details in the table. This field further controls the document number that can be displayed in Transactions CO09 and MD04. If you keep this field blank, then an ATP check won't be performed; however, there will be no effect on the requirement generation and passing of the data to MRP.
- **TotDlvReqs**
  This field (total delivery requirements) determines how you can transfer the data from delivery documents to MRP for planning. You can set an individual requirement or summarized requirement based on your needs. The settings in the total sales fields are also applicable in the total delivery requirement field as well.
- **Block QtRq**
  In the business scenario, there may be an instance where the two users are performing the availability check for the same material at the same time. This can lead to inconsistency in the confirmation of the quantities. To avoid this, you can check this material block checkbox.
- **No PAC**
  You can check this field to turn off the availability check for the materials. This check will be on the KP (no check) availability check group by default.
- **Accum...**
  This field is used to set the cumulative confirmed quantity logic in the sales order and production order, that is, whether the system should take already confirmed quantities or planned incoming inventory quantities. SAP has provided the following choices while setting up the accumulation:
  - **0**: No cumulation.
  - **1**: Check to take cumulated confirmed quantities into account. When calculating the cumulated ATP quantity in the sales order availability check, the system

considers the sum of all previously confirmed quantities. The new sales orders can be confirmed only if the total cumulative value of receipts is greater than the cumulated confirmed quantities.

- **2**: Check to take cumulated requirements quantities into account. When calculating the cumulated ATP quantity in the sales order availability check, the system considers the sum of all open requirements quantities to date; that is, the new sales order can be confirmed only if the total cumulative value of all receipts is greater than the cumulated requirement quantities.

- **RelChkPlan**
  This field acts as an indicator that determines whether the availability of a material must be checked against planned independent requirements generated from the various business processes.

- **Advanced ATP**
  To use the SAP S/4HANA for advanced ATP capabilities during the availability check, you have to activate it by choosing **Active**.

Note

For activating the advanced availability check, you have to purchase an additional license from SAP (*www.sapstore.com/solutions/80117/SAP-S-4HANA-for-advanced-ATP*).

Configure Default Values for Availability Check Group

You can default the checking group based on the material type and plant combination. Follow menu path **Sales and Distribution • Basic Functions • Availability Check and Transfer of Requirements • Availability Check with ATP Logic or Against Planning • Configure Default Values for Availability Check Group**. You'll arrive at the screen in Figure 4.18, which shows the configuration of availability check groups based on material type and plant. In this configuration, assign the availability check group configured earlier (**02**, in this example) to the combination of material type (**Ma...**) and **Plant**. This configuration will default the availability check group while creating the material master record for the given material type and plant combination.

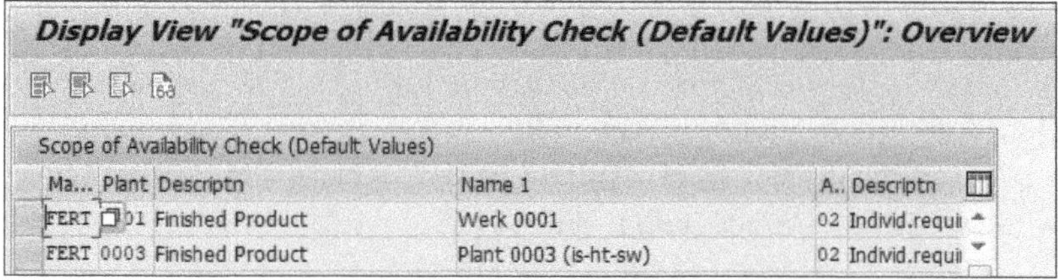

Ma...	Plant	Descriptn	Name 1	A..	Descriptn
FERT	0001	Finished Product	Werk 0001	02	Indivd.requi
FERT	0003	Finished Product	Plant 0003 (is-ht-sw)	02	Indivd.requi

Figure 4.18 Configure Default Values for Availability Check Groups

Configuring the Scope of Availability Check

The *availability check scope* governs the logic of which stocks must be considered when calculating ATP quantities. By referring to the scope of availability check, the system determines the ATP quantity. Several functionalities are available in the scope of availability check configuration that you can use to fine-tune the ATP quantity calculation.

You can configure the scope of the availability check with Transaction OVZ9 or by navigating to menu path **Sales and Distribution • Basic Functions • Availability Check and Transfer of Requirements • Availability Check with ATP Logic or Against Planning • Configure Scope of Availability Check**. You'll arrive at the screen shown in Figure 4.19, where you can see that the scope of availability check is defined using two parameters: **Availability Check** (the checking group) and **Checking Rule**. The checking group was configured in the previous section, so you can select it here.

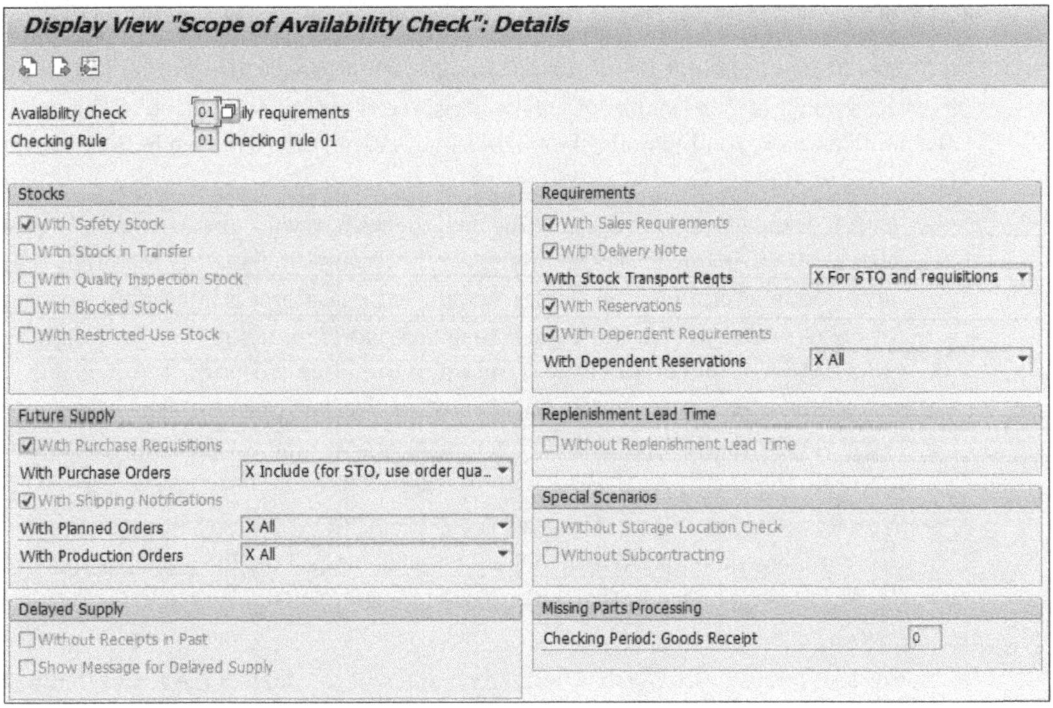

Figure 4.19 Scope of Availability Check

Checking rules are used by different applications such as sales, inventory management, process order processing, and so on. In terms of SAP S/4HANA sales and distribution, you can't define the checking rule; however, it can be freely defined for the production planning processes.

Now, let's walk through the remaining key fields for the availability check scope:

- **Stocks**
  You can control different kinds of stocks to include or exclude them in the product availability check. Let's explore each of the checkboxes as follows:
  - **With Safety Stock**: If you want to include safety stocks during the availability check, select this checkbox. If you uncheck this checkbox, safety stock won't be included to determine the availability of the material.
  - **With Stock in Transfer**: This checkbox refers to the good movement between one storage location to the other storage location. It doesn't include the STO movements, which consist of the purchase order, outbound delivery, and goods receipt. If you check this box, the quantities in the transit will be used for the availability check. If you uncheck the box, the materials or stocks that are in transit are ignored completely while doing the product availability check.
  - **With Quality Inspection Stock**: If you check this box, you'll allow the system to consider the stocks which are flagged for the quality inspection. In some companies, the outbound delivery is also managed by a quality inspection lot. During the availability check, this lot will be considered for the calculation of the availability check. You maintain the quality inspection stock with the help of movement type 503.
  - **With Blocked Stock**: If you check this box, the system will consider the materials with block stock for the availability check. This won't include the materials that have goods receipt blocked stock from the purchase orders. Materials received into goods receipt block stock will be displayed in Transaction CO09 as purchase order items. It's not an industry standard to use block stocks for the availability check. However, if the business sells the return products as refurbished products, then they can use the checkbox to include the stocks in the availability check. You maintain the quality block stock with the help of movement type 505.
  - **With Restricted-Use Stock**: This field corresponds to the stock that is managed by batch management in SAP S/4HANA. If you check this box, then batches that are flagged as restricted will also be considered for the availability check.
- **Future Supply**
  In this section, you can control when the system will consider all the stocks that will become the future supply. You have the following options:
  - **With Purchase Requisitions**: If you check this field, then purchase requisition quantities will also be considered in the availability check. However, the purchase requisition is a request, and based on the circumstances, it can be accepted or rejected. You can jeopardize the availability check's credibility by including purchase requisition supplies in it. Therefore, it's recommended to not include it in the ATP logic.
  - **With Purchase Orders**: You can include the incoming purchase orders stocks in the availability check. You can also confirm the STO for the target date or the

confirmation date. SAP has provided the following three options to choose from if you want to include the purchase order stocks:

- Choose **X** if you want the system to consider standard purchase order stocks for the specified date. It will include all purchase order stocks in the available inventory.
- Choose **A** if you want the system to examine standard purchase orders for the chosen date and STOs based on the verified data.
- Choose blank if you don't want the system to consider incoming purchase order stocks.

Note

SAP hasn't provided the functionality for choosing the document type that you want for ATP. Hence, if you check the **With Purchase Orders** box, it will include all the purchase order types, including STOs.

- **With Shipping Notifications**: If you check this field, the system will take into account advanced shipping alerts received by suppliers when doing the ATP check. When compared to purchase orders, the reliability of delivery dates is higher in shipment notifications.
- **With Planned Orders**: If you check this checkbox, then receipts from planned orders will be included in the ATP check. Planned orders are frequently created automatically by the MRP process; therefore, this option should be carefully considered. SAP has provided three options that you can choose from:
  - **X**: Check all planned orders: All scheduled orders are included, whether they are MRP generated, manually prepared, firmed, confirmed, or capacity planned.
  - **A**: Check firmed planned orders only: When you don't want certain planned orders to change during subsequent MRP runs, you activate the firming indicator in the planned order.
  - **B**: Only check planned orders that are completely confirmed: This includes only scheduled orders that have been checked for availability to ensure component availability.
- **With Production Orders**: This checkbox will control whether you can include production order receipts for the ATP check. SAP has provided two options to choose from:
  - **X**: Take all production orders into account: All open production orders will be included in this option.
  - **F**: Only take released production orders into account: Only receipts for open production orders that have been released for production will be included in this option.

- **Requirements**
  This consists of the orders that include outward movement. You have the following options:
  - **With Sales Requirements**: This checkbox should be on by default for all the checking groups. If you select this checkbox, the system will consider demand created through sales orders, scheduling agreements, and other types of sales and distribution documents, excluding deliveries. Stock that has already been allocated to sales documents won't be used for further allocation.
  - **With Delivery Note**: This includes the delivery documents that are created by sales and distribution, excluding the STO deliveries or inbound purchase-related deliveries. If you check this checkbox, the system won't consider stocks that are already assigned to the delivery document. If you remove the check, the stocks assigned to the delivery documents will also be taken into account for the ATP check. The same stocks will be allocated to the new sales order, causing inconsistency during order processing.
  - **With Stock Transport Reqts**: This checkbox is related to the stocks that have been assigned for the STO and stock transfer requisitions. If you check this checkbox, the system won't consider the quantities of stock that have been assigned to these objects. SAP has provided three options for this checkbox:
    - **Exclude:** Exclude the stock transport and requisition from the scope of availability check.
    - **X For STO and requisitions**: Include releases for both STO and requisitions.
    - **A For STO only**: Only include the releases for STO.
  - **With Reservations**: In MRP and product availability check, reservations are crucial because the system reserves needed quantities before they are posted. Reservations are system documents that identify a need for a specific quantity of an item for manufacturing, cost center, or any other purpose. This is created in Transaction MB21. When you make a reservation, the system prohibits you from using any other document to reserve the items for a different purpose. This is also dependent on the MRP/ATP system parameters. You could grant reservations the right to remove products off the shelf at any time, even if they are already reserved by a sales order or delivery. If you uncheck the checkbox, then you give permission to the system to consider the stocks that have been allocated with the material reservation functionality from the procure-to-pay side. If you check this checkbox, then material reservations will be considered before doing the allocation to the sales order with ATP logic.
  - **With Dependent Requirements**: This checkbox indicates whether the system considers dependent requirements during an availability check. Mark the field if you want the system to take dependent requirements into account.

- **With Dependent Reservations**: A component tied to a scheduled order is referred to as a dependent need. The dependent demand for this component becomes a reserve when the planned order is changed to a production order. SAP has provided two options to choose between:
  - **A**: Withdrawable only: Only requirements linked to release production orders will be included in this option. Order reservations for orders that haven't yet been released will be ignored.
  - **X**: All: All reservations will be included for production orders.

- **Replenishment Lead Time**

  This is the total time required for procuring raw materials and producing assemblies for the finished product. It's calculated by adding all planned delivery times or in-plant production times of the longest production process.

  Let's walk through the calculation logic for the RLT:

  - For externally procured materials: If it's external procurement, then the system calculates the RLT by taking four parameters into consideration:
    - Purchasing processing time maintained in Transaction OPPQ
    - The reference calendar for the date calculation from the factory calendar
    - The planned delivery time from the **MRP 2** view of the material master with the reference calendar taken from the standard calendar
    - Goods receipt processing time from the **MRP 2** view of the material master

    The formula for the total RLT value for externally produced material is as follows:

    Total RLT = Purchasing processing time + Planned delivery time + Goods receipt processing time

  - For internally produced materials: The system checks if the RLT is maintained in the material master **MRP 2** view; if so, then that time is considered as total RLT. If the RLT value isn't maintained in the **MRP 2** view, then the system calculates the total RLT values as follows:

    Total RLT value = In-house production time + Goods processing time

    If these two categories aren't satisfied and neither time is maintained in the material master, then the system calculates the total RLT value based on in-house production time of lot size, and the calculation for the RLT is as follows:

    Total RLT value = Setup time for the production lot + Interoperation time from routing process + Processing time

  - For both: If the material master is maintained with both procurement types, that is, procured externally and in-house production, then the system calculates the RLT value by considering it as internally produced without taking into account purchasing processing time and planned delivery time.

  If you wanted to calculate the RLT value for the product availability check as discussed, you have to keep the checkbox unchecked. If you check this checkbox, during the nonavailability of stock scenario, the system won't confirm any quantities. If you uncheck the checkbox, then the system will confirm the quantities based on the RLT. If the date falls outside the range of the RLT, the system will confirm all the ordered quantities.

- **Special Scenarios**
  The **Special Scenarios** section is newly introduced as a scope item in SAP S/4HANA and covers the business scenarios associated with storage location and subcontracting. It includes the following options:
  - **Without Storage Location Check**: Storage location determination is configured in the delivery type in Transaction OVLK (see Section 4.2.2 for details).

> **Note**
>
> Because the determination happens at the delivery document level, unless you enter the storage location manually in the sales order, the **Storage Location** field in the sales order will be blank. The storage location isn't determined at the sales order, so the system calculates the availability check at the plant level. However, you can populate the storage location field in the sales order by using user exit MV45AFZZ. If the **Storage Location** field is populated at the sales order level, then the system calculates the ATP check at the specified storage location in the sales order.

  If you check the **Without Storage Location Check** checkbox, then the system doesn't consider the storage location stock but rather considers the total plant stock for the availability check logic. If you uncheck the checkbox, then the system considers the storage location mentioned in the sales order for the calculation of the allocated availability stock.
  - **Without Subcontracting**: Subcontracting is the process where the semifinished products or raw materials are sent to the vendor. The vendor converts the semifinished material into a finished product or the raw material into the semifinished product and delivers it back to the company.

    If you select the checkbox, the subcontracting stock available in the system won't be considered for the availability check. This also removes the corresponding dependent requirements from the ATP logic.
- **Checking Period: Goods Receipt**
  The checking period is used in inventory management for goods receipt posting to specify how many times in the future the system will check for missing parts. During the checking period, inventory management sends an e-mail to the MRP controller noting that a goods receipt for a missing part was completed. The checking period entered in the field initiates the workflow. You have to maintain the checking period for the inventory management checking rule because there is no impact on the other checking rules. This is a pure production planning functionality,

and it doesn't have any impact on sales. The functionality will only be triggered if you check with replenishment time.

Advanced Availability Check Extensions in Other Functionalities

SAP S/4HANA for advanced ATP has an impact on transactional documents from other functionalities, such as production orders, STOs, reservations, and stock movements, in addition to sales orders. Let's explore the configuration extension for these document types:

- **Advanced ATP functionality in production and process orders**

  Availability in production orders ensures that only those orders are released for which material quantity is available on the calculated requirement date. This check can be triggered automatically by Transaction COMAC or manually via Customizing settings. The ATP technique is used to dynamically check all receipts and issue elements to be considered. The system marks the order as a material shortfall if the total needed amount of material components isn't available by the material required date. The result of the availability check is recorded in the availability log.

  Availability checks are carried out according to the checking rules that are dependent on Customizing with reference to the material. The scope of the check is specified for each plant and order type. The fields in the configuration work similarly to the other fields in the availability check configuration. Availability can be checked at the creation of the production order or during its release.

  For configuration of the SAP S/4HANA for advanced ATP functionality in production and process orders, you must follow menu path **Cross-Application Components • Advanced Available-to-Promise (aATP) • Configuration Activities for Specific Document Types • Planned and Production Orders • Configure Scope of Availability Check for Production and Process Orders.**

  You'll arrive at Figure 4.20, which shows the configuration elements for the scope of availability check for production and process orders.

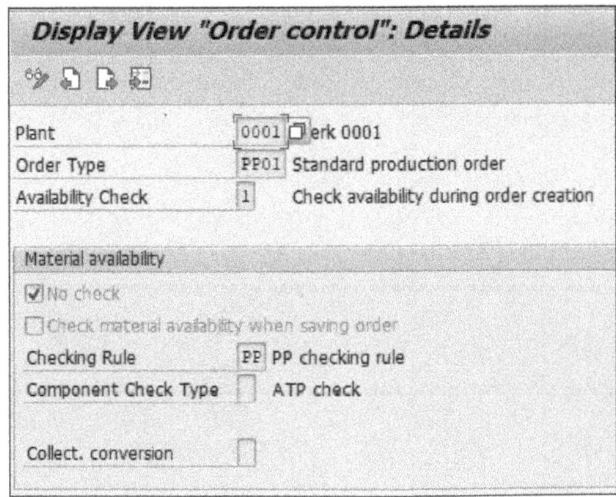

Figure 4.20 Configure Scope of Availability Check for Production and Process Orders

- **Advanced ATP functionality in the reservation and stock movements**
  In inventory management, the advanced ATP check happens in two areas: during entry of reservation and during entry of goods movement. You can configure the scope of availability check based on the stock movement types. To configure the advanced ATP functionality in reservation and stock movements, follow menu path **Cross-Application Components • Advanced Available-to-Promise (aATP) • Configuration Activities for Specific Document Types • Stock Movements • Configure Scope of Availability Check.**

  You'll arrive at the screen shown in Figure 4.21. To make changes to the movement type click on **Movement Type**; and to make changes to the transaction code, click on **Transaction Code**.

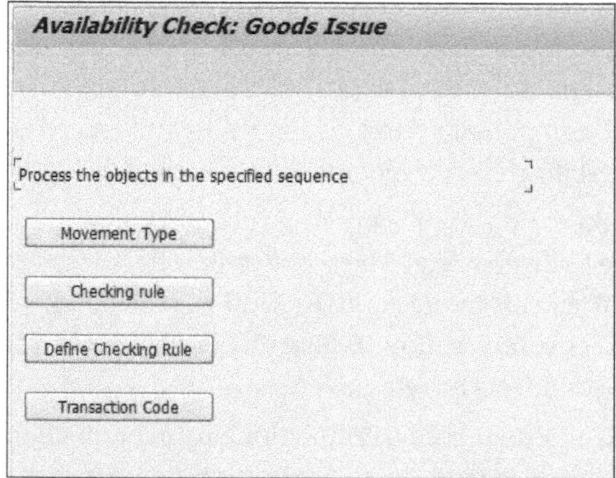

Figure 4.21 Configure the Scope of Availability Check

As shown in Figure 4.22, you can configure the movement type to set the messages in case of availability check failure. By default, SAP set message type **A** (warning for nonavailability) for all the movement types in the **Dynamic avail. check** field.

Change View "Dynamic Availability Check": Overview

M...	Movement Type Text	Val	Q...	S	Mvt	Rec	Cns	Dynamic avail. check
201	GI pipel.for cst cnt	☐	☐	P				
201	GI for cost center	☐	☑					A
201	GI cst cnt.fm consgt	☐	☑	K				A
201	GI pipel.for cst cnt	☐	☑	P				
201	GI for cost center	☑	☐					
201	GI for cost center	☑	☑					A
201	GI cst cnt.fm consgt	☑	☑	K				A
201	GI pipel.for cst cnt	☑	☑	P				
202	RE pipel.for cst cnt	☐	☐	P				
202	RE for cost center	☐	☑					
202	RE cst cnt.fm consgt	☐	☑	K				

Figure 4.22 Availability Check Configuration for Movement Type

You can also assign the checking rule to the transaction code for the underlying document, as shown in Figure 4.23. For inventory management-related transactions, checking rule **03** is assigned by default to the **ChR** field.

We'll explore the movement type configurations and their impact on sales and distribution in Section 4.3.

Change View "Checking Rule": Overview

TCo...	Transaction text	ChR	Checking Rule
CO27	Picking list		
MB11	Goods Movement		
MB1A	Goods Withdrawal	03	Checking rule 03
MB1B	Transfer Posting		
MB26	Picking list		
MIGO...	Goods Movement		
MIGO...	Transfer Posting		

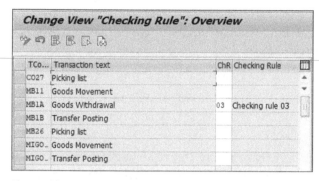

Figure 4.23 Transaction-Specific Checking Rule

- **Advanced ATP functionality in the STO**
  You can configure the scope of availability check based on the STO types. The advanced ATP functionality in an STO is configured in menu path **Cross-Application Components • Advanced Available-to-Promise (aATP) • Configuration Activities for Specific Document Types • Stock Transport Orders • Configure Delivery Type & Availability Check Procedure by Plant.**

  While performing the availability check for STOs, the system performs a stock check in the supplying plant. After arriving at the screen shown in Figure 4.24, you must maintain the availability checking rule (**CRl**) against the supplying plant (**SPl**). With the combination of the checking group maintained in the material master **MRP 3** view and the checking rule assigned to the plant, the system checks the availability check parameters in the scope of availability check. You can control the system reaction by choosing an appropriate message in case stock unavailability occurs.

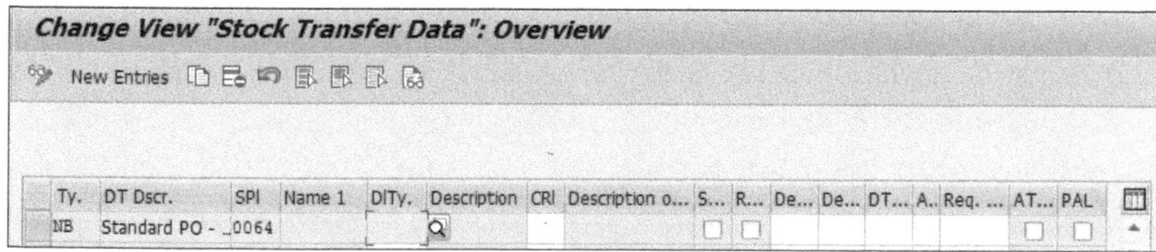

Figure 4.24 Configure Delivery Type and Availability Check Procedure by Plant

In this section, we've discussed ATP as a concept, along with its implementation in SAP S/4HANA. The integration of ATP with materials management is crucial for calculating dates, demand, and supply.

4.2 Stock Transport Order

Stock transfer is the process of transferring material between two plants, as shown in Figure 4.25. These plants can either belong to the same company code or to a different company code. The process is mainly used in manufacturing companies or companies that sell tangible products to the end customer. Due to the business complexity of having plants located in different geographical locations, multinational corporations must transfer material from one plant to another. There might be various other reasons to deploy the STO process in the organization.

Let's explore some of the important business reasons for deploying the STO process:

- An organization is doing the manufacturing in certain plants, and delivery is configured in the other plants. In this case, the STO process will happen between the manufacturing plant and delivering plant.
- Stock shortage occurs between the delivery plants. Due to an increase in demand or because of supply chain constraints, there is a shortage of material in the plant. In such a case, the STO is performed between two plants.
- From a raw material procurement standpoint, it's common practice that the material is procured in one plant and then distributed to the other plants via the STO process.

Figure 4.25 Stock Transport Process

We'll dive into the STO functionality in the following sections.

4.2.1 What Is a Stock Transport Order?

STOs can be divided into two major types—intercompany STO and intracompany STO—as shown in Figure 4.26.

Let's explore each type in detail:

- **Intracompany STO**
  The STO between plants belonging to the same company code is called an intracompany STO. In both cases, the goods receiving plant is created as a customer, and the goods delivering plant or supplying plant is created as a vendor. The purchase order document type used for intracompany STOs is UB. In most cases, a pro forma invoice is created for the customer or receiving plant.

- **Intercompany STO**
  The STO between plants belonging to different company codes is called an intercompany STO. The purchase order document type you use for the process is NB. For intercompany STOs, the intercompany invoicing will be created to the intercompany receiving plant.

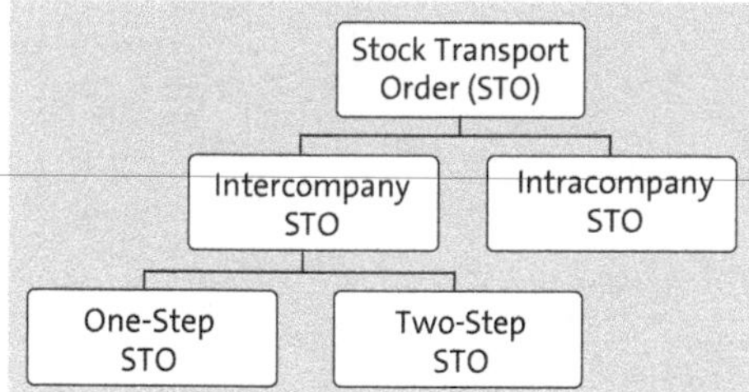

Figure 4.26 Types of STO

The STO process can be divided into five steps, as shown in Figure 4.27. These steps can be executed differently based on the requirement, but the core logic remains the same:

1. **The receiving plant creates the purchase order**
   The purchase order is created with the purchase order document type UB or NB based on whether the delivering plant belongs to the same company code or not. You can create the purchase order document type using Transaction ME21N.
2. **The replenishment delivery document is executed with respect to the STO**
   The purchase order document is performed via Transaction VL10B. The delivery document used for the intercompany STO process is NLCC and that used for intracompany STO is NL. We'll explore the configuration related to it in Section 4.2.2.
3. **The billing document is created with respect to the delivery created for STO**
   The intercompany invoice will be created for intercompany STO. The pricing related to the invoice will either flow from the purchase order or the delivery based on the configurations you've made.
4. **Goods receipt is made through Transaction MIGO**
   The receiving plant will perform Transaction MIGO and record the receipt of the goods against the replenishment delivery. Movement type 101 will be used to record the transaction. Stock will be updated from in transit to unrestricted-use stock at the receiving plant, and the material document is created.
5. **Invoice receipt is done through Transaction MIRO**
   The receiving plant creates the vendor invoice from the supplying company code. After the quantity and quality check, the invoice is posted for payment to the supplying plant.

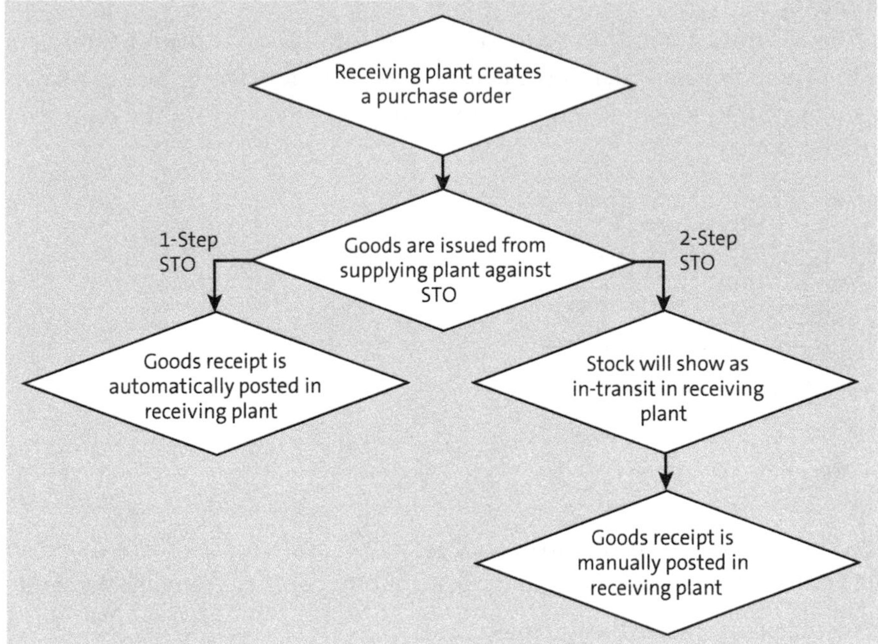

Figure 4.27 STO Steps

You can break down these steps into either a "one-step" process or a "two-step" process. The control for either workflow is based on the movement type that has been assigned to the schedule line category:

- **STO one-step process**
  You use movement type 647 for one-step process and assign it in the schedule line category. When the supplying plant creates the replenishment delivery, the movement type causes the stock to be added at the receiving plant without the goods receipt through Transaction MIGO.
- **STO two-step process**
  You use movement type 641 for the two-step process. When the supplying plant creates the replenishment delivery, the movement type causes the stock not to be added at the receiving plant without the receipt of the goods through Transaction MIGO. The receiving plant needs to perform the receipt of the goods through Transaction MIGO; until it's executed, the stock will show as in-transit in inventory management.

4.2.2 Configuration of Stock Transport Orders

We've explored the process overview of STO in the previous section. Now, let's walk through the configuration related to STO in further sections.

Shipping Data for Plants

You must first configure the plant as a customer and vendor before setting up the shipping data configuration. In the STO scenario, one plant will behave as a vendor (supplier), and the other will behave as a customer. To define shipping data for a plant, execute Transaction SPRO and follow menu path **Materials Management • Purchasing • Purchase Order • Set up Stock Transport Order • Define Shipping Data for Plants.**

You'll arrive at the screen shown in Figure 4.28, where you assign the supplying plant sales area, that is, sales organization (**SlsOrg.Int.B**), distribution channel (**DistChannelIB**), and division (**Div.Int.Billing**) to the plant, which will act as a vendor. For the plant to identify as a receiving plant or customer, you have to assign the plant as a customer number to the plant in the **Customer No. Plant** field. In this case, the material used for stock transfer should be extended to both the sales area and the plant. Click the **Save** button or press [Ctrl]+[S] after filling out the required details.

To summarize, you must perform the following configuration:

- Assign this customer number in the receiving plant details.
- Assign the supplying sales area in the supplying plant details.

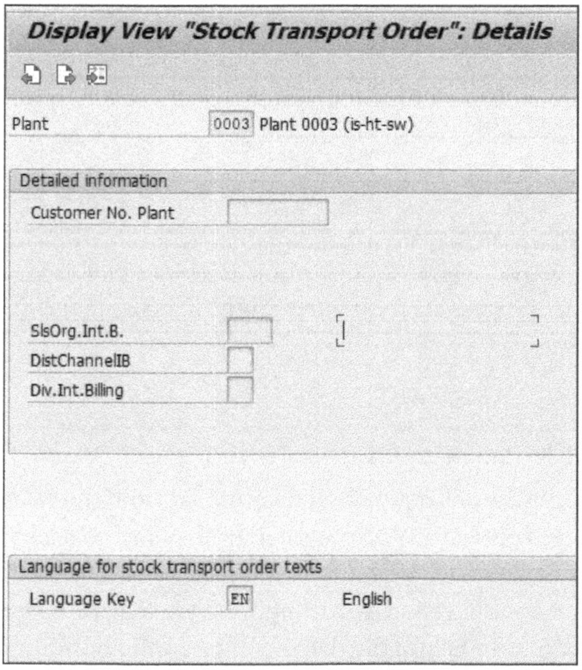

Figure 4.28 Define Shipping Data for Plants

The effect of this configuration can be seen in the purchase order, which can be viewed in Transaction ME23N with the **Shipping** tab enabled, as shown in Figure 4.29. You have to maintain the sales area (i.e., sales organization [**Sales Org.**]), distribution channel (**Distr. Channel**), and **Division** for the supplying plant (i.e., the plant from which the stock will be supplied). For the receiving plant (i.e., the plant where the goods are received), you have to assign the **Customer** number, as shown previously in Figure 4.28. The customer that you assign for the receiving plant is used in the sales and distribution shipping process to identify the goods receipt.

To ship the goods to the receiving plant, the **Shipping Point** must be determined in the supplying plant area. The shipping condition (**Shp.Cond.**) maintained in the customer master helps in determining the shipping point for the STO deliveries. With the help of shipping conditions, transportation zones, and delivery plants, the system determines the route in the STO delivery process.

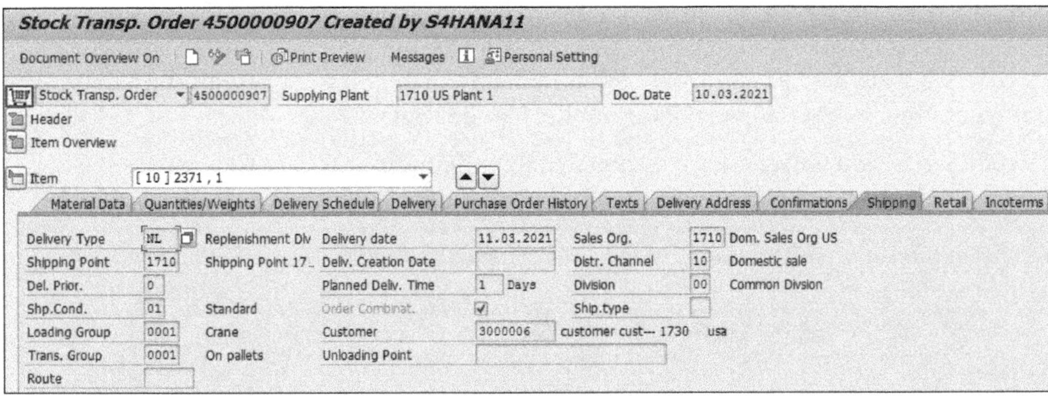

Figure 4.29 Shipping Tab in the Purchase Order

> **Note**
>
> In most implementations we've seen, the separate STO sales area is defined and used for the STO business process. This decision strictly comes from the business as to how they want to set up the reporting aspects for the STO deliveries.

Delivery Type and Availability Check Procedure by Plant

In a normal sales and distribution flow, the delivery type is determined from the sales order document type configuration. However, in STO, it gets determined from the purchase order document type and the delivery document that you assign in the preceding configuration. You maintain the configuration according to the purchase order document type and supplying plant. We'll explore the delivery type configuration in the next sections.

To configure a plant's delivery type and availability check procedure, navigate to menu path **SAP Customizing Implementation Guide • Materials Management • Purchasing • Purchase Order • Set Up Stock Transport Order • Configure Delivery Type & Availability Check Procedure by Plant**. You'll arrive at the screen shown in Figure 4.30.

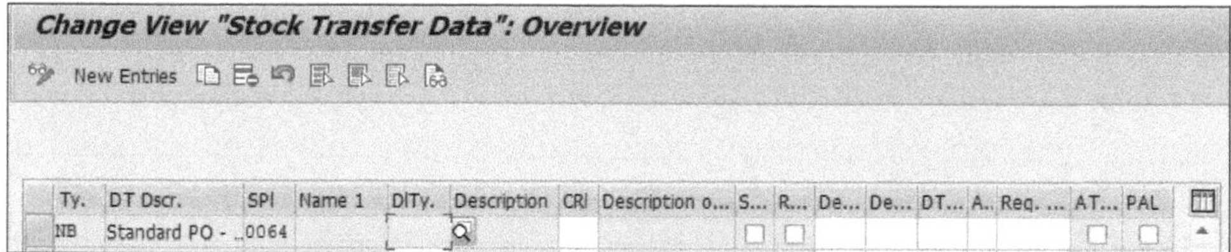

Figure 4.30 Configure Delivery Type and Availability Check Procedure by Plant

The standard purchase order document type (**Ty.**) you use for intracompany STOs is **UB**, whereas the purchase order document type for intercompany STOs is **NB**. In the configuration shown in Figure 4.30, you must maintain the delivery type (**DlTy.**) associated with the purchase order type (**Ty.**) and supplying plant (**SPl**).

As explained in Section 4.1, you can perform the product availability check during STOs as well. You can assign the availability check rule (**CRl**), which will help the system access the scope of the availability check (see Section 4.1.4). You can create shipment documents for the STO purpose. This shipment scheduling checkbox (**S...**) acts as an integration point between the STO, shipment, and warehouse management functionality. The **Shipment Scheduling** checkbox is used to process warehouse management shipment–related scheduling performed on the STO deliveries. To perform the warehouse management scheduling, your material master needs to be extended to the warehouse management views. Weekly client deliveries from a single shipping point to a number of product recipients and unloading locations along a route are planned. The goods issue time spot is an important component of the route schedule. All deliveries with the same products issue time spot on a route schedule depart the shipping location at the same time and along the same route. To enable this functionality, you have to select the route checkbox (**R...**).

Delivery Types

You use different delivery types based on the underlying business process. Table 4.3 exhibits the delivery types based on business processes. The configuration in the delivery type is different for each subprocess.

Business Process	Delivery Type
Normal sales order	LF
Cash sales	BV
STO	NL
Intercompany STO	NLCC

Table 4.3 Delivery Types

Business Process	Delivery Type
STO returns	NLR
Intercompany STO returns	NLCR

Table 4.3 Delivery Types (Cont.)

For delivery type configuration, you must execute Transaction SPRO and navigate to menu path **Logistics Execution • Shipping • Deliveries • Define Delivery Types**. You can also use Transaction OVLK to define the delivery types.

You'll arrive at the screen shown in Figure 4.31, where you should select the desired delivery type and click the **Details** icon to land on the screen in Figure 4.32, which, in this example, shows the configuration of delivery type **NL**.

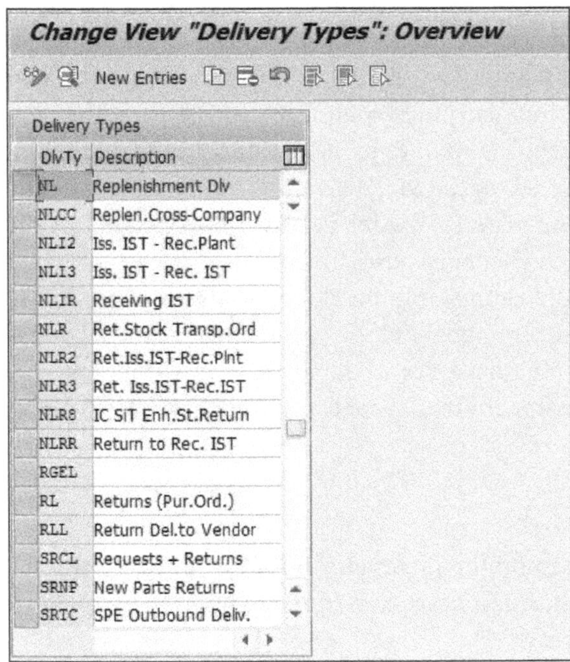

Figure 4.31 Delivery Types

Let's explore each important field in detail:

- **Document Cat.**

  The document category governs the backend logic or the functionality for the individual delivery type. The standard delivery type has the document category as **J**. The return delivery type is identified with the document category as **T**. The document category defines whether the system should propose the **Post Goods Issue** button during the goods issue or the **Post Goods Receipt** button during the goods receipt for the return delivery document creation. The **Document Cat.** field is also used for the status of the sales document; that is, it enables the system to provide information on the status of delivery processing, billing, and invoicing.

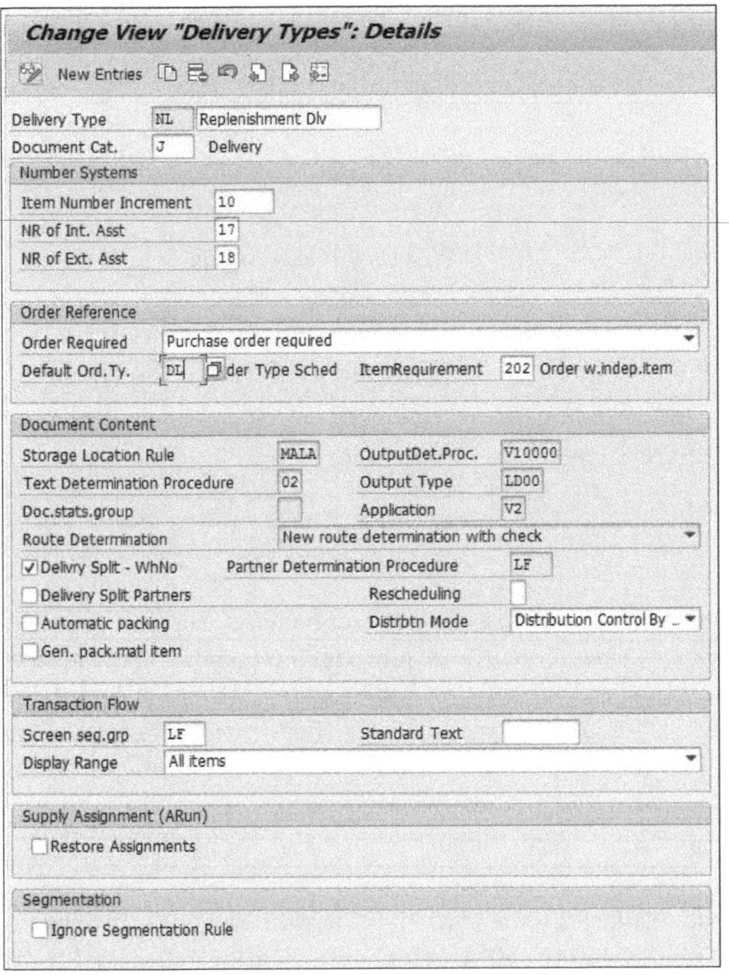

Figure 4.32 Delivery Type NL

- **Number Systems**
  This set of fields control the attribute for the number range. You can use the internal number range or external number range for the delivery document. It also controls how the line number should be incremented in the delivery document.
- **Order Required**
  This field determines whether or not any previous documents are necessary to create a delivery document. The STO delivery will require a purchase order.

  There are cases where you need to create a delivery document without reference to any order. The standard delivery type you can use in those cases is **LO**. You use this delivery type for the sample to be sent to the existing customer and if the customer is hesitant to raise an order for the same. You have to manually input the ship-to party in the delivery document if the delivery document is created without reference to any order. Standard SAP has provided various options for the **Order Required** field, as shown in Table 4.4.

Business Process	Preceding Document Option
Standard order-to-cash process	**X** (sales order required)
STO	**B** (purchase order required)
Delivery for subcontracting	**L** (delivery for subcontracting)
Return delivery to the supplier	**R** (return delivery to the supplier)
Project-specific delivery integrated with a work breakdown structure (WBS)	**P** (project required)
No preceding document required	Blank

Table 4.4 Order Required Options

- **Default Ord. Ty.**
  When the **Order Required** field is set to **No sales order required**, this field is usually set for STO and delivery with reference. The system uses the default order type **DL** to maintain the copy control between purchase orders to the delivery document, as there is no provision in SAP S/4HANA to maintain the copy control here. The default order type is also used for the pricing procedure determination for pro forma invoices in the intracompany STO process. We'll discuss the copy control setting in detail in later sections.
- **ItemRequirement**
  This is the ABAP code that needs to be created in Transaction VOFM. The code is called a routine, and it's used in SAP S/4HANA for any custom logic changes. For the delivery type configuration, two major routines are used as follows:
  - **201**: After creating the document, if you want to add a new line item in the delivery document, then you have to maintain routine 202 in the delivery type configuration.
  - **202**: If not then you have to maintain 201 routines in the delivery document.
- **Storage Location Rule**
  Storage location is determined based on the storage location rule that you specify in the delivery type configuration. The storage location determination is always done in the delivery document. You must leverage the user exit to do the automatic storage location determination at the sales order level. If not, usually you can mention

the storage location at the order level manually, and then it gets carried to the delivery document as well with the help of copy control. For automatic storage location determination, SAP has provided three rules from which you can choose and assign them in the delivery document:

- **MALA**: The storage location is determined based on the combination of shipping point (determined from Transaction OVL2), plant, and storage condition (will be picked from the **Sales: General/Plant** view). The configuration can be done in Transaction OVL3.
- **RETA**: This rule states that the storage location should be determined based on the shipping point, storage condition, and situation (which you can define in the Transaction SPRO path). This rule is selected based on if the organization is operating in the retail space. The path to determine the storage location with the **RETA** rule is **Logistics Execution • Shipping • Picking • Determine Picking Location • Storage Location • Determination with Situation.**
- **MARE**: You can choose this rule if you want the system to give priority to the **MALA** rule, but if the storage location isn't found, then the system can choose the **RETA** rule to find the storage location. When the storage location isn't found by both rules, the system won't populate the storage location field in the delivery and keeps the field blank.

Note

The following are prerequisites for the storage location determination:

- The material should be maintained for the **Sales: General/Plant** view with storage conditions.
- The **Relevant for Picking** and **Determine Storage Location** checkboxes in the delivery item category should be checked. The delivery item categories can be viewed in Transaction OVLP.
- The delivering plant and movement types should be activated for the storage location automatic determination via Transaction OMJ8.

- **OutputDet.Proc.**

  You'll assign the output determination procedure in this field. You can define the output determination procedure by following menu path **Logistic Execution • Shipping • Basic Shipping Functions • Output Control • Output Determination • Maintain Output Determination for Outbound Deliveries • Maintain Output Types.** To print the output type automatically during the creation of the delivery document, you have to maintain the delivery output type condition records by using Transaction VV21.

- **Text Determination Procedure**
  The text determination procedure for sales document type can be configured in Transaction VOTXN. You'll assign the configured text determination procedure in this field. The information can be exchanged with the different stakeholders in the order-to-cash cycle with the help of text determination. The **Text** tab in the delivery document item will be populated with the required information.
- **Output Type**
  This is the default output type that appears while triggering the output for the delivery document. If you don't maintain the output type here, the system will prompt you to choose the output type from the procedure. The standard **Output Type** maintained for the delivery document is **LD00**.
- **Doc.stats.group**
  The document statistic group is used purely from the reporting standpoint. You can create your document statistic group and assign that group to the field. The system will use the field to push the values to the Logistics Information System (LIS).
- **Application**
  Outputs are configured based on the application type. The application type typically used for the delivery process is **V2**. Similarly, the sales order is **V1**, and the invoice is **V3**. You must assign the application type in this field. **Application** isn't a freely definable field; it's provided by SAP as a standard.
- **Route Determination**
  We've discussed route determination in Chapter 3, Section 3.1. Normally, the route determination happens at the sales order level, and the same is copied to the delivery document. SAP has provided you with an option to redetermine the routes on the delivery document level. You must choose the appropriate option to either redetermine the route or keep it the same as the sales order. The system does a validation check against standard table TROAL, where you maintain the actual route and proposed route.
- **Delivery Split – WhNo**
  As the name suggests, if you select this checkbox, you prompt the system to do the delivery document split based on the warehouse number assigned for each delivery document line item. You can configure the system so that deliveries within a single warehouse are automatically created for specific warehouse numbers and delivery types, and so that a delivery split is performed if necessary.
- **Delivery Split Partners**
  The standard system uses the split criteria as the ship-to party. However, if you want the system to take additional partner functions into consideration while performing the delivery split, you can select this checkbox. For example, if the partner functions in any of the line items is different, then the default delivery split will happen in the system.

- **Automatic packing**
  The packing process is performed during delivery processing where you assign the delivery line item to the packaging material. This whole combination of packaging material and delivery items is called a handling unit. In outbound delivery, packing can be done both manually and automatically: manual packing is done by manually selecting the **Pack** button, whereas automatic packing uses the condition technique to automatically identify the material to be packed and create handling units. One of the prerequisites to automatically pack the goods is the delivery type control for automatic packing. You can select the checkbox if you want the automatic packing functionality to be enabled.
- **Gen. pack.matl item**
  If you want to charge the customer for the packaging material, you must input separate material as packaging material in the delivery document. If you select this checkbox, the packaging material will be automatically entered in the delivery document and then copied in the billing document that will be used to bill the customer.
- **Partner Determination Procedure**
  You can assign the partner determination procedure in the delivery type. Usually, the partner determination happens at the order level, but, in some cases, where the additional partners need to be determined at the delivery document level, you can use this field. You can determine the partner determination using Transaction VOPAN.
- **Screen seq.grp**
  You can control the tabs and views that are displayed in the delivery document with the help of the screen sequence group. The configuration for the screen sequence group is usually handled by technical consultants based on customer requirements.
- **Standard Text**
  This is the standard text that can be used to display texts in the delivery output documents. This text can be used in SAP scripts for output.

Delivery Item Categories

Now that we've covered delivery type configuration, let's explore the delivery item category configuration that determines the behavior of the delivery document line item. In most scenarios, the sales order item category gets copied into the delivery document, but the behavior has to be configured separately for the delivery item category.

You can configure delivery item categories with Transaction OVLP or by navigating to menu path **Logistics Execution • Shipping • Deliveries • Define Delivery Item Categories**. You'll arrive at Figure 4.33 where, in this example, we've used the item category **NLN**, which is used for the intercompany STO scenario.

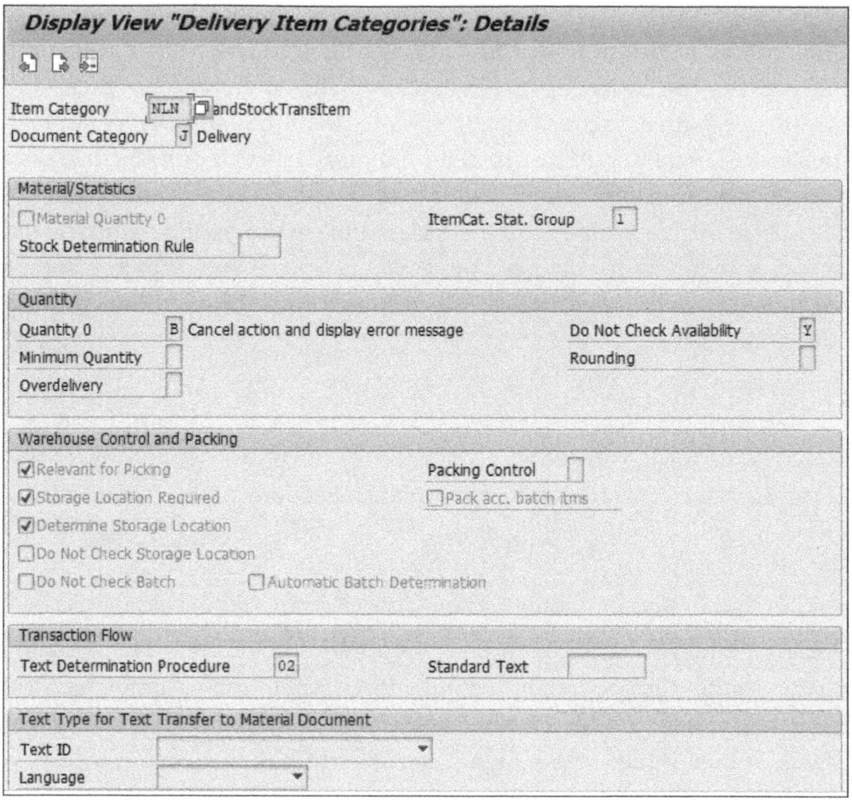

Figure 4.33 Delivery Item Category

Let's explore each field in the delivery document category in detail:

- **Document Category**
  This field governs the backend logic or the functionality for the individual delivery type. The standard delivery type has the document category as **J**. The return delivery type is identified with the document category as **T**. The document category defines whether the system should propose the **Post Goods Issue** button during the goods issue or the **Post Goods Receipt** button during the goods receipt for the return delivery document creation. The **Document Category** field is also used for the status of the sales document; that is, it enables the system to provide information on the status of delivery processing, billing, and invoicing.
- **Material Quantity 0**
  This field controls whether the system allows creating the delivery document without the delivery quantity. We've seen this functionality implemented in cases of subscription-based software products where the quantity is measured in terms of the contract data. The functionality is also used for the text items.
- **ItemCat. Stat. Group**
  This field is used to set the system for the LIS reporting.

- **Stock Determination Rule**
  The stock determination strategy is an alternative way to perform the availability check in the system. The main prerequisite of the stock determination strategy is plant, stock determination group (you assign it in the material master), and stock determination rule in the delivery item category type. The stock determination strategy also defines which stock type can be used for the stock determination, such as unrestricted stock, sales order stock, vendor consignment stock, and so on.
- **Quantity 0**
  This field controls the system response when the delivery is created with zero quantities. SAP has provided the following messages:
  - Blank: No system response.
  - **A**: Display warning message.
  - **B**: Display error message when a delivery is created or changed.
  - **C**: Display error message only when a delivery is created.
- **Do Not Check Availability**
  You can turn off the availability check in the delivery item category level. The effect of this configuration is that even if the stocks aren't available, the system will allow the delivery document to be created with the quantity mentioned in the sales order.
- **Minimum Quantity**
  This field specifies how the system should react if the quantity in the delivery document is less than the minimum delivery quantity specified in the material master, that is, whether to display a warning message, an error message, or no message.
- **Overdelivery**
  You can define the system behavior if the delivery quantity is more than the sales order quantity. The prerequisite for the overdelivery is that you must select the **Overdelivery Tolerance** checkbox in the material master. You don't have to maintain the unlimited over delivery tolerance in the customer master.
- **Rounding**
  If the delivery quantities are in decimals, you can round them up or down based on the settings maintained in the delivery item category.
- **Relevant for Picking**
  This checkbox must be selected if you've integrated the warehouse management functionality. This checkbox indicates that the delivery line item is relevant for picking. In certain item categories relevant for quotation, return consignment pickup, and consignment return, this checkbox isn't selected.
- **Storage Location Required**
  If you deselect this checkbox, you can process the deliveries without storage location.

- **Determine Storage Location**
  As mentioned in an earlier section, this is one of the prerequisites for the automatic storage location determination.
- **Do Not Check Storage Location**
  If certain materials aren't extended to the storage location extension view, the system by default checks if the material is extended to the storage location or not. If you select this checkbox, the system bypasses the logic. You can configure the movement type to create the material for the storage location, which we'll discuss further in a later section.
- **Automatic Batch Determination**
  This field is the prerequisite for the automatic batch determination procedure.
- **Text Determination Procedure**
  You can assign the text determination procedure in the delivery item category.
- **Standard Text**
  This is the standard text that can be used to display texts in the delivery output documents. This text can be used in SAP scripts for the output.

Delivery Item Category Determination

Item category determination happens in the sales order with the help of Transaction VOV4. However, there are certain scenarios where you have to either determine the item category or redetermine the delivery item category. For example, for an STO, the sales order document is absent in this business process. Here, you must determine the delivery item category with the help of the delivery document. Let's explore the delivery item category determination in detail.

To determine the delivery item category determination, execute Transaction SPRO and navigate to menu path **Logistic Execution • Shipping • Deliveries • Define Item Category Determination in Deliveries**. You'll arrive at the screen shown in Figure 4.34.

As shown in Figure 4.34, the delivery item category determination is based on the following four parameters. Similar to the sales order item category determination, there are 11 manual item categories that you can maintain in this setup.

- **DlvT**
  The delivery type will be determined from the sales order document type in a normal business process; however, in the STO process, this will be determined from the configuration that you've done for the STO delivery type.
- **ItCG**
  The item category group will be maintained in the material master.
- **Usge**
  You can maintain the usage indicator in the customer material info record. SAP has provided some standard usage indicators such as **SEIN** (delivery item relevant for billing), **FREE** (free goods), and so on.

- **ItmC (farthest right)**
  This is basically the item category of the previous line item. It's typically used in the bill of materials (BOM) scenario where the item category of the main item is considered a higher-level item category.

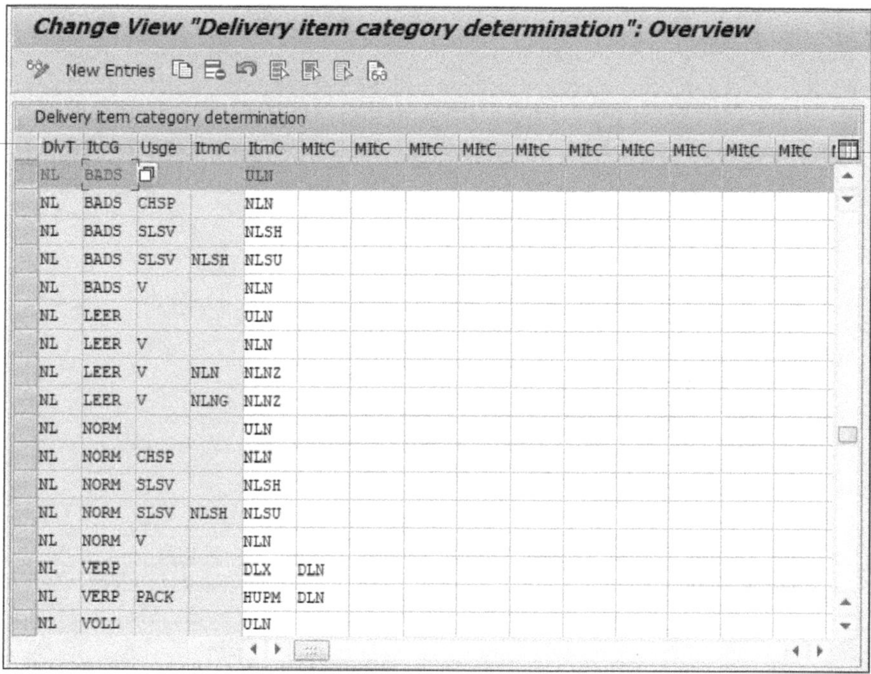

Change View "Delivery item category determination": Overview

New Entries

Delivery item category determination

DlvT	ItCG	Usge	ItmC	ItmC	MItC	MItC	MItC	MItC	MItC	MItC	MItC	MItC	MItC	MItC
NL	BADS			ULN										
NL	BADS	CHSP		NLN										
NL	BADS	SLSV		NLSH										
NL	BADS	SLSV	NLSH	NLSU										
NL	BADS	V		NLN										
NL	LEER			ULN										
NL	LEER	V		NLN										
NL	LEER	V	NLN	NLNZ										
NL	LEER	V	NLNG	NLNZ										
NL	NORM			ULN										
NL	NORM	CHSP		NLN										
NL	NORM	SLSV		NLSH										
NL	NORM	SLSV	NLSH	NLSU										
NL	NORM	V		NLN										
NL	VERP			DLX	DLN									
NL	VERP	PACK		HUPM	DLN									
NL	VOLL			ULN										

Figure 4.34 Delivery Item Category Determination

Document Type for Stock Transport Orders

The configuration of the document type for STOs enables the system to have the cross-company code stock transfer transactions. The configuration node for the settings is **Materials Management • Purchasing • Purchase Order • Set Up Stock Transport Order • Assign Document Type, One-Step Procedure, Underdelivery Tolerance.** You'll arrive at the screen shown in Figure 4.35, which illustrates the default document type for STOs.

Let's explore each field of the configuration in detail:

- **Doc. Category**
  The purchasing document category distinguishes between various types of purchasing documents, such as purchase requests, requests for quotations, purchase orders, scheduling agreements, and so on. They are further divided into purchase order types.
- **SPlt**
  This is the supplying plant from which the stock will be transferred to the plant where the goods will be received and a purchase order is created.

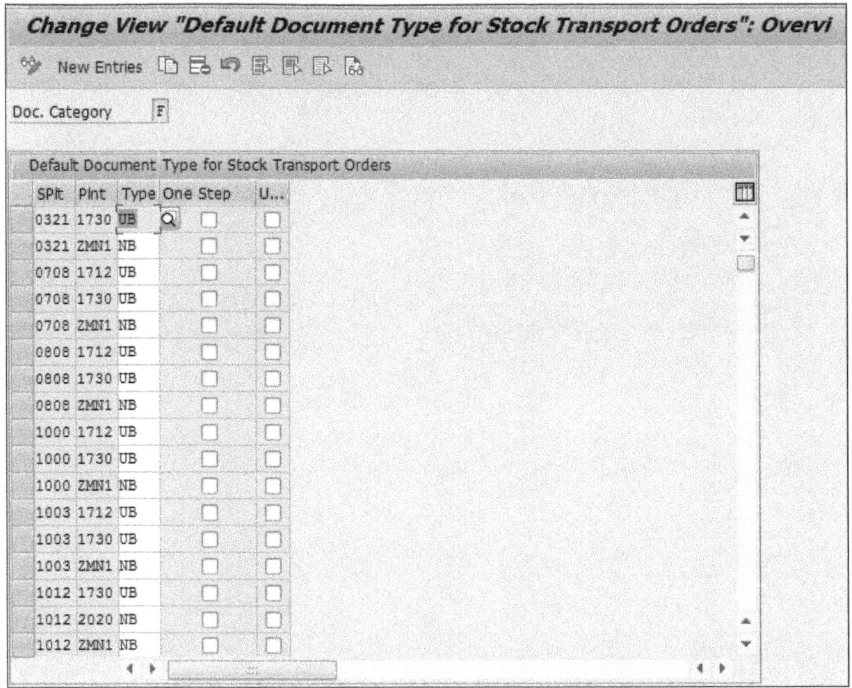

Figure 4.35 Assign Document Type, One-Step Procedure, Underdelivery Tolerance

- **Plnt**
  This refers to the delivery plant where the stocks will be delivered in the STO process.
- **Type**
  In this field, you have to mention the purchase order document type that will be used for the STO. For intracompany STO, you use purchase order type **UB**, and for intercompany STO, you use purchase order type **NB**.
- **One Step**
  This checkbox will govern the logic for the one-step process or two-step process, which we introduced in Section 4.2.1. Let's explore the processes:
  - One step: In a one-step process, once the delivery is created from the supplying plant and goods issue has been posted, then the stock will be available in the receiving plant as unrestricted stock with no need for the goods receipt (Transaction MIGO) in the receiving plant. This process is also called an automatic STO. The movement type used in this case is 647, and the schedule line category determined is NN.
  - Two step: If the **One Step** checkbox is unchecked, then the system by default considers it the two-step STO process. In a two-step process, the post-delivery document is created, and a goods issue has been posted by the supplying plant. The stock will be shown as stock in transit in the receiving plant. You have to manually perform the goods receipt, and then the stock will be moved from the stock in

transit to the unrestricted stock. The logic is configured in movement type 641, which will be determined for the two-step process. The movement type used for the Transaction MIGO process is 101. The schedule line category that will be determined in this case will also be NN. The determination happens based on the item category and MRP type in Transaction VOV4.

In the STO process, the schedule line category determination is as follows:

NLN (item category) + MRP type = NN (schedule line category)

We'll explore the schedule line category determination in Section 4.4.4.

- **U...**
  This checkbox will enable the system to have an underdelivery tolerance. If the quantity mentioned in the purchase order doesn't match the delivery document under the specified limit, the purchase order will be marked as **Completed** because you've activated the checkbox. The table level entry EKPO-EKPZ (delivery completed) field will be marked as X (yes).

Activate the Stock Transfer by Storage Location

Stock transfer between storage locations can be performed in two ways: transfer posting and stock transfer between storage locations. While performing the transfer posting, you must provide the movement type in Transaction MIGO. In this case, you'll use movement type 311 for the one-step process and 313 for the two-step process. However, if storage locations are located in different geographical locations, you have to perform the stock transfer between storage locations. The prerequisite of this process is that the material should be extended to both storage locations. As the stock has been transferred to the same plant's storage locations, the accounting entries won't be created in this case.

Let's explore the configuration related to the stock transfer between storage locations:

- **Activate stock transfer by storage location**
  Activate the stock transfer between storage locations by following menu path **Materials Management • Purchasing • Purchase Order • Set Up Stock Transport Order • Set Up Stock Transfer between Storage Locations • Activate Stock Transfer between Storage Locations**. You'll arrive at the screen shown in Figure 4.36, where you have to activate by checking the **Issuing Storage Location Active** checkbox. This will enable the **Shipping** tab in the delivery line item just like the stock transfer between two different plants.
- **Configure delivery type and availability check procedure by storage location**
  To configure the delivery type and availability check procedure, follow menu path **Materials Management • Purchasing • Purchase Order • Set Up Stock Transport Order • Set Up Stock Transfer between Storage Locations • Configure Delivery Type & Availability Check Procedure by Storage Location**. You'll arrive at the screen shown

in Figure 4.37, where you need to select the appropriate purchase document category (**Purch. Doc. Category**) **F** for purchase order and click the green checkmark.

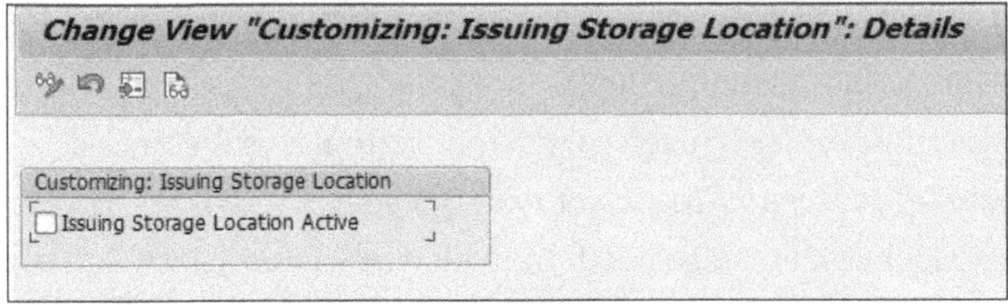

Figure 4.36 Activate Stock Transfer between Storage Locations

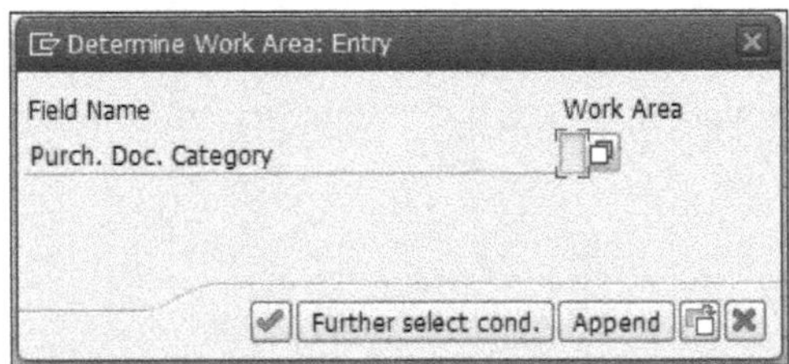

Figure 4.37 Configure Delivery Type and Availability Check Procedure by Storage Location: Initial Screen

You'll arrive at the screen shown in Figure 4.38, where you assign the delivery type (**DlvTy**) to the combination of purchase order type (**Type**), supplying plant (**SPlt**), and issuing storage location (**IStLoc**). We've already discussed the other configuration elements in the STO process configuration between the plants.

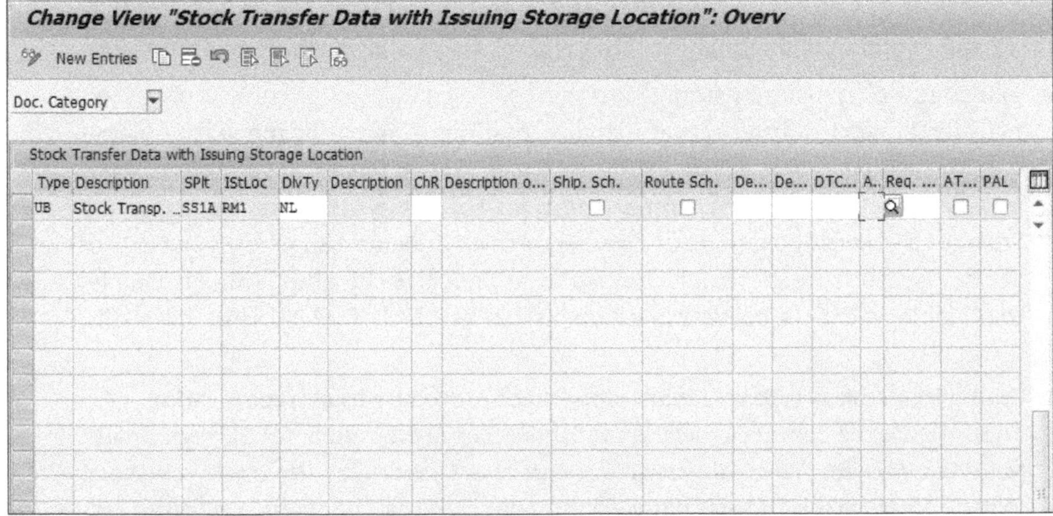

Figure 4.38 Configure Delivery Type and Availability Check Procedure by Storage Location

- **Define the shipping data for the plant**
  To define the shipping data for the plant, follow menu path **Materials Management • Purchasing • Purchase Order • Set Up Stock Transport Order • Set Up Stock Transfer between Storage Locations • Define Shipping Data for Stock Transfers between Storage Locations.**

  You'll arrive at the screen shown in Figure 4.39, where you'll define the shipping data for the STO between storage locations. You have to assign the storage location to the combination of plant (**Plnt**), sales organization (**Sales Org.**), distribution channel (**Distrib. Channel**), **Shipping Point**, and **Division**.

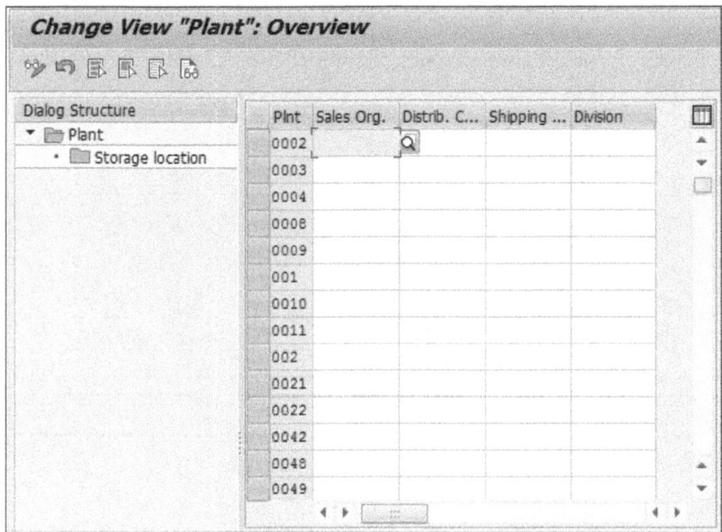

Figure 4.39 Define Shipping Data for Stock Transfers between Storage Locations

Automatic Delivery Creation

For the configuration related to automatic delivery creation in STOs, you must execute Transaction SPRO and follow menu path **Materials Management • Purchasing • Purchase Order • Set Up Stock Transport Order • Activate Automatic Delivery Creation and CRM Billing.** You'll arrive at the screen shown in Figure 4.40. SAP has provided functionality to automatically create the delivery document after creation of the STO purchase order. On this screen, you must activate the automatic delivery creation function with a combination of purchase order document categories (the **Cat** column). For STOs, you'll select the purchase order document category as **Purchase order**, select the purchase order **Type** as **ENB**, and enter the supplying plant (**SPlt**). You can activate auto delivery or keep it as inactive by choosing the appropriate option in the **Auto Delv.** field. To disable auto delivery, choose the blank option, and to activate the auto delivery, choose **auto delivery create active**.

When you use this function, the system doesn't perform an availability check when creating the delivery. It's assumed that the availability was already checked during the

STO processing. The billing can be executed in the SAP Customer Relationship Management (SAP CRM) system if you select the **CRM Bill** checkbox.

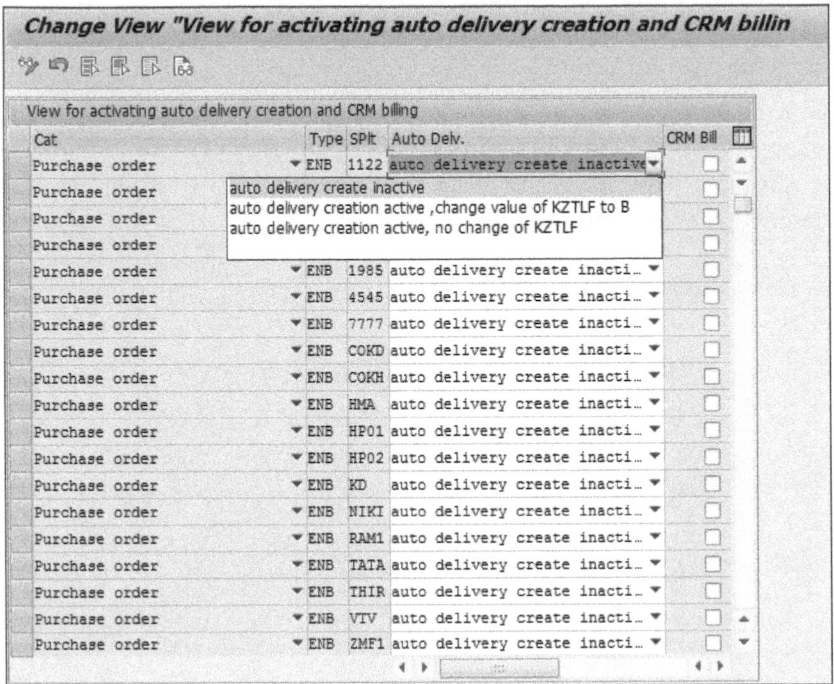

Figure 4.40 Automatic Delivery Creation

Copy Control Settings

Three document types will be generated during the STO depending on the intercompany STO or intracompany STO: purchase order for STO, delivery, and pro forma invoice. You have to copy the material, quantity, plant, and other important fields to the delivery document and from the delivery document to the invoice. SAP has provided standard functionality called *copy control* to copy these fields from one document type to another.

To configure the copy control setting between the purchase order and the delivery document, follow menu path **Logistics Execution • Shipping • Copying Control • Specify Copy Control for Deliveries**. You can also use Transaction VTLA for the same. You'll arrive at the screen shown in Figure 4.41, where you can choose the sales order document type (**SalesDocType**), select the target delivery type (**Delivery type**), and then click on the **Details** icon to arrive at the screen shown in Figure 4.42.

As mentioned in the previous section, there is no copy control setting directly between the purchase order and delivery. For the purchase order-related copy controls, you use the default order type **DL**, which you've maintained in the delivery type controls.

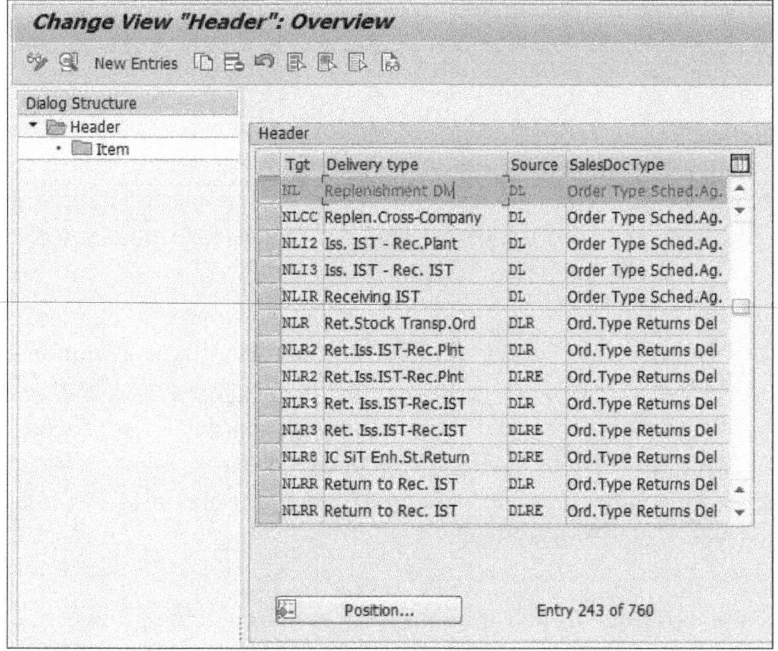

Figure 4.41 Copy Control: Initial Screen

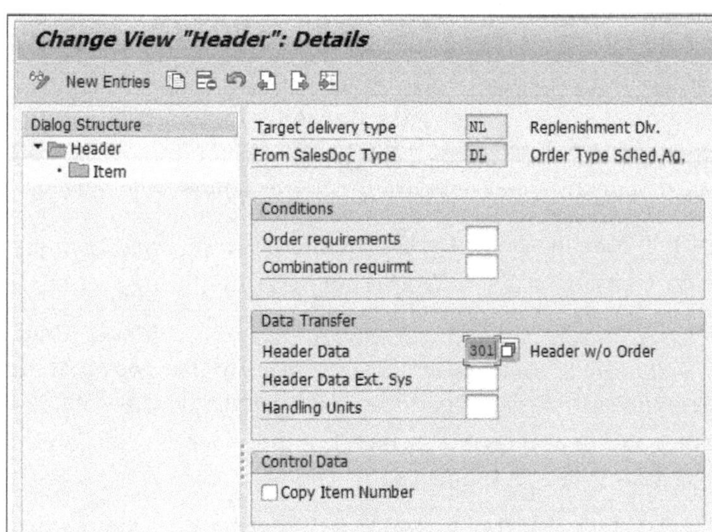

Figure 4.42 Copy Control Settings

As shown in Figure 4.42, you have to select the document type from which you have to copy the fields and the document type where the fields have to be copied. In this example of the stock transfer copy control, you must copy from default document type **DL** to delivery document type **NL**.

Let's explore some important fields in copy controls as follows:

- **Order requirements**
  When copying the order details to the delivery document, you can give specific requirements or logic to the system, which will be adhered to by the system every time the delivery document is created with reference to the sales document type. SAP has provided standard routines that you can identify and choose to achieve the desired requirements. You can create your own routine with the help of Transaction VOFM and assign the routine in the transaction.
- **Combination requirmt**
  While performing the sales order combination for deliveries, that is, combining multiple sales orders into a single delivery document, you need the system to make basic checks before performing the order combination. Standard SAP has provided routine **051** to accomplish this requirement. It checks the requirements, such as whether the delivery document type and billing document type are the same across all the orders that will need to be combined.
- **Data Transfer**
  This routine helps you transfer the data from the source document to the target document. In certain scenarios, you want some of the data to be redetermined at the delivery document level. You can pass the same logic in the routine and achieve the desired results. You can set the logic if you're copying the data from external sources such as any non-SAP solutions.
- **Copy Item Number**
  If you select this checkbox, the system copies the line-item number of the source document to the target document; otherwise, the system redetermines the item increment based on the document type configuration of the delivery document.

You can maintain the setting for copy control at the line-item level as well when you click on the **Item** folder in Transaction VTLA. You'll land in the following section, as shown in Figure 4.43.

As shown in Figure 4.43, displayed item categories are permitted for the copy requirement from the sales order type **DL** to the delivery document type **NL**. If you double-click on the line-item category, you can see the next screen that provides controls on the finer aspects of the line item, as shown in Figure 4.44.

As shown in Figure 4.44, most of the fields are the same as the header level copy control settings. For STO copy controls between purchase order and delivery, you must maintain the copy routine **302** in the **Item Data** field, which will be used when deliveries are created without a sales order. If you want to add an extra layer of logic, you can create your own copy routine in Transaction VOFM (with the help of a technical consultant) and assign it here.

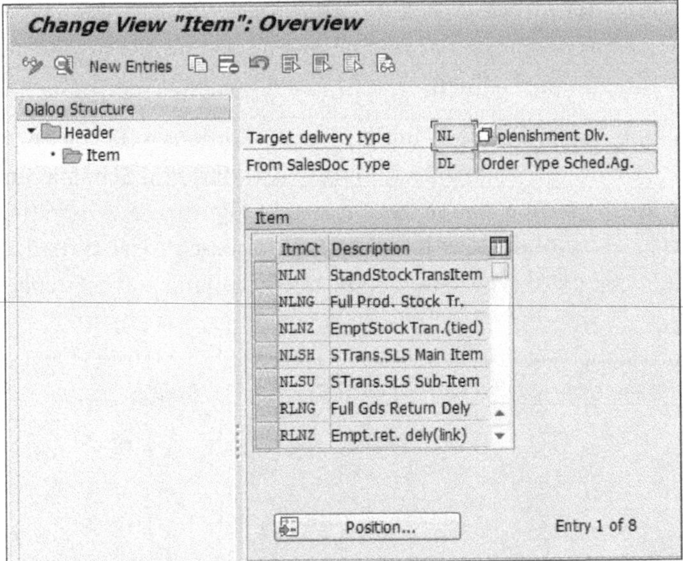

Figure 4.43 Copy Control at the Line-Item Level

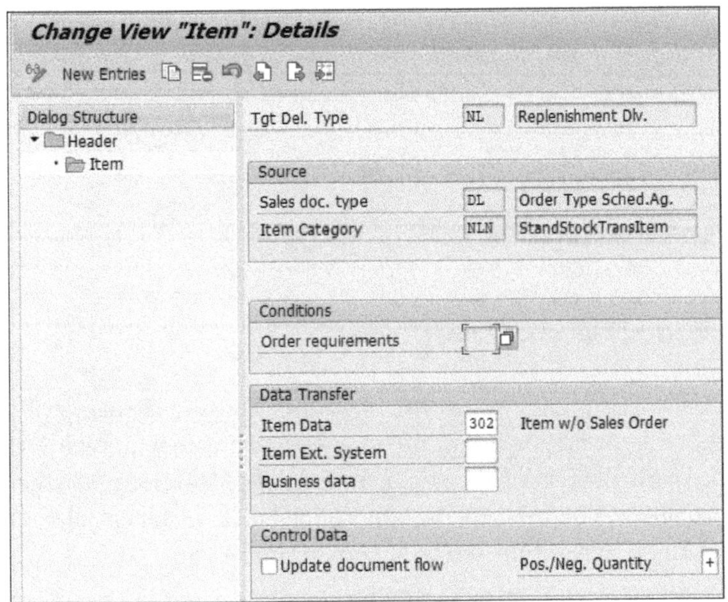

Figure 4.44 Copy Control Settings at the Line-Item Level

Integration with the Materials Management Pricing Procedure

While creating the pro forma invoice or intercompany invoice, the system needs the prices to flow into the invoice. The prices will flow from the purchase order to the invoice. You need to configure the materials management pricing procedure to do the same. We'll discuss the pricing procedures in sales and distribution in Chapter 5, Section 5.1.

Let's review the important steps in setting up the STO pricing procedure:

1. Follow menu path **Materials Management • Purchasing • Conditions • Define Price Determination Process • Define Schema Determination • Determine Schema for Stock Transport Orders**. You'll arrive at the screen shown in Figure 4.45, where the pricing procedure needs to be maintained with the combination of purchase organization (**Schema GrpPOrg**), document type (**Doc. Type**), and supplying plant (**Supplying**).

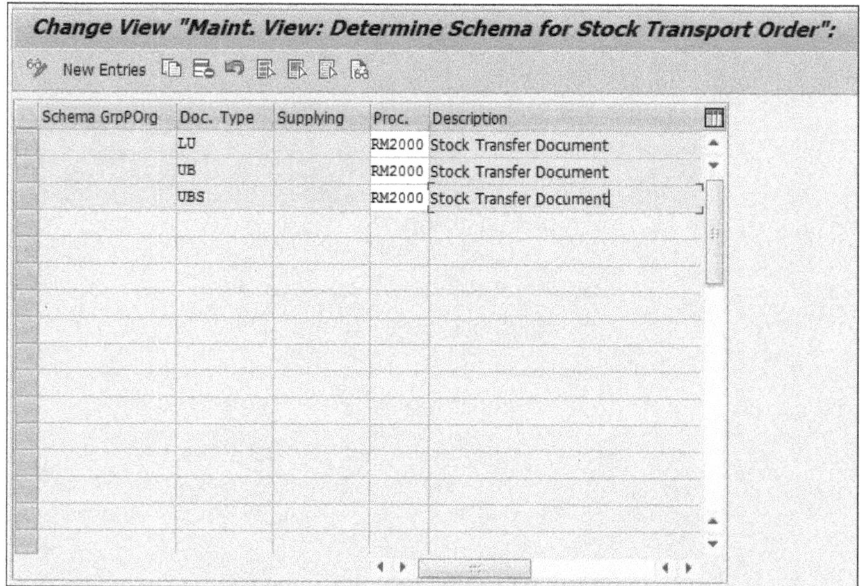

Figure 4.45 Determine the Schema for Stock Transport Orders

2. SAP provides a standard STO pricing procedure, **RM2000**. For any client-specific changes, you can use the same pricing procedure to copy and create your own STO pricing procedure. The path for creating the pricing procedure is **Materials Management • Purchasing • Condition • Define Price Determination Process • Set Calculation Schema – Purchasing**. You'll arrive at the screen shown in Figure 4.46.
3. Here, select the procedure (**Proc...**), and click on **Control data** to arrive at the screen shown in Figure 4.47, which displays the control data for the pricing schema of the stock transfer document.

> **Note**
>
> In SAP S/4HANA materials management, the pricing procedure is called a pricing schema.

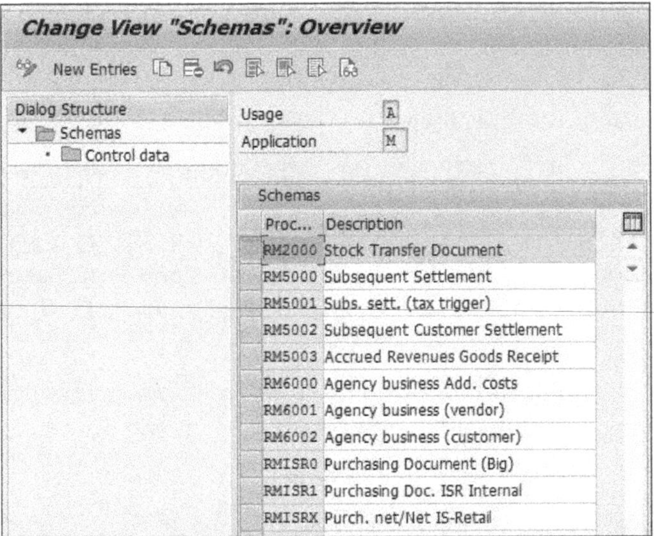

Figure 4.46 Pricing Schema: Initial Screen

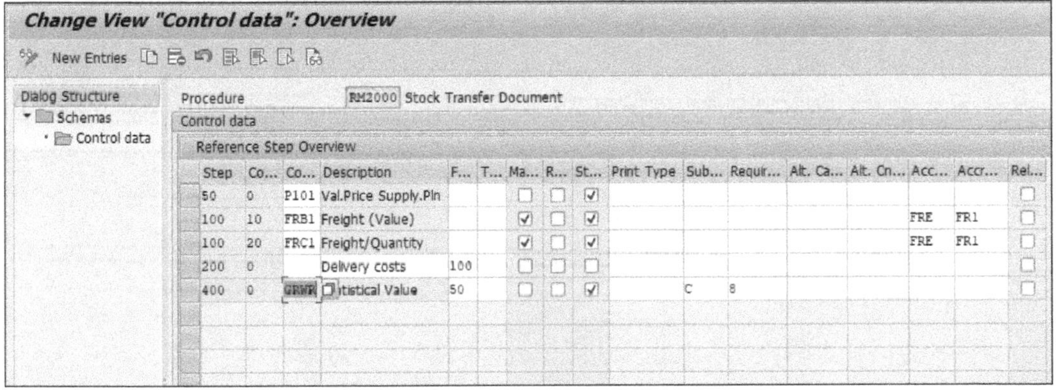

Figure 4.47 Pricing Schema

4. You have to create a condition type in sales and distribution with the help of Transaction V/06. The controls of the condition type should be the same as the PI01 condition type in the STO pricing procedure. We'll discuss the condition type controls in Chapter 5.

   The condition type that has been created in sales and distribution needs to be assigned in the STO pricing procedure (in the **Co...** field) along with the activation of the manual (**Ma...**) checkbox, as shown in the seventh column of Figure 4.47.

5. The document pricing procedure determination for STO can be achieved in two ways: based on the default order type (DL) or by maintaining the document pricing

procedure in the invoice document type with Transaction VOFA. The priority will be first given to the invoice document type; if the document pricing procedure isn't maintained in the invoice document type, then the system searches the same in the default order type from the sales document type.

6. You also have to maintain the pricing schema (that was configured in materials management) in the sales and distribution for the STO process with the following combination in Transaction OVKK (as shown in Figure 4.48). You can also follow the path for the pricing procedure determination **Sales and Distribution • Basic Functions • Pricing • Pricing Control • Define and Assign Pricing Procedures • Set Pricing Procedure Determination.**

   Maintain the pricing procedure (**Pricing Pro...**) along with the combination of sales area data, document pricing procedure (**Do...**), and customer pricing procedure (**Co...**).

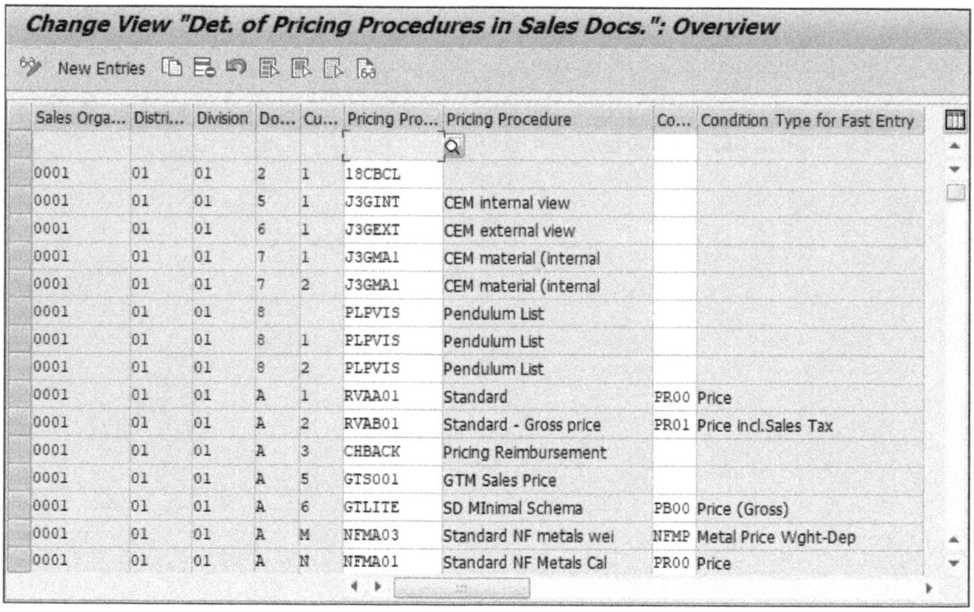

Change View "Det. of Pricing Procedures in Sales Docs.": Overview

New Entries

Sales Orga...	Distri...	Division	Do...	Cu...	Pricing Pro...	Pricing Procedure	Co...	Condition Type for Fast Entry
0001	01	01	2	1	18CBCL			
0001	01	01	5	1	J3GINT	CEM internal view		
0001	01	01	6	1	J3GEXT	CEM external view		
0001	01	01	7	1	J3GMA1	CEM material (internal		
0001	01	01	7	2	J3GMA1	CEM material (internal		
0001	01	01	8		PLPVIS	Pendulum List		
0001	01	01	8	1	PLPVIS	Pendulum List		
0001	01	01	8	2	PLPVIS	Pendulum List		
0001	01	01	A	1	RVAA01	Standard	PR00	Price
0001	01	01	A	2	RVAB01	Standard - Gross price	PR01	Price incl.Sales Tax
0001	01	01	A	3	CHBACK	Pricing Reimbursement		
0001	01	01	A	5	GTS001	GTM Sales Price		
0001	01	01	A	6	GTLITE	SD MInimal Schema	PB00	Price (Gross)
0001	01	01	A	M	NFMA03	Standard NF metals wei	NFMP	Metal Price Wght-Dep
0001	01	01	A	N	NFMA01	Standard NF Metals Cal	PR00	Price

Figure 4.48 Pricing Procedure Determination

7. You must maintain the copy control between delivery and invoice in Transaction VTFL. In the **Copying Requirements** field, use **009**, which corresponds to the pro forma invoice, as shown in Figure 4.49.

8. As shown in Figure 4.50, you can then navigate to the **Item** folder, where you need to maintain the **Copying Requirements** as **010** and **Pricing Type** as **A** to copy the pricing from the purchase order for the pro forma invoice. For intercompany invoices, you can maintain the **Pricing Type** as **B**.

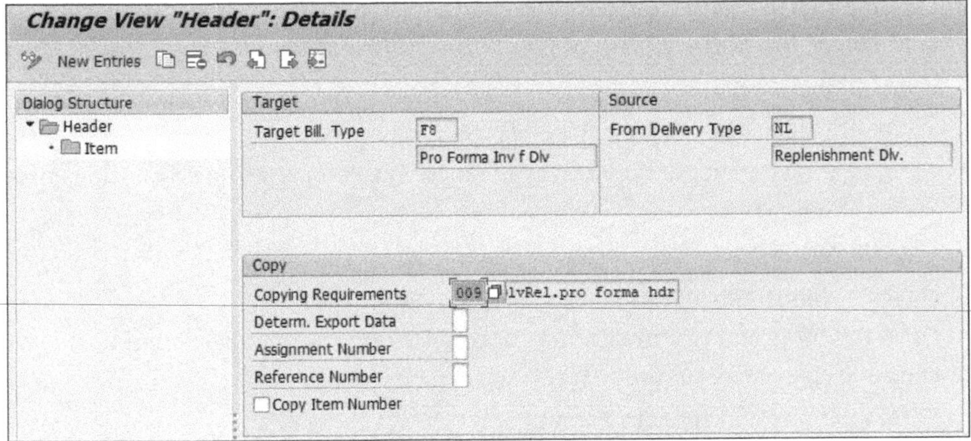

Figure 4.49 Copy Control Settings between Delivery and Invoice: Header

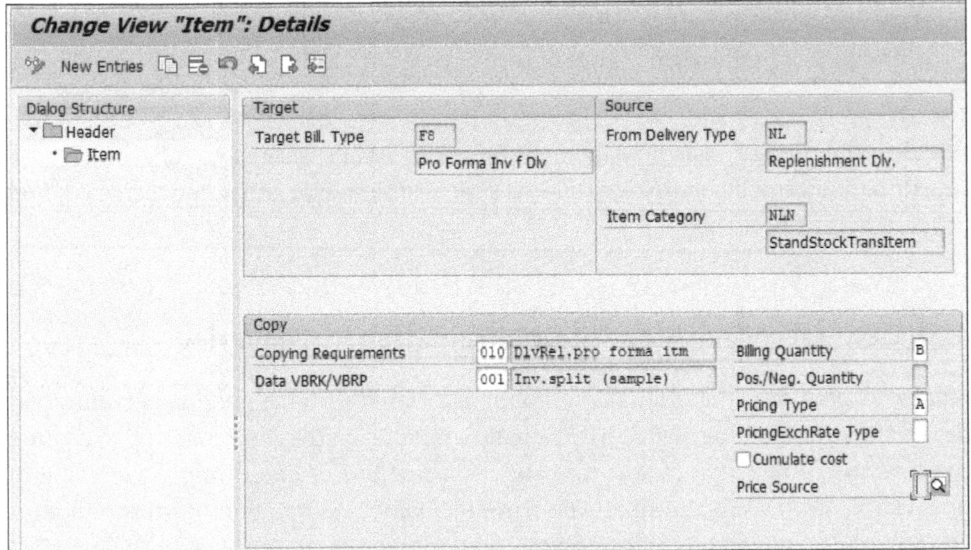

Figure 4.50 Copy Control Settings between Delivery and Invoice: Item

4.2.3 Accounting Entries in Stock Transport Orders

There is no impact on accounting entries during STO creation and outbound delivery creation. The accounting impact starts after the post goods issue (PGI).

Accounting entries in intercompany stock transfer are as follows:

- After PGI, you see an impact on the accounting side as the stocks are getting reduced from the supplier plant side. The accounting entry will be as follows:
  - Debit: Cost of goods sold (COGS)
  - Credit: Inventory account

- On the receiving plant side, once the goods are received and Transaction MIGO is performed, then the accounting entry impact is as follows:
  - Debit: Inventory
  - Credit: Supplier goods receipt/invoice receipt (GR/IR)
- After creating the supplier invoice by the receiving company, the accounting entry will be as follows:
  - Debit: GR/IR clearing account
  - Credit: Intercompany supplier
- Once the intercompany invoice has been raised by the supplier account, the accounting entry will be as follows:
  - Debit: Intercompany sales account
  - Credit: Intercompany revenue account
- Accounting entries in an intracompany stock transfer are as follows:
  - Debit: Stock inward movement account
  - Credit: Stock outward movement account

The STO process is a major area of integration between the sales and distribution functionality and the materials management functionality. Because of its reliance on both functionalities, responsibility for the STO process frequently shifts between sales and procurement consultants.

4.3 General Ledger Account Determination in Deliveries

Material valuation is the monetary amount associated with the goods in inventory at the end of an accounting period. The valuation is based on the costs incurred to acquire the inventory and to prepare it for sale. It's a method of determining the value of unsold inventory when a company prepares its financial statements. It must be appropriately valued at the end of the reporting period, such as the fiscal year. The valuated inventory will then be included in the financial statements. The valuation is based on the costs of acquiring the inventory or the cost of producing the inventory, as well as the costs of selling the inventory. Inventory is one of the biggest assets in the balance sheet statement for organizations. Inventory valuation allows you to determine your COGS and, ultimately, your profitability.

In SAP S/4HANA, material valuation is configured at the material type level. You can categorize materials as valuated or nonvaluated based on their material type. The stock of valuated material has a monetary value assigned to it; whereas the stock of nonvaluated material has no monetary value. You can also maintain the material type as nonstock. Nonvaluated material is maintained based on quantity rather than value, whereas nonstock items are consumed immediately after production and aren't kept in stock.

Nonvaluated materials of standard SAP material type UNBW are materials that you want to keep in stock but not in value. The best example is office stationery, where the stock (quantity) is kept, but when purchased, the amount goes to the office account as consumption.

Nonstock materials of standard SAP material type NLAG are those materials for which neither stock nor valuation is maintained, which means that when you do goods receipt on these materials, the quantity and amount are consumed. These are essentially one-time purchases.

After deciding that the material type needs to be valuated, the next course of action is to choose at what price the materials are valuated. The price controls in SAP S/4HANA are S (standard price) and V (moving average price). You can default the price control by making the appropriate setting while creating the material type. You can also choose the price control at the material master level.

Let's take a closer look at the impact of the price control:

- **Standard price (S)**
  When a material is assigned a standard price (S), its value is always calculated at that price. If the price of goods movement or invoice receipts differs from the standard price, the difference is recorded in a price difference account. The variance isn't considered in the valuation. You update the material price as a year-start or year-end activity using Transaction MR21. It updates the standard price in the material master record. The total stock value for materials with standard price control is calculated as follows:

  Total value = Standard price (per base unit of measure) × Total stock

- **Moving average price (V)**
  When a material is assigned a moving average price, the price in the material master record is automatically adjusted when price variances occur. If goods movements or invoice receipts are posted at a price that differs from the moving average price, the difference is posted to the stock account, and the moving average price and stock value change as a result.

  For each goods movement, the system automatically calculates the moving average price as follows:

  Moving average price = Total stock value ÷ Total stock quantity.

In the following sections, we'll explore the account determination concept in delivery creation. For every stock movement in SAP S/4HANA, a material document is generated along with the financial entries. The account determination for these financial entries happens through a systematic configuration in Transaction OBYC.

4.3.1 What Is Account Determination?

Account determination is a technique used in SAP to determine general ledger accounts automatically. You use condition pricing in both sales and distribution and in materials management. In Chapter 5, Section 5.2.2, we'll dive into the condition technique. SAP has provided another method—the transaction key technique—for determining general ledger accounts for inventory management transactions. A business transaction is identified by a three-character transaction key. Account determination is accomplished by associating the transaction key with one or more general ledger accounts. As shown in Figure 4.51, there are three main blocks: material, transaction, and movement type.

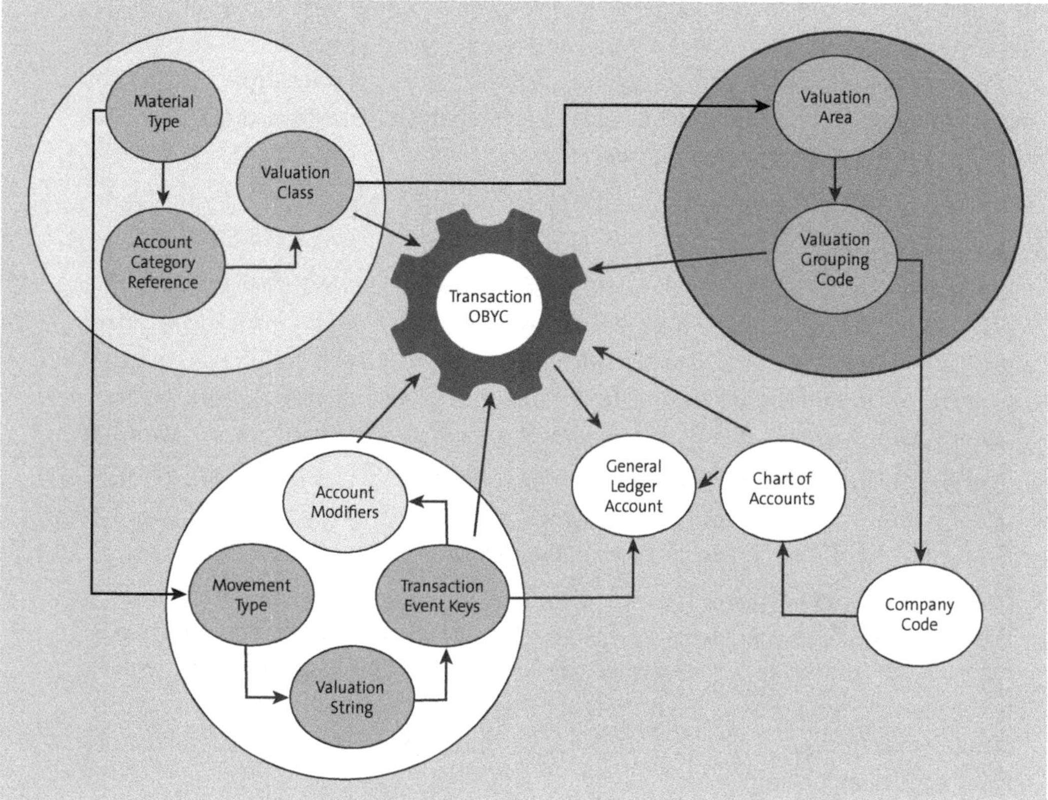

Figure 4.51 Account Determination Flow

In SAP, the *chart of accounts* is a collection of general ledger accounts that control the name of the general ledger master, the number of general ledger master records, and other control information. It's linked to the company code in Transaction OB62. The system determines the chart of accounts from the company code of the plant in inventory management.

The first material block shows that each material is associated with the material type. You can default the valuation class based on the material type. However, there is no direct link between the material type and valuation class. They both are linked together with an account category reference and linked together in Transaction OMSK. With this, you can default multiple material types with the same valuation class.

The second block shows the linkage between valuation area and valuation grouping code. Valuation areas are grouped to simplify management of the standard accounts table by reducing the number of entries.

The valuation grouping code, along with other factors, determines the general ledger accounts to which a goods movement is posted (automatic account determination). The valuation grouping code simplifies the automatic account determination process. You assign the valuation areas to the same valuation grouping code within the chart of accounts because you want to assign them to the same general ledger account.

The third block shows the linkage between movement type, valuation string, transaction key, and account modifier. It's not possible to define new valuation strings or transaction event keys in SAP S/4HANA, but account modifiers can be edited with any movement type; if GBB, PRD, or KON transaction keys are set off, then only the account modifier triggers. Based on the movement type, the system generates a valuation string, which then generates several transaction keys.

4.3.2 Prerequisites for Account Determination

Inventory can be valuated at two levels: plant level or company code level. In most projects, plant-level valuation is usually recommended compared to company code. When you choose valuation at the company code level, the same materials in all plants corresponding to that company code will have the same material price because valuation is only at the company code level. However, if you choose valuation at the plant level, you can have a different material price for the same material at different plants.

To configure the valuation level, execute Transaction SPRO and follow menu path **Enterprise Structure • Definition • Logistics – General • Define Valuation Level**. You'll arrive at the screen shown in Figure 4.52, where we've maintained the valuation area at the plant level.

> **Note**
>
> It's extremely difficult to switch back from one valuation area to another; consultants need to be very cautious while setting up the valuation area, whether it's at the company code level or plant level.

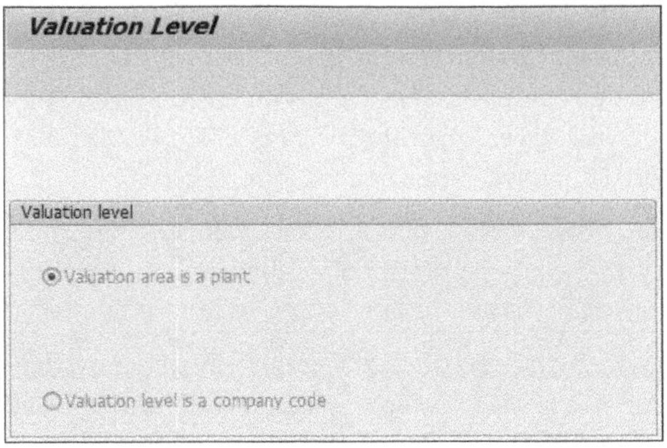

Valuation Level

Valuation level

Valuation area is a plant

Valuation level is a company code

Figure 4.52 Valuation Level

Material type is used to group the materials with shared attributes and features. It's basically a classification of materials into material styles based on characteristics. FERT is the standard material type for finished goods, HALB for semifinished products, and ROH for raw materials.

You must configure the material type in the system before creating a material master record because while making the material master record, you need to select a specific material type.

You can configure the material type with Transaction OMS2 or by navigating to menu path **Logistics – General • Material Master • Basic Settings • Material Types • Define Attributes of Material Types**. Further detail is beyond the scope of this book.

4.3.3 Configuration of Automatic Account Determination

Let's explore the various configuration elements to achieve automatic account determination.

Define Valuation Grouping Code

The account determination can be simplified by grouping together similar valuation areas. SAP has provided a standard functionality for grouping the valuation areas called a *valuation grouping code* (aka *valuation category*). This setting enables the functionality to use the same general ledger account for different valuation areas corresponding to different material types.

To activate the valuation control, follow menu path **Materials Management • Valuation and Account Assignment • Account Determination • Account Determination without Wizard • Define Valuation Control**. You'll arrive at the screen in Figure 4.53, which shows the configuration of the valuation grouping code. Select **Valuation grouping code active**.

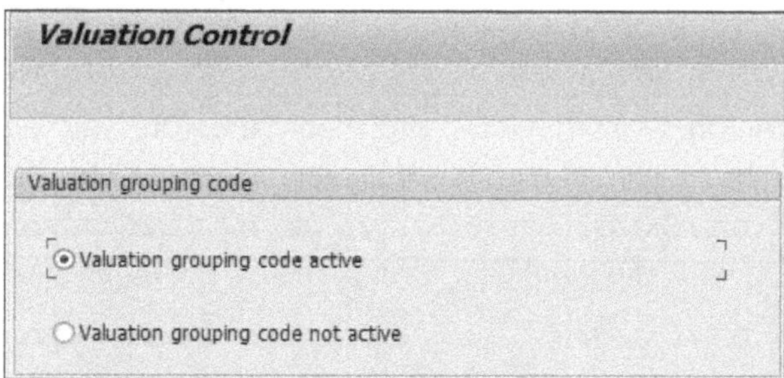

Figure 4.53 Valuation Grouping Code

Assign Valuation Grouping Codes to Valuation Areas

The setting you maintained earlier needs to be implemented in the given node. You must assign the valuation grouping code to each combination of the valuation area, company code, and chart of accounts. This enables you to assign the same general ledger account to multiple company codes and valuation areas. If the setting isn't enabled, then you have to assign the general ledger account for each valuation area separately, increasing the count in maintenance.

To group valuation areas together, follow menu path **Materials Management • Valuation and Account Assignment • Account Determination • Account Determination without Wizard • Group Together Valuation Areas**. You'll arrive at the screen shown in Figure 4.54, where we've assigned the same valuation grouping code (**9000**, in this example) to all the combinations of similar company codes.

Change View "Acct Determination for Val. Areas": Overview

Val. area	CoCode	Chrt/Accts	Val.Grpg Code
0021	2323	T	9000
0022	2323	INT	9000
0025	0025	YCOA	
0026	0025	YCOA	
003	301	333	
0033	301	333	IE00
0048	3105		
0049	2323	INT	9000
004P	0004		
0050	3118		
0062	0061	0055	
0064	0063	YCOA	
006A	0006	0006	0006
009A	0009	0009	009A
00SB	00ST	YCOA	
0100	SRSR		

Figure 4.54 Valuation Area Grouping

Define Valuation Classes

A *valuation class* is one of the important parameters to determine the general ledger accounts. You maintain the **Valuation Class** field for the material master in the **Accounting 1** view. Multiple materials can be assigned to the same valuation class. It acts as a key to grouping different materials that have the same account determination. The material types can be defaulted with the valuation class based on the configurations we'll discuss here.

To configure the valuation class, execute Transaction SPRO and follow menu path **Materials Management • Valuation and Account Assignment • Account Determination • Account Determination without Wizard • Define Valuation Classes.** You'll arrive at the screen shown in Figure 4.55.

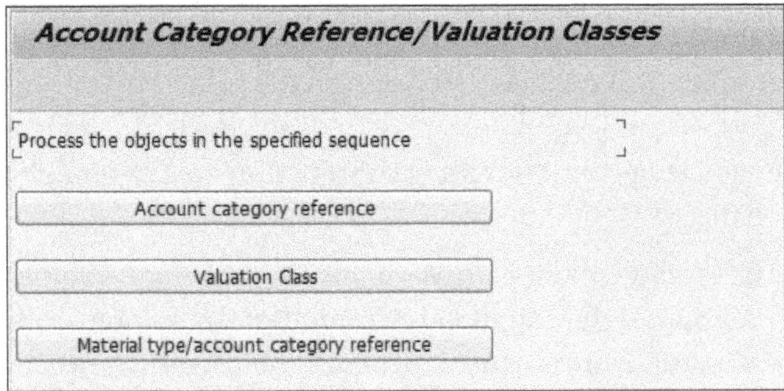

Figure 4.55 Valuation Classes

As shown in Figure 4.55, the configuration involves three objects. Let's explore each object in detail:

- **Account category reference**
  ARef is a four-digit freely definable field, as shown in Figure 4.56. You can create your own account category reference per the business requirement. There is no functionality associated with the field; it's only used as a linkage object. The account category reference can be defined as a group of valuation classes. It allows flexibility in linking material types with valuation classes. You must assign a valuation class with an account category reference, and the account category reference is linked to a material type, thus creating a linkage between the two.
- **Valuation Class**
  The second object is the valuation class. Assign the account category reference (**ARef**) to the valuation class (**ValCl**), as shown in Figure 4.57.
- **Material Type/account category reference**
  The third and last object is the material type. Assign the account category reference (**ARef**) defined earlier to the material type (**M...**), as shown in Figure 4.58. This configuration will have an impact on the selection of the allowed valuation class while

creating the material for the **Accounting 1** view. The account reference category will have a list of valuation classes, and this category is assigned to the material type, so the material can be maintained with the valuation classes that have been assigned to the account reference category.

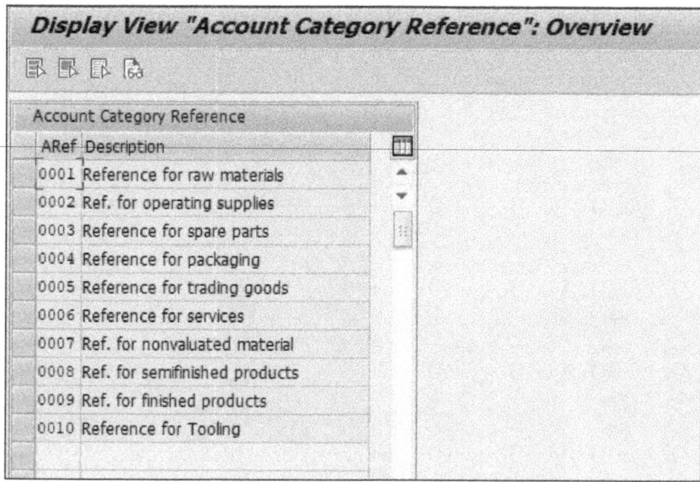

Display View "Account Category Reference": Overview

Account Category Reference

ARef	Description
0001	Reference for raw materials
0002	Ref. for operating supplies
0003	Reference for spare parts
0004	Reference for packaging
0005	Reference for trading goods
0006	Reference for services
0007	Ref. for nonvaluated material
0008	Ref. for semifinished products
0009	Ref. for finished products
0010	Reference for Tooling

Figure 4.56 Account Category Reference

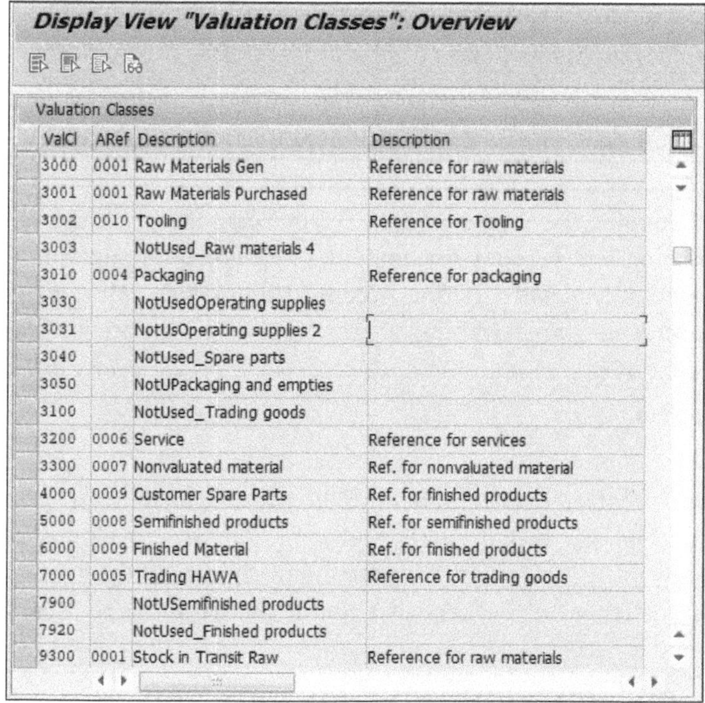

Display View "Valuation Classes": Overview

Valuation Classes

ValCl	ARef	Description	Description
3000	0001	Raw Materials Gen	Reference for raw materials
3001	0001	Raw Materials Purchased	Reference for raw materials
3002	0010	Tooling	Reference for Tooling
3003		NotUsed_Raw materials 4	
3010	0004	Packaging	Reference for packaging
3030		NotUsedOperating supplies	
3031		NotUsOperating supplies 2	
3040		NotUsed_Spare parts	
3050		NotUPackaging and empties	
3100		NotUsed_Trading goods	
3200	0006	Service	Reference for services
3300	0007	Nonvaluated material	Ref. for nonvaluated material
4000	0009	Customer Spare Parts	Ref. for finished products
5000	0008	Semifinished products	Ref. for semifinished products
6000	0009	Finished Material	Ref. for finished products
7000	0005	Trading HAWA	Reference for trading goods
7900		NotUSemifinished products	
7920		NotUsed_Finished products	
9300	0001	Stock in Transit Raw	Reference for raw materials

Figure 4.57 Assign Valuation Class to Account Category Reference

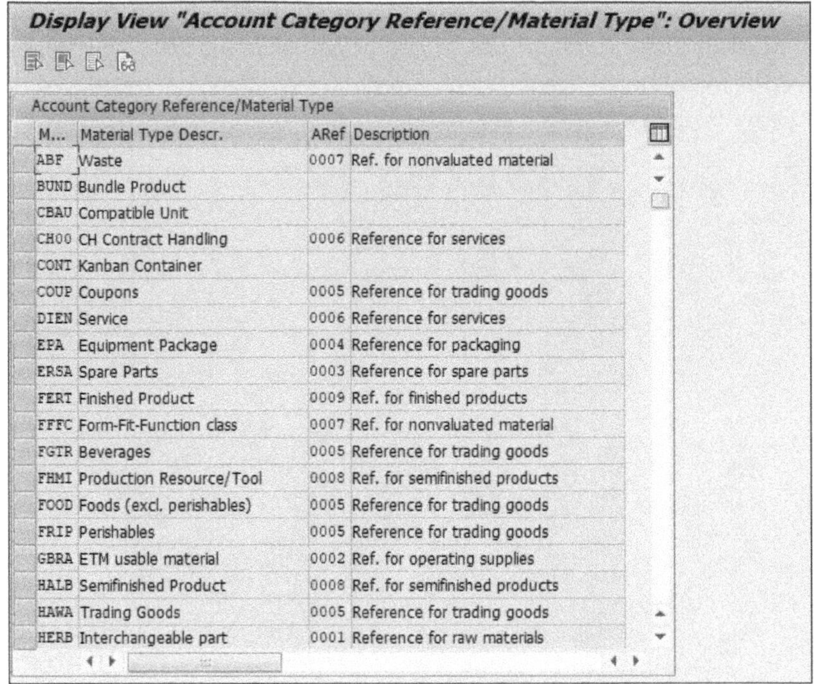

Display View "Account Category Reference/Material Type": Overview

Account Category Reference/Material Type

M...	Material Type Descr.	ARef	Description
ABF	Waste	0007	Ref. for nonvaluated material
BUND	Bundle Product		
CBAU	Compatible Unit		
CH00	CH Contract Handling	0006	Reference for services
CONT	Kanban Container		
COUP	Coupons	0005	Reference for trading goods
DIEN	Service	0006	Reference for services
EPA	Equipment Package	0004	Reference for packaging
ERSA	Spare Parts	0003	Reference for spare parts
FERT	Finished Product	0009	Ref. for finished products
FFFC	Form-Fit-Function class	0007	Ref. for nonvaluated material
FGTR	Beverages	0005	Reference for trading goods
FHMI	Production Resource/Tool	0008	Ref. for semifinished products
FOOD	Foods (excl. perishables)	0005	Reference for trading goods
FRIP	Perishables	0005	Reference for trading goods
GBRA	ETM usable material	0002	Ref. for operating supplies
HALB	Semifinished Product	0008	Ref. for semifinished products
HAWA	Trading Goods	0005	Reference for trading goods
HERB	Interchangeable part	0001	Reference for raw materials

Figure 4.58 Assign Material Type to Account Category Reference

Define Account Grouping for Movement Types

Account grouping configuration can be performed for transaction keys GBB, PRD, and KON only. However, the configuration changes are allowed for transaction key GBB only.

To configure the account grouping, use Transaction OMWN or follow menu path **Materials Management • Valuation and Account Assignment • Account Determination • Account Determination without Wizard • Define Account Grouping for Movement Types**. You'll arrive at the screen shown in Figure 4.59, which illustrates the accounting grouping for movement type **601**.

Let's explore each field in detail:

- **M...**
  Movement type is a three-character field that defines the material movements performed during goods receipt, goods issue, STOs, and so on. All inventory transactions are accompanied by movement types. They are indirectly used in the general ledger account determination with the help of account grouping. We'll discuss movement types in detail in Section 4.5.2.
- **S**
  The special stock indicator indicates the type of stock. It helps to manage the inventory of the same material separately. Some of the most used special stock indicators

are consignment stocks (**K**), customer orders in hand stock (**E**), and project-specific stocks (**Q**).

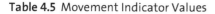

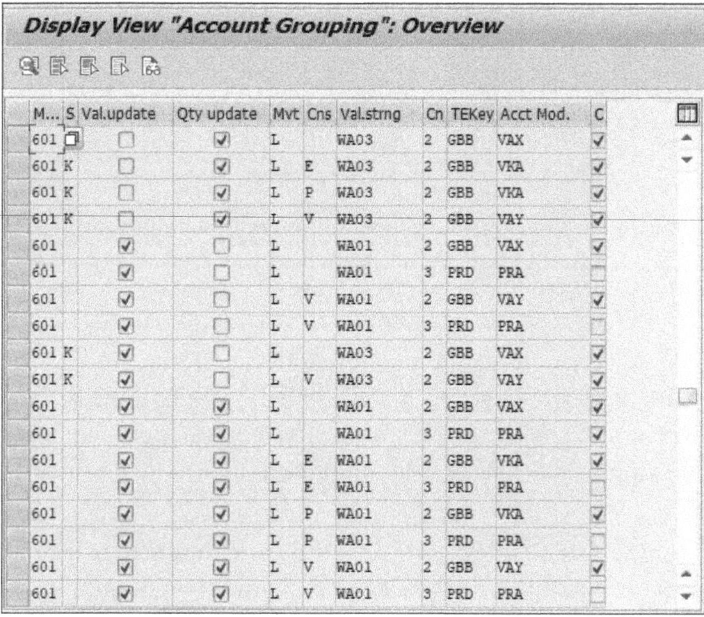

M...	S	Val.update	Qty update	Mvt	Cns	Val.strng	Cn	TEKey	Acct Mod.	C
601		☐	☑	L		WA03	2	GBB	VAX	☑
601	K	☐	☑	L	E	WA03	2	GBB	VKA	☑
601	K	☐	☑	L	P	WA03	2	GBB	VKA	☑
601	K	☐	☑	L	V	WA03	2	GBB	VAY	☑
601		☑	☐	L		WA01	2	GBB	VAX	☑
601		☑	☐	L		WA01	3	PRD	PRA	☐
601		☑	☐	L	V	WA01	2	GBB	VAY	☑
601		☑	☐	L	V	WA01	3	PRD	PRA	☐
601	K	☑	☐	L		WA03	2	GBB	VAX	☑
601	K	☑	☐	L	V	WA03	2	GBB	VAY	☑
601		☑	☑	L		WA01	2	GBB	VAX	☑
601		☑	☑	L		WA01	3	PRD	PRA	☑
601		☑	☑	L	E	WA01	2	GBB	VKA	☑
601		☑	☑	L	E	WA01	3	PRD	PRA	☐
601		☑	☑	L	P	WA01	2	GBB	VKA	☑
601		☑	☑	L	P	WA01	3	PRD	PRA	☐
601		☑	☑	L	V	WA01	2	GBB	VAY	☑
601		☑	☑	L	V	WA01	3	PRD	PRA	☐

Figure 4.59 Account Grouping

- **Val.update**
  This specifies that the material is managed on a value basis in the material master record for that specific valuation area. The values are updated in the respective general ledger accounts at the same time.
- **Qty update**
  This specifies that the materials are managed on a quantity basis. Both the field's value and quantity are configured in the material type configuration and can't be edited in the section.
- **Mvt**
  The movement indicator indicates the type of document used for the material movement. It's determined based on the underlying transaction that you're performing with the help of a movement type. Some examples of movement indicator values are shown in Table 4.5.

Movement Indicator	Description
Blank	Goods movement without reference
B	Goods movement for purchase order

Table 4.5 Movement Indicator Values

Movement Indicator	Description
F	Goods movement for production order
L	Goods movement for delivery note
K	Goods movement for Kanban requirement (warehouse management, internal only)
O	Subsequent adjustment of material-provided consumption
W	Subsequent adjustment of proportion/product unit material

Table 4.5 Movement Indicator Values (Cont.)

- **Cns**
  The consumption posting indicator specifies if the goods movement needs to be posted for consumption or not. The option tells you where you can post consumption if it's recorded, for example, sales order (**E**), project (**P**), and asset (**A**).
- **Val.strng**
  The posting string for value is an SAP internal key that can't be configured or created by consultants. This provides the linkage between the movement type and transaction key. It contains all the posting transactions possible for certain events.
- **Cn**
  The counter identifies the values for the configuration transaction.
- **TEKey**
  Every business transaction performed in SAP is associated with a three-character field called a transaction key. Along with the account modifier, you assign general ledger accounts for account determination.
- **Acct Mod.**
  The account modifier is a three-character field used to differentiate the offsetting accounts for consumption posting. These keys are uniquely defined in SAP and can't be changed or created.
- **C**
  This checkbox indicates whether the account assignment is checked or not. If this indicator is set, the system checks the item screen to see if a general ledger account or an account assignment has been specified. If this is the case, the system copies the data to the posting line. If this indicator isn't set, the system will always use the default general ledger accounts or account assignments.

Configure Automatic Postings

Let's configure the account determination for the transactions associated with inventory management and invoice verification. To perform the general ledger account assignment to the objects that we've explored, you can use Transaction OMWB or follow menu path **Materials Management • Valuation and Account Assignment • Account Determination • Account Determination without Wizard • Configure Automatic Postings.** You'll arrive at the screen shown in Figure 4.60.

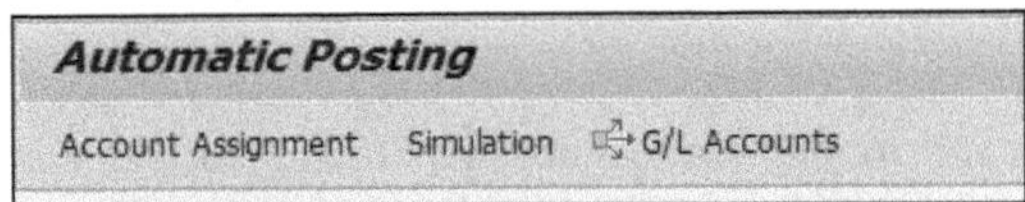

Figure 4.60 Configure Automatic Posting

The three buttons that are shown in Figure 4.60 have the following objectives:

- **Account Assignment**
  You can assign the general ledger accounts to the transaction key.
- **Simulation**
  The accounts assigned to the transaction key can be simulated with the help of the **Simulation** button. This helps you solidify the scenarios before commencing with the whole testing process.
- **G/L Accounts**
  The list of general ledger accounts assigned for the particular company code and valuation area, that is, plant or company code, can be viewed by clicking on the button.

Now let's explore the fields associated with the **Account Assignment** button. After clicking it, you'll arrive at the screen shown in Figure 4.61.

Configuration Accounting Display : Automatic Posts - Procedures

Group RMK Materials Management postings (MM)

Procedures

Description	Transaction	Account Determ.
Rev.from agency bus.	AG1	☑
Sales fr.agency bus.	AG2	☑
Exp.from agency bus.	AG3	☑
Expense/revenue from consign.mat.consum.	AKO	☑
Expense/revenue from stock transfer	AUM	☑
VF: Bonus Accrual	BAC	☑
Subsequent settlement of provisions	BO1	☑
Subsequent settlement of revenues	BO2	☑
Provision differences	BO3	☑
Inventory posting	BSD	☑
Inventory Value Adjustment	BSK	☑
Change in stock account	BSV	☑
Inventory posting	BSX	☑
Revaluation of other consumables	COC	☑
Del credere	DEL	☑
Materials management small differences	DIF	☑
Purchase account	EIN	☑
Purchase offsetting account	EKG	☑

Figure 4.61 Automatic Posting: Account Assignment

As shown in Figure 4.61, you must assign the general ledger account in association with the transaction key. These transaction keys are predefined in SAP S/4HANA according to the underlying business process and its accounting impacts. When you perform the goods issue or the goods receipt, the transaction keys are automatically determined based on the movement type.

Let's explore some of the important transaction keys used during the integration scenarios with respect to the sales and distribution business process:

- **GBB (offsetting entry for stock posting)**
  This transaction key is used for any of the transactions that have an impact on inventory management. It's dependent on the account grouping assigned to the movement type in the earlier Transaction OMWN. The business processes around inventory management are very complex, and the general ledger account determination needs to be flexible enough to accommodate all these changes and complexity. SAP has provided a further differentiating factor called account grouping codes that can be used to determine the general ledger accounts for the inventory posting. Transaction key GBB uses this account grouping code extensively to determine the general ledger accounts.

  Some of the important and widely used account grouping codes are as follows:

  - **VAX**: This account grouping code is used to determine the general ledger account for a delivery document created with respect to sales orders whose stocks are valuated; that is, no cost element is associated with the material.
  - **VAY**: This acts similar to VAX; however, it's used for the sales order where the sales order items carry cost and revenue, such as make to order (MTO) where the business wants to analyze the cost of sales orders based on the in-house production or when you want to collect and analyze the costs of a service on a sales order item.
  - **VBR**: This is used when the goods issue has been performed and it's expensed out for a cost center or an internal order. The goods issue can be done with the help of Transaction MIGO as well as with sales orders with account assignment of any cost center. The cost center can be assigned to the sales order by configuring the order reason and assigning the reason with the cost center in Transaction OVF3.
  - **VKA**: This is used for general ledger account determination with respect to the individual purchase order business process.
  - **VNG**: This is used for the business process used for scrapping material.
  - **BSA**: This account grouping code is used for general ledger determination during the initial stock posting in SAP S/4HANA.

  You'll perform the account assignment for the goods issue performed through the delivery document created by the sales order. The accounting entry for the transaction is as follows:

  - Debit: COGS
  - Credit: Inventory account

The COGS account needs to be assigned in transaction key **GBB**. Click on the transaction key, and you'll see the screen shown in Figure 4.62.

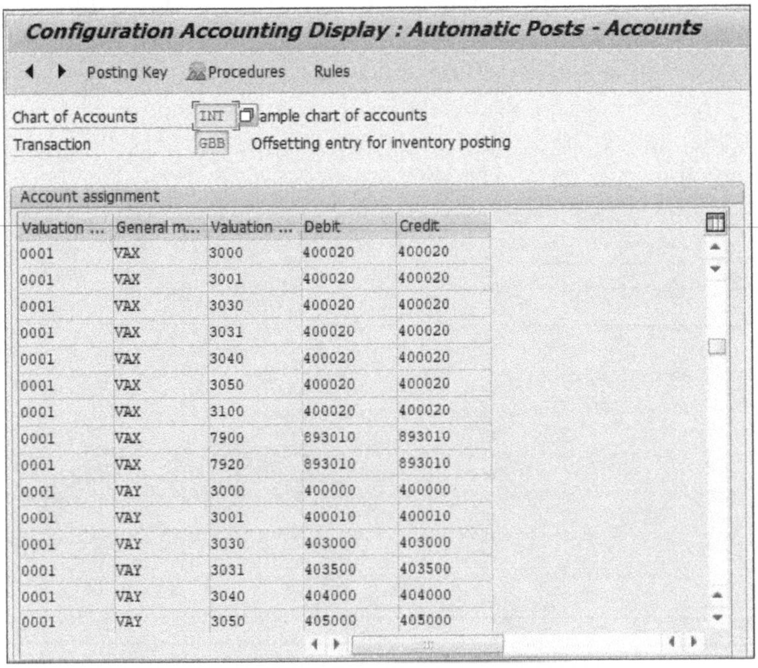

Configuration Accounting Display : Automatic Posts - Accounts

Posting Key Procedures Rules

Chart of Accounts INT Sample chart of accounts

Transaction GBB Offsetting entry for inventory posting

Account assignment

Valuation ...	General m...	Valuation ...	Debit	Credit
0001	VAX	3000	400020	400020
0001	VAX	3001	400020	400020
0001	VAX	3030	400020	400020
0001	VAX	3031	400020	400020
0001	VAX	3040	400020	400020
0001	VAX	3050	400020	400020
0001	VAX	3100	400020	400020
0001	VAX	7900	893010	893010
0001	VAX	7920	893010	893010
0001	VAY	3000	400000	400000
0001	VAY	3001	400010	400010
0001	VAY	3030	403000	403000
0001	VAY	3031	403500	403500
0001	VAY	3040	404000	404000
0001	VAY	3050	405000	405000

Figure 4.62 Automatic Posting: Transaction Key GBB

As you can see, we've used the fields for the valuation modifier (**Valuation ...** in first column), general modifier (**General m...**), and valuation class (**Valuation ...** in third column) to determine both the debit and credit general ledger accounts.

You can select the parameters based on which you want to perform the account determination by clicking on the **Rules** button. As shown in the Figure 4.63, we've selected all four parameters.

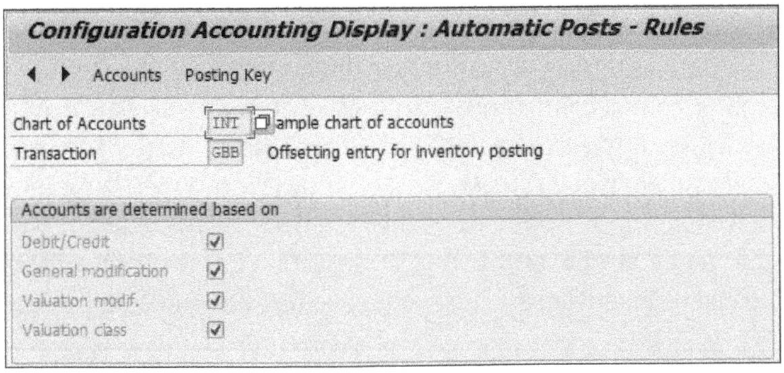

Configuration Accounting Display : Automatic Posts - Rules

Accounts Posting Key

Chart of Accounts INT Sample chart of accounts

Transaction GBB Offsetting entry for inventory posting

Accounts are determined based on

Debit/Credit	☑
General modification	☑
Valuation modif.	☑
Valuation class	☑

Figure 4.63 Automatic Posting: Rules

- **BSX (inventory posting)**
  Let's now set the general ledger account for the inventory. This is completed by using transaction key BSX, which is used to post values to stock accounts. The stock accounts represent the value of the total stocks owned by the organization. This transaction key is used when you're posting goods receipts to your own stock or goods issue from your own stock. As a general rule of thumb, you should use transaction key BSX to determine the stock account. No manual postings should be allowed on stock accounts. As shown in Figure 4.64, we've assigned the general ledger account in association with the valuation modifier and valuation class.

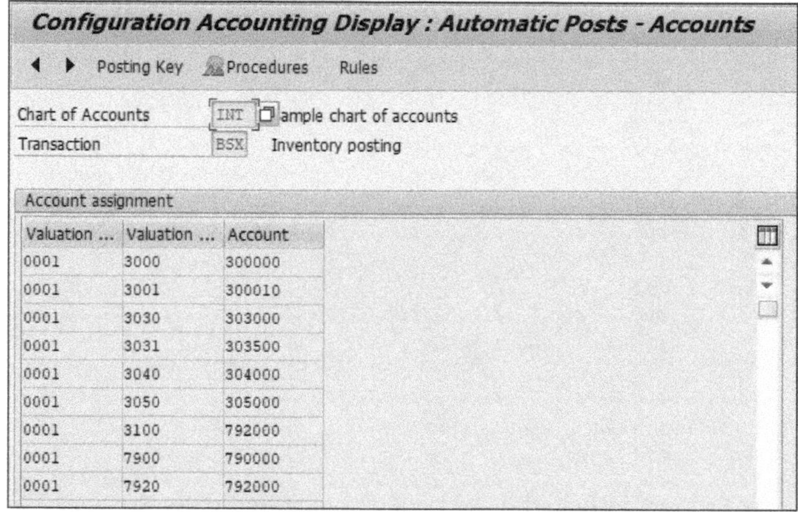

Valuation ...	Valuation ...	Account
0001	3000	300000
0001	3001	300010
0001	3030	303000
0001	3031	303500
0001	3040	304000
0001	3050	305000
0001	3100	792000
0001	7900	790000
0001	7920	792000

Figure 4.64 Automatic Posting: Transaction Key BSX

- **WRX (GR/IR clearing account)**
  The analysis of the GR/IR account is crucial during the period-end activities. SAP determines the general ledger account for GR/IR clearing with transaction key WRX. Discrepancies between goods receipt and quantity invoiced for a purchase order are common in the business processes. These differences result in an erroneous debit or credit balance. The GR/IR clearing account compares the number of goods received to the quantity of goods invoiced before posting a positive or negative balance. As a result, the GR/IR clearing account acts as a "buffer" between the inventory and vendor accounts, reducing confusion and the risk of accounting errors. When the goods receipt is posted, the accounting entry created by the system creates a credit entry to the general ledger account determined by the WRX transaction key while the offsetting debit entry is posted to the inventory account determined by the BSX transaction key.

  During the creation of the invoice receipt through Transaction MIRO, the general ledger account maintained for the WRX transaction key receives the debit posting while the offsetting entry is posted to the vendor account.

4.4 Third-Party Processing

A *third-party business process* is also referred to as a *drop shipment*. In a third-party process, order fulfillment happens from the vendor side. The seller doesn't store inventory; rather, it sends the customer's order and shipment information to the vendor, who then ships the goods directly to the customer. As a result, the seller doesn't have to handle the goods or products directly. The ordering company makes a profit on the price difference between the vendor price and the retail price.

We'll dive into third-party processing (drop shipping) in the following sections.

4.4.1 What Is Third-Party Processing?

First, let's walk through some of the benefits of deploying third-party processes in your organization:

- Inventory management isn't required. Inventory management can be difficult and time-consuming. Without having to keep track of stock, reorder it, and process it, the business can focus on other aspects of achieving growth for the organization.
- There will be fewer losses on unsellable goods as the goods aren't stored in the company's location.
- Businesses can offer multiple varieties of products under a single order.
- The cost associated with order fulfillment, such as packaging and shipping, is reduced.

The drop shipment process can be further categorized in two ways:

- **Third-party process with shipping notification**
  This is one of the variations in the third-party business process. In this case, the vendor sends you the advanced shipping notification (ASN), which can be captured through EDI inbound IDocs. As shown in Figure 4.65, the customer has raised an order to the company, and the system configuration will kick in and create a purchase requisition and purchase order to the vendor. Then the vendor performs the fulfillment activity and ships the goods or products to the customer location. At the same time, the vendor will send you the ASN and you'll capture the ASN as part of the statistical goods receipt. Based on the quantities captured through Transaction MIGO, the invoice will be raised to the customer.

  The configuration changes that need to be done are as follows:

  - The **Billing Relevance** field in the item category should be set to **G**. This will enable the system to check if Transaction MIGO is performed on the purchase order before invoicing to the end customer.
  - In Transaction VTFA, which controls the copy control between sales order and invoice, you have to maintain the **Billing Quantity** field as **E** in the item folder for

the corresponding item category. This will enable the system to copy the quantity from the goods receipt while performing the billing to the end customer.

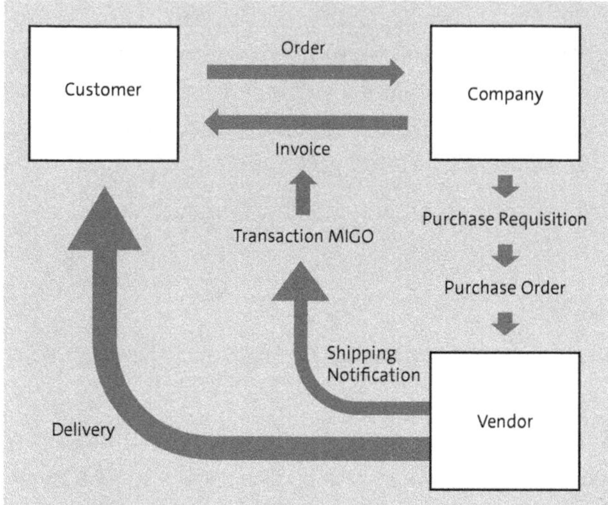

Figure 4.65 Third-Party Process with Shipping Notification

- **Third-party process without shipping notification**
  The other variation of the third-party process is if the vendor won't send the ASN to the ordering company. In this case, as shown in Figure 4.66, the other process remains the same; however, instead of the statistical goods receipt in Transaction MIGO, an invoice receipt in Transaction MIRO is created. In other words, the vendor will send the invoice to the ordering company, and it will be captured as an invoice receipt by the ordering company.

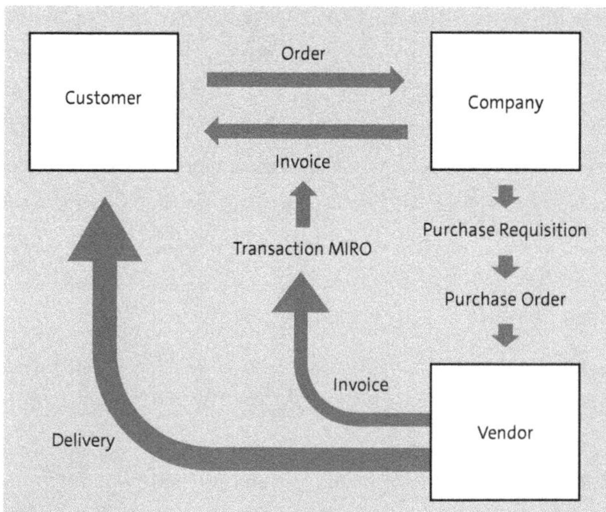

Figure 4.66 Third-Party Process without Shipping Notification

The configuration changes that need to be adjusted are as follows:

- The item category **Billing Relevance** needs to be set as **F** (status according to the invoice receipt) quantity. This won't allow the system to create an invoice to the end customer before the invoice receipt isn't created for the vendor.
- In Transaction VTFA, which controls the copy control between sales order and invoice, you have to maintain the **Billing Quantity** field as **F**. This will enable the system to copy the quantity from the invoice receipt while performing the billing to the end customer.

Before we move on to the prerequisites and configuration, let's explore the third-party process overview from creation of the sales order to customer billing. Figure 4.67 illustrates the third-party process flow.

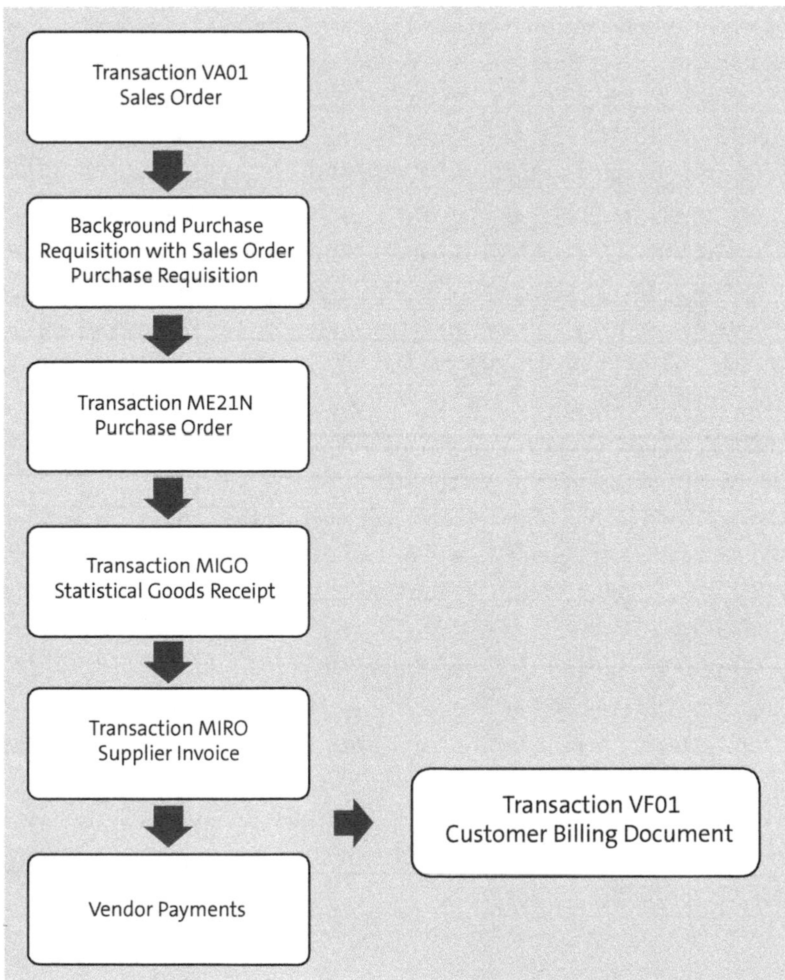

Figure 4.67 Third-Party Process Overview

The third-party process includes the following steps:

1. **Create the sales order for the third-party material**
   If the material is pure third-party material, then based on the item category determination, the item category TAS will be populated. You can create your own item category based on the business requirement, but fields related to the billing relevance should be appropriately chosen based on whether the third-party process is without shipping notification or with shipping notification.
2. **Review the purchase requisition automatically created with reference to the line item in the sales order**
   The automatic purchase requisition will be created, which can be achieved by the schedule line category configuration.
3. **Review the purchase order creation**
   If automatic purchase order creation is enabled, then the purchase order will be created automatically; otherwise, a manual intervention is needed for purchase order creation. The purchase requisition needs to be converted to a purchase order with Transaction ME21N.
4. **Statistical goods receipt is performed with respect to the purchase order**
   In this process, the goods aren't delivered by the ordering company but by the vendor to whom the purchase order is raised. However, if the business requirement is to document the receipt of the goods, you can achieve the requirement. The schedule line category fields **Account Assignment** and **Item Category** can be set as **1** and **5**, respectively, which will have an impact on the goods receipt. Statistical goods receipt can be recorded as well, which won't have any impact on the stock level or on the accounting side.
5. **Send a supplier invoice or perform invoice verification**
   Once the goods have been delivered to the end customer by the vendor, the vendor will raise an invoice to the company. This will be recorded as invoice verification in Transaction MIRO. After invoice receipt, the purchase order history is updated along with the vendor invoice.
6. **After the vendor invoice is posted, the customer can be billed**
   As outbound delivery isn't created in this case, the order-related billing will be performed. The item category configuration of billing relevance will derive from whether the quantities in the billing document will be picked from the goods receipt or the invoice receipt. The copy control setting VTFA, which we've briefly discussed earlier, also helps in not allowing the system to create a customer invoice until Transactions MIRO or MIGO are performed.

4.4.2 Prerequisites for Third-Party Processing

To perform the third-party process, you have to follow these prerequisites:

- The material needs to be created with item category group as BANS, and it should be extended to the purchasing views: **Purchasing** view and **Purchase Order Text** view.
- The vendor master needs to be created for the required third-party vendors, and the vendor source list needs to be created for the automatic vendor determination.
- Required configuration for an item category, schedule line category, and their respective determinations should be completed.

4.4.3 Item Category Controls

Item categories play a vital role in determining the behavior of material entered in the sales order. Mastering various controls in the item category gives an edge to integrate sales and distribution with other functionalities seamlessly. We'll explain configuration and determination for item categories in the following sections.

Define Item Categories

Now let's explore the item category controls by executing Transaction SPRO and navigating to menu path **Sales and Distribution • Sales • Sales Documents • Sales Document Item • Define Item Categories**. You'll arrive at the screen shown in Figure 4.68 and Figure 4.69, which illustrate the item category controls for item category **TAS**.

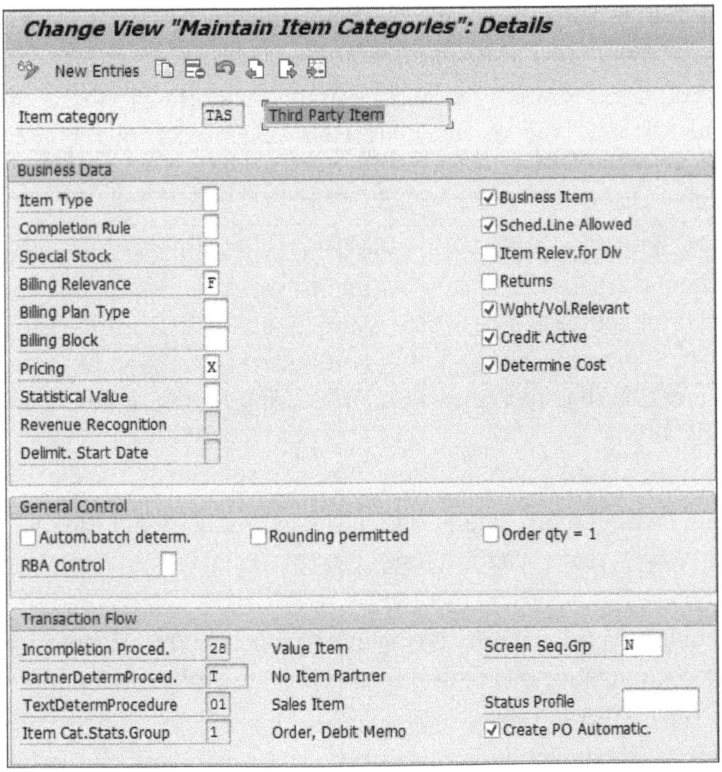

Figure 4.68 Item Category Controls (1 of 2)

We'll explore the configuration elements for item category TAS in this section, which is given as a default item category for third-party processes by SAP S/4HANA. You can also create a custom item category per the business requirement by copying the existing one.

Let's explore each field in item category control in detail:

- **Item Type**
  This field determines how the items need to be classified. SAP has provided the following options to choose from:
  - Blank (standard item): This is applicable to all the item categories that are relevant for pricing.
  - **A** (value item): To keep the customer's loyalty toward the products, companies offer certain incentives in the form of coupons, which customers can redeem while purchasing the products or services. These materials are configured as value items that the organization doesn't sell to the end customer but adds to the existing sales order as incentives. You can configure the item category and set the item type as a value item for those item categories.
  - **B** (text item): While buying any electronic equipment, you generally receive a booklet or catalog that provides the details about the products you've bought. Organizations usually don't sell these products as standalone items, but they are bundled with the products. You can create item categories with item types as text. The standard item category to achieve this is TATX.
  - **C** (packing item): You need materials that will be used to pack the products and deliver them to the customer; this specific material is called packaging material. The item category associated with these materials will have item type as **C**.
- **Completion Rule**
  This field determines whether the quotation or sales contract is complete or not and whether or not the quantities in the source documents, such as the quotation or sales contract, have been fully referenced. The completion rule is mostly used between sales quotations, sales contracts, and sales orders. You have to activate the **Update Document Flow** checkbox in Transaction VTAA. Let's explore some of the completion rules in detail:
  - Blank: Not relevant for completion.
  - **A** (item is completed with the first reference): This is generally used if the sales document is created with reference to the inquiry. For example, item category AFN uses this rule for an inquiry sales document.
  - **B** (item is completed if the full quantity has been referenced): This is generally used for the sales document created with reference to the quotation. Standard item category AGN can be used in this case.
  - **C** (item is completed if the target quantity is fully referenced): This is used for a quantity contract as a source document; that is, the sale document will be

completed only when all the quantity mentioned in the **Target Quantity** field has been referenced to create the sales order.

- **D** (item is referenced via contract release): This is used to set the document status as **Complete** via a contract release document.
- **E** (item is completed after the full target value is referenced): This is used to create the sales document with reference to the value contract. The standard item category for value contracts is WKN.

- **Special Stock**
  The stock managed separately and not owned by the company are called special stock. We'll explain more details about special stock in Section 4.5.5. For item categories that are relevant for the consignment process and MTO process, you'll set the field with the relevant stock type. Let's explore some of the item categories that will have special stock indicators:
  - Special stock indicator **E**: This indicator is also called orders in hand. It will be available in the item category related to the individual purchase order (IPO) and MTO process (e.g., item categories TAB and TAK).
  - Special stock indicator **W**: This indicator is also called customer consignment. It will be available in the item categories related to the consignment process. For example, standard item categories with indicator **W** include KEN (consignment issue) and KRN (consignment return).
- **Billing Relevance**
  This field signifies how the billing needs to be performed on the line items. SAP has given numerous options to choose from to bill the particular line item in the sales document. Let's explore some of the important billing relevance options:
  - Blank: It's not relevant for billing. Item categories that aren't relevant for billing are AFN, AGN, WKN, and TATX.
  - **A** (delivery-related billing document): The billing can be created with respect to the delivery document. The status of billing will be updated in the delivery document.
  - **B** (relevant for order-related billing status according to order quantity): The billing will be created with respect to the sales order document and with the requested delivery quantity. This is used in cases such as cash sales and returns.
  - **C** (relevant for order-related billing status according to target quantity): It's similar to indicator **B**; however, the billing status is dependent on the target quantity. It's used across business processes such as credit memos and debit memos.
  - **D** (relevant for pro forma invoicing): You use this indicator for configuring the item categories for pro forma invoicing or free-of-charge deliveries.
  - **F** (order-related billing document status according to invoice quantity): To configure the third-party process, the item category that needs to be configured should

have the billing relevance as **F**. While creating an invoice for the third-party material, the system will check if Transaction MIRO has been created. The system won't allow the creation of the invoice unless Transaction MIRO has been performed on the material. The quantity in the invoice receipt will get copied to the billing document, and for those quantities, you'll be able to raise an invoice. You have to make an additional setting for copy control along with it. We'll discuss those settings in Section 4.4.5.

- **G** (order-related billing of the delivery quantity): You can create an invoice in the third-party process with respect to the quantity that has been delivered to the customer. You must set the billing relevance as **G** and maintain the same copy controls in Transaction VTFA.
- **I** (order-relevant billing-billing plan): You can use the billing relevance if the item material is to be billed with respect to the billing plans and their corresponding status. You must configure the billing plans and assign the billing plans to the respective item category.
- **K** (delivery-related invoices for partial quantity): You can use this for creating a partial invoice corresponding to a single delivery document. You have to configure the item category with billing relevance as **K** for creating an invoice for partial delivered quantity.

- **Billing Plan Type**
  You can bill the customers based on the predetermined billing frequencies, which can be achieved by configuring the billing plans. There are two types of billing plans: **Milestone Billing (01)** and **Periodic (02)**. If you assign the billing plan in the item category, then the plan will be limited to only the specific line item in the sales document. You can also apply the same billing plan to the entire sales document type by assigning the billing plan to the document type.
- **Billing Block**
  The system won't be able to create the billing for the line item if the billing block has been set for the particular line item in the sales document. You can default the billing block during sales document creation in the line item if you assign the billing block in the item category configuration. You can set the billing block at the header level as well.
- **Pricing**
  You can control the relevance of the pricing to the particular line item in the sales order. If the line item is relevant for pricing, maintain the item category with **X**; if not, then you can keep the field blank. If the line item is related to free goods, then you can maintain the option as **B** for free goods. An example item category for free goods is TANN.
- **Statistical Value**
  For certain business scenarios, such as BOMs, the requirement is to have the pricing at the line-item level instead of header pricing. To achieve the requirement, you

have to set the item category associated with the main item as a statistical value. This won't update the line-item value, but will be used as the statistical value.

- **Revenue Recognition**
  These fields are related to the sales and distribution-based revenue recognition system; that is, if you want to drive the revenue recognition process through Transactions VF44 and VF45, you have to make the item categories relevant to the revenue recognition process. If a particular item category is driven by time-based revenue recognition or event-based revenue recognition, then you must maintain those fields in the **Revenue Recognition** field. However, SAP has announced that the newer revenue recognition capability will be addressed through the SAP Revenue Accounting and Reporting functionality. You'll configure a new object called performance obligation (POB) type, and you'll maintain the events and important characteristics for how you recognize the revenue in the POB type. If you're using revenue accounting and reporting (RAR), then you don't have to maintain these two fields. For more information about RAR, see Chapter 6.

- **Business Item**
  The business data in the sales order comprises the data which you maintain in the sales area data of the business partner. If you select this checkbox, you allow the system to change the data related to business data, and you can deviate the fields from the header data. If you leave the checkbox unchecked, the system won't allow changing the business data fields in the sales document.

- **Sched.Line Allowed**
  You can check the field schedule to determine the schedule lines in the sales order. The schedule lines will be allowed for all the delivery-relevant item categories. For order-related billing, the item categories associated with order-relevant billing won't have this checkbox checked. Standard SAP doesn't allow item categories that aren't relevant for schedule lines to be copied over to the delivery document.

- **Item Relev.for Dlv**
  In business scenarios where the line items associated with the text and value item are relevant for delivery, you have to select this checkbox.

- **Returns**
  The checkbox controls the accounting entries when the billing has been created for the order. The checkbox is activated for the return process as well as for the credit memo process; that is, the standard item categories where the **Returns** checkbox is selected are REN and G2N.

- **Wght/Vol.Relevant**
  In business scenarios where the routes are determined based on the weight of the line items, you have to make a system to calculate the weight and volume of the line items. Activating the checkbox system calculates the weight and volume of the line item.

- **Credit Active**
  To update the line items in credit management, one of the prerequisites is to select this checkbox in the item category. Along with this checkbox, you also have to maintain the subtotal as A in the pricing procedure control in Transaction V/08. We'll discuss the pricing procedure in detail in Chapter 5, Section 5.1. The business processes where the **Credit Active** checkbox is unchecked are quotation, returns, consignments, cash sales, and credit memos.
- **Determine Cost**
  This checkbox is a prerequisite to determining the cost condition types in the pricing procedure. The cost condition types are EK01 and VPRS.
- **Autom.batch determ.**
  The checkbox allows the system to automatically determine the batch for the sales order line item.
- **Rounding permitted**
  You can allow the system to do the rounding for the quantities in the sales order line item. Usually, this is achieved by configuring the rounding profiles and assigning it in the customer material info record or material master. If you want some particular item categories to be excluded from the rounding, you can achieve the requirement by not selecting the checkbox.
- **Order qty = 1**
  In a business scenario where the products have a unique identification number (UID) for each unit of material, you can't have two materials with the same UID. To avoid the issues related with identification, select this checkbox for the item category associated with the line item. This won't allow the system to enter more than one quantity in the line item.
- **Incompletion Proced.**
  The incompletion procedure consists of a list of mandatory fields that the user must fill in when creating a sales document. If any of the mandatory fields are missing, the system will either not allow saving the sales document, or, if saving is permitted, the document's status will be **Incomplete**, and it won't be allowed to proceed further with the business process. You have to create the incompletion procedure by adding appropriate fields in it and assigning the incompletion procedure to the item category. The configuration path for creating the incompletion procedure is **Sales and Distribution • Basic Functions • Log of Incomplete Items • Define Incompleteness Procedures**. Alternatively, you can use Transaction OVA2.
- **PartnerDeterm.Proced.**
  You can specify the partner functions that are allowed for the line items by configuring the appropriate partner determination procedure via Transaction VOPAN and assigning it to the item category.

- **TextDeterm.Procedure**
  In business scenarios, you have certain customer-specific instructions or requirements that need to be passed to the organization; you can use the text determination functionality in SAP S/4HANA to achieve these requirements. The text procedure that you configure can be assigned to the item category.
- **Item Cat.Stats.Group**
  This field is no longer used in SAP S/4HANA because online analytical processing (OLAP) and online transactional processing (OLTP) have been performed at the same time in the SAP S/4HANA database. In the earlier version, you use this field as part of LIS.
- **Screen Seq.Grp**
  You can control the look and feel of transactions with the help of the screen sequence group. You'll need help from an ABAP consultant to perform the changes in the screen sequence group.
- **Status Profile**
  The status profile acts as a workflow for the business processes. The status in SAP is classified in two ways: system status and user status. You can't do any optimizations in system status; however, you can play around with respect to the custom requirements through the user status. You can also create authorizations for specific activities. The modus operandi for the status profile setup is the configuration of the status profile and then assignment to the respective document type or item categories.
- **Create PO Automatic.**
  This is one of the prerequisites to create the automatic purchase order with respect to the purchase requisition in a third-party sales scenario. This check comes in handy when you have only a single vendor for the outgoing purchase requisitions; however, if the number of vendors is more, then it's better to only create an automatic purchase requisition and edit the vendors in it.
- **Billing form**
  This field specifies how you must charge the customer, either by a **Fixed rate (01)** or **Costs (02)**, as shown in Figure 4.69.
- **DIP Prof.**
  This is the integration between sales and the Project System functionality, which is used for resource-related billing (RRB). See Chapter 7 for more information.

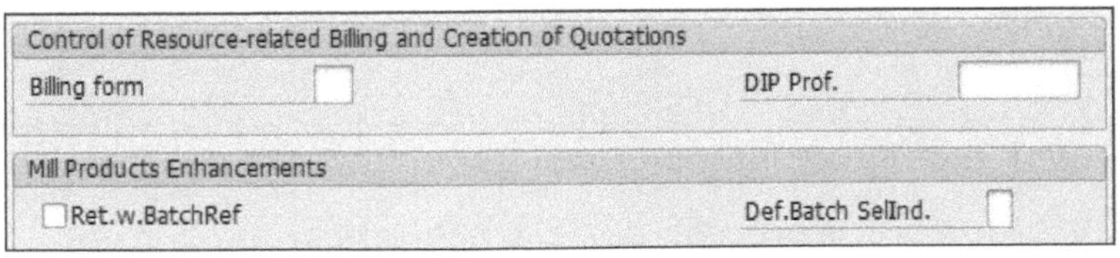

Control of Resource-related Billing and Creation of Quotations
Billing form | DIP Prof.
Mill Products Enhancements
Ret.w.BatchRef | Def.Batch SelInd.

Figure 4.69 Item Category Controls (2 of 2)

Item Category Determination

The item categories that you define need to be automatically determined in the sales order for efficient order management process. The item category determines the behavior of the line item.

The item category determination can be done with Transaction VOV4 or by following menu path **IMG • Sales and Distribution • Sales • Sales Documents • Sales Document Item • Assign Item Categories**. You'll arrive at the screen shown in Figure 4.70, where you must maintain the combination of four parameters for item category determination.

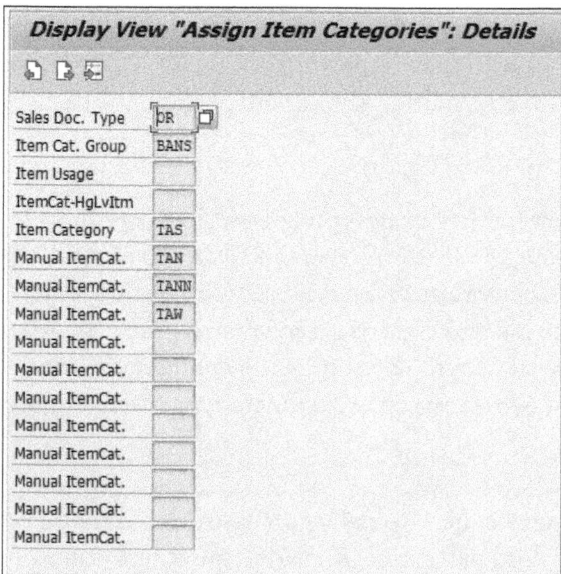

Figure 4.70 Item Category Determination

The parameters for determining the item category are as follows:

- **Sales Doc. Type**
  There are two ways the field will be updated: The first way is that the value will be entered by the user during the creation of the sales order. The second way is that it will be updated in the system by the upstream process by leveraging the solution capabilities of SAP CRM or any other configure price, and quote (CPQ) system. For automatic creation of the sales order, usually these values are passed in the sales order creation program.
- **Item Cat. Group**
  During the order creation process, users will input the material in the sales order creation screen. This material will have a field called **Item Category Group** in the **Sales: sales org 2** view of the material master data. You can differentiate the item categories based on the item category group. It adds an extra layer for creating multiple

combinations for the same material. Some of the important item category groups are listed in Table 4.6.

Business Process	Item Category Group
Standard business process	NORM
Individual purchase order	BANC
Third-party process	BANS
MTO	0001
BOM header pricing	ERLA
BOM item pricing	LUMF

Table 4.6 Item Category Groups

- **Item Usage**
  Item usage is the third parameter that can be used to determine the default and manual item categories in the sales order. The different scenarios where the usage can come into the picture are shown in Table 4.7.

Business Process	Usage
Free goods	FREE
Cross-selling	CSEL
Batch split	CHSP
Material determination	PSHP

Table 4.7 Usage

- **ItemCat-HgLvItm**
  The higher-level item category field is used in BOM pricing. To determine the item category for a subitem, the system considers the higher-level item category.

4.4.4 Schedule Line Category Controls

The schedule line category control is one of the important functions of the third-party process. The schedule line data contains the delivery date and exact quantity that needs to be delivered to the customer for each line item. The data in the schedule line can be controlled using the schedule line category configuration, which we'll explore in the following sections.

Define Schedule Line Categories

To configure the schedule line category, you can use Transaction VOV6 or follow menu path **IMG • Sales and Distribution • Sales • Sales Documents • Schedule Lines • Define Schedule Line Categories.** You'll arrive at the screen shown in Figure 4.71. Choose the schedule line category, and click on the **Details** icon to land on the screen in Figure 4.72, which shows the standard schedule line category **CS** for third-party processing.

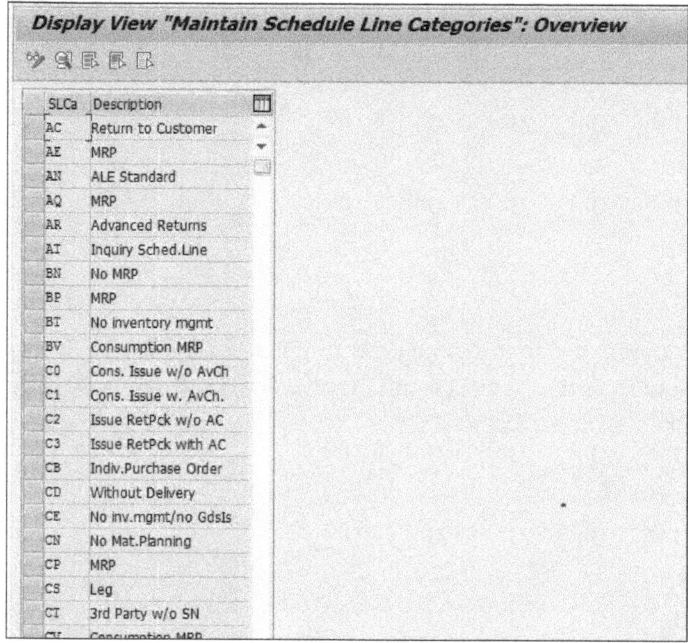

Figure 4.71 Schedule line Category: Initial Screen

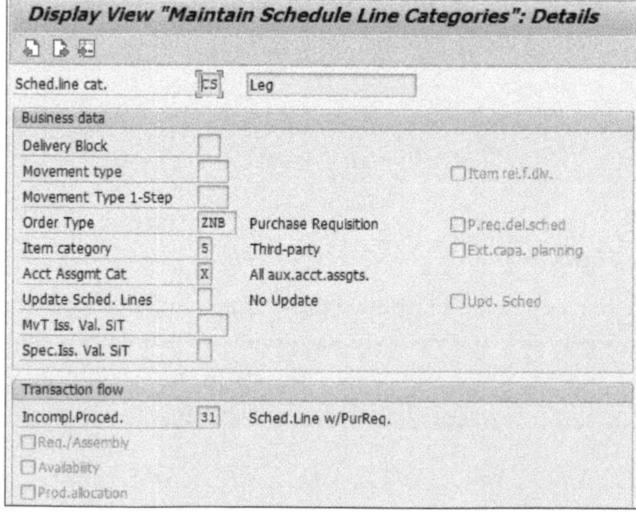

Figure 4.72 Schedule Line Category

Let's explore each field of the schedule line in detail:

- **Delivery Block**
  You can use a delivery block for a specific schedule line category. Delivery blocks can be set on sales document type, schedule line category, delivery type, and billing plan type. If you set the default delivery block for a particular schedule line, it will be applicable only to that schedule line. However, if the material is redetermined, then the same delivery block will be carried forward to the redetermined material as well.

  You can configure the user-specific delivery block by following menu path **IMG • Logistics Execution • Shipping • Deliveries • Define Reasons for Blocking in Shipping.** Blocking reasons configured in the system are shown in Figure 4.73.

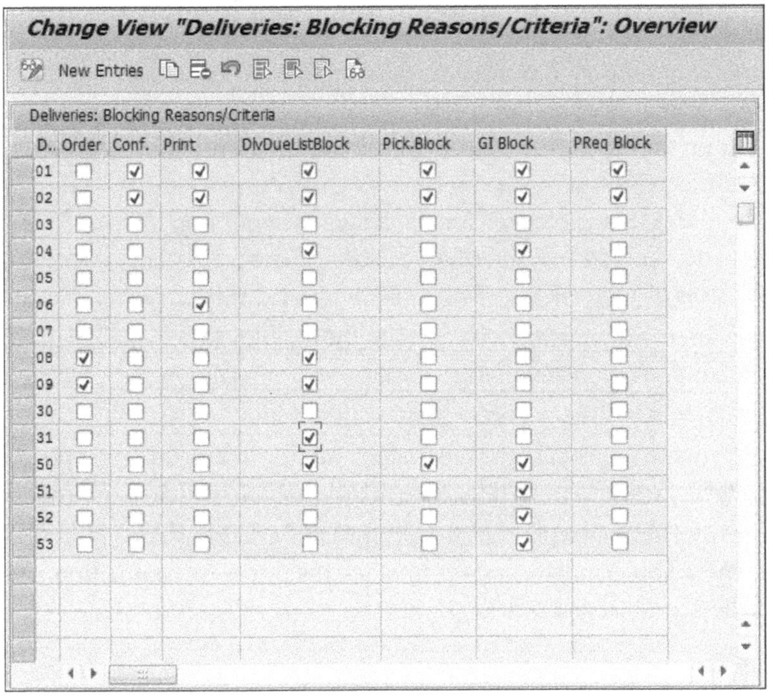

Change View "Deliveries: Blocking Reasons/Criteria": Overview

New Entries

Deliveries: Blocking Reasons/Criteria

D..	Order	Conf.	Print	DlvDueListBlock	Pick.Block	GI Block	PReq Block
01	☐	☑	☑	☑	☑	☑	☑
02	☐	☑	☑	☑	☑	☑	☑
03	☐	☐	☐	☐	☐	☐	☐
04	☐	☐	☐	☑	☐	☑	☐
05	☐	☐	☐	☐	☐	☐	☐
06	☐	☐	☑	☐	☐	☐	☐
07	☐	☐	☐	☐	☐	☐	☐
08	☑	☐	☐	☑	☐	☐	☐
09	☑	☐	☐	☑	☐	☐	☐
30	☐	☐	☐	☐	☐	☐	☐
31	☐	☐	☐	☑	☐	☐	☐
50	☐	☐	☐	☑	☑	☑	☐
51	☐	☐	☐	☐	☐	☑	☐
52	☐	☐	☐	☐	☐	☑	☐
53	☐	☐	☐	☐	☐	☑	☐

Figure 4.73 Deliveries: Blocking Reasons/Criteria

  Let's take a brief detour to explore some of the important fields in setting up the delivery block:

  - **DB.**: You can create your own delivery block and do the necessary configuration for it for the default delivery block.
  - **Order**: You can set the delivery block in the customer master. You must select the checkbox in scenarios where you want to copy over the delivery block that was assigned to the customer master to the sales order. Further processing of the sales document is only possible after the block has been removed from the sales order. There won't be any instant changes that will be applied to sales orders if you

remove the block in the customer master. You have to individually remove the delivery block from each sales order for the corresponding customer.

- **Conf.**: By selecting the checkbox, you allow the system to cancel the confirmation of the quantities that have been assigned after the availability check in the system. There might be requirements from clients specific to certain delivery blocks that they should also cancel the confirmed quantities and allocate the confirmed quantities to the other sales orders until the order is released. You can achieve the requirement by selecting the checkbox. Note that the changes will get triggered after you click the **Save** button in the sales order. The system commits the quantity if you don't select the checkbox.
- **Print**: For sales orders that are blocked for delivery, the system won't allow you to send the order confirmation via print if you select the checkbox.
- **DlvDueListBlock**: The delivery due list can be viewed in Transaction VL10. For automatic delivery creation, you can leverage the transaction and set up a daily job that will pick up the sales order which appears in the transaction and create the delivery document. If for some business reason, you don't want the system to include the sales order that is blocked for the delivery to not pop up in Transaction VL10, then you can activate the **DlvDueListBlock** checkbox. This checkbox will prevent the sales order from populating the delivery due list.
- **Pick.Block**: The system won't allow you to pick the materials if you select this checkbox in the configuration. If you uncheck it, even if the sales order is blocked for delivery, the system will allow you to pick the quantity.
- **GI Block**: If you activate the checkbox, the system won't allow you to post goods issues for the delivery document that has been created with the delivery block.
- **PReq Block**: The block is used in the third-party process and individual purchase order process where you want the system to block the purchase requisition creation for the delivery of blocked orders.

- **Movement type**
  While performing the goods issue, the system updates the stock level in inventory management and creates the accounting document corresponding to the goods movement. These activities are controlled by movement type. We'll briefly discuss the movement type and its impact in Section 4.5.2. For third-party business processes, because the vendor is supplying the goods to the customer, you don't maintain the movement type.
- **Movement Type 1-Step**
  As discussed in the stock transfer section, for one-step STO; you have to set the movement type as **647**.
- **Order Type**
  For the third-party scenario, you must create the purchase requisitions for the vendor. You can achieve it by configuring the **Order Type** field and maintaining the

required purchase requisition type. This will generate the purchase requisition automatically with the desired purchase requisition type.

- **Item category**
  The configuration of this field in the schedule line category is done by the materials management consultant. You generally use the standard item categories. While creating the purchase requisition, the user must input the item category. Similar to the sales and distribution item category, the materials management item categories control the behavior of line items in the sales order. As in the third-party process, you're creating the automatic purchase requisition, so you also must feed the item category associated with the line item. The system picks the item category you've maintained in the schedule line category and passes it during the purchase requisition generation. The standard item category used in a third-party process is **5**. It controls how the purchase requisition should update the values of stocks in the Transaction MIGO process of a third party. In the third-party process, you don't have to update the value of stocks; this will be achieved by item category **5**.
- **Acct Assmgt Cat**
  The account assignment category is only related to the schedule line for which the purchase requisition is created. It corresponds to the account assignment category in the purchase order and determines against which object you have to perform the purchase requisition, that is, the cost collector for the purchase order.
- **Update Sched. Lines**
  In a third-party scenario, you can update the schedule lines with the information received from the vendor related to the delivery of the materials mentioned in the purchase requisitions. It will allow the system to populate the data in the schedule line with the information received from the delivery notification from the vendor.
- **P.req.del.sched**
  In an individual purchase order scenario, the vendor delivers the goods to the company location, and then the company will send the goods to the customer. This will cause a lead time in the delivery processing that can be calculated and updated in the delivery schedule by selecting this checkbox.
- **Ext.capa. planning**
  This field is a prerequisite to performing the external capacity planning for certain materials for which you set up third-party processing. If you want to perform material capacity planning outside of the SAP S/4HANA system, you can use this field.
- **Incompl.Proced.**
  This field controls the mandatory fields that need to be populated in the sales order without which you can't save the sales order.
- **Req./Assembly**
  The requirements that get generated in the sales order can be transferred to MRP. One of the prerequisites to do that is the **Req./Assembly** field in the schedule line category. If you select the checkbox, then the requirements will be transferred to MRP.

- **Availability**
  To perform the availability check in the system, you must check this **Availability** checkbox in the schedule line category.

Schedule Line Category Determination

The schedule line category that you defined earlier should be determined automatically in the system. You can use Transaction VOV5 for schedule line category determination or follow menu path **Sales and Distribution • Sales • Sales Documents • Schedule Lines • Assign Schedule Line Categories**. You'll arrive at the screen shown in Figure 4.74.

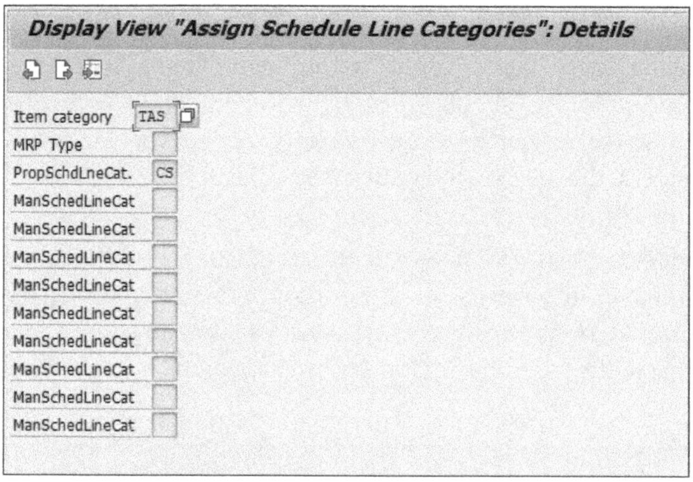

Display View "Assign Schedule Line Categories": Details

Item category	TAS
MRP Type	
PropSchdLneCat.	CS
ManSchedLineCat	
ManSchedLineCat	
ManSchedLineCat	
ManSchedLineCat	
ManSchedLineCat	
ManSchedLineCat	
ManSchedLineCat	
ManSchedLineCat	
ManSchedLineCat	

Figure 4.74 Schedule Line Category Determination

The parameters that have been taken into consideration for schedule line category determination are as follows:

- **Item category**
  The item category is determined in the sales order line item with the help of configuration related to item category determination. It can also be updated manually provided the allowed manual item categories are maintained with the desired combination.
- **MRP Type**
  The field comes from the material master. It determines how the material is planned for production.

With the help of these two fields, the system determines the default schedule line category. SAP has also provided you with the option to enter the manual schedule line category. By default, you can configure nine manual schedule line categories. For third-party scenarios, we've maintained the schedule line category determination with the combination of the item category **TAS** and **MRP Type** as blank (as shown in Figure 4.74), which means that for any combination with the **TAS** item category, the system will determine the schedule line category as **CS**, provided there is no other combination maintained for TAS item category and MRP type. The system will give the first preference to both the item category and MRP type; if the values aren't found for the combination, then it gives a second preference to the item category.

4.4.5 Copy Control Settings

Now let's explore the copy control settings between the sales order and invoice in the third-party process. The copy control setting is needed to copy the billing quantity from the goods receipt to the invoice; it also helps to apply the compliances for the third-party process.

To do the copy control setting between the sales order and invoice, you can use Transaction VTFA or follow menu path **IMG • Sales and Distribution • Billing • Billing Documents • Maintain Copying Control for Billing Documents • Copying Control: Sales Document to Billing Document.**

You'll arrive at the screen shown in Figure 4.75, where we've input the source document with sales document type **OR** and target document with billing document type **F2**.

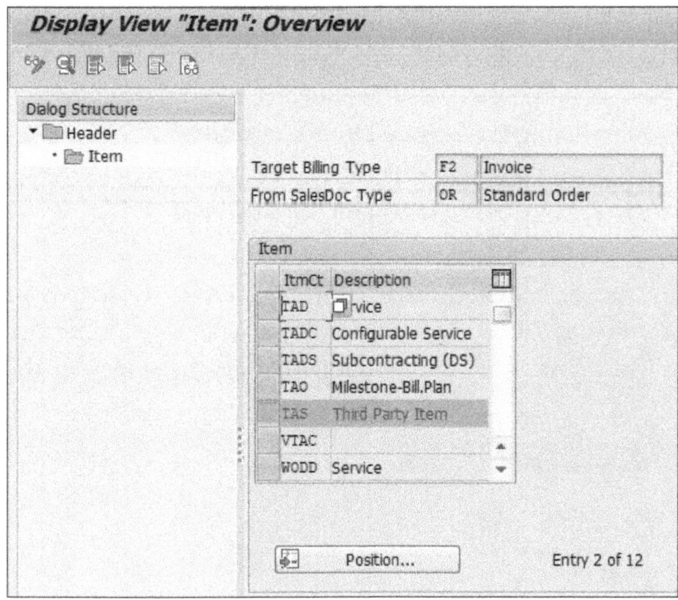

Figure 4.75 Copying Control: Sales Document to Billing Document

In a normal sales order, you can have all types of material and item categories included in it. For item category-specific changes, you have to click the item category (**ItmCt**) associated with it and then click on the **Details** icon . The system will take you to the screen shown in Figure 4.76.

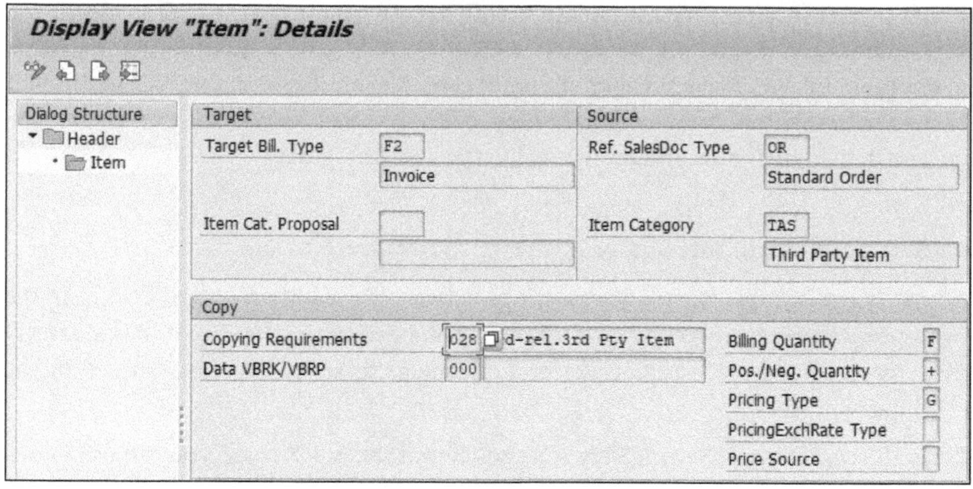

Figure 4.76 Copy Control Settings at the Item Level

Let's explore the important fields in the copy control at the item level:

- **Copying Requirements**
  This is the ABAP code that needs to be created in Transaction VOFM. This routine is used in SAP for any custom logic changes. For the third-party process, two important routines play a major part:
  - **012**: In a third-party process, if Transaction MIRO (invoice receipt) isn't created, then the system won't allow billing to be created for the customer.
  - **028**: In a third-party process, if Transaction MIGO (goods receipt) isn't created, then the system won't allow billing to be created for the customer.
- **Billing Quantity**
  This specifies the quantity that the system needs to copy from the source document or any other documents such as GR/IR. SAP has provided you with numerous options to choose from while determining the billing quantity, as shown in the Table 4.8.

Billing Quantity	Business Significance
A	Order-related billing
B	Delivery-related billing
C and D	Pro forma invoice
E and F	Third-party business scenarios
G and H	Batches

Table 4.8 Billing Quantity in Copy Control Settings

In the third-party process, you can choose either **E** or **F** depending on the business requirement. In a scenario where the billing quantity needs to be copied from the goods receipt, that is, for a third-party scenario with shipping notification, you have to maintain the billing quantity as **E**. For third-party scenarios without shipping notification, you have to maintain the billing quantity as **F**. This will allow the system to copy the billing quantities from the invoice receipt that has been created after Transaction MIRO execution.

- **Pos./Neg. Quantity**
  When you create a document that refers to another document, the reference quantity is subtracted from the open quantity of the source document. This is called a positive effect and will be applicable to the open quantity of the source document.

  The negative effect is applicable in return scenarios where the return quantities get added to the original document or source document.

- **Pricing Type**
  The field controls the way in which the price elements or values get copied over to the target document. SAP has provided multiple options to choose from. For the third-party scenario, keep the pricing type as **G** to copy the pricing from the source document and redetermine the taxes.

- **PricingExchRate Type**
  You can redetermine the exchange rate with the field in the target document. Some of the important options provided by SAP are listed in Table 4.9.

Exchange Rate Type	Significance
A	Copy from sales order
B	Price exchange rate = accounting rate
C	Exchange rate determination according to the billing date
D	Exchange rate determination according to the pricing date
E	Exchange rate determination according to current date
F	Exchange rate determination according to date of service rendered

Table 4.9 Exchange Rate Type

- **Price Source**
  You can allow the system to take prices from multiple sources, including orders, purchase orders, deliveries, shipments, and so on.

4.5 Inventory Management

Inventory management plays a vital role in all ERP software. In SAP S/4HANA, inventory management is used throughout multiple logistic functionalities. From the integration perspective, it's very important to have an idea of the commonly used inventory management concepts. In this section, we'll discuss the concept of movement types and some of the commonly used movement types in core business processes. Then we'll dive into the concept of goods issue and goods receipt, along with the stock overview functionality.

4.5.1 What Is the Document Concept?

The established document principle for any inventory management software is that you can't submit any transaction unless the document is generated. SAP S/4HANA, in accordance with the *document principle*, generates a document and stores it in the system for each transaction/event that results in a change in stock or value. The document principle simply states that the SAP S/4HANA system keeps track of at least one document for each business transaction. In other words, with the help of a document number, each transaction in SAP S/4HANA can be traced back to a unique document. The system can assign the document number automatically using internal number ranges, or users can assign the document number manually using external number ranges. Every document is identified by a document number, company code, and fiscal year. Some business events necessitate the creation of multiple SAP documents. The SAP S/4HANA system determines which documents are required based on the type of business transaction.

For example, when you post a goods movement, the following documents are created:

- **Material document**
  When a goods movement is posted in the inventory management system, a material document is generated that serves as proof of the movement as well as a source of information for any applications that follow.
- **Accounting document**
  If the goods movement is important for financial accounting, an accounting document is created in addition to the material document. For a single material document, several accounting documents may be created in some cases. This could be the case if you have two material document items with different plants that are assigned to different company codes. An automatic account assignment is used to update the general ledger accounts involved in a goods movement.

The procurement process begins with the gathering of requirements and ends with the acquisition of goods from vendors. Once the goods have been purchased from a vendor, they must be stored in the proper location on the company's premises so that they can be consumed when needed. Inventory management is concerned with the placement and handling of stock received from vendors within the company's premises.

The sales process or order-to-cash process exhibits the same requirements but on the opposite side. Once the orders are created for the customer, delivery is posted along with goods issue, and the stock gets reduced from the system.

4.5.2 Movement Types

Movement type plays an important role in inventory management in terms of updating quantity fields in stock and consumption accounts, controlling the fields of Transaction MIGO, and performing message determination.

The *material document* is created once the stock movement happens in the SAP landscape, and the stock movement is governed by the movement type. Therefore, the material document acts as a data point for any other application involved.

The system performs the following activities once the material document is posted:

- If the movement has financial accounting effects, one or more accounting documents are generated.
- The quantity of materials in stock is updated.
- The stock value in the material master is updated.

SAP provides standard movement types; however, custom movement types are created in the following cases:

- **For reporting purposes**
  If the business wants to procure the special material with a different movement type such as dangerous goods, you can create a new movement type by copying the existing one.
- **General ledger account determination**
  In general ledger account determination for inventory management, the movement type plays a critical role. When the business doesn't want to pick the general ledger based on a predetermined modifier assigned to the movement type, then you can create a new valuation modifier. For example, if there is a business requirement that account modifier VBR should not be used to pick the general ledger account, you can create a new valuation modifier and assign it to the movement type. You can post the values in a different consumption account by making these appropriate settings in the movement type and in Transaction OBYC, as discussed in Section 4.3.
- **Field selection**
  If the business wants to control any field selection or allowed transaction at the movement type level, then you can configure the movement type accordingly.

> **Note**
> To display the general ledger account mapped via Transaction OBYC, you can execute Transaction SE16N for table T030.

The following impacts on the material document can result:

- A material document is created as proof of the movement and as a source of data for any other applications that may be involved.
- If the movement is relevant for financial accounting, then one or more accounting documents are generated.
- Material stock quantities are revised in the stock overview. The stock values in the material master record, as well as the stock and consumption accounts, are updated.

Movement types can be classified based on the underlying business process or type of material movement. As shown in Table 4.10, the movement types can be categorized based on the initial number associated with the movement type.

Movement Types	Usage
1XX	Goods receipt from purchasing, production, and returns
2XX	Good issue for consumption
3XX/4XX	Transfers
5XX	Goods receipt without reference to purchase order or production planning order
6XX	Logistics execution – shipping movement types
7XX	Physical inventory

Table 4.10 Classification of Movement Types

We'll explore the configuration of movement types and explain how they're used in sales and distribution integration in the following sections.

Movement Type Configuration

Movement types have a critical impact on all logistic functionalities such as materials management, production planning, quality management, sales and distribution, and some of the finance functionality such as financial accounting and controlling. Therefore, consultants should be extremely cautious when configuring movement types or when making any changes in existing movement types. The goal of this section is to give an overview of the various capabilities of movement types and their impacts on other functionalities.

Note

Keep in mind that this is only an introduction to movement type configuration. Typically, movement type configuration is handled by the materials management consultant.

Let's explore the movement type configuration by using Transaction OMJJ or by following Customizing menu path **Materials Management • Inventory Management and Physical Inventory • Movement Types • Copy, Change Movement Types**.

To copy the specific movement type, you have to select the **Movement type** checkbox and click the green checkmark (or press `Enter`), as shown in Figure 4.77. You'll then be taken to the screen shown in Figure 4.78.

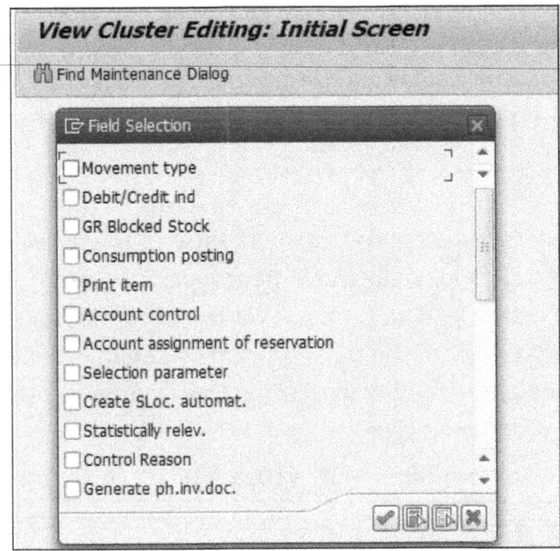

Figure 4.77 Movement Types: Initial Screen

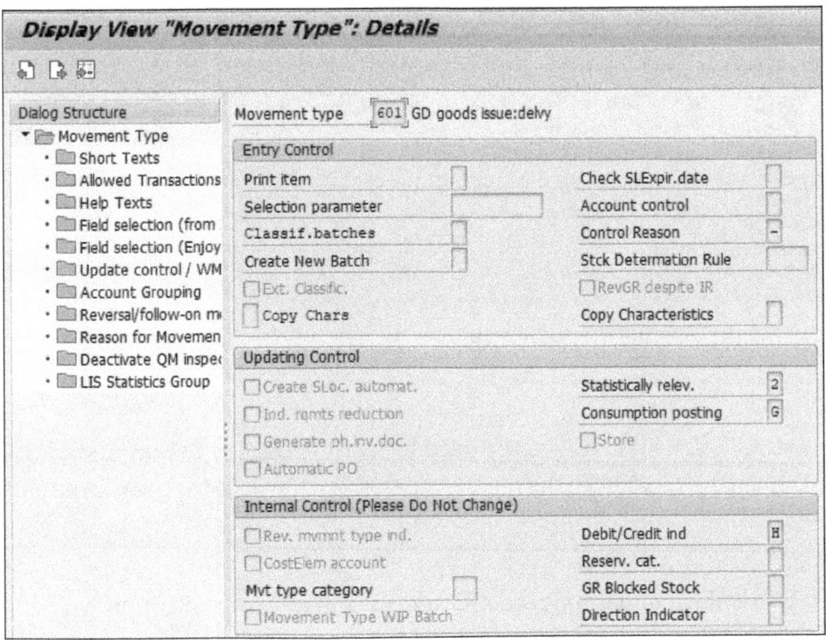

Figure 4.78 Movement Type: 601

As explained earlier, we won't deep dive into each and every field of the movement type as the configuration is quite exhaustive. As an SAP consultant from the integration perspective, you should know what major customization is possible for the movement type.

As shown in Figure 4.78, you can see various dialog structures. Each dialog structure corresponds to a detailed configuration screen. Let's proceed with an overview of these dialog structures:

- **Short Texts**
  You can log in to SAP S/4HANA with a variety of language options. In the event that you need to create a new movement type, you can keep transaction short text for different languages.
- **Allowed Transactions**
  A very common business requirement is for users to restrict the use of the movement type in some transactions. A special goods issue movement type, for example, can only be posted via sales order and delivery document, not via Transaction MIGO. You can include the transactions associated with the movement type and maintain them in the list. Allowed transactions are simply transactions that can be maintained and are permitted to post this movement type.

  Figure 4.79 shows the allowed transactions, including **MB11**, **VL01N**, **VLPOD**, and so on.

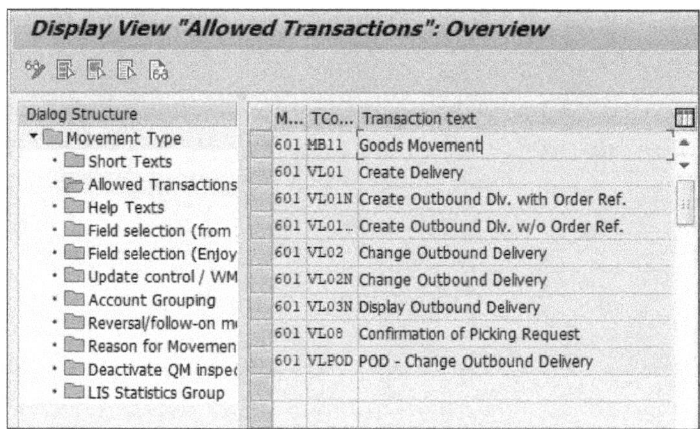

Figure 4.79 Movement Type: Allowed Transactions

- **Help Texts**
  In SAP S/4HANA, F1 help is frequently used to learn about the details associated with the fields. You can maintain the text that describes the uses for the movement type.
- **Field selection**
  You can make a field mandatory/required and optional for a specific movement

type before executing the underlying business transaction based on the business requirements. Before executing any inventory transactions, the system reads the field selection for the underlying business transaction, such as a sales order or a goods receipt, which is applicable to all movement types associated with the transaction. However, if you set a field required from the field selection movement type, this will be applicable only to that specific movement type.

- **Update control / WM**
  The dialog structure can be used to configure the availability check for the movement type as well as the warehouse management controls associated with the reference movement type.
- **Account Grouping**
  This is the same field covered in Section 4.3.3 when you defined account groups for movement types. Account modification keys can be defined in this dialog structure. The key is used to distinguish between account determinations for goods movement. This key's values are predefined by SAP and can't be changed.
- **Reversal/follow-on movement type**
  Every movement type has a reversal movement type that reverses the changes caused by the movement type. For example, the reversal movement type for **601** is **602** (see Figure 4.80). With customized movement type creation, you must also assign the reversal movement type in the dialog structure.

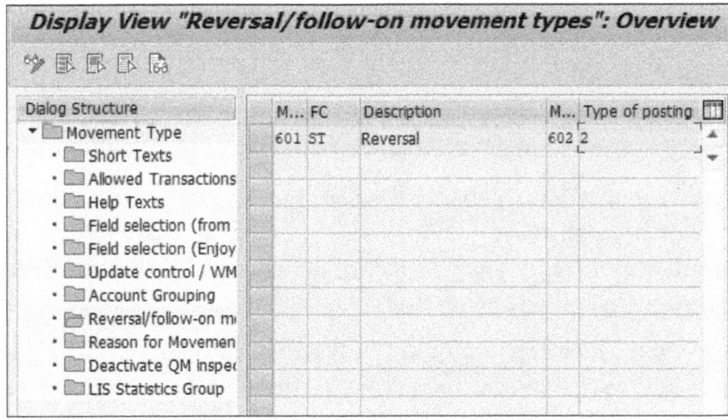

Figure 4.80 Reversal Movement Type

- **Reason for Movement**
  From a reporting standpoint, you can use this field to differentiate the various scenarios in which you use the movement type.
- **Deactivate QM inspection**
  You can specify whether or not a specific movement type is activated for quality inspection. As a result, no inspection lots for an inspection process will be created.

- **LIS Statistics Group**
  You can use this dialog box for LIS reporting purposes.

Standard Movement Types in Sales and Distribution Integrations

Let's explore important movement types from the perspective of sales and distribution integration with materials management:

- **101 (goods receipt)**
  This movement type is used for goods receipt against a purchase order. The stock will be added in the unrestricted stock with this movement type. The accounting entry will be as follows:
  - Debit: Goods receipt
  - Credit: Inventory account
- **102 (goods receipt for purchase order reversal)**
  Movement type 102 is a reversal of movement type 101. You can cancel the goods movement with this movement type.
- **103 (goods receipt for blocked stock)**
  This movement type is used for goods receipt of blocked stock against a purchase order. The stock in blocked stock will be increased as a result of this movement type. There will be no accounting documents generated.
- **104 (goods receipt for blocked stock reversal)**
  This movement type is a reversal of movement type 103.
- **301 (transfer from plant to plant)**
  This movement type is used to transfer the quantity from a supplying plant's unrestricted stock to a receiving plant's unrestricted stock.
- **321 (transfer from quality inspection to unrestricted stock)**
  You maintain this movement type in the quality view of a material master record to transfer the material quantity from quality inspection stock to unrestricted stock. There will be no accounting documents generated.
- **323 (transfer between storage locations for quality inspection stock)**
  This movement type is used to transfer the quality inspection stock from supplying storage location to receiving storage location's quality inspection stock.
- **325 (transfer between storage locations for blocked stock)**
  This movement type is used to transfer the blocked stock from the supplying storage location to the blocked stock of the receiving storage location.
- **401 (transfer of sales order stock to company stock)**
  This movement type is used to transfer the quantity from nonvaluated unrestricted stock of sales order to valuated unrestricted storage stock.

- **403 (transfer of consignment stock to company stock)**
  This movement type is used to transfer the quantity from unrestricted consignment stock to unrestricted storage stock.
- **561 (initial stock entry into unrestricted stock)**
  This movement type is used to make the stock entry into unrestricted stock. With Transaction MIGO, you can enter this movement type along with material, plant, and storage location to create the stock entry.
- **562 (reversal of initial stock entry)**
  This movement type is used to reverse the initial entry stock.
- **601 (goods issue for delivery)**
  This movement type is mainly used in sales and distribution to PGI with reference to the outbound delivery. The stock will be reduced from unrestricted stock with the use of this movement type. The accounting document entry will be as follows:
  - Debit: COGS account
  - Credit: Inventory account
- **602 (goods issue for delivery reversal)**
  This movement type is a reversal of movement type 601. When PGI is reversed for outbound delivery, then this movement type comes in the picture for the reversal entry, and stock will be added to unrestricted stock. The accounting entry will be as follows:
  - Debit: Inventory account
  - Credit: COGS account
- **651 (returns from customer – damage stock)**
  This movement type is used in the return process. In case of damage stock that is returned by the customer, this movement type is used to add the stock in return stock. The inventory accounting document isn't generated in this case.
- **653 (return from customer – overdelivery)**
  If there is an overdelivery for any material, for example, a customer returns the overdelivered quantity, then this stock will be added back to unrestricted stock. The inventory accounting document entry will be as follows:
  - Debit: Inventory account
  - Credit: COGS
- **655 (return from customer – defect stock)**
  If there is a return delivery of defective stock from the customer, then this stock will be added to quality stock with the use of this movement type. The inventory accounting document is generated with the following entry:
  - Debit: Inventory account
  - Credit: COGS

- **657 (return from customer – blocked stock)**
  If expired stock is returned by the customer, the stock will be added to blocked stock by using this movement type. The inventory accounting document entry will be as follows:
  - Debit: Inventory account
  - Credit: COGS
- **631 (transfer from unrestricted stock to consignment stock)**
  With this movement type, stock is transferred from unrestricted stock to consignment stock, which means stock will be reduced from unrestricted stock and will be added to consignment stock. The inventory accounting document won't generate in this case.
- **632 (transfer from consignment stock to unrestricted stock)**
  This is the reversal of movement type 631, which will transfer the stock from consignment stock to unrestricted stock. There is no accounting impact in this case.
- **633 (goods issue from customer consignment)**
  This movement type is used in the consignment issue process, which will reduce the stock from consignment stock and add it to the consignee's stock. The inventory accounting document generates in this case, and the accounting entry will be as follows:
  - Debit: COGS account
  - Credit: Inventory account
- **634 (goods issue receipt from customer consignment)**
  When the consignee returns the goods, then the stock will be added back to consignment stock. This movement of material quantity will be captured by movement type 634. The inventory accounting document entry will be as follows:
  - Debit: Inventory account
  - Credit: COGS account
- **641 (goods issue for two-step STO)**
  This movement type is used in the two-step STO process where the quantity is transferred from unrestricted stock of the supplying plant to stock in transit of the receiving plant. The stock will be reduced from the supplying plant and then displayed in transit at the receiving plant. The inventory accounting document will generate with the following accounting entries:
  - Debit: Stock inward movement account
  - Credit: Stock outward account
- **643 (goods issue for two-step intercompany STO)**
  The movement type is used for intercompany STO with the two-step process. The quantity is reduced from the unrestricted stock of the supplying plant; however, stock in transit isn't created. The goods receipt is entered at the receiving plant in the second step.

- **645 (goods issue for one-step intercompany STO)**
  For one-step intercompany STO, this movement type is used, which will reduce the stock from unrestricted stock in the supplying plant. Goods receipt will be posted in the receiving plant automatically.
- **647 (goods issue for one-step STO)**
  This movement type is used in one-step STO. The stock will be reduced from unrestricted stock in the supplying plant, and stock will be added in the receiving plant automatically. Inventory accounting document entries will be as follows:
  - Debit: Stock inward movement account
  - Credit: Stock outward account
- **671 (goods issue for two-step STO return)**
  This is the reversal of movement type 641. Movement type 671 reduces the stock in transit of the receiving plant and increases the unrestricted stock of the supplying plant.
- **673 (goods issue for two-step intercompany STO return)**
  This movement type is used for the two-step intercompany STO return process where the return stock will be transferred to the supplying plant in the second step.
- **675 (goods issue for one-step intercompany STO return)**
  This movement type is used in the one-step intercompany STO return process. The return stock is transferred to the unrestricted stock of the supplying plant.
- **677 (goods issue for one-step STO return)**
  This movement type is the reversal of movement type 647, which is used in the one-step STO return process. The return stock will post as a goods receipt in the unrestricted stock of the supplying plant with the use of movement type 677.

4.5.3 Goods Issue

A *goods issue* is defined as a physical outbound movement of goods or materials from the warehouse. It results in a decrease in stock from the plant, warehouse, or storage location. In SAP S/4HANA, you can perform goods issues either through Transaction MIGO or standard delivery document creation through Transaction VL01N.

Let's explore some of the important activities where goods issue is performed:

- **Goods issue with reference to a sales order**
  Sales and distribution handles the withdrawal, picking, and shipping of goods to customers. You perform the goods issue with reference to the sales order in Transaction VL01N. When you enter a goods issue into inventory management, the system generates a transfer request as a request to pick up goods from the warehouse. Based on the transfer request, you create a transfer order and remove the goods from storage. In an event where the sales are performed on another non-SAP system or the sales and distribution functionality isn't implemented, then the inventory management

system provides two movement types for posting goods issues to customers: consumption to sales order and consumption to sales, which can be performed in Transaction MIGO.

- **Goods issue to production order**
  A goods issue occurs in production planning scenarios when raw material is consumed to produce material in accordance with the production order. Goods issue against a production order is performed using movement type 261 whenever you consume component materials to produce another material. After goods are issued, the system reduces the component inventory at the relevant storage location. You can also automate the goods issuance process for the production order through backflushing. You can perform the goods issue with Transaction MIGO. After executing the transaction, you'll arrive at the screen shown in Figure 4.81, where you select the reference document as **R08 Order** for the production order.

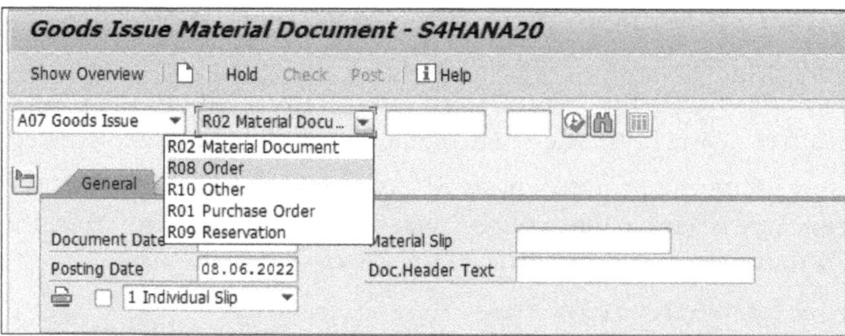

Figure 4.81 Goods Issue

- **Goods issue for sampling**
  Sample withdrawal is a product or goods issue that is typically associated with quality control. The SAP sampling procedure ensures that the testing sample is drawn from existing stock. The sampled goods are treated as destroyed; that is, the system assumes the material can no longer be used following the quality inspection. In this sense, sampling is analogous to scrapping, with the exception that the value of the sampled material is transferred from the material stock account to the quality inspection expense account. To check the material deterioration, often manufacturing companies deploy the periodic sampling process, which is executed by the quality management department. For the sampling process, you use Transaction MIGO, and the movement types are as follows: If the sample is provided from unrestricted stock, you must use movement type 333; for quality stock, you must use movement type 331; and for blocked stock, you must use movement type 335.
- **Goods issue for scrapping**
  Materials that have exceeded their shelf life, have been damaged, can't be used, or can't be reworked are classified as scrap in SAP S/4HANA. Scraps are generated in most industries during the manufacturing or assembly process. The scrapping

process in SAP S/4HANA can be linked to production planning or materials management functionalities. If the material is destroyed, this information must also be entered into the SAP S/4HANA system. You can scrap material from unrestricted-use stock, quality inspection stock, and blocked stock. Movement type 551 is used to scrap from unrestricted stock, movement type 553 is used for quality inspection stock, and movement type 555 is used for blocked stock. When you post material for scrapping, the system reduces the relevant stock, transfers the value of the scrapped material from the stock account to a scrap account, and debits the cost center entered.

Major impacts of the goods issue process on the system are as follows:

- A material document is created that serves as the audit proof for the material movements.
- Stock updates are performed: as the movement of goods is taking place in the goods issue, the stock will get reduced in the system; if the goods issue reversal is performed, then the stock is increased in the system.
- As stocks are removed from inventory, the corresponding valuation for the stocks should be updated. This is accomplished through the automatic generation of the financial accounting document, which describes the financial movement associated with the issuance of goods.
- A goods issue posting not only updates the inventory in the material master record but also updates the consumption statistics if the material is planned with MRP.
- When goods are issued, an inspection lot is created if inspection processing is enabled in the quality management system. This inspection lot is used by the quality management system to carry out the inspection.
- When goods are issued in response to an order, the quantities withdrawn for the components are updated in the order.

4.5.4 Goods Receipt

The physical movement of goods into the warehouse from outside vendors is referred to as *goods receipt*. It's primarily used by businesses to replenish semifinished goods, raw materials and supplies, and finished goods. In the warehouse management system (WMS), a goods receipt is the physical inbound movement of goods or materials into the warehouse. It's a type of goods movement that is used to transport goods received from external vendors or manufactured in house. All goods receipts result in an increase in warehouse stock. It always increases the amount of inventory in your warehouse. You can plan and manage your goods receipts, as well as keep track of the stock of ordered and manufactured materials.

Steps involved in a typical goods receipt process are as follows:

1. A purchase order is issued along with a request for goods receipt by the purchasing department.

2. When goods are received at the goods receiving point, the person receiving them inspects them for any potential damage.
3. After inspection, if the packaging is satisfactory, the recipient forwards the goods to the department that ordered them.
4. The purchasing department checks the goods; if they are satisfied with the ordered goods suitability and condition, they issue a goods receipt referencing the purchase order.
5. The finance department then pays the invoice for the received goods.

Figure 4.82 shows the goods receipt screen. The goods receipt can be made against various documents, such as inbound delivery, purchase order, and production order, and without any reference.

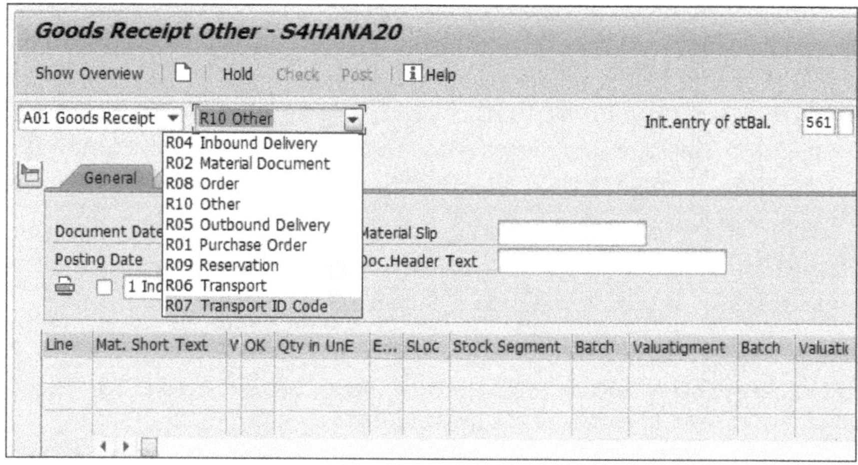

Figure 4.82 Goods Receipt

Let's explore some of the important reference documents:

- **Goods receipt for production order**
  Companies may manufacture their own goods as well as obtain goods from outside sources. Most manufacturing clients obtain raw materials and then use these raw materials to produce finished products. Following the completion of production, the manufactured goods must be entered into inventory via a related goods receipt. Goods receipt against order is performed with movement type 101, which occurs when the material is manufactured. After receiving the goods, the system replenishes the material stock at the appropriate storage location. The system's stock will be increased with goods receipt.
- **Goods receipt for purchase order**
  This is a standard business process where the goods receipt is made against the purchase order. Standard movement type 101 is used to post stock against the purchase

order. After goods receipt, the purchase history gets updated and the material document is posted.

- **Goods receipt without reference**
  You can't reference a purchase order from the SAP S/4HANA system when entering a goods receipt if your company doesn't use the purchasing component. In this case, the external goods receipt is entered as a miscellaneous (other) goods receipt. Sometimes there is no reference document or document number available, but the related goods have arrived and must be placed in inventory to proceed with dependent inventory management processes. In this case, as described in this section, a goods receipt without a reference may be posted.
- **Initial stock upload**
  This task is carried out during the cutover phase of a new SAP S/4HANA implementation. The stocks will be updated in the system with movement type 561 if you want to post them in unrestricted stocks, movement type 563 if you want to post them in quality inspection, and movement type 565 if you want to post them in blocked stock.

Impacts of goods receipt on the system are as follows:

- A material document is created that serves as the audit proof for the material movements.
- As the movement of goods is taking place in the goods receipt, the stock will get increased in the system; if the goods receipt reversal is performed, then the stock is decreased in the system.
- As stocks are added into the inventory, the corresponding valuation for the stocks should be updated. This is accomplished through the automatic generation of the financial accounting document, which describes the financial movement associated with the receipt of goods.

4.5.5 Stock Overview

In this section, we'll discuss the stock overview, which can be executed with Transaction MMBE and is used to display the material stock at various levels such as company code, plant, and storage location. This transaction provides detailed information about the material stock availability in a particular plant or storage location, as well as the information in which stock the material quantity is available, such as unrestricted stock, quality stock, blocked stock, and so on.

To display the stock overview, you can execute Transaction MMBE or navigate to menu path **Logistics • Materials Management • Inventory Management • Environment • Stock • MMBE – Stock Overview**. You'll be directed to the screen shown in Figure 4.83, where you can enter the selection parameters and click the **Execute** icon to display the stock overview.

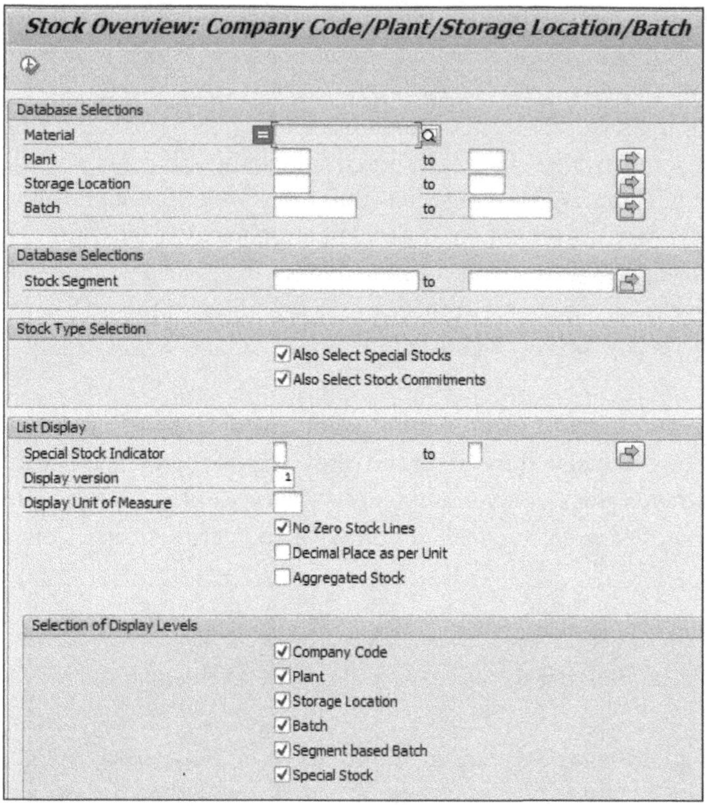

Figure 4.83 Stock Overview: Initial Screen

Let's discuss these selection parameters in detail:

- **Material**
  In this field, you specify the material for which the stock overview should be displayed.
- **Plant**
  You can select the plant for which the stock overview should be published in this field. If no plant is specified here, the stock for all applicable plants for that material will be listed.
- **Storage Location**
  You can enter the storage location in this field, just like you do in the **Plant** field, so that the stock overview will be displayed for that specific storage location. If you leave this field blank, the stock overview of all applicable storage locations will be shown.
- **Batch**
  If you enter a batch number in this field, the stock overview will be categorized by batch. If no values are entered in this field, an overview of all relevant batches will be displayed.

- **Stock Segment**
  If you enter stock segment in this field, then the stock overview will be displayed with that specific stock segment. You can define the stock segment in the segmentation strategy, and the strategy is assigned in the material master record.
- **Also Select Special Stocks**
  If you check this indicator, then the special stocks, such as consignment stock, sales order stock, project stock, and so on, are included in the stock overview.
- **Also Select Stock Commitments**
  If this indicator is set, then the stock overview will display the stock commitments such as open purchase order quantities, reservations, stock in transit, open deliveries, and so on.
- **Special Stock Indicator**
  If you want to see a stock overview of a special stock, you should use this field option to choose the appropriate special stock indicator. For example, special stock indicator **B** for customer stock, **E** for orders on hand, **K** for consignment stock, and so on.
- **Display version**
  This field is used to display the stock overview according to the display version configured in the Customizing of inventory management. The path for this Customizing is **Inventory Management and Physical Inventory • Reporting • Define Stock List Display**.
- **Display Unit of Measure**
  The field is used to display the material quantity in a specific unit of measure (UoM).
- **No Zero Stock Lines**
  With this indicator enabled, if the stock quantity at any storage location is zero, the line for that storage location will be hidden from the stock overview.
- **Decimal Place as per Unit**
  Generally the stock quantity is shown with three decimal places in the stock overview. You can, however, set this indicator to display no decimal places if that is the requirement.
- **Aggregated Stock**
  If this checkbox is activated, the cumulative stock of material is displayed in the stock overview. For example, if the stock is maintained at various storage locations in one plant, the cumulated quantity of all storage location stock is displayed at the plant level.
- **Selection of Display Levels**
  This selection pane contains a number of factors that can be used to display the stock, such as the company code, plant, storage location, and so on. You'll be able to choose which organizational levels the stock overview is displayed on by setting up these parameters.

After setting the selection parameters in the initial screen of the stock overview, execute the transaction. The screen shown in Figure 4.84 will appear.

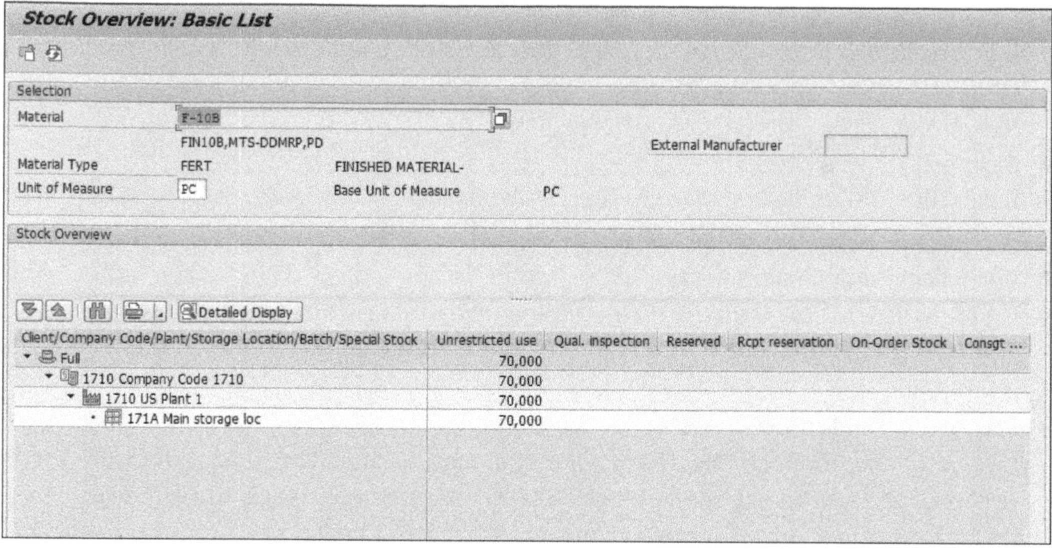

Figure 4.84 Stock Overview: Basic List

This screen displays the material for which you've requested the stock overview. In addition, it contains the material type and UoM details. In the bottom section of the **Stock Overview: Basic List** screen, you can see the stock at the organizational level, such as the company code level, plant level, and storage location level, with the respective stock types.

If you click the **Detailed Display** button on this screen, you'll be able to see the detailed display of stock types with the stock quantity, as shown in Figure 4.85.

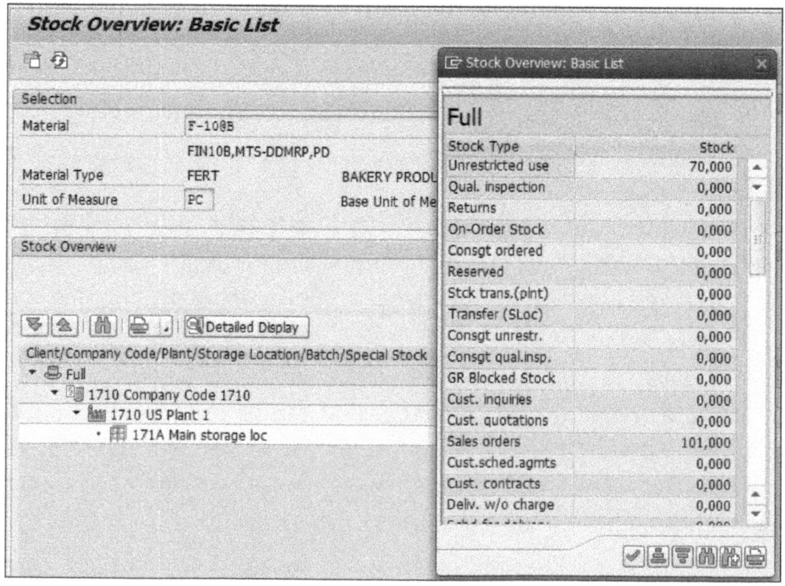

Figure 4.85 Stock Types

Let's briefly discuss the sales and distribution-related stock types, as described in Table 4.11.

Stock Type	Description
Unrestricted	Unrestricted stock is ready for use without any restrictions.
Quality inspection	The stock planned for quality inspection is stored in quality inspection stock and isn't available for use.
Returns	The stock returned by the customer for any reason is stored in the returns stock.
On-order stock	This stock specifies the open order quantity that is yet to be delivered.
Reserved	This stock indicates the reserved quantity against particular use, such as sales order or production order.
Sales orders	The sales order stock is allocated with the sales orders, which mean the stock reserved for a specific sales order is sales order stock.
Blocked	The defective materials are stored in the blocked stock.
Consignment	The consignment stock is used in the consignment process in which the stock is moved from unrestricted stock to consignment stock.
Stock in transit (plant)	This stock corresponds to the stocks that are in transit from one plant to another during the STO process.
Delivery without charge	This is the stock received for movement type 511 (free delivery).
Scheduled for delivery	If you create a delivery and save it without performing PGI, you can see the corresponding stock in Transaction MMBE under this tab.

Table 4.11 Stock Types

We've discussed inventory management in this section, including the document concept, movement types, and the effect of movement types on the system and its configuration. Then we covered the impacts of goods issue and goods receipt process. At the end of the section, we explored the stock overview Transaction MMBE and stock types from a sales and distribution perspective.

4.6 Summary

In this chapter, we've talked about the integration between the sales and distribution and materials management functionalities.

We started the discussion in Section 4.1 with the ATP concept and its implications in the SAP S/4HANA landscape. We briefly touched on the different solution offerings with respect to SAP advanced availability check and dove into the details of the product availability check functionality offered by SAP S/4HANA for advanced ATP. We explored the different configuration elements and the corresponding impacts on the system, as well as the peripheral processes around delivery scheduling and the associated configurations.

Then we moved on to Section 4.2 for the STO process and explored the important business variations of the STO process such as intercompany, intracompany, one step, and two step. We talked briefly about configuration aspects such as plant, customer, document type, delivery type, storage locations, and copy control settings. Then we discussed the materials management pricing procedure and its integration with STO. We also briefly touched on the accounting implications of the STO process.

In Section 4.3, we discussed the concept of account determination in inventory management. We started our discussion around material valuation and understood the implication of material valuation on the business process. Then we took a deep dive into the transaction key-specific account determination technique in SAP S/4HANA and explored the associated configurations to achieve automatic general ledger account determination in inventory transactions.

In Section 4.4, we got into the details of the third-party process where we discussed third party as a business concept, its benefits, its variations in terms of with and without shipping notification, and its prerequisites. Then we went over the configuration elements of the third-party process, such as item category controls and their determination, schedule line category controls and their determination, and respective copy control settings.

In Section 4.5, we started our discussion on inventory management with its importance in business processes. We briefly discussed the document concept in SAP S/4HANA and how it's leveraged. Then we took a detailed look at movement types, the effect of movement types on the system, and the need for configuring a custom movement type. We briefly touched on the overview of movement type configurations and discussed important movement types from an integration standpoint. Then we discussed the impacts of goods issue and goods receipt processes. At the end of the section, we touched on the stock overview Transaction MMBE and stock types.

Now, let's move on to our next integration point with sales and distribution: finance.

Chapter 5
Finance

The ultimate goal of a business is to create value for its customers and generate profit for its stakeholders in a sustainable way. The finance functionality in SAP S/4HANA plays a very crucial role in the entire record-to-report business process. The data fed into the record-to-report process often originates from the order-to-cash flow.

5

The sales and distribution functionality in SAP S/4HANA integrates seamlessly with finance in various business processes. The tight integration between these functionalities prevents revenue leakage in the organization. It's very important to understand the integration points between the sales and distribution functionality and the finance functionality to effectively implement SAP S/4HANA in the enterprise.

In this chapter, we'll explain pricing and taxation, along with how they can be configured in the system with the condition technique. Then, we'll walk you through account determination in billing and provide a comprehensive, step-by-step understanding of each process involved. We'll describe the credit management functionality in general, and then walk through the specific credit management based on sales and distribution and the specific credit management based on financial supply chain management (FSCM). We'll also discuss profitability analysis, along with its associated configurations and data flow. Finally, we'll cover intercompany billing, its configurations, and an example of intercompany sales flow.

5.1 Pricing and Taxation

Pricing and *taxation* are critical interfaces between the sales and distribution functionality and the finance functionality. Accounting documents generated after invoicing contain finance-related data that is used to generate end reporting from both compliance and internal reporting perspectives. In this section, we'll first explain the pricing concept and its implementation in SAP S/4HANA, and then we'll look at how taxes flow through the system and interact with sales and distribution.

5.1.1 Condition Technique

The *condition technique* is the most widely used and adaptable methodology used by SAP to assist consultants in configuring complex business rules associated with pricing determination, output determination, text determination, revenue account determination, and so on. This is widely used in sales and distribution, materials management, and controlling. In materials management, its used for determining the pricing schema, that is, the pricing procedure from the materials management side.

The condition technique describes how the system determines prices based on information stored in condition records. you set up and control the various elements used in the condition technique with Customizing in sales and distribution. The condition technique is used by the system during sales order processing to determine a variety of important pricing information. For example, given the conditions, the system automatically determines which gross price the customer should be charged and which discounts and surcharges are applicable.

As shown in Figure 5.1, it consists of the following major components:

- **Field catalog**
  The field catalog contains every possible set of fields that can be used to determine business rules. If the associated field isn't present in the field catalog, then you can append the pricing structure with the help of an ABAP consultant and include the desired fields in the field catalog.
- **Condition table**
  A condition table is a database table that is created as part of the customization process from a small subset of the field catalog.
- **Access sequence**
  An access sequence is a search strategy used by the system to locate valid data for a specific condition type. The order of the accesses determines which condition records take precedence over others. The accesses instruct the system on where to look first, second, and so on, until a valid condition record is found. The condition tables that you'll create in the previous step needs to be assigned in the access sequence of most specific to most general.
- **Condition type**
  Each condition type represents one of the condition technique's logical components. Excise tax, for example, could be one of the logical components of pricing and could be represented by one condition type or a combination of multiple condition types. The access sequence created earlier needs to be assigned in the condition type.
- **Pricing procedure**
  A pricing procedure is a combination of multiple condition types. The condition type that you configured in the previous step needs to be assigned in the pricing procedure with the sequential order. Finally, the pricing procedure is assigned to the

final document type that the business rule affects. In some cases, the determination happens at the document type level, that is, in revenue account determination, output determination, and cash account determination. You must assign the procedure to the document type. In sales pricing, you have to set up the determination of pricing procedure based on the sales area, document pricing procedure, and customer pricing procedure.

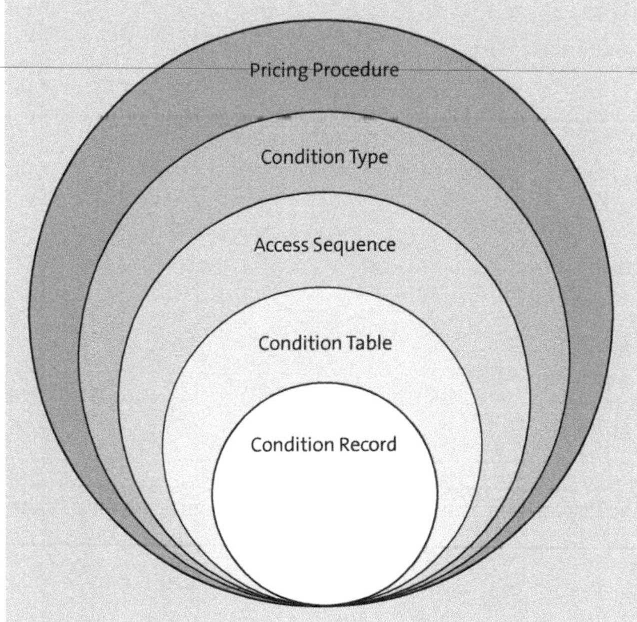

Figure 5.1 Condition Technique

We'll walk through the key configuration activities in the following sections.

Condition Tables

A condition table is a three-digit number that can be generated after the following steps are completed. You can only use a number higher than 500 to create custom tables because SAP has reserved the numbers 1 to 500 for internal tables created by SAP. You must ensure that the table you're attempting to create doesn't already exist in the standard tables. There is no need to create the table if it already exists; you can use the existing table for further configurations.

You can create the condition table by navigating to menu path **Sales and Distribution • Basic Functions • Pricing • Pricing Control • Condition Tables and Field Catalog • Create Condition Tables.** You can also use Transaction V/03 for creating condition tables. After following the given path, you'll end up on the screen shown in Figure 5.2, where you should enter the condition **Table Number** in the field and press `Enter` to arrive at the screen shown in Figure 5.3.

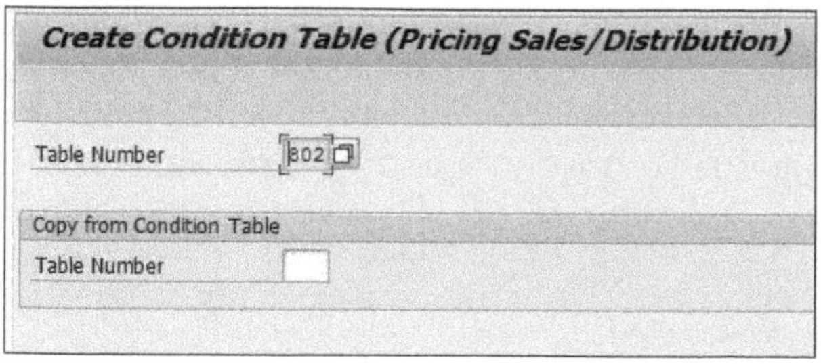

Create Condition Table (Pricing Sales/Distribution)

Table Number 802

Copy from Condition Table

Table Number

Figure 5.2 Create Condition Table: Initial Screen

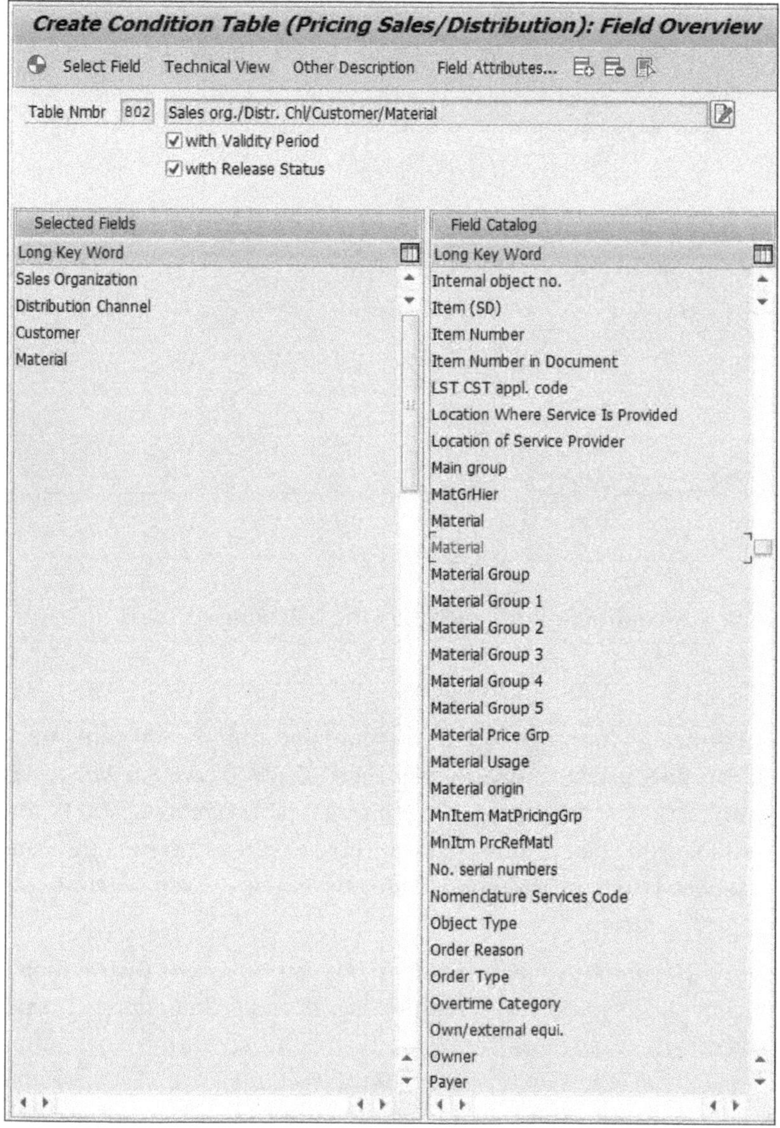

Figure 5.3 Create Condition Table

If you want the condition table to be stored with a validity period, that is, the period in which the condition records are valid, you can select the **with Validity Period** checkbox. The effect of this configuration is that the **From** date and **To** date fields will populate automatically while creating the condition records in Transaction VK11.

The **with Release Status** checkbox determines whether or not a condition record can be used in the pricing calculation. When you check this box, the additional field **Status** gets activated, and you can select the appropriate status based on the requirement in the condition record. The statuses given by SAP are **Released**, **Blocked**, **Released for pricing simulation**, and **Released for planning and pricing simulation**.

The **Field Catalog** is the list of fields provided by SAP to create the condition tables. When creating condition tables, you must select the fields from the field catalog by selecting the field and clicking on the **Select Field** button at the top of the screen. It will populate the selected field in the **Selected Fields** section. In the example shown in Figure 5.3, you can see table **802** with the fields as **Sales Organization**, **Distribution Channel**, **Customer**, and **Material**. After selecting the fields, you have to click the **Generate** icon (the red wheel in the upper-left corner).

Because the changes associated with the condition tables are cross-client, you need to store the changes in the workbench request. The access sequence and the condition table maintenance are stored in workbench requests. In some cases, you need to create a condition table by using customized fields. These customized, or Z, fields are absent in the field catalog, so you need to append these fields in the field catalog with the help of an ABAP consultant.

Note

Cross-client data isn't unique to any one client; it's data that all clients have access to such as cross-client customization and all repository objects that have an impact on the entire SAP system.

Access Sequence

The access sequence is the system's search strategy for identifying valid data for a specific condition type. During the pricing in the sales document, it assists the system in determining the valid condition records from the condition tables. It's defined for each condition type for which the condition records are maintained. The access sequence checks on which table the prices are stored in and populates the correct price in the sales document. The changes associated with the access sequence are also cross-client by nature, so they are stored in the workbench request. An access sequence can have single or multiple condition tables depending on the business requirement. The same access sequence can be used by multiple condition types.

You can create the access sequence by navigating to menu path **Sales and Distribution • Basic Functions • Pricing • Pricing Control • Access Sequences • Set Access Sequences**. You can also use Transaction V/07 to define the access sequence. You'll arrive at the screen shown in Figure 5.4. You can create your own access sequence by clicking on the **New Entries** button. Select the access sequence (**Ac...**) and click on the **Accesses** folder to arrive at the screen shown in Figure 5.5. The example shows the standard access sequence for price **PR00**.

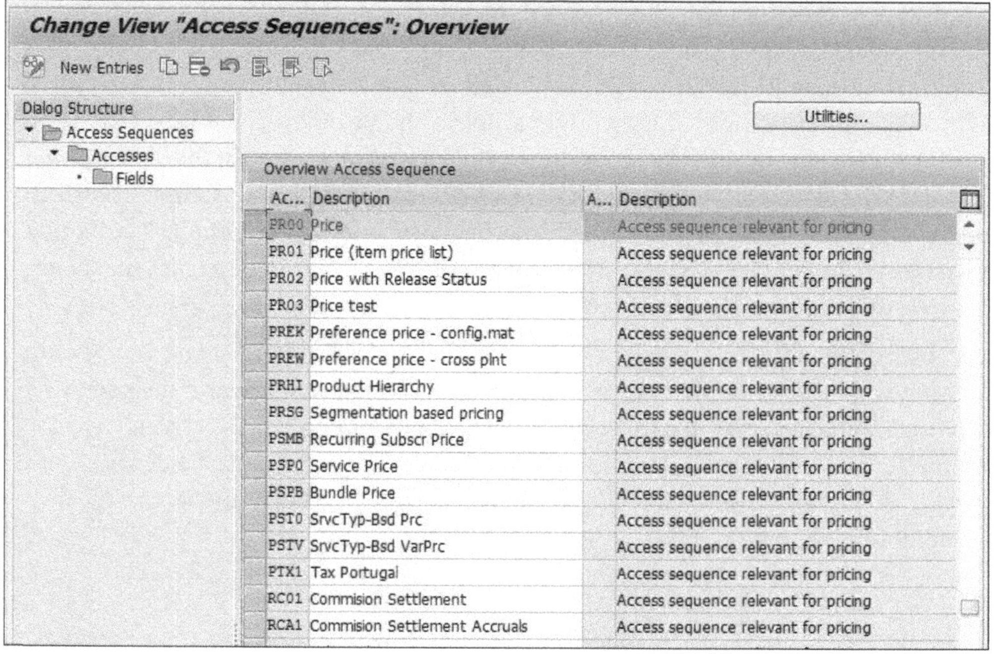

Figure 5.4 Create Access Sequence

Display View "Accesses": Overview

Dialog Structure
- Access sequences
  - Accesses
    - Fields

Access Sequence KOFI Account determination

Overview Accesses

No.	T...	Description	Requirement
5	017	Sales Org./Item Cat./Acct Key	0
10	001	Cust.Grp/MaterialGrp/AcctKey	0
20	002	Cust.Grp/Account Key	0
30	003	Material Grp/Acct Key	0
40	005	Acct Key	0
50	004	General	0

Figure 5.5 Access Sequence

Let's explore each field in the access sequence setup:

- **Access Sequence**
  You must give the newly created access sequence a suitable name. Typically, the name of the condition type for which the access sequence being created is provided in this field. Generally, organizations have their own nomenclature set, which the implementation partner uses to assign names to pricing objects such as the access sequence.
- **No.**
  The sequence of condition tables in the access sequence will be specified by step number. It's a three-digit number that is used to define the sequence of conditions within the pricing procedure. It's always best to leave a space between the two numbers when configuring steps to allow for the addition of an intermediate step later if necessary.
- **T...**
  The second field is the table. The table defined in Transaction V/03 can be maintained in the table field. The description will be auto-populated in the **Description** field.
- **Requirement**
  This is an ABAP code written in Transaction VOFM by the ABAP consultant. Certain business requirements want you to determine the condition records from the table only if a certain condition is met. You can achieve the changes by creating the appropriate logic with the business, writing it in the form of ABAP code, and assigning the routine in the **Requirement** field. If the requirement is fulfilled, then only the values from the table will be populated in the sales order.
- **Exclusive**
  This checkbox (not shown) is the last column in the access sequence, to the right of the **Requirement** field. It governs the logic in the condition technique to stop searching for the condition record once the successful condition record for the condition type has been found within an access sequence. In this case, as shown in Figure 5.5, let's say condition records are maintained for all combinations, that is, **10**, **20**, **30**, and **40** steps. When the **Exclusive** checkbox is selected, the system will stop searching for condition records if the values are found in any of the combinations from step 10 to 40.

  However, if the **Exclusive** checkbox isn't selected, the system will populate all the values maintained for all the combinations in the sales document, which may result in condition type values being duplicated. As a result, in most cases, the checkbox is activated; however, in some special cases, you can use the **Exclusive** checkbox to satisfy any custom requirement associated with the duplicity of the condition record values.

Following the addition of each individual table, you must double-click on the **Fields** button in the **Dialog Structure** while selecting the created line. This results in the screen shown in Figure 5.6. The automatic mapping of the technical field happens after you click on the **Fields** folder. In this example, the first line of the access sequence, step number **10**, is selected. The technical fields associated with the selected field are shown in Figure 5.6.

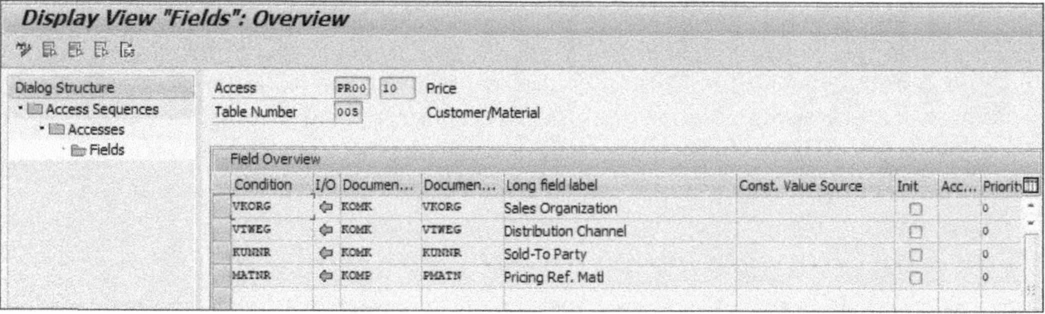

Figure 5.6 Access Sequence Fields

You can now save the access sequence by clicking the **Save** button on the toolbar or by pressing Ctrl+S.

Condition Types

Condition types represent pricing elements in the pricing procedure. Pricing elements can include prices, surcharges, taxes, freight, discounts, and so on. These elements are represented in the system as condition types. You can define a separate condition type for each pricing element.

You can configure the condition type by following the path **Sales and Distribution • Basic Functions • Pricing • Pricing Control • Define Condition Types • Set Condition Types for Pricing**. You can also use Transaction V/06.

You'll arrive at the screen shown in Figure 5.7, where you can create your own condition type by clicking on the **New Entries** button. It's always recommended to create a new condition type by copying an existing one. You can do so by selecting the existing condition type and clicking on the **Copy As** button in the application toolbar. In the example, we've described the standard base condition type **PR00** in the display mode, as shown in Figure 5.8.

The condition type configuration is split between several sections: **Control Data 1**, **Group Condition**, **Changes which can be made**, **Master Data**, **Scales**, and **Control Data 2**. Let's walk through all the key fields.

Change View "Conditions: Condition Types": Overview

New Entries

Condition type	Description	Condition Class	Calculation Type
PR00	Price	Prices	Quantity
PR01	Price incl.Sales Tax	Prices	Quantity
PR02	Graduated Price	Prices	Quantity
PR03	Price (AECMA AUC)	Discount or surcharge	Quantity
PR04	Price (test)	Discount or surcharge	Quantity
PR33	PINAS Price	Prices	Quantity
PR99	Price	Prices	Quantity
PRA0	Promo SP wholesale 1	Prices	Quantity
PRA1	Promo SP wholesale 2	Prices	Quantity
PRMM	Price mmsd	Prices	Quantity
PRPP	PProtection Adjust	Prices	Formula
PRRP	Repair Price	Prices	Quantity
PRSG	Seg. based Price	Prices	Quantity
PSAM	Standalone (Mat.)	Prices	Quantity
PSCO	MtrPr.in Serv.Cntr	Prices	Quantity
PSI1	Price f.Srv.Cntr.Itm	Prices	Quantity - Monthly Price
PSP0	Service Price	Prices	Quantity
PSPM	Discount	Discount or surcharge	Percentage (Travel Costs)
PSPR	Profit	Discount or surcharge	Percentage
PSVB	Sales price basis	Prices	Quantity
PTAM	American Express	Discount or surcharge	Fixed amount
PTBL	Invoice amount	Discount or surcharge	Fixed amount
PTCH	Payment Type - Check	Discount or surcharge	Fixed amount
PTCI	PE Tx Collect Indic	Discount or surcharge	Percentage
PTCO	PE Tx Collect Offset	Taxes	Percentage

Figure 5.7 Condition Type: Initial Screen

Display View "Conditions: Condition Types": Details

Condition Type	PR00 Price	Access Sequence	PR02 Price with Release Status
			Records for Access

Control Data 1

Condition Class	B Prices	Plus/Minus	positive and negative
Calculation Type	C Quantity		
Condition Category			
Rounding Rule	Commercial		
Structure Condition	None		
Condition Function			
Dat.Rec.Source	Condition Technique (old)		

Group Condition

Group Condition	☐	Group Cond. Routine	0
RoundDiffComp	☐		

Changes which can be made

Manual Entries	C Manual entry has priority	Amount/Percent	☑
Header Condition	☐	Quantity Relation	☐
Item Condition	☑	Value	☐
Delete	☐	Calculation Type	☐

Master Data

Proposed Valid-From	Today's date	Pricing Procedure	PR0000
Proposed Valid-To	31.12.9999	Delete from DB	Do not delete (set the deletion flag o...
Ref. Condition Type		Condition Index	☐
Ref. Application		Condition Update	☐
Obsolete	Maint. of cond. recs allowed		

Figure 5.8 Condition Type

First, the **Control Data 1** section contains the following fields:

- **Condition Class**
  The condition class specifies how a condition type, such as prices, surcharges, discounts, and taxes, can be used. It's a distinguishing feature that defines the purpose and behavior of condition types. It defines the condition type's structure and allows you to control each condition type based on its functionalities. Some condition types have functionality hard-coded into them. If you use condition class **B** (prices), for example, you'll be unable to have two base prices active in a single sales document line item. Table 5.1 lists some of the most important condition classes.

Condition Class	Description
A	Discount or surcharge
B	Prices
C	Expense reimbursement
D	Taxes
E	Extra pay
G	Tax classification
H	Determining sales deal
W	Wage withholding tax

Table 5.1 Condition Class

- **Condition Category**
  A condition type is further classified within a condition class by its condition category. The condition category categorizes condition types into predefined groups. For example, **PR00** and **EDI1** are both pricing condition types, so they both have **B** for condition class; however, **PR00** is used as the base price, and **EDI1** is used as the customer expected price. This difference is accounted for by the condition category, where the condition category for **PR00** will be **H** (basic price) and **EDI1** will be **J** (customer expected price). Some of the most-used condition types have the condition categories listed in Table 5.2.

Condition Type	Condition Category
KF00	F (freight)
MWST	D (tax)
VPRS	G (internal price)
EK01/EK02	Q (costing)

Table 5.2 Condition Category

- **Calculation Type**
  This specifies how the system calculates prices, discounts, and surcharges in a given condition type. For example, based on quantity, volume, or weight, the system can calculate a discount as a fixed amount or as a percentage. While maintaining the condition records for the condition types, the system populates the calculation type automatically during the maintenance of Transaction VK11. Finally, it converts the amount to the condition type value.

  Let's explore some of the important calculation types in Table 5.3 that are widely used across industries.

Calculation Type	Usage
A	It's usually maintained for discount and surcharge condition types. The condition record contains percentage values, which are applied to the condition base value to calculate the condition type value.
B	By configuring the condition type with the calculation type as **B**, you can maintain the condition record for the fixed currency value. It should be noted that these condition types are typically configured as header condition types. If you make this a condition for an item, the system attempts to divide the total value by the total quantity.
C	For the base price condition type, this is the most commonly used calculation type. You can maintain the condition records for the currency value by configuring the condition type as calculation type **C**. The condition value will then be calculated by multiplying the quantity specified in the sales order by the currency value from the condition records.
D	This corresponds to the freight condition type. You maintain condition records based on currency value. The condition value is calculated by multiplying the currency value by the line item's total weight.
E	This corresponds to the net weight used in the freight condition type configuration. In case you want to calculate the freight value excluding the packaging material weight, then you can use the calculation type as **E**.
F	To calculate the condition value based on the volume, keep the calculation type set to **F** for the required condition type.
G	If the business requirement is to calculate the condition value based on some custom formula, you can maintain the calculation type as **G**.
H	This calculation type can be used for reverse tax calculations. In retail clients, it's common for sales agents to enter the value into the system, including tax. To separate the tax amount from the net value, configure the tax condition types with the calculation type set to **H**.

Table 5.3 Calculation Types

Calculation Type	Usage
M	The monthly prices must be configured in subscription business scenarios. In this case, you can use the calculation type as **M**. This condition type is used when the line item is relevant to the billing plans. Based on the contract start and end dates specified in the sales order contract data, the system computes the billing plan frequencies. The total condition value for the line item will be calculated by multiplying the number of months in the contract duration by the amount of the one-month price.
N	The preceding logic mentioned for the calculation type holds true for **N** as well. In this case, this price corresponds to the yearly price. The contract start date and end date are mandatory to calculate the yearly price.
O	If you want to calculate the price based on the number of days consumed or used, you can maintain the calculation type set to **O**. The condition value will be calculated by multiplying the number of days specified in the contractual period by the price maintained for the single day.
P	The same logic applies to calculation type **P**; the only difference is that the calculated price is maintained for the week.

Table 5.3 Calculation Types (Cont.)

- **Plus/Minus**
  This field is applicable to the surcharge and discount condition type, that is, the condition type with calculation type as **A**. If the value in the **Plus/Minus** field in condition type (discount) is **X** (negative), the amount will be subtracted from the other reference condition type. If the value in the **Plus/Minus** field is **A** (positive) condition type (surcharge), the amount is added to the other reference condition types.
- **Rounding Rule**
  In the system, the field is linked to the condition value. It determines whether commercial rounding, rounding up, or rounding down is performed. If the condition value is 10.543, for example, the commercial rounding rule will round it to 10.54. If it had been rounded up, the value would have been 10.55, and if it had been rounded down, the value would have been 10.54.
- **Structure Condition**
  This field is used when you're configuring the condition type for a bill of material (BOM) or configurable material. A blank field indicates that the condition type isn't relevant for the accumulation of values in a BOM, nor is it applicable for the distribution of values at the item level. If you maintain the value as **B**, it will help to cumulate the value of components and display it in the main item.

- **Condition Function**
  For accumulating condition values, you can use the *condition function*. The condition function can be used to separate or identify condition types based on business importance. To check the tolerance of the standalone selling price (SSP) range for SSP calculation in revenue accounting and reporting (RAR), you can use the condition function (see Chapter 6 for more information on RAR). Some of the condition functions provided by SAP are standalone (**Mat.**), **Tolerance for Expected Value**, and so on.
- **Dat.Rec.Source**
  This field is used to set the system to leverage the old condition technique to determine the condition records or any other technique to determine the records in the system. This can also be used to configure the system to fetch the condition values from the pricing procedure configured in the SAP Customer Relationship Management (SAP CRM) system.

Next, the **Group Condition** section contains the following fields:

- **Group Condition**
  A discount based on the material group is a very common business requirement across multiple industries. The requirement can be met by configuring the discount condition type with the **Group Condition** checkbox. If you check the group condition, the group condition amount will be distributed among all the line items in proportion to the line item's value. This works based on the group condition routine selected for the condition type.

  The business requirement can have any of the two or both variations:

  - Total document value: If the total document value hits a specific limit, then an automatic discount condition type should be populated, which will reduce the total document value.

    The solution is to configure a condition type with the **Group Condition** checkbox selected. Because the requirement is based on the value and should be applicable to the total document value, you have to select the appropriate scale basis, that is, in the scale basis (**B**) and group condition routine as **1** (total document value). (We'll discuss both fields later in this list.) From the master data side, you have to maintain the condition records with appropriate scales.
  - Particular material group's value: If the discount should be populated only for materials with a specific material group, material pricing group, or any other characteristics, the discount should be applied only to the materials related to that characteristic.

    As a solution, SAP has provided a separate group condition routine **3** (material pricing group). You must select it for the condition type and select the scale basis as **B** (quantity basis). (We'll discuss both fields later in this list.) From the master data side, you have to maintain the condition records with appropriate scales.

- **Group Cond. Routine**
  The group condition routine specifies whether the total document value or group of materials value should be considered. If you want to consider the total document value, leave the group condition routine at **1**. If you want to consider a group of material's values, keep the group condition routine set to **3**.
- **RoundDiffComp**
  If you check the rounding difference comparison, then in scenarios such as while distributing group condition amount among all line items, any left-out amount will be added to the highest value item.

Let's continue to the **Changes which can be made** section, which contains the following fields:

- **Manual Entries**
  This field control whether you can allow the users to change or modify the condition values during the order processing. SAP has given four options to choose from for the manual entry as follows:
  - **A**: There are no limitations, so you can either manually edit it or automatically populate it with the help of condition records or condition routine.
  - **B**: Automatic entry has priority; that is, if the condition records are maintained, then values will be populated through condition records, and you can't edit the conditions manually.
  - **C**: The manual entry takes precedence. When you manually enter the condition, the system doesn't check to see if a condition record exists.
  - **D**: You can't process the condition records manually. You can set this for the condition type where the values are populated with the help of any condition routine.
- **Header Condition**
  By activating the checkbox, you set the condition type as the header condition type. Header conditions are applied to all items in the document and are distributed to them automatically. Header conditions don't have an access sequence and must be processed manually. They can be based on a percentage or an absolute amount. If you enter a percentage-based header condition, the system will automatically apply that percentage to all items in the document. If the header condition is an absolute amount, the system has two options for distributing the amount:
  - The amount is distributed proportionately among the items
  - The amount entered at the header level is duplicated for each item.
- **Item Condition**
  By activating the checkbox, you signify the condition type as an item condition. The item conditions are applicable to the particular line items, and they will have an access sequence assigned to them.

- **Delete**
  You can allow users to delete the condition type from the sales document post activating the deletion checkbox in the condition type.
- **Amount/Percent**
  If the requirement is that for certain condition types end users or customer representative should modify the condition amount or the percentage, then you can achieve the requirement by activating the checkbox.
- **Quantity Relation**
  This field indicates that users can alter the quantity for the condition type. If the checkbox isn't selected, and the sales units or condition units are not the same and differ from the base unit of measure (UoM), then the system carries the quantity conversion twice (for example, from the sales unit to the base unit and then from the base unit to the condition unit).
- **Value**
  If the user wants to manually change the condition value, you can check the **Value** checkbox for the condition type, which will allow the user to change the condition value in relation to the condition type.
- **Calculation Type**
  You can enable this functionality for the condition type of a specific business requirement, such as users wanting to manually edit the calculation type during document processing.

Next, the **Master Data** section contains the following fields:

- **Proposed Valid-From**
  You can default the valid-from date while maintaining the condition records by defaulting the settings in the field. If you leave the field blank, the system will use today's date as the valid date by default. Users can edit the date field while maintaining the condition records.
- **Proposed Valid-To**
  By defaulting the settings in the field, you can set the valid-to date while maintaining the condition records. If you leave the field blank, the system will set the valid-to date to **31.12.9999** as the default end date. Users can make changes to the date field while keeping the condition records.
- **Pricing Procedure**
  This field will be used for the concept of condition supplement. It's essentially the concept of adding a condition record for an existing condition record. The system controls the use of condition supplements in records of this condition type by using the pricing procedure that you enter here. Discounts defined in the pricing procedure can be applied as condition supplements during pricing. If the main condition record is found, the system will find the supplement condition records.

- **Delete from DB**
  This field controls whether you can permanently delete the condition records from the database or mark the condition records with a deletion indicator. SAP has provided three options to choose from:
  - **Do not delete (set the deletion flag only)**: You can configure an indicator to prevent the condition record from being used in pricing. In the archiving run, the condition record is then archived.
  - **With popup**: Users can delete condition records from the database. They will see a popup asking if the condition record should be deleted or if the deletion indicator should simply be set.
  - **Without popup**: Users can delete condition records from the database. They will see a popup message only if condition supplements are available.
- **Ref. Condition Type**
  This is common when configuring the intercompany sales process. We'll cover this process extensively in Section 5.5. You maintain a condition record for PI01 in intercompany sales, and this will be applicable to the IV01 condition type. You don't need to maintain separate condition records for each condition type if you maintain the reference condition type in the field. You only need to maintain the condition record for the reference condition type, and it will apply to all condition types that share the same reference condition type. When users attempt to maintain the condition record for the main condition type, an error message appears informing them that they must maintain the condition records for the reference condition type.
- **Ref. Application**
  A condition technique is condition record maintenance that is also used in other application components of SAP S/4HANA. In certain scenarios, there might be a need to pull the values from the different application components other than sales. For example, to pull the values from the settlement management application component, you can use the value **WR**. In this case, you can use the reference application. This field is used in close collaboration with the reference condition type.
- **Condition Index/Condition Update**
  You can maintain condition records by using condition indexes for specific condition types. Condition indices need to be activated for each condition table. You can activate the condition index for a specific table by going to Transaction SPRO and following menu path **Sales and Distribution • Basic Functions • Pricing • Maintain Condition Index**. You can limit the use of the condition type during sales order processing by combining it with condition update (e.g., per specific sales order or based on total condition value). This option restricts your user's ability to make manual changes to the pricing procedure during sales order entry.

Let's continue with the condition type configuration fields shown in Figure 5.9, starting with the **Scales** section.

Scales
Scale Basis | C Quantity scale | Scale Routine | 0
Check Scale | A Descending | Scale Unit
Scale Type | can be maintained in condition record

Control Data 2
Currency Conversion | Exclusion
Pricing Date | Standard (KOMK-PRSDT; tax and reb...
Accruals
Variant Condition | Rel. for Acct Assigt | Relevant for account assignment
Invoice List Cond.
Quantity Conversion
Intercomp.Billing | ServChgeSettlem
Zero Value Proc.

Text Determination
TextDetermProcedure | Price | Text ID | 0001 Internal comment

Figure 5.9 Condition Type

This is a common requirement for clients in retail space to maintain product prices based on the predetermined slabs. Let's consider the example in Table 5.4.

Quantity	Price
1	$2,000
100	$1,900
200	$1,800
300	$1,700
400	$1,600

Table 5.4 Scales

If the customer places an order for 1 to 99 units, the product price should be $2,000. If the customer orders 100 to 199 units, the product price should be $1,900, and so on. This scale is known as the normal scale.

Let's explore each field in the **Scales** section:

- **Scale Basis**
  The slab that we discussed earlier can be defaulted while maintaining the condition records by selecting the appropriate scale basis in the condition type. You can choose from a variety of options such as quantity scale (**C**), value scale (**B**), or gross weight scale (**D**). It determines the basis on which you'll maintain prices in the condition records.
- **Check Scale**
  You can set the condition type based on how you want to distribute the prices based

on the scale basis, that is, whether the slab price should increase or decrease. The option given by SAP S/4HANA are **Descending (A)** and **Ascending (B)**.

- **Scale Type**
  The field controls the behavior of the scale, that is, if you have to maintain the normal scale or graduated scale.
- **Scale Routine**
  If the users want to calculate the scale value by custom logic, then you can write a code and assign it to the alternate calculation routine in Transaction VOFM.
- **Scale Unit**
  You can maintain the UoM in the field that will be used for condition record maintenance.

Next, the **Control Data 2** section contains the following fields:

- **Currency Conversion**
  This field plays an important role for currency conversion scenarios. The system multiplies the amount resulting from the condition record by the item quantity to calculate a condition value in a document. This indicator determines whether the system performs currency conversion before or after multiplication. If you activate the checkbox, the system multiplies the condition value by the document currency. If you leave the checkbox blank, the system converts the condition value to the document currency before multiplying it.
- **Accruals**
  The accruals accumulation is common in the rebate process; the amount posted as accruals in the invoice will be stored in a general ledger account maintained in the **Account Assignment** setting in Transaction VKOA against the accruals account key. The accumulated amount will be retrieved during settlement, and the amount to be settled will be finalized and settled through the invoice. You can set the condition type for accruals relevant by checking the **Accruals** checkbox.
- **Variant Condition**
  This checkbox indicates that the condition type is used for the variant configuration price setup. The variant configuration functionality is explained in Chapter 8, Section 8.3.
- **Invoice List Cond.**
  The invoice list is where you can send an invoice, debit memo, or credit memo to a payer on a specific date. All billing documents must be assigned to the invoice list using Transaction OVV7. An invoice list must have a factory calendar assigned to it. The factory calendar will determine when the invoice list must be created. When you select this checkbox, the condition type will be populated in the invoice list billing document.
- **Quantity Conversion**
  Quantity conversion is only relevant for condition types with calculation type **C**. It's

applied if the sales quantity unit and the quantity unit maintained in the condition records are the same and those differ from the stock quantity unit or base unit maintained in the material master. If you activate the **Quantity Conversion** checkbox and the sales quantity unit and condition quantity unit are identical, the document item quantity is used during sales order processing. If the checkbox isn't selected, then the condition basis quantity is converted to the stock keeping unit (SKU) via the quantities of the SKU. Any changes to the conversion factors in the delivery or order are ignored during quantity conversion.

- **Intercomp. Billing**
  If a specific condition type is configured for intercompany billing, then you can check the checkbox for intercompany billing for that specific condition type. You use standard condition type IV01 and PI01 for the intercompany sales process.
- **Exclusion**
  This field plays an important role in the condition exclusion configuration. If you maintain the condition type with the **Exclusion** group as **X**, then all the conditions that have the same condition routine assigned as **2** will be excluded from the sales order pricing. **Exclusion** can be maintained at the condition type configuration level, or it can be maintained at the condition record maintenance level in Transaction VK11.
- **Pricing Date**
  Pricing condition records are accessed or searched based on the pricing date. You can default the pricing date on the sales order in two ways:
  - Document type configurations (Transaction VOV8): While defining the sales document type, you can default the pricing date with the field proposal for the pricing date, which will cause a pricing date to be determined on the header level, and it will be applicable across all the line items.
  - Condition type configuration (Transaction V/06): SAP has provided several options to choose from, as shown in Table 5.5. Based on the business requirements for the condition type, you can default the option and determine the pricing date for the condition type. For example, if you want the pricing date the same as the order creation date in the sales document, then you have to maintain option **E** in the **Pricing Date** field of the condition type configuration.

Option	Dates
Blank	Standard tax and rebate
A	Date of services rendered
B	Price date
C	Billing date

Table 5.5 Pricing Date Options

Option	Dates
D	Creation date
E	Order date

Table 5.5 Pricing Date Options (Cont.)

Note

If the pricing date logic isn't fulfilled in these two ways, you also have an option to enhance the SAP code through user exit MV45AFZZ from USEREXIT_MOVE_FIELD_TO_VBKD to update field VBKD-PRSDT (**Pricing Date**).

- **Rel. for Acct Assigt**
  This checkbox is used for the account determination, that is, to automatically determine the general ledger account for the values in the condition type. If you leave this field blank, then account determination takes place as standard account determination configured in Transaction VKOA. However, if you maintain the value **B** (**Account assignment with accounting indicator**), then the system also includes the accounting indicator while determining the general ledger accounts. This is commonly used when you want to book the cost against any of the accounts.
- **ServChgeSettlem**
  You check the condition type for the service charge settlement in the business scenario where the source document is trading contracts. By marking the checkbox, you limit the condition types to those that are only relevant for service settlement.
- **Zero Value Proc.**
  You can use this indicator to control how conditions with values equal to zero are handled. If you leave this field empty, the following will happen: When a condition's value is zero, it's ignored by the condition exclusion logic. If the amount and value of the price conditions are both zero, they are deactivated during the price calculation.

  If you set this indicator's value to **A** for this condition type, then even if their value is zero, conditions of this type will be considered in the exclusion logic. If this is a condition type with the condition class **Price**, conditions of this type won't be deactivated during the price calculation.

Pricing Procedure

The *pricing procedure* plays a crucial role in the condition technique. It acts like a schema to hold all the condition types in the sequential manner. You can configure the pricing procedure by following menu path **Sales and Distribution • Basic Functions • Pricing • Pricing Control • Define and Assign Pricing Procedures • Set Pricing Procedures.**

Alternatively, you can also use Transaction V/08. You'll arrive at the screen shown in Figure 5.10, where you can create your own pricing procedure by clicking on the **New Entries** button. After which, you select the pricing procedure (**Proc...**) and click on the **Procedures – Control** folder to arrive at the screen in Figure 5.11. Here, the standard pricing procedure **RVAA01** is used.

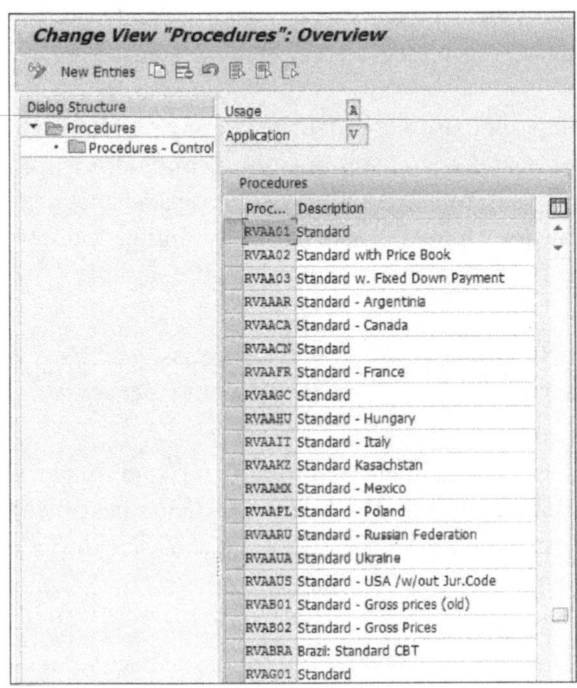

Figure 5.10 Pricing Procedure: Initial Screen

Display View "Procedures - Control Data": Overview

Dialog Structure
- Procedures
  - Procedures - Control

Procedure RVAA01 Standard

Procedures - Control Data

Reference Step Overview

Step	Co...	Co...	Description	Fro...	To ...	Ma...	R...	St...	Rel...	Print T...	Subtotal	Requir...	Alt. Ca...	Alt. Cn...	Accou...	Accruals
905	0	BO05	Hierarchy rebate/mat	400			☐	☐	☐			24			ERB	ERU
908	0		Net Value 3	0	0	☐	☐	☐	☐			0	0	0		
909	0	PI02	Inter-company %	0	0	☐	☐	☑	☐		B	22	0	0	ERL	
910	0	PI01	Inter-company Price	0	0	☐	☐	☑	☐		B	22	0	0	ERL	
914	0	SKTV	Cash Discount	0	0	☐	☐	☑	☐		D	14	0	2		
915	0	MWST	Output Tax	0	0	☐	☐	☐	☐	S		10	0	16	MWS	
919	0	DIFF	Rounding Off	0	0	☐	☑	☐	☐			13	16	4	ERS	
920	0		Total	0	0	☐	☐	☐	☐		A	0	4	0		
930	0	SKTO	Cash Discount	0	0	☑	☐	☐	☐			9	0	11		
932	0	RL00	Factoring Discount	0	0	☐	☐	☑	☐			23	0	2	ERS	
933	0	MW15	Factoring Disc. Tax	932	0	☐	☐	☑	☐			21	0	0	MWS	
935	0	GRWR	Statistical value	0	0	☐	☐	☑	☐		C	8	0	2		
940	0	VPRS	Internal price	0	0	☐	☐	☑	☐		B	4	0	0		
941	0	EK02	Calculated costs	0	0	☑	☐	☑	☐		B	0	0	0		
942	0	EK03	Calculated ship.cost	0	0	☑	☐	☑	☐			0	0	0		
950	0		Profit Margin	0	0	☐	☐	☐	☐			0	11	0		

Figure 5.11 Pricing Procedure

Let's take a closer look at each field for the pricing procedure:

- **Step**
  The sequence of condition types in the pricing procedure will be specified by step number. It's a three-digit number used to define the sequence of conditions within the pricing procedure. It's always best to leave a space between two numbers when configuring steps to allow for the addition of an intermediate step later if necessary. Step numbers will also be used in **From** and **To** fields to calculate the base value.
- **Co... (Counter)**
  If there is no space between two steps, you use a counter to add one or more condition types. It's a two-digit access number used to define a series of conditions within a single-step number. During pricing determination, the system considers both the step number and the counter. If you don't have a specific need for multiple counters within a step, leave the field blank. The counter will be set to **0** by the system.
- **Co... (Component)**
  The condition types that you've defined in the earlier section are assigned here. It specifies the type of pricing component, such as base price, taxes, or surcharge.
- **Description**
  The description will be auto-populated using the description of the condition type from Transaction V/06. The **Description** field can also be used to divide the pricing procedure into sections such as gross value, net value, and total. If you leave the field empty, the pricing procedure line will function as the subtotal.
- **Fro.../To...**
  The pricing procedure uses the value fields to calculate the condition base value. A **From** field is referred to as a standard base. It will aid in determining the starting point for calculating the condition type value in sales document pricing. The **To** field is used to add the values of multiple sequential steps. If you leave the **From** and **To** value fields blank, the system will use the immediate preceding value.
- **Ma... (Manual)**
  The **Manual** checkbox indicates whether or not the specific condition type can be determined manually during sales order processing. If you check the field, the entry will be manual; if you uncheck it, the entry will be automatic. Even if the condition records for the condition type are maintained, if you check the checkbox, it won't appear in the sales order. It will appear once you manually enter the condition type in the sales order. The condition type configuration setting affects the **Manual** checkbox. If the condition type is set as manual entry **D** (not possible to process manually), it will take precedence and won't allow you to enter the condition manually in the sales order because the condition is blocked for manual entries.
- **R... (Required)**
  The **Required** checkbox indicates that the condition type is required for the pricing procedure. If the condition type isn't present in the sales order pricing procedure,

the system won't allow users to save the order. If the condition type is checked with the **Required** checkbox, the value for the condition type must be maintained or the system won't allow the users to process the document. Tax condition types are mostly set as required in the pricing procedure.

- **St... (Statistical)**
  The **Statistical** checkbox is used to indicate the condition type that will be used for statistical purposes. If the checkbox is marked as statistical, it won't be considered for account determination. As a result, there is no need to assign an account key to such a condition type. It's commonly used for the VPRS and SKTO condition types. In standard SAP, the pricing dividing steps are also marked as a statistical condition.
- **Rel... (Relevant)**
  This field determines whether the condition type is relevant for account determination. Specifically, it determines whether or not the values associated with the condition type should be posted to accounting.
- **Print T...**
  This field determines whether or not the condition type is printed in the output printout. If you don't want to print, you should leave the field blank. If you want to print, keep either **X** or **S**. If you want to print at the item level, you use **X**. If you want to print at the header level, use **S**. For all header conditions, set the field as **S**. This only applies to the standard output condition type BA00. You can build user-specific logic to print the outputs for any custom development for print programs.
- **Subtotal**
  Subtotal is an alphanumeric single-character field used to store the condition type's value in some temporary tables and fields for later calculation. You can compute condition values using an alternate calculation type and an alternate base type. The field's value determines where the field's value should be captured. If you use the same field to store different condition amounts, the system will add up all the individual amounts. **Subtotal** will also be used to update the credit management value of the sales document by using option **A**. The subtotal will also be used to update the billing document's value in the rebate agreement by using the **Subtotal 7**. It's used to store statistical condition values such as VPRS with a **Subtotal B**.
- **Requir... (Requirement)**
  This is ABAP code from Transaction VOFM. You assign a code to a specific number and enter it in the **Requirement** field. A requirement is a condition that the system checks every time the condition type in a sales document is determined. If the condition is met, the sales document will include the condition type. This enables you to perform additional validation before executing a specific condition type. SAP has provided some standard requirement conditions that you can leverage as listed in Table 5.6.

Requirement	Description/Uses
2	Verifies that the **Pricing** field in the item category is set to **X** or **B**.
4	Verifies that the **Determine Cost** field in the item category is checked.
9	Verifies that the **Cash Discount** field in the material master **Accounting 1** view is checked.
22	For intercompany billing condition type PI01, you assign the routine, and it checks that the ordering company and delivery company should be different.
24	You deploy the requirement in the rebate conditions. It checks to ensure that the document is a billing document, so the rebate conditions are applied on the billing documents.

Table 5.6 Standard Pricing Requirements

- **Alt. Ca... (Alternate Calculation)**
  You must assign an ABAP code to the condition type in the pricing procedure if the calculation logic of the condition type is based on a custom requirement. Based on the business requirements, ABAP consultants use Transaction VOFM to create any custom routine. If you need to calculate the value of the condition type based on custom logic rather than condition records, you use the alternate calculation type in this field. The condition type routine will compute the condition type's total value. You don't need to maintain condition records for the condition type that has the alternate calculation type routine assigned to it.
- **Alt. Cn... (Alternate Base Value)**
  The alternate base value is the pricing routine created by the ABAP consultant in Transaction VOFM. In most cases, the base value of the condition type is taken from the **From** field in the pricing procedure. However, if the business requirement is to calculate the base value of the condition using a custom formula, you assign the base condition routine in the **Pricing Procedure** field. Unlike the alternate calculation routine, where you don't need to keep the condition record for the condition type for the alternate base value, you must maintain the condition records for the alternate base value to convert the base value into the condition value. For example, for freight-related condition types where the value is calculated based on the material's gross weight and volume, you use the alternate base value to calculate the base value from which the freight value is calculated.
- **Accou... (Account Key)**
  The account key is one of the integration points that link the invoice values to the finance functionality. When posting invoice values into accounting, it's one of the parameters used to determine the revenue general ledger accounts. If the condition type isn't statistical, you must maintain it along with the account key. If the account

key isn't maintained, the values won't be passed to accounting. In rebate condition types where both the account key and the statistical field are checked, the **Statistical** field will take precedence over the accounting key. In this case, the values of the condition type won't be recorded in accounting. For more details on the account key, see Section 5.2.2.

- **Accruals**
  The accruals key is used to post amounts into accrual accounts instead of revenue accounts. It will track all earnings and expenses whenever a sale or transaction occurs, whether or not it's paid.

The pricing procedure that you've configured must be assigned in the configuration for it to be determined automatically in the sales documents. To assign the pricing procedure, follow menu path **Sales and Distribution • Basic Functions • Pricing • Pricing Control • Define and Assign Pricing Procedures • Set Pricing Procedure Determination.** Alternatively, you can also use Transaction OVKK to land on the same configuration, as shown in Figure 5.12. Click the **New Entries** button to determine the pricing procedure.

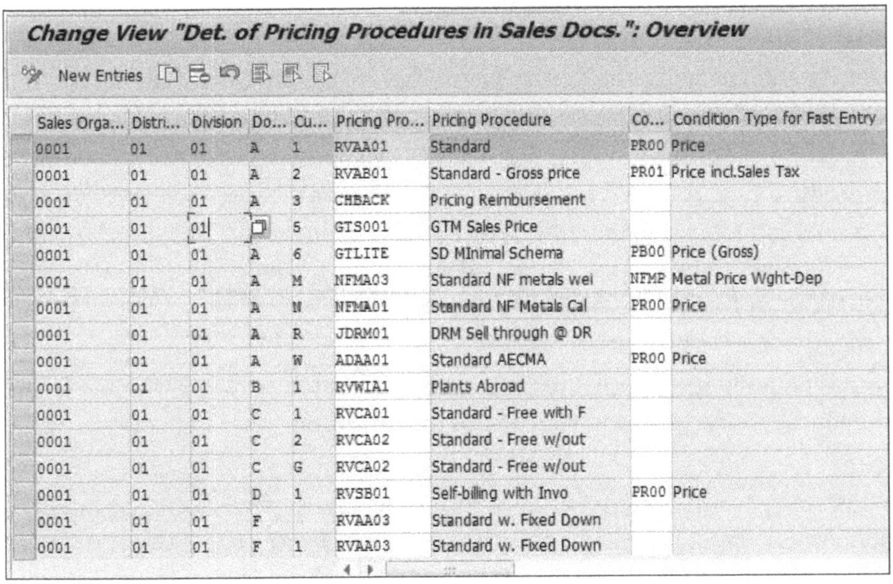

Change View "Det. of Pricing Procedures in Sales Docs.": Overview

New Entries

Sales Orga...	Distri...	Division	Do...	Cu...	Pricing Pro...	Pricing Procedure	Co...	Condition Type for Fast Entry
0001	01	01	A	1	RVAA01	Standard	PR00	Price
0001	01	01	A	2	RVAB01	Standard - Gross price	PR01	Price incl.Sales Tax
0001	01	01	A	3	CHBACK	Pricing Reimbursement		
0001	01	01		5	GTS001	GTM Sales Price		
0001	01	01	A	6	GTLITE	SD MInimal Schema	PB00	Price (Gross)
0001	01	01	A	M	NFMA03	Standard NF metals wei	NFMP	Metal Price Wght-Dep
0001	01	01	A	N	NFMA01	Standard NF Metals Cal	PR00	Price
0001	01	01	A	R	JDRM01	DRM Sell through @ DR		
0001	01	01	A	W	ADAA01	Standard AECMA	PR00	Price
0001	01	01	B	1	RVWIA1	Plants Abroad		
0001	01	01	C	1	RVCA01	Standard - Free with F		
0001	01	01	C	2	RVCA02	Standard - Free w/out		
0001	01	01	C	G	RVCA02	Standard - Free w/out		
0001	01	01	D	1	RVSB01	Self-billing with Invo	PR00	Price
0001	01	01	F		RVAA03	Standard w. Fixed Down		
0001	01	01	F	1	RVAA03	Standard w. Fixed Down		

Figure 5.12 Pricing Procedure Determination

Fill in the sales organization (**Sales Orga...**), distribution channel (**Distri...**), and **Division**, along with document pricing procedure (**Do...**) and customer pricing procedure (**Cu...**).

Let's explore the origin of the following mentioned fields in the sales document:

- **Cu...**
  The customer pricing procedure data will come from the customer master sales area data.

- **Do...**
  The document pricing procedure is assigned to the sales document type in Transaction VOV8.

The condition type (**Co...**) field is optional and can be left blank. If you assign a condition type, the system will automatically display a value associated with it at the sales order line-item level. This allows users to view the condition type value without having to go into the line item's **Conditions** tab. To process transactions, use the scroll bar to move to the right of the line item. If the field is left blank, the system will display the current price condition's value.

5.1.2 Taxation

Taxation is tightly linked to the sales process because accounts receivable triggers the accounts receivable taxes by sales document. In this section, we'll look at how taxes are configured in the SAP S/4HANA system.

Taxation involves the following key concepts:

- **Tax classification**
  Tax classification is determined by the customer master and the material master, while *tax jurisdiction* is determined by the plant and the business partner. The country is determined by the location of the delivery plant.
- **Tax procedure**
  The tax configuration is maintained based on the country that delivers the plant. Based on local tax compliances, SAP provides a sample tax procedure for each country. The tax procedure is assigned to the country.
- **Tax category**
  The same condition technique is used to configure the tax pricing procedure in the finance functionality. However, you refer to the condition type as a tax category.
- **Tax rates**
  Tax rates can be maintained in SAP S/4HANA using Transaction FTXP. The rates are maintained for the country, tax code, and tax jurisdiction code. General ledger accounts are maintained using Transaction OB40, which is determined by the account key assigned in the sales and distribution pricing procedure against the tax condition type.
- **Tax codes**
  The tax is calculated using the tax code and the tax procedure. The tax codes are derived from the condition records maintained in the VK11 condition record.

To summarize the tax flow, as shown in Figure 5.13, the condition record pushes the tax code, and the tax rates are fetched from the tax code, along with the country and jurisdiction code, and fetched from Transaction FTXP for the relevant account key and condition type maintained in the sales and distribution pricing procedure. Transaction OB40 for the relevant account key is used to determine the general ledger accounts.

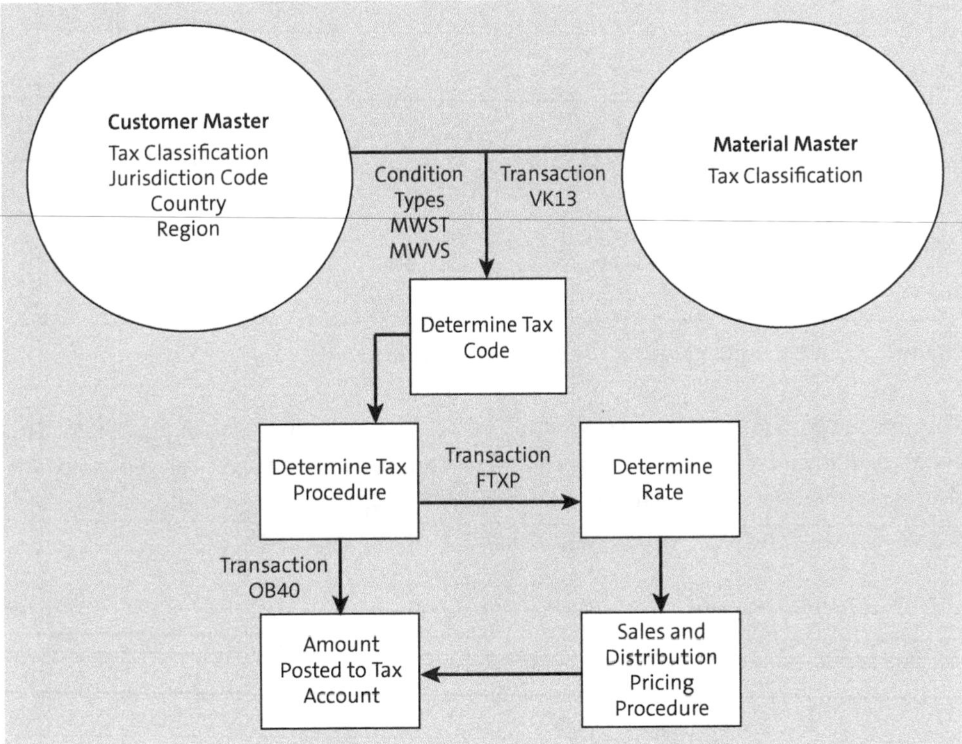

Figure 5.13 Tax Calculation

We'll walk through the key configuration activities in the following sections.

Tax Determination Procedure

The tax determination is based on the condition technique. The tax category is simply the tax condition type, such as MWST/MWVS, that you use in the pricing procedure. In the finance functionality, this is known as a *tax category*. A tax category should be assigned to a specific country, and then it can be used in the customer or material master.

To create the tax category, you have to follow menu path **Financial Accounting • Financial Accounting Global Settings • Tax on Sales/Purchases • Basic Settings • Check Calculation Procedure.**

As you click on the **Check Calculation Procedure**, you get the following three options, as shown in Figure 5.14, which you need to follow to configure the tax pricing procedure: **Access Sequences**, **Define Condition Types**, and **Define Procedures**.

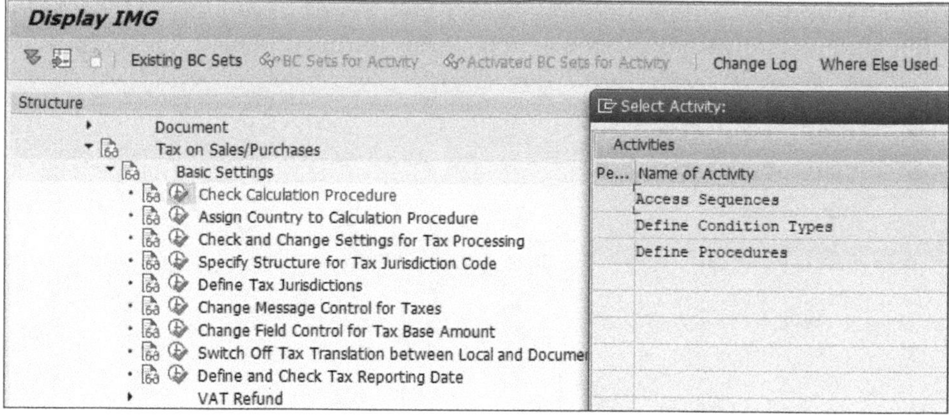

Figure 5.14 Configuration Steps for Tax Pricing Procedure

You first have to create the access sequence based on the business requirement. This access sequence can also be created in Transaction V/07 as the sales-related tax condition types must be assigned in the sales and distribution pricing procedure. After clicking on **Access Sequences**, you get the screen shown in Figure 5.15.

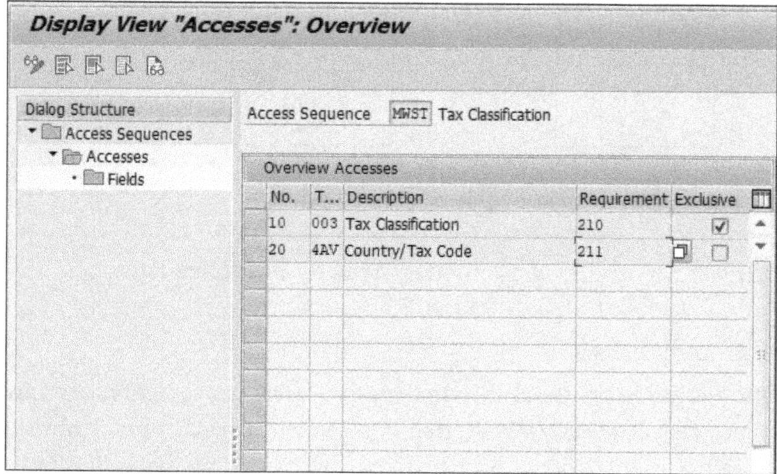

Figure 5.15 Access Sequence MWST

The screen elements are the same as discussed in Section 5.1.1 for pricing, so you can follow the same workflow and steps to configure the access sequence for taxation.

After creation of the access sequence, you have to create the tax condition type and assign the access sequence in the condition type. You can click on **Define Condition Types** and the screen shown in Figure 5.16 will appear.

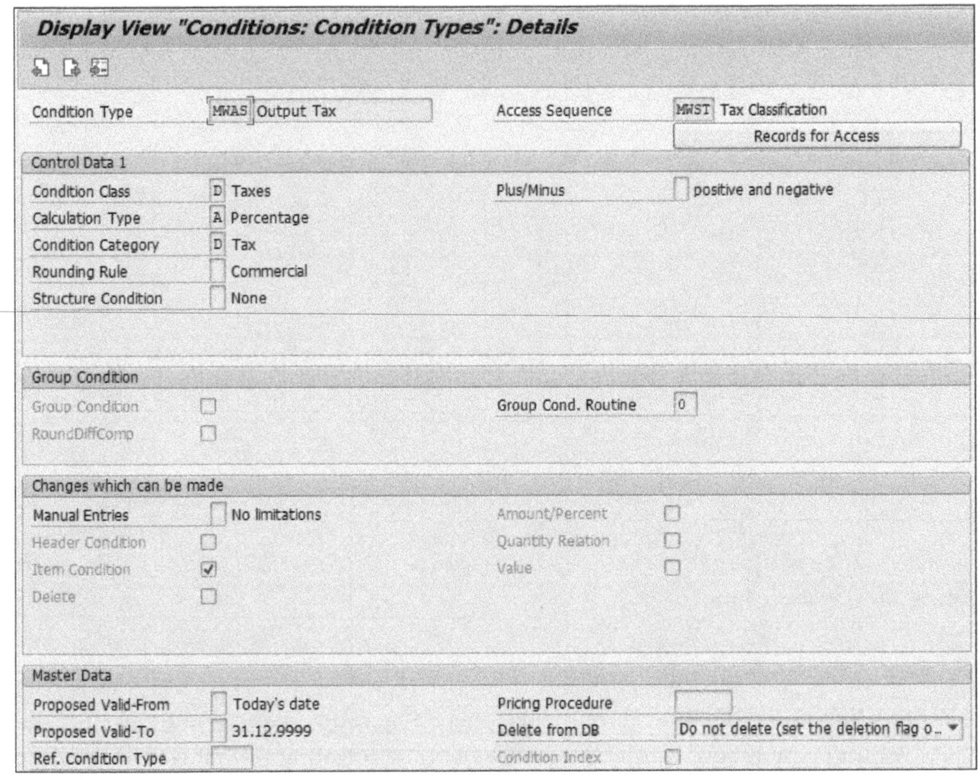

Figure 5.16 Condition Type MWAS

The condition type fields are the same as discussed in Section 5.1.1 for pricing, so you can follow the same workflow. Remember that any condition type that you're creating for the tax procedure should have **Condition Class** as **D**.

The next step in the tax setup is the creation of the tax pricing procedure. You can copy the standard tax procedure provided by SAP to create a new tax procedure, or you can enhance the standard tax procedure to include the custom condition type if created to address the business requirement. After double-clicking **Define Procedure**, you get the various tax procedures out of which you can choose the tax procedure to copy or enhance from, as shown in Figure 5.17.

The fields in the tax procedure are the same as those in the pricing procedure (refer to Section 5.1.1). The **Accou...** (**Account Key**) column is a link between the tax procedure and the general ledger accounts where tax data is to be posted. This aids in the automatic assignment of tax accounts.

Display View "Control Data": Overview

Dialog Structure
- Procedures
  - Control Data

Procedure TAXUSJ Sales Tax USA w. Jurisdictions

Control Data

Reference Step Overview

Step	Co...	Co...	Description	Fro...	To ...	Ma...	R...	St...	Print T...	Subtotal	Requir...	Alt. Ca...	Alt. Cn...	Accou...	Accruals
100	0	BASB	Base Amount	0	0	☐	☐	☐			0	0	0		
120	0		Subtotal	0	0	☐	☐	☑			0	0	0		
200	0		Distributed to G/L	100	110	☐	☐	☑			0	0	0		
210	0	JP1I	A/P Sales Tax 1 Inv.	120	0	☐	☐	☐			0	0	0	NVV	
220	0	JP2I	A/P Sales Tax 2 Inv.	120	0	☐	☐	☐			0	0	0	NVV	
230	0	JP3I	A/P Sales Tax 3 Inv.	120	0	☐	☐	☐			0	0	0	NVV	
240	0	JP4I	A/P Sales Tax 4 Inv.	120	0	☐	☐	☐			0	0	0	NVV	
300	0		Expensed	0	0	☐	☐	☑			0	0	0		
310	0	JP1E	A/P Sales Tax 1 Exp.	120	0	☐	☐	☐			0	0	0	VS1	
320	0	JP2E	A/P Sales Tax 2 Exp.	120	0	☐	☐	☐			0	0	0	VS2	
330	0	JP3E	A/P Sales Tax 3 Exp.	120	0	☐	☐	☐			0	0	0	VS3	
340	0	JP4E	A/P Sales Tax 4 Exp.	120	0	☐	☐	☐			0	0	0	VS4	
400	0		Self-assessment	0	0	☐	☐	☑			0	0	0		
410	0	JP1U	A/P Sales Tax 1 Use	210	0	☐	☐	☐			0	0	0	MW1	
420	0	JP2U	A/P Sales Tax 2 Use	220	0	☐	☐	☐			0	0	0	MW2	
430	0	JP3U	A/P Sales Tax 3 Use	230	0	☐	☐	☐			0	0	0	MW3	

Figure 5.17 Tax Procedure

Assign Tax Determination Procedure to the Country Code

After creation of the tax procedures, you have to assign the tax procedure to the individual country by following menu path **Financial Accounting • Financial Accounting Global Settings • Tax on Sales/Purchases • Basic Settings • Assign Country to Calculation Procedure**. You'll arrive at the screen shown in Figure 5.18, where you can make the assignment of country to calculation procedure by assigning the procedure (**Proc.**) to the country key (**Ctr**).

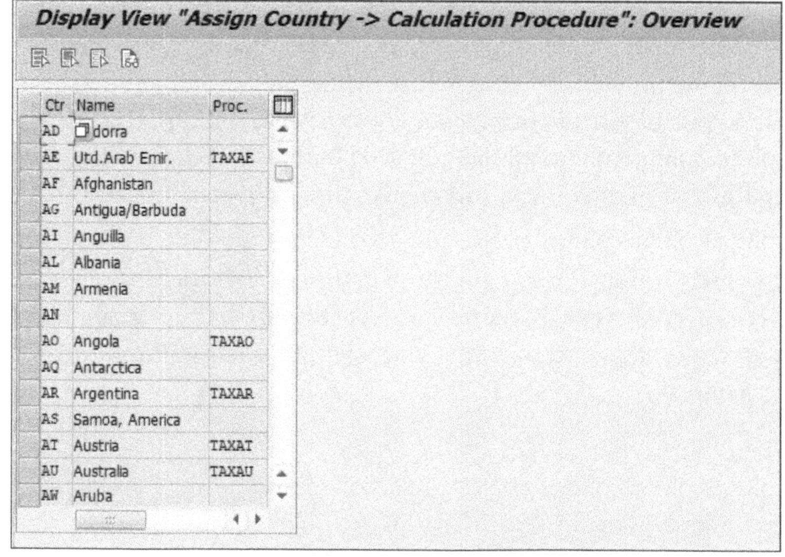

Display View "Assign Country -> Calculation Procedure": Overview

Ctr	Name	Proc.
AD	Andorra	
AE	Utd.Arab Emir.	TAXAE
AF	Afghanistan	
AG	Antigua/Barbuda	
AI	Anguilla	
AL	Albania	
AM	Armenia	
AN		
AO	Angola	TAXAO
AQ	Antarctica	
AR	Argentina	TAXAR
AS	Samoa, America	
AT	Austria	TAXAT
AU	Australia	TAXAU
AW	Aruba	

Figure 5.18 Assign Country to Calculation Procedure

In the sales and distribution side of configuration, you have to assign the tax category or tax condition type to the country by following menu path **Sales and Distribution • Basic Functions • Taxes • Define Tax Determination Rules**. You can also use Transaction OVK1 for the same. As shown in Figure 5.19, tax determination rules can be configured by clicking on the **New Entries** button and assigning **Tax count.** with **Tax Categ.**

Change View "Taxes: Tax Categories by Country": Overview

New Entries

Tax count.	Name	Seq.	Tax Categ.	Name
IN	India	0	MWST	Output Tax

Figure 5.19 Define Tax Determination Rules

Regional taxation exists in some countries. As a result, it's critical to define all cities or county regions within the country. Divide the county and region entries into country codes based on the applicable criteria. You can perform regional bifurcation by following menu path **Sales and Distribution • Basic Functions • Taxes • Define Regional Codes**.

Figure 5.20 shows the regional codes classification in the tax procedure. Here, you have to assign the county code (**Cnty Code**) to the combination of **Country** and **Region**.

Display View "County": Overview

Country	Region	Cnty Code	Description
US	NV	001	County in NV
US	NY	001	County in NY
US	OH	001	County in OH
US	OK	001	County in OK
US	OR	001	County in OR
US	PA	001	County in PA
US	PR	001	County in PR
US	RI	001	County in RI
US	SC	001	County in SC
US	SD	001	County in SD
US	TN	001	County in TN
US	TX	001	County in TX
US	UT	001	County in UT
US	VA	001	County in VA
US	VI	001	County in VI
US	VT	001	County in VT

Figure 5.20 Define Regional Codes

Tax Jurisdiction

In the United States, different areas have their own tax authority, which determines the tax percentage in that area. As a result, the tax percentage applicable to a business transaction is determined by the transaction's classification. In SAP, the requirement is achieved by utilizing the *tax jurisdiction code* concept. Each taxing authority is defined as a tax jurisdiction code.

Business users should be able to identify the area by looking at the tax jurisdiction code because the purpose of the tax jurisdiction code is to identify the exact area or the tax authority involved in a business transaction. The tax jurisdiction code consists of codes for the state, county, city, and district. Prior to creating a tax jurisdiction code, you must define the tax jurisdiction structure. Tax percentages are maintained against tax condition types using a combination of tax code and tax jurisdiction code. Tax jurisdiction codes are maintained in vendor masters, customer masters, internal order masters, cost center masters, and profit center masters.

You can define the tax jurisdiction by navigating to menu path **Financial Accounting • Financial Accounting Global Settings • Tax on Sales/Purchases • Basic Settings • Define Tax Jurisdictions.** After executing this path, you'll arrive at the screen shown in Figure 5.21, where you must enter the **Costing Sheet**, which is the tax procedure configured for the country. In this example, the values are maintained for costing sheet **TAXUSJ**. After entering the **Costing Sheet** value, click on the green check to arrive at the screen shown in Figure 5.22.

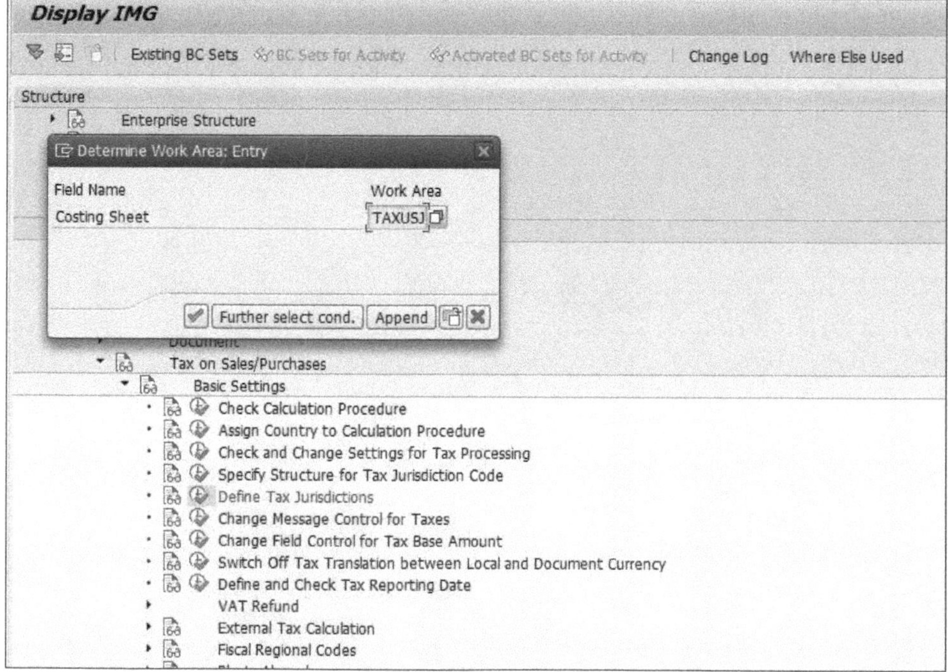

Figure 5.21 Tax Jurisdiction: Initial Screen

Figure 5.22 shows the tax jurisdictions for **TAXUSJ**.

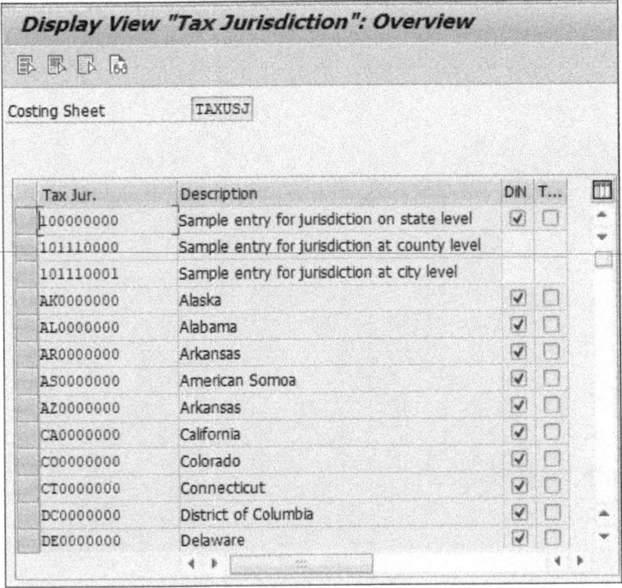

Figure 5.22 Tax Jurisdiction

You can maintain tax codes and their rates in Transaction FTXP. After executing this transaction, you'll arrive at the screen shown in Figure 5.23, where you'll input the **Country Key** and **Tax Code** and then press Enter.

Figure 5.23 Maintain Tax Code

Next, the popup in Figure 5.24 will appear to input the **Tax type**. Here, you can maintain tax type as **A** for output tax and **V** for input tax. Click the green checkmark to arrive at the screen shown in Figure 5.25.

You can maintain the tax rates in the **Tax Percent. Rate** column with the combination of **Tax Type**, **Acct Key**, and **Cond. Type**.

Maintain Tax Code: Initial Screen

Copy

Country Key	US	USA
Tax Code	A0	

Properties

Tax Code	A0
Tax type	☑
CheckID	☐
EU Code / Code	
Target tax code	
Tol.per.rate	
Relevant to tax	
Tax category	
Product code	

Figure 5.24 Maintain Tax Code

Maintain Tax Code: Tax Rates

Properties Tax accounts Deactivate line

Country Key	US	USA
Tax Code	A0	
Procedure	TAXUSX	
Tax type	A	Output tax

Percentage rates

Tax Type	Acct Key	Tax Percent. Rate	Level	From Lvl	Cond. Type
Base Amount			100	0	BASB
Calculated Call			105	0	
Shared with G/L			200	0	
A/P Sales Tax 1 Inv.	NVV		210	100	XP1I
A/P Sales Tax 2 Inv.	NVV		220	100	XP2I
A/P Sales Tax 3 Inv.	NVV		230	100	XP3I
A/P Sales Tax 4 Inv.	NVV		240	100	XP4I
A/P Sales Tax 5 Inv.	NVV		250	100	XP5I
A/P Sales Tax 6 Inv.	NVV		260	100	XP6I
Expensed			300	0	
A/P Sales Tax 1 Exp.	VS1		310	100	XP1E
A/P Sales Tax 2 Exp.	VS2		320	100	XP2E
A/P Sales Tax 3 Exp.	VS3		330	100	XP3E
A/P Sales Tax 4 Exp.	VS4		340	100	XP4E
A/P Sales Tax 5 Exp	VS4		350	100	XP5E
A/P Sales Tax 6 Exp	VS4		360	100	XP6E
Self-assessment			400	0	
A/P Sales Tax 1 Use	MW1		410	210	XP1U
A/P Sales Tax 2 Use	MW2		420	220	XP2U
A/P Sales Tax 3 Use	MW3		430	230	XP3U
A/P Sales Tax 4 Use	MW4		440	240	XP4U

Figure 5.25 Maintain Tax Code: Tax Rates

Prerequisites for Taxation

We've discussed configuration and setup of the tax determination procedure in the previous section. Now let's explore the prerequisites for taxation.

After the configuration of taxation, you must assign the tax category in the business partner and material master data. The tax category is used to determine the taxes in the sales document. Let's walk through the assignment process:

- **Business partner**
  To assign the tax category to the business partner, enter Transaction BP, and select the **Customer** role in the **Display in BP role** field. Click on the **Sales and Distribution** button to display the **Sales Area** data. On this screen, choose the **Billing** tab, and under the **Output Tax** section, you have to assign the tax category, as shown in Figure 5.26.

  You can maintain multiple countries in this section and assign the tax category along with the tax classification, which implies the tax liability for the customer based on the customer country. Tax classification **1** specifies that the customer is liable for taxes; however, tax classification **2** specifies that the customer is exempted from taxes.

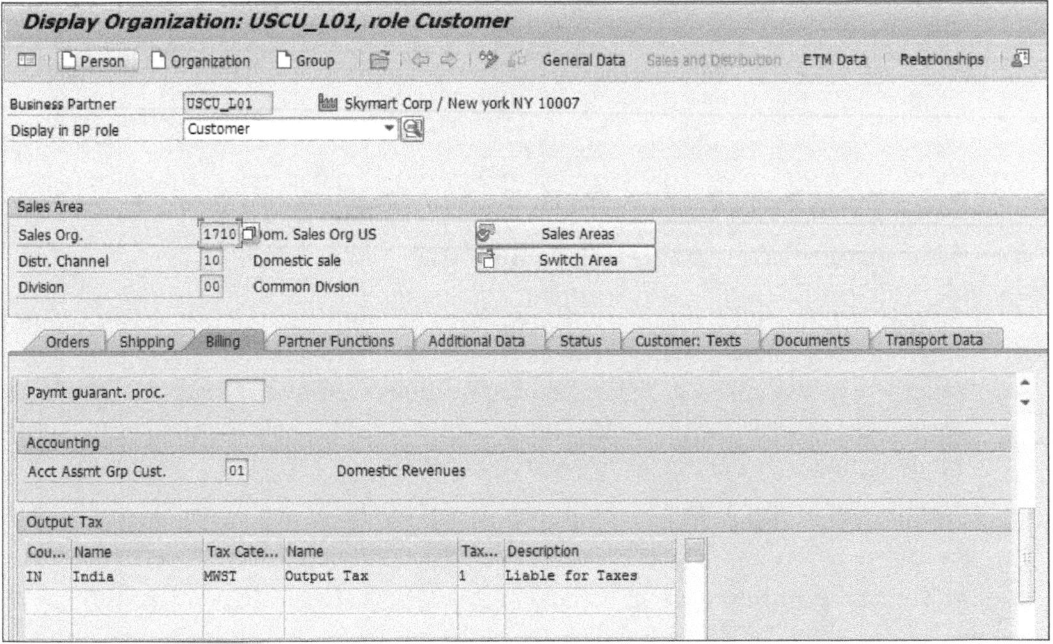

Figure 5.26 Business Partner: Tax Category

- **Material master**
  In the material master record in Transaction MM02, the tax category is assigned in the **Sales: sales org. 1** view under the **Tax data** section, as shown in Figure 5.27.

Similar to business partners, you can assign multiple countries to a **Tax Category** in the material master along with a **Tax Classification**, which determines whether the material is liable for full tax or no tax. Tax classification **1** specifies full tax; however, tax classification **0** specifies no tax.

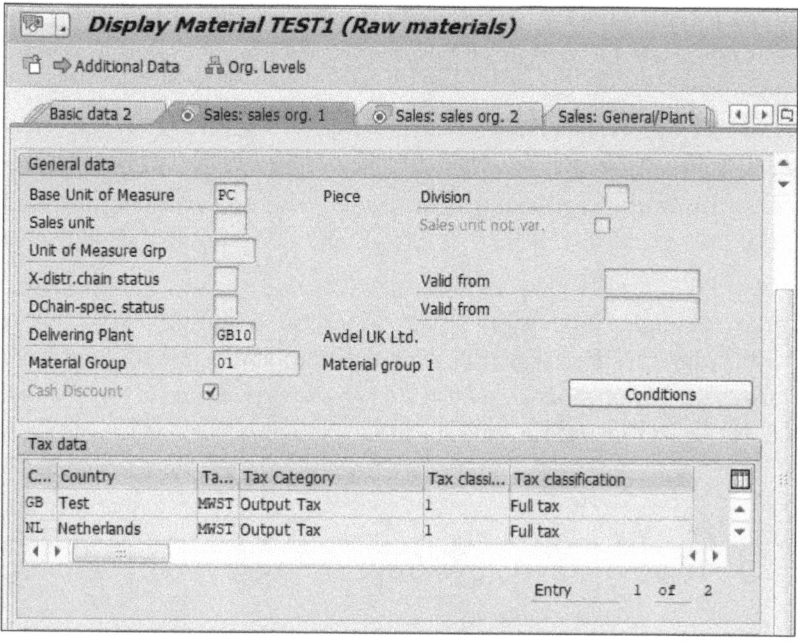

Figure 5.27 Material Master: Tax Category

5.2 Account Determination in Billing

Account determination is a search strategy used to identify the general ledger account when posting billing documents to accounting subledgers. It's a critical integration point where sales and distribution condition amounts are transferred to the financial accounting general ledger. The account determination also follows the condition technique approach to identify the revenue accounts.

The account determination that happens when the billing document is created has two parts:

- The customer subledger account determination (aka reconciliation account)
- The revenue accounts determination for sales revenue, discount, freight, and so on

The revenue account is determined by Transaction VKOA settings. The reconciliation account in the business partner master data is used to determine the customer subledger. However, you can also use the condition technique to determine the reconciliation account. We only discuss revenue account determination in this section, but reconciliation account determination follows the same condition technique process that we covered in Section 5.1.1. The revenue account determination condition technique consists of the following major steps:

1. The first step is to set up the condition tables. Based on the business requirements, fields from the field catalog are added, and condition tables are created.
2. These condition tables, which you created in the previous step, must be assigned in the access sequence from most specific to most general. SAP provides the standard access sequences KOFI and KOFK. You primarily use KOFI for financial posting without any cost object. You can use the access sequence KOFK to use the account assignment object while posting revenue accounts.
3. The access sequence must then be assigned to the account determination type.
4. The next-to-last step in the account determination process is to create the account determination procedure and assign it an account determination type.
5. The procedure is then assigned to the billing document type as the final step. The billing document type determines the account determination procedure.

Let's explore the configuration for account determination in the following sections step by step.

5.2.1 Account Assignment Groups

In the first step, you have to define the account assignment groups for the customer master and material master. Once they are defined, you can assign them in the customer master and material master record.

The account assignment group in the material master is used to group the materials to post the revenue for that group of materials into one general ledger account. For example, the revenue generated from finished goods should be posted to a different general ledger account than that of semifinished goods.

To define the account assignment groups of material master data, navigate to menu path **Sales and Distribution • Basic Functions • Account Assignment/Costing • Revenue Account Determination • Check Master Data Relevant for Account Assignment • Materials: Account Assignment Groups**. After executing the given path, you can create the account assignment group of material by clicking on the **New Entries** button. Figure 5.28 shows the account assignment groups of material. Click the **Save** button or press [Ctrl]+[S] when you're done.

Once the account assignment group of material is defined, you should assign it in the material master by navigating to Transaction MM02, selecting the **Sales: sales org. 2** view, and maintaining the value in the **Acct Assmt Grp Mat.** field, as shown in Figure 5.29.

Change View "Materials: Account Assignment Groups": Overview

New Entries

Acct Assmt Grp Mat.	Description
01	Trading Goods
02	Performances
03	Finished Products
Y2	Returnable goods

Figure 5.28 Account Assignment Groups of Material

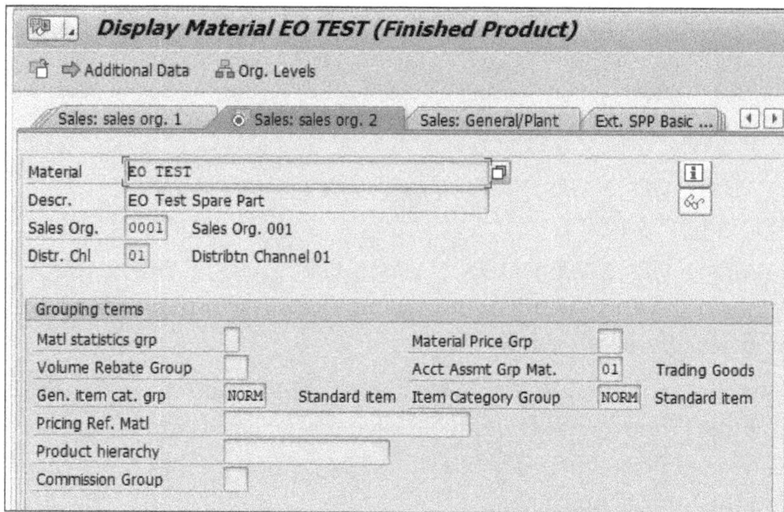

Figure 5.29 Material Master: Account Assignment Group

Similarly, the customer account assignment group is used for grouping customers to post the revenue from that group into one general ledger account. For example, the revenue from domestic customers should be posted to a different general ledger account than that of foreign customers.

To define the account assignment group of customers, follow menu path **Sales and Distribution • Basic Functions • Account Assignment/Costing • Revenue Account Determination • Check Master Data Relevant for Account Assignment • Customers: Account Assignment Groups.** Here, you can define the account assignment group for domestic customers as **01** and for foreign customers as **02**, as shown in Figure 5.30, similar to the account assignment group of material explained earlier.

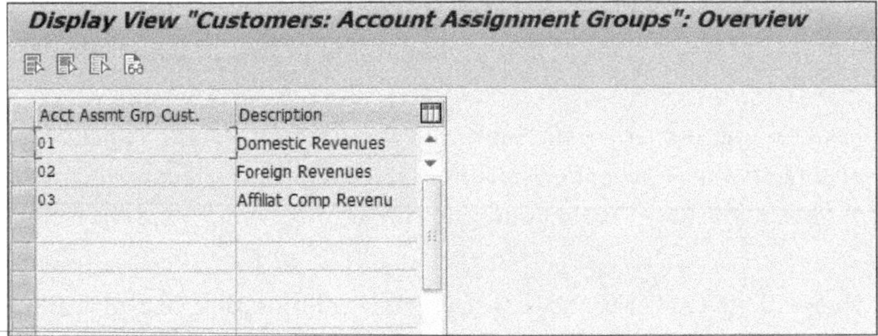

Figure 5.30 Account Assignment Group of Customer

After defining the customer account assignment group, you must assign it to the business partner by executing Transaction BP, selecting the **Customer** role, and clicking on the **Sales and Distribution** button to display the sales area data. On this screen, choose the **Billing** tab, as shown in Figure 5.31, and assign the account assignment group in the **Acct Assmt Grp Cust** field.

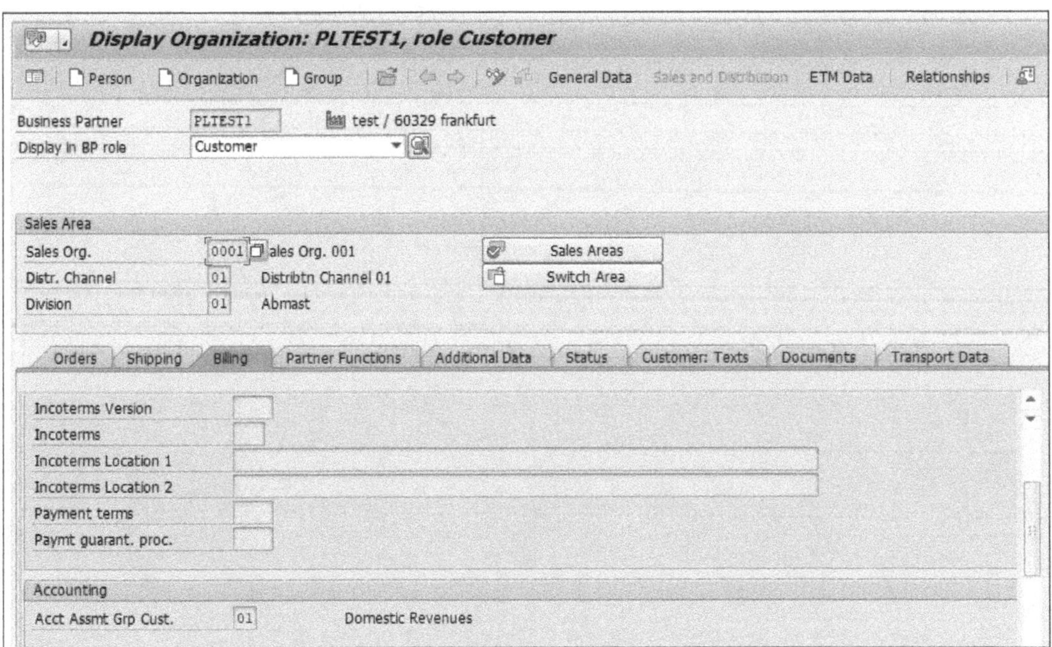

Figure 5.31 Business Partner: Account Assignment Group

5.2.2 Condition Technique

The next steps for account determination mirror the condition technique flow we discussed for pricing in Section 5.1.1. We'll walk through the key activities in the following sections.

Dependencies of Revenue Account Determination

In the next step, you need to create condition tables with the required combination of fields, which you can choose from the field catalog. To create a condition table, execute Transaction SPRO, and follow menu path **Sales and Distribution • Basic Functions • Account Assignment/Costing • Revenue Account Determination • Dependencies of Revenue Account Determination • Create Condition Tables for Revenue Account Determination.**

The condition table setup is similar to the condition table creation that you've done in Section 5.1.1. As shown in Figure 5.32, the condition table is created with the combination of sales organization, customer account assignment group, material account assignment group, and account key.

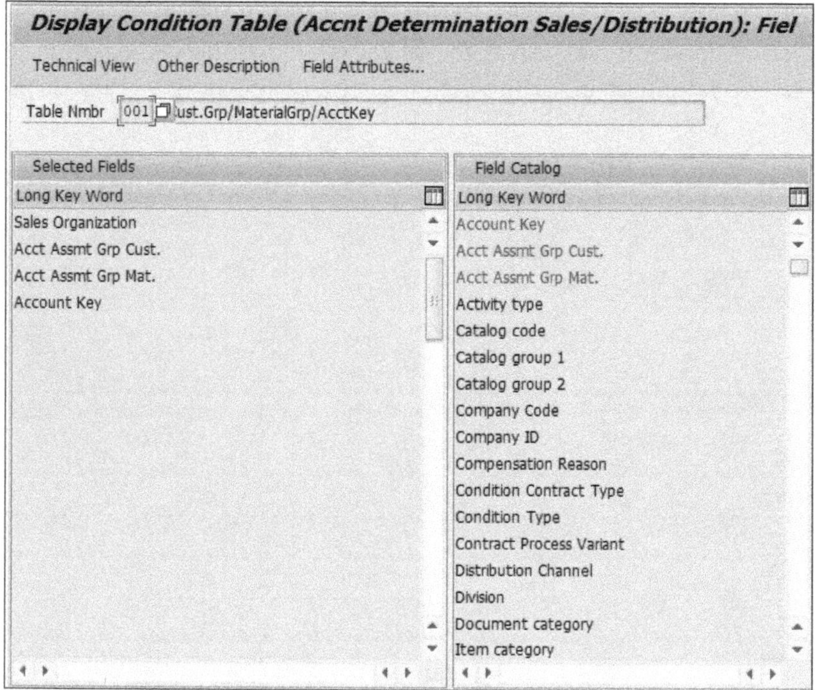

Figure 5.32 Condition Table

Define Access Sequences and Account Determination Types

After defining the condition tables, you need to set up the access sequence where condition tables are assigned sequentially per the requirement. To set up the access sequence, follow menu path **Sales and Distribution • Basic Functions • Account Assignment/Costing • Revenue Account Determination • Define Access Sequences and Account Determination Types • Define Access Sequences.**

Select access sequence **KOFI**, which is the standard access sequence for account determination, as shown in Figure 5.33.

Display View "Accesses": Overview

Access Sequence KOFI Account determination

Overview Accesses

No.	T...	Description	Requirement
5	017	Sales Org./Item Cat./Acct Key	0
10	001	Cust.Grp/MaterialGrp/AcctKey	0
20	002	Cust.Grp/Account Key	0
30	003	Material Grp/Acct Key	0
40	005	Acct Key	0
50	004	General	0

Figure 5.33 Access Sequence

After setting up the access sequence, the account determination condition type should be configured by following menu path **Sales and Distribution • Basic Functions • Account Assignment/Costing • Revenue Account Determination • Define Access Sequences and Account Determination Types • Define Account Determination Types**. After executing the given path, click on the **New Entries** button to assign the condition type (**CTyp**) with the access sequence (**AS**). Standard account determination types **KOFI** and **KOFK** are shown in Figure 5.34.

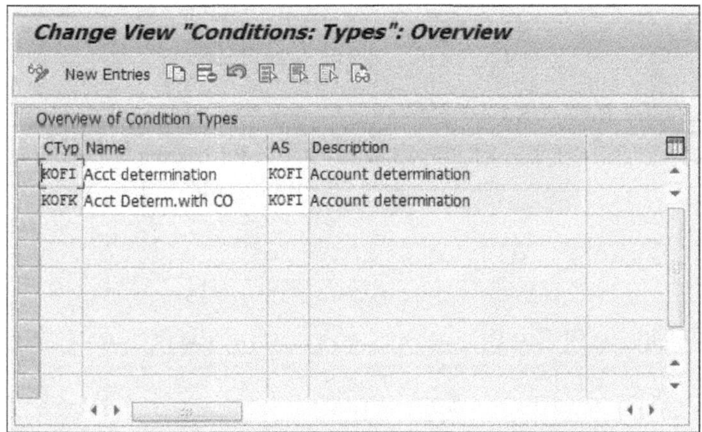
Change View "Conditions: Types": Overview

Overview of Condition Types

CTyp	Name	AS	Description
KOFI	Acct determination	KOFI	Account determination
KOFK	Acct Determ.with CO	KOFI	Account determination

Figure 5.34 Account Determination Types

Define and Assign Account Determination Procedures

Once the condition type is set up, you can create an account determination procedure by following menu path **Sales and Distribution • Basic Functions • Account Assignment/Costing • Revenue Account Determination • Define and Assign Account Determination Procedures**. You'll arrive at the screen in Figure 5.35, where you can create your own procedure by clicking on the **New Entries** button. Select the procedure (**Proc...**), and click the **Control data** folder to arrive at the screen in Figure 5.36. This procedure contains a list of account determination types, which you configured in the previous section.

Figure 5.36 shows the standard account determination type **KOFI00** with account determination types **KOFI** and **KOFK**.

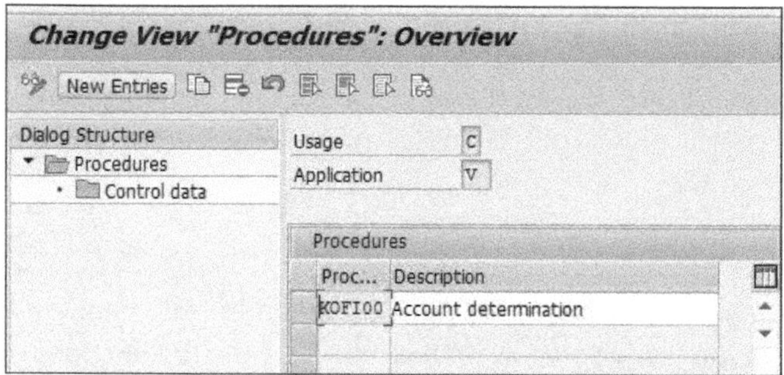

Figure 5.35 Account Determination Procedure: Initial Screen

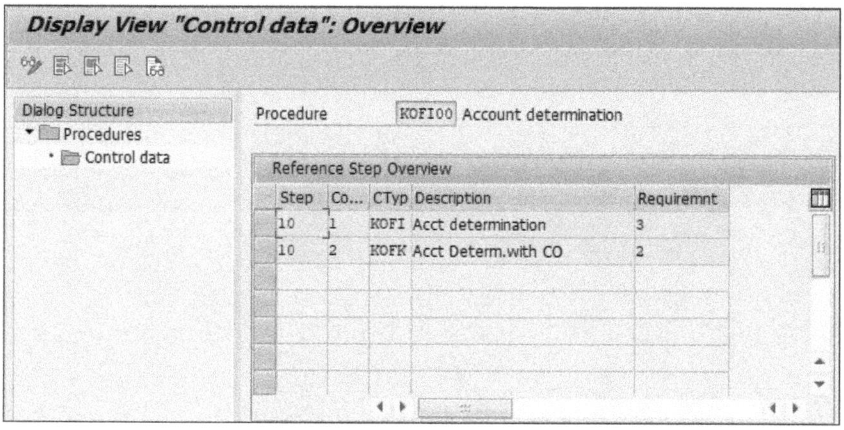

Figure 5.36 Account Determination Procedure

After the account determination procedure is defined, navigate to menu path **Sales and Distribution • Basic Functions • Account Assignment/Costing • Revenue Account Determination • Define and Assign Account Determination Procedures • Assign Account Determination Procedure**, where you need to assign this procedure to the billing type. As shown in Figure 5.37, we've assigned account determination procedure (**ActG/L**) **KOFI00** with standard billing type (**BillT**) **F2**.

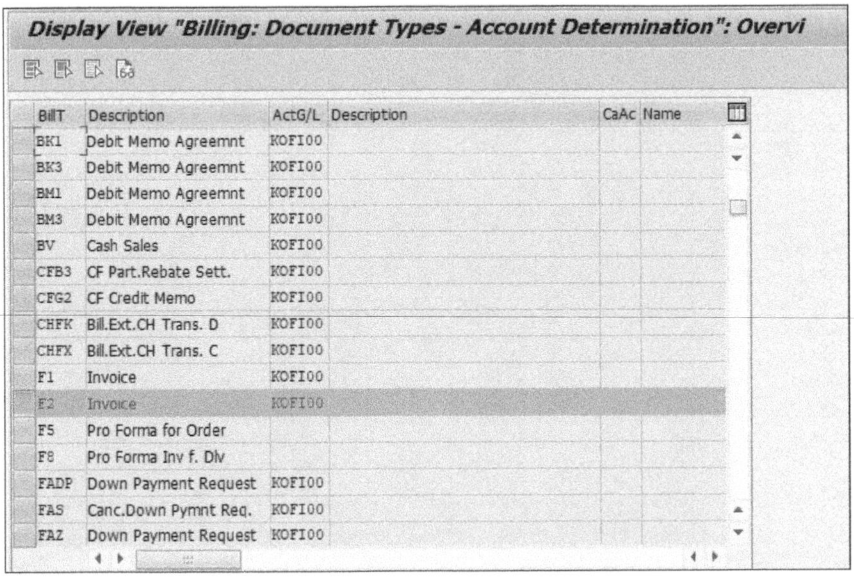

Display View "Billing: Document Types - Account Determination": Overvi

BillT	Description	ActG/L	Description	CaAc	Name
BK1	Debit Memo Agreemnt	KOFI00			
BK3	Debit Memo Agreemnt	KOFI00			
BM1	Debit Memo Agreemnt	KOFI00			
BM3	Debit Memo Agreemnt	KOFI00			
BV	Cash Sales	KOFI00			
CFB3	CF Part.Rebate Sett.	KOFI00			
CFG2	CF Credit Memo	KOFI00			
CHFK	Bill.Ext.CH Trans. D	KOFI00			
CHFX	Bill.Ext.CH Trans. C	KOFI00			
F1	Invoice	KOFI00			
F2	Invoice	KOFI00			
F5	Pro Forma for Order				
F8	Pro Forma Inv f. Dlv				
FADP	Down Payment Request	KOFI00			
FAS	Canc.Down Pymnt Req.	KOFI00			
FAZ	Down Payment Request	KOFI00			

Figure 5.37 Assign Account Determination Procedure to Billing Type

Define and Assign Account Keys

Account key is the parameter assigned with condition types in the pricing procedure to identify the general ledger account for posting calculated values from the condition type. You have different account keys for different condition types; a few examples are shown in Table 5.7.

Condition Type	Account Key
Price	ERL
Discount	ERS
Tax	MWS

Table 5.7 Account Key

You can define and assign account keys by navigating to menu path **Sales and Distribution • Basic Functions • Account Assignment/Costing • Revenue Account Determination • Define and Assign Account Keys • Define Account Keys**. As shown in Figure 5.38, you can create your own account keys by clicking on the **New Entries** button and entering an **ActKy** code and **Name**. Configured account keys in the system are shown in Figure 5.38.

After defining the account keys, follow menu path **Sales and Distribution • Basic Functions • Account Assignment/Costing • Revenue Account Determination • Define and Assign Account Keys • Assign Account Keys**, arriving at the screen shown in Figure 5.39. Click the **New Entries** button and assign account keys (**ActKy**) with the combination of pricing procedure (**Proc.**), **Step**, and condition types (**CTyp**) in the pricing procedure.

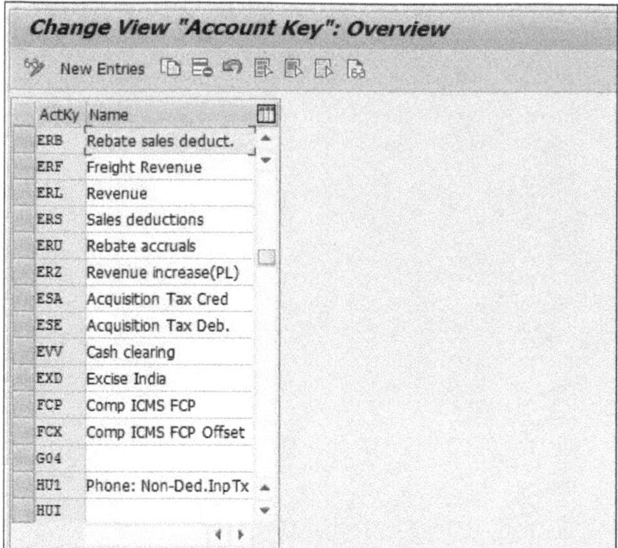

Change View "Account Key": Overview

New Entries

ActKy	Name
ERB	Rebate sales deduct.
ERF	Freight Revenue
ERL	Revenue
ERS	Sales deductions
ERU	Rebate accruals
ERZ	Revenue increase(PL)
ESA	Acquisition Tax Cred
ESE	Acquisition Tax Deb.
EVV	Cash clearing
EXD	Excise India
FCP	Comp ICMS FCP
FCX	Comp ICMS FCP Offset
G04	
HU1	Phone: Non-Ded.InpTx
HUI	

Figure 5.38 Account Keys

Change View "Pricing Procedures: Revenue Account Determination": Overv

New Entries

Proc.	Step	Cntr	CTyp	Name	ActKy	Name	Accrls	N:
RVAA01	8	0	EK01	Actual Costs	ERL	Revenue		Re
	11	0	PR00	Price	ERL	Revenue		
	13	0	PB00	Price (Gross)	ERL	Revenue		
	20	0	VA00	Variant Price	ERL	Revenue		
	101	0	KA00	Sales deal	ERS	Sales deductions		
	102	0	K032	Price Group/Material	ERS	Sales deductions		
	103	0	K005	Customer/Material	ERS	Sales deductions		
	104	0	K007	Customer Discount	ERS	Sales deductions		
	105	0	K004	Material	ERS	Sales deductions		
	106	0	K020	Price Group	ERS	Sales deductions		
	107	0	K029	Material pricing grp	ERS	Sales deductions		
	108	0	K030	Customer/Mat.Pr.Grp	ERS	Sales deductions		
	109	0	K031	Price Grp/Mat.Pr.Grp	ERS	Sales deductions		
	110	1	RA01	% Disc.from Gross	ERS	Sales deductions		
	110	2	RA00	% Discount from Net	ERS	Sales deductions		
	110	3	RC00	Quantity Discount	ERS	Sales deductions		

Figure 5.39 Assign Account Keys to Pricing Procedure

5.2.3 Assign General Ledger Accounts

After configuration of the account determination procedure, you need to assign general ledger accounts to the condition tables. This step is similar to the condition records maintenance in pricing.

> **Note**
>
> The general ledger accounts will be created by the financial accounting consultant with Transaction FS00.

For assignment of general ledger accounts, follow menu path **Sales and Distribution • Basic Functions • Account Assignment/Costing • Revenue Account Determination • Assign G/L Accounts**. You can also use Transaction VKOA. You'll arrive at the screen shown in Figure 5.40, where you should choose the required combination of tables (**Tab**) for which you have to assign the general ledger accounts and click on **Details** icon . Then you'll arrive at the general ledger account maintenance screen shown in Figure 5.41, where you'll assign the general ledger accounts with the combination of selected tables.

Assign G/L Accounts

Selections

Assign G/L Accounts

Tab	Description
001	Cust.Grp/MaterialGrp/AcctKey
002	Cust.Grp/Account Key
003	Material Grp/Acct Key
004	General
005	Acct Key

Figure 5.40 Assign Account Keys: Initial Screen

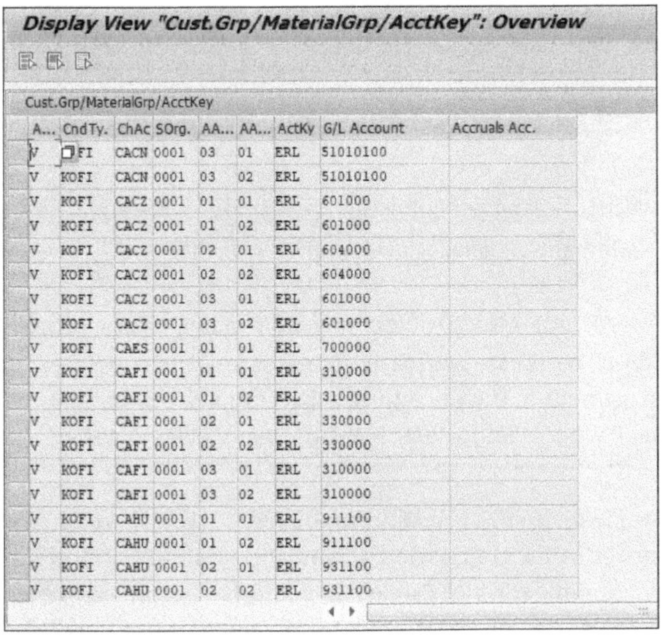

Display View "Cust.Grp/MaterialGrp/AcctKey": Overview

Cust.Grp/MaterialGrp/AcctKey

A...	CndTy.	ChAc	SOrg.	AA...	AA...	ActKy	G/L Account	Accruals Acc.
V	FI	CACN	0001	03	01	ERL	51010100	
V	KOFI	CACN	0001	03	02	ERL	51010100	
V	KOFI	CACZ	0001	01	01	ERL	601000	
V	KOFI	CACZ	0001	01	02	ERL	601000	
V	KOFI	CACZ	0001	02	01	ERL	604000	
V	KOFI	CACZ	0001	02	02	ERL	604000	
V	KOFI	CACZ	0001	03	01	ERL	601000	
V	KOFI	CACZ	0001	03	02	ERL	601000	
V	KOFI	CAES	0001	01	01	ERL	700000	
V	KOFI	CAFI	0001	01	01	ERL	310000	
V	KOFI	CAFI	0001	01	02	ERL	310000	
V	KOFI	CAFI	0001	02	01	ERL	330000	
V	KOFI	CAFI	0001	02	02	ERL	330000	
V	KOFI	CAFI	0001	03	01	ERL	310000	
V	KOFI	CAFI	0001	03	02	ERL	310000	
V	KOFI	CAHU	0001	01	01	ERL	911100	
V	KOFI	CAHU	0001	01	02	ERL	911100	
V	KOFI	CAHU	0001	02	01	ERL	931100	
V	KOFI	CAHU	0001	02	02	ERL	931100	

Figure 5.41 Assign General Ledger Accounts

5.3 Credit Management

A business extends credit to customers by selling goods and collecting payment from them after a set period. This is referred to as credit management. *Credit management* is a critical task in every organization. It's concerned with ensuring that the customers pay organizations on time for the products or services they purchase. Giving credit to clients or customers puts them at risk of not being paid. However, the majority of business-to-business (B2B) firms must grow in the cutthroat competitive environment, and, to do so, they have to extend credit to their customers. Everything directly related to the processes of approving customers for onboarding, extending payment terms, setting credit and payments policy, issuing credit or financing, and monitoring business cash flow is referred to as credit management. Credit management is essential because it strengthens a company's liquidity. If done correctly, it will increase cash flow and decrease costs.

Classic credit management is a functionality that assists businesses in monitoring, evaluating, and controlling credit issues and credit allocations. It enables you to extend credit to the company's clients and conduct credit checks on their purchases. When we talk about the new credit management solution in SAP S/4HANA, we're referring to a system that helps companies implement a company-wide credit policy and run central credit management in a distributed system landscape.

Classic credit management can connect with multiple systems through Central Finance and central payment functionalities of SAP S/4HANA. This scenario necessitates using system landscape transformation and intermediate document (IDoc)/ Application Link Enabling (ALE), among other things. The credit manager can monitor a customer's credit exposure in one centralized system. These customers may reside in several separate instances.

Note

Credit management and collections management aren't synonymous. They are, however, closely related and are frequently managed by the same department.

This section will discuss how SAP S/4HANA handles the credit management process and its associated configuration. We'll explore many new innovations compared to standard SAP ERP credit management in the upcoming subsections. We'll first discuss the overall credit management process and then dive into the associated configurations.

Credit management can be implemented in two ways in the SAP S/4HANA world. The first approach is to use the functionalities of classic sales and distribution-based credit management and keep the credit limit and risk categories static. The second approach is to leverage the solution capabilities of FSCM credit management and make the credit limit and credit risk categories dynamic based on formulas.

5.3.1 What Is Credit Management?

Let's explore how the credit management process works in SAP S/4HANA. Credit management is always done on only three documents, that is, the sales order, delivery, and goods issue. After the goods are issued from the company's location, you don't have any control over them, and ownership is transferred to the customer. Once any of the mentioned operational documents are created, the credit management process kicks in. The relevant master data associated with the credit management process is explained in Chapter 3. This master data consists of fields such as credit control area, credit segment, risk classes, and credit limit. You configure the credit management process in the SAP landscape based on these parameters. Sales orders, deliveries, and post goods issues (PGIs) feed the master data elements into the configuration. You map your organization's credit policies into the credit management application when you implement it in your SAP S/4HANA instance. Customers are aligned with these credit policy rules based on information gathered from various sources, such as the customer's previous transnational history, credit reports available from credit agencies (e.g., Dun & Bradstreet [D&B]), the customer's market financial stability, the geographical and political situations of the regions where the goods are sold, and so on.

As shown in Figure 5.42, after operational document creation, the credit limit check initiates. A *credit check* is essentially a comparison of the customer's credit exposure to the customer's available credit limit set up in the business partner.

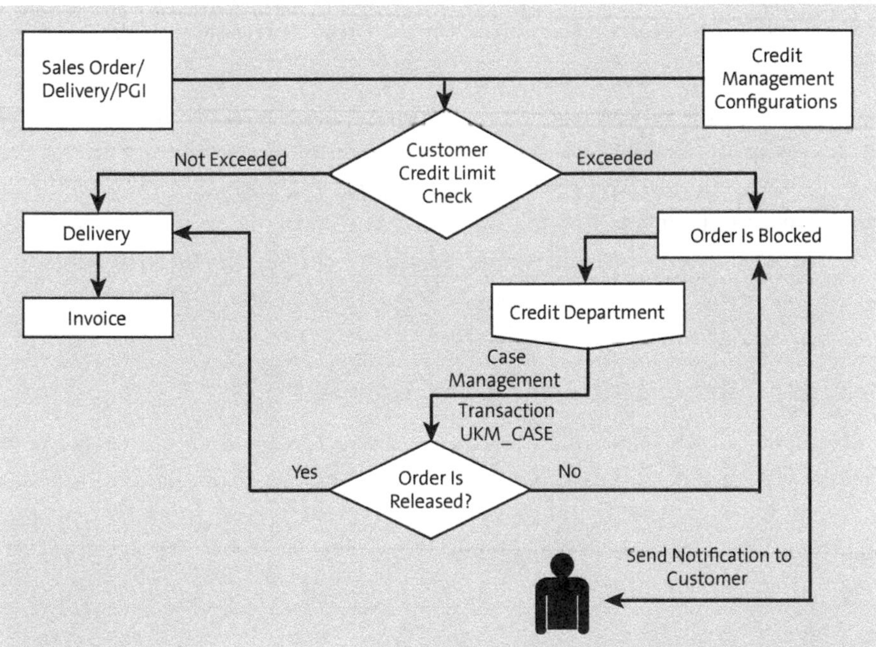

Figure 5.42 Credit Management Flow

Note

The total amount of open orders, open deliveries, open billings, open receivables, and open special liabilities is used to calculate credit exposure. You can see the credit exposure in the business partner or by entering Transaction UKM_COMMITMENTS.

FSCM includes credit management and consists of the following four functionalities:

- **Credit management**
  Monitors and controls credit risk from a centralized system.
- **Dispute resolution**
  Resolves disagreements between organizations and customers.
- **Collections management**
  Manages collections issues in risk management and customer relations.
- **Direct biller**
  Performs e-payments and integration of customers with financial services.

The *credit limit* is the maximum amount an organization will allow its customers to purchase goods on credit. When you create a new document relevant for credit checks, SAP S/4HANA calculates the customer's current credit exposure and compares it to the customer's available credit limit, which is maintained in the business partner's UKM role. If the exposure exceeds the credit limit, the credit check fails, and the order is held for credit management. This blocked sales order can be found in Transaction UKM_CASE.

Once the order has been blocked due to exceeding the credit limit, the *documented credit decision (DCD)* document is generated, which contains all the data associated with the creditworthiness failed credit check. The credit manager can then review the document in Transaction UKM_CASE. The manager has two options: either release or reject the document. If the document is approved, the subsequent operational documents are created; if the document is rejected, the next operational documents are blocked.

5.3.2 Sales and Distribution-Based Credit Management

In this section, we'll look at the configuration required to set up the credit management functionality. As previously discussed, there are two approaches to implementing credit management in SAP S/4HANA. In this section, we'll go over the configuration for classic sales and distribution-based credit management first.

Note

The organizational elements such as sales area, company code, and so on were already covered in Chapter 2. This chapter will only cover the configuration related to credit management.

Credit Control Area

The *credit control area* is a four-digit alphanumeric key required for the credit management process. It's used to specify and check the customer's credit limit for credit management in sales and distribution and in accounts receivable. It can be classified based on the areas of responsibility for credit monitoring.

To define the credit control area, follow menu path **Enterprise Structure • Definition • Financial Accounting • Define Credit Control Area**. You can also use Transaction OB45. You'll arrive at the screen shown in Figure 5.43, where you can create your own credit control area by copying the existing one via the **Copy As** button. You'll then arrive at the screen shown in Figure 5.44.

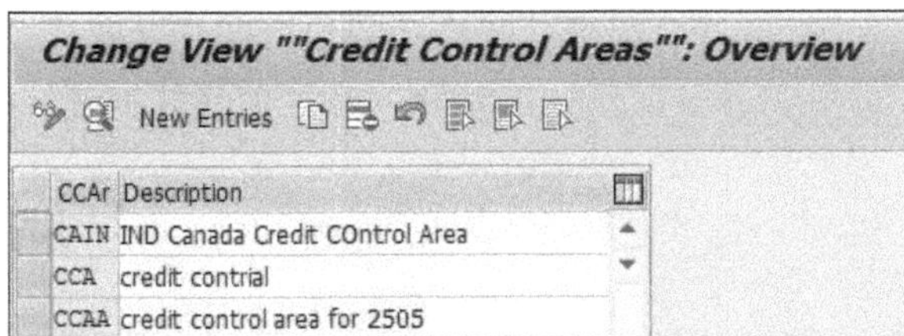

Figure 5.43 Credit Control Area: Initial Screen

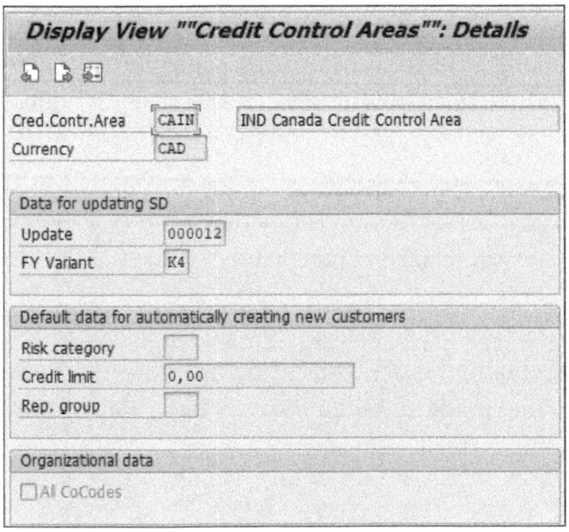

Figure 5.44 Credit Control Area

As shown in Figure 5.44, you must define the credit control area with an appropriate description, currency, and credit update.

Each credit controlling area in SAP S/4HANA includes a **Currency** that is used to manage the customer credit. The system converts receivable transactions from transaction currencies to the currency of the credit controlling area. A customer for each company code can only have one credit control area.

The **Update** groups are used to determine what values should be updated and when in relation to credit management. In the credit control area, you have four options for setting the update group:

- **Blank**
  If the field is left empty, the sales and distribution documents are ignored, and only open receivables and open special general ledger items are used to calculate credit exposure.
- **000012**
  The open order value is added to the credit exposure when a new order is created. When the same order is delivered, the open order value is subtracted from the exposure, and the open delivery value is added. When billing the delivery document, the open delivery value is subtracted from the exposure, and the open billing value is added. When a billing document is posted to accounting, the open billing value is subtracted from the exposure, and the open accounts receivable value is added. When the cash is applied against open accounts receivable, the exposure is finally reduced.
- **000015**
  This calculates exposure without considering the value of open sales orders. The open delivery value is added to the exposure when the order is delivered. When billing the delivery, the open delivery value is subtracted from the exposure, and the open billing value is added. When billing posts to accounting, the open billing value is subtracted from the exposure, and the open accounts receivable value is added. When the cash is applied against open accounts receivable, the exposure is finally reduced.
- **000018**
  This only applies to nondelivery-related orders. The open delivery value is added to the credit exposure when a new order is created. When the order is billed, the open delivery value is subtracted from the exposure, and the open billing is added. When billing posts to accounting, the open billing value is subtracted from the exposure, and the open accounts receivable value is added. When the cash is applied against open accounts receivable, the exposure is finally reduced.

Note

If a document can't be processed using the update group you specify, the system determines the next update that can be performed. For example, if you select update group **000012**, the open order value is reduced while the open delivery value is increased at delivery. Assume that one of the items in the order is irrelevant to delivery. In this case, the system determines update group **000018** for this item automatically. Update group **000018** raises the order item's open delivery value. The system updates the order value based on the confirmed quantity of delivery-relevant schedule lines.

Next, you'll assign the relevant credit control area to the company code. For assignment of the credit control area with the company code, follow menu path **Enterprise Structure • Assignment • Financial Accounting • Assign Company Code to Credit Control Area**. You'll arrive at the screen shown in Figure 5.45.

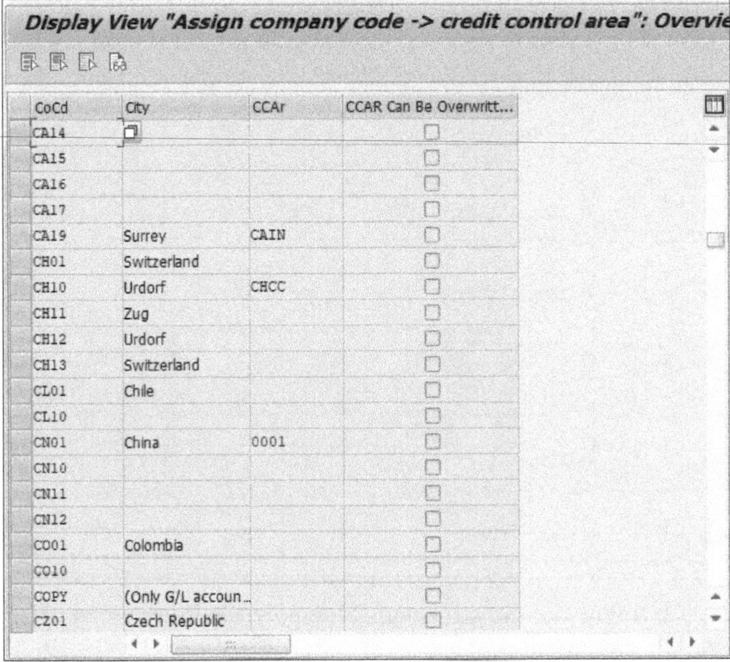

Display View "Assign company code -> credit control area": Overvie

CoCd	City	CCAr	CCAR Can Be Overwritt...
CA14			
CA15			
CA16			
CA17			
CA19	Surrey	CAIN	
CH01	Switzerland		
CH10	Urdorf	CHCC	
CH11	Zug		
CH12	Urdorf		
CH13	Switzerland		
CL01	Chile		
CL10			
CN01	China	0001	
CN10			
CN11			
CN12			
CO01	Colombia		
CO10			
COPY	(Only G/L accoun...		
CZ01	Czech Republic		

Figure 5.45 Assignment of Credit Control Area to Company Code

The relationship between a company code and a credit control area is 1:1; that is, one company code can only have one credit control area. However, you can assign the same credit control area to multiple company codes. Figure 5.45 illustrates the assignment of a credit control area with company code. Here, you have to assign the credit control area to the company code in the transaction. If you select the **CCAR Can Be Overwritt...** checkbox, then you can overwrite the determination of the credit control area.

The credit control area can be determined based on the following flow:

1. First, the system tries to find the credit control area from the user exit. You can write custom logic to determine the credit control area inside user exit EXIT_SAPFV45K_001.
2. If the credit control area isn't found in the first step, then the system tries to pick up the credit control area from the business partner.
3. If the credit control area isn't maintained in the business partner, then the system checks the credit control area maintained with the combination of sales area data. We'll explore this configuration in subsequent sections.
4. If all these steps fail, then the credit control area is determined from the company code assigned in the preceding configuration.

Credit Segment

Credit segment is the organizational unit in FSCM. In SAP S/4HANA, credit segment is the highest organizational element of credit management. Credit segments are required to calculate the credit limit and to conduct detailed checks at the business partner level. The relationship between credit segment and credit control area is shown in Figure 5.46.

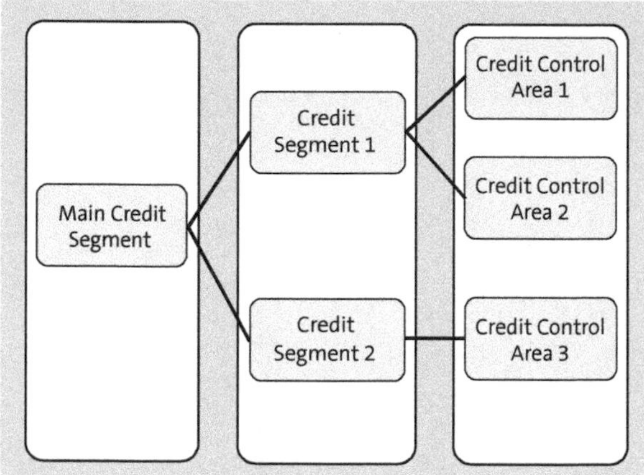

Figure 5.46 Credit Segment

To create a credit segment, follow menu path **Financial Supply Chain Management • Credit Management • Credit Risk Monitoring • Master Data • Create Credit Segments.** You'll arrive at the screen shown in Figure 5.47. Click on the **New Entries** button to create a new credit segment (**6110**, in the example), arriving at the screen shown in Figure 5.48.

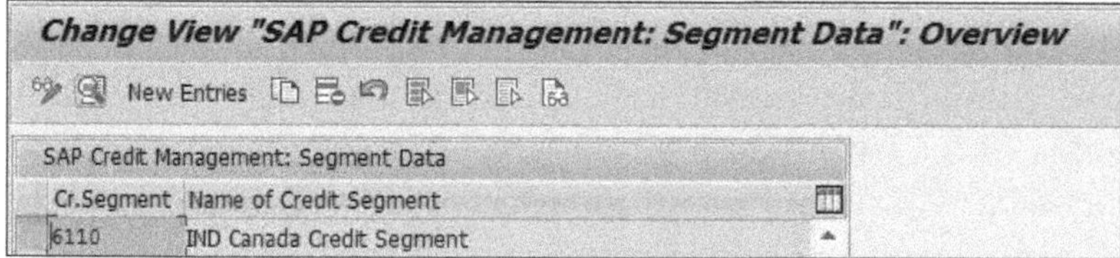

Figure 5.47 Create Credit Segment: Initial Screen

As shown in Figure 5.48, you have to add the appropriate description for the credit segment in the field. Let's now discuss the fields from the credit segment screen:

- **Currency**
  You have to maintain the transaction currency in this field. The amount in the exposure list will be reflected in the credit segment's currency. The conversion is performed based on the transaction date of the sales order, using the exchange rate specified in the credit segment definition.

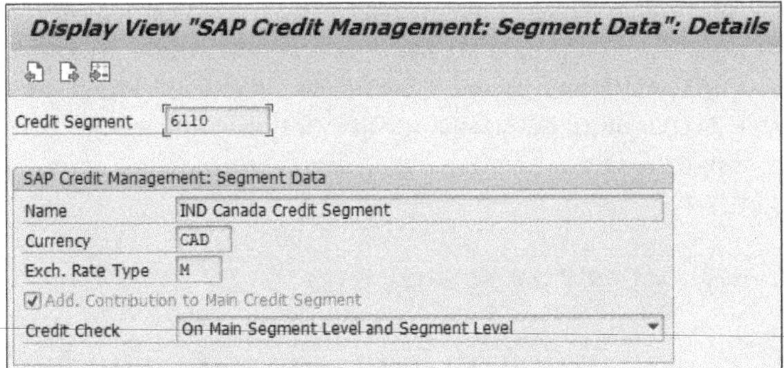

Figure 5.48 Create Credit Segment

- **Add. Contribution to Main Credit Segment**
  If you check this checkbox, the liability of the business partner is added up in the main credit segment.
  The following liabilities are included in the main credit segment's liability:
  - Directly updated liabilities for the primary credit segment
  - Liabilities for all other credit segments for which this indicator is selected
- **Credit Check**
  You can use the **Credit Check** field to specify the segment used for the credit check independently of the liability calculation. The following options are available:
  - **On Main Segment Level Only**: If you select this option, then the liability of only the main credit segment is considered for the credit check.
  - **On Segment Level Only**: If you activate this option on the credit segment, then only the liability of the given credit segment is taken into consideration for the credit check.
  - **On Main Segment Level and Segment Level**: If you choose this option in the configuration of the credit segment, then the liability of the main credit segment and the liability of a given credit segment are considered in the credit check.

> **Note**
>
> You have to create the credit segment at two levels: the FSCM level and the client level. To create the credit segment at the client level, follow menu path **Financial Supply Chain Management • Credit Management • Integration with Accounts Receivable Accounting and Sales and Distribution • Integration with Sales and Distribution • Define Credit Segment**. You only have to maintain the credit segment, which you created in an earlier section. There is no field level configuration that needs to be performed in this node.

Once the credit segment is configured, you have to assign the credit segment to the credit control area. To assign the credit segment with the credit control area, follow menu path **Financial Supply Chain Management • Credit Management • Integration with Accounts Receivable Accounting and Sales and Distribution • Integration with Sales and Distribution • Assign Credit Control Area and Credit Segment**. You'll arrive at the screen shown in Figure 5.49.

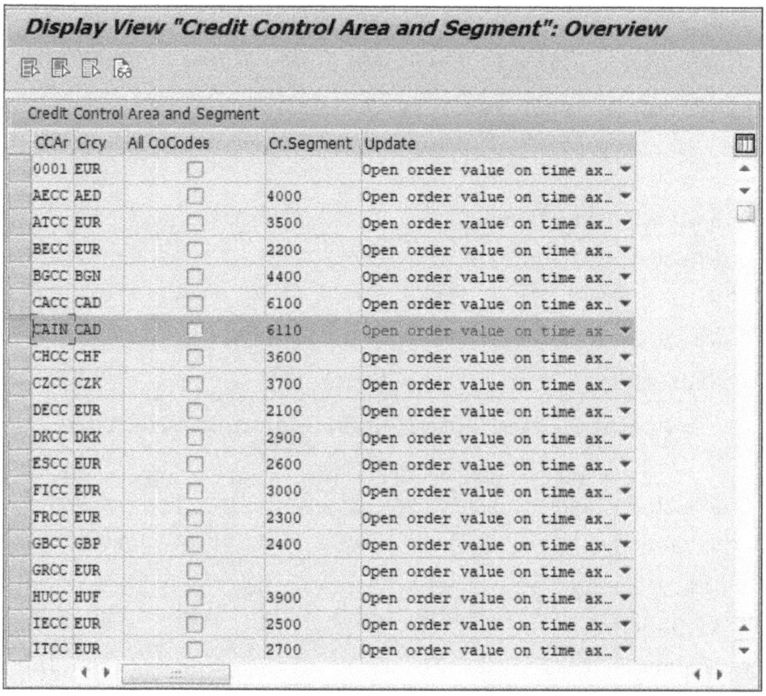

Display View "Credit Control Area and Segment": Overview

Credit Control Area and Segment

CCAr	Crcy	All CoCodes	Cr.Segment	Update
0001	EUR	☐		Open order value on time ax...
AECC	AED	☐	4000	Open order value on time ax...
ATCC	EUR	☐	3500	Open order value on time ax...
BECC	EUR	☐	2200	Open order value on time ax...
BGCC	BGN	☐	4400	Open order value on time ax...
CACC	CAD	☐	6100	Open order value on time ax...
CAIN	CAD	☐	6110	Open order value on time ax...
CHCC	CHF	☐	3600	Open order value on time ax...
CZCC	CZK	☐	3700	Open order value on time ax...
DECC	EUR	☐	2100	Open order value on time ax...
DKCC	DKK	☐	2900	Open order value on time ax...
ESCC	EUR	☐	2600	Open order value on time ax...
FICC	EUR	☐	3000	Open order value on time ax...
FRCC	EUR	☐	2300	Open order value on time ax...
GBCC	GBP	☐	2400	Open order value on time ax...
GRCC	EUR	☐		Open order value on time ax...
HUCC	HUF	☐	3900	Open order value on time ax...
IECC	EUR	☐	2500	Open order value on time ax...
ITCC	EUR	☐	2700	Open order value on time ax...

Figure 5.49 Assignment of Credit Control Area to Credit Segment

As you can see in Figure 5.49, you have to assign the credit control area configured earlier (**CAIN**, in the example) to the credit segment (**6110**, in the example). The relation between credit control areas to credit segment is 1:1; that is, every credit control area can be assigned to only one credit segment.

Parameters such as currency and update rules will be auto-populated from the credit control area. The **All CoCodes** checkbox will enable the system to post in every company code that you've defined.

As mentioned in the previous section, the credit control area can also be assigned based on the sales area. You assign the credit control area to sales organizations because one company code can have multiple credit control areas. If you want the segregation based on the sales organization, you can do this assignment by following menu path **Financial Supply Chain Management • Credit Management • Integration with Accounts Receivable Accounting and Sales and Distribution • Integration with Sales and Distribution • Assign Sales Area to Credit Control Area**.

You'll arrive at the screen shown in Figure 5.50, where you can assign credit control area (**CCAr**) with a combination of sales organization (**SOrg.**), distribution channel (**DChl**), and division (**Dv**).

Display View "Sales Area: Allocation to Credit Control Area": Overview

SOrg.	DChl	Dv	CCAr
0001		01	
0002	01	01	
0003	01	01	
CA19	10	67	
CA19	10	82	
CA19	10	83	
CA19	10	84	
CA19	10	ZZ	CAIN
DE11	10	01	
DE11	10	02	
DE11	10	03	
DE11	10	04	
DE11	10	05	
DE11	10	06	

Figure 5.50 Assignment of Sales Area to Credit Control Area

Pricing Procedure Changes

There are also other configurations that you must complete to fully integrate sales and distribution with credit management. Let's explore the cross-functional prerequisites for credit management now.

The pricing procedure needs to be tuned to send the values to the credit management component to calculate the total exposure. To make these relevant changes, follow menu path **Financial Supply Chain Management • Credit Management • Integration with Accounts Receivable Accounting and Sales and Distribution • Integration with Sales and Distribution • Enter Settings**. You'll arrive at the screen shown in Figure 5.51.

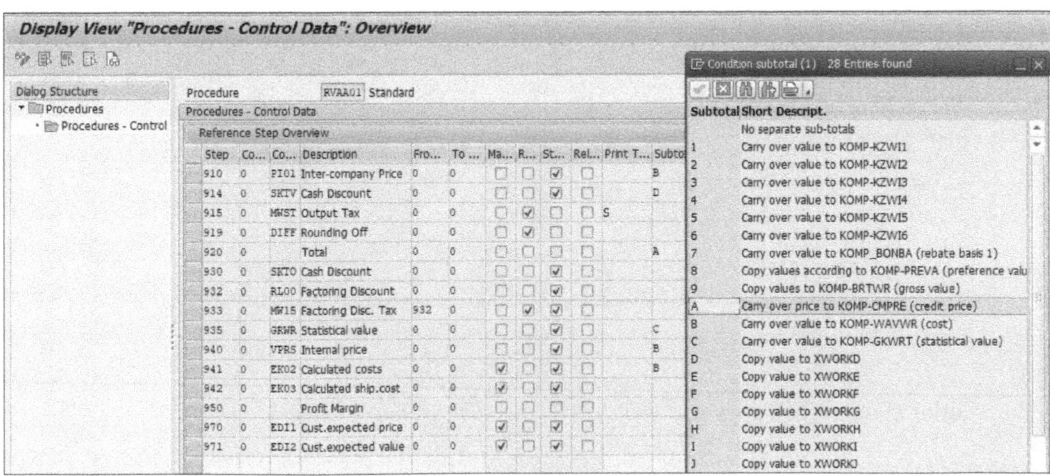

Display View "Procedures - Control Data": Overview

Dialog Structure
Procedures
Procedures - Control

Procedure RVAA01 Standard

Procedures - Control Data

Reference Step Overview

Step	Co...	Co...	Description	Fro...	To ...	Ma...	R...	St...	Rel...	Print T...	Subto
910	0	PI01	Inter-company Price	0	0			✓			B
914	0	SKTV	Cash Discount	0	0			✓			D
915	0	MWST	Output Tax	0	0		✓			S	
919	0	DIFF	Rounding Off	0	0		✓				
920	0		Total	0	0						A
930	0	SKTO	Cash Discount	0	0			✓			
932	0	RL00	Factoring Discount	0	0			✓			
933	0	MW15	Factoring Disc. Tax	932	0		✓	✓			
935	0	GRWR	Statistical value	0	0			✓			C
940	0	VPRS	Internal price	0	0			✓			B
941	0	EK02	Calculated costs	0	0	✓		✓			B
942	0	EK03	Calculated ship.cost	0	0	✓		✓			
950	0		Profit Margin	0	0						
970	0	EDI1	Cust.expected price	0	0	✓		✓			
971	0	EDI2	Cust.expected value	0	0	✓		✓			

Condition subtotal (1) 28 Entries found

Subtotal	Short Descript.
	No separate sub-totals
1	Carry over value to KOMP-KZWI1
2	Carry over value to KOMP-KZWI2
3	Carry over value to KOMP-KZWI3
4	Carry over value to KOMP-KZWI4
5	Carry over value to KOMP-KZWI5
6	Carry over value to KOMP-KZWI6
7	Carry over value to KOMP_BONBA (rebate basis 1)
8	Copy values according to KOMP-PREVA (preference valu
9	Copy values to KOMP-BRTWR (gross value)
A	Carry over price to KOMP-CMPRE (credit price)
B	Carry over value to KOMP-WAVWR (cost)
C	Carry over value to KOMP-GKWRT (statistical value)
D	Copy value to XWORKD
E	Copy value to XWORKE
F	Copy value to XWORKF
G	Copy value to XWORKG
H	Copy value to XWORKH
I	Copy value to XWORKI
J	Copy value to XWORKJ

Figure 5.51 Pricing Procedure: Subtotal

This can be achieved by the **Subtotal** field from the 17 fields of the pricing procedure. Maintain the subtotal as **A** for the total net price row in the pricing procedure, as shown in Figure 5.51.

Credit Active for Item Category

You can enable or disable credit management based on the item categories. There may be business scenarios in which the company doesn't want to update the value in credit management for certain materials, such as free-of-charge promotional items or returnable packaging. You can disable the credit management functionality for such materials by item category.

To deactivate or activate credit management based on item categories, follow menu path **Financial Supply Chain Management • Credit Management • Integration with Accounts Receivable Accounting and Sales and Distribution • Integration with Sales and Distribution • Determine Active Receivables Per Item Category.**

You'll arrive at the screen shown in Figure 5.52, where you can select the **Credit Active** checkbox if the item category is relevant for the credit check.

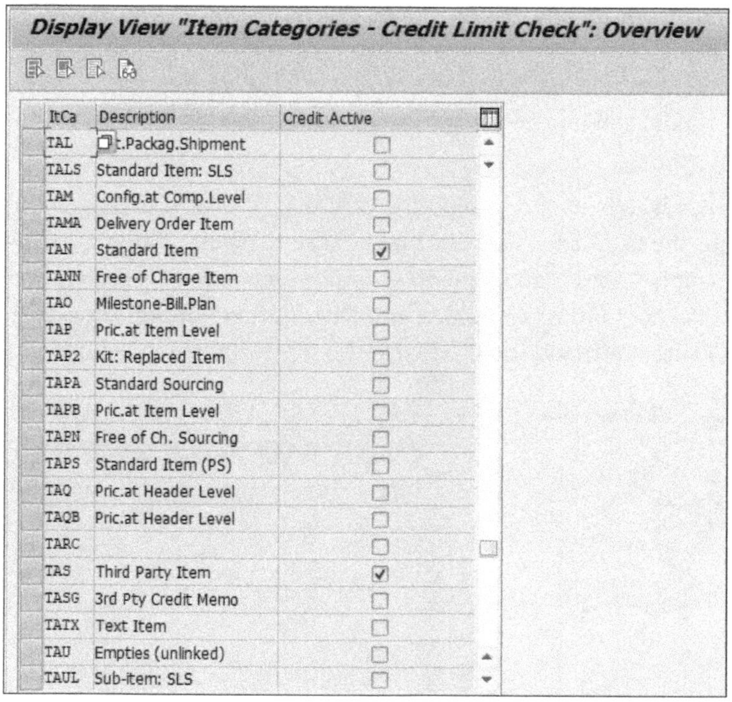

Display View "Item Categories - Credit Limit Check": Overview

ItCa	Description	Credit Active
TAL	t.Packag.Shipment	☐
TALS	Standard Item: SLS	☐
TAM	Config.at Comp.Level	☐
TAMA	Delivery Order Item	☐
TAN	Standard Item	☑
TANN	Free of Charge Item	☐
TAO	Milestone-Bill.Plan	☐
TAP	Pric.at Item Level	☐
TAP2	Kit: Replaced Item	☐
TAPA	Standard Sourcing	☐
TAPB	Pric.at Item Level	☐
TAPN	Free of Ch. Sourcing	☐
TAPS	Standard Item (PS)	☐
TAQ	Pric.at Header Level	☐
TAQB	Pric.at Header Level	☐
TARC		☐
TAS	Third Party Item	☑
TASG	3rd Pty Credit Memo	☐
TATX	Text Item	☐
TAU	Empties (unlinked)	☐
TAUL	Sub-item: SLS	☐

Figure 5.52 Item Categories: Credit Active

Sales Document Types and Delivery Types (Credit Limit Check)

The next step is to configure the sales and delivery document types relevant for credit management. To activate the sales document type and delivery type for credit management, follow menu path **Financial Supply Chain Management • Credit Management • Integration with Accounts Receivable Accounting and Sales and Distribution • Integration with Sales and Distribution • Assign Sales Documents and Delivery Documents.** You can also use Transaction OVAK (for sales document type) and Transaction OVAD (for delivery document type) to perform this activity.

You'll arrive at the screen shown in Figure 5.53, where you need to assign the check credit and credit group to the corresponding sales document type:

- **Credit group**
  Based on the credit group, you can control the credit check at different times during order processing. You can choose from the following options:
  - **01**: Credit group for sales order
  - **02**: Credit group for delivery
  - **03**: Credit group for goods issue
- **Check credit**
  Based on the credit check, you can instruct the system whether to perform credit management or not for the order types or delivery type. Maintain option **D** (credit management: automatic credit control). You can also keep it blank if you don't want any credit check.

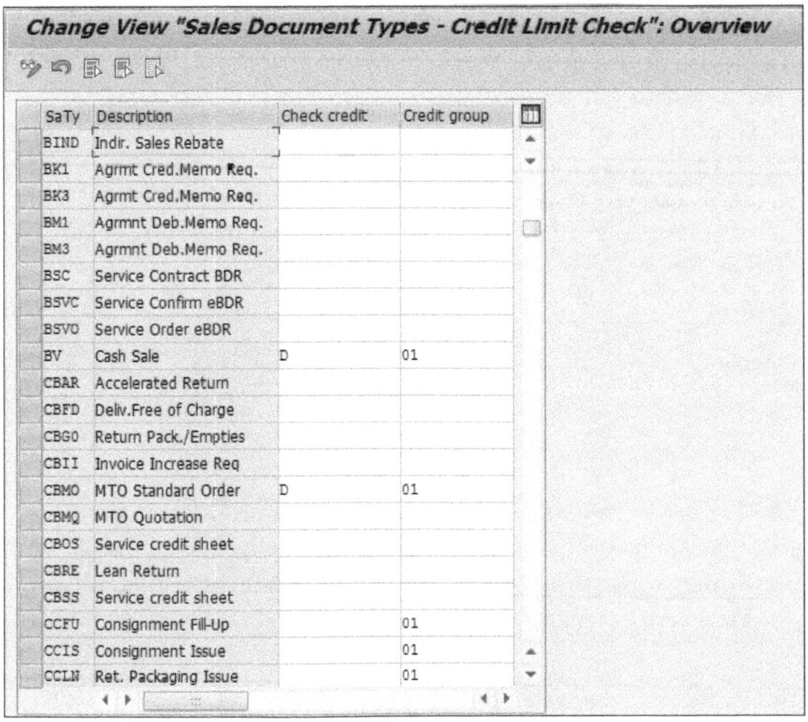

Change View "Sales Document Types - Credit Limit Check": Overview

SaTy	Description	Check credit	Credit group
BIND	Indir. Sales Rebate		
BK1	Agrmt Cred.Memo Req.		
BK3	Agrmt Cred.Memo Req.		
BM1	Agrmnt Deb.Memo Req.		
BM3	Agrmnt Deb.Memo Req.		
BSC	Service Contract BDR		
BSVC	Service Confirm eBDR		
BSVO	Service Order eBDR		
BV	Cash Sale	D	01
CBAR	Accelerated Return		
CBFD	Deliv.Free of Charge		
CBGO	Return Pack./Empties		
CBII	Invoice Increase Req		
CBMO	MTO Standard Order	D	01
CBMQ	MTO Quotation		
CBOS	Service credit sheet		
CBRE	Lean Return		
CBSS	Service credit sheet		
CCFU	Consignment Fill-Up		01
CCIS	Consignment Issue		01
CCLN	Ret. Packaging Issue		01

Figure 5.53 Sales Document Type: Credit Limit Check

Risk Category

Customers can be segregated based on the financial risk associated with them. This is called risk category in FSCM credit management and risk class in classic credit management. Based on the past payment behavior of the customer, you can categorize them as high-risk, medium-risk, or low-risk customers. In SAP S/4HANA, you can create a risk category and risk class for the segregation and assign or determine them in the business partner.

To define the risk category, follow menu path **Financial Supply Chain Management • Credit Management • Integration with Accounts Receivable Accounting and Sales and Distribution • Integration with Sales and Distribution • Define Risk Categories**. You'll arrive at the screen shown in Figure 5.54. In this step, assign the **Risk Category** with credit control area (**CCAr**).

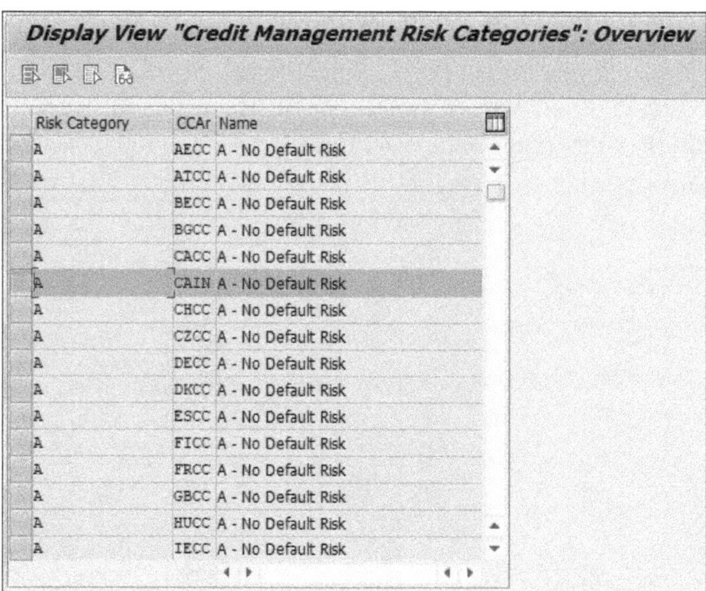

Risk Category	CCAr	Name
A	AECC	A - No Default Risk
A	ATCC	A - No Default Risk
A	BECC	A - No Default Risk
A	BGCC	A - No Default Risk
A	CACC	A - No Default Risk
A	CAIN	A - No Default Risk
A	CHCC	A - No Default Risk
A	CZCC	A - No Default Risk
A	DECC	A - No Default Risk
A	DKCC	A - No Default Risk
A	ESCC	A - No Default Risk
A	FICC	A - No Default Risk
A	FRCC	A - No Default Risk
A	GBCC	A - No Default Risk
A	HUCC	A - No Default Risk
A	IECC	A - No Default Risk

Figure 5.54 Risk Category

> **Note**
>
> The risk category in sales and distribution is distinguished from the risk class in classic credit management. To define the risk class in FSCM credit management, you have to first define the risk categories in sales and distribution. After defining the risk classes and risk categories, you have to assign the risk class to the relevant business partner.

For the automatic credit check, the system proceeds as follows:

1. It refers to the business partner's risk class in classic credit management.

2. Then, it automatically converts the risk class to the risk category (sales and distribution).
3. Lastly, it carries out the automatic credit control as specified in the relevant risk category (sales and distribution).

Automatic Credit Control

In this configuration, you have to set the credit control based on the parameters that you configured earlier. This configuration acts like a trigger to enable the credit check rule maintained in FSCM nodes.

For configuring automatic credit management, follow menu path **Financial Supply Chain Management • Credit Management • Integration with Accounts Receivable Accounting and Sales and Distribution • Integration with Sales and Distribution • Define Automatic Credit Control.** You can also use Transaction OVA8 to perform the activity. You'll arrive at the screen shown in Figure 5.55.

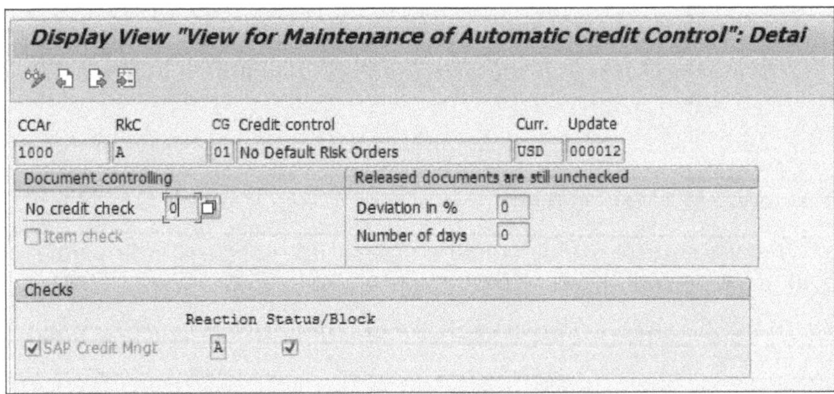

Figure 5.55 Automatic Credit Control

As shown in Figure 5.55, you need to enter the credit control area (**CCAr**), risk category (**RkC**), and credit group (**CG**). The currency (**Curr.**) and update group (**Update**) will populate automatically from the credit control area.

Let's explore the fields from automatic credit control settings:

- **No credit check**
  You can assign the routine or any custom logic in this field. SAP has provided standard routine **1** (order) and **2** (delivery). You can copy the routines and write your own custom logic in the routine to drive the credit check.
- **Item check**
  You can allow the system to check the credit limit as soon as you enter the line item in the sales order. If the line item exceeds the credit limit value, it will populate the error or warning message as configured in the system. If the item check isn't active, then it gives you warning or error messages while saving the sales order or delivery.

- **Deviation in %**
  You can give a threshold value for the deviation in credit limit check or an upward tolerance percentage in the field. For example, if the credit limit isn't exceeded by more than 5%, the system won't block the order or delivery of credit checks.
- **Number of days**
  You can specify the number of days after a changed operational document must be rechecked for credit management. If the value of the changed operational document exceeds the approved value, the credit management block will be reapplied to the sales document.
- **SAP Credit Mngt**
  The checkbox will enable the system to trigger the credit management configuration completed in the FSCM functionality.
- **Reaction**
  You can set the reaction, that is, whether to give warning message or error message if the credit limit is exceeded.
- **Status/Block**
  You need to activate the checkbox if you want the system to block the sales order in the event of an exceeded credit limit.

5.3.3 FSCM-Based Credit Management

The previous configurations are all that is required for the first approach to implementing classic credit management. However, if you want the credit limit and risk class to be calculated dynamically based on certain parameters, you must maintain the configurations we'll look at next.

Risk Class

You can maintain or calculate the risk class in the credit profile of the UKM role (**SAP Credit Management**) in the business partner (Transaction BP), as shown in Figure 5.56.

If you want to use the advanced functionalities of FSCM and calculate the risk class and credit limit automatically, then you have to perform the following configurations.

You can calculate credit risk class and credit limit with the help of formulas in FSCM credit management. The formula that you set up in the configuration needs to be assigned in the rule, which we'll discuss in the next section.

To define formulas, follow menu path **Financial Supply Chain Management • Credit Management • Credit Risk Monitoring • Master Data • Define Formulas.** You can also use Transaction UKM_FORMULAS. You'll arrive at the screen shown in Figure 5.57.

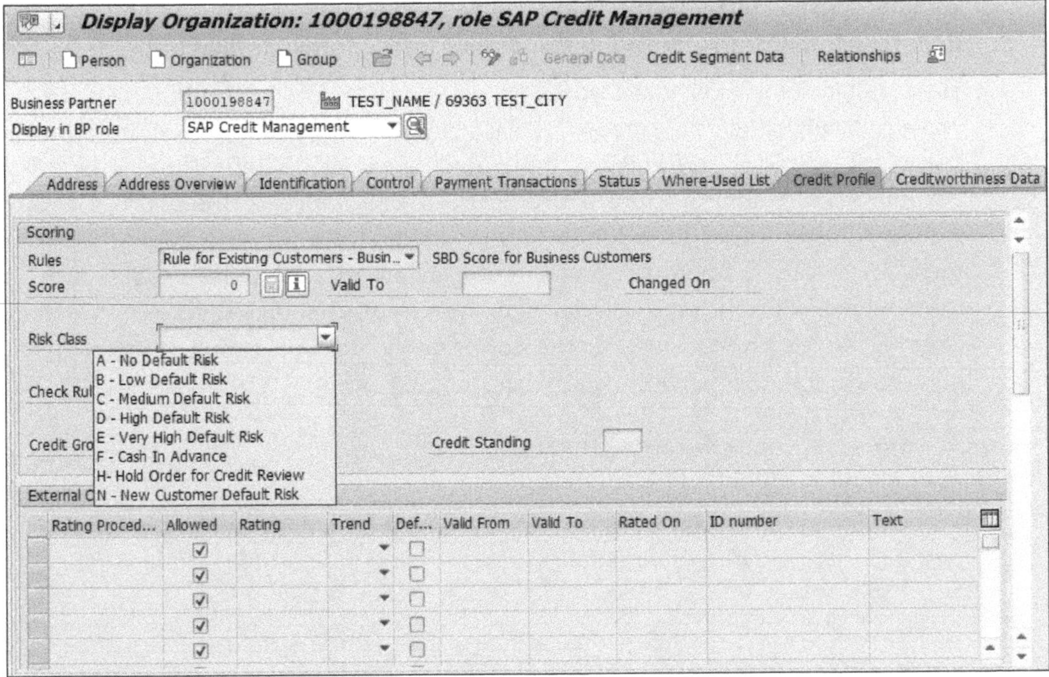

Figure 5.56 Business Partner: Risk Class

Display View "SAP Credit Management: Formulas": Overview

BC Set: Field Value Origin   Formula Editor

SAP Credit Management: Formulas

Formula	Formula Name	Result Type
LIMIT_B2B	Credit Limit for Business Customers	Calculation of Cr
LIMIT_B2C	Credit Limit for Private Customers	Calculation of Cr
SAP_LIMIT_DEFAULT	Credit Limit Default	Calculation of Cr
SAP_SCORE_ALL	Score with ALL Agencies	Calculation of Sc
SCORE_B2B	Score for Business Customers	Calculation of Sc
SCORE_B2C	Score for Private Customers	Calculation of Sc
YLIMIT_DEFAULT	Credit Limit Default	Calculation of Cr
YSCORE_DEFAULT	Credit Score Default	Calculation of Sc

Figure 5.57 Credit Management: Formulas

As shown in Figure 5.57, SAP S/4HANA provides the option to calculate score and credit limit with the help of formulas. You have to define individual formula for both score and credit limit. The scores can be assigned to the risk classes, so the risk class can be automatically populated in the SAP S/4HANA business partner. You can enter the formula by selecting the **Formula** row and clicking on the **Formula Editor** button.

The formula setup looks like Figure 5.58. You need to set up the steps, which we'll explain at a high level (this configuration is typically performed by FSCM consultants). The logic checks each step and determines the score or credit limit. The credit scoring formula acts as a numerical tool to measure the risk and creditworthiness of an organization. The editor tool provides an easy-to-use interface for entering logical statements. You can combine customer master data and transactional data, such as payment behavior. The scoring is based on the formula that the user can freely define. External ratings can be included in the scoring method. To make multiple external ratings comparable, they can be mapped to an internal rating.

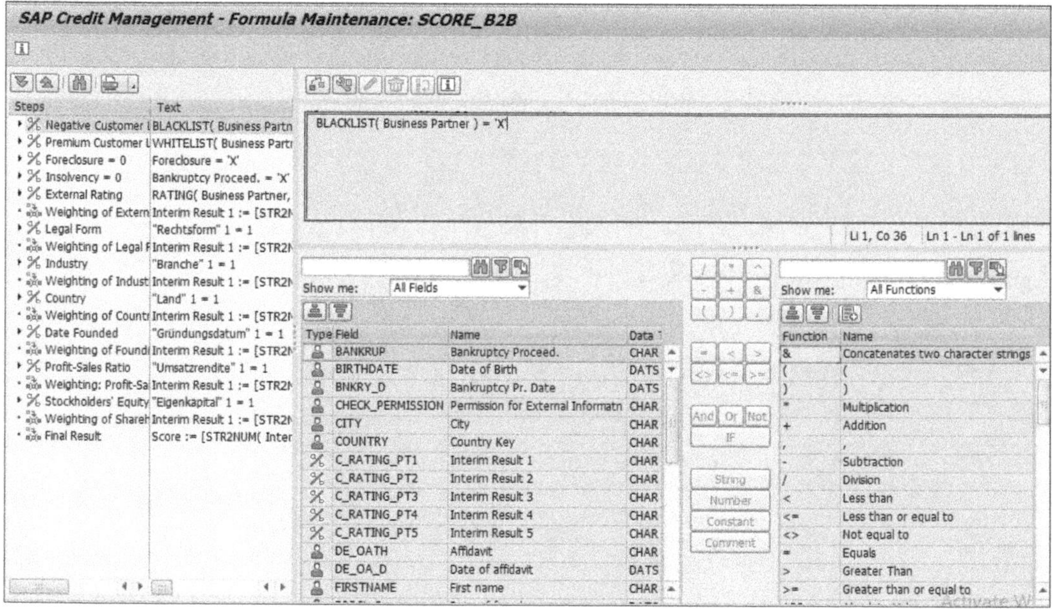

Figure 5.58 Formula Setup

Rule for Scoring and Credit Limit Calculation

As part of the credit management in FSCM, you have to maintain the rules in the business partner. The rule contains the formula associated with the credit limit and risk score, and it also contains the external rating procedure.

Create rules for scoring and credit limit calculation by following menu path **Financial Supply Chain Management • Credit Management • Credit Risk Monitoring • Master Data • Create Rule for Scoring and Credit Limit Calculation**. You'll arrive at the screen shown in Figure 5.59.

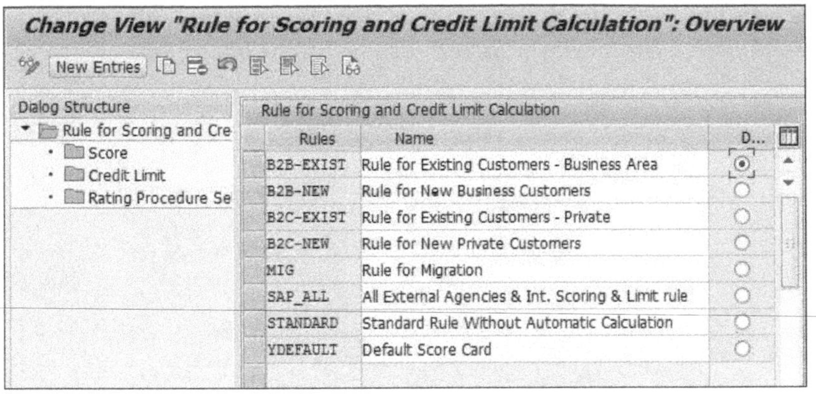

Change View "Rule for Scoring and Credit Limit Calculation": Overview

New Entries

Dialog Structure
- Rule for Scoring and Cre
  - Score
  - Credit Limit
  - Rating Procedure Se

Rule for Scoring and Credit Limit Calculation

Rules	Name	D...
B2B-EXIST	Rule for Existing Customers - Business Area	(•)
B2B-NEW	Rule for New Business Customers	○
B2C-EXIST	Rule for Existing Customers - Private	○
B2C-NEW	Rule for New Private Customers	○
MIG	Rule for Migration	○
SAP_ALL	All External Agencies & Int. Scoring & Limit rule	○
STANDARD	Standard Rule Without Automatic Calculation	○
YDEFAULT	Default Score Card	○

Figure 5.59 Rule for Scoring and Credit Limit Calculation

As shown in Figure 5.59, you have to first create the rule. You can create the custom rule by copying the existing one. In the example, select **B2B-EXIST**, and click on **Copy As** icon at the top of the screen. The default (**D...**) radio button is used to default the rule while creating the business partner.

After creation of the rule, you have to select the rule row, and click on the **Score** folder. You can see the screen after clicking the folder, as shown in Figure 5.60. You have to assign the **Score Formula** that you created earlier. You can also see the **Validity...** (validity days) this will be used to calculate the validity date in the business partner. By activating the trace for the formula (**Tr...** checkbox), you can view the actual working of the formula in business partner master data in Transaction BP by clicking on the **Information** button (i) shown previously in Figure 5.56.

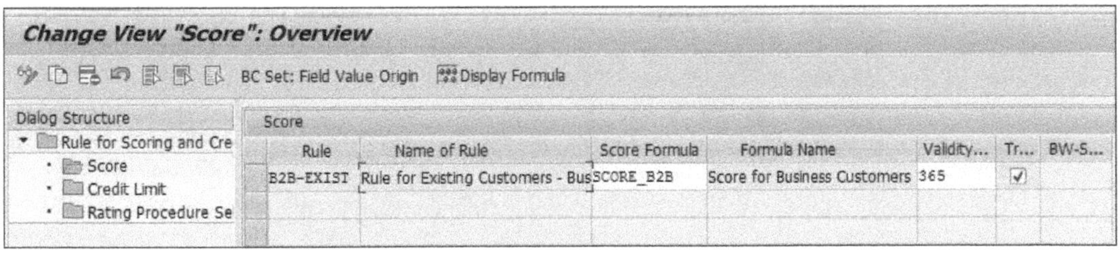

Change View "Score": Overview

BC Set: Field Value Origin   Display Formula

Dialog Structure
- Rule for Scoring and Cre
  - Score
  - Credit Limit
  - Rating Procedure Se

Score

Rule	Name of Rule	Score Formula	Formula Name	Validity...	Tr...	BW-S...
B2B-EXIST	Rule for Existing Customers - Bus	SCORE_B2B	Score for Business Customers	365	☑	

Figure 5.60 Score

Similar to the score formula, you have to assign the formula to calculate the credit limit, as shown in Figure 5.61, by navigating to the **Credit Limit** folder. If the credit department prefers to set the credit limit manually, then you don't have to input any credit limit formula and leave the **Credit Limit** folder blank for a specific rule. However, if you want the credit limit to be determined automatically, then you have to maintain the formula. You must assign each credit segment (**Credit...**), as well as the validity date

(**Vali...**). You can view the actual working of the formula in the business partner master data by activating the trace for the formula and clicking on the **Information** button (i) shown previously in Figure 5.56.

Display View "Credit Limit": Overview

BC Set: Field Value Origin Display Formula

Dialog Structure
- Rule for Scoring and Cre
  - Score
  - Credit Limit
  - Rating Procedure Sel

Rule B2B-NEW Rule for New Business Customers

Credit Limit

Credit...	Credit Limit ...	Formula Name	Vali...	...	Maximu...
01	LIMIT_B2B	Credit Limit for Business ...	180	☑	0
02	LIMIT_B2B	Credit Limit for Business ...	180	☑	0
03	LIMIT_B2B	Credit Limit for Business ...	180	☑	0

Figure 5.61 Credit Limit

In some cases, the business requirement is to integrate with the external rating agency for credit ratings of the business partner. You can assign the external rating procedure in the **Rat. Proc.** field in the **Rating Procedure Selection** folder, as shown in Figure 5.62.

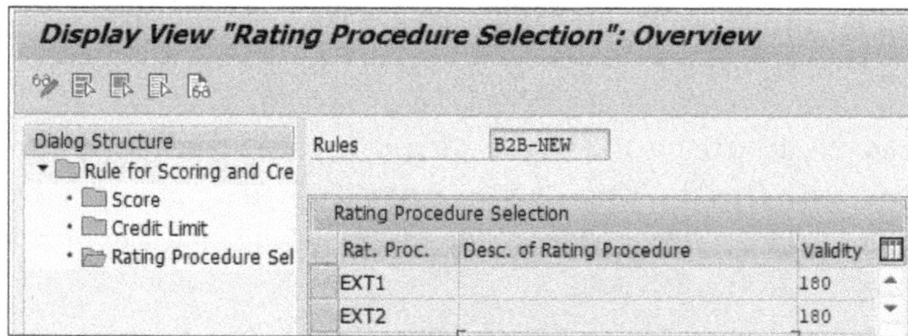

Figure 5.62 External Rating Procedure

Assignment of Risk Class to Score

The score that will be calculated with the help of a formula is used to determine the risk class in FSCM credit management. You can achieve it by assigning the scores to the risk class. To assign scores to the risk class, follow menu path **Financial Supply Chain Management • Credit Management • Credit Risk Monitoring • Master Data • Create Risk Classes**. You'll arrive at the screen shown in Figure 5.63. To make the assignments, click on the **New Entries** button, and provide the **Score From** and **Score To** for the individual **Risk Class**.

For example, you have to maintain the score of 80 to 100 for **Risk Class 001**. If the calculated credit score is 85 for a business partner, then the risk class calculated for the business partner will be **001**.

Change View "SAP Credit Management: Assignment of Risk Class to Score"

New Entries

SAP Credit Management: Assignment of Risk Class to Score

Risk Class	Name of Risk Class	Score From	Score To
001	Risk category 001	80	100
A	No Default Risk A	60	79
B	Low Default Risk B	40	59
C	Medium Default Risk C	20	39
D	High Default Risk D	1	19

Figure 5.63 Assignment of Risk Class to Score

5.3.4 Case Management

When you create a sales document for a credit-controlled customer, credit checks can be performed in a variety of ways based on the credit checking rules setup. If a credit check yields a negative result, the system generates a DCD based on the setup. The DCDs can be checked by a credit analyst or processor using Transactions SCASE, UKM_CASE, or UKM_MY_DCDS. They have the option to recheck, release, or reject the sales document and put a note on the DCD.

With Transaction UKM_CASE, the case document can be refused or released. After executing the transaction code, expand the **Cases** folder, and double-click on **Documented Credit Decision – Search**, which will open the screen shown in Figure 5.64.

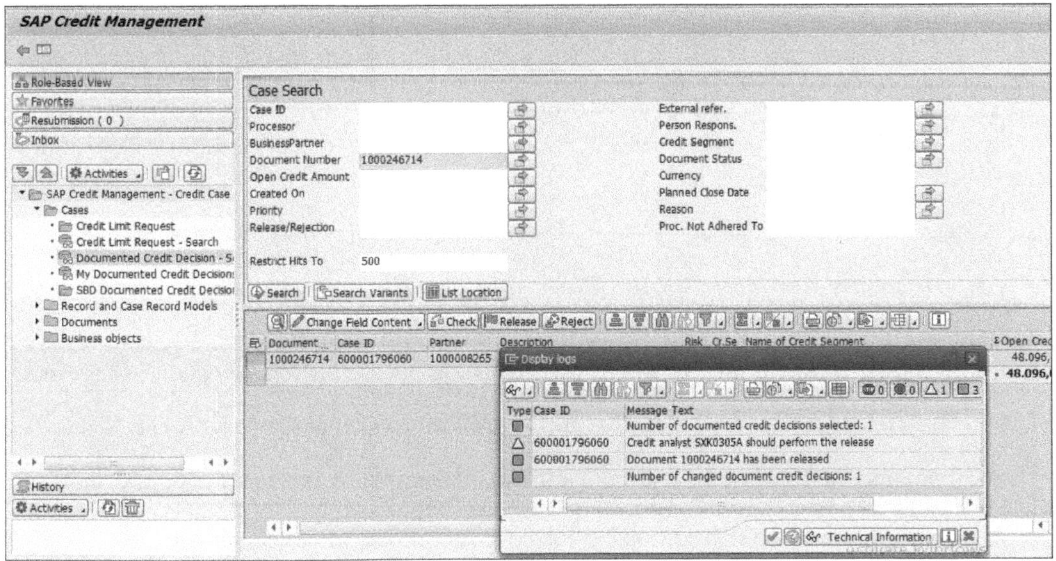

Figure 5.64 Credit Case

You can input the sales document in the case search **Document Number** field and click the **Search** button. Once the document is obtained, the credit manager can release or reject the credit case by clicking on the **Release** or **Reject** button, and it will open the **Display logs** screen. When rejecting a document, the credit manager can enter the appropriate reason in the text field. The credit case is closed once it has been rejected or released.

5.3.5 Tables and Transactions

In this section, a few important tables and transactions relevant for credit management are illustrated. Table 5.8 compares the SAP ERP transactions that are replaced in SAP S/4HANA. Table 5.9 explains the important new transactions and SAP Fiori apps. Table 5.10 summarizes important tables in SAP ERP as well as SAP S/4HANA.

Description	SAP ERP Transaction	Corresponding SAP S/4HANA Transaction
Credit account master data	Transaction FD32	Transaction UKM_BP
Credit blocked sales and distribution documents	Transaction VKM1/4 (still available although as work-around cases)	Transaction UKM_MY_DCDS
Releasing credit blocked sales orders	Transaction VKM3	Transaction UKM_CASE

Table 5.8 Credit Management Transactions

Transactions/SAP Fiori Apps	Description
Analyze Credit Exposure app	Analyze the risk exposure
Credit Limit Utilization app	Monitor the credit limit use of the business partner
Transaction UKM_COMMITMENTS	Analyze the credit exposure to one or more business partner
Transaction UKM_B_W_LIST	Maintain customers based on their credit performance
Transaction UKM_PM_BALANCE	Use for classic credit management: liability totals
Transaction UKMBP_VECTOR_IT	Use for classic credit management: credit segment

Table 5.9 New SAP Fiori Apps and Transactions for FSCM Credit Management

SAP ERP Tables	Corresponding SAP S/4HANA Tables
Table KNKA (Credit Management: Central Data)	Table UKMBP_VECTOR_IT (Credit Segment)
Table KNKK (Credit Management: Control Area Data)	▪ Table UKMBP_CMS (Credit Profile) ▪ Table UKMBP_CMS_SGM (Credit Segment) ▪ Table UKM_ITEM (Credit Commitments)

Table 5.10 Credit Management Tables

5.4 Profitability Analysis

Profitability analysis helps business executives and stakeholders find strategies to maximize profitability when it comes to various projects, plans, or goods. Profitability analysis is a methodical examination of corporate earnings derived from various revenue sources. Business stakeholders and leaders can monitor a company's performance by analyzing earnings. For a variety of reasons, understanding the nature of a company's earnings is critical. To maximize profits, business executives must first understand the factors that contribute to their profitability. This improves the efficiency of revenue-generating procedures and endeavors. As a result, it forces leaders to constantly look for ways to reduce overhead and other expenses that have an impact on profitability.

Profitability analysis aids in determining some important business concerns, as follows:

- How to improve product mixes to increase earnings in the short and long term. As leaders seek to set realistic goals and outline their implementation strategies, this makes it useful for budgeting.
- The ability to recognize both short-term and long-term product mixes assists management in determining whether or not to make changes to the company.
- When studying a variety of products, the most and least profitable items are identified, which is a useful insight. When deciding whether or not to discontinue a particular product, business decision-makers may occasionally consider this information.
- As a result, it's possible to predict sales and provides information on customer demographics, regional factors, and product categories that can be used to assess profit potential.

Finally, profitability analysis considers the various connections with clients and suppliers. These aid in determining which customers are the most and least profitable, as well as which vendors have the greatest impact on profitability. This is especially useful when dealing with customers and vendors.

In subsequent sections, we'll explore table ACDOCA, discuss the basics of profitability analysis, and walk through the configuration elements.

5.4.1 Universal Journal

Prior to the introduction of SAP HANA as a database solution, SAP Business Warehouse (SAP BW) was the go-to solution for business reporting. A scheduled job was used to transfer data from profitability analysis to the SAP BW system. Financial accounting and controlling were thought to function independently of one another from a business standpoint, even though they shared some fundamental business operations. As a result, each area has its own database table. The system was used to store general ledger, customer and vendor balances, and open items in various database tables to support reporting in the SAP ERP world.

The benefits of having all this information in one place were obvious:

- No required reconciliation activities
- Eliminated data redundancies
- No line-item duplication

All of this reduces the memory footprint and increases the throughput of the system. The finance and controlling components were also unified into one physical table (table ACDOCA) with the introduction of the SAP HANA database technology.

As shown in Figure 5.65, financial accounting and controlling, which were formerly separate components, are combined into one pool of business data by the Universal Journal. All accounting-related transactions are gathered in this single table, and it acts as a single source of truth that is made accessible to all pertinent application components, including financial accounting, controlling, asset accounting, profitability analysis, and the Material Ledger. Table ACDOCA helps to keep reports and tables in one database table itself. There is no need to store balanced and open items separately.

When you post a journal entry in SAP S/4HANA Finance, the header record is posted in table BKPF, and the line-item record is posted in table ACDOCA. In special scenarios, such as carrying forward, migration adjustments, and other activities, the line-item records in table ACDOCA are written without the corresponding document header data.

Some salient features of table ACDOCA are as follows:

- Table ACDOCA contains more than 360 different fields required for the general ledger, controlling, asset accounting, Material Ledger, and profitability analysis. The table also includes some of the fields that weren't part of table BSEG in SAP ERP.
- Customer-specific new general ledger fields are also stored in table ACDOCA.
- The old or redundant tables are still available as views.

- Table BSEG still exists, and it's used by several applications, including those for sales and purchasing, and SAP hasn't yet converted all of these programs to divert to table ACDOCA from table BSEG. In the future, table BSEG will likely be only used to store open item management.
- The Universal Journal has the ability to save data centrally as a single source of truth. It makes life easy for users and developers because it adheres to the on-the-fly calculating process.
- The year-end process is greatly accelerated and considerably smoother.
- There is no limitation of 999 document line items. Table BSEG is often aggregated due to the posting limitation of 999 document line items. Table ACDOCA doesn't have this restriction.

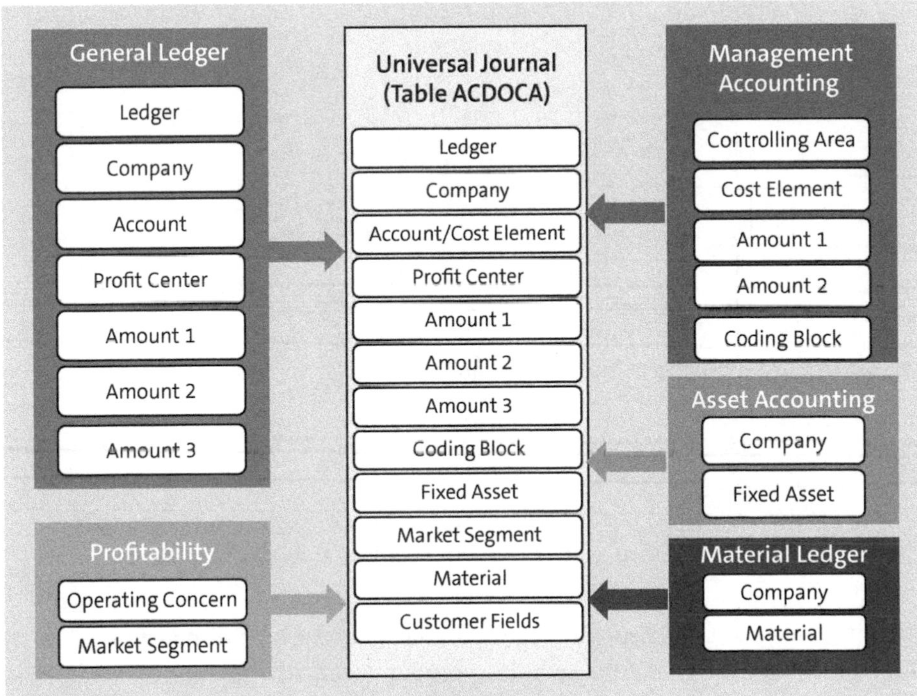

Figure 5.65 Financial Accounting and Controlling Components

As you can see, table ACDOCA is the most significant SAP S/4HANA innovation in the finance space, and it has had a significant impact on how financial data is stored in database tables.

5.4.2 What Is Profitability Analysis?

Let's first explore the organization structure for setting up profitability analysis in SAP S/4HANA. The operating concern is the highest organizational element in controlling.

All profitability reporting is performed on the operating concern. The controlling area is the highest level of an organization at which costs and revenues are recorded in SAP S/4HANA. Each controlling area can be assigned one or more company codes. As shown in Figure 5.66, the relationship between controlling area and operating concern is many to one, that is, many controlling areas can be assigned to one operating concern. The controlling area can be assigned with multiple company codes, but one company code can't be assigned with multiple controlling area.

In the example, you can see the operating concern is assigned to two company codes: NL01 and PL01. The cost center, profit center, and internal orders are assigned to the controlling area.

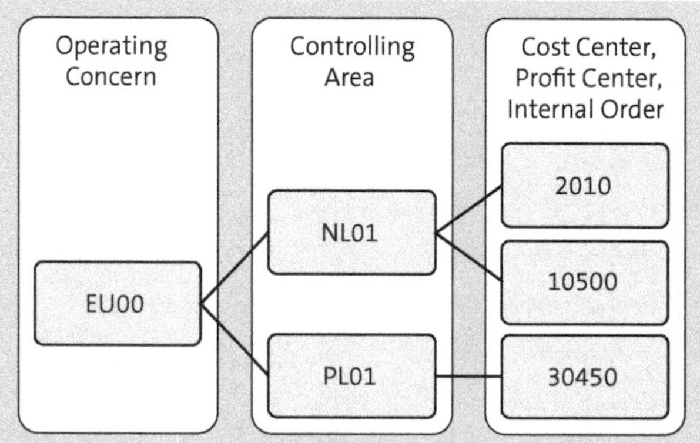

Figure 5.66 Organizational Structure for Profitability Analysis

Note

You can transfer costs from one cost center to another cost center that belong to the same controlling area; the same applies for profit centers and internal orders.

Profitability analysis provides a view of profitability for various dimensions. *Dimensions* are simply the parameters by which a company wants to assess its profitability. These dimensions are determined by the characteristics. You can examine the profitability of a combination of dimensions. Dimensions include sales group, customer group, material, material group, countries, regions, and states.

Profit can be seen in the *profit and loss (P&L)* statement generated at the company code level by financial accounting. However, to see the performance across multiple subunits or parameters for internal management reporting, you need a robust system in place that can provide you with the exact data that the business requires to access the financial health of the organization internally. For example, how the business is performing on a regional, state, or product level. The P&L statement is also used for external compliance reporting.

As shown in Figure 5.67, the basic calculation of profit is *P&L = Revenue – Expenses – Taxes*. As you can see in the diagram for company code IN01, the profit generated is *20,000 – 8,000 = 12,000*. The basic P&L statement only captures the total P&L across the organization.

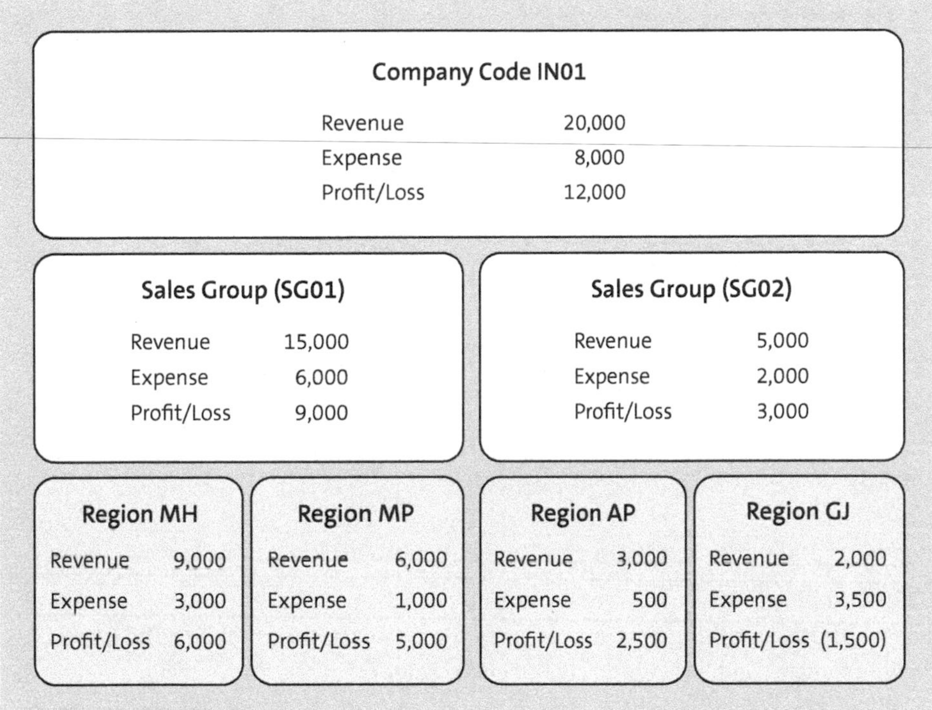

Figure 5.67 Example of P&L

However, the segment reporting isn't done through P&L. As you can see, the same P&L statement is first segregated based on the sales group. If you reconcile the data between the sales group and P&L, it will match with the original P&L statement. The P&L can also be segregated based on the geographical region. Thus, it provides a powerful capability to internal reporting, and reporting can be performed across multiple dimensions.

The profitability of the enterprise can only be analyzed if the finance-relevant data across all the components or the areas is passed to the central component. In SAP S/4HANA, this central component is profitability analysis. As shown in Figure 5.68, the finance-relevant data across multiple functionalities is passed to profitability analysis in the form of *characteristics*.

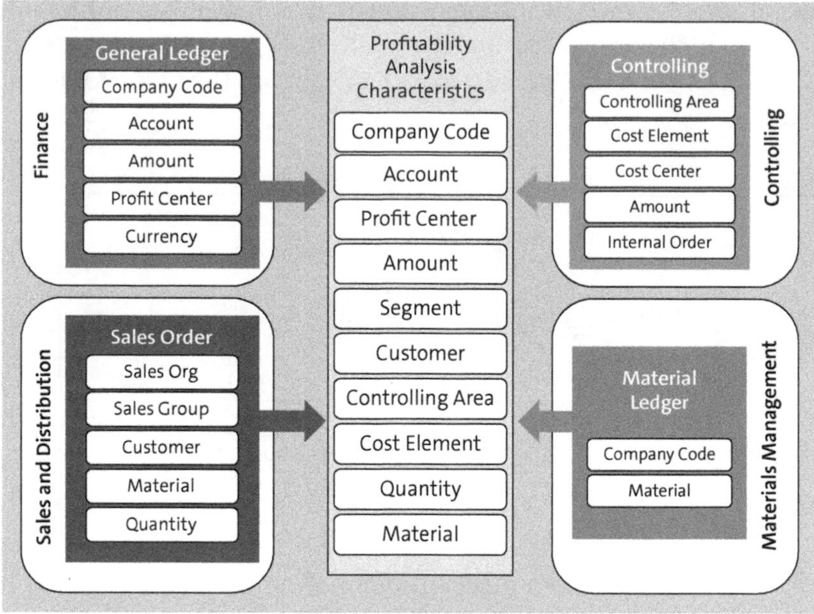

Figure 5.68 Characteristics in Profitability Analysis

The important data sources across multiple functionalities are as follows:

- **Sales and distribution**
  Sales orders and billing documents carry the values associated with the quantities, revenues, sales deduction, and cost of goods sales from the delivery document; that is, all information about the customer is derived from sales and distribution.
- **Materials management**
  Expenses are derived from materials management, especially the expenses coming from the Material Ledger.
- **General ledger**
  Expenses coming from the general ledger and controlling functionality such as advertising, marketing, and salary expenses.
- **Production planning**
  Production orders and variances.
- **Project System**
  The values from the workbench structure elements and the research and development (R&D) cost associated with the projects.

All these functionalities are very tightly integrated, and characteristics are derived for profitability analysis. The majority of profitability analysis characteristics are derived from the logistics functionality, so setting up master data is very important for creating a smooth flow of characteristics values.

One of the first steps in configuring profitability analysis is to identify, create, and assign the characteristics to the operating concern. SAP S/4HANA has provided predefined characteristics, but you also have the option to create custom characteristics in SAP S/4HANA. This character's nomenclature should begin with WW***.

The values in the characteristics are derived from the sender component, which could be sales and distribution, materials management, or any other logistic or finance-related functionality where profitability analysis is enabled. You can derive the value of custom characteristics through a configuration called *derivation*, which forces the system to choose predefined values based on business requirements.

Characteristics are determined automatically from the sales order or material master. However, if the expenses are booked for the material based on the journal entry, then the user has to choose the characteristics manually while posting the journal entry.

As a rule of thumb, you generally assign five characteristics to the profitability segment because more than five can compromise the data that has been entered while posting the journal entry by the user.

Another key concept for profitability analysis is the value field. *Value fields* are criteria that can be used to track and assess an organization's profitability, which groups cost and revenue elements into value fields in amount and quantity. Similar to characteristics, you have to set the value fields. You can create custom value fields with a prefix of VV****. However, value fields are only relevant in costing-based profitability analysis, which we'll discuss further next.

There are two types of profitability analysis approaches: costing-based and account-based. For a comparison of account-based versus costing-based profitability analysis, see Table 5.11.

Account-based profitability analysis, now called *margin analysis* in SAP S/4HANA, is the recommended approach because it's permanently reconciled with financial accounting. Costing-based profitability analysis functionalities are now available in margin analysis. The Universal Journal (table ACDOCA) combines margin analysis characteristics with financial accounting, controlling, and the Material Ledger in a single table.

Account-Based Profitability Analysis (Margin Analysis)	Costing-Based Profitability Analysis
Uses characteristics	Uses characteristics and value fields
Uses cost and revenue elements so its P&L is very similar to the company P&L	Primarily designed to allow analysis of profit quickly for the purpose of sales management; can analyze a margin quickly

Table 5.11 Differences between Account-Based and Costing-Based Profitability Analysis

Account-Based Profitability Analysis (Margin Analysis)	Costing-Based Profitability Analysis
Permanently reconciled with financial accounting.	Reconciliation based on timing
Cost of goods sold (COGS) calculated at the time of goods issue	COGS calculated at the time of billing

Table 5.11 Differences between Account-Based and Costing-Based Profitability Analysis (Cont.)

5.4.3 Configuration for Margin Analysis

The key configurations required to set up profitability analysis are described in this section. Keep in mind that configurations are often conducted by controlling consultants and can become quite complicated depending on the business requirements. As a result, it's recommended that the following activities be performed with the assistance of a controlling expert.

Define Characteristics

Definition of characteristics is one of the prerequisites for profitability analysis in SAP S/4HANA. You have to maintain characteristics for account-based as well as costing-based profitability analysis. Let's explore how to create characteristics in SAP S/4HANA.

To create characteristics, follow menu path **Controlling • Profitability Analysis • Structures • Define Operating Concern • Maintain Characteristics**. You can also use Transaction KEA5 for creation of characteristics.

You'll arrive at the screen shown in Figure 5.69, where you can choose between three functions:

- **All Characteristics**
  You can view all the characteristics that are created in the system.
- **Chars from operating concern**
  You can only view the predefine characteristics that are created for the operating concern.
- **Characteristics that are not used in operating concern**
  You can view the characteristics that aren't used in any of the created operating concerns.

Then, you have to click on the **Display** button to view the characteristics maintained in the system, as shown in Figure 5.70. SAP has provided the standard characteristics such as customer, material, cost center, company code and so on, as shown in Figure 5.70. You can get business requirements to create your own custom characteristics. However, SAP has given the limit of 60 characteristics in SAP S/4HANA. Custom characteristics can be created with the prefix WW. The entire configuration that you perform in the characteristic's node is cross-client; that is, once the changes are made in one client, they will be available across all the other clients.

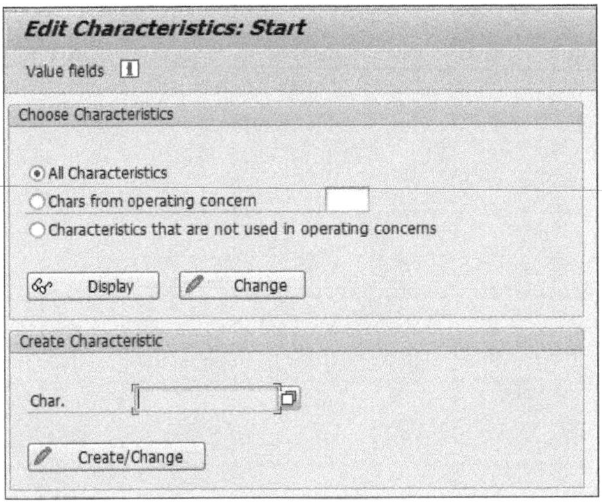

Edit Characteristics: Start

Value fields

Choose Characteristics

- All Characteristics
- Chars from operating concern
- Characteristics that are not used in operating concerns

Display | Change

Create Characteristic

Char.

Create/Change

Figure 5.69 Characteristics

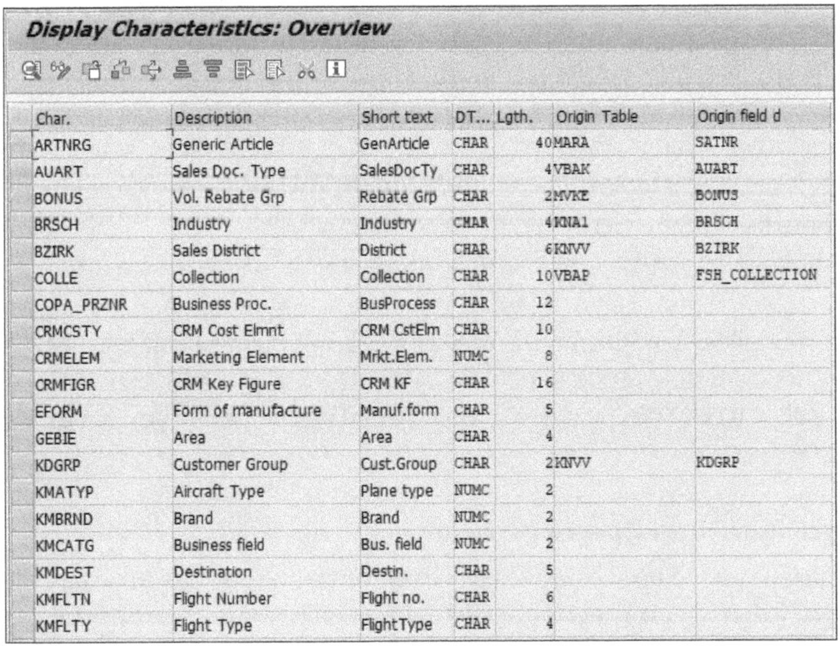

Display Characteristics: Overview

Char.	Description	Short text	DT...	Lgth.	Origin Table	Origin field d
ARTNRG	Generic Article	GenArticle	CHAR	40	MARA	SATNR
AUART	Sales Doc. Type	SalesDocTy	CHAR	4	VBAK	AUART
BONUS	Vol. Rebate Grp	Rebate Grp	CHAR	2	MVKE	BONUS
BRSCH	Industry	Industry	CHAR	4	KNA1	BRSCH
BZIRK	Sales District	District	CHAR	6	KNVV	BZIRK
COLLE	Collection	Collection	CHAR	10	VBAP	FSH_COLLECTION
COPA_PRZNR	Business Proc.	BusProcess	CHAR	12		
CRMCSTY	CRM Cost Elmnt	CRM CstElm	CHAR	10		
CRMELEM	Marketing Element	Mrkt.Elem.	NUMC	8		
CRMFIGR	CRM Key Figure	CRM KF	CHAR	16		
EFORM	Form of manufacture	Manuf.form	CHAR	5		
GEBIE	Area	Area	CHAR	4		
KDGRP	Customer Group	Cust.Group	CHAR	2	KNVV	KDGRP
KMATYP	Aircraft Type	Plane type	NUMC	2		
KMBRND	Brand	Brand	NUMC	2		
KMCATG	Business field	Bus. field	NUMC	2		
KMDEST	Destination	Destin.	CHAR	5		
KMFLTN	Flight Number	Flight no.	CHAR	6		
KMFLTY	Flight Type	FlightType	CHAR	4		

Figure 5.70 Characteristics

Click the **Details** icon to arrive at the screen in Figure 5.71, which shows the characteristics sales document type **AUART**.

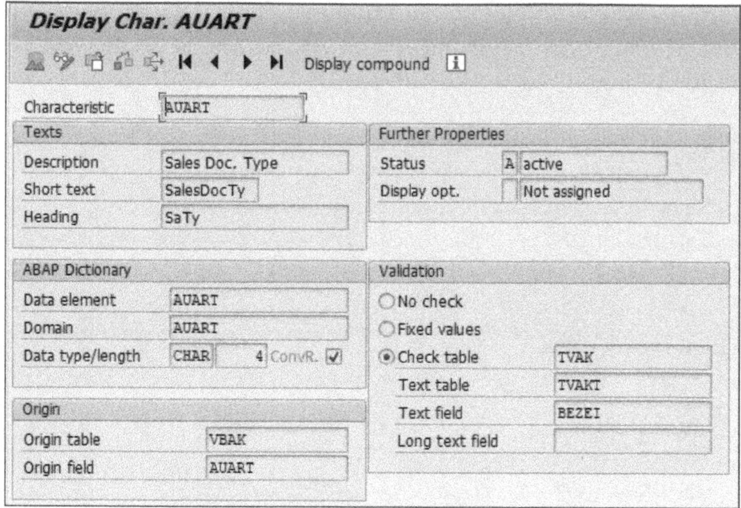

Figure 5.71 Characteristics Fields

Let's explore fields in characteristics:

- **Texts**
  You can define the description of the characteristics in this section. Custom characteristics need to be created with prefix as **WW**.
- **ABAP Dictionary**
  This section displays the technical name of the characteristics. In the event of creation of the custom characteristics with the help of ABAP consultant, you have to append the structure and add your custom field in the ABAP dictionary.
- **Further Properties**
  This section gives the status of the characteristics (active or inactive state).
- **Validation**
  This section provides insight into the type of characteristic. You can transfer the characteristics from the SAP standard table or create a custom characteristic with prefix as **WW**. You can also create your own check table from where you can derive the characteristics.

Assign Characteristics to the Operating Concern

The created characteristics need to be assigned to the operating concern. To assign the characteristics, follow menu path **Controlling • Profitability Analysis • Structures • Define Operating Concern • Maintain Operating Concern**. You can also use Transaction KEA0 for this assignment.

When you click the **Data Structure** button, you get the screen shown in Figure 5.72. In the **Data structure**, you can find the characteristics that you activated for the operating concern. As shown in Figure 5.72, there are two columns, **Transfer from** and **Data**

structure. You can move the characteristics field from the **Transfer from** column to the **Data structure** column by clicking on the **Transfer fields** button ◀. After assigning the characteristics field, activate the fields by clicking on the **Activate** button.

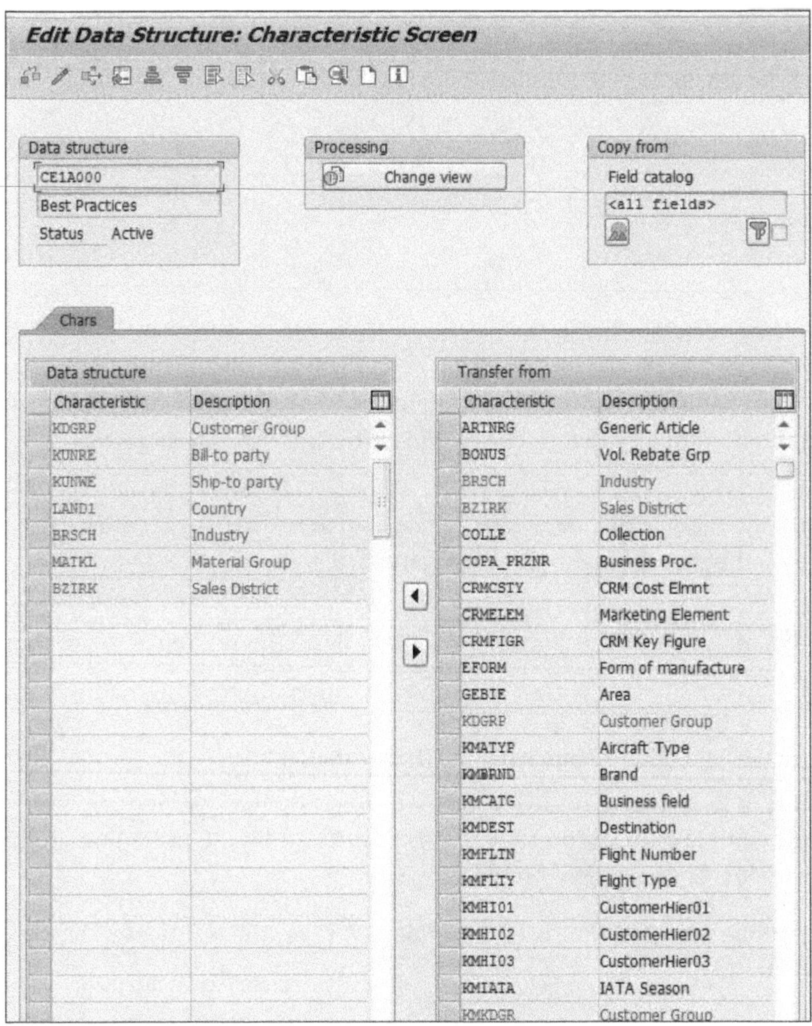

Figure 5.72 Characteristics: Data Structure

Any custom characteristics created based on the business requirements can be populated with a fixed set of possible values. After activating the user-defined characteristics, the system automatically generates a check table that can be used to check the characteristics values permitted, as shown in Figure 5.73.

To navigate here, follow the menu path for maintaining characteristic values: **Controlling • Profitability Analysis • Master Data • Characteristic Values • Maintain Characteristic Values**.

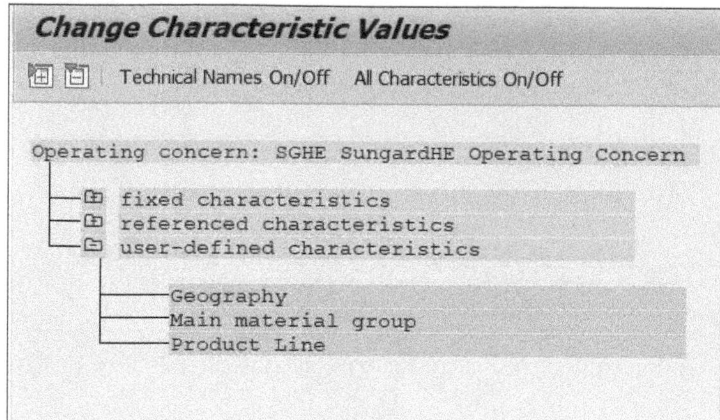

Figure 5.73 Maintain Characteristic Values

You can derive the characteristics in the document based on the derivation rule. SAP has provided four different ways by which you can derive the characteristics value:

- **Derivation rule**
  You can derive the value of the characteristic based on the if-then logic, which can be configured by setting up the appropriate derivation rule.
- **Table lookup**
  You can derive the value of the characteristics by taking the reference to another table.
- **Move**
  You can move the value of the source field to the target field.
- **Enhancement**
  To drive some complex derivation logic that isn't fulfilled by the preceding methods, you can use the enhancement provided by SAP.

Further detail on this configuration is beyond our scope, as this is done by the controlling consultant.

Maintain Operating Concern

The prerequisite of setting up profitability analysis reporting is to create the operating concern, which is handled by the SAP financial accounting consultant or controlling consultant (usually, the latter). An operating concern is the highest organizational unit for which you want to report overall profitability. It houses the profitability analysis data model and stores data for reporting purposes.

To create or display the operating concern, follow menu path **Controlling • Profitability Analysis • Structures • Define Operating Concern • Maintain Operating Concern**. You can also use Transaction KEA0 for the same. You'll arrive at the screen shown in Figure 5.74. You generally create the new operating concern by clicking on the **Create** icon.

Changes for configurations associated with the operating concern are cross-client. Let's explore each screen for the operating concern.

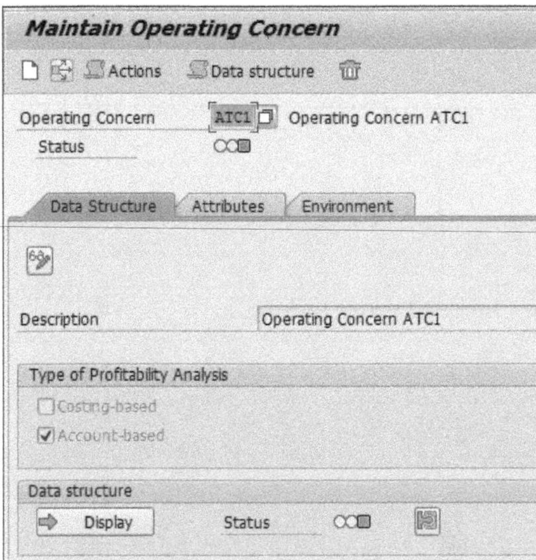

Figure 5.74 Maintain Operating Concern: Data Structure

As shown in Figure 5.74, some of the important fields in the operating concern **Data Structure** tab are as follows:

- **Description**
  Give the appropriate description for the operating concern.
- **Type of Profitability Analysis**
  As previously stated, you can set up two different methods of profitability analysis: **Account-based** and **Costing-based**. SAP S/4HANA also allows using both profitability analysis techniques. Profitability is determined by the value and characteristic fields. However, reconciliation of costing-based profitability analysis is difficult. SAP recommends using the account-based method to calculate profitability analysis values (margin analysis) because it includes a built-in general ledger reconciliation. Table ACDOCA (the Universal Journal) contains all the necessary features, making reconciliation with financial accounting easier.
- **Data structure**
  The characteristics that we've discussed earlier need to be assigned in the data structure. We'll cover the configuration of characteristics in a later section.

The next screen in the operating concern configuration is the **Attributes** tab, as shown in Figure 5.75.

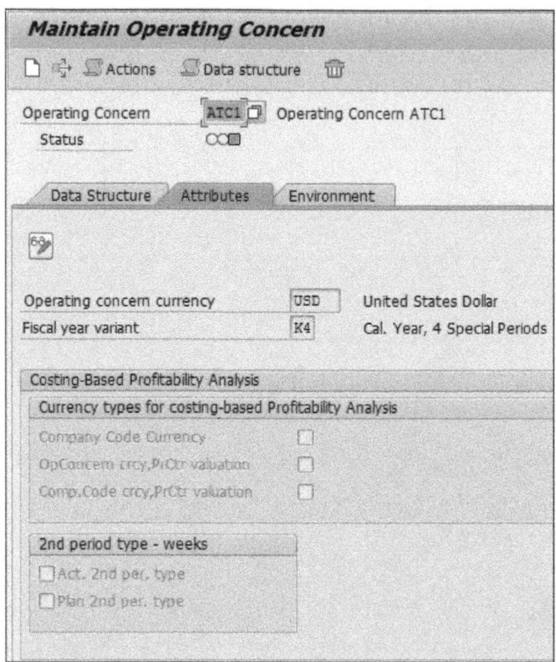

Figure 5.75 Maintain Operating Concern: Attributes

Let's dive into each field, as follows:

- **Operating concern currency**
  This is the currency in which the data transferred to profitability analysis is converted and updated.
- **Fiscal year variant**
  The defines the period structure of the operating concern. The fiscal year variant includes the total number of posting periods and the total number of special periods. A fiscal year may have up to 16 posting periods defined in the controlling functionality, represented by the **CO** value. For each company code, the fiscal year variant must be specified. You must also include the fiscal year variant when creating a controlling area. The sole difference between the governing area and business code fiscal year variations is the number of special periods used. All controlling areas that are assigned to the operating concern have to be assigned to the same fiscal variant.
- **Currency types for costing-based Profitability Analysis**
  This field is applicable only if you activate costing-based profitability analysis. You can define the additional currency types to store the values associated with costing-based profitability analysis.
- **2nd period type – weeks**
  You can also store actual and planned data in costing-based profitability analysis in weeks after activating the indicator.

After completing the configuration of the operating concern, you have to activate the operating concern in the **Environment** tab by clicking on the **Activate** (match) icon, as shown in Figure 5.76. The operating concern is enabled and ready to use if both the **Status** of the **Cross-client part** and the **Status** of the **Client-specific part** are green.

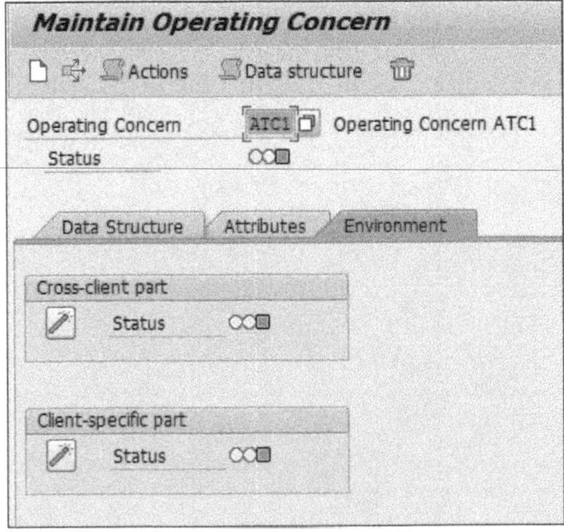

Figure 5.76 Maintain Operating Concern: Environment

Assigning Controlling Areas to the Operating Concern

To generate the profitability segment once the document is posted, you have to assign the company code to the newly created operating concern via menu path **Enterprise Structure • Assignment • Controlling • Assign Controlling Area to Operating Concern**. You'll arrive at the screen shown in Figure 5.77.

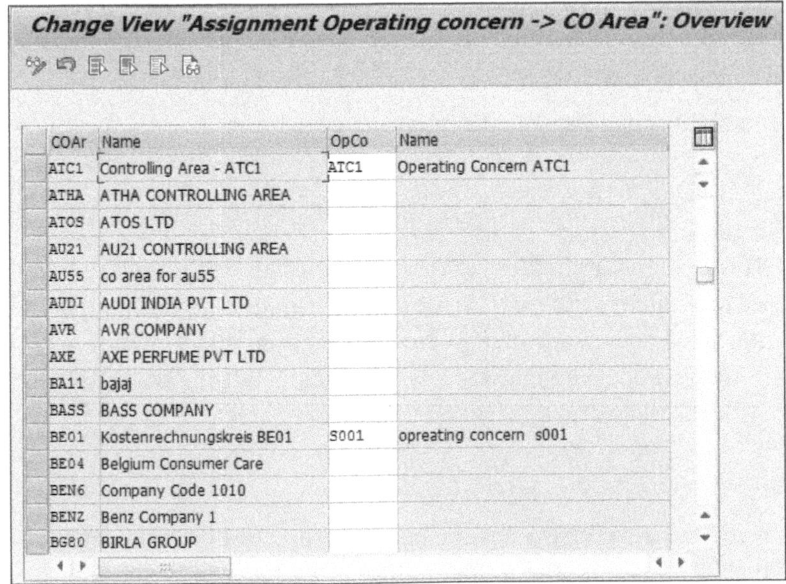

Figure 5.77 Assignment Operating Concern to Controlling Area

As shown in Figure 5.77, you have to assign the controlling area (**COAr**) to the operating concern (**OpCo**). You can assign multiple controlling areas to a single operating concern. However, you must make sure that the fiscal year variant is the same for the controlling area as the operating concern.

After assigning the operating concern to the controlling area, the next step is to activate profitability analysis/margin analysis. To activate profitability analysis for the controlling area, follow menu path **Controlling • Profitability Analysis • Flows of Actual Values • Activate Profitability Analysis**. You'll arrive at the screen shown in Figure 5.78.

Change View "CO-PA: Active Flag for Profitability Analysis": Overview

COAr	Name	From FY	Op....	costing-based	account-based
ATC1	Controlling Area - ATC1	2021	ATC1	☐	☑
ATHA	ATHA CONTROLLING AREA	2021		☐	☐
ATOS	ATOS LTD	2002		☐	☐
AU21	AU21 CONTROLLING AREA	2021		☐	☐
AU55	co area for au55	2022		☐	☐
AUDI	AUDI INDIA PVT LTD	2021		☐	☐
AXE	AXE PERFUME PVT LTD	2021		☐	☐
BA11	bajaj	2022		☐	☐
BE01	Kostenrechnungskreis BE01	1995	S001	☐	☐
BE01	Kostenrechnungskreis BE01	1997	S001	☐	☐
BE04	Belgium Consumer Care	2022		☐	☐
BENZ	Benz Company 1	1999		☐	☐
BENZ	Benz Company 1	2021		☐	☐
BG80	BIRLA GROUP	2021		☐	☐
BHCO	Bharath Mobiles	2022		☐	☐
BHE1	POWER TRANS(BHEL)	2022		☐	☐

Figure 5.78 Activate Profitability Analysis

The controlling area must be activated in conjunction with the combination of fiscal year (**From FY**) and operating concern (**Op...**).

After activating profitability analysis, operating concerns can be used.

5.4.4 Data Flow

In this section, we'll discuss the flow of the values for account-based profitability analysis and costing-based profitability analysis. The flow of the values is determined in the following Transaction SPRO node: **Controlling • Profitability Analysis • Flows of Actual Values**. Profitability analysis doesn't generate any of the data, but the data is passed through several logistics as well as financial functionalities.

Invoice Value Flow

As discussed earlier, you can use both the costing-based and account-based approach to pass values to profitability analysis. The primary differences between the approaches are as follows:

- **Account-based profitability analysis (margin analysis)**
  You use general ledger accounts to transfer the value into profitability analysis; that is, the prerequisite to use account-based profitability analysis is the revenue account determination and Transaction OBYC settings for the COGS account. The general ledger accounts are mapped as cost elements while the general ledger accounts are created in Transaction FS00. As shown in Figure 5.79, you'll map the general ledger account used for the revenue account determination with cost element category as **11** for revenue and **12** for discounts.

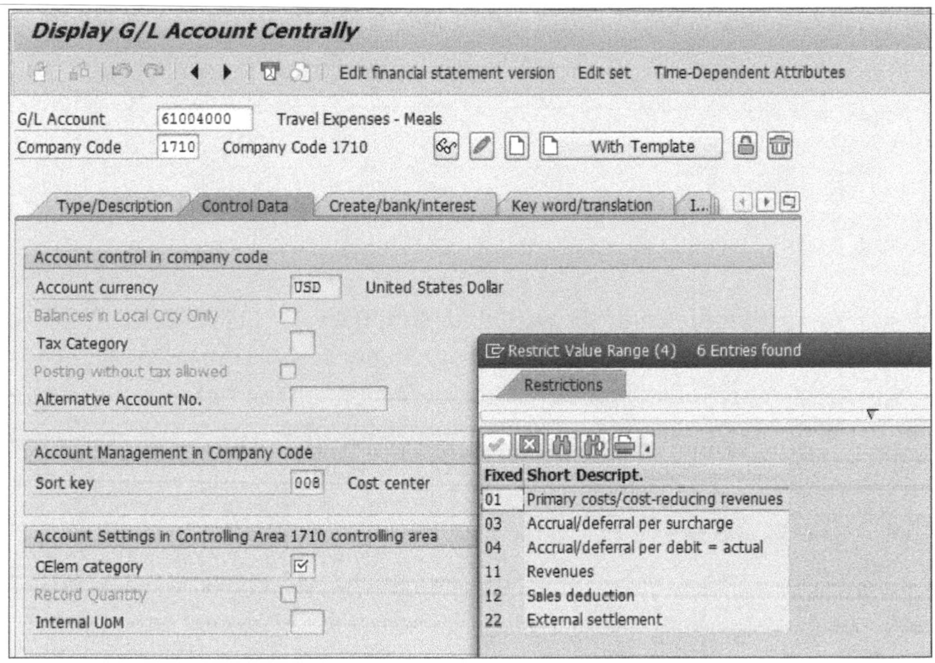

Figure 5.79 General Ledger Account

  After creation of the billing document on the sales and distribution side, the accounting document gets generated once the values are passed to accounting. The general ledger account determination happens via the revenue account determination condition technique that you've configured in Section 5.2. There won't be any value fields in the account-based profitability analysis document.

- **Costing-based profitability analysis**
  In this technique, the values are transferred via value fields that you'll assign to the condition types in menu path **Controlling • Profitability Analysis • Flows of Actual Values • Transfer of Billing Documents • Assign Value Fields • Maintain Assignment of SD Conditions to CO-PA Value Fields.**

  You'll arrive at the screen shown in Figure 5.80, where you must map the sales and distribution condition type (**CTyp**) that you've included in the sales and distribution pricing procedure to the value fields (**Val. fld**) in controlling. You can create your own value fields based on the business requirement similar to custom characteristics. The standard value field provided by SAP is ERLOS for revenue.

Display View "CO-PA: Assignment of SD Conditions to Value Fields": Ove

Op. concern BDOC B&D Operating Concern

CTyp	Name	Val. fld	Description	Transfer +/-
AMIZ	Minimum ValueSurchrg	VV427	Delivery Surcharges	☐
DIFF	Rounding Off	VV110	Price Discount	☑
NETD	Diff. clearing	VV110	Price Discount	☐
NETP	Price	VV105	Customer List Price	☑
NRAB	Free goods	VV110	Price Discount	☑
R100	100% discount	VV109	List Price Reversal	☐
RA00	% Discount Manual	VV110	Price Discount	☐
RA02	% Discount Manual	VV110	Price Discount	☐
SKTO	Cash Discount	VV112	Cash Discount (PA)	☐
SKTV	Cash Discount	VV112	Cash Discount (PA)	☐

Figure 5.80 Assignment of Sales and Distribution Conditions to Value Fields

For costing-based profitability analysis, along with the value fields, you also have to assign the quantity fields to the relevant profitability analysis quantity field by following menu path **Controlling • Profitability Analysis • Flows of Actual Values • Transfer of Billing Documents• Assign Quantity Fields**. In the screen that appears, as shown in Figure 5.81, assign **SD qty field** to **CO-PA qty field**.

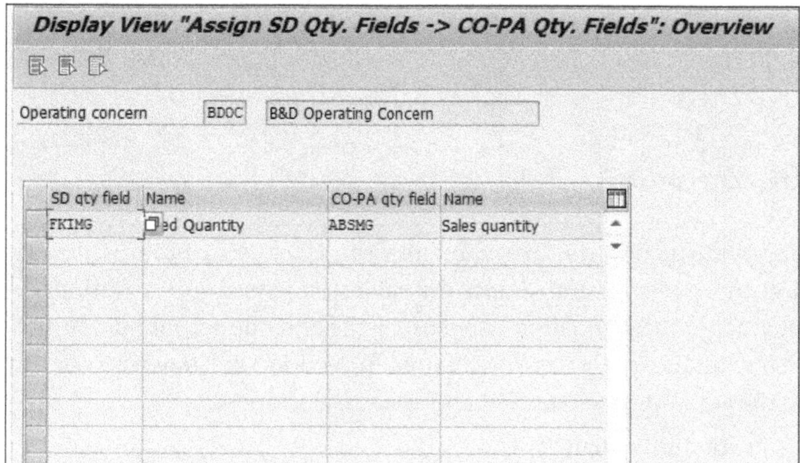
Display View "Assign SD Qty. Fields -> CO-PA Qty. Fields": Overview

Operating concern BDOC B&D Operating Concern

SD qty field	Name	CO-PA qty field	Name
FKIMG	[illegible]ed Quantity	ABSMG	Sales quantity

Figure 5.81 Assign Quantity Fields

Cost of Goods Sold and Cost of Sales

The flow of COGS and cost of sales values is different in both profitability analysis approaches, which we'll explore in subsequent sections:

- **Account-based profitability analysis (margin analysis)**
  After creation of the deliveries in the sales and distribution landscape, along with the delivery document, financial documents will also get generated that post the COGS values to accounting. Table ACDOCA gets updated with the production cost along with the profitability segment.
- **Costing-based profitability analysis**
  Posting to profitability analysis doesn't happen during delivery creation; that is, posting to profitability analysis happens after the invoice has been created for the customer, which means both COGS and revenue are posted at the same time. This causes problem in the reconciliation of the values. From the sales and distribution side, the condition type VPRS corresponds to the COGM value. The value in the VPRS condition type is derived based on the material cost maintained in the **Accounting 1** tab of the material master. For costing-based profitability analysis, this condition type is assigned to the value field.

In SAP S/4HANA, you can segregate COGS into smaller components; that is, you can split the COGS amount. As we've covered in Chapter 4, Section 4.3, the general ledger account determination for COGS is done through the transaction key GBB-VAX combination. In the SAP S/4HANA world, you can further differentiate the general ledger accounts based on the cost component.

5.5 Intercompany Billing

Intercompany accounting is the process of recording and managing financial transactions between different legal entities within the same parent company. These entities' transactions aren't "independent" because they are related. As a result, companies are unable to record a profit or loss from these transactions in their consolidated financial statements. Each company can use the *intercompany billing* process to match costs to revenue and determine profitability. This automated process also generates intercompany receivable and payable entries in the general ledger, ensuring that each company's balance sheets are balanced.

In this section, we'll take a deep dive into how intercompany sales transactions are performed and configured in the SAP landscape. We'll first cover the transaction overview and steps, and then we'll look at the configurations and their impact on the SAP S/4HANA system.

5.5.1 What Is Intercompany Billing?

Figure 5.82 shows the typical intercompany sales transaction between plants of two company codes. Corporations frequently incorporate multiple legal entities to manage a complex business. In the SAP S/4HANA organization structure, each legal entity could be represented by a separate company code. These company codes could be established in different geographies or countries. As shown in Figure 5.82, a customer places an order with a plant associated with company code ZINO. Due to unforeseen circumstances, the plant doesn't have the material that the customer requires. So, in the sales order, the customer representative creates the sales order with the different plant associated with company code ZDE1 where the stock is available. The system examines the sales organization entered in the sales order, as well as the company code associated with it, and compares the company code of the sales organization to the company code of the delivering plant. If the company codes are different, the system classifies the sales transaction as intercompany sales.

The order is fulfilled, and the goods are delivered to the customer by the company code ZDE1. The invoice is raised by the company code ZINO to the end customer who receives the goods. The company code associated with the delivering plant sends the ordering company an intercompany invoice. The pricing for the affiliate intercompany invoice and the end customer is different. It's triggered by the PI01 condition type, which appears only in the billing document.

The intercompany sales process prevents the company from stockpiling goods in its own warehouse and allows the company to choose which plant and company code can deliver the goods to the customer. It allows all company codes to share inventory information, track intercompany shipments, and view finance postings and settlements automatically. Account reconciliation and settlement between companies is done automatically.

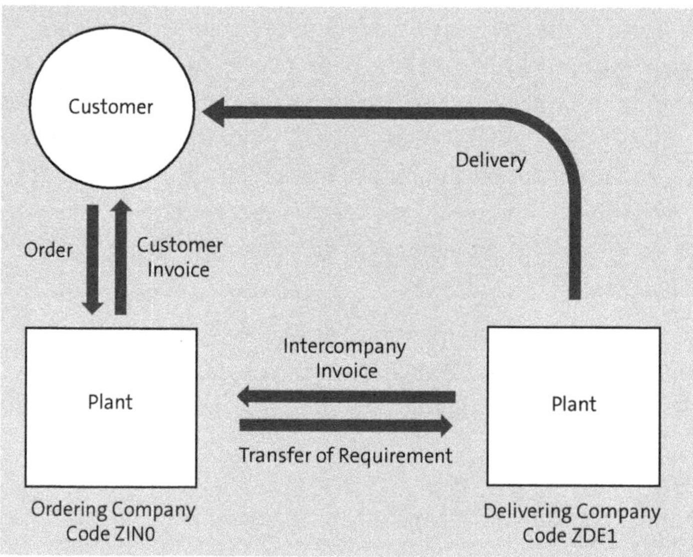

Figure 5.82 Intercompany Sales

5.5.2 Prerequisites for Intercompany Billing

The prerequisite for intercompany setup is that the material should be extended to both sales organizations involved in intercompany sales. The plant you'll use for the intercompany transactions needs to be assigned with the sales organizations associated with the transactions. To make this assignment, follow menu path **Enterprise Structure • Assignment • Sales and Distribution • Assign Sales Organization – Distribution Channel – Plant.**

You'll arrive at the screen shown in Figure 5.83, where you'll assign **SOrg.** and **DChCust/Mt** with **Plnt**. In the example, we've assigned sales organizations **ZDE1** and **ZINO** with plant **ZDE1**.

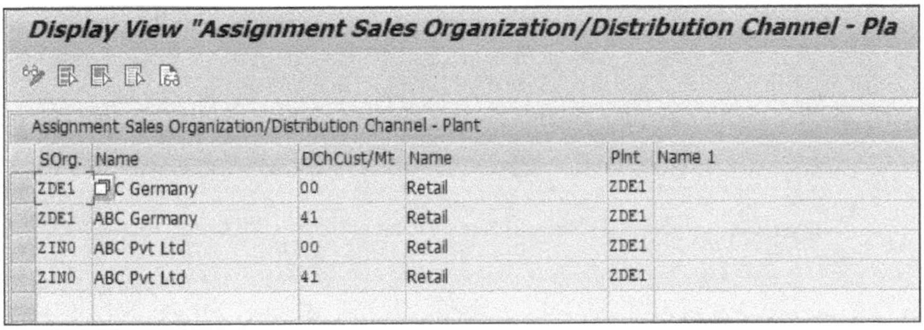

Display View "Assignment Sales Organization/Distribution Channel - Pla

Assignment Sales Organization/Distribution Channel - Plant

SOrg.	Name	DChCust/Mt	Name	Plnt	Name 1
ZDE1	C Germany	00	Retail	ZDE1	
ZDE1	ABC Germany	41	Retail	ZDE1	
ZINO	ABC Pvt Ltd	00	Retail	ZDE1	
ZINO	ABC Pvt Ltd	41	Retail	ZDE1	

Figure 5.83 Assignment of Sales Organization/Distribution Channel to Plant

5.5.3 Configuration for Intercompany Billing

To perform intercompany sales, a series of configurations must be implemented. Let's go through each configuration one by one.

Define Order Types for Intercompany Billing

The intercompany billing document type must be assigned to the sales document types that are applicable for the intercompany billing transaction. To define order types for intercompany billing, follow menu path **Sales and Distribution • Billing • Intercompany Billing • Define Order Types for Intercompany Billing.** You'll arrive at the screen shown in Figure 5.84.

Assign the intercompany billing document type **IV** (the SAP-defined standard billing type for intercompany billing) with respect to the sales document type **ZIOR**.

You can also create a custom billing type by copying the existing **IV** billing type for the creation of intercompany billing document types. To create the billing document type, follow menu type **Sales and Distribution • Billing • Billing Documents • Define Billing Types.** You can also use Transaction VOFA to perform the same activity. You'll arrive at the screen shown in Figure 5.85, where you can select billing type **IV** and click on the **Details** icon to arrive at the screen shown in Figure 5.86.

Display View "Sales Order Types for Inter-Company Billing": Overview

SalesDocTy	Sales Document Type	Interco.	Intercomp. Bill.Type
ZIOR	IN Std Order	IV	Intercompany Billing
ZJBV	Cash Sale mar s.dac	IV	Intercompany Billing
ZJOR	Standard Order cyc	IV	Intercompany Billing
ZLQT	Quotatio		
ZOOR	Standard Order GB	IV	Intercompany Billing
ZOR	Standard Order	IV	Intercompany Billing
ZORD	Standard Order_NPSG	IV	Intercompany Billing
ZQHT	Quote		
ZQT	Quotation		
ZQTO	Quotation_NPSG		
ZSIN	SCM Inquiry		
ZSOR	Standard Order	IV	Intercompany Billing
ZSQT	Quotation		
ZYOR	Standard Order	IV	Intercompany Billing
ZYQT	Quotation		
ZZOR	Sales Order	IV	Intercompany Billing
ZZCR	Credit Mem Req S&m		

Figure 5.84 Define Order Types for Intercompany Billing

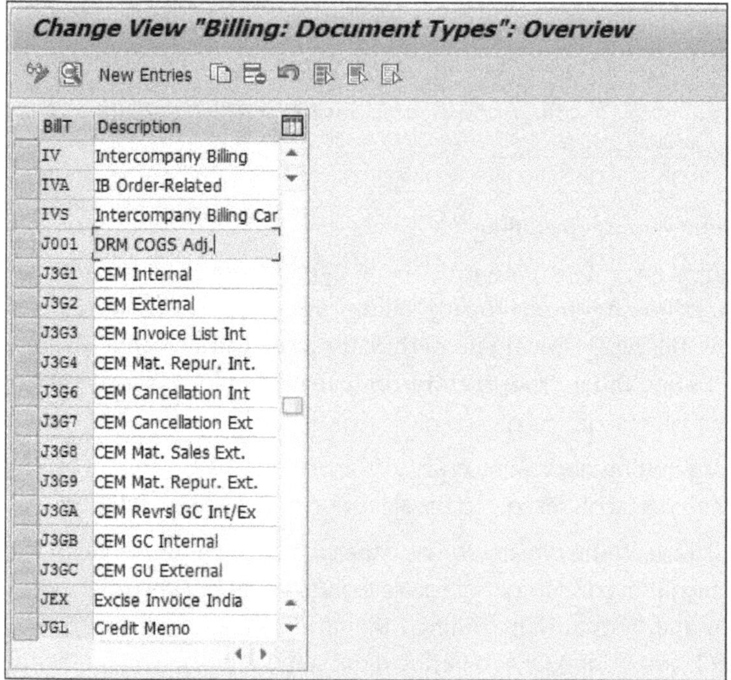

Change View "Billing: Document Types": Overview

New Entries

BillT	Description
IV	Intercompany Billing
IVA	IB Order-Related
IVS	Intercompany Billing Car
J001	DRM COGS Adj.
J3G1	CEM Internal
J3G2	CEM External
J3G3	CEM Invoice List Int
J3G4	CEM Mat. Repur. Int.
J3G6	CEM Cancellation Int
J3G7	CEM Cancellation Ext
J3G8	CEM Mat. Sales Ext.
J3G9	CEM Mat. Repur. Ext.
J3GA	CEM Revrsl GC Int/Ex
J3GB	CEM GC Internal
J3GC	CEM GU External
JEX	Excise Invoice India
JGL	Credit Memo

Figure 5.85 Billing Document Type: Overview

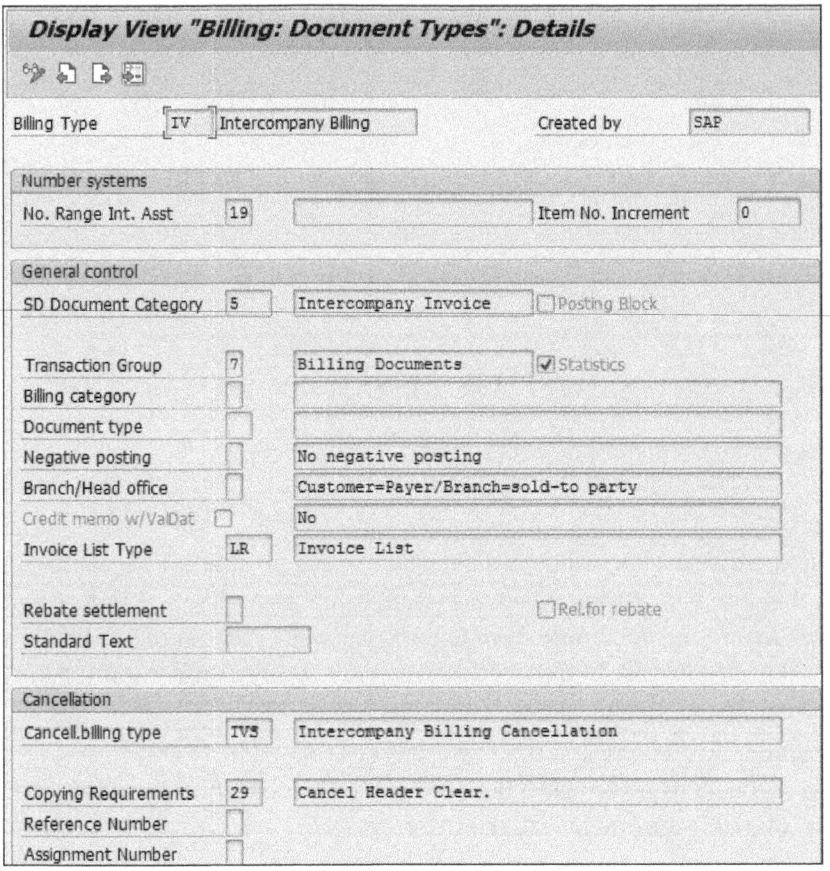

Figure 5.86 Billing Document Type: Details

Figure 5.86 and Figure 5.87 show the fields in intercompany billing document type **IV**. Let's explore each field in the billing document type configuration:

- **No. Range Int. Asst**
  You can assign the number range to the billing document type. Billing document types are limited to an internal number range by law, which mandates that billing document numbers should always be consecutive.
- **Item No. Increment**
  This is used to increase the number associated with each line item in the billing document. In most business scenarios, the copy control configuration is set up so that the line-item numbers are populated the same as the source document.
- **SD Document Category**
  The system identifies the billing document type, that is, whether it's based on an invoice, credit memo, or debit memo. It also controls the accounting behavior of the document types. Table 5.12 shows the standard sales and distribution document categories with respect to document types.

Process	Document Type	Document Category
Invoice	F2	M
Credit memo	G2	O
Debit memo	L2	P
Pro forma invoice	F8	U
Intercompany invoice	IV	5
Intercompany debit memo	IG	6
Invoice cancellation	S1	N

Table 5.12 Sales and Distribution Document Category

- **Posting Block**
  You can use the checkbox to validate the invoice before posting it to accounting. This allows the system to prevent the invoice from being released to accounting and prevents the accounting document from being created. By going into Transaction VF02 and clicking the **Release** button, you can manually release the accounting document. You can also do the same thing with Transaction VFX3.
- **Transaction Group**
  You can use this field to govern specific aspects of transaction flow for sales order (**0**), delivery (**6**), billing documents (**7**), and so on.
- **Billing category**
  The field can be used to group billing document types for printing, creation, and accounting transfer. For example, SAP has provided the options **P (Down Payment Request)**, **U (Billing Request)**, and **W (POS billing document)** for this field.
- **Document type**
  Here, you must assign the financial accounting document type. **RV** is the accounting document type for sales and distribution-based billing.
- **Negative posting**
  This field should be activated only when the company code is activated for the negative posting. The functionality of the field is to flip the sign of the amount associated with the billing document. For cancellation and credit memos, that is, for sales and distribution document categories **O**, **P**, and **N**, you don't need to activate the negative posting. By default, the document categories will flip the signs.
- **Credit memo w/ValDat**
  You can check or uncheck this checkbox based on the business requirement. If you check this checkbox, then when a credit memo is created with a reference to an unpaid billing document whose payment deadline date is later than the credit

memo's billing date, the payment deadline baseline date of the base billing document is populated in the credit memo request's field VALDT (fixed value date). This doesn't happen if the payment deadline for the reference billing document falls before the credit memo's current billing date.

- **Invoice List Type**
  An invoicing list allows you to consolidate all invoices for a specific period or month and send them to the payer in a single invoice list document. To run the invoice list, you can use Transactions VF21 and VF24. You have to list the invoice list type for the billing document type. The standard invoice list type provided by SAP is **LR**.
- **Rel. for rebate**
  The field is used when the billing document type is used for rebate processing. SAP has provided the document type options shown in Table 5.13 to choose from.

Option	Description
A	Final rebate settlement
B	Rebate correction document
C	Partial settlement for a rebate agreement
D	Manual accruals for a rebate agreement

Table 5.13 Relevant for Rebate Options

- **Standard Text**
  This field isn't used in SAP S/4HANA.
- **Cancell.billing type**
  When you cancel the billing document, it creates the cancellation billing document to offset the accounting entries. The cancellation billing document type **IVS** needs to be assigned in the field for intercompany billing type **IV**. Usually, you use the **S1** cancellation document type for the **F2** billing types.
- **Copying Requirements**
  You can maintain the copy requirement routine in the field. The routine is associated with copying billing documents to cancellation documents. Though SAP has provided Transaction VTFF to maintain the copy control settings between billing documents, the copy control setting between any billing document types to cancellation billing document type is grayed out. Any copy requirement settings with respect to billing documents and cancellation documents need to be maintained in this field.
- **Reference Number**
  The accounting document that is generated following the creation of the cancellation invoice contains the reference number, which can be viewed at the table level at the BKPF-XBELNR field. By selecting the appropriate options, such as sales order

number, delivery number, invoice number, and current billing document number, you can select the reference number that needs to be populated in the field.

- **Assignment Number**
  The behavior of the assignment is similar to the reference number. The reference field as well the assignment field is used to build internal reports.
- **Act Det.G/L Act**
  You have to assign the account determination procedure in the billing document type. The procedure will be used to determine the general ledger accounts while posting invoices values to accounting. The account determination procedure configurations are covered in Section 5.2. This field and the following fields are shown in Figure 5.87.
- **Doc. Pricing Proc.**
  The document pricing procedure field is one of the prerequisites to determine the pricing procedure in the sales order. Normally, the pricing is carried from the sales order to invoices, but in special cases where the operation document isn't a sales order or to redetermine prices, you can assign the billing document type with the document pricing procedure. In an intercompany sales scenario, the pricing procedure needs to be redetermined while creating the intercompany invoice. You can do that by maintaining the separate document pricing procedure in the billing document type. We've covered the document pricing procedure creation step in Section 5.1.1.
- **Acc. det. rec. acc.**
  The reconciliation account is usually picked from the customer master data. However, in some business scenarios, the requirement might be to determine the reconciliation account based on some parameters. You can achieve it by configuring the reconciliation account determination, which is the same as the configuration of the revenue account determination.
- **Acc. det. cash. set.**
  When creating an invoice for a cash transaction, cash settlement accounts need to be determined. You have to assign the cash settlement account determination procedure in this field. You only use this field if the billing type is **BV**.

  Following are the accounting entries for a cash sale:
  - Debit: Cash settlement account
  - Credit: Revenue account
- **Acc. det. pay. cards**
  You determine the payment card general ledger account with the help of payment card account determination. This is used only when the payment card functionality is activated in the system. Payment card functionality is nothing but payment of invoices through credit and debit cards.

Account assignment/pricing		
Act Det.G/L Act	KOFI00	Account determination
Doc. Pricing Proc.	Y1	Standard-BL
Acc. det. rec. acc.		
Acc. det. cash. set.		
Acc. det. pay. cards		

Figure 5.87 Billing Document Type

Assign Organizational Units by Plant

In this step, you'll assign the sales organization to a plant via **Sales and Distribution • Billing • Intercompany Billing • Assign Organizational Units by Plant**. You'll arrive at the screen shown in Figure 5.88.

Display View "Organizational Units for Internal Costing Per Plant": Ov

Organizational Units for Internal Costing Per Plant

Plant	SOrg	Descriptn	DstCh	Descriptn
Z223				
Z666				
ZAIN				
ZCP				
ZDE1	ZDE1		00	Retail
ZGB				
ZKT1				
ZKT2				
ZMSN				
ZNAV				
ZPPL				
ZXCV				
ZYX2				

Figure 5.88 Assign Organizational Units by Plant

As shown in Figure 5.88, you have to assign the delivery plant (**Plant**) with sales organization (**SOrg**) and distribution channel (**DstCh**). The sales area that you maintain here will be populated in the intercompany billing document. The system gets to know the sales area of the plant from this configuration.

Define Internal Customer Number by Sales Organization

In this configuration, you'll assign an internal customer number to the sales organization. In intercompany billing, the intercompany billing document is created for this customer number as payer. You have to create a customer number that represents the sales organization and assign the customer in the configuration. Internal customers can have separate customer pricing procedure maintained for the determination of intercompany billing.

To assign a sales organization unit to an intercompany customer, follow menu path **Sales and Distribution • Billing • Intercompany Billing • Define Internal Customer Number by Sales Organization**. You'll arrive at the screen shown in Figure 5.89, where you'll assign the internal customer number (**CustInterC**) to the sales organization (**Sales org.**). In the example, the internal customer number **50000000** is assigned to sales organization **ZINO**.

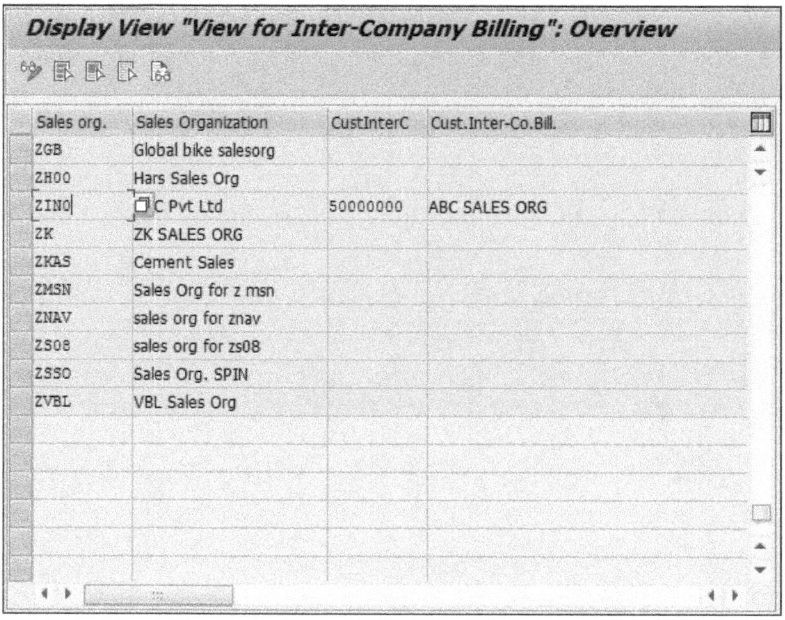

Display View "View for Inter-Company Billing": Overview

Sales org.	Sales Organization	CustInterC	Cust.Inter-Co.Bill.
ZGB	Global bike salesorg		
ZH00	Hars Sales Org		
ZINO	C Pvt Ltd	50000000	ABC SALES ORG
ZK	ZK SALES ORG		
ZKAS	Cement Sales		
ZMSN	Sales Org for z msn		
ZNAV	sales org for znav		
ZS08	sales org for zs08		
ZSSO	Sales Org. SPIN		
ZVBL	VBL Sales Org		

Figure 5.89 Internal Customer Number by Sales Organization

Pricing Procedure Changes

There are two billing documents created in an intercompany scenario: one is from the ordering company code to the end customer, and the other is from the supplying company code to the ordering company code. You map the ordering company code as an internal customer in SAP S/4HANA and assign it to the plant.

When an ordering firm submits a billing document using pricing process RVAA01, the ordering company's costs are represented by condition PI01. It will only populate in the condition tabs if the plant is an intercompany plant controlled by routine 22.

In this case, you can set up two pricing procedures. The ordering company code determines the pricing procedure for the invoice sent to the end customer. In the pricing procedure configuration (refer to Section 5.1.1), you must maintain condition type **PI01** with the **Statistical** checkbox selected and the requirement (**Requir...**) as **22**, as shown in Figure 5.90. The **Statistical** checkbox ensures that the values are only used for statistical purposes, have no impact on accounting, and aren't posted to the accounting document. Requirement **22** necessitates that the ordering and delivering company codes be different and that the values not be populated in the invoicing document.

Additionally, condition type IV01, which is part of pricing procedure ICAA01 and assigned to intercompany billing document IV, displays the revenue of the providing company when the supplying business sends a bill to the ordering company, that is, when the intercompany invoice has been sent.

Display View "Procedures - Control Data": Overview

Dialog Structure
- Procedures
  - Procedures - Control

Procedure RVAA01 Standard

Procedures - Control Data

Reference Step Overview

Step	Co...	Co...	Description	Fro...	To ...	Ma...	R...	St...	Rel...	Print T...	Subtotal	Requir...	Alt. Ca...	Alt. Cn...	Accou...	Accruals
905	0	B005	Hierarchy rebate/mat	400			☐	☐	☐			24			ERB	ERU
908	0		Net Value 3	0	0	☐	☐	☐	☐			0	0	0		
909	0	PI02	Inter-company %	0	0	☐	☐	☑	☐		B	22	0	0	ERL	
910	0	PI01	Inter-company Price	0	0	☐	☐	☑	☐		B	22	0	0	ERL	
914	0	SKTV	Cash Discount	0	0	☐	☐	☑	☐		D	14	0	2		
915	0	MW3I	Output Tax	0	0	☐	☐	☐	☐	S		10	0	16	MWS	
919	0	DIFF	Rounding Off	0	0	☐	☑	☐	☐			13	16	4	ERS	
920	0		Total	0	0	☐	☐	☐	☐		A	0	4	0		
930	0	SKTO	Cash Discount	0	0	☑	☐	☐	☐			9	0	11		
932	0	RL00	Factoring Discount	0	0	☐	☐	☑	☐			23	0	2	ERS	
933	0	MW15	Factoring Disc. Tax	932	0	☐	☐	☑	☐			21	0	0	MWS	
935	0	GRWR	Statistical value	0	0	☐	☐	☑	☐		C	8	0	2		
940	0	VPRS	Internal price	0	0	☐	☐	☑	☐		B	4	0	0		
941	0	EK02	Calculated costs	0	0	☑	☐	☑	☐		B	0	0	0		
942	0	EK03	Calculated ship.cost	0	0	☑	☐	☑	☐			0	0	0		
950	0		Profit Margin	0	0	☐	☐	☐	☐			0	11	0		

Figure 5.90 Pricing Procedure

For intercompany billing, you need to redetermine the pricing procedure shown in Figure 5.91 with the combination of sales organization, distribution channel, division, document pricing procedure, and customer pricing procedure. To do so, you can maintain separate customer pricing procedures in the ordering company code internal customer. You have to maintain the document pricing procedure in the intercompany billing document type. The system will redetermine the pricing procedure while creating an intercompany invoice.

The condition records need to be maintained for the **PI01** condition type, which will automatically populate in the intercompany billing invoice via the **IV01** condition type because the **PI01** condition type is maintained as a reference condition type in **IV01**.

Display View "Det. of Pricing Procedures in Sales Docs.": Overview

Sales Orga...	Distri...	Division	Do...	Cu...	Pricing Pro...	Pricing Procedure	Co...	Condition Type for Fast Entry
ZDE1	00	02	A	1	RVAA01	Standard	PR00	Price
ZDE1	00	02	Y1	3	ICAA01	Intercompany Billing		
ZDE1	41	02	A	1	RVAA01	Standard	PR00	Price
ZDE1	41	02	Y1	3	ICAA01	Intercompany Billing		
ZGB	10	00	A		A17J02	Materials (US)	PPR0	Price
ZGB	10	00	A	01	A17J02	Materials (US)	PPR0	Price
ZGB	10	00	A	02	A17J02	Materials (US)	PPR0	Price
ZGB	10	00	A	1	RVAA01	Standard		
ZGB	10	00	AS		A17J10	Materials and Service		
ZGB	10	00	AS	01	A17J10	Materials and Service		
ZGB	10	00	AS	02	A17J10	Materials and Service		
ZGB	10	00	C		A17J02	Materials (US)	PPR0	Price
ZGB	10	00	C	01	A17J02	Materials (US)	PPR0	Price
ZGB	10	00	01		Y17101	Materials (US)	PPR0	Price
ZGB	10	00	01	01	Y17101	Materials (US)	PPR0	Price
ZGB	10	00	01	02	Y17J01	Materials (US)	PPR0	Price

Figure 5.91 Pricing Procedure Determination

Copy Control Settings

You can't create an intercompany invoice unless a billing invoice is created for the customer. This is controlled by the *copy control routine*. Copy control routines also govern the logic of price redetermination, that is, the prices in the intercompany invoice won't be taken from the sales order but will be redetermined during the creation of the intercompany invoice.

The copy control routine you maintain for intercompany billing is between delivery documents and the intercompany billing document. You can navigate to the copy control setting between a delivery document and billing document with Transaction VTFL.

As shown in Figure 5.92, set the **Pricing Type** as **B**, which redetermines the prices in the intercompany billing document.

Once you give the same delivery document in Transaction VF01, the IV billing type will be fetched. In an intercompany billing document, the sales area comes from the configuration that you made earlier.

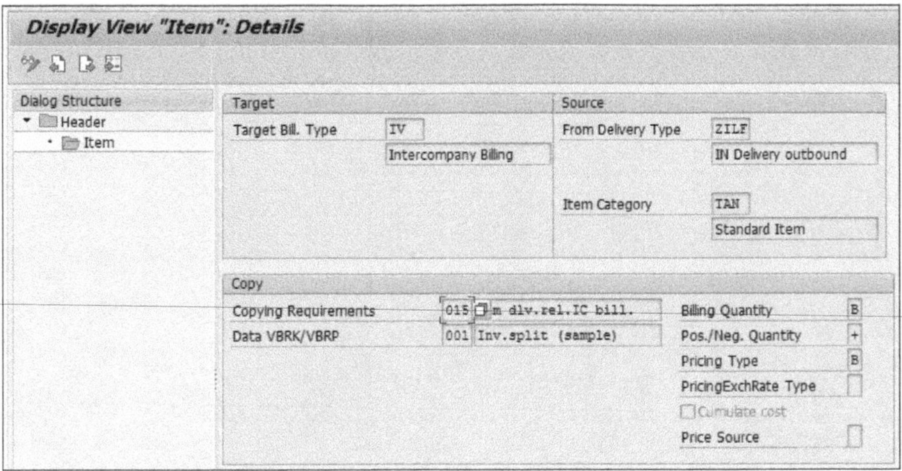

Figure 5.92 Copy Control Settings

5.5.4 Document Flow

In this section, we'll explore the document flow for the intercompany sales process. As shown in Figure 5.93, sales order **0066000010** is created for sales organization ZINO by using Transaction VA01. With reference to the sales order, outbound delivery **0080002696** is created with Transaction VL01N, so the picking and PGI are done with Transaction VL02N. Once the PGI is completed, customer invoice **0090002347** is created using Transaction VF01 with respect to the delivery. After the customer invoice, intercompany invoice **0090002348** is created with Transaction VF01.

Document Flow

Status Overview | Display Document | Service Documents

Business Partner 0011000000 Domestic customer
Material 000000003000000051 Grains- Batch Manged

Document	Quantity	Unit	Ref. Value	Currency	On	Time
IN Std Order 0066000010 / 10	2	KG	280.000,000	INR	07.01.2022	00:26:50
IN Delivery outbound 0080002696 / 10	2	KG			07.01.2022	00:35:13
Picking Request 20220107 / 10	2	KG			07.01.2022	00:35:27
GD goods issue:delvy 7300000010 / 1	2	KG	0,00	EUR	07.01.2022	00:36:55
INInvoice 0090002347 / 10	2	KG	285.714,286	INR	07.01.2022	00:38:04
Intercompany Billing 0090002348 / 10	2	KG	1.200,00	EUR	07.01.2022	00:38:43

Figure 5.93 Intercompany Billing Document Flow

You can see in Figure 5.94, based on the configuration that you've done earlier, the **Payer 50000000** is determined in the intercompany billing document, the **Sales Organization** is **ZDE1**, and the **Pricing Procedure ICAA01** is determined at the header level of the intercompany billing document. In the **Conditions** tab, the condition type **IV01** is determined, as shown in Figure 5.95.

Billing Intercompany Billing 90002348 (IV) Display : Header Data

Items Accounting Output

Intercompany ...	90002348				
Payer	50000000	ABC SALES ORG / 400001 Mumbai			
Created by	S4LOG17	Created on	07.01.2022	Time	00:38:43

Header Detail | Header Partners | Conditions | Header Texts

Incoterms Location 2	
Pricing Procedure	ICAA01 Intercompany Billing

Taxes

Destination Country	IN	Region	13
TaxClass1-Cust.		County Code	
VAT Registration No.		City code	
Country Sls Tax No.	IN		
Origin Sls. Tax No.	A Ship-to party	EU Triangular Deal	☐

General Information

Sales Organization	ZDE1	Inv. List Type	LR
Distribution Channel	00 Retail	Billing Date	
Division	02 Retail	Canceld Bill.Dc	
Sales District		Canceled	☐
Shipping Conditions	Standard	Man. Invoice Maint.	☐

Figure 5.94 Intercompany Billing Document

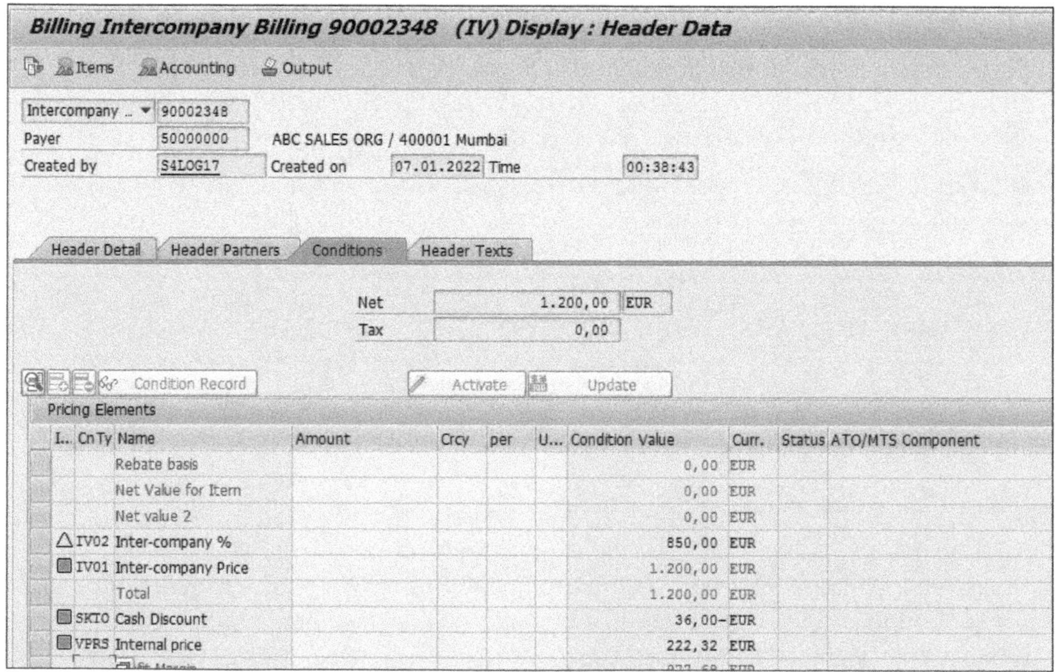
Billing Intercompany Billing 90002348 (IV) Display : Header Data

Items Accounting Output

Intercompany ...	90002348				
Payer	50000000	ABC SALES ORG / 400001 Mumbai			
Created by	S4LOG17	Created on	07.01.2022	Time	00:38:43

Header Detail | Header Partners | Conditions | Header Texts

Net	1.200,00	EUR
Tax	0,00	

Condition Record | Activate | Update

Pricing Elements

I...	CnTy	Name	Amount	Crcy	per	U...	Condition Value	Curr.	Status	ATO/MTS Component
		Rebate basis					0,00	EUR		
		Net Value for Item					0,00	EUR		
		Net value 2					0,00	EUR		
△	IV02	Inter-company %					850,00	EUR		
■	IV01	Inter-company Price					1.200,00	EUR		
		Total					1.200,00	EUR		
■	SKTO	Cash Discount					36,00-	EUR		
■	VPRS	Internal price					222,32	EUR		

Figure 5.95 Intercompany Billing Document: Conditions

5.6 Summary

In this chapter, we covered the integration between the sales and distribution functionality and the financial accounting functionality.

We started the discussion in Section 5.1 with the introduction of the condition technique and the conceptual implication of the condition technique on pricing. Then we explored the important configuration to set up the pricing in sales and distribution. In the subsequent section, we explored the tax determination methodology in SAP and the configurations associated with it.

Then we moved on to Section 5.2, where we discussed revenue accounting determination and how the condition technique is used to achieve the automatic determination of general ledger accounts in the billing document. We explored configuration activities for the access sequence, account determination type, account determination procedure, account keys, and Transaction VKOA settings.

In Section 5.3, we discussed the concept of credit management in the sales and distribution functionality and in FSCM. We started our discussion with the credit management flow and understood the implication of that data flow on the business process. Then we dove into the configurations associated with the credit management process, including credit control area, credit segment, risk category, risk class, rules for scoring and credit limit calculation, and so on. We concluded the section with an overview of case management and important tables and transactions.

In Section 5.4, we explored the importance of profitability analysis and its benefits for organizations. We explored profitability analysis as a concept and the important configuration associated with characteristics, value fields, and organizational elements such as operating concerns and controlling areas.

In Section 5.5, we started our discussion on intercompany billing by going through the business scenario related to two company codes. Then we dove into the configurations needed for the intercompany sales process. We concluded the section with an example of the intercompany sales flow.

In the next chapter, we'll continue our coverage of key sales and distribution integration points with a deep dive into revenue recognition.

Chapter 6
Revenue Recognition

In an ideal world, a sales process must always be followed by a revenue recognition process. Revenue recognition is a process by which businesses calculate and post revenues to their general ledger following a revenue recognition model, which we'll discuss in detail in this chapter.

In this chapter, we'll begin our discussion by walking through revenue recognition concepts from a business process standpoint. We'll talk about International Financial Reporting Standards (IFRS) compliance and explain how revenue treatment works in an SAP S/4HANA system. We'll also share our knowledge about price allocation and depict how it plays a key role in revenue accounting and reporting (RAR), specifically in the services industry.

Next, we'll dive into SAP Revenue Accounting and Reporting, where we'll show you step-by-step how RAR components are configured in SAP S/4HANA through the lens of sales and distribution integration. We'll provide an in-depth discussion of the transactions you can perform from the SAP Business Client (Transaction NWBS) screen, and we'll also walk through the use of Business Rule Framework plus (BRFplus) extensively.

We'll conclude this chapter by giving you detailed information about optimized contract management (OCM), including how to activate this feature in SAP S/4HANA using contract categories, the benefits of using OCM, the limitations, the enhanced functionality OCM brings, and the system impact implications.

6.1 What Is Revenue Recognition?

Revenue recognition is a process by which companies recognize revenue on the sales they make with their customers. At a high level, the formula to calculate revenue is *Revenue = (Number of products sold) × (Cost per product)*. Depending on the kind of sales made and the type of revenue recognition model a business follows, their revenue recognition process can either be a time-based process or an event-based process.

In this section, we'll look at concepts of revenue recognition as they relate to IFRS 15 compliance standards, and we'll dive into how revenue is treated in SAP systems, whether it's the traditional sales and distribution way or the new RAR way. We'll also shed light on what price allocation is and how it impacts revenue recognition.

6.1.1 IFRS 15 Compliance

The IFRS 15 standard deals with how contractual revenues are recognized, accounted, and reported. IFRS 15 insists on having standard principles for reporting revenues that are universal across various industries and domains. Back in 2015, SAP launched *SAP Revenue Accounting and Reporting* to support IFRS 15 standards. To make sure all the principles of IFRS 15 were followed thoroughly, SAP built its RAR solution based on this five-step model. Let's walk through these five steps, as shown in Figure 6.1:

1. **Identify the customer contract**
   The customer contract in SAP S/4HANA is an attested document (physical or virtual) that highlights the following:
   - Products or services sold to a customer
   - Terms of payment of the contract
   - Price at which the company closed the contracted deal with the customer

   Let's consider an example: SAP sold a disclosure report bundled solution to company S4 Foods at USD 2,200 for the first year. The bundled solution included one license product and one maintenance product (12-month maintenance). SAP offered 30-day payment terms on this contract.
2. **Identify the individual performance obligations (POBs)**
   POBs are the line items or products sold via the contract. Basically, all lines items of a contract are obligations that must be performed by the company for their customer. In this example, the license product has one POB (let's call it License POB), and the maintenance product has another POB (let's call it Maintenance POB).
3. **Determine the transaction price**
   The transaction price is the total contracted price of the bundled product. There is another concept in SAP Revenue Accounting and Reporting called the *standalone selling price (SSP)*. SSP is the price of individual components of the bundled product if they were sold as standalone products. So, in this example, the transaction price of the disclosure report bundle product is USD 2,200, the SSP of the license component is USD 1,500, and the SSP for the maintenance component is USD 1,700.
4. **Allocate the price**
   This is the core step that differentiates sales and distribution revenue recognition from the RAR functionality in SAP S/4HANA. In this step, based on the SSP value of individual products of a bundle, the price is allocated to each POB. Sticking with this example, based on the SSP value of USD 1,500 and USD 1,700 for License POB and Maintenance POB, respectively, the allocated price for License POB is USD 1,031.25 and for Maintenance POB is USD 1,168.75. The formula to calculate the allocated price is as follows:

   Allocated price = SSP percentage × Total transaction price where *SSP percentage = (Individual SSP ÷ Total SSP) × 100*

5. **Recognize the revenue**
   Once the price allocation is complete, the POB is ready to be fulfilled. In our example, fulfillment for License POB is event based, and fulfillment for Maintenance POB is time based. This means that as soon as the license is provisioned, revenue on that POB is recognized, and as soon as the first day of the contract month begins, revenue on the Maintenance POB is recognized (depending on the POB type configuration).

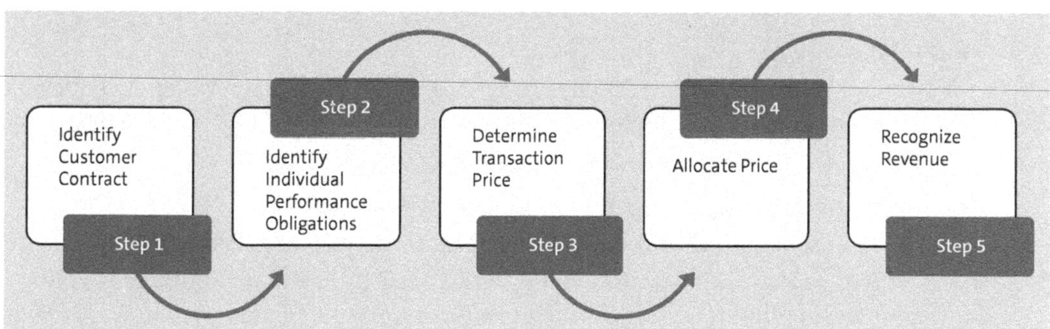

Figure 6.1 IFRS 15 Five-Step Model

Table 6.1 explains the five-step model in a tabular format.

POB	Transaction Price (USD)	SSP (USD)	Allocated Price (USD)	Fulfillment Type	First Month (USD)	Second Month (USD)	Third Month (USD)	Fourth Month (USD)
License POB	1,000	1,500	1,031.25	Event-based	1,031.25	N/A	N/A	N/A
Maintenance POB	1,200	1,700	1,168.75	Time-based	97.39	97.39	97.39	97.39
Total	2,200	3,200	2,200		1,128.64	97.39	97.39	97.39

Table 6.1 Allocate Price Table

Let's walk through the example steps represented by the columns in this table:

- **POB**
  This represents the two POBs in this example: License POB and Maintenance POB.
- **Transaction price**
  This represents the transaction price of the total bundled product and individual POBs. The transaction price for the RAR disclosure bundled product (total) is USD 2,200, for License POB is USD 1,000, and for Maintenance POB is USD 1,200.

- **SSP**
  This represents the SSP of each POB. The SSP for License POB is USD 1,500, for Maintenance POB is USD 1,700, and total SSP is *USD 1,500 + 1,700 = 3,200*.
- **Allocated price**
  This represents the price allocation value for each POB. The allocated price for License POB is USD 1,031.25, the allocated price for Maintenance POB is USD 1,168.75, and in total, *Allocated price = 1,031.25 + 1,168.75 = 2,200*.
- **Fulfillment type**
  This represents the type of fulfillment tied to each POB, based on which revenue recognition happens. The fulfillment type for License POB is event based, and the fulfillment type for Maintenance POB is time based.
- **Month (first through fourth)**
  This represents month over month revenue recognition for each POB. The entire allocated amount for License POB is recognized in the first month as it follows event-based fulfillment. The allocated amount for Maintenance POB is evenly split across 12 months because it's a 12-month contract and follows time-based fulfillment. Each month's revenue number is recognized on the first of every month. So, USD 1,168.75 is evenly split across 12 months, making one month's revenue number to be USD 97.39, which is recognized on the first of the first month, second month, third month, fourth month, and so on for 12 months.

Note

SAP has always been IFRS compliant. Following are solutions SAP introduced in response to various IFRS standards in the recent past:

- IFRS 9: SAP Treasury and Risk Management
- IFRS 10: SAP Business Planning and Consolidation (SAP BPC) and group reporting
- IFRS 16: SAP Real Estate Management
- IFRS 17: SAP for Insurance

6.1.2 Revenue Treatment in SAP Systems

In this section, we'll talk about how revenue treatment happens within an SAP system. We'll look at how revenue recognition happens in the traditional sales and distribution revenue recognition process and compare it to how revenue recognition happens in SAP Revenue Accounting and Reporting.

Note

While the RAR functionality can work very well with SAP ERP, to make the best use of its holistic capabilities, you should use it with SAP S/4HANA. The finest results for RAR have been seen when used with SAP S/4HANA.

Classic Revenue Recognition

In the sales and distribution revenue recognition methodology, the triggers for revenue recognition are either an event or start date of a contract. Depending on the item category configuration, a material would either follow an event-based revenue recognition or a time-based revenue recognition.

Let's consider an example: Dell Inc. sells a server to company S4 Foods along with a five-year support contract. It's a bundle package for which revenue on the server is recognized as soon as it's delivered to S4 Foods (because it has an event-based item category tied to it), and revenue on the support years (Supp Year 1, Supp Year 2, Supp Year 3, Supp Year 4, and Supp Year 5) is recognized on the first day of every month of the contract period, depending on the item category configuration and revenue recognition configuration (see Table 6.2).

Material	Amount (USD)	Delivered On	Contract Dates	Revenue Amount (USD)	Revenue Recognition Date
Server	1,000	01/31/2022	01/01/2022 – 12/31/2026	1,000	01/31/2022
Supp Year 1	100	N/A	01/01/2022 – 12/31/2022	100/yearly	01/01/2022, 02/01/2022 . . .
Supp Year 2	120	N/A	01/01/2023 – 12/31/2023	120/yearly	01/01/2023, 02/01/2023 . . .
Supp Year 3	140	N/A	01/01/2022 – 12/31/2024	140/yearly	01/01/2024, 02/01/2024 . . .
Supp Year 4	160	N/A	01/01/2022 – 12/31/2025	160/yearly	01/01/2025, 02/01/2025 . . .
Supp Year 5	180	N/A	01/01/2022 – 12/31/2026	180/yearly	01/01/2026, 02/01/2026 . . .

Table 6.2 Sales and Distribution: Revenue Recognition

Table 6.2 has the following columns:

- **Material**
  This column represents materials sold by Dell Inc. (Server and Supp Years).
- **Amount**
  This column represents the transaction price of Server and Supp Years.
- **Delivered on**
  This column represents the post goods issue (PGI) date of the delivery document created for Server. The Supp Years don't have a delivery document, so they are denoted by N/A.

- **Contract dates**
  This column represents the contract term (start date and end date) for Server and Supp Years.
- **Revenue amount**
  This column represents the revenue amount recognized for Server and Supp Years on a yearly basis. In the system, based on the revenue cycle, revenue recognition for Server happens one time on the date the server is provisioned, and revenue recognition for Supp Years happens monthly. Revenue amount for Server is still USD 1,000, but revenue amount for Supp Year 1 is calculated as *100 ÷ 12 = 8.33*.
- **Revenue recognition date**
  This column represents the date on which the revenue is recognized for Server and Supp Years. The revenue recognition date for Server is the delivered-on date, which is 01/31/2022. The 8.33 revenue amount calculated for Supp Year 1 in the previous point is recognized on the first of every month for year 2022 (01/01/2022, 02/01/2022, etc.). The same concept applies to other Supp Years shown in Table 6.2.

SAP Revenue Accounting and Reporting

In the SAP Revenue Accounting and Reporting methodology, the trigger for revenue recognition is fulfillment data (explained in Section 6.2.1). Depending on the POB type configuration, a material would follow an event-based revenue recognition, a time-based revenue recognition, or a percentage of completion recognition.

Let's explore the example in the same way we did in the previous section: Dell Inc. sells a Server to company S4 Foods along with a five-year support contract. It's a bundle package for which revenue on the Server is recognized as soon as it's delivered to S4 Foods (because it has an event-based POB tied to it), and revenue on the Support Years (Supp Year 1, Supp Year 2, Supp Year 3, Supp Year 4, and Supp Year 5) are recognized on the first day of every month of the contract period depending on the POB type configuration. The difference between RAR and sales and distribution revenue recognition is that within RAR, there is a price allocation between Server and Supp Years, and for each Supp Year, revenue is calculated and recognized equally (see Table 6.3). This is the core fundamental of the IFRS 15 standard, where revenue is recognized equally when products are sold as a bundle depending on SSP, transaction price, and the ratio between them.

Material	Amount (USD)	Delivered On	Contract Dates	Revenue Amount (USD)	Allocation Effect	Revenue Recognition Date
Server	1,000	01/31/2022	01/01/2022 – 12/31/2026	1,000	N/A	01/31/2022

Table 6.3 SAP Revenue Accounting and Reporting

Material	Amount (USD)	Delivered On	Contract Dates	Revenue Amount (USD)	Allocation Effect	Revenue Recognition Date
Supp Year 1	100	N/A	01/01/2022 – 12/31/2022	140/ yearly	+40	01/01/2022, 02/01/2022 ...
Supp Year 2	120	N/A	01/01/2023 – 12/31/2023	140/ yearly	+20	01/01/2023, 02/01/2023 ...
Supp Year 3	140	N/A	01/01/2024 – 12/31/2024	140/ yearly	0	01/01/2024, 02/01/2024 ...
Supp Year 4	160	N/A	01/01/2025 – 12/31/2025	140/ yearly	-20	01/01/2025, 02/01/2025 ...
Supp Year 5	180	N/A	01/01/2026 – 12/31/2026	140/ yearly	-40	01/01/2026, 02/01/2026 ...

Table 6.3 SAP Revenue Accounting and Reporting (Cont.)

Table 6.3 has the following columns:

- **Material**
  This column represents materials sold by Dell Inc. (Server and Supp Years).
- **Amount**
  This column represents the transaction price of Server and Supp Years.
- **Delivered on**
  This column represents the PGI date of the delivery document created for Server. Supp Years don't have delivery documents, so they are denoted by N/A.
- **Contract date**
  This column represents the contract term (start date and end date) for Server and Supp Years.
- **Revenue amount**
  This column represents the allocated revenue amount recognized for Server and Supp Years on a yearly basis. In the system, based on the revenue cycle, revenue recognition for Server happens one time on the date the server is provisioned, and revenue recognition on the Supp Years happens monthly. Revenue amount for Server is still USD 1,000, but revenue amount for Supp Year 1 is calculated as *USD 140 ÷ 12 = USD 11.66*.

- **Allocation effect**
  This column represents the allocation effect number for the material line item (allocation effect and price allocation are explained in detail in Section 6.1.3).
- **Revenue recognition date**
  This column represents the date on which the revenue is recognized for Server and Supp Years. Revenue recognition date for Server is the delivered-on date, which is 01/31/2022. The USD 11.66 revenue amount calculated for Supp Year 1 earlier in this list is recognized on the first of every month for year 2022 (01/01/2022, 02/01/2022, etc.). The same concept applies to other Supp Years shown in Table 6.3.

6.1.3 Price Allocation Impact

Simply put, *price allocation* is the distribution of price between components of a bundle where the net total price of the bundle remains the same, but the component allocated price defers from its original SSP. Let's look at Table 6.4 (which uses the same numbers as Table 6.1) to understand the concepts of price allocation and allocation effect and how they contribute to revenue recognition.

POB	Transaction Price (USD)	SSP (USD)	Allocated Price (USD)	Allocated Effect	First Month	Second Month	Third Month	Fourth Month
License POB	1,000	1,500	1,031.25	+ 31.25	1,031.25	N/A	N/A	N/A
Maintenance POB	1,200	1,700	1,168.75	- 31.25	97.39	97.39	97.39	97.39
Total	2,200	3,200	2,200	0	1,128.64	97.39	97.39	97.39

Table 6.4 Allocate Price Table

The License product, if sold standalone, has a selling price of USD 1,500. The Maintenance product, if sold standalone, has a selling price of USD 1,700. When both are sold together as a bundle, License POB's transaction price is USD 1,000 and Maintenance POB's transaction price is USD 1,200. Because they are sold as a bundle and their SSPs and transaction prices are different, following the principles of the IFRS 15 standard, there is a price allocation between License and Maintenance. The License POB has an allocation price of USD 1,031.25, and the Maintenance POB has an allocation price of USD 1,168.75. The formula is *Allocation effect = Allocation price – Transaction price*; therefore, the allocation effect on License POB is +31.25 and on Maintenance POB is -31.25.

Note

The total allocation effect should always be equal to 0. This is because you don't add or subtract numbers to a contract; you just move numbers around between POBs to adhere to the revenue recognition guidelines.

When fulfillment happens on the contract, USD 1,031.25 revenue is recognized on the License POB and USD 1,168.75 is ready for revenue recognition on the Maintenance POB. But the billing amount of License and Maintenance is based on the transaction price, so for the first month at the POB level, revenue amount and billing amount won't match because the billing amount on License is USD 1,000 and billing amount on Maintenance is USD 1,200. That is where the concept of contract asset and contract liability comes into the picture:

- **Contract asset position**
  This is created when the revenue number is greater than the billing number. The example License POB, at the end of the first month, will have a contract asset residual.
- **Contract liability position**
  This is created when the billing number is greater than the revenue number. The example Maintenance POB, at the end of the first month, will have a contract liability residual.

When a contract matures (i.e., comes to an end), contract asset and contract liability get washed out. Remember, the total transaction price and total allocation price are always the same. Therefore, at the contract level, when all POBs are completely fulfilled, contract asset and contract liability zero out. In the example, at the end of the 12-month contract, transaction price = allocation price = revenue amount, which is equal to USD 2,200—the contracted deal with the customer. From the customer standpoint, nothing changed: they paid USD 2,200, they received goods and services worth USD 2,200, and they were invoiced for USD 2,200. From the company standpoint, at the end of the contract term, the company sold products worth USD 2,200, billed the customer USD 2,200, and recognized revenue for USD 2,200.

6.2 SAP Revenue Accounting and Reporting

In the previous section, you learned about IFRS 15 regulations, revenue treatment in SAP, and price allocation. In this section, we'll dive into SAP Revenue Accounting and Reporting to see how it's configured around the IFRS 15 five-step model. To make sure different organizations are compliant with IFRS 15 standards, SAP allows them to configure their systems seamlessly using out-of-the-box RAR functionality in SAP S/4HANA.

Typically, sales are the source for any revenue, so, in most scenarios, RAR connects with the sales and distribution functionality in SAP S/4HANA. Sales and distribution feeds all the relevant sales information into RAR, and RAR calculates revenue per the regulations/standards and then sends accounting and posting data to the general ledger. This closes the loop of a RAR process in the finance functionality. The offset of the revenue posting in finance comes from the sales and distribution invoice. Figure 6.2 shows how data moves from sales and distribution to RAR and then to finance in a common sales-revenue scenario.

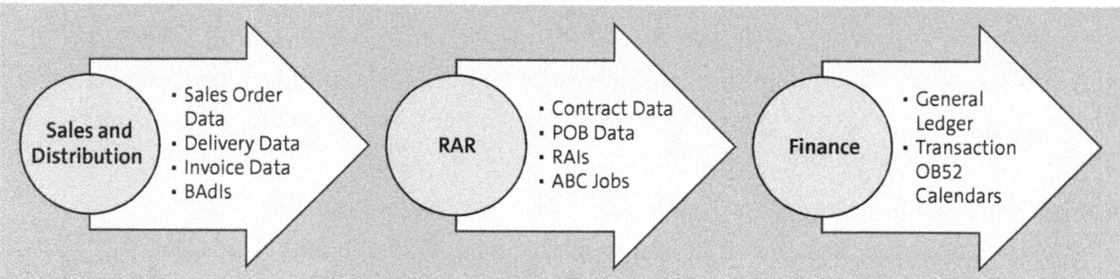

Figure 6.2 Sales and Distribution to RAR Data Flow

In the following sections, we'll go through specific configuration steps required for a sales and distribution–RAR integration. All steps of the integration are critical because if not done correctly, the RAR functionality will be in limbo with no value added to the business. There are steps you must perform in RAR, steps you must do in sales and distribution, and a couple of steps in BRFplus to have a successful sales and distribution–RAR integration.

6.2.1 Configuration of the RAR Node

In this section, we'll walk you through the configuration steps to set up RAR functionality in SAP S/4HANA. We'll dive into key configurations of revenue accounting items (RAIs), RAI management, and revenue accounting contracts. All configuration is done in Transaction FARR_IMG or Transaction SPRO. For ease of understanding, we'll use the Transaction SPRO menu path to show different configurations. Keep in mind that we'll focus on configuration needed for sales and distribution integration only.

Further Reading

To get more information on configuration that isn't related to sales and distribution in Transaction FARR_IMG, refer to *SAP Revenue Accounting and Reporting and IFRS 15*, written by Dayakar Domala and Koti Tummuru (SAP PRESS, 2017).

Revenue Accounting Items

RAIs are entities that help the system transfer data from sales and distribution to RAR. There are mainly three categories of RAIs: order RAIs, fulfillment RAIs, and invoice RAIs.

Any transaction on a sales order triggers an RAI. Depending on what kind of transaction it is, the RAI can either be an order RAI, a fulfillment RAI, or an invoice RAI. RAIs are created as processable or raw depending on the upload rule configuration discussed later in this chapter. RAI generation looks at all items of a contract for a header ID or a sales order number, and if one item on the contract is in error, then the entire contract fails and sits in a raw state until the error on that single RAI is fixed.

> **Warning!**
>
> Don't trick the system and force un-errored RAIs of a failed batch to go over to RAR. They might process successfully, but you'll potentially break the contract in RAR because of partial processing, which you don't want.

Let's look at the different configuration steps involved in setting up RAIs. We'll start with interface component configuration, then move onto RAI class maintenance, and finally conclude by seeing how modifiable fields are defined in RAIs.

Interface Components

SAP has a standard list of interface components you can use to define RAI classes. For the most part, SAP has covered all standard components, but you can add new components if needed. SAP has done a good job with their standard components, so the need to add new components is very rare. If your business still requires you to add a new component, you can reach out to SAP for guidance or copy an existing component and name it "ZComponent".

To get to the list of standard interface components, follow IMG menu path **Financial Accounting • Revenue Accounting • Inbound Processing • Revenue Accounting Items • Define Interface Components**. You'll arrive at the screen shown in Figure 6.3.

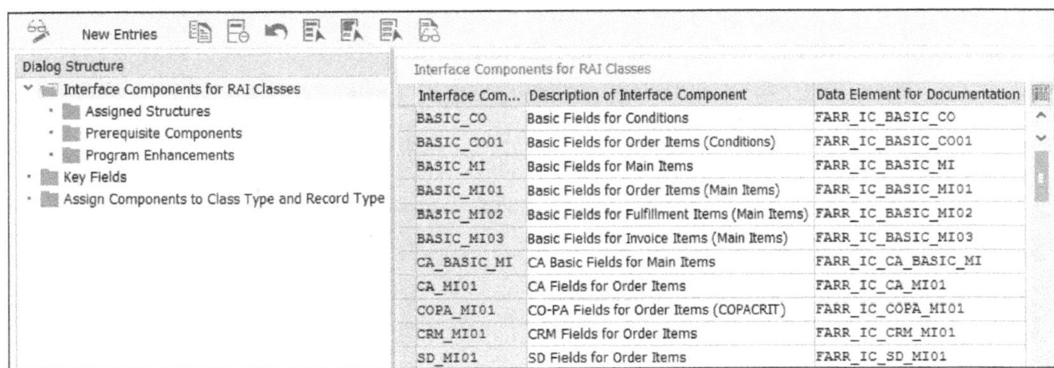

Interface Com...	Description of Interface Component	Data Element for Documentation
BASIC_CO	Basic Fields for Conditions	FARR_IC_BASIC_CO
BASIC_CO01	Basic Fields for Order Items (Conditions)	FARR_IC_BASIC_CO01
BASIC_MI	Basic Fields for Main Items	FARR_IC_BASIC_MI
BASIC_MI01	Basic Fields for Order Items (Main Items)	FARR_IC_BASIC_MI01
BASIC_MI02	Basic Fields for Fulfillment Items (Main Items)	FARR_IC_BASIC_MI02
BASIC_MI03	Basic Fields for Invoice Items (Main Items)	FARR_IC_BASIC_MI03
CA_BASIC_MI	CA Basic Fields for Main Items	FARR_IC_CA_BASIC_MI
CA_MI01	CA Fields for Order Items	FARR_IC_CA_MI01
COPA_MI01	CO-PA Fields for Order Items (COPACRIT)	FARR_IC_COPA_MI01
CRM_MI01	CRM Fields for Order Items	FARR_IC_CRM_MI01
SD_MI01	SD Fields for Order Items	FARR_IC_SD_MI01

Figure 6.3 RAR Interface Components

Note

You can add more components from this screen too, but, as mentioned, we recommend reaching out to SAP and get their sign-off before you do so.

As shown in Figure 6.3, the interface component configuration screen is divided into two parts: the left part represents the **Dialog Structure** of an interface component (discussed later in the section), and the right part has the following three fields:

- **Interface Com...**
  This field represents the interface component name for an RAI class.
- **Description of Interface Component**
  This field is used to describe the interface component in a few words.
- **Data Element for Documentation**
  This field represents the data element of the interface component name for an RAI class.

In a rare scenario, if after consulting with SAP, you decide to create a new component, then these three fields should be filled out. For each component type you configure, it's recommended to go through the entire dialog structure even if you don't intend to use a few components within it. For a standard interface component, you can define **Assigned Structures**, **Prerequisite Components** (optional), and **Program Enhancements**.

As shown in Figure 6.4, start by selecting the **SD_MI01** component and navigating to the **Assigned Structures** folder. **Assigned Structures** has the following fields:

- **Rec. Type**
  This field represents the record type for an RAI. There are three standard record types provided by SAP S/4HANA:
  - **All Record Types**: Any new record type added within a component by default has its record type as **All Record Types**. This basically mean this record type is universal and can be used as a main item or condition item. You should only select this option in the rare instance that you're unsure what record type the RAI should be assigned to.
  - **Main Item**: This record type is used to tag an RAI as a main item. **Main Items** are mandatory for RAI data processing.
  - **Condition Item**: This record type is used to tag an RAI as a condition item. **Condition Items** are dependent on main items and can only be processed once the underlying main items are processed.
- **Status**
  This field represents possible statuses for an RAI. By default, there are the following status options available:

- **All Statuses**: This is a default catchall status. Any new record type you create in the system will have this status assigned to it as default. It's recommended to seldomly use this status and always use one of the specific statuses that we'll discuss next.
- **0 (Raw)**: An RAI with raw status is modifiable for errors or inconsistencies. Raw RAIs aren't processable to be sent over for data processing.
- **1 (Raw – Exempted)**: If a raw RAI is completely broken and unusable for data processing, you can exempt that RAI.
- **2 (Processable)**: An RAI with status **Processable** is ready and validated by the system to be used for data processing. Data seen in a processable RAI should match one-to-one to document data in the source system.
- **3 (Processable – Exempted)**: If a processable RAI is broken or has bad data and is unusable for data processing, you can exempt that RAI.
- **4 (Processed)**: An RAI that is fully processed and has been used to create/update a RAR contract for revenue recognition will have the status **Processed**.

- **Structure**
  This field represents the structure with fields for the interface component.
- **Condit. Active**
  This checkbox is used to conditionally activate the structure of an interface component. The following two conditions must be fulfilled for a structure to be conditionally active:
  - The RAI class to which the structure belongs must use the interface component.
  - The record type of the assigned structure is active in the RAI class.

Component: SD_MI01
Description: SD Fields for Order Items

Assigned Structures

Rec. Type	Status	Structure	Condit. Active	ndit. Active
MI Main Item	All Statuses	FARR_S_ICMI01_SD	☐	☐
MI Main Item	0 Raw	FARR_S_ICMI01_SD0	☐	☐
MI Main Item	1 Raw - Exempted	FARR_S_ICMI01_SD0	☐	☐

Figure 6.4 Assigned Structures

Next, we'll go to the **Prerequisite Components** folder, which is optional. As shown in Figure 6.5, **Prerequisite Components** includes two fields:

- **Component**
  This field represents the interface component that needs to be activated first, as a prerequisite, for the post-requisite component to be activated seamlessly. For example, let's say in your SAP S/4HANA system, you have an interface component for bill

plans. But as a prerequisite, you always want the sales order component to be activated before the bill plan component because technically no bill plans can exist without sales order line items. In this case, under the bill plan component configuration, you'll maintain sales order **Component** as the prerequisite.

- **Description of Interface Component**
  This field is used to describe the prerequisite component in a few words.

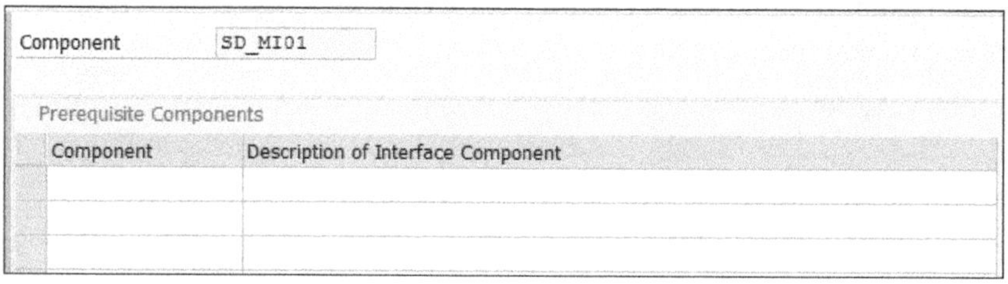

Component SD_MI01

Prerequisite Components

Component	Description of Interface Component

Figure 6.5 Prerequisite Components

Next, we'll go to the **Program Enhancements** folder, which has the following fields, as shown in Figure 6.6:

- **Ev**
  This field represents the event when a program enhancement is triggered. SAP S/4HANA provides three standard events:
  - **0E Enrich Raw Data Items**: If you want to add a validation or any other kind of enhancement on the raw data items, you can do so by selecting this event type.
  - **2E Enrich Processable Items**: If you want to add error handling or any other kind of enhancement on the processable RAIs, you can do so by selecting this event type.
  - **2C Final Check Before Saving Processable Items**: If you want to do any final checks or add any other kind of enhancement on the processable RAIs, you can do so by selecting this event type.
- **No**
  This field represents the sequence number of method calls for an event. If you have more than one event set up in this configuration, you can decide the sequence of how you want to trigger the event enhancements by assigning a number to them. The lower the number, the higher the priority. In this example, because there is only one event, we've assigned sequence number **0** to it.
- **Method for Interface Component**
  This field represents the method name of an interface component.
- **Prio.**
  This fields represents the priority of functions within an event.

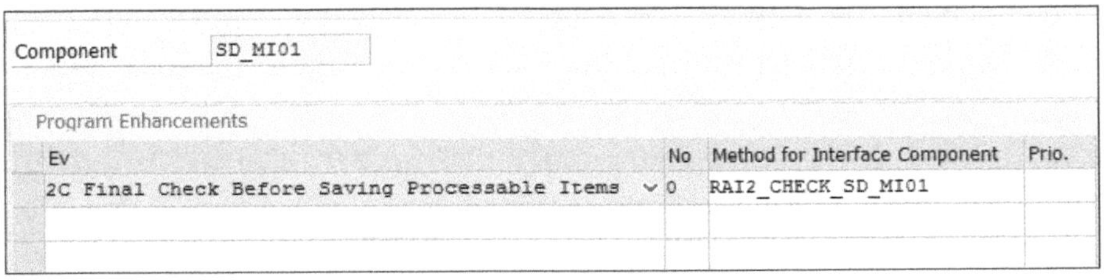

Component	SD_MI01		

Program Enhancements

Ev	No	Method for Interface Component	Prio.
2C Final Check Before Saving Processable Items	0	RAI2_CHECK_SD_MI01	

Figure 6.6 Program Enhancements

The next step in the **Dialog Structure** for interface components is setting up key fields by proceeding to the **Key Fields** folder. The key field is a combination of **Rec Type**, **Status**, and **Structure**, as shown in Figure 6.7. We explained these fields when we discussed the **Assigned Structures** folder. Based on business requirements as to how you want RAIs to be set up, you should add those entries as key fields within this step. For instance, the example business need was to generate main items and condition items for every change made to sales documents in the source system, and for the main item and condition item, we wanted to allow all the SAP-provided statuses. Thus, we created the combinations shown in Figure 6.7.

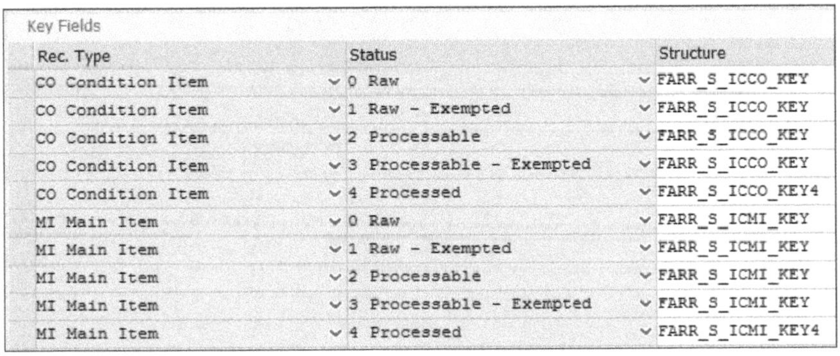

Key Fields

Rec. Type	Status	Structure
CO Condition Item	0 Raw	FARR_S_ICCO_KEY
CO Condition Item	1 Raw - Exempted	FARR_S_ICCO_KEY
CO Condition Item	2 Processable	FARR_S_ICCO_KEY
CO Condition Item	3 Processable - Exempted	FARR_S_ICCO_KEY
CO Condition Item	4 Processed	FARR_S_ICCO_KEY4
MI Main Item	0 Raw	FARR_S_ICMI_KEY
MI Main Item	1 Raw - Exempted	FARR_S_ICMI_KEY
MI Main Item	2 Processable	FARR_S_ICMI_KEY
MI Main Item	3 Processable - Exempted	FARR_S_ICMI_KEY
MI Main Item	4 Processed	FARR_S_ICMI_KEY4

Figure 6.7 Key Fields

The final step in the **Dialog Structure** of defining interface components is to go to the **Assign Components to Class Type and Record Type** folder. As shown in Figure 6.8, the assignment screen has the following fields:

- **Class Type**
  This field represents the RAI data class type. SAP S/4HANA provides three default class types:
  - **01 Order item**: This class type is used for order items, for example, sales order line items from the source SAP S/4HANA sales and distribution system.
  - **02 Fulfillment item**: This class type is used for fulfillment items, for example, delivery document items from the source SAP S/4HANA sales and distribution system.

  - **03 Invoice item**: This class type is used for invoice items, for example, billing and credit memo items from the source SAP S/4HANA sales and distribution system.
- **Rec. Type**
  This field represents the record type for an RAI. There are three standard record types provided by SAP S/4HANA: **All Record Types**, **MI Main Item**, and **CO Condition Item**.
- **Interface Component**
  This field represents the interface component name for an RAI class.
- **Description of Interface Component**
  This field is used to describe the interface component in just a few words.
- **Mandatory**
  This checkbox is used to tell the system if an interface component is mandatory or not.

Assign Components to Class Type and Record Type

Class Type	Rec. Type	Interface Component	Description of Interface Component	Mandatory
01 Order Item	CO Condition Item	BASIC_CO	Basic Fields for Conditions	☑
01 Order Item	CO Condition Item	BASIC_CO01	Basic Fields for Order Items (Conditions)	☑
01 Order Item	MI Main Item	BASIC_MI	Basic Fields for Main Items	☑
01 Order Item	MI Main Item	BASIC_MI01	Basic Fields for Order Items (Main Items)	☑
01 Order Item	MI Main Item	CA_BASIC_MI	CA Basic Fields for Main Items	☐
01 Order Item	MI Main Item	CA_MI01	CA Fields for Order Items	☐
01 Order Item	MI Main Item	COPA_MI01	CO-PA Fields for Order Items (COPACRIT)	☐
01 Order Item	MI Main Item	CRM_MI01	CRM Fields for Order Items	☐
01 Order Item	MI Main Item	SD_MI01	SD Fields for Order Items	☐
02 Fulfillment Item	CO Condition Item	BASIC_CO	Basic Fields for Conditions	☐
02 Fulfillment Item	MI Main Item	BASIC_MI	Basic Fields for Main Items	☑
02 Fulfillment Item	MI Main Item	BASIC_MI02	Basic Fields for Fulfillment Items (Main Items)	☑
02 Fulfillment Item	MI Main Item	CA_BASIC_MI	CA Basic Fields for Main Items	☐
03 Invoice Item	CO Condition Item	BASIC_CO	Basic Fields for Conditions	☑
03 Invoice Item	MI Main Item	BASIC_MI	Basic Fields for Main Items	☑
03 Invoice Item	MI Main Item	BASIC_MI03	Basic Fields for Invoice Items (Main Items)	☑
03 Invoice Item	MI Main Item	CA_BASIC_MI	CA Basic Fields for Main Items	☐

Figure 6.8 Assign Components to Class Type and Record Type

Tip

Use the **Mandatory** checkbox wisely. In most cases, the basic field's interface components are mandatory, while others aren't.

After filling out the relevant fields, click the **Save** button or press Ctrl+S to finish setting up interface components.

Revenue Accounting Item Classes

In this section, we'll dive into the configuration of RAI classes. An *RAI class* houses technical details of an RAI. For example, a sales order RAI class will determine database tables and function modules for sales order RAIs. Similarly, an invoice RAI class will determine database tables and function modules for invoice RAIs, and a fulfillment RAI class will determine database tables and function modules for fulfillment RAIs.

There are three main activities that we'll cover:

- **Maintain Revenue Accounting Item Classes**
  We'll show you how to configure and maintain RAI classes, which is very important for sales and distribution integration.
- **Generate Interfaces for Revenue Accounting Item Classes**
  We'll show you how to generate an interface for RAI classes, which you use to transfer RAI information from sales and distribution to RAR.
- **Assign Upload Rules to Revenue Accounting Item Classes**
  We'll provide guidance as to how you should configure upload rules for RAI classes.

To maintain an RAI class, follow IMG menu path **Financial Accounting • Revenue Accounting • Inbound Processing • Revenue Accounting Items • Maintain Revenue Accounting Item Classes**. Next, click the **New Class** button to create a new class, or double-click on an existing class to make modifications. We double-clicked on an existing **SD Order Item** class to arrive at the screen shown in Figure 6.9.

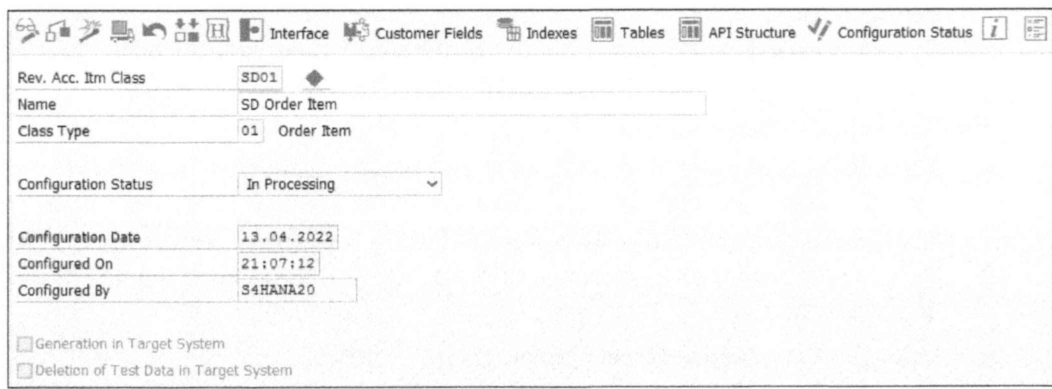

Figure 6.9 Maintain Revenue Accounting Item Class

RAI classes have mainly two sections: header-level data and field-level data. Let's first look at field-level data:

- **Rev. Acc. Itm Class**
  This field represents the unique ID for an RAI class. It's a four-character alphanumeric value.
- **Name**
  This field represents the name for an RAI class.
- **Class Type**
  This field represents the RAI data class type. SAP S/4HANA provides three default class types: **01 (Order Item)**, **02 (Fulfillment Item)**, and **03 (Invoice Item)**.

- **Configuration Status**
  This field represents the configuration status for an RAI class. By default, SAP S/4HANA has three possible statuses:
  - **In Processing**: This is the first status an RAI class takes when created new. In this status, changes are allowed to an RAI class but can't be transported to a different system.
  - **Transportable**: Once all needed changes are made to the RAI class, you can move it to **Transportable** status, which means SAP S/4HANA will allow you to move changes to another system.
  - **Released as Productive**: An RAI class is moved to this status when all changes are configured and tested successfully. Although there are a few changes that the system will allow you to do in this status, it's recommended not to make any changes when the RAI class is released as productive.
- **Configuration Date**
  This field represents the date when the last change was made on an RAI class.
- **Configured On**
  This field represents the time when the last change was made on an RAI class.
- **Configured By**
  This field represents the person's SAP user ID who last made a change on an RAI class.
- **Generation in Target System**
  This checkbox indicates if an RAI class is automatically generated in the target system. We recommend selecting this checkbox for all configured classes. You don't want a situation where the classes have moved to the target system correctly but haven't been activated. RAR configurations won't work correctly if the RAI classes aren't activated.
- **Deletion of Test Data in Target System**
  This checkbox indicates if test data from an RAI class is automatically deleted in the target system. You should typically also have this selected for all classes to ensure you don't test with old data that doesn't have the new changes incorporated.

Next, let's look at the header-level data points for the RAI class. The following buttons are important from the sales and distribution integration standpoint:

- **Interface**
  You can activate the interface components shown previously in Figure 6.3 using this configuration step. After clicking the **Interface** button, you'll arrive at the screen shown in Figure 6.10. In this example, you can see that RAI class **SD01** has the following fields:
  - **Active**: This checkbox is used to activate an interface component.
  - **Interface Component**: This field represents the interface component name for an RAI class.

- **Information**: This field represents SAP-provided information for the selected interface component.
- **Field Overview**: This field helps control the default status and display fields for the selected interface component.

Check the **Active** checkboxes for the interface components you want to activate and then click the green checkmark button. In this example, we activated the following components: **Basic Fields for Conditions, Basic Fields for Order Items (Conditions), Basic Fields for Main Items, Basic Fields for Order Item (Main Items), CO-PA Fields for Order Items (COPACRIT),** and **SD Fields for Order Items.** You can see the **Active** checkbox is checked for all these interface components in Figure 6.10.

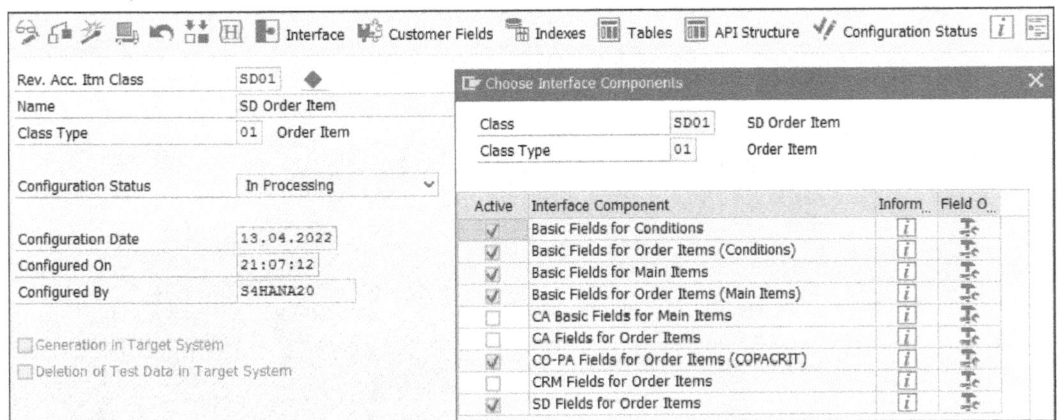

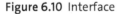

Figure 6.10 Interface

- **Indexes**
  This data point helps with selecting the default status for indexes of an RAI class. Indexes in general are used to set up default values for repetitive transactions to make life easy for end users by not having them go through an extra manual step. After clicking the **Indexes** button, you'll arrive at the screen shown in Figure 6.11, where you can choose an option under **Status Selection**. In this example, the default index status for RAI class **SD01** is set to **Raw**. So, whenever a new SD01 RAI is created in the system, it by default has the status **Raw**.

After filling out the relevant fields, click the **Save** button or press Ctrl + S to finish setting up the RAI class.

Now we can move on to the next activity. To generate an interface for an RAI class, follow IMG menu path **Financial Accounting • Revenue Accounting • Inbound Processing • Revenue Accounting Items • Generate Interfaces for Revenue Accounting Item Classes.** You'll arrive at the screen shown in Figure 6.12. From this screen, you can either view existing upload rules or create new ones by clicking on the **New Entries** button (not shown).

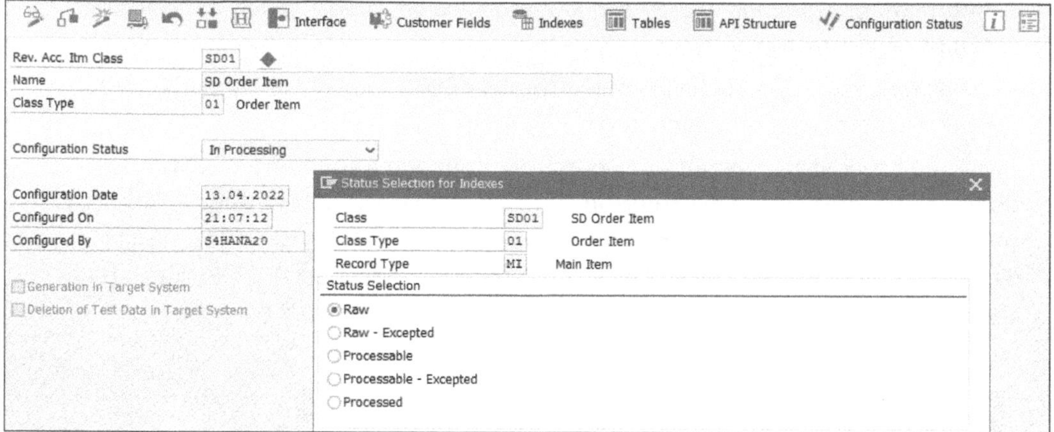

Figure 6.11 Indexes

Generate Interfaces for Revenue Accounting Item Classes

Generate | Objects | History | Log | Configuration

Classes of Revenue Accounting Items

Generation ...	Re...	Class Type	Name	Release Status	Generation Date	Generated On	Generated By
	SD01	Order Item	SD Order Items		05/13/2020	17:49:07	
	SD02	Fulfillment Item	SD Fulfillment Items		05/13/2020	22:57:39	
	SD03	Invoice Item	SD Invoice Item		05/13/2020	17:50:48	

Figure 6.12 Generate Interface for RAI Class

There is a one-to-one relationship between RAI classes and interfaces. Once you set up an interface component and configure an RAI class, an entry gets automatically added to this screen. The only task you need to do in this step is to generate the interface entry. In Figure 6.12, you can see for the **SD01** RAI class you created, an interface has been successfully generated, which is indicated by the green box under the **Generation** field.

Via the **Generate Interfaces for Revenue Accounting Item Classes** configuration screen, as shown in Figure 6.12, you can do the following (corresponding to the icons at the top of the screen, from left to right):

- Check generation of a class (Ctrl+F2)
- Generate a class (Ctrl+F3)
- Delete generated objects (Shift+F2)
- Display generated objects (F5)
- Display generation history (F6)
- Display generation log (F7)
- Display active configuration (F8)

- Compare with current configuration (Shift+F6)
- Lock class for usage (Shift+F5)
- Release class for usage (Shift+F4)
- View information (Ctrl+F8)
- View legend (Ctrl+F12)

The **Generate Interfaces for Revenue Accounting Item Classes** configuration screen also has the following fields:

- **Generation ... (Generation Status)**
  This field represents the generation status of an interface for an RAI class. SAP S/4HANA provides the following default generation statuses:
  - **Not Generated**: This status is represented by a blue diamond symbol indicating that the interface isn't yet generated.
  - **Generation Error**: This status is represented by a red circle symbol indicating the interface generation ran into errors.
  - **Regeneration Required**: This status is represented by a yellow triangle symbol indicating the interface requires regeneration.
  - **Generated Completely**: This status is represented by a green square symbol indicating the interface generation is successfully completed.
  - **Configuration Already Deleted**: This status is represented by a yellow lightning symbol indicating that the configuration required for interface generation has been deleted.
- **Re... (Rev. Acc. Itm Class)**
  This field represents the unique ID for an RAI class. It's a four-character alphanumeric value.
- **Class Type**
  This field represents the RAI data class type. SAP S/4HANA provides three default class types that we've discussed previously.
- **Name**
  This field represents the name for an RAI class.
- **Release Status**
  This field represents the release status of an RAI. SAP S/4HANA provides three default release statuses: **Not Released for Use**, **Released for Productive Use**, and **Released for Test Use.**
- **Generation Date**
  This field represents the date when the RAI class was last generated.
- **Generated On**
  This field represents the time when the RAI class was last generated.

- **Generated By**
  This field represents the person's SAP user ID who last generated the RAI class.

This brings us to the final activity for RAI classes: upload rules. To assign upload rules to an RAI class, follow IMG menu path **Financial Accounting • Revenue Accounting • Inbound Processing • Revenue Accounting Items • Assign Upload Rules to Revenue Accounting Item Classes**. You'll arrive at the screen shown in Figure 6.13. From this screen, you can either view existing modifiable fields or create new ones by clicking on the **New Entries** button.

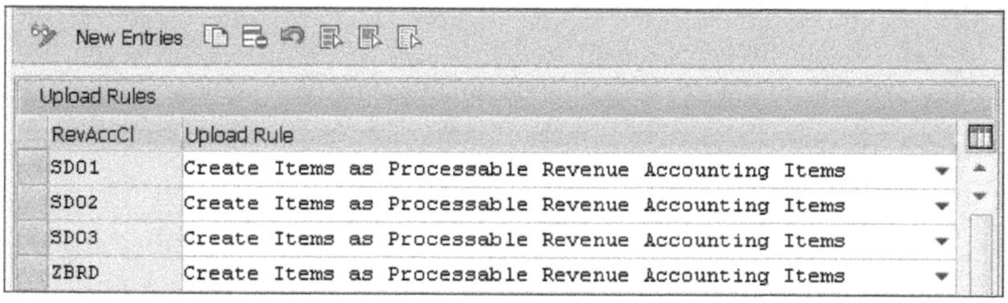

New Entries

Upload Rules

RevAccCl	Upload Rule
SD01	Create Items as Processable Revenue Accounting Items
SD02	Create Items as Processable Revenue Accounting Items
SD03	Create Items as Processable Revenue Accounting Items
ZBRD	Create Items as Processable Revenue Accounting Items

Figure 6.13 Assign Upload Rules to RAI Classes

The **Upload Rules** screen has two fields:

- **RevAccCl**
  This field represents the unique ID for an RAI class. It's a four-character alphanumeric value.
- **Upload Rule**
  This field represents the upload rules tied to an RAI class. Upload rules helps you control how RAIs should be generated on creation. There are two options available by default:
  - **Create Items as Processable Revenue Accounting Items**: If you select this option for the upload rule, all RAIs for sales and distribution changes are created in the ready state, and when the RAI monitor job runs, RAIs get sent over to RAR without any manual intervention.
  - **Create Items as Raw Revenue Accounting Items**: If you select this option for the upload rule, all RAIs for sales and distribution changes are created in the raw state. You must manually transfer raw RAIs to processable, and then when the RAI monitor job runs, RAIs get sent over to RAR. This rule is used if business users want to review RAIs before sending them over to RAR.

Define Modifiable Fields

As a standard, SAP S/4HANA doesn't allow any fields to be modifiable on an RAI. This makes sense because RAIs are outcomes of changes made to source documents (e.g., sales orders in sales and distribution). So, if you really want to change an RAI, you should make the modification on the source document and let it naturally flow over to RAI.

There may be business-approved reasons for end users to modify certain fields on a RAI. If that is true in your case, then this configuration step will help you achieve the requirement. The control parameters of making a field modifiable are RAI class, record type, status, and field name. A combination of these four parameters determines if a field on the RAI is modifiable, display only, or hidden.

To define modifiable fields, follow IMG menu path **Financial Accounting • Revenue Accounting • Inbound Processing • Revenue Accounting Items • Define Modifiable Fields for Revenue Accounting Items**. You'll arrive at the screen shown in Figure 6.14. From this screen, you can either view existing modifiable fields or create new ones by clicking on the **New Entries** button.

New Entries

Maintain Changeable Fields of Rev. Accounting Item Classes

RevAccCl	Rec. Type	Status	Field Name	FieldAttr
SD01	Condition Item	Raw	CATEGORY	
SD01	Condition Item	Raw	MAIN_COND_TYPE	
SD01	Condition Item	Raw	STATISTIC	
SD01	Condition Item	Processable	CATEGORY	
SD01	Condition Item	Processable	MAIN_COND_TYPE	
SD01	Condition Item	Processable	PL_ACCOUNT	
SD01	Condition Item	Processable	STATISTIC	
SD01	Main Item	Raw	REFERENCE_ID	Hide
SD01	Main Item	Raw	WERKS	
SD01	Main Item	Processable	BUKRS	
SD01	Main Item	Processable	END_DATE	Hide
SD01	Main Item	Processable	INITIAL_LOAD	
SD01	Main Item	Processable	PREDOC_ID	
SD01	Main Item	Processable	PREDOC_TYPE	
SD01	Main Item	Processable	REFERENCE_ID	
SD01	Main Item	Processable	REFERENCE_TYPE	Display only
SD01	Main Item	Processable	START_DATE	
SD01	Main Item	Processable	WERKS	
SD02	Main Item	Raw	HWAE2	
SD02	Main Item	Raw	HWAE3	Display only
SD02	Main Item	Raw	HWAER	
SD02	Main Item	Raw	WAERS	
SD03	Condition Item	Raw	CATEGORY	
SD03	Condition Item	Raw	MAIN_COND_TYPE	
SD03	Condition Item	Raw	STATISTIC	

Figure 6.14 Modifiable Fields

The modifiable fields configuration screen has the following fields:

- **RevAccCl**
  This field represents the unique ID for an RAI class. It's a four-character alphanumeric value.
- **Rec. Type**
  This field represents the record type for an RAI. There are three standard record

types provided by SAP S/4HANA that we've discussed: **All Record Types**, **MI Main Item**, and **CO Condition Item**.

- **Status**
  This field represents possible statuses for an RAI. By default, there are five status options available that we've already discussed: **All Statuses**, **0 (Raw)**, **1 (Raw – Exempted)**, **2 (Processable)**, **3 (Processable – Exempted)**, and **4 (Processed)**.
- **Field Name**
  This field represents the technical name of the field you would like to make modifiable.
- **FieldAttr**
  This field represents the attribute you want the modifiable field to inherit. SAP S/4HANA provides three default attributes: blank for modifiable, - for hidden, and * for display only.

Revenue Accounting Item Management

In the previous section, you learned about RAIs in terms of their core setup, including interface components, RAI classes, and modifiable fields. In this section, we walk you through supplementary RAI management components such as source document types, logical systems, sender components, reference condition types, and SSP condition types. All of these are extremely important from the sales and distribution–RAR integration standpoint within SAP S/4HANA.

Source Document Item Type

Within this configuration, you define the different item types of the source system documents, which are used when revenue accounting is performed in the RAR system. Source systems can be SAP S/4HANA, SAP Customer Relationship Management (SAP CRM), or any third-party system. You can technically add item types for all connecting systems or only one system depending on your business needs. Because our source system is sales and distribution in SAP S/4HANA, the item types we defined in this configuration are SAP order items, SAP fulfillment items, SAP bill plan items, and SAP invoice items. The order item type links to the sales and distribution sales order, the fulfillment item type links the sales and distribution delivery, the bill plan item type links to the sales and distribution sales order billing plans, and the invoice item type links to the sales and distribution sales invoices.

To define source document item types, follow IMG menu path **Financial Accounting • Revenue Accounting • Inbound Processing • Revenue Accounting Item Management • Define Source Document Item Types**. You'll arrive at the screen shown in Figure 6.15. From this screen, you can either view existing source item types or create new ones by clicking on the **New Entries** button (not shown here).

Source Item Types

SrcItmType	Class Type	Item Type Description
SDFI	02 Fulfillment Item	SAP Fulfillment Item
SDII	03 Invoice Item	SAP Invoice Item
SDOI	01 Order Item	SAP Order Item
SDPI	03 Invoice Item	SAP Billing Plan Item

Figure 6.15 Source Document Item Types

The screen has three fields, as shown in Figure 6.15:

- **SrcItmType**
  This field represents the unique alphanumeric key for a source document item type.
- **Class Type**
  This field represents the RAI data class type. SAP S/4HANA provides three default class types: **01 (Order Item)**, **02 (Fulfillment Item)**, and **03 (Invoice Item)**.
- **Item Type Description**
  This field describes a source document item type in a few words.

Logical Systems

Within this configuration, you should define the logical system or system from where the source data for revenue accounting originates. Because SAP S/4HANA is the source system for RAR, we'll define all systems within the SAP S/4HANA landscape as logical systems in this configuration step.

To define logical systems, follow IMG menu path **Financial Accounting • Revenue Accounting • Inbound Processing • Revenue Accounting Item Management • Define Logical Systems**. You'll arrive at the screen shown in Figure 6.16. From this screen, you can either view existing logical systems or create new ones by clicking on the **New Entries** button (not shown).

As shown in Figure 6.16, **Logical Systems** only includes two fields:

- **Log.System**
  This field represents the unique alphanumeric key for a logical system.
- **Name**
  This field represents the name given to a logical system.

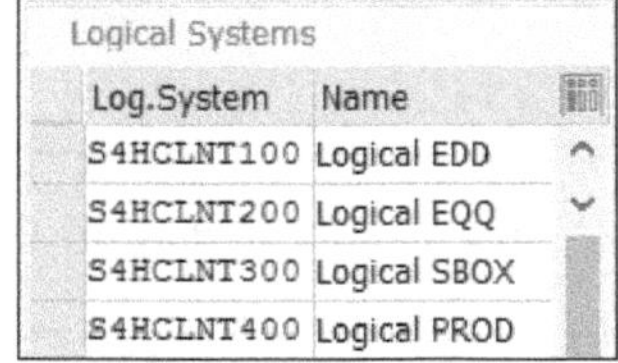

Logical Systems

Log.System	Name
S4HCLNT100	Logical EDD
S4HCLNT200	Logical EQQ
S4HCLNT300	Logical SBOX
S4HCLNT400	Logical PROD

Figure 6.16 Logical Systems

Sender Components

Within this configuration, you determine the true connection between RAR and the source system. The sender component connects with the logical systems and item types to send data from the source system to RAR.

To define sender components, follow IMG menu path **Financial Accounting • Revenue Accounting • Inbound Processing • Revenue Accounting Item Management • Define Sender Components**. You'll arrive at the screen shown in Figure 6.17. From this screen, you can either view existing sender components or create new ones by clicking on the **New Entries** button.

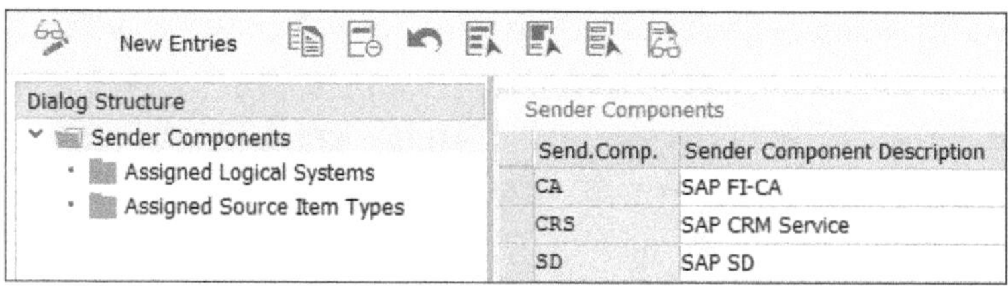

Figure 6.17 Sender Components

The **Sender Components** main screen has two fields, as shown in Figure 6.17:

- **Send.Comp.**
  This field represents the unique key of the sender component, for example, **SD**, which stands for SAP sales and distribution.
- **Sender Component Description**
  This field describes a sender component in just a few words.

To assign logical systems to sender components, select a sender component from the right section of the screen (refer to Figure 6.17), and then double-click on the **Assigned Logical Systems** dialog structure folder on the left. We selected **SD** and assigned four logical systems to it by clicking the **New Entries** button on the top-left side of the screen. As shown in Figure 6.18, the screen has the following fields:

- **SourceSys.**
  This field represents the unique alphanumeric key for a logical source system.
- **+**
  This fields represents the name of the logical source system.
- **RFC Destination of Sender**
  This field represents the remote function call (RFC) name of the sender destination. This field is used when you want to extract and match RAI data with source system data.
- **Description**
  This field represents the description of RFC destinations.

Sender Comp. SD

Assigned Logical Systems

SourceSys.	+	RFC Destination of Sender	Description
S4HCLNT100	Logical EDD		
S4HCLNT200	Logical EQQ		
S4HCLNT300	Logical SBOX		
S4HCLNT400	Logical PROD		

Figure 6.18 Sender Component Logical Systems

After filling out the relevant fields, click the **Save** button or press Ctrl+S to finish assigning the logical systems.

To assign source item types to sender components, select a sender component from the right section of the screen (refer to Figure 6.17), and then double-click on the **Assigned Source Item Types** dialog structure folder on the left. We selected **SD** and assigned four item types to it by clicking the **New Entries** button on the top-left side of the screen. As shown in Figure 6.19, the screen has two fields:

- **SrcItmType**
  This field represents the unique alphanumeric key for a source document item type.
- **Item Type Description**
  This field describes a source document item type in just a few words.

Sender Comp. SD

Assigned Source Item Types

SrcItmType	Item Type Description
SDFI	Fulfillment Item
SDII	Invoice Item
SDOI	Order Item
SDPI	Billing Plan Item

Figure 6.19 Assigned Source Item Types

After filling out the relevant fields, click the **Save** button or press Ctrl+S to finish the source item type assignment.

Reference Types

Reference types, along with reference IDs, control how RAIs combine on a RAR contract. Both reference type and reference ID are fields on the RAIs that can be seen from the RAI monitor. The *RAI monitor* is an interface used to move RAIs from the sales and distribution side of SAP S/4HANA to the RAR side. To open the RAI monitor, use Transaction FARR_RAI_MON.

As shown in Figure 6.20, reference type is the fourth field from the right (**Ref. Type**) and **Reference ID** is the third field from the right. All RAIs with the same reference type and reference ID combine on one contract in RAR, and this logic is defined in business add-in (BAdI) FARR_BADI_CONTRACT_COMBINATION.

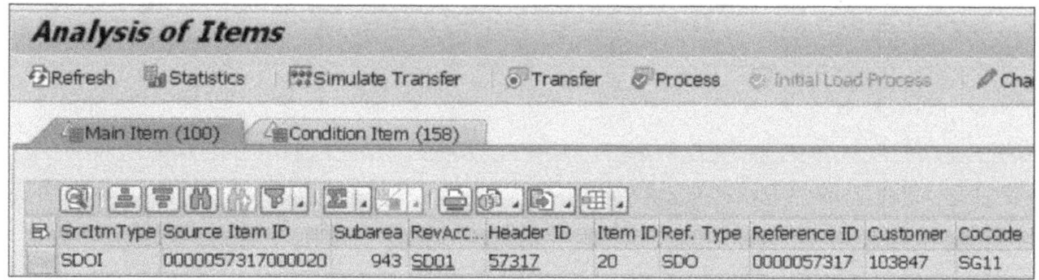

Figure 6.20 RAI Monitor

To define reference types, follow IMG menu path **Financial Accounting • Revenue Accounting • Inbound Processing • Revenue Accounting Item Management • Define Reference Types**. You'll arrive at the screen shown in Figure 6.21. From this screen, you can either view existing reference types or create new ones by clicking on the **New Entries** button.

The **Reference Types** screen has two fields:

- **Ref. Type**
  This field represents the type of reference ID. For example, at the example company, we use sales order as the reference ID, so the reference type is **SDO**. You can see this in the RAI monitor (refer to Figure 6.20).
- **Reference Type Text**
  This field represents a short text description for the **Ref. Type** field.

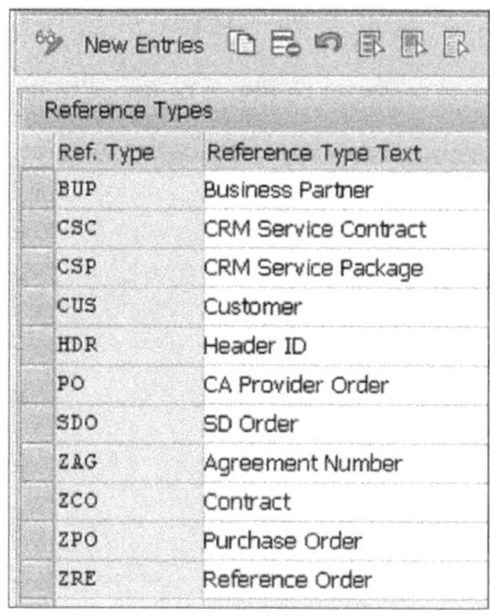

Ref. Type	Reference Type Text
BUP	Business Partner
CSC	CRM Service Contract
CSP	CRM Service Package
CUS	Customer
HDR	Header ID
PO	CA Provider Order
SDO	SD Order
ZAG	Agreement Number
ZCO	Contract
ZPO	Purchase Order
ZRE	Reference Order

Figure 6.21 Reference Types

Condition Type for Standalone Selling Price and Right of Return

Condition type data is transferred from the source system to RAR via the RAIs. The data passes through BRFplus first and then enters the RAR contract. BRFplus makes certain decisions on the condition type data based on the rules you set up within the decision tables and other attributes within it. Ideally, SSP and right of return should naturally flow over from the source system without being amended. That is why RAR gives you this specific configuration, where the condition types defined in this step won't go over to BRFplus and will directly go into the RAR contract untouched.

To define the condition type for SSP and right of return, follow IMG menu path **Financial Accounting • Revenue Accounting • Inbound Processing • Revenue Accounting Item Management • Define Condition Type for Standalone Selling Price and Right of Return**. You'll arrive at the screen shown in Figure 6.22. From this screen, you can either view existing condition types or create new ones by clicking on the **New Entries** button.

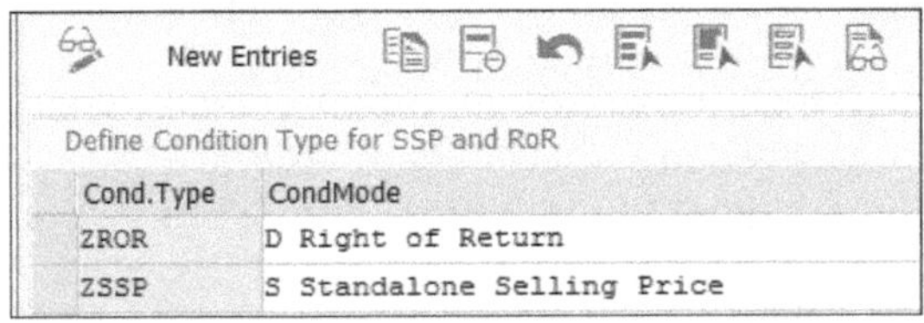

Cond.Type	CondMode
ZROR	D Right of Return
ZSSP	S Standalone Selling Price

Figure 6.22 Condition Type for SSP and Right of Return

As shown in Figure 6.22, the condition type for SSP and right of return has two fields:

- **Cond.Type**
  This field represents the unique condition which you want to tag as an SSP or right of return condition type.
- **CondMode**
  This field classifies the **Cond.Type** field as **S Standalone Selling Price**, **D Right of Return**, or **T Standalone Selling Price Tolerance**. Tolerance is the buffer you can add on top of your regular SSP, within which if there is allocation, the system will ignore it and proceed with a regular revenue recognition as if there was no allocation.

  Let's consider an example where ZSSP is your regular SSP without the buffer, which can have **CondMode S**, while ZSSPT is the tolerance SSP with the buffer, which can have **CondMode T**. If ZSSP = 10, the approve tolerance is 5, and ZSSPT comes in at 15, SAP S/4HANA will treat the contract as a regular contract and not allocate. But if the ZSSPT comes in at 20, then there is true allocation on the contract, and SAP S/4HANA will perform allocation across the RAR contract and move numbers accordingly.

Revenue Accounting Contracts

In the previous section, you learned everything about RAIs, from configuration to usage and how they are critical integration components from sales and distribution to RAR. In this section, we'll look at what revenue accounting contracts are and how they are configured from the sales and distribution integration standpoint.

Revenue accounting contracts are core entities in RAR that store contract data from source system that is relevant for RAR. For example, if sales and distribution sends sales order data along with bill plans, invoices, and general ledger information to RAR, all of this is housed under the revenue accounting contract. The formula is as follows:

Revenue accounting contracts = Contract information (from sales and distribution) + Performance obligations

Since SAP S/4HANA 1909, SAP introduced the concept of optimized contract management (OCM). For the most part, OCM works in the same way as traditional contract management with a few key changes and benefits. We'll look at OCM in Section 6.3, but we wanted to mention it here because after the introduction of OCM, SAP started referring to the traditional contract management as classic contract management (CCM). In this section, we'll only focus on CCM, but we'll pivot to OCM in Section 6.3.

At the end of this section, you'll have a good understanding of the following:

- Accounting principles and company code assignments
- How to exclude currency calculation if needed
- How to open and close RAR calendars
- Configuration of POB types and other condition types
- Configuration of fulfillment types and review reasons

Let's dive right in.

Assign Company Codes to Accounting Principles

Accounting principles are legal standards based on which financial statements are composed and furnished. Examples of accounting principles include International Accounting Standard (IAS) and Generally Accepted Accounting Principles (GAAP). All company codes configured within your source sales and distribution functionality should exist in this configuration step, pointing to a minimum of one accounting principle each. If a company follows more than one accounting principle, then they should assign each principle to each company code entity depending on their requirement.

To assign company codes to accounting principles, follow IMG menu path **Financial Accounting • Revenue Accounting • Revenue Accounting Contracts (Classic) • Assign Company Codes to Accounting Principles**. You'll arrive at the screen shown in Figure 6.23. From this screen, you can either view existing assignments or create new ones by clicking on the **New Entries** button (not shown).

Supported Company Codes per Accounting Principle

AccP	CoCd	Company Name	Transf.Dat	Status	Adopt.Date	Src.Acc.Pr	Ext.Acc.Pr
606	0001		11/30/2015	Productive	01/01/2019		☑
605	0001		11/30/2015	Productive	01/01/2019		☑
606	SG11		11/30/2015	Migration	01/01/2019		☐

Figure 6.23 Assign Company Codes to Accounting Principles

The assignment screen for company codes to accounting principles includes the following fields:

- **AccP**
  This field represents the unique code of the accounting principle within the SAP S/4HANA system.
- **CoCd**
  This field represents the company code that must be assigned to the accounting principle.
- **Company Name**
  This field represents the name associated with the company code.
- **Transf.Dat**
  This field represents the transfer date for historic data. In this example, the company went live in 2018, but from a reporting standpoint, we went retrospective and stated data from 2015 onwards. That is why the adoption date is 2019, but the transfer date is 2015. For companies who don't go retrospective, their adoption date and transfer date are the same.
- **Status**
  This field represents the revenue accounting status of an accounting principle and company code combination. By default, SAP S/4HANA provides four statuses:
  - **Migration**: This is the first status an accounting principle should have when set up new. While performing data migration or data cleanup for the accounting principle, SAP S/4HANA recommends having this status.
  - **Transition**: This is the logical next status after migration activities are completed for an accounting principle. Before changing the status to transition, you should make sure all open reconciliation keys are closed for the migration activities. RAIs before transfer date are processed in the **Transition** status.
  - **Adoption Preparation**: RAIs after transfer date, which are copied back to **Processable** status, are processed in the **Adoption Preparation** status. Within this status, you're preparing the accounting principle and the underlying data to be ready for go-live.
  - **Productive**: This is the go-live RAI status for the newly configured accounting principle once all the migration and transition activities are completed. When an accounting principle is in **Productive** status, it naturally fits in to the RAR process, and any new RAIs getting created for the revenue recognition process get attached to this principle depending on configuration.
- **Adopt.Date**
  This field represents the adoption date when a company goes live with their RAR.
- **Src.Acc.Pr**
  This field represents the source accounting principle if you're transitioning from an old accounting principle to a new one.

- **Ext.Acc.Pr**
  This checkbox is checked if there is no source accounting principle, and you're adopting an external accounting principle for revenue accounting. Because we did a fresh RAR implementation and didn't adopt an existing configured accounting principle, this checkbox is checked for all company code/accounting principle entries within the configuration.
- **End.D.Usg.**
  This field (not shown) represents the end date after which RAIs won't be processed for that company code/accounting principle combination.
- **App.Ear.OP**
  This checkbox (not shown) is checked if you want to apply contract changes to the earliest open RAR period for a company code.

Exclude Local Currency Calculation

There are use cases where companies set up multiple local currencies for a company code in Transaction OB22. For such companies, if they want to exclude specific currencies from revenue accounting, they can do so via this configuration. For example, the US company code (SG11) at the organization has CAD as local currency 2. For revenue accounting purposes, we only want USD to be considered and not CAD. To achieve this, we've added an entry to this configuration step to exclude CAD.

To exclude local currency calculation from revenue accounting, follow IMG menu path **Financial Accounting • Revenue Accounting • Revenue Accounting Contracts (Classic) • Exclude Local Currency Calculation from Revenue Accounting**. You'll arrive at the screen shown in Figure 6.24. From this screen, you can either view existing exclusion entries or create new ones by clicking on the **New Entries** button.

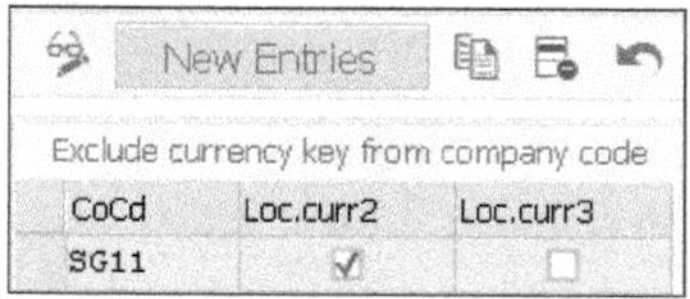

Figure 6.24 Exclude Local Currency Calculation from Revenue Accounting

As shown in Figure 6.24, the exclude local currency configuration has three fields:

- **CoCd**
  This field represents the company code for which you want alternate local currency to be excluded.
- **Loc.curr2**
  This field represents local currency 2 of a company code in case you want that to be excluded from revenue accounting.

- **Loc.curr3**
  This field represents local currency 3 of a company code in case you want that to be excluded from revenue accounting.

Open and Close Revenue Accounting Periods

Just like financial accounting periods can be controlled via Transaction OB52, revenue accounting periods can be controlled by this configuration. Generally, financial accounting and revenue accounting periods go together; that is, they will follow the same opening and closing schedules. When an account's team is done performing all transactions for the month end, they move both finance and revenue accounting periods together.

To open and close revenue accounting periods, follow IMG menu path **Financial Accounting • Revenue Accounting • Revenue Accounting Contracts (Classic) • Open and Close Revenue Accounting Periods**. You'll arrive at the screen shown in Figure 6.25. From this screen, you can either view existing period close entries or create new ones by clicking on the **New Entries** button (not shown).

Revenue Accounting Period Close

CoCd	AccP	Fr. F.Year	Fr. Period	Status
SG11	606	2020	4	Open
SG13	606	2020	4	Open
SG14	606	2020	4	Open
SG15	606	2020	4	Open
SG24	606	2020	4	Open
SG30	606	2020	4	Open
SG31	606	2020	4	Open
SG32	606	2020	4	Open

Figure 6.25 Open and Close Revenue Accounting Periods

As shown in Figure 6.25, the **Revenue Accounting Period Close** screen has the following fields:

- **CoCd**
  This field represents the company code for which you want to open or close revenue accounting periods.
- **AccP**
  This field represents the unique code of the accounting principle within the SAP S/4HANA system.
- **Fr. F.Year**
  This field represents the from fiscal year of a revenue accounting period.
- **Fr. Period**
  This field presents the from period of a revenue accounting period.

- **Status**
  This field represents the status of a revenue accounting period. SAP S/4HANA standard has three default statuses: **Open**, **In-Closing**, and **Close**.

Performance Obligation Types

Just like item categories are the heart of sales and distribution, *POB types* are the heart of RAR. The core behavior of line-item data in RAR is controlled by POB type configuration. As explained in Chapter 2, Section 2.5.1, each sales order line item flowing over from sales and distribution to RAR gets converted to a POB. The POB controls allocation and fulfillment, which are the two core fundamentals of revenue accounting.

To configure POB types in SAP S/4HANA, follow IMG menu path **Financial Accounting • Revenue Accounting • Revenue Accounting Contracts (Classic) • Define Performance Obligation Types**. To create a new POB, click on the **New Entries** button, or double-click on an existing POB type, and you'll arrive at the screen shown in Figure 6.26. This screen shows that POB types comprise four sections: header section, **General Data**, **Fulfillment Data**, and **Allocation Data**.

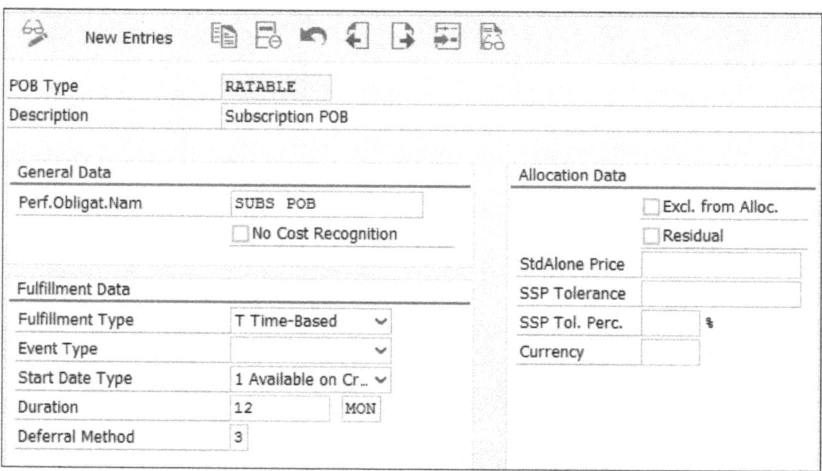

Figure 6.26 Performance Obligation Types

The header section has two fields:

- **POB Type**
  This field is used to identify the POB type for the POB.
- **Description**
  This field describes the POB type in just a few words.

Next, the **General Data** section has two fields:

- **Perf.Obligat.Nam**
  This field represents the name given to the POB.

- **No Cost Recognition**
  You should only check this checkbox if you don't want cost recognition to be active for a POB type. Cost recognition is useful when you recognize cost portion along with revenue for a third-party sale. For example, say your company sells an SAP license to its customer. SAP charges you USD 2,000 for the license, and you sell it to your customer for USD 2,500. In this scenario, for the revenue recognition process, you'll have a pricing condition of USD 2,500 on your RAR contract and a cost condition of USD 2,000. That way, you're recognizing cost and revenue appropriately based on purchase and sale.

The next section is **Fulfillment Data**, which has the following fields:

- **Fulfillment Type**
  This field represents the fulfillment type for a POB. Fulfillment type is the trigger for revenue recognition. Whenever a POB is fulfilled, it's technically ready for revenue recognition. By default, SAP S/4HANA provides three standard fulfillment types:
  - **Event-Based**: This fulfillment type is triggered when an underlying event occurs, for example, delivery, resource-related billing (RRB), and so on.
  - **Time-Based**: This fulfillment type is triggered after regular time intervals, for example, monthly maintenance, yearly support, and so on.
  - **Percentage of Completion**: This fulfillment type is triggered when a percentage of a task is completed, for example, at inception, halfway through a full task completion, and so on.
- **Event Type**
  This field represents the event type for fulfillment on a POB. There is a list of standard event types available, or you can add custom ones if needed (see the next section).
- **Start Date Type**
  This field represents the start date type for a POB. This field is only active for time-based POBs. By default, SAP S/4HANA provides three standard date types:
  - **Available on Creation of Performance Obligation**: If you select this setting, then the system will force you to enter a start date for POB at the time of POB creation.
  - **Available After Creation of Performance Obligation**: If you select this setting, then the system will allow you to enter a start date for POB any time after POB creation.
  - **Is Always the Event Date**: If you select this setting, then the system will default the start date of the POB to the event date.
- **Duration**
  This field represents the duration for a POB. This field is only active for time-based POBs.

- **Deferral Method**
  This field represents the deferral method for a POB. This field is only active for time-based POBs.

Finally, the **Allocation Data** section has the following fields:

- **Excl. from Alloc.**
  This checkbox is only checked if you want the POB to be excluded from allocation.
- **Residual**
  This checkbox is only checked is you want the POB to be active for residual allocation.
- **StdAlone Price**
  This field represents the SSP of a POB.
- **SSP Tolerance**
  This field represents the SSP tolerance for a POB.
- **SSP Tol. Perc.**
  This field represents the SSP tolerance percentage for a POB.
- **Currency**
  This field represents the default currency for a POB.

Condition Types

There are three standard condition type configuration steps available in CCM in SAP S/4HANA:

- **Define Reserved Condition Types**
- **Define Condition Types Not Requiring Allocation**
- **Define Roles for Condition Types**

As condition types are important integration components between sales and distribution and RAR, paying special attention to configuration specific to condition types in this section will be very beneficial. Condition types are carriers of revenue data from sales and distribution in SAP S/4HANA to RAR. Within this configuration, you have the flexibility to make condition type-specific settings that will help you meet your complex business requirements. Examples of more commonly used condition types in this configuration are allocation difference condition type, exchange rate difference condition type, third-party condition type, and cost condition type.

To define reserved condition types, follow IMG menu path **Financial Accounting • Revenue Accounting • Revenue Accounting Contracts (Classic) • Condition Types • Define Reserved Condition Types**. You'll arrive at the screen shown in Figure 6.27.

SAP S/4HANA provides you with four **Reserved Condition Types** options to assign:

- **Allocation Difference**
  This field represents the condition type that stores the allocation effect number for a revenue account contract.

- **Right-of-Return Revenue Adjustment**
  This field represents the condition type that stores the right-of-return adjustment number for a revenue account contract.
- **Right-of-Return Cost Adjustment**
  This field represents the condition type that stores the right-of-return cost adjustment number for a revenue account contract.
- **Exchange Rate Difference**
  This field represents the condition type that stores the exchange rate difference number for a revenue account contract.

Reserved Condition Types	
Allocation Difference	ZALL
Right-of-Return Revenue Adjustment	ZRRA
Right-of-Return Cost Adjustment	ZRRC
Exchange Rate Difference	ZED

Figure 6.27 Reserved Condition Types

After filling out the relevant fields for the four condition types, click the **Save** button or press [Ctrl]+[S] to finish setting them up.

Fulfillment Event Type

Revenue recognition happens when the underlying POB is fulfilled. Fulfillment of POB is controlled by events such as delivery, RRB, invoicing, and so on. The driver for events in RAR is the corresponding action performed in sales and distribution (the source system). For example, if a sales order line item is delivered in sales and distribution, it creates a delivery fulfillment event in RAR, thus making the corresponding POB available for revenue recognition. SAP S/4HANA provides you with a standard list of event types that you can associate with a fulfillment activity. You also have the flexibility to add new event types if needed.

To view the standard available fulfillment event types, follow IMG menu path **Financial Accounting • Revenue Accounting • Revenue Accounting Contracts (Classic) • Define Fulfillment Event Types**. You'll arrive at the screen shown in Figure 6.28. You can also add a new event type by clicking the **New Entries** button.

As shown in Figure 6.28, the fulfillment event type screen has two fields:

- **Event Type**
  This field represents the event type for fulfillment on a POB.
- **Description**
  This field describes the event type in just a few words.

Customizing of Event Type

Event Type	Description
AD	Acceptance Date
CC	Contract Acquisition Cost
CI	Customer Invoice
CS	Consumption
GI	Goods Issue
IB	Inter-company Billing Process
MA	Manual fulfillment
PD	Proof of Delivery
PI	Purchase Invoice (Drop Shipping)
RO	Contract Release Order (Call Off)
ZB	BRD

Figure 6.28 Fulfillment Event Type

Review Reasons

Like we have blocks on sales orders (delivery block, billing block, or revenue block), we have review reasons in RAR. *Review reasons* temporarily put a POB on hold. Business users then come in and review the POB and, if is everything is good, remove the review reason and make it ready for revenue recognition.

There are standard reports or worklists in RAR that a business user can run to get a list of POBs held with a review reason. At the example company, we've mapped the revenue block from sales and distribution to review reasons in RAR. All revenue block codes are mapped one-to-one with review reason codes. We have logic in BRFplus to read revenue block reasons from sales order RAIs and accordingly add review reason codes to POBs in RAR. More information on BRFplus is provided in Section 6.2.4.

To define review reasons, follow IMG menu path **Financial Accounting • Revenue Accounting • Revenue Accounting Contracts (Classic) • Define Review Reasons**. You'll arrive at the screen shown in Figure 6.29. From this screen, you can either view existing review reasons or create new ones by clicking on the **New Entries** button (not shown).

View for Review Reason

ReviewReas	Set Review	SusPstg	Query Description
RB1	☐	☑	Overall Rev. Block
RB2	☐	☑	Exp.Payment >120days
RB3	☐	☑	Contract Clauses
RB4	☐	☑	Until Cust. Payment
RB5	☐	☑	Del. of future Funct
RB6	☐	☑	Contract Contingen.
RB7	☐	☑	Significant open A/R
RB8	☐	☑	Re-Bill in Process
RB9	☐	☑	Credit Pending
RBC	☐	☑	Conversion
ZC	☐	☑	Conversion
ZRR	☑	☑	Revenue Rec Review

Figure 6.29 Review Reasons

This screen provides the following fields:

- **ReviewReas**
  This field represents the unique alphanumeric code for review reasons.
- **Set Review**
  This checkbox is checked if you want to set a POB as reviewed when the review reason is attached to it.
- **SusPstg**
  This checkbox is checked when you want to suspend a POB from posting when the review reason is attached to it.
- **Query Description**
  This field describes the review reason in just a few words.

6.2.2 SAP Business Client (Transaction NWBC)

We've now covered all the necessary information from the RAR side of the configuration when it comes to sales and distribution–RAR integration. In this section, we'll look at SAP Business Client and how it plays an important role in in the whole sales and distribution–RAR cycle.

SAP has built an SAP Business Client interface to support its SAP Revenue Accounting and Reporting solution. Each time you send RAIs from sales and distribution to RAR, the impact of those RAIs can be viewed in the SAP Business Client interface. Within SAP Business Client, you can view RAR contracts and RAR POBs, run revenue posting jobs, execute reports, and do much more. You can use Transaction NWBC to launch SAP Business Client.

In this section, we'll focus on the following Transaction NWBC features, which are important from the sales and distribution–RAR integration standpoint:

- **Contract view**
  Contract view is the screen in Transaction NWBC where you can search and display one or more contracts in RAR.
- **POB view**
  POB view is the screen in Transaction NWBC from where you can display all the fields of a POB of a revenue contract in RAR.
- **Worklists**
  Worklist are programs in RAR you can run from the Transaction NWBC screen to identify and track issues related to POBs or contracts.
- **Revenue posting jobs**
  Revenue posting jobs are used to transfer, calculate, and post revenue postings to RAR and general ledger tables.

Contract View

Contract view is the screen in Transaction NWBC where you can search and display one or more contracts in RAR. To get to the contract view, execute Transaction NWBC, and choose **Contract Management • Revenue Manager • Contract Search**. Type in the contract number you're looking for in the selection screen, and click on the contract record from the results list once you find it. Figure 6.30 shows a resulting contract view.

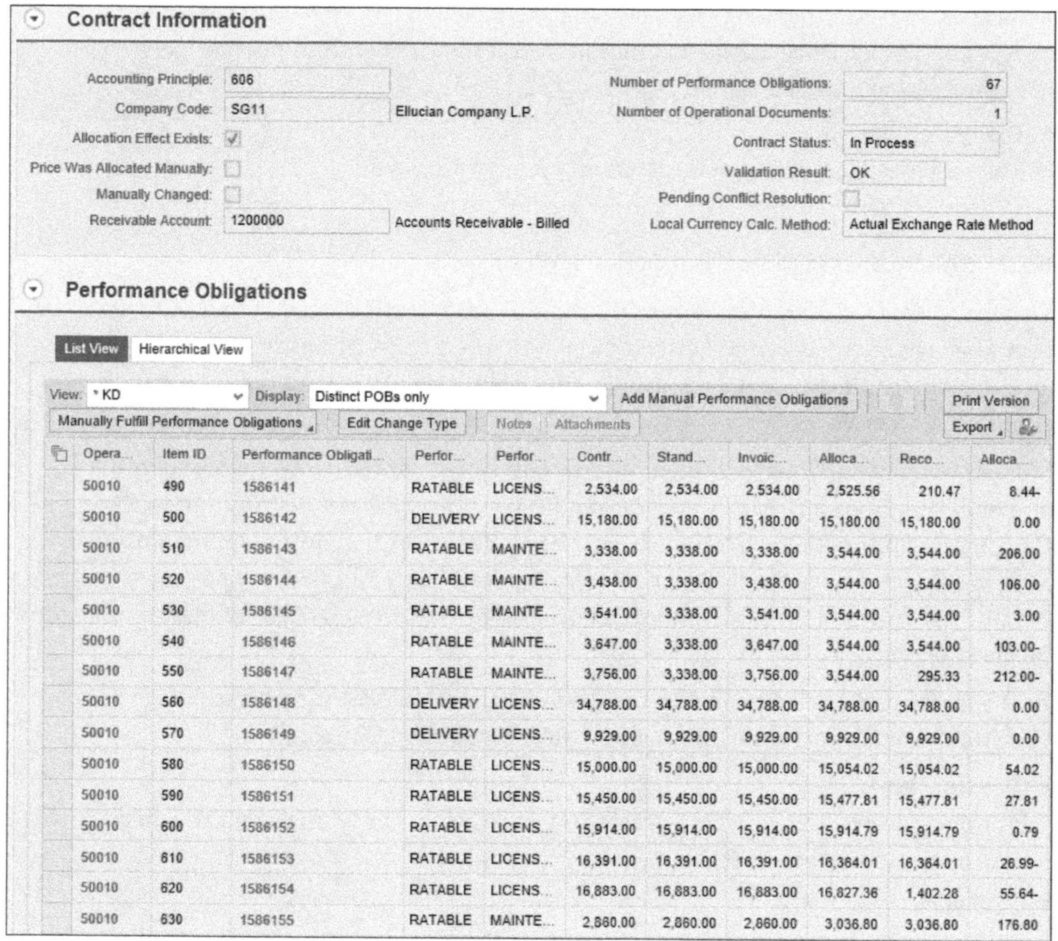

Opera...	Item ID	Performance Obligati...	Perfor...	Perfor...	Contr...	Stand...	Invoic...	Alloca...	Reco...	Alloca...
50010	490	1586141	RATABLE	LICENS...	2,534.00	2,534.00	2,534.00	2,525.56	210.47	8.44-
50010	500	1586142	DELIVERY	LICENS...	15,180.00	15,180.00	15,180.00	15,180.00	15,180.00	0.00
50010	510	1586143	RATABLE	MAINTE...	3,338.00	3,338.00	3,338.00	3,544.00	3,544.00	206.00
50010	520	1586144	RATABLE	MAINTE...	3,438.00	3,338.00	3,438.00	3,544.00	3,544.00	106.00
50010	530	1586145	RATABLE	MAINTE...	3,541.00	3,338.00	3,541.00	3,544.00	3,544.00	3.00
50010	540	1586146	RATABLE	MAINTE...	3,647.00	3,338.00	3,647.00	3,544.00	3,544.00	103.00-
50010	550	1586147	RATABLE	MAINTE...	3,756.00	3,338.00	3,756.00	3,544.00	295.33	212.00-
50010	560	1586148	DELIVERY	LICENS...	34,788.00	34,788.00	34,788.00	34,788.00	34,788.00	0.00
50010	570	1586149	DELIVERY	LICENS...	9,929.00	9,929.00	9,929.00	9,929.00	9,929.00	0.00
50010	580	1586150	RATABLE	LICENS...	15,000.00	15,000.00	15,000.00	15,054.02	15,054.02	54.02
50010	590	1586151	RATABLE	LICENS...	15,450.00	15,450.00	15,450.00	15,477.81	15,477.81	27.81
50010	600	1586152	RATABLE	LICENS...	15,914.00	15,914.00	15,914.00	15,914.79	15,914.79	0.79
50010	610	1586153	RATABLE	LICENS...	16,391.00	16,391.00	16,391.00	16,364.01	16,364.01	26.99-
50010	620	1586154	RATABLE	LICENS...	16,883.00	16,883.00	16,883.00	16,827.36	1,402.28	55.64-
50010	630	1586155	RATABLE	MAINTE...	2,860.00	2,860.00	2,860.00	3,036.80	3,036.80	176.80

Figure 6.30 Transaction NWBC: Contract View

The contract view has two sections: **Contract Information** and **Performance Obligations.**

The **Contract Information** section has the following fields:

- **Accounting Principle**
  This field represents the accounting principle code configured in the sales and distribution–RAR system.

- **Company Code**
  This field represents the company code from the sales and distribution system to which the RAR contract belongs.
- **Allocation Effect Exists**
  This checkbox gets automatically checked when an allocation effect exists on an RAR contract.
- **Price Was Allocated Manually**
  This checkbox gets automatically checked if a user allocates the price manually on an RAR contract.
- **Manually Changed**
  This checkbox gets automatically checked if a user makes manual changes to an RAR contract (and doesn't let it flow naturally over from sales and distribution).
- **Receivable Account**
  This field represents the accounts receivable general ledger account mapped from the sales and distribution system.
- **Number of Performance Obligations**
  This field represents the total number of POBs present on a contract. The number of POBs equals the number of line items of the operational document from the source sales and distribution system.
- **Number of Operational Documents**
  This field represents the total number of operational documents present on the RAR contract. The operational document is the sales order if your source system is SAP S/4HANA sales and distribution.
- **Contract Status**
  This field represents the status of the RAR contract. SAP S/4HANA has three standard statuses: **In Process**, **Completed**, and **Pending Review**.
- **Validation Result**
  This field represents the validation status of the RAR contract. Validation status can be **Error**, **Warning**, or **OK**.
- **Pending Conflict Resolution**
  This checkbox gets automatically checked when there is a conflict existing on a contract that needs to be administered and fixed. A worklist in RAR lists all contracts waiting for contract resolution.
- **Local Currency Calc. Method**
  This field represents the calculation method you want the system to use to calculate local currency exchange rates. There are two methods available by default:
  - **Fixed Exchange Rate Method**: In this method, the system calculates the exchange price based on a fixed rate. Fixed can be a rate a finance user maintains in the system or the first or last of every month, depending on the business requirement.

- **Actual Exchange Rate Method**: In this method, the system calculates exchange prices based on the actual conversion rate for that day.

The **Performance Obligations** section summarizes POB fields in a tabular format. It displays all POBs existing on a RAR contract. You can configure the number of columns and rows you want to see, as a preview, in the POB settings section. You can get to the POB settings screen from the contract view by clicking the **Open Settings** icon. We've set the count to 15 rows and 11 columns, as shown in Figure 6.30. You can also choose which fields you want to show versus hide in the same settings section. Once you've selected your settings, you can save the view as your default view, so the next time you're in a contract view, your default layout will automatically open. The fields you see in Figure 6.30 are relevant to sales and distribution, which is why they are displayed in the default layout.

POB View

POB view is the screen in Transaction NWBC where you can display all the fields of a POB for a revenue contract in RAR. After clicking on one of the POBs from the contract view, you'll arrive at the POB view screen. The POB view screen is broadly segregated into two areas: **General Information** and **Details**.

As shown in Figure 6.31, the **General Information** area has the following fields:

- **Performance Obligation**
  This field represents the ID of a POB whose general information you're viewing.
- **Performance Obligation Name**
  This field represents the name of a POB whose general information you're viewing.
- **Sales Organization**
  This field represents the sales organization ID to which the POB belongs. Sales organization is an entity from the source sales and distribution system.
- **Operational Document**
  This field represents the operational document numbers from the source sales and distribution system.
- **Pending Conflict Resolution**
  This checkbox gets automatically checked when there is a conflict existing on a POB that needs to be administered and fixed. There is a worklist in RAR that lists all POBs waiting for contract resolution. We'll discuss worklists further in the next section.

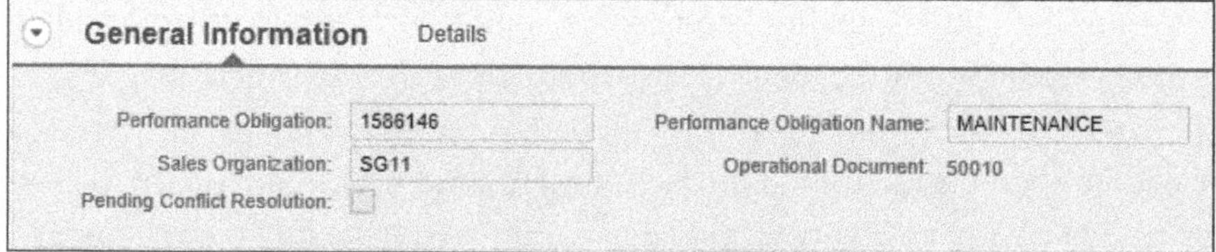

Figure 6.31 Transaction NWBC: POB General Information

The **Details** section is made up multiple sections: **General Data, Allocation Data, Fulfillment Data, Account Assignment Data, Status Data**, and **Administration Data**. Figure 6.32 shows the fields in the **General Data** and **Allocation Data** sections:

- **Performance Obligation Name**
  This field represents the name of a POB whose details information you're viewing.
- **Higher-Level Performance Obligation**
  This field represents the higher-level POB ID in case it exists for the POB you're viewing, such as the POB of the parent line item of a BOM material from the sales and distribution system.
- **Leading Performance Obligation**
  This field represents the leading POB ID in case it exists for the POB you're viewing. If there is a linked POB in your system, then this ID would be the POB ID for the first POB in the link.
- **Value-Relevant**
  This checkbox is automatically checked when the POB is value relevant. Value-relevant means fulfillment of a POB would be done in amount instead of quantity. All the time-based POBs generally have this checkbox selected.
- **Quantity**
  This field represents the actual quantity of the material associated with the POB. This information flows from the source sales and distribution system.
- **Effective Quantity**
  This field represents the effective quantity of the material associated with the POB. This information flows from the source sales and distribution system and normally is blank for time-based POBs. Effective quantity should exist for event-based POBs, especially if the event for fulfillment is delivery.
- **Estimated Quantity**
  This checkbox is selected if the POB contains an estimated quantity.
- **Leading/Linked**
  Leading or linked are two different POB roles. In a scenario when two POBs are linked together (let's say we manually link them from two separate RAR contracts), then this field would show the POB number of the other linked POB. Alternatively, in a scenario where separate POBs are created for delivery line items and separate POBs are created for sales order line items, the **Leading/Linked** field on the delivery POB general data will have the sales order line-item POB number. We don't have leading/linked scenarios at the example client, so this field is blank.
- **Performance Obligation Type**
  This field represents the type of POB.
- **Performance Obligation Category**
  This field represents the category of POB.

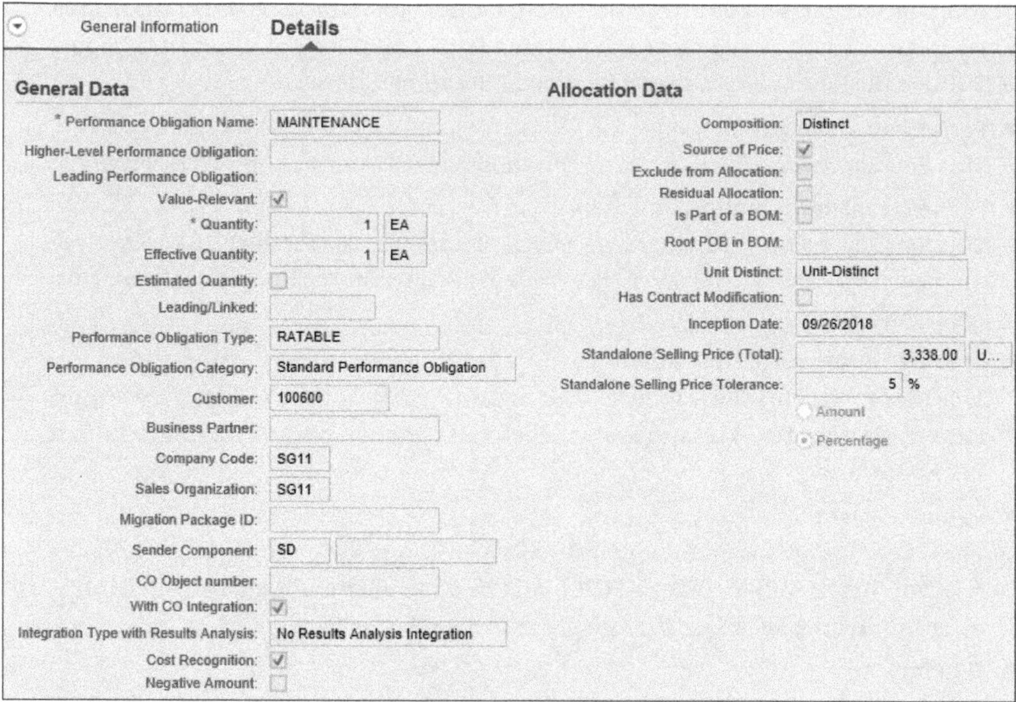

Figure 6.32 Transaction NWBC: Details Tab Showing General Data and Allocation Data

- **Customer**
  This field represents the customer to which the POB belongs. At the example client, the customer field is mapped to the sold-to party from **SD**.
- **Business Partner**
  This field represents the business partner to which the POB belongs.
- **Company Code**
  This field represents the company code to which the POB belongs. Company code information is mapped from the source sales and distribution system.
- **Sales Organization**
  This field represents the sales organization to which the POB belongs. Sales organization information is mapped from the source sales and distribution system.
- **Migration Package ID**
  This field represents the ID of a migration package in case you used one to migrate data over to RAR. If your source system is sales and distribution, which is the case with the example client, then this field is blank.
- **Sender Component**
  This field represents the description of the sender component that feeds data into RAR.

- **CO Object number**
  This field represents the controlling object numbers in case you're doing results analysis integration. We don't have this at the example client, so the field is blank.
- **With CO Integration**
  This checkbox automatically gets checked when a POB is enabled for controlling integration.

Note

Cost object controlling integration can be enabled by following IMG menu path **Financial Accounting • Revenue Accounting • Integration with Cost Object Controlling**. You then assign the revenue accounting version and currency type to the company code and accounting principle, and specify revenue accounting keys and versions relevant for revenue accounting integration.

- **Integration Type with Results Analysis**
  This field is used in conjunction with controlling object number if you're doing results analysis integration. RAR provides three default values for this field:
  - **No Results Analysis Integration**: This type indicates there is no integration between RAR and results analysis.
  - **PoC based Integration**: This type indicates that integration between RAR and results analysis is based on the percentage of completion method.
  - **Revenue Based Integration**: This type indicates that integration between RAR and results analysis is based on the revenue accounting method.
- **Cost Recognition**
  This checkbox is checked if cost recognition is permitted for a POB. If you don't want cost recognition on a POB, you can disable that option from POB type configuration.
- **Negative Amount**
  This checkbox is checked if a negative amount is allowed for POB.
- **Composition**
  This field indicates the composition of a POB. There are three possible composition values:
  - **Distinct**: The POB is unique with no dependencies or commonness.
  - **Non-Distinct**: The POB may have dependencies or redundancies.
  - **Compound**: The POB is part of a bigger group of compound POBs.
- **Source of Price**
  This checkbox is checked if the source of the POB pricing is based on the pricing condition from the operational document. At the example client, pricing is based on a pricing condition from the sales order line item in sales and distribution, so this checkbox is checked for all POBs.

- **Exclude from Allocation**
  This checkbox is checked when a POB is excluded from cross allocation on a contract. This feature is controlled in the POB type configuration.
- **Residual Allocation**
  This checkbox is checked when a POB has residual allocation or is allowed to have residual allocation on a RAR contract. This feature is also controlled in the POB type configuration. Residual allocation only comes into the picture when certain POBs within a contract don't have an SSP.
- **Is Part of a BOM**
  This checkbox is checked when a POB is part of a BOM material bundle.
- **Root POB in BOM**
  This field represents the POB ID of the root POB in a BOM material bundle.
- **Unit Distinct**
  This field tells you if a POB does prospective or retrospective revenue and allocation adjustment. If the field value is unit-distinct, it will only do prospective adjustments; if the field value isn't unit-distinct, then it will do retrospective adjustments (if needed). These are system-driven values but can be modified by the user if needed.
- **Has Contract Modification**
  This checkbox is checked if there is a contract modification entry in the contract history table for the POB's parent contract.
- **Inception Date**
  This field represents the date when the POB was added to the contract.
- **Standalone Selling Price (Total)**
  This field represents the SSP associated with a POB. At the example client we've sent over the SSP value to RAR via a pricing condition from the sales order.
- **Standalone Selling Price Tolerance**
  This field represents the SSP tolerance value. This can be set up as percentage or amount. The underlying configuration for this is within Transaction FARR_IMG. At the example client, SSP tolerance is set to 5%.

Figure 6.33 shows the **Fulfillment Data** and **Account Assignment** sections of a POB view. Here are all the fields under those sections:

- **Fulfillment Type**
  This field represents the fulfillment type for a POB. By default, SAP S/4HANA provides three standard fulfillment types: **Event-Based**, **Time-Based**, and **Percentage of Completion**. The value of this field is derived from the POB type configuration (see Section 6.2.1).
- **Event Type**
  This field represents the event type for fulfillment on a POB.

- **Spreading Manually Changed**
  SAP Revenue Accounting and Reporting allows you to manually change allocation amounts across months for a time-based POB. When any such change happens, this checkbox gets automatically checked, indicating to the end user that revenue spreading has manually changed on the POB.
- **Start Date Type**
  This field represents the start date type for a POB. This field is only active for time-based POBs. By default, SAP S/4HANA provides three standard date types: **Available on Creation of Performance Obligation**, **Available After Creation of Performance Obligation**, and **Is Always the Event Date**. The value of this field is derived from the POB type configuration.
- **Start Date**
  This field represents the start date of the revenue cycle on a POB.
- **End Date**
  This field represents the end date of the revenue cycle on a POB.
- **Duration**
  This field represents the total duration of the revenue cycle on a POB. Ideally, you should only have a value in the **Start Date/End Date** field or in the **Duration** field. If you have values in both, it will conflict and result in an error.
- **Deferral Method**
  This field represents the deferral method for a POB. This field is only active for time-based POBs. The value of this field is derived from the POB type configuration.

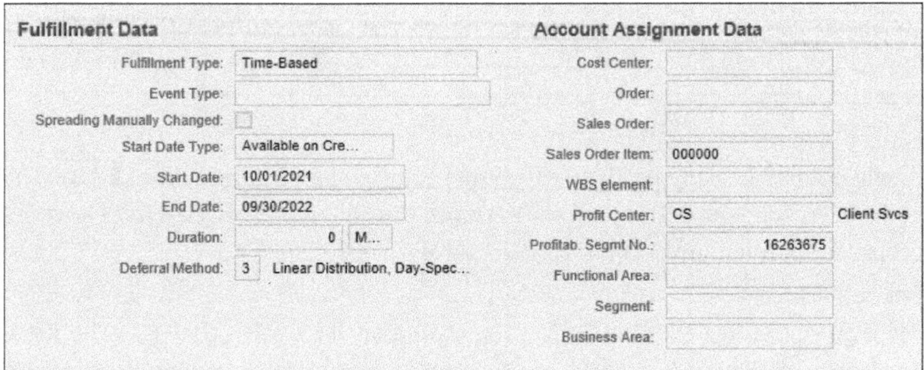

Figure 6.33 Transaction NWBC: Fulfillment Data and Account Assignment Data

- **Cost Center**
  This field represents the cost center number associated with the POB. The cost center information flows from the source system. At the example client, we don't send cost center information to RAR based on how the account assignment is configured on the sales order side.

- **Order**
  This field represents the order number from the source system associated with the POB.
- **Sales Order**
  This field represents the sales order number associated with the POB. The sales order information flows from the source system. At the example client, we don't send sales order information to RAR from the **Account Assignment** section. We've mapped sales orders to the **Operational Document** field, which is why the **Sales Order** field is blank in Figure 6.33. But you'll see a sales order number in the **Operational Document** field, which can be seen later in Section 6.2.5.
- **Sales Order Item**
  This field represents the sales order item number associated with the POB. The sales order item information flows from the source system. At the example client, we don't send sales order item information to RAR from the **Account Assignment** section. That is why the **Sales Order Item** field is blank in Figure 6.33. But you'll see the sales order item number in the **Operational Document Item ID** field, which can be seen later in Section 6.2.5.
- **WBS element**
  This field represents the work breakdown structure (WBS) ID associated with the POB. The WBS information flows from the source system based on how the account assignment is configured on the sales order side. For the example shown in Figure 6.33, there is no WBS on the sales order line item, so the field is blank in RAR.
- **Profit Center**
  This field represents the profit center number associated with the POB. The profit center information flows from the source system based on how the account assignment is configured on the sales order side.
- **Profitab. Segmt No.**
  This field represents the profitability segment number associated with the POB. The profitability segment information flows from the source system based on how the account assignment is configured on the sales order side.
- **Functional Area**
  This field represents the functional area code associated with the POB. The functional area information flows from the source system. At the example client, we don't send functional area information to RAR as there is no reporting need based on functional areas.
- **Segment**
  This field represents the segment number associated with the POB. The segment information flows from the source system. At the example client, we don't send segment information to RAR as there is no reporting need based on segments.

- **Business Area**
  This field represents the business area code associated with the POB. The business area information flows from the source system. At the example client, we don't send business area information to RAR as there is no reporting need based on business areas.

Figure 6.34 shows the **Status Data** and **Administration Data** sections of a POB view. Here are all the fields under those sections:

- **Suspend Posting**
  This checkbox is checked when you want to suspend revenue posting on a POB. What that basically means is you can still perform transactions on the POB such as fulfillment, but nothing will move forward even if you run posting jobs until the suspension is removed. A suspend posting check should ideally have a review reason code attached to it for the end user to know why a POB is suspending for posting.
- **Pending Conflict Resolution**
  This checkbox automatically gets checked when there is pending conflict on a POB. The check is removed when the conflict is resolved. To find out a list of POBs sitting in **Pending Conflict Resolution** status, you can run a worklist program, which will be discussed in the next section.
- **Attribute conflict**
  This checkbox is selected automatically when either of the attributes on a POB have a conflict. We haven't seen this happen very often because, ideally, attribute conflict is caught as an exception in the source system itself or during RAI monitoring.

Status Data

Suspend Posting:
Pending Conflict Resolution:
Attribute conflict:
Spreading conflict:
Structure Changed:
Validation Result: OK
Performance Obligation Status: In Process
Last Change: 10/02/2018
Review Reason:
Review Reason Changed By: 10/02/2018
Review Date:
Finalization Date:
Manually Created:
Manually Changed:
Fully Fulfilled:
Final Invoice:
Billing Plan Invoice:
Simplified Invoice:
Has Billing Plan: ✓
Invoice Effect on Price: Debit/credit memo changes prices immediately

Administration Data

Created by: Production Backgroun...
Created On: 09/27/2018
Changed by: Production Backgroun...
Changed on: 09/09/2019

Figure 6.34 Transaction NWBC: Status Data and Administration Data

- **Spreading conflict**
  This checkbox gets checked automatically when the spreading of revenue across a time-based POB has a conflict. When a POB has either of the conflict checkboxes checked, no RAIs for that POB transfer from sales and distribution to RAR until the conflicts are resolved.
- **Structure Changed**
  Each POB has a structure associated to it. The structure comprises different sections (**General Data** section, **Status Data** section, etc.), different fields under each section (**Suspend Posting**, **Fulfillment Type**, etc.), and so on. If a change is made to this structure (in BRFplus) after a POB is created in RAR, then this checkbox gets automatically checked, indicating to the end user that the structure of the POB was changed after the POB got created under the RAR contract.
- **Validation Result**
  This field represents the validation result status of a POB. As a default, RAR functionality in SAP S/4HANA has three statuses: **Error**, **Warning**, and **OK**.
- **Performance Obligation Status**
  This field represents the POB status of a POB. As a default, RAR functionality in SAP S/4HANA has four statuses: **In Process**, **Completed**, **Pending Review**, and **Manually Completed**.
- **Last Change**
  This field represents the name of the user who last made a change on the POB along with the date when the change was made.
- **Review Reason**
  This field represents the review reason code associated with a POB (if any). At the example company, we've mapped revenue blocks from sales and distribution to review reason codes in RAR. Within the review reason configuration in Transaction FARR_IMG, you can force the system to automatically suspend posting if a review reason code is selected on a POB. **Performance Obligation Status** should be changed to **Pending Review** before adding a review code.
- **Review Reason Changed By**
  This field represents name of the user who last changed review reason on POB along with the date when the change was made.
- **Review Date**
  This field represents the date on which the POB will be reviewed. If a POB has status **Pending Review** and you selected a review reason code, you can along with that also select **Review Date** based on which end user would know when the POB is due for review.
- **Finalization Date**
  This field represents the end date of a POB. Any bill plans or revenue after that date won't show up in the revenue schedule of the POB.

- **Manually Created**
  This checkbox automatically gets checked when a POB is manually created in RAR.
- **Manually Changed**
  This checkbox automatically gets checked when a POB is manually changed in RAR.
- **Fully Fulfilled**
  This checkbox automatically gets checked when a POB is fully fulfilled in RAR.
- **Final Invoice**
  This checkbox automatically gets checked when the final invoice is issued for a POB in RAR, that is, no further bill plans are pending in RAR, or the POB is marked as completed manually.
- **Billing Plan Invoice**
  This checkbox is checked when you want to allow RAR to automatically calculate and post invoice correction entries for a bill plan on a POB.
- **Simplified Invoice**
  This checkbox is checked when you want to allow a simplified invoice feature for a POB. The simplified invoice feature enables businesses to create billing documents based on revenue realized on that POB. Revenue realization can be either time based or event based.
- **Has Billing Plan**
  This checkbox gets automatically checked when a POB has billing plans flowing in from the source system.
- **Invoice Effect on Price**
  This field tells you when a debit memo or a credit memo would impact the transaction price on a POB. As a default, RAR has three options available: **Debit/credit memo doesn't change prices immediately**, **Debit/credit memo changes prices immediately**, and **Adjust price only at Final invoice**.
- **Created by**
  This field represents the name of the user who created the POB. At the example client, a background job sends RAIs from sales and distribution to RAR and creates the POBs. That is why you see the **Created by** value as **Production Background Processing** in Figure 6.34.
- **Created On**
  This field represents the date on which the POB was created.
- **Changed by**
  This field represents the name of the user who changed the POB.
- **Changed on**
  This field represents the date on which the POB was changed.

The POB view has a small section at the bottom, right after the **General Information** and **Details** section, which is shown in Figure 6.35.

Figure 6.35 Transaction NWBC: Condition Types and Accounts

This section shows the following data:

- **Related Performance Obligations**
  If you're using BOMs at your client, this section is very useful for you. It shows you details about related POBs and how they are linked to the main POB under which this section exists. It also gives you details about distinct and nondistinct POBs. BOMs aren't used at the example client, so this section is blank and void.
- **Linked Performance Obligations**
  If you have the linked POBs feature activated at your client, this section is very useful for you. It will give you details of POBs linked to the parent POB and when they were created. You can add and delete linked POBs through this section. Again, this feature isn't used at the example client, so this section is void.
- **Right of Return**
  The right of return feature allows you to define return policies at the POB level of an RAR contract. You can configure the percentage of allowed return as well as duration within which the return can be honored. You can define the duration in month/days or any other unit of measure (UoM), or you can add a start and end date.

  For example, let's say your company allows a full refund on a product sale for 30 days. You go into the **Right of Return** section of the product POB and add an entry where you define percentage for value deferral as 100% and duration as 30 days. Or you can add a start date of 01/01/2022 and an end date of 01/30/2022 to define the 30-day duration.

Right of return isn't allowed for time-based POBs, linked POBs, and nondistinct POBs. The example shown in Figure 6.35 is of a time-based POB, so the **Right of Return** section is blank.

- **Condition Type and Accounts**
  This section is very important from the sales and distribution–RAR integration standpoint. Within this section, you can find details of sales condition types flowing from the sales and distribution sales order line item to the RAR POB. This section also shows you details of the receivable adjustment general ledger account, as well as static and nonstatic cost condition types coming in from the source sales and distribution system. This section has helped us at many client engagements to respond to support tickets where users complained about sales and distribution and RAR account determination entries not matching or POB revenue postings not going to the correct general ledger.

Worklists

Worklists in RAR are programs that, when executed, help you identify POBs sitting in error or waiting for IT intervention. We recommend scheduling a job daily to run these programs or having someone in IT execute programs manually make sure that any POBs needing attention are looked at promptly. Worklists are important for sales and distribution–RAR integration because we don't often process RAIs manually or watch each newly created or modified contract. So having these worklists is a handy tool to make sure you have good quality checkpoints and error controls in place. It helps you proactively identify and address issues rather than waiting for revenue jobs to catch it or a business user to identify it as a month-end reconciliation activity. SAP Revenue Accounting and Reporting calls these worklists *pending review worklists*. To get to the pending review worklist, go to Transaction NWBC to reach the SAP Business Client interface. Then under the **Revenue Manager** tab, click on **Pending Review Worklist** to open the program dropdown list.

There are six programs available, as shown in Figure 6.36:

- **Regular Monitoring**
  This is one of the most helpful worklists in our experience. It gives you details of all contracts and POBs that need your attention. RAR has a few predefined rules it uses to validate contracts and POBs for inconsistencies. And if RAR finds an inconsistency, it will flag those contracts and POBs as ready for review and display them within this worklist. You can customize queries within this worklist based on your clients' requirements so that you review only the contracts important for your business processes. Once you've reviewed the contracts and made the fixes, you can manually mark them as reviewed. This is important if there are multiple users supporting RAR for a client.

- **Contracts with Errors**
  This is another key worklist query we use often. The query returns a list of contracts sitting in error with details such as number of errors on a contract, company code to which the contract belongs, and customer and accounting principle details. RAR allows you to customize queries and layouts for this worklist too.
- **Contract manual change detail**
  This worklist displays errors specifically introduced by manual changes on a contract. There are three categories of errors that show up under this worklist: attributes conflicts, revenue schedule conflicts, and price allocation conflicts. You can directly fix errors from the worklist page or individually go into a contract and fix the error from there.
- **Contracts with Conflicts**
  This worklist displays contracts that are specifically sitting in error because of conflicting data. Conflicts are differences in data within RAR when compared to the source system. There are two ways you can resolve conflicts:
  - Take advantage of the **Use Value From** field and let the system know which value to choose as the source of truth, whether it's the RAR system or the sales and distribution system. You can see the **Use Value From** field under the POB view of the contract in conflict.
  - Go into the contract and determine and fix the issue from there by either manually changing the field value or resending RAIs from the source system to update field values.

Pending Review Worklists
A collection of worklists that allows you to monitor performance obligations that require review and follow-up action.
• Regular Monitoring
Here you can review revenue accounting contracts and performance obligations that are newly created and require review and confirmation.
Items are sent to this worklist for review because of predefined reasons.
• Contracts with Errors
Here you can review and resolve errors that are found in revenue accounting contracts and performance obligations when they are created or updated.
• Contract manual change detail
• Contracts with Conflicts
Here you can review and resolve conflicts that result from changes made from difference sources but to the same target, including changes manually made from the user interface and automatically made from the back-end operational system.
• Contract Completed View
• Manual Contract Combination

Figure 6.36 Transaction NWBC: Pending Review Worklists

The final two worklists are nice to have, but not necessary features. **Contract Completed View** is used to list a comprehensive view of a contract and then perform any actions to it from there, and **Manual Contract Combination** is used when you want to directly combine contracts in RAR.

Revenue Posting Jobs

Revenue posting jobs are crucial for sales and distribution–RAR integration as they post revenue data from RAR to the sales and distribution general ledger. Think of this as reverse integration because in all the other sections, we mostly talk about data flowing from sales and distribution to RAR, but in this section, we'll focus on how processed revenue data from RAR flows to sales and distribution (and finance).

Three steps occur in RAR to calculate revenue postings and then post them to RAR and sales and distribution tables. The sequence of steps is three posting jobs that run one after the other and are referred to as ABC jobs (A, Transfer Revenue; B, Calculate Contract Liabilities and Assets; and C, Revenue Posting Run). To get to the revenue posting job list, go to Transaction NWBC to reach the SAP Business Client interface. Then under the **Revenue Manager** tab, click on **Revenue Posting** to view and run ABC jobs. You can see these jobs as the top three shown in Figure 6.37:

1. **Transfer Revenue**
   This program is normally run for a selected period. When you run this program, SAP Revenue Accounting and Reporting calculates and transfers all revenue transactions for that selected period to a revenue posting table called the revenue subledger table in RAR. Running this program is the first step of the ABC schedule and is recommended to run daily. You can either run this job manually or schedule it as a background job. This program has various selection parameters such as accounting principle, contract, POB, company code, operational document, and so on.

   You can run the program from Transaction NWBC using the option shown in Figure 6.37 or execute Transaction FARR_REV_TRANSFER.

2. **Calculate Contract Liabilities and Assets**
   This program is also executed for a selected period. If you're running it as a part of the ABC schedule, then you should select the same period as the Transfer Revenue job period. When you run this program, SAP Revenue Accounting and Reporting calculates the contract asset and contract liability position of all contracts transferred via the A job and then stages the data in a posting table for the next posting job (C job or Revenue Posting Run) to pick it up. Like the transfer revenue job, you can either run this job manually or schedule it as a background job. This program has various selection parameters as well, such as accounting principle, contract, POB, company code, operation document, and so on, and the job can be run for a specific value date.

   You can run the program from Transaction NWBC using the option shown in Figure 6.37 or execute Transaction FARR_LIABILITY_CALC.

3. **Revenue Posting Run**
   This is the third step of the ABC schedule and the job that completes the revenue posting to RAR tables. Revenue data transferred and calculated from jobs A and B is posted to the general ledger and other dependent ledgers in job C. There is an option

to simulate revenue posting in job C, which is good because it gives you an opportunity to fix the contract in case you see an error in simulation. This job also can be run manually or scheduled in the background. The C job has the same selection parameters as the A and B jobs.

We like that the C job can be run for specific company codes or contracts. This reduces the load on the system and increases productivity. In addition, when it comes to debugging, having the flexibility to only run C jobs by contract or company code really helps. When you're ready to execute the revenue posting job, you should enter a date, which is used as the posting date for all entries executed during that run.

You can run the program from Transaction NWBC using the option shown in Figure 6.37 or execute Transaction FARR_REV_POST.

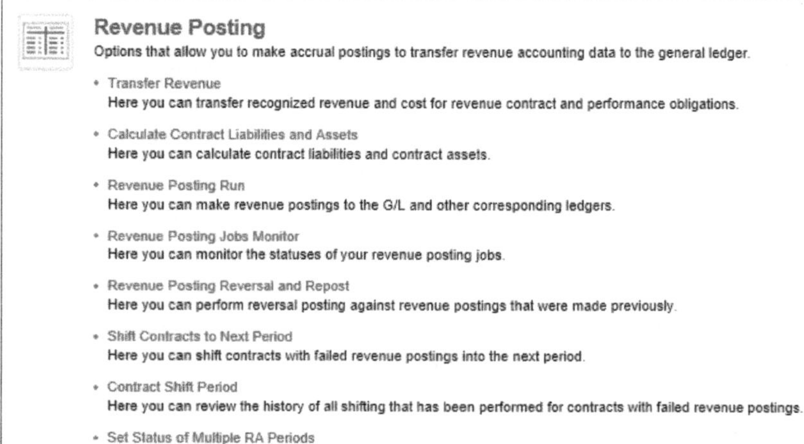

Figure 6.37 Transaction NWBC: Revenue Posting Jobs

There are also a handful of other options that you can execute for revenue posting:

- **Revenue Posting Jobs Monitor**
  This interface is used to monitor the performance of revenue posting jobs. We used this a lot in conjunction with ABC jobs. Each time we run the ABC jobs manually, we use the job monitor to see if everything is going per plan or if we're seeing errors. When the job monitor finds errors, it will give you a description of the error message and direct you to instructions for fixing the error.
- **Revenue Posting Reversal and Repost**
  This program is used to reverse a revenue posting and repost in case you find an error or a business reason to do so. It's recommended that you judiciously use this option and try to use it in the same period as the original revenue posting. We normally don't use this program a lot with our clients. If there is a need to reverse postings, we recommend it originate from the source system as a delta entry, or you can

reverse the posting directly in the general ledger and make an equivalent adjustment entry.

- **Shift Contracts to Next Period**
  This program is used when you want to move contracts from one period to the next one. This program should also be used sparingly. We've only used this program when it was recommended by SAP through an SAP OSS note. You can shift contracts by company code, accounting principle, and/or contract number.
- **Contract Shift Period**
  This program is used to monitor error history for failed shifted contracts.
- **Set Status of Multiple RA Periods**
  This program is used to mass update revenue accounting periods. The program can be run for company code, accounting principle, fiscal year, posting period, and/or status. For the most part, we use Transaction FARR_IMG to update revenue accounting periods, but we've used this program a lot as well.

6.2.3 Configuration of Sales and Distribution

Now that you're an expert with configurations of the RAR node and Transaction NWBC, let's discuss the different steps on the sales and distribution side after which you'll be a sales and distribution–RAR integration expert. In this section, you'll learn how to perform the following configurations:

- Integrate sales and distribution to RAR
- Activate functions to integrate with revenue accounting
- Maintain RAI settings
- Create a POB for the sales and distribution billing item
- Exclude billing plan items

All these steps are activation steps and therefore are very important to be performed thoroughly. Let's jump right in.

Integrate Sales and Distribution with Revenue Accounting and Reporting

This configuration is used to activate the integration component of RAR. Only when this step is complete, will your configuration from the previous chapter and this chapter work successfully. Normally, this is one of the final configuration steps we do once everything else is completed.

To activate the integration component of sales and distribution to RAR, follow IMG menu path **Sales and Distribution • Revenue Accounting and Reporting • Integrate with Revenue Accounting and Reporting**. You'll arrive at the screen shown in Figure 6.38.

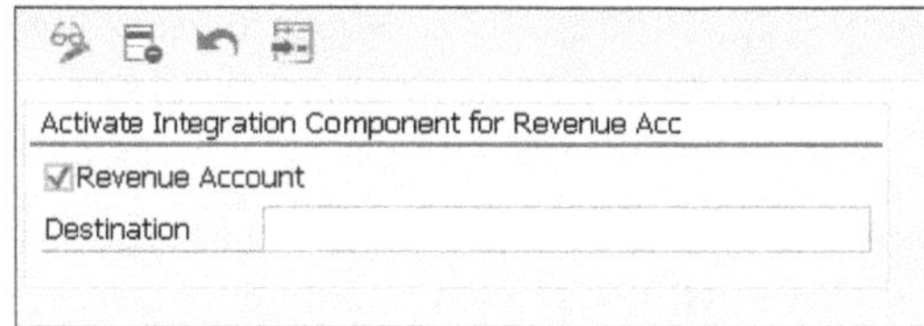

Figure 6.38 Integrate with Revenue Accounting and Reporting

As shown in Figure 6.38, the screen has two fields:

- **Revenue Account**
  This checkbox is checked when you're ready to start using RAR. This checkbox controls activation of sales and distribution to RAR integration. Once activated, all your integration configuration will kick in, and RAIs will start to generate and process over to RAR.
- **Destination**
  If you're using an RFC, then this is the place where you'll mention the destination name. RFCs would normally be used if your source system for RAR isn't standard SAP S/4HANA sales and distribution. For example, let's say you're using Oracle as your sales ERP system; in this case, you would mention the RFC destination name for your Oracle system in the **Destination** field. At the example company, we use SAP S/4HANA sales and distribution with no need for an RFC, so the field is blank.

Activate Functions to Integrate with Revenue Accounting

The second-most important step, after component activation, is activation of functions for revenue accounting integration. Integration functions are activated per sales organization. Depending on which functions you activate within this configuration, bill plan RAIs and/or fulfillment RAIs get generated. Generation of functions has a date control parameter, meaning only after that date will any transactions performed on the sales order generate bill plan or fulfillment RAIs.

To activate the integration functions for RAR, follow IMG menu path **Sales and Distribution • Revenue Accounting and Reporting • Activate Functions to Integrate with Revenue Accounting**. You'll arrive at the screen shown in Figure 6.39. From this screen, you can either view existing entries or create new ones by clicking on the **New Entries** button.

Activate functions configuration has six checkboxes, one for each function you want to activate, and six date fields that control function activation. Functions are activated per sales organization, so in total there are 13 fields within this configuration step:

- **SOrg.**
  This field represents the sales organization for which you want to activate the integration functions.

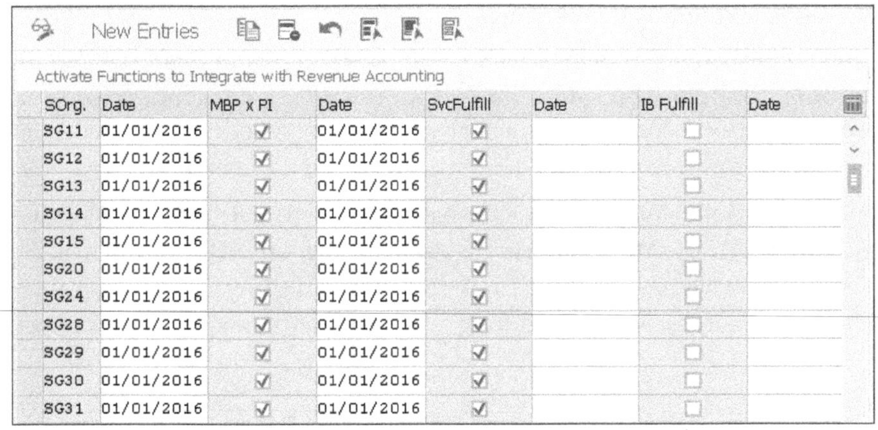

New Entries

Activate Functions to Integrate with Revenue Accounting

SOrg.	Date	MBP x PI	Date	SvcFulfill	Date	IB Fulfill	Date
SG11	01/01/2016	☑	01/01/2016	☑		☐	
SG12	01/01/2016	☑	01/01/2016	☑		☐	
SG13	01/01/2016	☑	01/01/2016	☑		☐	
SG14	01/01/2016	☑	01/01/2016	☑		☐	
SG15	01/01/2016	☑	01/01/2016	☑		☐	
SG20	01/01/2016	☑	01/01/2016	☑		☐	
SG24	01/01/2016	☑	01/01/2016	☑		☐	
SG28	01/01/2016	☑	01/01/2016	☑		☐	
SG29	01/01/2016	☑	01/01/2016	☑		☐	
SG30	01/01/2016	☑	01/01/2016	☑		☐	
SG31	01/01/2016	☑	01/01/2016	☑		☐	

Figure 6.39 Activate Functions to Integrate with Revenue Accounting

- **MBP x PI**
  This field represents the milestone billing plan planned invoice RAIs function in case you want to activate it for your business.
- **SvcFulfill**
  This field represents the nonstock material transfers fulfillment RAIs function in case you want to activate it for your business.
- **IB Fulfill**
  This field represents the intercompany invoice fulfillment RAIs function in case you want to activate it for your business.
- **PI Fulfill**
  This field represents the vendor invoice fulfillment RAIs function in case you want to activate it for your business.
- **POD Fulfill**
  This field represents the proof of delivery fulfillment RAIs function in case you want to activate it for your business.
- **AD Fulfill**
  This field represents the acceptance date fulfillment RAIs function in case you want to activate it for your business.
- **Date**
  This field represents the date when you want a function to be activated; that is, RAIs for a function will only generate when the underlying document is created on or after the mentioned date. For example, say the service fulfillment date is set to 01/01/2016. Any delivery document with a PGI date on or after 01/01/2016 will generate fulfillment RAIs. Any documents with a PGI date before 01/01/2016 won't generate RAIs.

Maintain Revenue Accounting Item Settings

Now that integration components and functions are activated, the next step is to active sales document types and item categories. Within this configuration step, you can make a combination of sales organization/sales document type/item category relevant for revenue accounting or not based on your business requirements.

To maintain RAI settings, follow IMG menu path **Sales and Distribution • Revenue Accounting and Reporting • Maintain Revenue Accounting Item Settings.** You'll arrive at the screen shown in Figure 6.40. From this screen, you can either view existing item category entries or create new ones by clicking on the **New Entries** button (not shown).

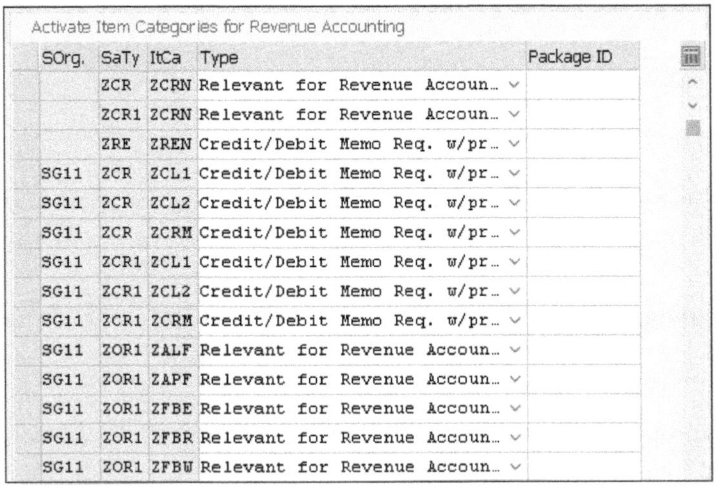

Activate Item Categories for Revenue Accounting

SOrg.	SaTy	ItCa	Type	Package ID
	ZCR	ZCRN	Relevant for Revenue Accoun...	
	ZCR1	ZCRN	Relevant for Revenue Accoun...	
	ZRE	ZREN	Credit/Debit Memo Req. w/pr...	
SG11	ZCR	ZCL1	Credit/Debit Memo Req. w/pr...	
SG11	ZCR	ZCL2	Credit/Debit Memo Req. w/pr...	
SG11	ZCR	ZCRM	Credit/Debit Memo Req. w/pr...	
SG11	ZCR1	ZCL1	Credit/Debit Memo Req. w/pr...	
SG11	ZCR1	ZCL2	Credit/Debit Memo Req. w/pr...	
SG11	ZCR1	ZCRM	Credit/Debit Memo Req. w/pr...	
SG11	ZOR1	ZALF	Relevant for Revenue Accoun...	
SG11	ZOR1	ZAPF	Relevant for Revenue Accoun...	
SG11	ZOR1	ZFBE	Relevant for Revenue Accoun...	
SG11	ZOR1	ZFBR	Relevant for Revenue Accoun...	
SG11	ZOR1	ZFBW	Relevant for Revenue Accoun...	

Figure 6.40 Maintain RAI Settings

As shown in Figure 6.40, the screen has the following fields:

- **SOrg.**
  This field represents the sales organization for which you want to activate revenue accounting.
- **SaTy**
  This field represents the sales document type for which you want to activate revenue accounting.
- **ItCa**
  This field represents the item category for which you want to activate revenue accounting.
- **Type**
  This field represents the type of revenue accounting activation you want for a sales organization/sales document type/item category combination. SAP S/4HANA provides five standard types:

- **Not Relevant**: If a combination of sales organization/sales document type/item category is tagged as **Not Relevant**, then no RAIs will be generated for that combination and that combination won't contribute to the revenue recognition process.
- **Relevant for Revenue Accounting**: If a combination of sales organization/sales document type/item category is tagged as **Relevant for Revenue Accounting**, then RAIs will be generated for that combination and that combination will always contribute to the revenue recognition process.
- **Credit/Debit Memo Req. w/predecessor**: If a combination of sales organization/sales document type/item category is tagged as **Credit/Debit Memo Req. w/predecessor**, then RAIs aren't generated for that combination of credit memo request/sales organization/item category or debit memo request/sales organization/item category, but RAIs are created for the actual credit memo or debit memo. This makes sense because the request for debit memo or credit memo doesn't impact revenue numbers, but the actual credit memo and debit memo do impact revenue.
- **Relevant for Revenue Accounting by Invoice**: If a combination of sales organization/sales document type/item category is tagged as **Relevant for Revenue Accounting by Invoice**, then RAIs by invoice will be generated for that combination and that combination will always contribute to the revenue recognition process.
- **Call-Off Order with predecessor**: If a combination of sales organization/sales document type/item category is tagged as **Call-off Order with predecessor**, then RAIs aren't generated for that combination of call-off order/sales organization/item category, but RAIs are created for the actual invoice of the call-off order.

- **Package ID**
  This field represents the package ID name in case you're migrating granular level data as a part of your initial data load into RAR.

Create Performance Obligation for Sales and Distribution Billing Item

As the name suggests, this configuration is used when you specifically want to create POBs for sales and distribution billing items. In a normal RAR scenario, sales order line items create POBs, and sales and distribution billing items either perform fulfillment or complete the billing for sales order POB.

You can use this configuration to activate POBs for sales and distribution billing items in the following scenarios: (1) the source document originates from an external system, but the billing originates from sales and distribution, or (2) the source document isn't relevant for revenue accounting, but the billing document is.

To create a POB for sales and distribution billing items, follow IMG menu path **Sales and Distribution • Revenue Accounting and Reporting • Create Performance Obligation**

for SD Billing Item. You'll arrive at the screen shown in Figure 6.41. From this screen, you can either view existing billing item entries or create new ones by clicking on the **New Entries** button (not shown).

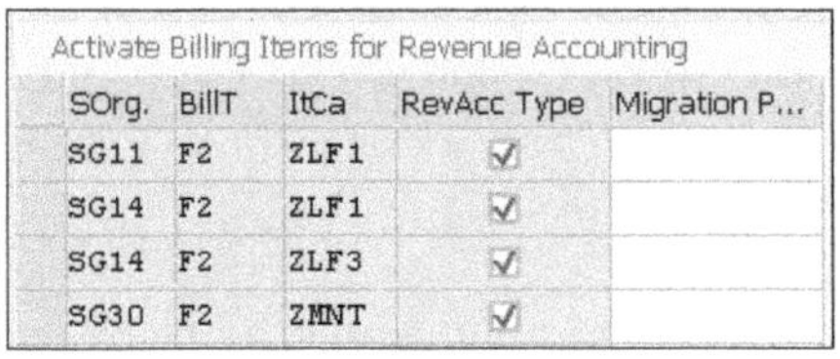

Activate Billing Items for Revenue Accounting

SOrg.	BillT	ItCa	RevAcc Type	Migration P...
SG11	F2	ZLF1	✓	
SG14	F2	ZLF1	✓	
SG14	F2	ZLF3	✓	
SG30	F2	ZMNT	✓	

Figure 6.41 POB for Sales and Distribution Billing Items

As shown in Figure 6.41, the **Activate Billing Items for Revenue Accounting** screen has the following fields:

- **SOrg.**
  This field represents the sales organization for which you want to activate billing items.
- **BillT**
  This field represents the billing type (**F2**, **G2**, **F5**, etc.) for which you want to activate billing items.
- **ItCa**
  This field represents the item category for which you want to activate billing items.
- **RevAcc Type**
  This checkbox is only checked when you want the combination of sales organization/billing type/item category to be activated for billing items.
- **Migration P...**
  This field represents the package ID name in case you're migrating granular data as a part of your initial data load into RAR. For example, if the business decision is to migrate an entire data set for a company code/accounting principle/item category combination, then you don't need to maintain a migration package in this configuration. But if the business need is to migrate specific data sets, let's say only a few material types and not all, then you should maintain the package ID name of the package here within which you'll add logic about which material type data should be migrated versus which should not.

Exclude Billing Plan Items

This configuration is used if you want to specifically exclude or include billing plan items from contributing to revenue accounting in RAR. You can set up exclusion or inclusion of RAIs by adding a block on the billing plan items (the same block codes you can configure in IMG path **Sales and Distribution • Billing • Billing Documents • Define Blocking Reason for Billing**).

To set up billing plan items exclusion, follow IMG menu path **Sales and Distribution • Revenue Accounting and Reporting • Exclude Billing Plan Items.** You'll arrive at the screen shown in Figure 6.42. From this screen, you can either view existing block codes or create new ones by clicking on **the New Entries** button (not shown).

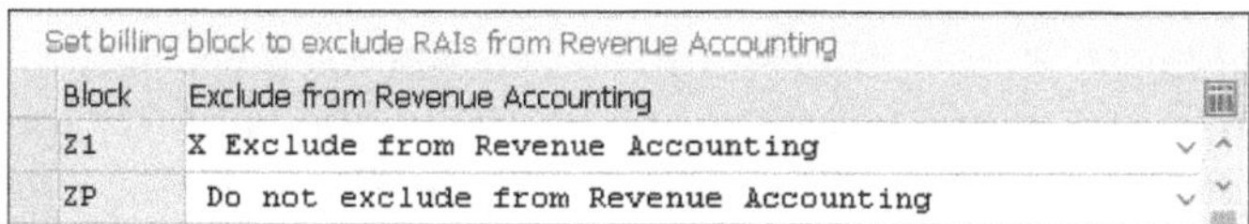
Set billing block to exclude RAIs from Revenue Accounting

Block	Exclude from Revenue Accounting
Z1	X Exclude from Revenue Accounting
ZP	Do not exclude from Revenue Accounting

Figure 6.42 Exclude Billing Plan Items

The screen shown in Figure 6.42 has two fields:

- **Block**
  This field represents the billing block codes configured in IMG path **Sales and Distribution • Billing • Billing Documents • Define Blocking Reason for Billing.**
- **Exclude from Revenue Accounting**
  This field helps you control if, for a block code, you want RAIs to be excluded from revenue allocation or not.

6.2.4 BRFplus Usage

A *BRFplus* application is used to set up frameworks for different business cases that are driven by rules or complex logic. A typical application for a RAR BRFplus is made up data objects, expressions, functions, and rulesets. Figure 6.43 shows the most common structure of RAR BRFplus objects.

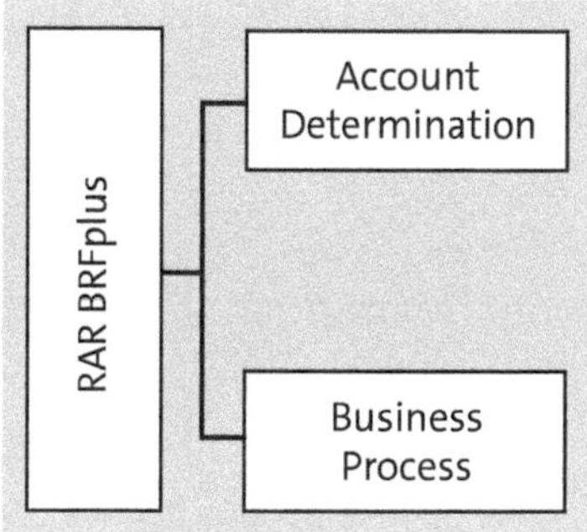

Figure 6.43 BRFplus Structure

An RAR BRFplus object comprises account determination and business process applications. In this section, we'll look at BRFplus through the lens of sales and distribution–RAR integration. We'll deep dive into account determination and business process applications of RAR for sample clients. We'll look at things such as these:

- General data for each application, including general texts and documentation
- Detail information for each application, including properties, default settings, contained objects, and miscellaneous
- What data objects, expressions, functions, and rulesets look like for each application

When configured correctly, all of these will help make the core foundation of sales and distribution–RAR integration strong and successful. The RAR functionality in SAP S/4HANA provides a standard list of applications and all components preconfigured within them. So, as in SAP S/4HANA sales and distribution, you copy over standard applications to Z applications in BRFplus and only make changes to them wherever needed. Once the applications are copied over, you can pick and choose the components you want to activate based on your project requirements.

Account Determination Application

The *account determination application* in BRFplus helps you configure account determination for POBs in terms of revenue, contract asset, contract liability, cost, allocation, right of return, unbilled, and deferred general ledgers. Just like you configure Transactions VKOA, OVUR, and OV64 in sales and distribution, you must configure BRFplus applications too. An advantage with BRFplus is that you can add not only the account determination entries but also supplementing expressions, functions, and rulesets.

To view an existing application, go to Transaction BRF+ in your SAP S/4HANA system. In the BRFplus portal page that opens, select **My Applications** from the **Show** dropdown list, and then click on the **Search** button under the **Repository** tab, as shown in Figure 6.44.

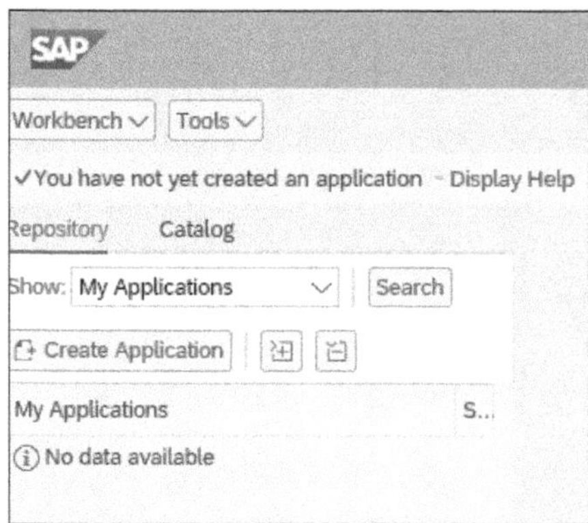

Figure 6.44 BRFplus Search Application

From here, you can create a new application as well by going to **Workbench • Create Application** or by simply clicking on the **Create Application** button under the **Show: My Applications** dropdown. To make sure you understand and comprehend all key fields for an account determination application, rather than creating a new application, we'll walk you through an existing application. Creating an application is straightforward and can be done easily once you understand the logic behind the key fields.

Moving on with the search for the account determination application, enter selection based on your requirement, and click **Search** as seen in Figure 6.45.

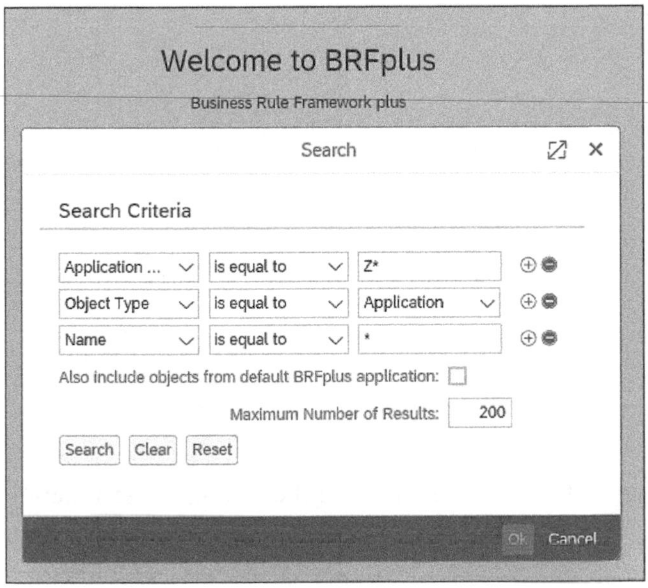

Figure 6.45 BRFplus Search Application Selection

In this example, we've searched all **Z*** applications with object type **Application**. As only one ZRAR account determination application is configured in BRFplus, it directly opened that application, as shown in Figure 6.46.

The main screen of the account determination application contains two sections: **General** and **Detail**. Figure 6.46 shows what the **General** section of an account determination application looks like in BRFplus. It has three sections: **General**, **Texts**, and **Documentation**.

The **General** section has the following fields:

- **Name**
  This field represents the name given to an account determination application.
- **ID**
  This field represents the unique system-generated ID for an account determination application.
- **Versioning**
  This field tells you if versioning is activated for an account determination application. If versioning is activated, you can compare or roll back to previous versions of an application if needed. In this example, we had switched this control off.

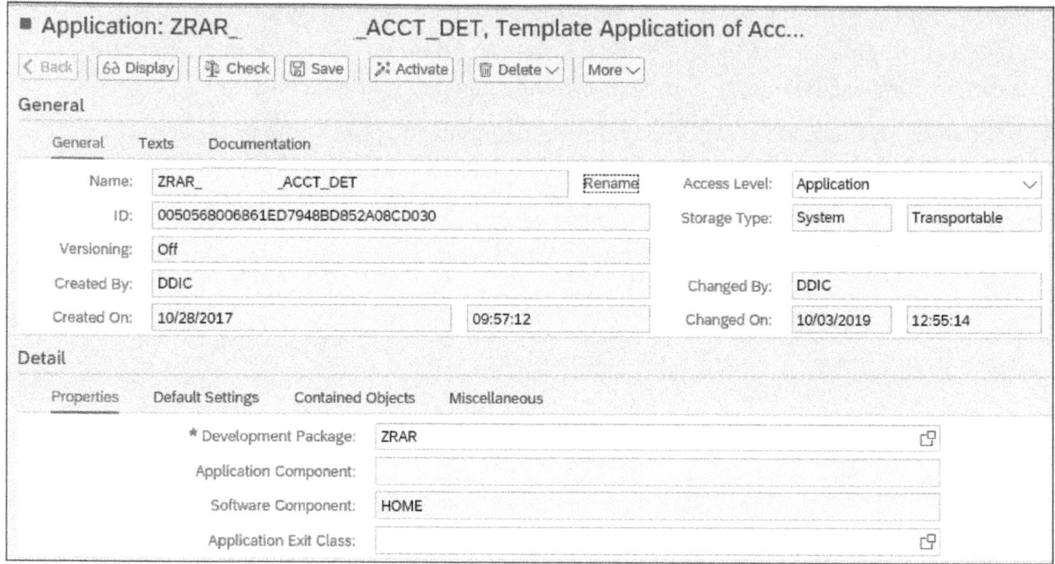

Figure 6.46 BRFplus Account Determination Application: General Section

- **Created By**
  This field represents the name of the user who created the account determination application.
- **Created On**
  This field represents the date and time when the account determination application was created.
- **Access Level**
  This field helps you control the access level you want to assign to an account determination application. By default, SAP S/4HANA provides five access levels:
  - **Application**: By selecting this option, you're allowing the object to be accessed by all other objects belonging to the same parent application.
  - **Application Component**: By selecting this option, you're allowing the object to be accessed by all other objects belonging to the same parent application assigned to the same component.
  - **Superordinate Component**: By selecting this option, you're allowing the object to be accessed by all other objects belonging to the same parent application assigned to the same component with the same superordinate component.
  - **Top Component**: By selecting this option, you're allowing the object to be accessed by all other objects belonging to the same top component.
  - **Global**: By selecting this option, you're allowing the object to be accessed by all other objects irrespective of any application or assigned component.

- **Storage Type**
  This field represents two things: where you logistically want to store data and whether the data is transportable between clients or is client specific.
- **Changed By**
  This field represents the name of the user who changed the account determination application most recently.
- **Changed On**
  This field represents the date and time when the account determination application was changed most recently.

As shown in Figure 6.47, we'll move to the **Texts** section, which has the following fields:

- **Source**
  This field represents the source of text for an account determination application. There are two options available by default: **Free text input** and **Text symbol**. We generally choose the option for free text as it gives you more flexibility on the text to maintain for an application.
- **Dependency**
  This field helps you control if you want the text to be dependent on a certain language or version. BRFplus provides you four options by default: **Independent of language and version**, **Language dependent but not version dependent**, **Version dependent but not language dependent**, and **Language and version dependent**.
- **Short Text**
  This field represents the short text given to an account determination application.
- **Text**
  This field represents the long text given to an account determination application.

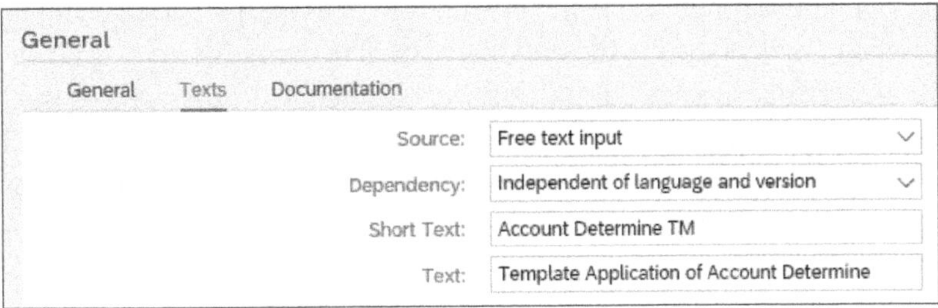

Figure 6.47 BRFplus Account Determination Application Texts

As shown in Figure 6.48, the next section, **Documentation**, has three fields:

- **Source**
  This field represents the source of documentation for an account determination application. There are two options available by default: **Free text input** and **SAPscript object**. Again, we generally choose the option for free text input as it gives you more flexibility on the text to maintain for an application.

- **Dependency**
  This field helps you control if you want the documentation to be dependent on a certain language or version. BRFplus provides you four options by default: **Independent of language and version**, **Language dependent but not version dependent**, **Version dependent but not language dependent**, and **Language and version dependent**.
- **Documentation**
  This field represents the actual documentation you want to associate with an account determination application.

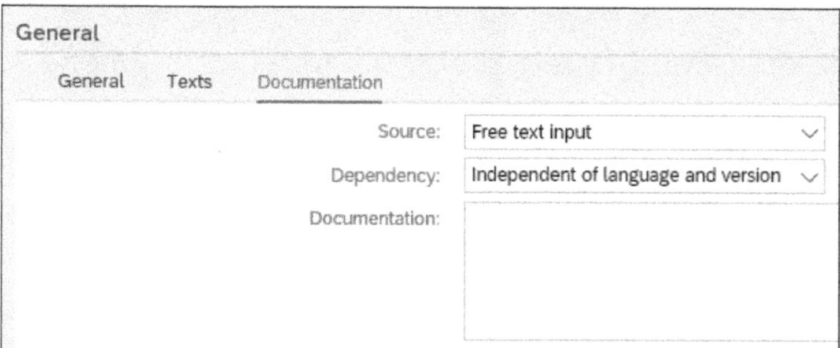

Figure 6.48 BRFplus Account Determination Application Documentation

Next, Figure 6.49 shows what the **Detail** section of an account determination application looks like in BRFplus. It has four sections: **Properties**, **Default Settings**, **Contained Objects**, and **Miscellaneous**.

The **Properties** section has the following fields:

- **Development Package**
  This field represents the development package associated with the account determination application. A development package is a standard or a custom package, under the ABAP Workbench, used to store information about developments and enhancements made to a particular object. All objects with similar patterns are grouped under one development package. For example, let's say you use BRFplus for RAR and billing. As a standard practice, you should create a separate development package for RAR objects and a separate package for billing objects. Any RAR-related changes or enhancements must be saved to the RAR package, and any billing-related changes or enhancements must be tagged to the billing package. In the future, if you want to roll back or refer to what changes were made, this package data will help you get the required information.
- **Application Component**
  This field represents the unique ID of a component in case you have more than one component for an account determination application. Application components are defined in the development package. For example, if you have one account determination application component for sales and another account component for supply chain management (SCM) in your BRFplus framework, then you should enter the

component name of "Sales" in this field to make sure the correct account determination is happening for revenue transactions.

- **Software Component**
  This field represents the unique ID of a software component in case you add one for an account determination application. Software components are objects, logically grouped together with the same delivery date. All objects within a software component must be delivered together or they won't work as expected. Software components are also a part of the development package. Both application component and software component get derived from the development package automatically, unless explicitly set by the user.
- **Application Exit Class**
  This field represents the exit class of an account determination application. Application exit classes are ABAP classes built to support special functions (calculations, validations, etc.) for an application. The RAR functionality in SAP S/4HANA offers a list of standard exit classes already defined for you, but you can create extra Z classes if needed based on business requirements.

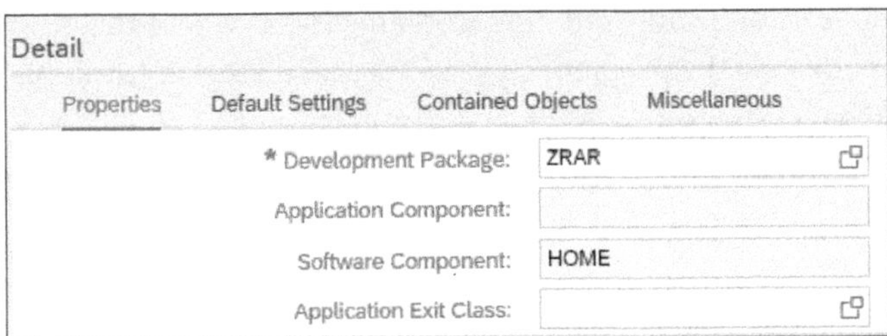

Figure 6.49 BRFplus Account Determination Application Detail and Properties

As shown in Figure 6.50, the **Default Settings** section has four subsections: **Application Log**, **Language Settings**, **Currency Settings**, and **Other Settings**.

The **Application Log** subsection has the following fields:

- **Application Log Object**
  This field represents the unique name of a log object for an account determination application. Application log objects record a series of events for an application.
- **Application Log Subobject**
  This field represents the unique name of a log subobject for an account determination application. Events recorded by an application log can be classified by objects or subobjects.
- **Default Enforcement**
  This field represents default settings you want to enforce on an application log for an account determination application. There are four default options available:
  - **No Constraints**: Choose this option if you don't want to add any constraints to the application log.

   - **Optional:** Choose this option if you want to allow modification of log settings for an application log.
   - **Mandatory:** Choose this option if you don't want to allow modification of log settings for an application.
   - **Mandatory and Hidden**: Choose this option if you don't want to allow modification of log settings and want to hide the option from within an application.
- **Allowed Message Types**
  This field represents the different message types allowed for a log for an account determination application. There are six default message types: **Abort**, **Error**, **Exit**, **Information**, **Status**, and **Warning**. You can either select one or all depending on your business requirements.
- **Save Log Data**
  This checkbox is checked if you want to save log data for an account determination application.
- **Show Problem Class**
  This checkbox is checked if you want to display the problem class of a log for an account determination application. Simply put, the problem class is where the error has occurred. If you want to display the problem class name and details in the application log, you should select this checkbox.

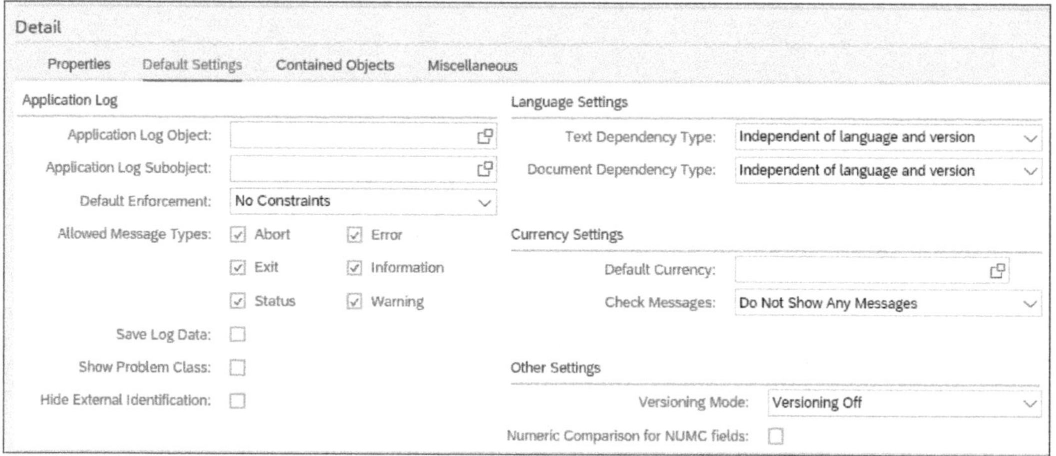

Figure 6.50 BRFplus Account Determination Application Default Settings

- **Hide External Identification**
  This checkbox is checked if you want to hide the external identification of a log for an account determination application. Message logs are universal and can be used for one than one application (account determination, sales process, finance reconciliation, etc.). Let's say you choose the option to have an external identification on the message log master, but for the account determination application only, you don't want to display the external identification. In that case, you'll check this checkbox

under the application log settings for the account determination application only. External identification will continue to show for other applications where this checkbox isn't checked.

Next, the **Language Settings** subsection has two fields:

- **Text Dependency Type**
  This field helps you control if you want the text to be dependent on a certain language or version. BRFplus provides you four options by default: **Independent of language and version**, **Language dependent but not version dependent**, **Version dependent but not language dependent**, and **Language and version dependent**.
- **Document Dependency Type**
  This field helps you control if you want the documentation to be dependent on a certain language or version. BRFplus provides you four options by default: **Independent of language and version**, **Language dependent but not version dependent**, **Version dependent but not language dependent**, and **Language and version dependent**.

Note

Both default dependency language settings can be overwritten by general dependency language settings if needed.

Next, the **Currency Settings** subsection has two fields:

- **Default Currency**
  This field represents the default currency code for an account determination application. This field is left blank because you want the account determination currency to flow over from sales and distribution (following the source documentation currency).
- **Check Messages**
  This field represents how you want the system to perform message checks for an account determination application log. Three different options are available for message checks: **Do Not Show Any Messages**, **Show Messages as Warning**, and **Show Messages as Error**.

Finally, the **Other Settings** subsection has two fields:

- **Versioning Mode**
  This field helps control if you want versioning to be on or off for an account determination application. Versioning helps with tracking changes made to an application since its inception. This is a very powerful feature from an audit and error control standpoint. The RAR functionality in SAP S/4HANA provides four default options:
  - **Versioning Off**: Choose this option if you want to turn versioning off.
  - **Versioning Triggered by Transport**: Choose this option if you want to track version changes in a transport.

- **Versioning On**: Choose this option if you want versioning to be on but versioning changes not tracked in transport.
- **Versioning Enforced**: Choose this option if you want versioning to be enforced for all technical objects already existing or newly created.

> **Note**
>
> **Versioning On** and **Versioning Enforced** aren't recommended options because you want to track changes and you don't want to force versioning on existing SAP standard objects. To make the best use of versioning, you should have it enabled for any new custom Z objects created by end users.

- **Numeric Comparison for NUMC fields**
  This checkbox is checked if you want to enable numeric comparisons for NUMC fields for an account determination application log. NUMC is a character data type in standard ABAP, which basically means you can use NUMC as numeric or alphanumeric depending on the need. If you want to use NUMC for calculations such as addition or subtraction, then it must be configured as alphanumeric, which can be done by checking this checkbox.

As you can see, most of the fields within the **Default Settings** sections are technically driven, so it's recommended to work with a technical person on your team while setting up the account determination application. As mentioned earlier, all settings are default as provided and recommended by SAP, so only change them if your business demands so.

Next, let's look at the **Contained Objects** section, as shown in Figure 6.51. This section helps you with creation, display, and maintenance of different objects contained in an application.

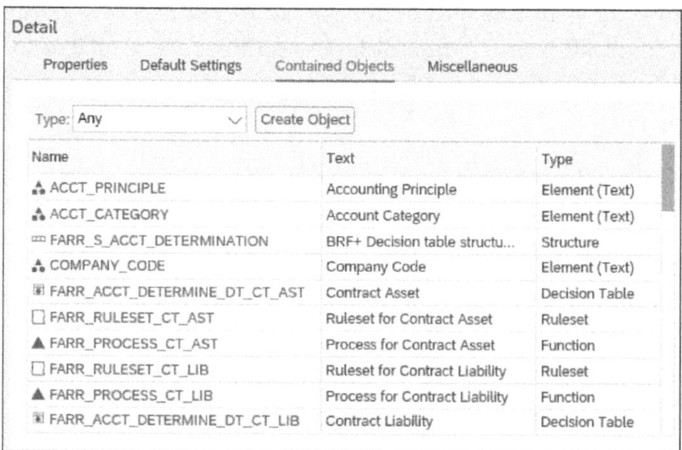

Figure 6.51 BRFplus Account Determination Application Contained Objects

An account determination application has the following object types available:

- Action
- Catalog
- Data object
- Expression
- Expression type
- Filter
- Function
- Rule
- Ruleset

Using these object types, you can create objects for an application depending on your project's functional design and business needs. To create an object, you simply select the type of object from the **Type** dropdown list, as shown in Figure 6.51, and click the **Create Object** button. For example, if your client needs to create an object for an accounting principle, you choose the **Data Object** option and set the data object type as **Element**. You'll understand more about these object types when we discuss the folder structure later in this section.

Now let's turn to the **Miscellaneous** section, which has two fields, as shown in Figure 6.52:

- **Restart Rulesets Enabled**
  This checkbox is checked if you want to enable the restarting of rulesets. There are scenarios in daily BRFplus processes where a ruleset has a primary condition and many dependent conditions. The normal logic in these scenarios is to exit the ruleset when the primary condition is met. But there is a secondary request in these scenarios where we want to restart the process from the same point, when more data comes in to support the process (rather than starting from scratch). To support these kinds of requests, you can select this checkbox in BRFplus, and the ruleset will resume its process from where it left off and not start from scratch.
- **Database Connection**
  This field represents the database name in case you're making a connection to an external database to drive any data for account determination. If you're connecting to any SAP source system (e.g., sales and distribution), then this field is left blank.

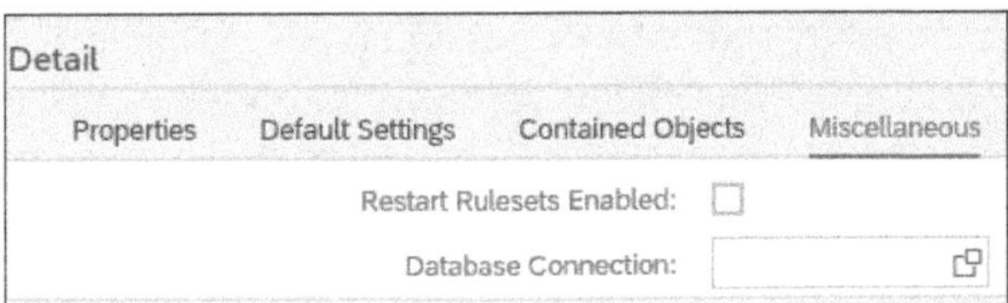

Figure 6.52 BRFplus Account Determination Application Miscellaneous

Now, let's look at the folder structures in an account determination application. We'll use an example implementation project to demonstrate. A few fields or data elements are intentionally grayed out for privacy reasons. Figure 6.53 shows the high-level folder structure for an account determination application. All components of the account determination application come over automatically when you copy a standard application to a Z application.

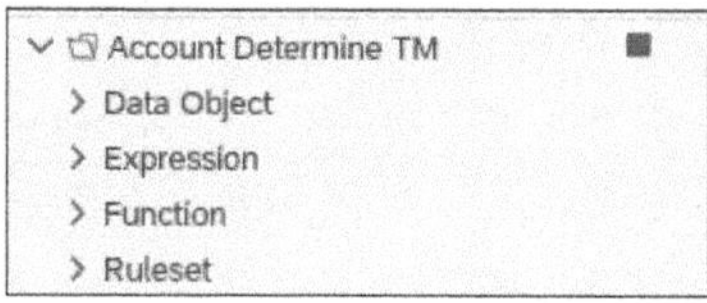

Figure 6.53 Account Determination Folder Structure

To copy an application to a new one, from the BRFplus Workbench screen, search for the application you're looking for by following the steps shown previously in Figure 6.44 and Figure 6.45. Once you find the application, click on it to select it, and then choose **More • Copy**, as shown in Figure 6.54.

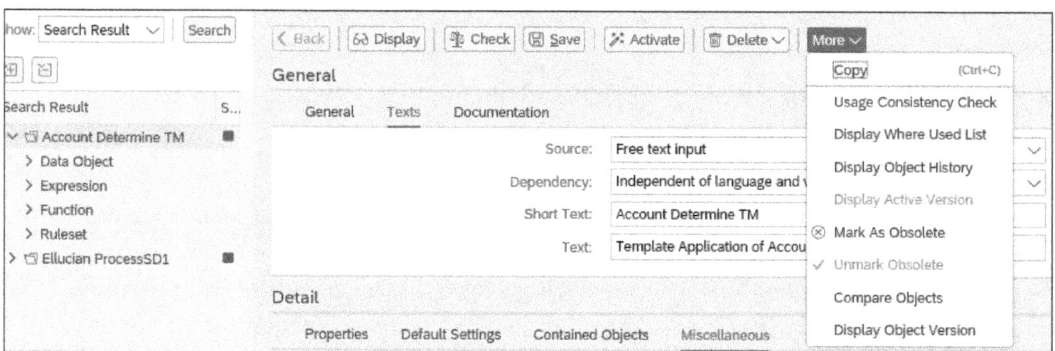

Figure 6.54 Application Copy

Data Object is defined as a carrier of data within an application. Data objects are used to describe data types, which can be either elements, structures, tables, or all three. Based on the example client's requirements, we copied and activated elements and structures as data objects for the account determination application. Figure 6.55 shows what the folder structure looks like for this example.

Expression or expression types are used to support various business rule usage scenarios for a BRFplus application. There are many standard expression types available, but the RAR functionality in SAP S/4HANA gives you the liberty to configure new ones if needed using BRFplus. The most common expressions we use are Boolean, decision table, procedure call, and table operation.

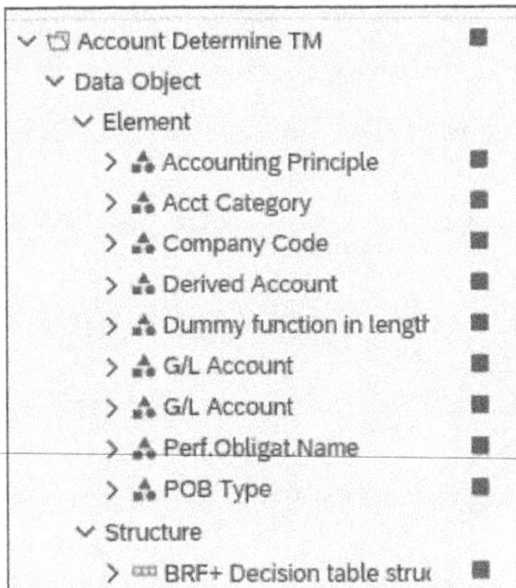

Figure 6.55 Account Determination Data Object Folder Structure

As shown in Figure 6.56, we only activated one decision table expression for the account determination application based on business needs, but within that one expression were various decision tables.

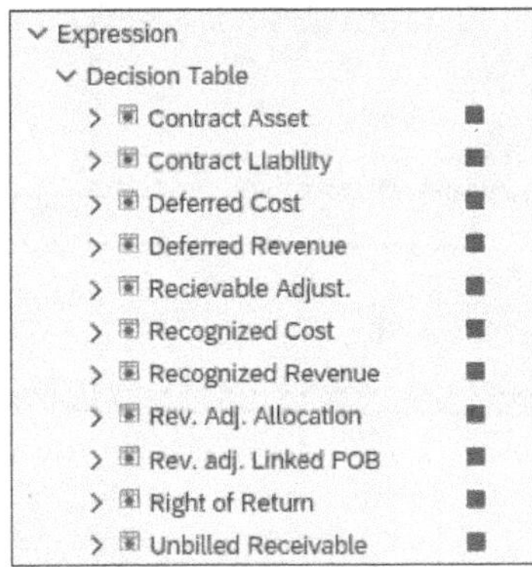

Figure 6.56 Account Determination Expression Folder Structure

Function can be defined as a mediator between a business application and a business framework that connects the two entities to perform a seamless business task. Functions have a signature and assigned rulesets. You can simulate a function in BRFplus before activating it for a live business task. Figure 6.57 shows the different functions activated for the account determination application for the example client. The list of functions matches the list of expressions one to one and are available as standard in BRFplus.

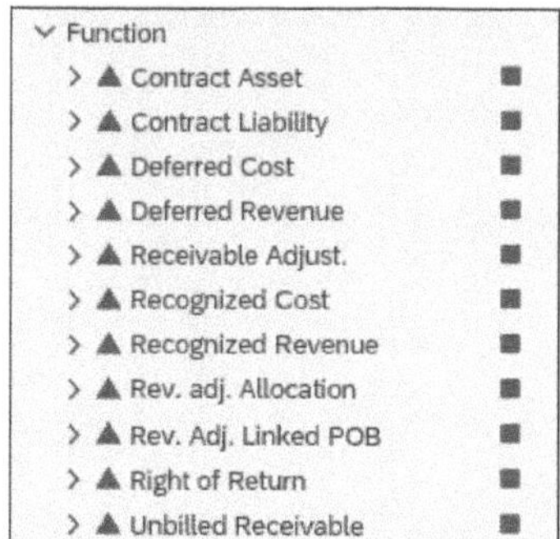

Figure 6.57 Account Determination Functions

Ruleset is assigned to functions. Ruleset is a box of rules a function uses to perform its job. Whenever a function is called, the underlying ruleset is called along with it. **Ruleset** is made up of a ruleset header and rules:

- **Ruleset header**
  The header stores supporting ruleset information details, such as function, precondition, number of rules, number of variables, priority, and if the ruleset is enabled or not.
- **Rules**
  Rules are the actual "change, from" statements written for the parent function to perform its task.

Figure 6.58 gives an overview of the different rulesets activated for the account determination application at the example client. Rulesets match the expressions and functions one to one.

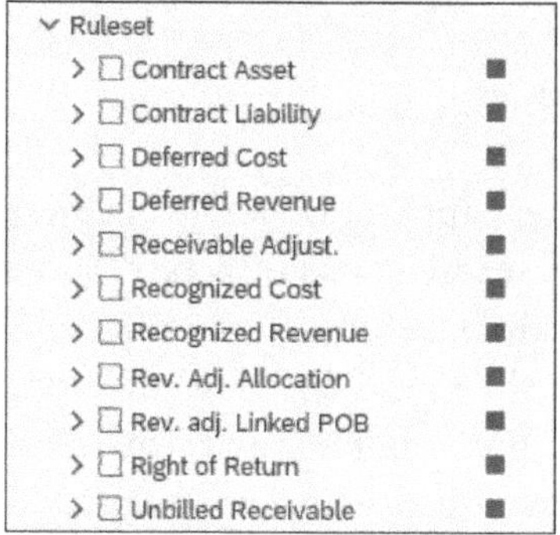

Figure 6.58 Account Determination Ruleset

Business Process Application

The *business process application* in BRFplus houses various configurations needed to support source business processes and fields (i.e., standard or Z fields for the source sales and distribution system). Consider this example: For a client we had worked for in the past, we had mapped revenue blocks from sales and distribution to review reasons in BRFplus. So, each time a sales order containing a revenue block was sent from sales and distribution, it got mapped to the relevant review reason code in RAR. Until the revenue block from sales and distribution was removed, and RAIs were sent over to RAR, revenue on a POB in RAR wasn't recognized even if revenue posting jobs were executed.

The high-level structure and fields of a business process application should be the same as the account determination application, considering we copied over the standard application to a Z application even in this case. You can follow the same steps to copy a business process application, as shown previously in Figure 6.54. The **General** and **Detail** section and the folder structure have the same fields and functionality, so we won't walk through every component in the business process application. Instead, in this section, we'll only focus on the fields and folder structure elements that are either built differently or have different information buried within them.

Note

Keep in mind that the information shared in this section is strictly based on the example client's requirements. It may not match one to one to your business needs. Think of these sections as a guideline that you can refer to when configuring applications for your own projects.

There are a few fields in the **General** and **Detail** sections of the business process application that have different values compared to the account determination application, so let's look at those fields first, as shown in Figure 6.59.

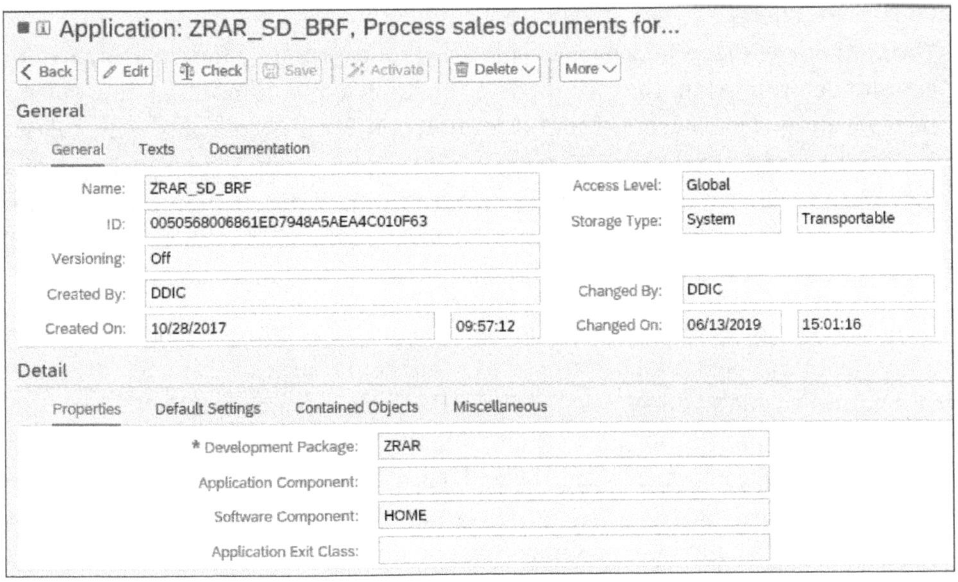

Application: ZRAR_SD_BRF, Process sales documents for...

Back | Edit | Check | Save | Activate | Delete | More

General

General | Texts | Documentation

Name:	ZRAR_SD_BRF	Access Level:	Global
ID:	0050568006861ED7948A5AEA4C010F63	Storage Type:	System, Transportable
Versioning:	Off		
Created By:	DDIC	Changed By:	DDIC
Created On:	10/28/2017 09:57:12	Changed On:	06/13/2019 15:01:16

Detail

Properties | Default Settings | Contained Objects | Miscellaneous

* Development Package:	ZRAR
Application Component:	
Software Component:	HOME
Application Exit Class:	

Figure 6.59 Business Process Application

If you compare this screen with Figure 6.46 (which is for the account determination application), you'll notice it matches for the most part. Following are the few fields that show different values:

- **Name**
  This field represents the name given to a business process application. We've named this field "ZRAR_SD_BRF" compared to the account determination application, which was named "ZRAR_ACCT_DET".
- **ID**
  This field represents the unique system generated ID for a business process application. Because the ID is unique and system generated, it would be different when compared to the account determination application.
- **Access Level**
  This field helps you control the access level you want to assign to a business process application. By default, SAP S/4HANA provides five access levels: **Application**, **Application Component**, **Superordinate Component**, **Top Component**, and **Global**. The **Access Level** set for the business process application is **Global** compared to the account determination application where **Access Level** is set to **Application**.
- **Short Text**
  This field represents the short text given to a business process application.
- **Text**
  This field represents the long text given to a business process application.
- **Documentation**
  This field represents the actual documentation you want to associate with a business process application.
- **Contained Objects**
  The **Contained Objects** for a business process application are different compared to account determination. The account determination application will contain objects relevant for general ledger account determination, such as company code, ruleset `FARR_PROCESS`, decision table `FARR_ACCT_DETERMINE`, and so on. The business process application will contain objects relevant for sales and distribution business processes, such as sales and distribution field elements (distribution channel, division), RAR exclude allocation logic procedure call, process BOM ruleset, and so on.

Let's move on to the differences in the folder structure now. While the folder structure and the definition of the folder structure components, such as element, structure, function, ruleset, and so on, remain the same, the subcomponents of the folder structure for business process applications are different. This is natural because account determination subcomponents are defined based on the account determination needs, and the business process subcomponents are defined based on the business process needs. Let's jump into the similarities and differences.

An account determination application has two data objects, element and structure, while a business process application has three data objects: element, structure, and table.

We activated several elements for the business process application data objects at the example client, as shown in Figure 6.60.

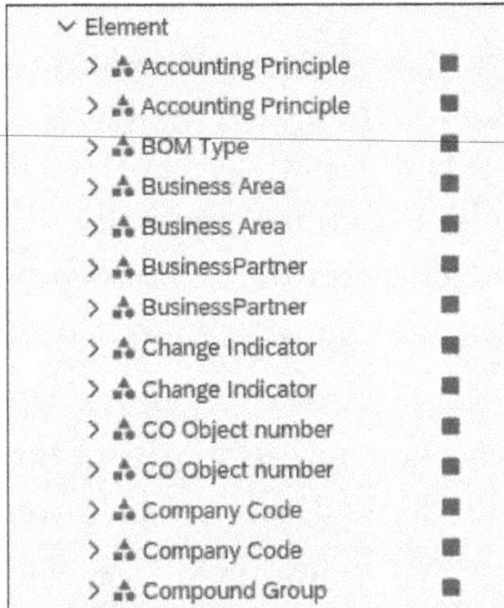

Figure 6.60 Business Process Element Folder Structure

Account determination data objects only have one structure, while a business process application has 10 structures, as shown in Figure 6.61. This is only because of the complex nature of business processes at the example client. There is no minimum or maximum for data objects. They depend purely on business requirements and process design.

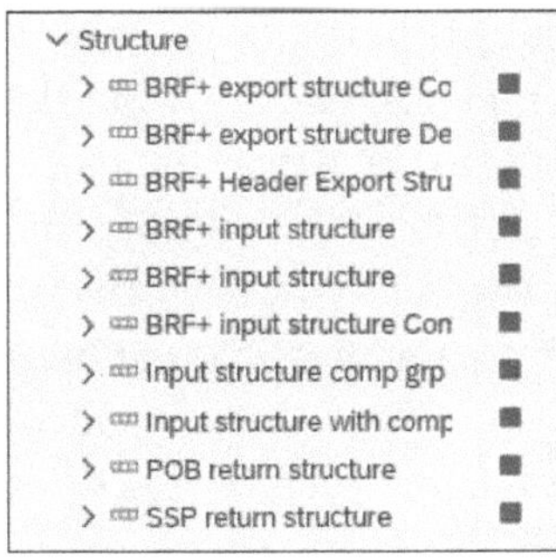

Figure 6.61 Business Process Structure Folder Structure

Table in BRFplus is a bucket of data grouped together with a common theme or a business process in mind. Within tables, you define the data binding type and table properties, and you list all components that construct the table. All of this is done automatically when you copy a standard application. While there were no tables required for the account determination application, we created four tables within the business process application based on client requirements, as shown in Figure 6.62.

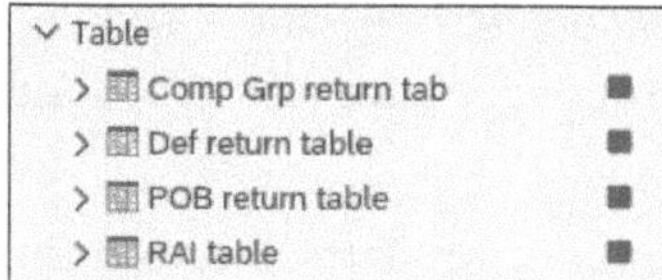

Figure 6.62 Business Process Table Folder Structure

Moving on to business process application **Expression**, there are four expressions in a business process application compared to an account determination application, which has only one expression. The common expression within both applications is the **Decision Table** expression, but the actual decision tables within the expression are still different. Figure 6.63 shows the **Expression** folder structure for the business process application activated at the example client, containing the following expressions:

- **Boolean**
  Boolean is used when there are two satisfying values for an expression. This is the typical if, then, else statement. For example, if the value is initial, then set the revenue block, else remove the revenue block. We activated one Boolean expression at the example client called **Rev Block Precondition**.
- **Decision Table**
  Decision Table is used to visually represent data used to perform a set of actions based on predefined conditions. For example, say a decision table shows that for accounting principle 606 and item category Lic, always determine License POB. We activated seven decision tables for the business process application to meet the example client's requirements.
- **Procedure Call**
  Procedure Call is used to call function modules or methods written in the source SAP S/4HANA sales and distribution ABAP system. For example, an exclude from the allocation procedure call is configured in BRFplus to call the exclude from the allocation function module written in SAP S/4HANA sales and distribution. In a procedure call, you configure the function module and the respective call type. You can also configure mapped parameters and any exception handling based on project requirements. Again, all of this comes readymade for you if you copy a standard BRFplus application instead of creating a new one from scratch. We activated three procedure calls for the Z business process application.
- **Table Operation**
  Table Operation is an expression that helps you connect data object tables to data object structures within a BRFplus application. For example, from the RAI table, you can get the first row and return the result to the BRFplus input structure. We've activated one table operation for the business process application, as shown in Figure 6.63.

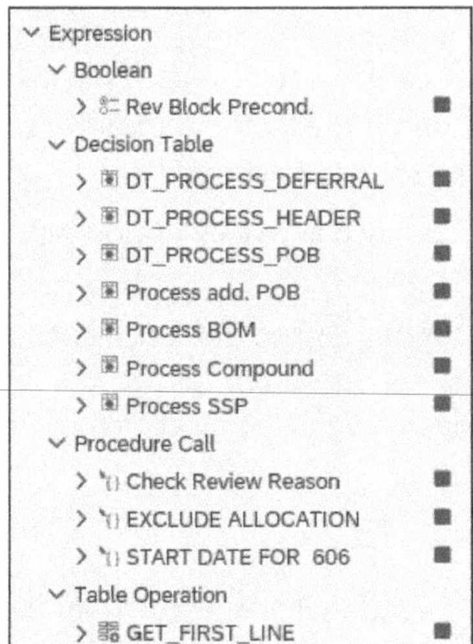

Figure 6.63 Business Process Expression Folder Structure

Next, we pivot to **Function** in the business process application. Figure 6.64 shows the seven different functions activated for the example client.

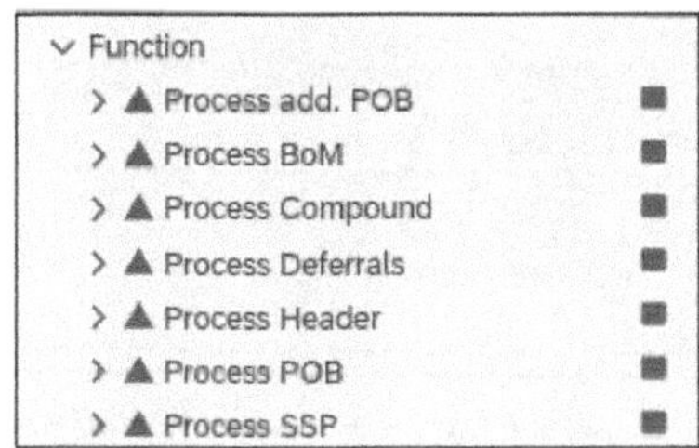

Figure 6.64 Business Process Function Folder Structure

Let's look at **Ruleset** next. Figure 6.65 shows the seven activated rulesets, matching the seven functions, for the Z business process application.

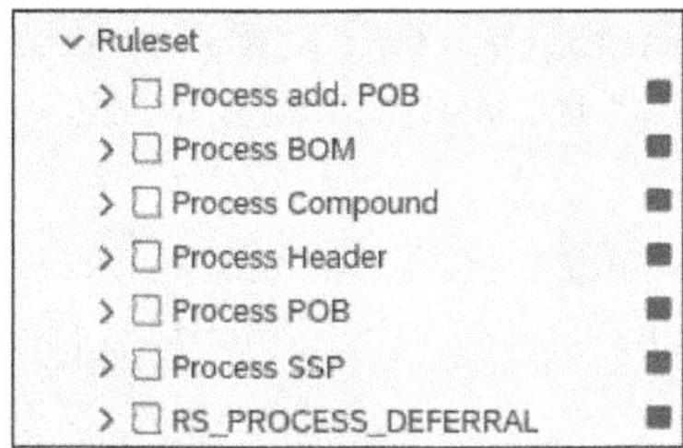

Figure 6.65 Business Process Ruleset Folder Structure

Kudos! You have successfully completed the BRFplus setup and are now ready to configure an end-to-end sales and distribution–RAR integration using the CCM techniques.

6.2.5 End-to-End Integration

In this section, we'll walk you through an end-to-end use case of a typical sales and distribution–RAR integration. It should be a good review for all the configuration we've covered in previous sections. We'll touch on topics such as the following:

- RAR touch points in sales and distribution sales orders, such as SSP condition type, revenue block, billing block, and so on
- Mapping of sales order and line items in sales and distribution to the contract and POBs in RAR
- Generation of RAIs in the RAI monitor
- Contract view and POB view in Transaction NWBC
- Price allocation
- Sales and distribution touch points in RAR, such as operational document, item ID, general ledger account, contract start and end dates, and so on
- ABC jobs
- Revenue posting and general ledger

> **Note**
>
> Due to the wide nature of many of the screens in the RAR functionality in SAP S/4HANA, you may find some images in this section difficult to parse. For better readability, you can download the particularly wide images from this book's webpage under the **Product supplements** section at *https://www.sap-press.com/5592*.

First, let's create a sales order in SAP S/4HANA sales and distribution via Transaction VA01, which has both event-based and time-based line items. For the example, Figure 6.66 represents a typical sales order with a professional services company. It has one license product along with five years of maintenance. Line 10 represents the License product and has item category **ZLF1**. This is the event-based line item. Note that there is a revenue block on the License line item, which we'll talk about later in this section. Lines 20–60 represent maintenance lines, one line item for each year of the five-year contract. The item category of the maintenance product is **ZMNT**, which is the time-based product.

Figure 6.67 shows the pricing conditions for the License line item. To get to the pricing condition, double-click on the License line item, and navigate to the **Conditions** tab. You'll see the following condition types:

- **ZPLF** is the primary condition type with **Amount 1,200.00.**
- **ZSSP** is the SSP condition type with **Amount 1,200.00.**

Other condition types in Figure 6.67 are tax condition types that aren't relevant for this use case.

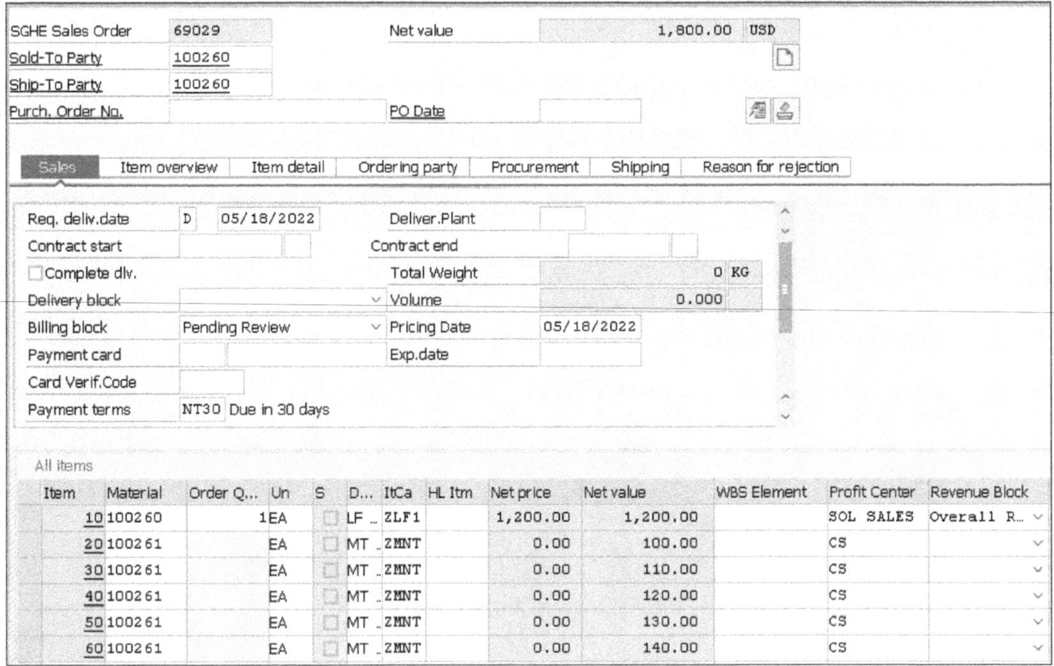

Figure 6.66 Sales Order

N..	CnTy	Description	Amount	Crcy	per	U...	Condition value	Curr.
	ZPLF	LF Software (Rev.)	1,200.00	USD	1	EA	1,200.00	USD
	ZSSP	SSP Condition	1,200.00	USD			1,200.00	USD
		Net Value	1,200.00	USD	1	EA	1,200.00	USD
	UTXD	US Tax per document	100.000	%			1,200.00	USD
	UTXE	US Tax per document	0.000	%			0.00	USD
	XR1	Tax Jur Code Level 1	4.000	%			0.00	USD
	XR2	Tax Jur Code Level 2		%			0.00	USD
	XR3	Tax Jur Code Level 3	4.500	%			0.00	USD
	XR4	Tax Jur Code Level 4		%			0.00	USD
	XR5	Tax Jur Code Level 5	0.375	%			0.00	USD
	XR6	Tax Jur Code Level 6		%			0.00	USD
		Total	1,200.00	USD	1	EA	1,200.00	USD

Figure 6.67 License Product Pricing Condition Types

Figure 6.68 shows the pricing conditions for the first **Maintenance** line item:

- **ZPMA** is the primary condition type with **Amount 100.00**.
- **ZLSP** is the list price condition type with **Amount 100.00**.
- **ZBSE** is the base price condition type with **Amount 100.00**.
- **ZSSP** is the SSP condition type with **Amount 100.00**.

Other condition types in Figure 6.68 are tax condition types that aren't relevant for this use case. All maintenance line items (20–60) have the same pricing structure but different amounts because the price for maintenance escalates year over year.

Pricing Elements

N..	CnTy	Description	Amount	Crcy	per	U...	Condition value	Curr.
	ZPMA	Maintenance	100.00	USD			100.00	USD
	ZLSP	List price	100.00	USD			100.00	USD
	ZBSE	Base amount	100.00	USD			100.00	USD
	ZSSP	SSP Condition	100.00	USD			100.00	USD
		Net Value	0.00	USD	1	EA	100.00	USD
	UTXD	US Tax per document	100.000	%			100.00	USD
	UTXE	US Tax per document	0.000	%			0.00	USD
	XR1	Tax Jur Code Level 1	4.000	%			0.00	USD
	XR2	Tax Jur Code Level 2		%			0.00	USD
	XR3	Tax Jur Code Level 3	4.500	%			0.00	USD
	XR4	Tax Jur Code Level 4		%			0.00	USD
	XR5	Tax Jur Code Level 5	0.375	%			0.00	USD
	XR6	Tax Jur Code Level 6		%			0.00	USD
		Total	0.00	USD	1	EA	100.00	USD

Figure 6.68 Maintenance Product Pricing Condition Types

Once the sales order is created, RAIs are generated for that sales order in the RAI monitor, which we'll go to using Transaction FARR_RAI_MON. You'll see **SDOI** for now as the sales order is only created and there is no delivery or invoice yet.

Figure 6.69 shows what the SDOIs look like for the sales order. Think of the RAI monitor as the true integration interface that reads sales and distribution data and then transfers it to the RAR system (in the form of RAIs). There are many fields available in the RAI monitor, but let's focus on the ones important for you and the sales and distribution–RAR integration.

Main Item (6) | Condition Item (12)

Error	Send.Com...	CoCode	SrcItmType	Source Item ID	RevAcc...	Header...	Item ID	Contract...	POB(606)	Quantity	Creation Date	Create Tim	Customer	Ref. Type	Reference ID	Sales Org.	Doc.Cat.
	SD	SG11	SDOI	0000069029000010	SD01	69029	10			1	05/18/2022	13:02:18	100260	SDO	0000069029	SG11	C
	SD	SG11	SDOI	0000069029000020	SD01	69029	20			0	05/18/2022	13:02:18	100260	SDO	0000069029	SG11	C
	SD	SG11	SDOI	0000069029000030	SD01	69029	30			0	05/18/2022	13:02:18	100260	SDO	0000069029	SG11	C
	SD	SG11	SDOI	0000069029000040	SD01	69029	40			0	05/18/2022	13:02:18	100260	SDO	0000069029	SG11	C
	SD	SG11	SDOI	0000069029000050	SD01	69029	50			0	05/18/2022	13:02:18	100260	SDO	0000069029	SG11	C
	SD	SG11	SDOI	0000069029000060	SD01	69029	60			0	05/18/2022	13:02:18	100260	SDO	0000069029	SG11	C

Figure 6.69 RAI Monitor: Main Items

As shown in Figure 6.69, the RAI monitor has two sections: **Main Item** and **Condition Item**.

First, the **Main Item** section has the following important fields:

- **Error**
  If there is an error in RAI creation, this field represents the process that generated the error and the status of that error. SAP S/4HANA provides three standard error statuses:

- 1 **When checking in Status Raw**: This status tells you that an error was found when the RAIs were in the raw status.
- 2 **When Transferring (from Raw to Processable)**: This status tells you that an error was found when the RAIs were transferred from raw to processable.
- 3 **When Processing (from Status Processable to Processed)**: This status tells you that an error was found when RAIs were moved from processable to processed.

The green traffic light (as shown in Figure 6.69) indicates there are no errors on the RAIs. A red traffic light signifies a hard error.

- **Send.Com...**
  This field represents the code of the sender component from where the RAIs originate. Our RAIs have sender component **SD**, which means the source system for RAIs is SAP S/4HANA sales and distribution (sender component configuration was discussed in Section 6.2.1 during our discussion of RAIs).
- **CoCode**
  This field represents the company code of the sales order for which RAIs are created.
- **SrcItmType**
  This field represents the unique alphanumeric key for a source document item type (source item type configuration was discussed in Section 6.2.1 during our discussion of RAIs).
- **Source Item ID**
  This field is a combination of technical field values for header ID + item ID.
- **RevAcc...**
  This field represents the unique ID for a RAI class. It's a four-character alphanumeric code (RAI class configuration was discussed in Section 6.2.1 during our discussion of RAIs).
- **Header ID**
  This field represents the sales order number from the source sales and distribution system.
- **Item ID**
  This field represents the sales order line-item number from the source sales and distribution system.
- **Contract...**
  This field represents the RAR contract ID for the sales and distribution sales order. The reason the field is blank for the order RAIs is because this is the first time the sales order is being sent to RAR, so no contract exists in RAR yet. Any further transactions on the sales order will generate RAIs that will have the contract ID populated on them.
- **POB (606)**
  This field represents the RAR POB ID for the sales and distribution sales order line items. The reason this field is blank for the order RAIs is because this is the first time

the sales order line items are being sent to RAR, so no POBs exist in RAR yet. Any further transactions on the sales order line items will generate RAIs that will have POB ID populated on them.

- **Quantity**
  This field represents the quantity of the sales order line item for which RAIs are created.
- **Creation Date**
  This field represents the creation date of the RAIs.
- **Creation Time**
  This field represents the creation time of the RAIs.
- **Customer**
  This field represents the sold to ID of the sales and distribution sales order for which RAIs are created.
- **Ref. Type**
  This field describes the type of reference ID (reference type configuration was discussed in Section 6.2.1 during our discussion of RAI management).
- **Reference ID**
  All RAIs with the same reference type and reference ID combine on one contract in RAR, and the combination logic is defined in BAdI `FARR_BADI_CONTRACT_COMBINATION`.
- **Sales Org.**
  This field represents the sales organization of the sales order for which RAIs are created.
- **Doc. Cat.**
  This field represents the sales and distribution document category of the sales order for which RAIs are created.

Next, as shown in Figure 6.70, the RAI monitor **Condition Item** section has the following relevant fields:

- **ItemStat**
  This field represents the status of the item RAIs. As default, SAP S/4HANA provides seven statuses: **Raw Data**, **Processable Items**, **Not Processed Items**, **Processed Items**, **Exempted Items**, **All Items**, and **Manual Selection**.
- **Error**
  If there is an error in RAI creation, this field represents the process that generated the error and the status of that error. SAP S/4HANA provides three standard error statuses: **1 When checking in Status Raw**, **2 When Transferring (from Raw to Processable)**, and **3 When Processing (from Status Processable to Processed)**. The green traffic light indicates there are no errors on the RAIs, while a red traffic light signifies a hard error.

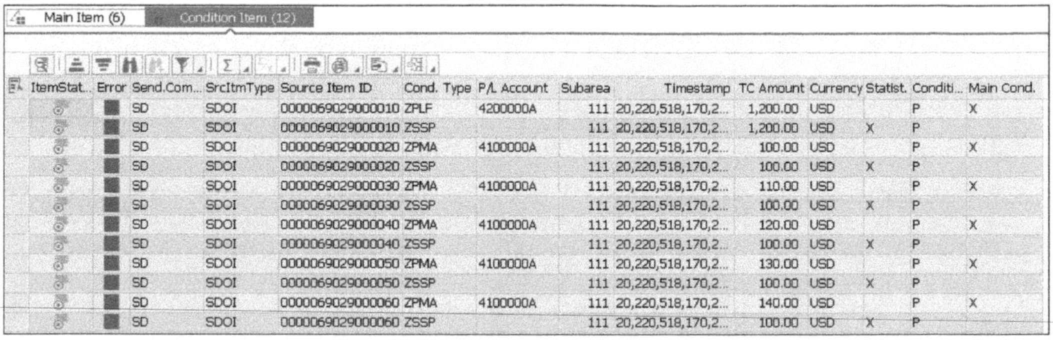

Main Item (6) | Condition Item (12)

ItemStat...	Error	Send.Com...	SrcItmType	Source Item ID	Cond. Type	P/L Account	Subarea	Timestamp	TC Amount	Currency	Statist.	Conditi...	Main Cond.
		SD	SDOI	0000069029000010	ZPLF	4200000A	111	20,220,518,170,2...	1,200.00	USD		P	X
		SD	SDOI	0000069029000010	ZSSP		111	20,220,518,170,2...	1,200.00	USD	X	P	
		SD	SDOI	0000069029000020	ZPMA	4100000A	111	20,220,518,170,2...	100.00	USD		P	X
		SD	SDOI	0000069029000020	ZSSP		111	20,220,518,170,2...	100.00	USD	X	P	
		SD	SDOI	0000069029000030	ZPMA	4100000A	111	20,220,518,170,2...	110.00	USD		P	X
		SD	SDOI	0000069029000030	ZSSP		111	20,220,518,170,2...	100.00	USD	X	P	
		SD	SDOI	0000069029000040	ZPMA	4100000A	111	20,220,518,170,2...	120.00	USD		P	X
		SD	SDOI	0000069029000040	ZSSP		111	20,220,518,170,2...	100.00	USD	X	P	
		SD	SDOI	0000069029000050	ZPMA	4100000A	111	20,220,518,170,2...	130.00	USD		P	X
		SD	SDOI	0000069029000050	ZSSP		111	20,220,518,170,2...	100.00	USD	X	P	
		SD	SDOI	0000069029000060	ZPMA	4100000A	111	20,220,518,170,2...	140.00	USD		P	X
		SD	SDOI	0000069029000060	ZSSP		111	20,220,518,170,2...	100.00	USD	X	P	

Figure 6.70 RAI Monitor: Condition Items

- **Send.Com...**
  This field represents the code of the sender component from where the RAIs originate. Our RAIs have sender component **SD**, which means the source system for RAIs is SAP S/4HANA sales and distribution (sender component configuration was discussed in Section 6.2.1 during our discussion of RAIs).
- **SrcItmType**
  This field represents the unique alphanumeric key for a source document item type (source item type configuration was discussed in Section 6.2.1 during our discussion of RAI management).
- **Source Item ID**
  This field is a combination of technical field values for header ID + item ID.
- **Cond. Type**
  This field represents the pricing condition type of the sales and distribution sales order line item.
- **P/L Account**
  This field represents the revenue profit and loss general ledger account for the sales and distribution sales order line item.
- **Subarea**
  This field represents the subarea code used for parallelization.
- **Timestamp**
  This field represents the timestamp on which the RAI was created.
- **TC Amount**
  This field represents the amount of the sales order line time in transaction currency.
- **Currency**
  This field represents the currency code, which supplements the **TC Amount** field.
- **Statist.**
  This field indicates if the condition type represented by the RAI is a statistical condition. Statistical conditions don't contribute to revenue numbers. The statistical feature of the condition is inherited from sales and distribution into RAR.

- **Main Cond.**
  This field indicates if the condition type represented by the RAI is the main condition. The main condition is the primary condition on the sales order (source document), which has a direct impact on revenue numbers. The main condition will always have a general ledger account associated with it as well.

Now that you've validated the RAIs and everything looks good, let's send them over to RAR. To do so, first select all RAIs from the RAI monitor, and then click the **Process** button from the main menu ribbon at the top, as shown in Figure 6.71.

Refresh · Statistics · Simulate Transfer · Transfer · Process · Initial Load Process · Change · Exempt

Main Item · Condition Item

Error	Send.Com...	CoCode	SrcItmType	Source Item ID	Subarea	RevAcc...	Header...	Item ID	Quantity	Creation Date	Create Tim	Customer	Sales Org.	Doc.Cat.
	SD	SG11	SDOI	0000069029000010	111	SD01	69029	10	1	05/21/2022	09:52:23	100260	SG11	C
	SD	SG11	SDOI	0000069029000020	111	SD01	69029	20	0	05/21/2022	09:35:59	100260	SG11	C
	SD	SG11	SDOI	0000069029000030	111	SD01	69029	30	0	05/21/2022	09:35:59	100260	SG11	C
	SD	SG11	SDOI	0000069029000040	111	SD01	69029	40	0	05/21/2022	09:35:59	100260	SG11	C
	SD	SG11	SDOI	0000069029000050	111	SD01	69029	50	0	05/21/2022	09:35:59	100260	SG11	C
	SD	SG11	SDOI	0000069029000060	111	SD01	69029	60	0	05/21/2022	09:35:59	100260	SG11	C

Figure 6.71 RAI Monitor: Process RAIs

To view the impact of RAIs in RAR, go to Transaction NWBC. When SAP Business Client opens, go to **Contract Management • Contract Search**. Enter the sales order number "69029" in the **Operational Document** selection criteria, and click **Search**. The RAR functionality in SAP S/4HANA directs you to the screen shown in Figure 6.72.

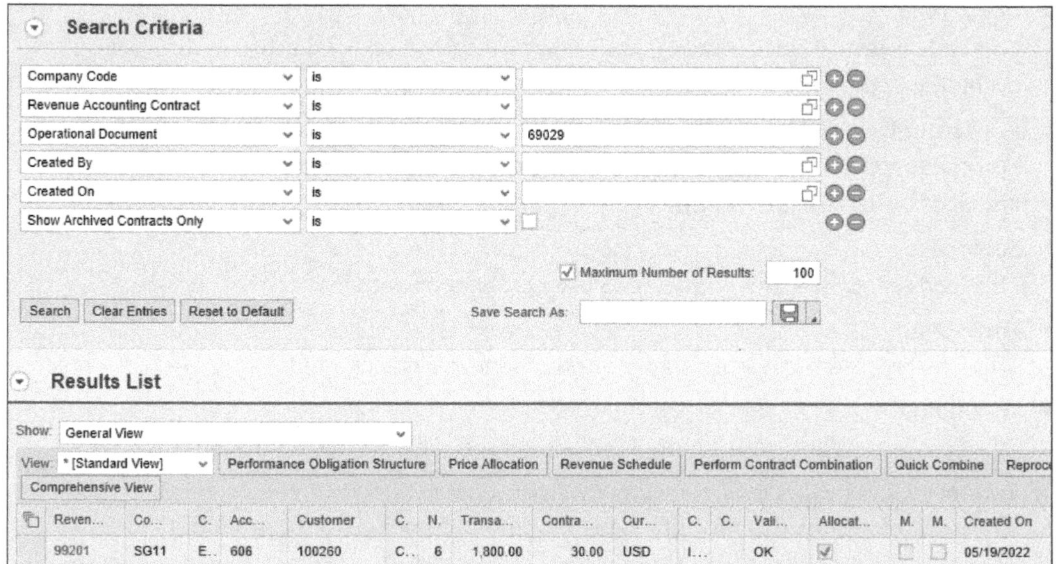

Figure 6.72 Transaction NWBC: Contract Search

Next, click on the revenue accounting contract **99201**, which takes you to the contract view screen as shown in Figure 6.73.

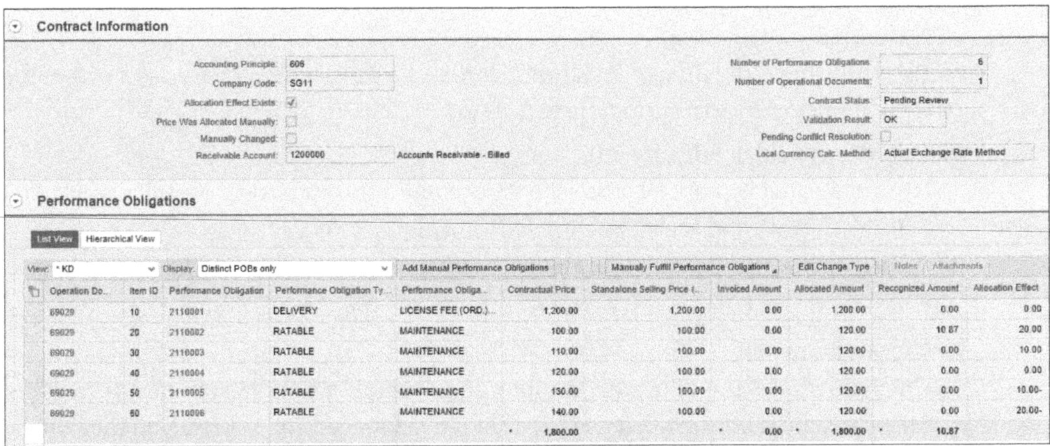

Operation Do...	Item ID	Performance Obligation	Performance Obligation Ty...	Performance Obliga...	Contractual Price	Standalone Selling Price (...	Invoiced Amount	Allocated Amount	Recognized Amount	Allocation Effect
69029	10	2110001	DELIVERY	LICENSE FEE (ORD.)...	1,200.00	1,200.00	0.00	1,200.00	0.00	0.00
69029	20	2110002	RATABLE	MAINTENANCE	100.00	100.00	0.00	120.00	10.87	20.00
69029	30	2110003	RATABLE	MAINTENANCE	110.00	100.00	0.00	120.00	0.00	10.00
69029	40	2110004	RATABLE	MAINTENANCE	120.00	100.00	0.00	120.00	0.00	0.00
69029	50	2110005	RATABLE	MAINTENANCE	130.00	100.00	0.00	120.00	0.00	10.00-
69029	60	2110006	RATABLE	MAINTENANCE	140.00	100.00	0.00	120.00	0.00	20.00-
					• 1,800.00		• 0.00	• 1,800.00	• 10.87	

Figure 6.73 Transaction NWBC: Contract View

Pay special attention to the following fields in Figure 6.73 as they will give you a visual representation of the core concepts you've learned, such as price allocation, SSP, review reason, revenue recognition, and so on.

Under the **Contract Information** section, the following fields are the most critical:

- **Allocation Effect Exists**
  This checkbox is checked because the allocation effect exists on the contract **99201**. There is allocation between the maintenance lines. They escalate year over year as shown in the contract and sales order. Per the IFRS 15 standard, if there is escalation on a contract, you should flatline all lines to have the same allocation amount for all years. The difference in the allocation amount and transaction price helps the system determine the allocation effect.
- **Number of Performance Obligations**
  There are six POBs on the contract, one for each line item of the sales order.
- **Number of Operational Documents**
  There is only one sales order on the contract for now, so the number of operational documents is one.
- **Contract Status**
  If you go back and look at Figure 6.66, you'll see there is a revenue block on line item 10. That is why status of the contract right now is **Pending Review**.

Under the **Performance Obligations** section, the following fields are the most critical:

- **Operation Doc...**
  This field shows the SAP S/4HANA sales and distribution sales order number, **69029**.

- **Item ID**
  This field shows the SAP S/4HANA sales and distribution sales order line-item IDs: **10**, **20**, **30**, and so on.
- **Performance Obligation**
  This field shows the unique POB number for each item ID. For every sales order line item in sales and distribution, there is a POB in RAR.
- **Standalone Selling Price (Total)**
  This field value is mapped from the ZSSP condition type from the sales order line item, as shown previously in Figure 6.67 and Figure 6.68.
- **Invoiced Amount**
  This field shows **0** because we haven't done invoicing in sales and distribution yet.
- **Allocated Amount**
  This field shows the allocated amount after applying IFRS 15 standard principles. Because there is only one license line that is event based and revenue on that will be recognized when the event is triggered, the allocation amount on the license line equals the transaction amount, which equals the revenue amount (i.e., USD 1,200 in this use case). For maintenance, the total five-year transaction amount is divided and allocated equally to each year. Therefore, the allocated amount on each of the maintenance lines is USD 120.
- **Recognized Amount**
  This field shows the amount recognized in the current period but not posted yet. Posting will happen when you run the ABC jobs. License line item 10 hasn't been delivered yet, so the **Recognized Amount** column is 0. Line 20, which is the current maintenance line, will recognize the amount of 10.87 when you run ABC jobs on this contract.
- **Allocation Effect**
  This field show the calculated allocation effect number based on escalation and flatlining as explained earlier in the section. At a high level, the formula to calculate allocation effect is *Allocation effect = Allocation amount – Transaction price.*
- **Start Date** and **End Date**
  These fields (not shown) represent the contract start and contract end date from the sales order line item.

The next step is to look at the revenue schedule for the License POB and Maintenance POB to make sure everything is okay. To do so, select the **License** or the **Maintenance** POB, and then click the **Revenue Schedule** button from the ribbon above the **Contract Information** section, as shown in Figure 6.74.

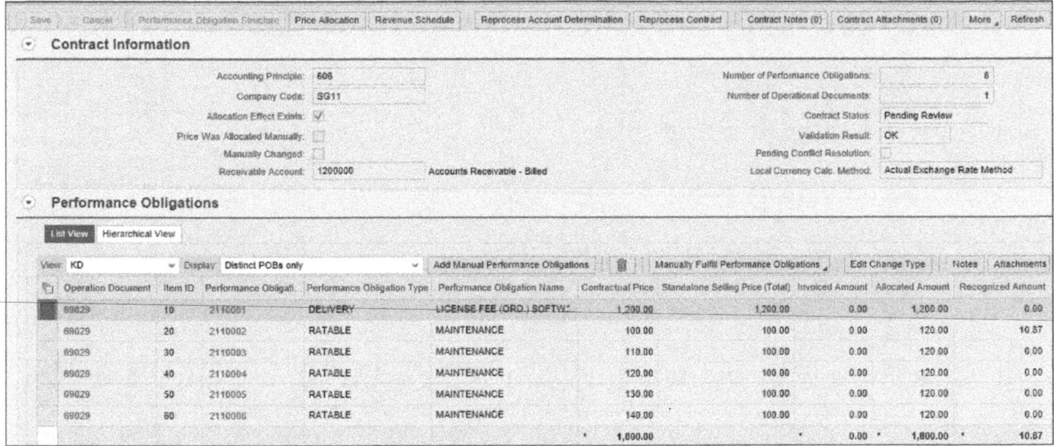

Figure 6.74 Transaction NWBC: Revenue Schedule Button

You'll arrive at the screen shown in Figure 6.75, which represents the License revenue schedule. Note that this is how the schedule looks before delivery is processed in SAP S/4HANA sales and distribution and before ABC jobs are run on the contract. Things will change once delivery and ABC is done, and we'll look at that later in the section.

Revenue Schedule

Summary

Recognized Revenue: 0.00 USD
Posted Revenue: 0.00 USD
Planned Revenue: 0.00 USD
Unscheduled Revenue: 1,200.00 USD
Total Revenue: 1,200.00 USD
Fulfilled Progress: 0 %

Recognized Cost: 0.00
Posted Cost: 0.00
Planned Cost: 0.00
Unscheduled Cost: 0.00
Total Cost: 0.00

View: KD | Display Fulfillment Details | Display Fulfil. Details for Non-Distinct Perf. Oblig. | Manually Fulfill Performance Obligations | Change Spreading | Notes | Attachments

Status	Performance O...	Accounting Period	Performance Obliga...	Allocated Amount	Effective Quantity	Quantity	Fulfillment Progr...	Cumulative Fulfillm...	Revenue	Unsuspended R...	Posted Revenue	Posting Price	Invoiced Amount
	2110001	2113005	LICENSE FEE (ORD...	1,200.00	1	0	0.00	0.00	0.00	0.00	0.00	0.00	0.00
△	2110001	Unscheduled	LICENSE FEE (ORD...	1,200.00	1	1	1.00	1.00	1,200.00	0.00	0.00	0.00	0.00
									• 1,200.00		0.00	•	0.00

Figure 6.75 Transaction NWBC: License Revenue Schedule before Delivery and ABC

Figure 6.76 represents the Maintenance revenue schedule for line item 10. For the most part, this will remain the same after ABC too, just that the gray light will change to a green light, indicating the scheduled revenue of 10.87 has been posted to RAR and general ledger tables.

Everything looks okay on the revenue schedule, so let's remove the revenue block on the license line and deliver it in sales and distribution. You'll also remove the header billing block and run billing on the maintenance and license lines. You can execute Transaction VL02N to run the delivery and Transaction VF04 to run billing.

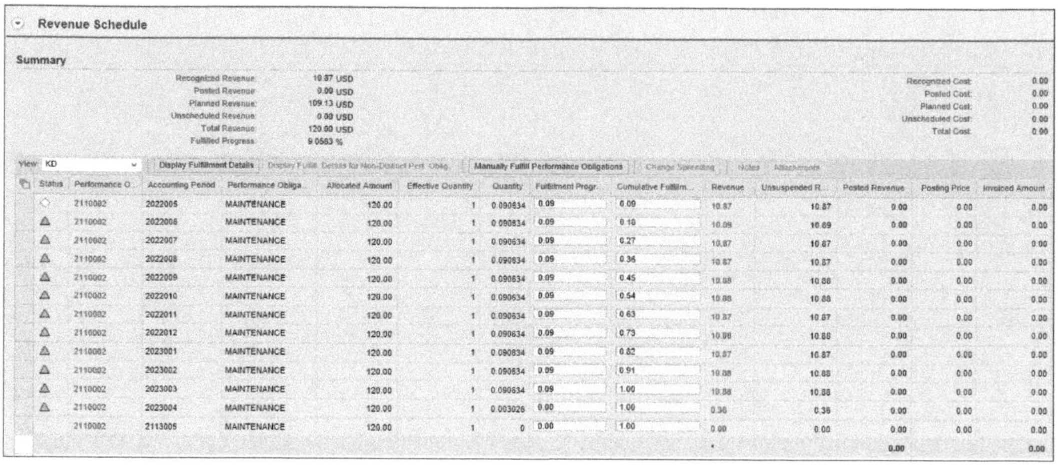

Revenue Schedule

Summary

Recognized Revenue:	10.87 USD	Recognized Cost:	0.00
Posted Revenue:	0.00 USD	Posted Cost:	0.00
Planned Revenue:	109.13 USD	Planned Cost:	0.00
Unscheduled Revenue:	0.00 USD	Unscheduled Cost:	0.00
Total Revenue:	120.00 USD	Total Cost:	0.00
Fulfilled Progress:	9.0583 %		

View: KD | Display Fulfillment Details | Display Fulfill. Details for Non-Distinct Perf. Oblig. | Manually Fulfill Performance Obligations | Change Spreading | Notes | Attachments

Status	Performance O...	Accounting Period	Performance Obliga...	Allocated Amount	Effective Quantity	Quantity	Fulfillment Progr.	Cumulative Fulfillm...	Revenue	Unsuspended R...	Posted Revenue	Posting Price	Invoiced Amount
◇	2110002	2022005	MAINTENANCE	120.00	1	0.090834	0.09	0.09	10.87	10.87	0.00	0.00	0.00
△	2110002	2022006	MAINTENANCE	120.00	1	0.090834	0.09	0.18	10.88	10.88	0.00	0.00	0.00
△	2110002	2022007	MAINTENANCE	120.00	1	0.090834	0.09	0.27	10.87	10.87	0.00	0.00	0.00
△	2110002	2022008	MAINTENANCE	120.00	1	0.090834	0.09	0.36	10.87	10.87	0.00	0.00	0.00
△	2110002	2022009	MAINTENANCE	120.00	1	0.090834	0.09	0.45	10.88	10.88	0.00	0.00	0.00
△	2110002	2022010	MAINTENANCE	120.00	1	0.090834	0.09	0.54	10.88	10.88	0.00	0.00	0.00
△	2110002	2022011	MAINTENANCE	120.00	1	0.090834	0.09	0.63	10.87	10.87	0.00	0.00	0.00
△	2110002	2022012	MAINTENANCE	120.00	1	0.090834	0.09	0.73	10.88	10.88	0.00	0.00	0.00
△	2110002	2023001	MAINTENANCE	120.00	1	0.090834	0.09	0.82	10.87	10.87	0.00	0.00	0.00
△	2110002	2023002	MAINTENANCE	120.00	1	0.090834	0.09	0.91	10.88	10.88	0.00	0.00	0.00
△	2110002	2023003	MAINTENANCE	120.00	1	0.090834	0.09	1.00	10.88	10.88	0.00	0.00	0.00
△	2110002	2023004	MAINTENANCE	120.00	1	0.003026	0.00	1.00	0.36	0.36	0.00	0.00	0.00
	2110002	2113005	MAINTENANCE	120.00	1	0	0.00	1.00	0.00	0.00	0.00	0.00	0.00
									•		0.00		0.00

Figure 6.76 Transaction NWBC: Maintenance Revenue Schedule before ABC

Figure 6.77 shows how the order, fulfillment, and invoice RAIs look after all four transactions are performed.

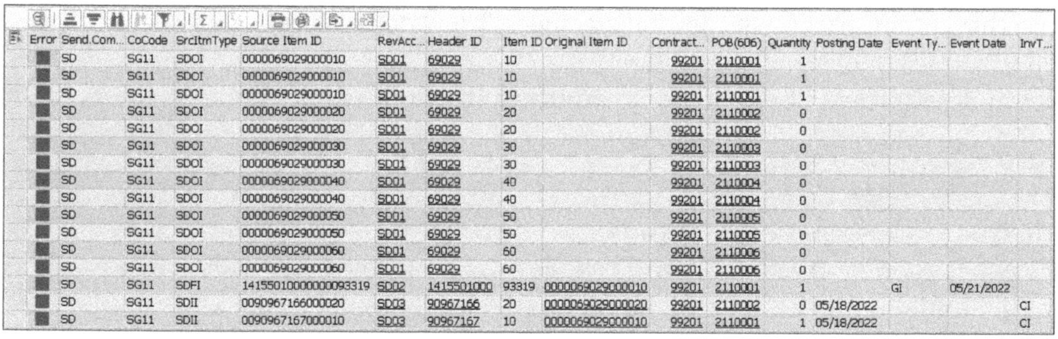

Error	Send.Com...	CoCode	SrcItmType	Source Item ID	RevAcc...	Header ID	Item ID	Original Item ID	Contract...	POB(606)	Quantity	Posting Date	Event Ty...	Event Date	InvT...
■	SD	SG11	SDOI	0000069029000010	SD01	69029	10		99201	2110001	1				
■	SD	SG11	SDOI	0000069029000010	SD01	69029	10		99201	2110001	1				
■	SD	SG11	SDOI	0000069029000010	SD01	69029	10		99201	2110001	1				
■	SD	SG11	SDOI	0000069029000020	SD01	69029	20		99201	2110002	0				
■	SD	SG11	SDOI	0000069029000020	SD01	69029	20		99201	2110002	0				
■	SD	SG11	SDOI	0000069029000030	SD01	69029	30		99201	2110003	0				
■	SD	SG11	SDOI	0000069029000030	SD01	69029	30		99201	2110003	0				
■	SD	SG11	SDOI	0000069029000040	SD01	69029	40		99201	2110004	0				
■	SD	SG11	SDOI	0000069029000040	SD01	69029	40		99201	2110004	0				
■	SD	SG11	SDOI	0000069029000050	SD01	69029	50		99201	2110005	0				
■	SD	SG11	SDOI	0000069029000050	SD01	69029	50		99201	2110005	0				
■	SD	SG11	SDOI	0000069029000060	SD01	69029	60		99201	2110006	0				
■	SD	SG11	SDOI	0000069029000060	SD01	69029	60		99201	2110006	0				
■	SD	SG11	SDFI	14155010000000093319	SD02	1415501000	93319	0000069029000010	99201	2110001	1		GI	05/21/2022	
■	SD	SG11	SDII	0090967166000020	SD03	90967166	20	0000069029000020	99201	2110002	0	05/18/2022			CI
■	SD	SG11	SDII	0090967167000010	SD03	90967167	10	0000069029000010	99201	2110001	1	05/18/2022			CI

Figure 6.77 RAIs after Delivery and Billing

There are a few important things to note on this screen:

- There are two sets of **SDOIs** (order RAIs) for all line items. This is because we removed the billing block in one transaction and adjusted the bill plans in another transaction. For line 10, we also removed the revenue block in a separate third transaction, which is why it has three SDOIs, one for each change transaction made.
- For **SDFI** (fulfillment RAI), **Event Ty...** and **Event Date** fields are populated. Event type **GI** is for goods issue, and event date **05/21/2022** is the PGI date.
- For **SDIIs** (invoice RAIs), the **Posting Date** field is populated, which maps to the bill plan date in sales and distribution. You'll also see **InvT** (invoice type) populated as **CI**, which stands for customer invoice. For the example client, you bill license and invoice separately, and that is why you see two separate invoices and invoice RAIs.

Next, you'll send these RAIs over to RAR and see what their impact is in the contract view and revenue schedule. To process the RAIs, either select all RAIs from the RAI monitor screen or choose the specific ones you want to process, and then click on the **Process** button (refer to Figure 6.71).

Tip

Always process RAIs in the same order as the underlying transactions were performed in the source sales and distribution system. In this example, you first processed the removal of block RAIs, then the delivery RAIs, then the bill plan adjustment RAIs, and finally the invoice RAIs. If the RAIs are processed out of order, they might have an unwanted impact in RAR, which could lead to errors or miscalculated numbers. For example, if you processed the invoice and delivery RAIs before the block removal RAIs, they would fail with the error stating the source line item is blocked for billing or revenue.

Figure 6.78 shows the updated contract view. When compared to Figure 6.73, Figure 6.78 shows the following updated fields:

- **Invoiced Amount**
  This field now shows a value for both License (line 10) and Maintenance (line 20).
- **Recognized Amount**
  This field now shows a value of 1,200 on the License line, as the event for revenue recognition (delivery) has happened in sales and distribution. The 1,200 will be posted to RAR and general ledger tables only when you run ABC jobs.
- **Completion Date**
  This field (not shown) represents the date when the POB is fully completed in RAR. Because the License line is fully delivered and invoiced, RAR marks this POB as complete, and because the latest transaction to complete the POB was performed on 05/21/2022, RAR flags this date as the completion date.

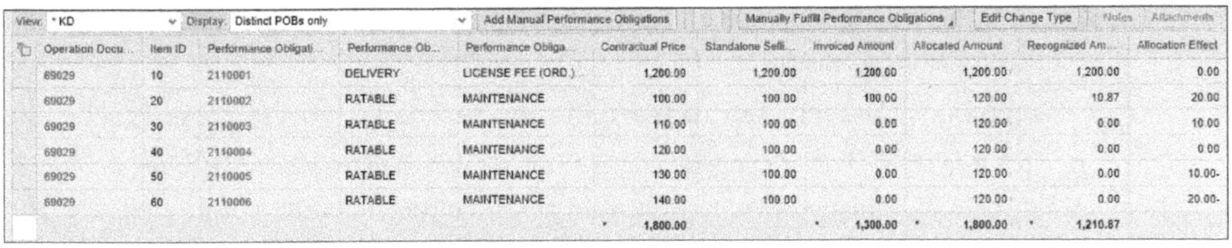

View: * KD | Display: Distinct POBs only | Add Manual Performance Obligations | Manually Fulfill Performance Obligations | Edit Change Type | Notes | Attachments

Operation Docu...	Item ID	Performance Obligati...	Performance Ob...	Performance Obliga...	Contractual Price	Standalone Selli...	Invoiced Amount	Allocated Amount	Recognized Am...	Allocation Effect
69029	10	2110001	DELIVERY	LICENSE FEE (ORD.)	1,200.00	1,200.00	1,200.00	1,200.00	1,200.00	0.00
69029	20	2110002	RATABLE	MAINTENANCE	100.00	100.00	100.00	120.00	10.87	20.00
69029	30	2110003	RATABLE	MAINTENANCE	110.00	100.00	0.00	120.00	0.00	10.00
69029	40	2110004	RATABLE	MAINTENANCE	120.00	100.00	0.00	120.00	0.00	0.00
69029	50	2110005	RATABLE	MAINTENANCE	130.00	100.00	0.00	120.00	0.00	10.00-
69029	60	2110006	RATABLE	MAINTENANCE	140.00	100.00	0.00	120.00	0.00	20.00-
					• 1,800.00		• 1,300.00	• 1,800.00	• 1,210.87	

Figure 6.78 Contract View after Processing RAIs

Figure 6.79 shows the updated revenue schedule for the License line. Take special note of the following fields in Figure 6.79, which have been updated because of the RAIs you just sent over to RAR:

- **Unsuspended R...**
  This field represents the revenue amount that is unblocked and ready to be recognized. Because we unblocked the license line and delivered it in sales and distribution, this field shows the value of 1,200.
- **Invoiced Amount**
  This field represents the invoiced amount value for a revenue schedule line. Because the License line has been fully billed, the invoiced amount shows as the full 1,200.

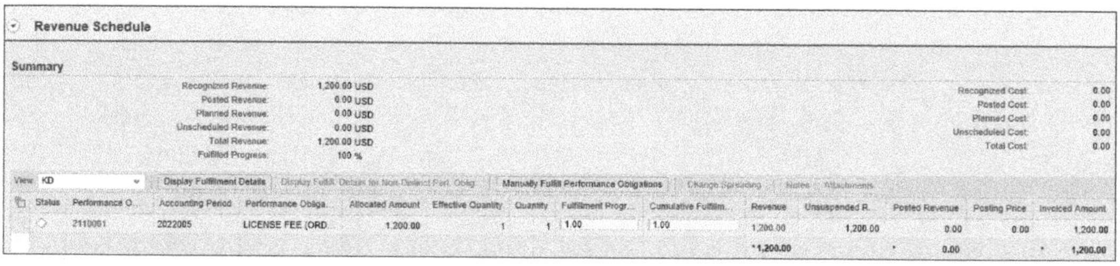

Figure 6.79 Transaction NWBC: License Revenue Schedule after Delivery

- **Status**
  This field represents the status of revenue for a revenue schedule line. By default, SAP S/4HANA provides five colored revenue status lights:
  - No light: Revenue schedule lines are for billing plan items only and have no revenue impact on the POB.
  - Orange light: Revenue schedule lines are a result of the initial data load from the legacy system.
  - Gray light: Revenue has been recognized but not yet posted for the revenue schedule lines.
  - Yellow light: Revenue for those revenue schedule lines is scheduled to be recognized in the future (either waiting for an event to happen or a period to be current).
  - Red light: ABC jobs were run for those revenue schedules lines, but the posting failed for some reason.
  - Green light: ABC jobs ran successfully, and revenue for those revenue schedule lines was posted to RAR and general ledger tables without any errors.

  In Figure 6.75, which previously showed the revenue schedule before delivery and unblock RAIs, you'll see there are two revenue schedule lines: one line with blank revenue status and one line with a yellow light as the revenue status. Compare it to Figure 6.79, which is for the revenue schedule after change RAIs are sent to RAR, and you'll see the revenue schedule only has one line with the gray light as revenue status.

  After the License line is delivered in sales and distribution, and the RAIs are sent to RAR, revenue is recognized in RAR but not posted, which is why you see a gray light in the revenue schedule.

Figure 6.80 shows the updated revenue schedule for the Maintenance line.

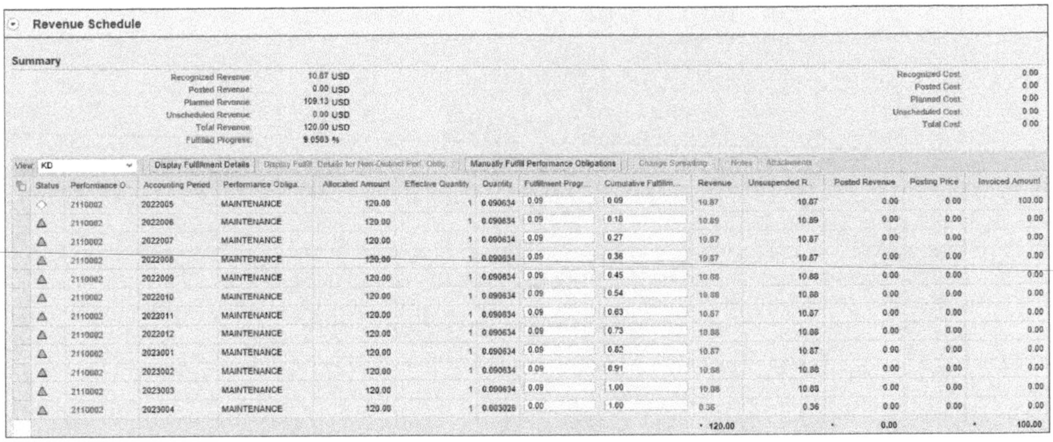

Revenue Schedule

Summary

Recognized Revenue: 10.87 USD
Posted Revenue: 0.00 USD
Planned Revenue: 109.13 USD
Unscheduled Revenue: 0.00 USD
Total Revenue: 120.00 USD
Fulfilled Progress: 9.0583 %

Recognized Cost: 0.00
Posted Cost: 0.00
Planned Cost: 0.00
Unscheduled Cost: 0.00
Total Cost: 0.00

View: KD | Display Fulfillment Details | Display Fulfill. Details for Non-Distinct Perf. Oblig. | Manually Fulfill Performance Obligations | Change Spreading | Notes | Attachments

Status	Performance O...	Accounting Period	Performance Obliga...	Allocated Amount	Effective Quantity	Quantity	Fulfillment Progr...	Cumulative Fulfillm...	Revenue	Unsuspended R...	Posted Revenue	Posting Price	Invoiced Amount
◇	2110002	2022005	MAINTENANCE	120.00	1	0.090634	0.09	0.09	10.87	10.87	0.00	0.00	100.00
△	2110002	2022006	MAINTENANCE	120.00	1	0.090634	0.09	0.18	10.89	10.89	0.00	0.00	0.00
△	2110002	2022007	MAINTENANCE	120.00	1	0.090634	0.09	0.27	10.87	10.87	0.00	0.00	0.00
△	2110002	2022008	MAINTENANCE	120.00	1	0.090634	0.09	0.36	10.87	10.87	0.00	0.00	0.00
△	2110002	2022009	MAINTENANCE	120.00	1	0.090634	0.09	0.45	10.88	10.88	0.00	0.00	0.00
△	2110002	2022010	MAINTENANCE	120.00	1	0.090634	0.09	0.54	10.88	10.88	0.00	0.00	0.00
△	2110002	2022011	MAINTENANCE	120.00	1	0.090634	0.09	0.63	10.87	10.87	0.00	0.00	0.00
△	2110002	2022012	MAINTENANCE	120.00	1	0.090634	0.09	0.73	10.88	10.88	0.00	0.00	0.00
△	2110002	2023001	MAINTENANCE	120.00	1	0.090634	0.09	0.82	10.87	10.87	0.00	0.00	0.00
△	2110002	2023002	MAINTENANCE	120.00	1	0.090634	0.09	0.91	10.88	10.88	0.00	0.00	0.00
△	2110002	2023003	MAINTENANCE	120.00	1	0.090634	0.09	1.00	10.88	10.88	0.00	0.00	0.00
△	2110002	2023004	MAINTENANCE	120.00	1	0.003026	0.00	1.00	0.36	0.36	0.00	0.00	0.00
									• 120.00		• 0.00		• 100.00

Figure 6.80 Transaction NWBC: Maintenance Revenue Schedule after Invoicing

Only one field got updated in the maintenance revenue schedule, which is for the invoiced amount of the first revenue schedule line. Everything else remains the same when compared to the revenue schedule before RAIs (refer to Figure 6.76).

Next, we'll run ABC jobs on this contract and then look at the revenue schedule and RAR tables to validate revenue postings. Let's use SAP transactions to run ABC jobs so you can get a flavor of those programs from SAP GUI too.

Start with the A job (Transfer Revenue) by executing Transaction FARR_REV_TRANSFER. You'll arrive at the screen shown in Figure 6.81, where you enter the **Company Code**, **Accounting Principle**, **Fiscal Year**, **Posting Period**, and **Contract** number of the RAR contract you want to run ABC jobs for.

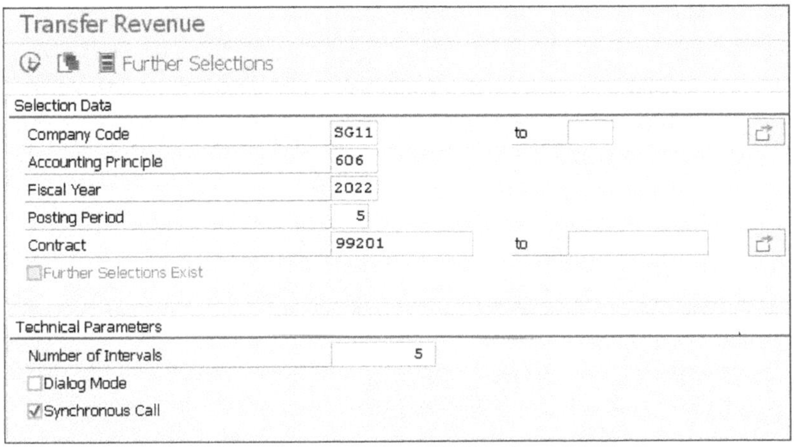

Transfer Revenue

Further Selections

Selection Data

Company Code	SG11	to	
Accounting Principle	606		
Fiscal Year	2022		
Posting Period	5		
Contract	99201	to	

☐ Further Selections Exist

Technical Parameters

Number of Intervals	5

☐ Dialog Mode
☑ Synchronous Call

Figure 6.81 Transfer Revenue Job

Click the **Execute** icon to see the job logs shown in Figure 6.82.

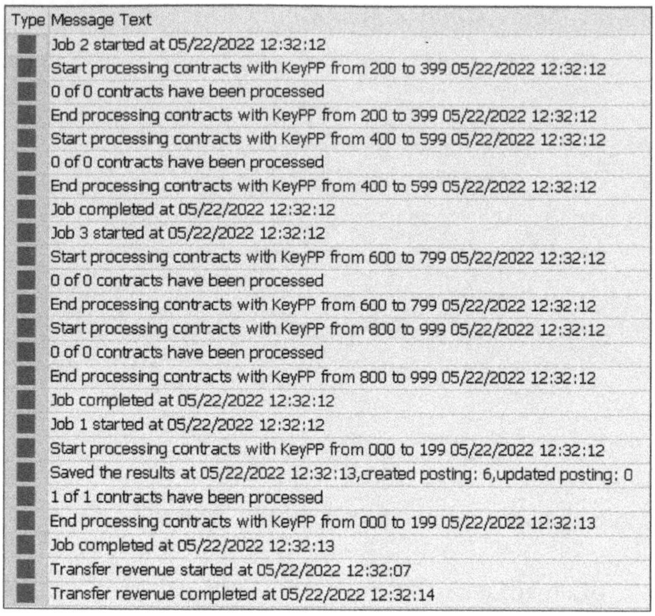

Type	Message Text
■	Job 2 started at 05/22/2022 12:32:12
■	Start processing contracts with KeyPP from 200 to 399 05/22/2022 12:32:12
■	0 of 0 contracts have been processed
■	End processing contracts with KeyPP from 200 to 399 05/22/2022 12:32:12
■	Start processing contracts with KeyPP from 400 to 599 05/22/2022 12:32:12
■	0 of 0 contracts have been processed
■	End processing contracts with KeyPP from 400 to 599 05/22/2022 12:32:12
■	Job completed at 05/22/2022 12:32:12
■	Job 3 started at 05/22/2022 12:32:12
■	Start processing contracts with KeyPP from 600 to 799 05/22/2022 12:32:12
■	0 of 0 contracts have been processed
■	End processing contracts with KeyPP from 600 to 799 05/22/2022 12:32:12
■	Start processing contracts with KeyPP from 800 to 999 05/22/2022 12:32:12
■	0 of 0 contracts have been processed
■	End processing contracts with KeyPP from 800 to 999 05/22/2022 12:32:12
■	Job completed at 05/22/2022 12:32:12
■	Job 1 started at 05/22/2022 12:32:12
■	Start processing contracts with KeyPP from 000 to 199 05/22/2022 12:32:12
■	Saved the results at 05/22/2022 12:32:13,created posting: 6,updated posting: 0
■	1 of 1 contracts have been processed
■	End processing contracts with KeyPP from 000 to 199 05/22/2022 12:32:13
■	Job completed at 05/22/2022 12:32:13
■	Transfer revenue started at 05/22/2022 12:32:07
■	Transfer revenue completed at 05/22/2022 12:32:14

Figure 6.82 Transfer Revenue Job Logs

Figure 6.82 shows the A job ran successfully!

Next, let's run the B job (Calculate Contract Assets and Liabilities) by executing Transaction FARR_LIABILITY_CALC. You'll arrive at the screen shown in Figure 6.83, where you'll enter the same details in the selection as the A job. Click the **Execute** icon to see the jobs log in Figure 6.84.

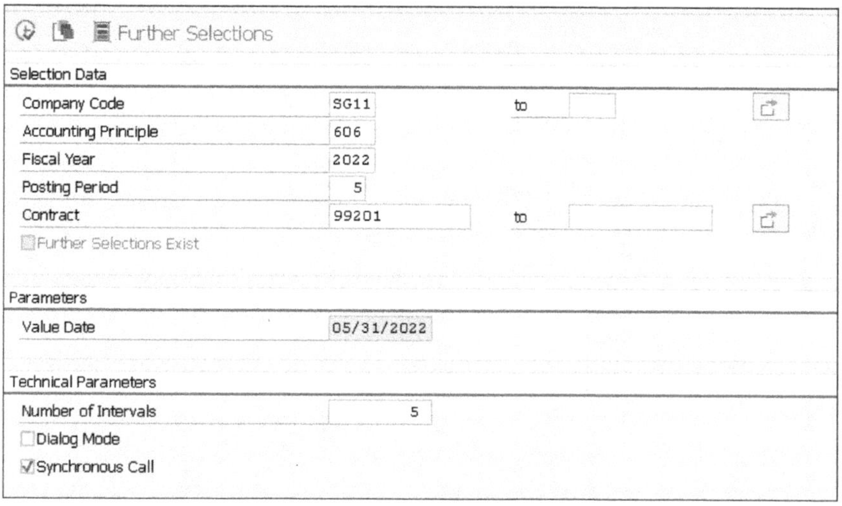

Further Selections

Selection Data

Company Code	SG11	to	
Accounting Principle	606		
Fiscal Year	2022		
Posting Period	5		
Contract	99201	to	

☐ Further Selections Exist

Parameters

Value Date	05/31/2022

Technical Parameters

Number of Intervals	5

☐ Dialog Mode

☑ Synchronous Call

Figure 6.83 Calculate Contract Assets and Liabilities Job

Figure 6.84 show the B job also ran successfully!

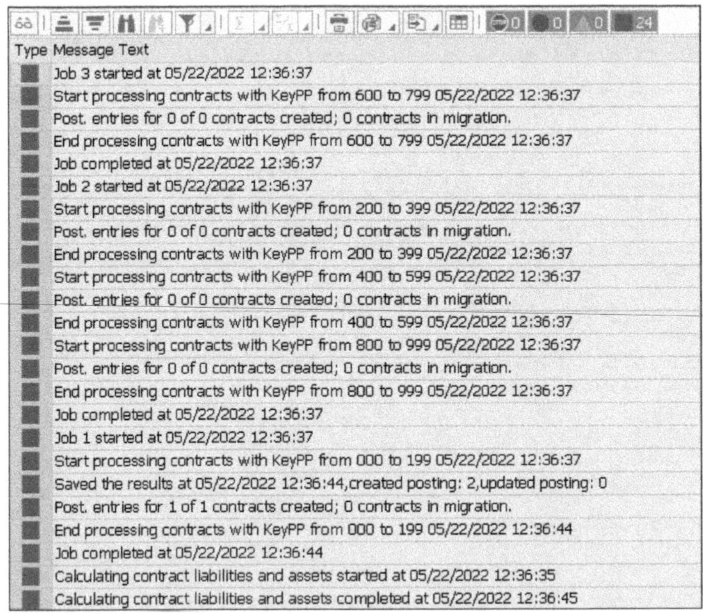

Type	Message Text
	Job 3 started at 05/22/2022 12:36:37
	Start processing contracts with KeyPP from 600 to 799 05/22/2022 12:36:37
	Post. entries for 0 of 0 contracts created; 0 contracts in migration.
	End processing contracts with KeyPP from 600 to 799 05/22/2022 12:36:37
	Job completed at 05/22/2022 12:36:37
	Job 2 started at 05/22/2022 12:36:37
	Start processing contracts with KeyPP from 200 to 399 05/22/2022 12:36:37
	Post. entries for 0 of 0 contracts created; 0 contracts in migration.
	End processing contracts with KeyPP from 200 to 399 05/22/2022 12:36:37
	Start processing contracts with KeyPP from 400 to 599 05/22/2022 12:36:37
	Post. entries for 0 of 0 contracts created; 0 contracts in migration.
	End processing contracts with KeyPP from 400 to 599 05/22/2022 12:36:37
	Start processing contracts with KeyPP from 800 to 999 05/22/2022 12:36:37
	Post. entries for 0 of 0 contracts created; 0 contracts in migration.
	End processing contracts with KeyPP from 800 to 999 05/22/2022 12:36:37
	Job completed at 05/22/2022 12:36:37
	Job 1 started at 05/22/2022 12:36:37
	Start processing contracts with KeyPP from 000 to 199 05/22/2022 12:36:37
	Saved the results at 05/22/2022 12:36:44,created posting: 2,updated posting: 0
	Post. entries for 1 of 1 contracts created; 0 contracts in migration.
	End processing contracts with KeyPP from 000 to 199 05/22/2022 12:36:44
	Job completed at 05/22/2022 12:36:44
	Calculating contract liabilities and assets started at 05/22/2022 12:36:35
	Calculating contract liabilities and assets completed at 05/22/2022 12:36:45

Figure 6.84 Calculate Contract Assets and Liabilities Job Logs

For the C job (Revenue Posting Run), you first run it in test mode to make sure everything is correct and then run it in posting mode. Let's start by executing Transaction FARR_REV_POST to arrive at the screen shown in Figure 6.85, where you'll enter again the same selection as the A and B jobs, and select the **Posting Date** as the current date and **Run Mode** as **Posting**. Click the **Execute** icon once more to view the job logs shown in Figure 6.86.

Revenue Posting Run

Further Selections

Selection Data

Company Code	SG11	to	
Accounting Principle	606		
Fiscal Year	2022		
Posting Period	5		
Contract	99201	to	

☐ Further Selections Exist

Parameters

Posting Date	05/22/2022
Run Mode	Test Only

☐ Close Period for Rev

☐ Posting Check

☐ Switch Off Parallel Posting

Technical Parameters

Number of Intervals	5

☐ Dialog Mode

Figure 6.85 Revenue Posting Run Job Test Mode

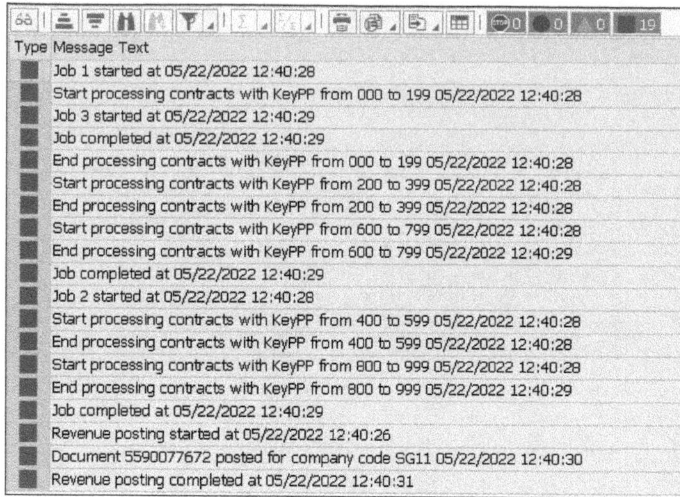

Figure 6.86 Revenue Posting Run Job Logs

Figure 6.85 and Figure 6.86 show that the C job also ran successfully, and document **5590077672** is posted to the general ledger. To view this accounting document, go to Transaction FB03 (see Figure 6.87).

Data Entry View

Document Number	5590077672	Company Code	SG11	Fiscal Year	2022
Document Date	05/22/2022	Posting Date	05/22/2022	Period	5
Reference		Cross-Comp.No.			
Currency	USD	Texts exist		Ledger Group	

CoCd	Item	Key	Account	Description	Cost Center	Profit Center	Σ	Amount	Currency
SG11	2	50	1200399A	FI Receivable Adjust		CS		100.00-	USD
SG11	3	50		FI Receivable Adjust		SOL SALES		1,200.00-	USD
SG11	7	40		FI Receivable Adjust		CS		1.81	USD
SG11	8	40		FI Receivable Adjust		CS		9.06	USD
SG11	9	40		FI Receivable Adjust		CS		89.13	USD
SG11	10	40		FI Receivable Adjust		SOL SALES		1,200.00	USD
			1200399A				•	**0.00**	**USD**
SG11	1	50	2190001A	Deferred Revenue - M		CS		89.13-	USD
			2190001A				•	**89.13-**	**USD**
SG11	5	50	4100000A	Software Maintenance		CS		1.81-	USD
SG11	6	50		Software Maintenance		CS		9.06-	USD
SG11	12	40		Software Maintenance		CS		100.00	USD
			4100000A				•	**89.13**	**USD**
SG11	4	50	4200000A	License Fee Revenue		SOL SALES		1,200.00-	USD
SG11	11	40		License Fee Revenue		SOL SALES		1,200.00	USD
			4200000A				•	**0.00**	**USD**

Figure 6.87 Accounting Document in the General Ledger

In this example, the **FI Receivable Adjust** account has net to 0, which is expected because the receivable adjustment is a temporary general ledger account where values are stored momentarily as you run through ABC jobs. The **Deferred Revenue – M** general ledger account has USD -89.13, which is also correct because when you ran ABC on the contract, revenue moved from the deferred general ledger to the **Software Maintenance** revenue general ledger account, which has the equivalent positive USD 89.13. Finally, the **License Fee Revenue** general ledger account also has the correct USD 1,200 as well.

Let's go back and look at how the revenue schedule has changed because of ABC jobs. Figure 6.88 shows the updated revenue schedule for the License line. The following three key fields have changed:

- **Status**
  The revenue status of the revenue schedule line changed from gray light to green light indicating revenue posting is successfully completed.
- **Posted Revenue**
  The **Posted Revenue** field now shows the value of 1,200 versus 0 (which it was showing before the ABC jobs).
- **Posting Price**
  The **Posted Price** field also shows the value of 1,200 versus 0 (which it was showing before the ABC jobs).

Recognized Revenue:	1,200.00 USD	Recognized Cost:	0.00
Posted Revenue:	1,200.00 USD	Posted Cost:	0.00
Planned Revenue:	0.00 USD	Planned Cost:	0.00
Unscheduled Revenue:	0.00 USD	Unscheduled Cost:	0.00
Total Revenue:	1,200.00 USD	Total Cost:	0.00
Fulfilled Progress:	100 %		

KD | Display Fulfillment Details | Display Fulfill. Details for Non-Distinct Perf. Oblig. | Manually Fulfill Performance Obligations | Change Spreading | Notes | Pri

Status	Perform...	Accounting...	Performan...	Allocate...	Effective Q...	Quantity	Fulfillme...	Cumulativ...	Revenue	Unsusp...	Posted Re...	Posting Price
■	2110001	2022005	LICENSE F...	1,200.00	1	1	1.00	1.00	1,200.00	1,200.00	1,200.00	1,200.00

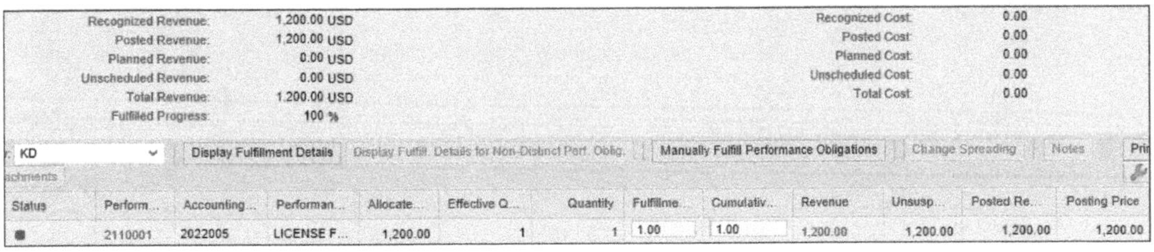

Figure 6.88 License Revenue Schedule after ABC Jobs

Figure 6.89 shows the updated revenue schedule for the Maintenance line. The same three fields have changed here too: **Status, Posted Revenue**, and **Posting Price**.

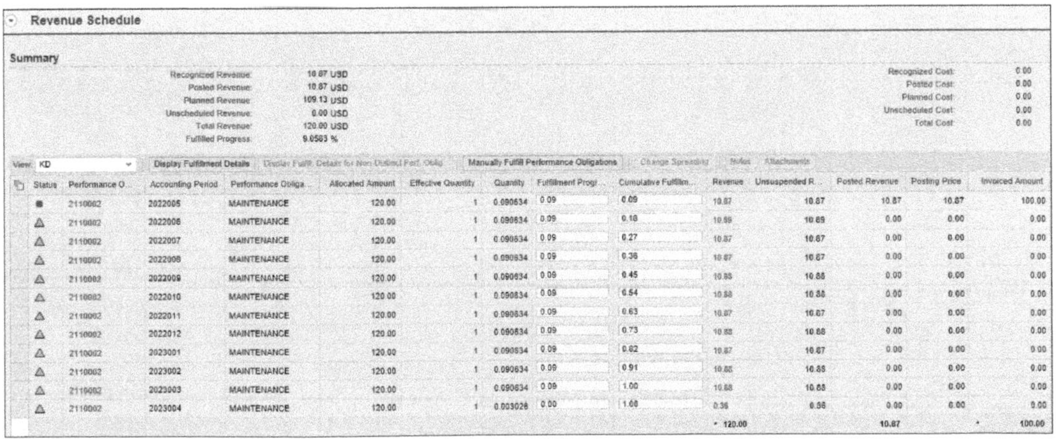

Revenue Schedule

Summary

Recognized Revenue:	10.87 USD	Recognized Cost:	0.00
Posted Revenue:	10.87 USD	Posted Cost:	0.00
Planned Revenue:	109.13 USD	Planned Cost:	0.00
Unscheduled Revenue:	0.00 USD	Unscheduled Cost:	0.00
Total Revenue:	120.00 USD	Total Cost:	0.00
Fulfilled Progress:	9.0583 %		

View: KD | Display Fulfillment Details | Display Fulfill. Details for Non-Distinct Perf. Oblig. | Manually Fulfill Performance Obligations | Change Spreading | Notes | Attachments

Status	Performance O...	Accounting Period	Performance Obliga...	Allocated Amount	Effective Quantity	Quantity	Fulfillment Progr...	Cumulative Fulfillm...	Revenue	Unsuspended R...	Posted Revenue	Posting Price	Invoiced Amount
■	2110002	2022005	MAINTENANCE	120.00	1	0.090634	0.09	0.09	10.87	10.87	10.87	10.87	100.00
△	2110002	2022006	MAINTENANCE	120.00	1	0.090634	0.09	0.18	10.89	10.89	0.00	0.00	0.00
△	2110002	2022007	MAINTENANCE	120.00	1	0.090634	0.09	0.27	10.87	10.87	0.00	0.00	0.00
△	2110002	2022008	MAINTENANCE	120.00	1	0.090634	0.09	0.36	10.87	10.87	0.00	0.00	0.00
△	2110002	2022009	MAINTENANCE	120.00	1	0.090634	0.09	0.45	10.88	10.88	0.00	0.00	0.00
△	2110002	2022010	MAINTENANCE	120.00	1	0.090634	0.09	0.54	10.88	10.88	0.00	0.00	0.00
△	2110002	2022011	MAINTENANCE	120.00	1	0.090634	0.09	0.63	10.87	10.87	0.00	0.00	0.00
△	2110002	2022012	MAINTENANCE	120.00	1	0.090634	0.09	0.73	10.88	10.88	0.00	0.00	0.00
△	2110002	2023001	MAINTENANCE	120.00	1	0.090634	0.09	0.82	10.87	10.87	0.00	0.00	0.00
△	2110002	2023002	MAINTENANCE	120.00	1	0.090634	0.09	0.91	10.88	10.88	0.00	0.00	0.00
△	2110002	2023003	MAINTENANCE	120.00	1	0.090634	0.09	1.00	10.88	10.88	0.00	0.00	0.00
△	2110002	2023004	MAINTENANCE	120.00	1	0.003026	0.00	1.00	0.36	0.36	0.00	0.00	0.00
									• 120.00		10.87	•	100.00

Figure 6.89 Maintenance Revenue Schedule after ABC Jobs

As a final step, we'll look at this contract in the revenue table. To do so, go to Transaction SE16N, and enter the table name "FARR_D_POSTING" (see Figure 6.90). Enter the **Company Code**, **Accounting Principle**, **Fiscal Year**, **Posting Period**, and **Contract** number we ran through the RAR cycle, and click **Execute**.

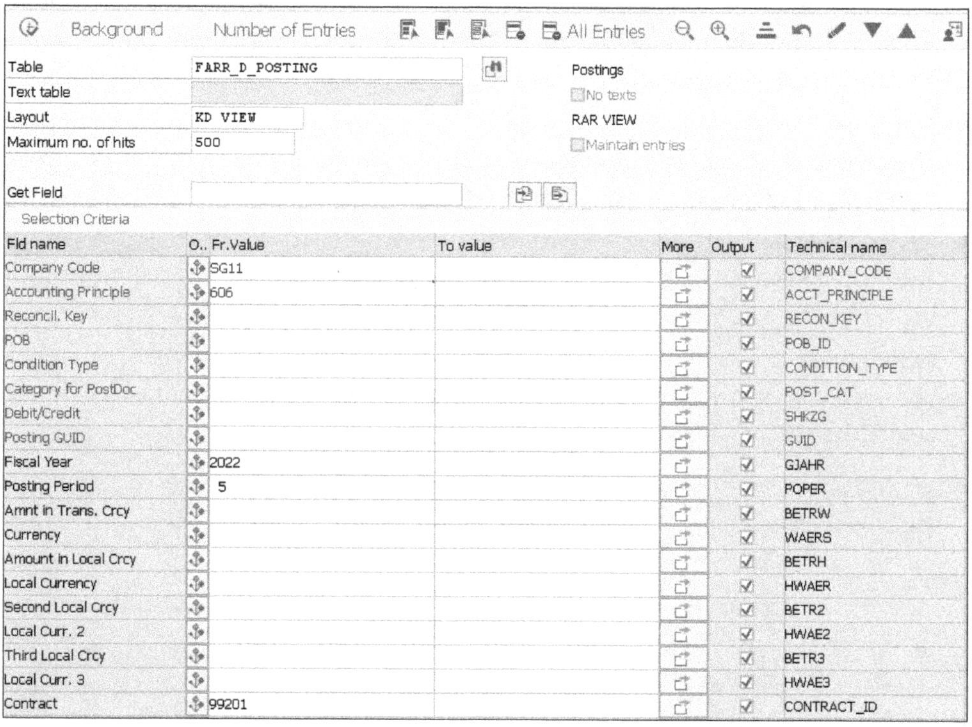

Background   Number of Entries   All Entries

Table	FARR_D_POSTING	Postings
Text table		No texts
Layout	KD VIEW	RAR VIEW
Maximum no. of hits	500	Maintain entries
Get Field		

Selection Criteria

Fld name	O.. Fr.Value	To value	More	Output	Technical name
Company Code	SG11			☑	COMPANY_CODE
Accounting Principle	606			☑	ACCT_PRINCIPLE
Reconcil. Key				☑	RECON_KEY
POB				☑	POB_ID
Condition Type				☑	CONDITION_TYPE
Category for PostDoc				☑	POST_CAT
Debit/Credit				☑	SHKZG
Posting GUID				☑	GUID
Fiscal Year	2022			☑	GJAHR
Posting Period	5			☑	POPER
Amnt in Trans. Crcy				☑	BETRW
Currency				☑	WAERS
Amount in Local Crcy				☑	BETRH
Local Currency				☑	HWAER
Second Local Crcy				☑	BETR2
Local Curr. 2				☑	HWAE2
Third Local Crcy				☑	BETR3
Local Curr. 3				☑	HWAE3
Contract	99201			☑	CONTRACT_ID

Figure 6.90 Table FARR_D_POSTING Selection

The data shown in Figure 6.91 matches the general ledger shown previously in Figure 6.87, which concludes that the use case is successful and all the configurations performed in this chapter are accurate. Congratulations!

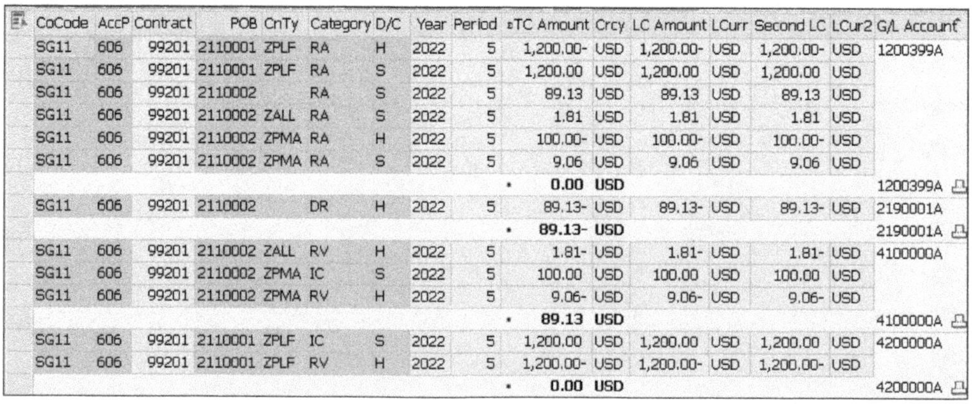

CoCode	AccP	Contract	POB	CnTy	Category	D/C	Year	Period	ΣTC Amount	Crcy	LC Amount	LCurr	Second LC	LCur2	G/L Account
SG11	606	99201	2110001	ZPLF	RA	H	2022	5	1,200.00-	USD	1,200.00-	USD	1,200.00-	USD	1200399A
SG11	606	99201	2110001	ZPLF	RA	S	2022	5	1,200.00	USD	1,200.00	USD	1,200.00	USD	
SG11	606	99201	2110002		RA	S	2022	5	89.13	USD	89.13	USD	89.13	USD	
SG11	606	99201	2110002	ZALL	RA	S	2022	5	1.81	USD	1.81	USD	1.81	USD	
SG11	606	99201	2110002	ZPMA	RA	H	2022	5	100.00-	USD	100.00-	USD	100.00-	USD	
SG11	606	99201	2110002	ZPMA	RA	S	2022	5	9.06	USD	9.06	USD	9.06	USD	
								•	**0.00**	**USD**					1200399A
SG11	606	99201	2110002		DR	H	2022	5	89.13-	USD	89.13-	USD	89.13-	USD	2190001A
								•	**89.13-**	**USD**					2190001A
SG11	606	99201	2110002	ZALL	RV	H	2022	5	1.81-	USD	1.81-	USD	1.81-	USD	4100000A
SG11	606	99201	2110002	ZPMA	IC	S	2022	5	100.00	USD	100.00	USD	100.00	USD	
SG11	606	99201	2110002	ZPMA	RV	H	2022	5	9.06-	USD	9.06-	USD	9.06-	USD	
								•	**89.13**	**USD**					4100000A
SG11	606	99201	2110001	ZPLF	IC	S	2022	5	1,200.00	USD	1,200.00	USD	1,200.00	USD	4200000A
SG11	606	99201	2110001	ZPLF	RV	H	2022	5	1,200.00-	USD	1,200.00-	USD	1,200.00-	USD	
								•	**0.00**	**USD**					4200000A

Figure 6.91 Table FARR_D_POSTING: Successful Use Case

6.3 Optimized Contract Management

OCM was introduced in SAP Revenue Accounting and Reporting with the rollout of SAP S/4HANA 1909. When SAP S/4HANA and SAP Revenue Accounting and Reporting merged in the 1909 version, SAP optimized few features within the RAR functionality to add a different flavor of contract management for their end users. While the core functionality of contract management remains the same, there are few key enhancements in OCM, which we'll look at in this section.

Note

SAP refers to OCM as just *contract management* and refers to the SAP S/4HANA 1809 version of contract management as classic contract management (CCM). In this book, for the ease of understanding, we'll clearly refer to them as OCM and CCM wherever needed. The previous section was based on CCM, and this section is based on OCM.

In this section, we'll look at the following:

- How OCM can be activated in SAP S/4HANA using contract categories
- Changes introduced in OCM and the resulting system impacts
- Benefits of newly introduced changes within OCM
- CCM features that are discontinued in OCM

6.3.1 Activation Using Contract Categories

OCM is an optional feature in the RAR functionality in SAP S/4HANA and can be activated by using contract categories. Activation of OCM is a two-step process:

1. Define the contract category.
2. Select contract management for contract categories.

To define contract categories, follow IMG menu path **Financial Accounting • Revenue Accounting • Revenue Accounting Contracts • Define Contract Categories.** You'll arrive at the screen shown in Figure 6.92.

Customizing of Contract Category

Contr. Cat	Description	No. Range
0001	Optimized Contract Management (OCM)	01

Figure 6.92 OCM Contract Category

As shown in Figure 6.92, the **Customizing of Contract Category** screen has three fields:

- **Contr. Cat**
  This field represents the unique code of the contract category in the RAR functionality in SAP S/4HANA.
- **Description**
  This field describes the contract category in just a few words.
- **No. Range**
  This field represents the number range code associated with a contract category. Number range codes assist with the numbering convention for contract categories.

After filling in the relevant fields, click the **Save** button or press Ctrl+S to finish setting up the contract category.

To select contract management for contract categories, follow IMG menu path **Financial Accounting • Revenue Accounting • Revenue Accounting Contracts • Select Contract Management for Contract Categories**. You'll arrive at the screen shown in Figure 6.93.

Select Contract Management for Contract Categories

CoCd	Company Name	Contr. Cat	Contract Category Description	Contract With CM Instead of CM Classic
1008	Company Code 1710	0001	Optimized Contract Management (OCM)	☑

Figure 6.93 Contract Management for Contract Categories

As shown in Figure 6.93, the **Select Contract Management for Contract Categories** screen has the following fields:

- **CoCd**
  This field represents the company code for which you want to assign a contract category.
- **Company Name**
  This field represents the company name for which you want to assign a contract category.
- **Contr. Cat**
  This field represents the unique code of contract category in the RAR functionality in SAP S/4HANA.
- **Contract Category Description**
  This field describes the contract category in just a few words.

- **Contract With CM Instead of CM Classic**
  This checkbox is checked when you want the system to use OCM instead of CCM for a company code/contract category combination.

After filling in the relevant fields, click the **Save** button or press Ctrl+S to finish setting up contract management for contract categories.

Simple, isn't it? OCM is now ready to be used within your RAR system.

6.3.2 Enhanced Functionality and System Impact

In this section, we'll look at the system impact of OCM enhancements in the RAR functionality in SAP S/4HANA. Table 6.5 lists the key features and objects enhanced in OCM. It also highlights the impact of those enhancements on system behavior and if there are any configurations involved to leverage the enhancements. (Data within Table 6.5 holds true per SAP Note 3075187 version 7, released on 08/04/2022.)

Enhanced Functionality	Enhanced Objects	System Impact	Configuration/ Development
Contract and POBs management	■ POB attributes ■ Leading/linked POBs ■ POB with hierarchies ■ POB with cost	Compound group and BOM functionality possible in OCM	Additional configuration steps needed to support compound groups and BOMs
Account determination	Accounts to support SAP Revenue Accounting and Reporting 1.3 derivation rules	Account redetermination with POB change in CCM; explicit use of the account redetermination functionality required for OCM	No additional configuration or development needed
Allocation	■ SSP determination ■ Exclude from allocation ■ SSP tolerance ■ Residual allocation ■ Manual price allocation	Consistent allocation from leading POBs with linked and nonlinked POBs in OCM	BAdI introduced: ■ FARR_BADI_PRICE_ALLOCATION BAdIs discontinued: ■ FARR_BADI_ALLOCATION_ENGINE ■ FARR_BADI_ALLOCATION_METHOD

Table 6.5 OCM Enhanced Functionality and System Impact

Enhanced Functionality	Enhanced Objects	System Impact	Configuration/ Development
Fulfillment	■ Event-based fulfillment with quantity fulfillment ■ Time-based POB with start date type 1 and 2 ■ Deferral methods 1, 2, S, F and L ■ Value-based fulfillments from customer invoice, release order, or consumption ■ Manual percentage of completion-based fulfillments ■ Freeze/unfreeze for time-based POBs	■ Fractions used to represent fulfillment quantity in CCM, but not in OCM ■ Days used as UoM for period in OCM ■ In OCM, for start date 3, customer invoice only able to be the triggering event, and duration only used as the selection parameter; for date 1 and 2, start and end dates allowed to be specified	BAdI introduced: ■ FARR_BADI_DEFERRAL_METHOD_V2 BAdI discontinued ■ FARR_BADI_DEFERRAL_METHOD
Contract modification	■ Contract modification change type ■ Contract modification change reason ■ Manual contract modification ■ Manual termination ■ POB cancellation	■ Day-based contract management available to be used in OCM ■ Manual POB reassignment possible in OCM ■ Changes tracked in table FARR_D_CHG_TYPE, and changes always period based in OCM ■ 50+ rules available for prospective and retrospective implementation in OCM ■ Catchup revenue calculated together with recognized revenue in OCM	BAdI introduced: ■ FARR_BADI_CHANGE_TYPE_DETN BAdIs discontinued: ■ FARR_CHANGE_MODE_DETERMINATION ■ FARR_BADI_TM_REMAINING_PERC
Cost recognition	■ Fulfillment cost ■ Contract acquisition cost at the contract level	■ Contract acquisition cost at POB level not possible in OCM ■ New posting category accrued cost introduced in OCM	BAdI discontinued: ■ FARR_BADI_COAC_DERIVE_TM_ATTR

Table 6.5 OCM Enhanced Functionality and System Impact (Cont.)

Enhanced Functionality	Enhanced Objects	System Impact	Configuration/ Development
Migration from legacy system	■ Migration from sales and distribution, SAP Billing and Revenue Innovation Management, and third-party system possible in OCM ■ Migration via the SAP S/4HANA migration cockpit possible	■ Transition between accounting principles not possible in OCM ■ Sender components not required to send legacy revenue under OCM ■ Status of company code and transfer date not mandatory for migration under OCM ■ Operational load and initial load combined together in OCM	N/A

Table 6.5 OCM Enhanced Functionality and System Impact (Cont.)

As you can see, there are very few changes in OCM, so the system impact is minimal.

6.3.3 Benefits

In this section, let's look at the perks OCM brings to the table:

- **Performance optimization**
  With OCM, SAP changed data types for contracts and POBs from NUMC to CHAR. This was primarily done for performance optimization and to make handling of temporary IDs easier.
- **Day-based contract modification**
  In CCM, contract modifications are tracked and recorded on a period-by-period basis, whereas in OCM, contract modifications are recorded on a daily or as-incurred basis. This is a great value add for the accounting folks as they can monitor contract modifications daily, such as what changed, what POB types were added, and so on. This is our favorite benefit of OCM.
- **SAP Fiori-based capabilities**
  The following is a list of SAP Fiori functionalities that are added by default to OCM:
  - Contract management
  - POB management
  - Revenue schedule
  - Contract combination using quick combine
  - Revenue accountant overview
  - Revenue disaggregation

The following SAP Fiori apps are exclusively developed in SAP S/4HANA 1909 and are made available with OCM only to support the preceding functionalities: Manual Fulfillment, Revenue Schedule, Manage Revenue Contracts, Overview Page for Revenue Accountant, Disaggregation of Revenue, Quick Combine for Revenue Contracts, and Manage Performance Obligation Details.

- **Parallel use of contract management**
  OCM and CCM can be used in parallel. For example, say you switch to OCM tomorrow and there are open contracts within your RAR system. Those open contracts can continue to use CCM, and any new contracts that get created can use OCM. This feature is possible and comes as a standard functionality in OCM.
- **Advance termination**
  Even though early termination is supported in CCM, it involves a lot of manual steps. OCM comes with standard condition type configuration for early termination, which can be used to automatically execute the advance termination process. This is a great perk of OCM that adds tremendous value.
- **Custom code adoption**
  While this isn't a benefit per se, it's something you should keep in mind if you decide to move to OCM. If you have custom code within your RAR landscape, which most of us do, then that custom code must be adopted to new contracts explicitly if they have had any transactions with CCM.

6.3.4 Limitations

In this section, let's look at CCM features not supported in OCM:

- **Contract combination between OCM and CCM**
  Let's say you have both sets of contracts, OCM and CCM, existing in your RAR system. The RAR functionality in SAP S/4HANA won't allow you to combine both contracts. You can combine OCM and OCM contracts, and you can combine CCM and CCM contracts.
- **Hierarchal POBs**
  The concept of hierarchical POBs isn't supported with OCM.
- **Cost POBs**
  Cost-based POBs aren't supported in OCM. Therefore, the cost recognition functionality doesn't exist either.
- **Manual price allocation and manual spreading**
  In CCM, you can manually allocate price and/or change spreading for time-based POBs. This feature isn't supported with OCM.
- **BAdIs**
  The following BAdIs aren't supported in OCM:

  - FARR_BADI_ALLOCATION_ENGINE
  - FARR_BADI_ALLOCATION_METHOD
  - FARR_BADI_DEFERRAL_METHOD
  - FARR_CHANGE_MODE_DETERMINATION
  - FARR_BADI_TM_REMAINING_PERC
  - FARR_BADI_RAIO
- **Time-based POB with start date type 3**
  For time-based POBs, the start date type 3 option isn't supported in OCM.
- **POC-based fulfillments with result analysis integration**
  Unfortunately, the POC fulfillment type with result analysis integration is discontinued in OCM.
- **Deferral methods 3 and 4**
  Deferral methods 3 and 4, which involve rounding adjustments, aren't supported with OCM.
- **Transition to new accounting principles**
  This functionality isn't available with OCM.
- **Results analysis integration**
  This functionality isn't supported in OCM.
- **Simplified invoicing**
  This functionality isn't supported in OCM.
- **Manual POB reassignment**
  Reassigning of POBs between contracts isn't possible with OCM.
- **Contract creation from sales and distribution invoices**
  Within CCM, you can create a RAR contract from sales and distribution invoices. This functionality isn't supported in OCM.
- **Drop shipment**
  This functionality isn't supported in OCM.
- **Intercompany billing**
  This functionality isn't supported in OCM.
- **Condition-based contract acquisition costs**
  This functionality isn't supported in OCM, although you can still create contract acquisition cost POBs.
- **Fixed exchange rate method**
  This functionality isn't supported in OCM.

Based on our experience working with SAP for many years, we feel if SAP sees a genuine need for any of these features in the future, they will implement those through feature packs or routine upgrades.

6.4 Summary

Congratulations! You can now confidently call yourself a sales and distribution and RAR integration expert.

Here is a summary of all the topics we dove into in this chapter:

- In Section 6.1, we touched on the general concepts of revenue recognition and talked about IFRS 15 compliance standards. We also compared traditional sales and distribution revenue recognition with SAP Revenue Accounting and Reporting and explored the key differences. Finally, we concluded the section by explaining price allocation and how it impacts revenue recognition in the RAR world.
- In Section 6.2, we jumped into the core sales and distribution–RAR integration topics. We looked at configuration steps in RAR and in sales and distribution needed to build a successful sales and distribution–RAR integration. You also learned about Transaction NWBC and how it can be used to monitor the impact of RAIs sent from sales and distribution to RAR. Transaction NWBC is also used to run worklist programs and revenue posting jobs. We walked you through different steps in BRFplus that must be performed to support sales and distribution and integrations, and finally we concluded the section by demonstrating a use case from an example client's sales and distribution–RAR system.
- In Section 6.3, we talked about the concept of OCM and how to activate it using contract categories. We also looked at the OCM enhanced functionalities and their impact on RAR in SAP S/4HANA. Finally, we concluded the section by comparing OCM to CCM to help you understand the benefits and limitations of OCM.

In the next chapter, we'll talk about resource-related billing (RRB) as one of the key integration points between sales and distribution and Project System.

Chapter 7
Resource-Related Billing

Resource-related billing (RRB) is a prime integration point between the sales and distribution functionality and Project System in SAP S/4HANA. It's an important topic to learn if you're working or plan to work in any service-based industry.

In this chapter, we'll talk about the core concepts of RRB, and how RRB helps the sales and distribution functionality and Project System functionality integrate with each other.

There are broadly two types of RRB functionalities available in standard SAP S/4HANA: the Project System RRB and the customer service RRB. In this chapter, we'll focus on the Project System solution for RRB as that is a more widely used functionality and naturally synchronizes with sales and distribution.

Figure 7.1 shows what an end-to-end Project System RRB solution looks like in SAP S/4HANA.

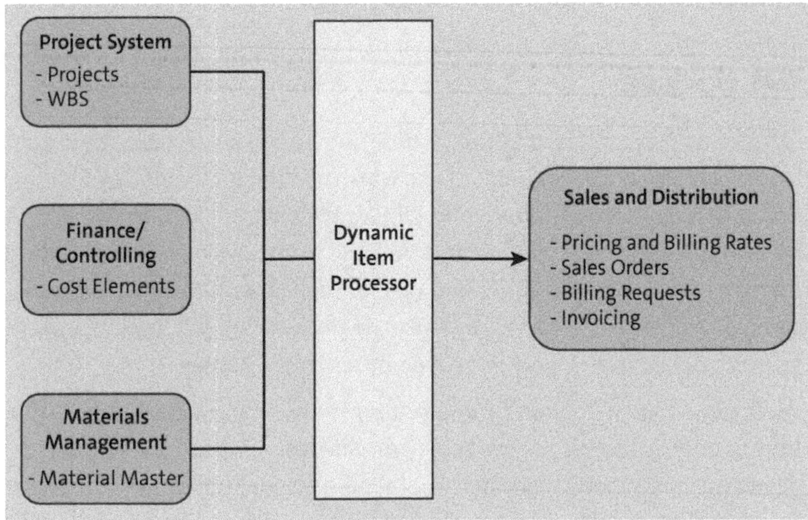

Figure 7.1 Project System RRB Solution

The middle box in Figure 7.1 represents the heart of an RRB process, called the *dynamic item processor (DIP) profile*, where the actual conversion of Project System to sales and distribution data happens. More details about the DIP profile are given in Section 7.2.1.

Toward the left are three functionalities that feed data into the DIP profile, namely Project System, finance/controlling, and materials management. Toward the right is the sales and distribution functionality, which accepts processed data from the configured DIP profile. Sales and distribution combines the processed DIP data with billing rates to create a billing request document that is ultimately invoiced to complete the RRB process.

With three functionalities feeding data into DIP, you may be wondering why RRB is referred to as the only integration point for the Project System–sales and distribution integration. The answer is that the cost elements from financial accounting/controlling and the master data from materials management are processed together and attached to a work breakdown structure (WBS) in DIP before they are sent over to sales and distribution. So truly it's the WBS that is driving the entire RRB process, and because WBS is a Project System component, RRB is referred to as a sales and distribution–Project System integration point.

In this chapter, we'll share our experience and knowledge about the following topics:

- Project System components—projects and WBSs—as they relate to RRB and sales and distribution–Project System integration
- DIP profile configuration and components
- Time sheet entry using cross-application time sheets (CATS) as an example
- Expense entry using SAP Concur as an example
- Working RRB use case

7.1 Project-Based Billing

RRB can be thought of as project-based billing, whereby you bill a customer based on resources consumed by a project stakeholder. Let's walk through an example of a Project System RRB scenario: Say a consultant worked on a project for 30 hours/week and was on-site while working. He charged meals and mileage to the project budget. Billing for the hours and expenses happened at the end of the week when the consultant systematically entered his expenses and hours against the project budget. Expenses were accompanied by receipts, and hours were approved by a project manager.

As you can see, hours and expenses aren't fixed prices, so they can't follow the simple sales and distribution billing process. Hours can be on-site, off-site, and so on, depending on project need and can only be recorded and billed once the project engagement is completed. Similarly, expenses are project dependent too, they can be travel, meals, and so on, depending on if and where consultant travels to fulfill project responsibilities. As both sets of information are on an as-incurred basis, SAP S/4HANA provides a standard solution to bill such scenarios: RRB.

Figure 7.2 shows a data flow diagram for a simple Project System RRB use case.

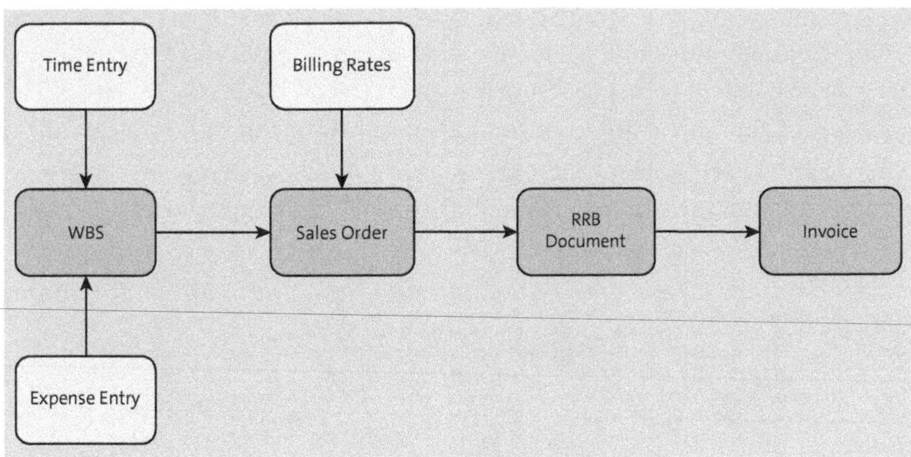

Figure 7.2 Project System RRB Data Flow Diagram

The dark tiles in Figure 7.2 are primary data points, and the light tiles are supporting data points. What we mean is that WBS, sales orders, and RRB documents drive the RRB process from end to end, while time entry, expense entry, and billing rates are input data points supporting WBS and sales orders. Invoices are outcomes of the RRB process.

In the following sections, we'll talk about Project System from the point of view of RRB and sales and distribution integration. We'll look at the two core components of Project System, project and WBS, as they help the RRB process function smoothly and help Project System connect with sales and distribution sales orders. Having information about these components will be useful in understanding later sections in this chapter.

7.1.1 Project System

Project System is SAP's project management solution, launched to address the project lifecycle. Project System naturally integrates with many other SAP S/4HANA functionalities to form a strong end-to-end solution. Project System also can integrate with non-SAP project management tools, thus making it one of SAPs most efficient project management solution.

Following are a few of the key tasks you can perform using Project System: projects and WBS creation and tracking, cost and revenue planning, and time schedule management and reporting. Out of these tasks, the projects and WBS creation and tracking task is crucial for RRB, so that's what we'll look at more closely in the next two sections.

7.1.2 Projects

Projects can be defined as a collection of tasks that are planned and organized in a strategic manner, as well as targeted to meet end goals of business requirements. Projects are time-, resource-, and cost-sensitive endeavors, meaning for a project to be successful, it should be completed within committed deadlines, should not exceed allocated resources, and should be within the estimated budget.

To create a project in SAP S/4HANA, execute Transaction CJ20N or follow SAP menu path **Logistics • Project System • Project • CJ20N – Project Builder**. From the Project Builder screen, navigate to **Project • New • Project**. You'll arrive at the screen shown in Figure 7.3.

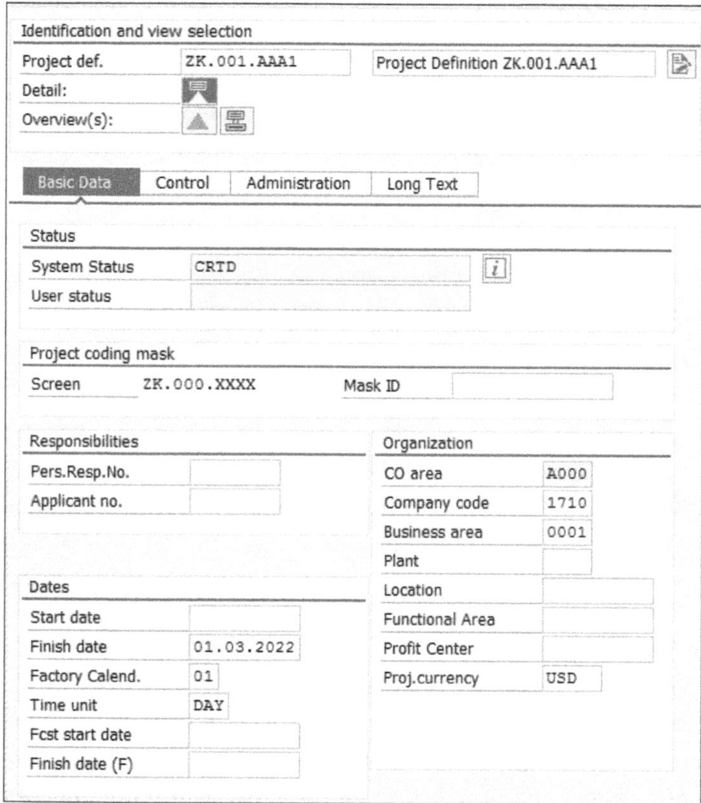

Figure 7.3 Project: Basic Data Tab

As shown in Figure 7.3, a project screen is divided into two sections: the **Identification and view selection** header section, and the detail section, which has tabs for **Basic Data**, **Control**, **Administration**, and **Long Text**.

The header section has three fields:

- **Project def.**
  This field has two parts: the first part represents the unique key for a project definition, and the second part represents the description associated with the project definition.

- **Detail**
  This button is used to toggle between the **Detail** view and **Overview** of a project. By clicking on this icon, you can see the **Detail** view.
- **Overview(s)**
  This button is used to toggle between the **Detail** view and **Overview** sections of a project. By using this icon, you can switch between different overviews. There are two standard overview options available:
  - **WBS Element Overview**: Display, change, or create multiple WBSs for the project in one go.
  - **Network Overview**: Display, change, or create multiple networks for the project in one go.

Keeping the scope of this book in mind, we'll only dive into those detail section tabs and fields that are relevant for sales and distribution–RRB integration. Let's start with fields under the **Basic Data** tab first (refer to Figure 7.3):

- **System Status**
  This field represents the system status of a project. Statuses on a project are configured and controlled by the status profile. A Project System consultant can help you configure the status profile.
- **User status**
  This field represents the user status of a project. In addition to the system status, SAP S/4HANA allows you to add user-defined statuses for a project. We've used this feature in previous projects to add an additional layer of control to differentiate which projects can be used for internal purposes only versus which can be released for external business purposes.
- **Screen**
  This field represents the coding mask configured for a project definition. Coding mask is the code format a project follows when newly configured. It helps users define which elements should be copied from a project to a WBS element.
- **Mask ID**
  This field represents the mask short ID for a project or a WBS element. **Mask ID** is used to search a project using a short string.
- **Pers.Resp.No.**
  This field represents the personal ID of the person who owns the project. Typically, this person is the project manager.
- **Applicant no.**
  This field represents the personal ID of the person who applies for a project. Typically, this person is the project requestor.
- **Start date**
  This field represents the start date of a project.

- **Finish date**
  This field represents the finish date of a project.
- **Factory Calend.**
  This field represents the factory calendar a project will follow.
- **Time unit**
  This field represents the time unit of measure (UoM) you want the project to follow. Examples include days, hours, minutes, and so on.
- **Fcst start date**
  This field represents the forecast start date of a project.
- **Finish date (F)**
  This field represents the forecast finish date of a project.

Next, we'll look at the **Organization** fields, which are especially important from the sales and distribution integration standpoint because they should match one to one with what is on the sales order or the RRB document. If they don't match, then you can't use the project for that specific sales order or RRB process. Said differently, if organization components on a project don't match the organization components within the RRB process, then that project doesn't qualify to be used for that RRB process. The following fields are available:

- **CO area**
  This field represents the controlling area code of a project.
- **Company code**
  This field represents the company code of a project.
- **Business area**
  This field represents the business area of a project.
- **Plant**
  This field represents the plant of a project.
- **Location**
  This field represents the location of a project. Location is a subentity under the main plant entity.
- **Functional Area**
  This field represents the functional area of a project.
- **Profit Center**
  This field represents the profit center of a project.
- **Proj.currency**
  This field represents the default currency of a project. All cost- or payment-related transactions performed on a project will always be in the project currency.

Next, let's look at some relevant fields under the **Control** tab, as shown in Figure 7.4:

- **Project Profile**
  This field represents the unique project profile of a project. Every project must be assigned to a project profile.
- **Transfer to proj.def**
  This checkbox is checked when you want to automatically create a project for a newly created WBS element. The project will have the same name as the WBS element.
- **Statistical**
  This checkbox if checked if you want a project and related WBS elements to be statistical only and not record actual costs.
- **Integrated Planning**
  This checkbox is checked when you want to tag a project to qualify for integrated planning.
- **Object Class**
  This field represents the object class associated with a project. Object classes are used to tag controlling objects to lines of business (LoBs). As a default, SAP S/4HANA provides you with four object classes:
  - **Investment**: Controlling objects belonging to the investment LoB should be classified under this class. Examples include the controlling internal order and controlling accrual order.
  - **Overhead**: Controlling objects belonging to the overhead LoB should be classified under this class. Examples include cost center and cost object hierarchy.
  - **Earning Sales**: Controlling objects belonging to the earning sales LoB should be classified under this class. Examples include profitability segment and WBS element order.
  - **Production**: Controlling objects belonging to the production LoB should be classified under this class. Examples include sales order and general cost object.
- **Tax Jurisdiction**
  This field represents the unique tax jurisdiction code for a project. Tax jurisdiction codes are used for US entities to determine tax rates.
- **WBS status profile**
  This field represents the WBS status profile for a project. Each WBS element created under a project will inherit this profile by default.
- **Sales Organization**
  This field is a sales pricing field and represents the sales organization a project belongs to.
- **Distr. Channel**
  This field is also a sales pricing field and represents the distribution channel a project belongs to.

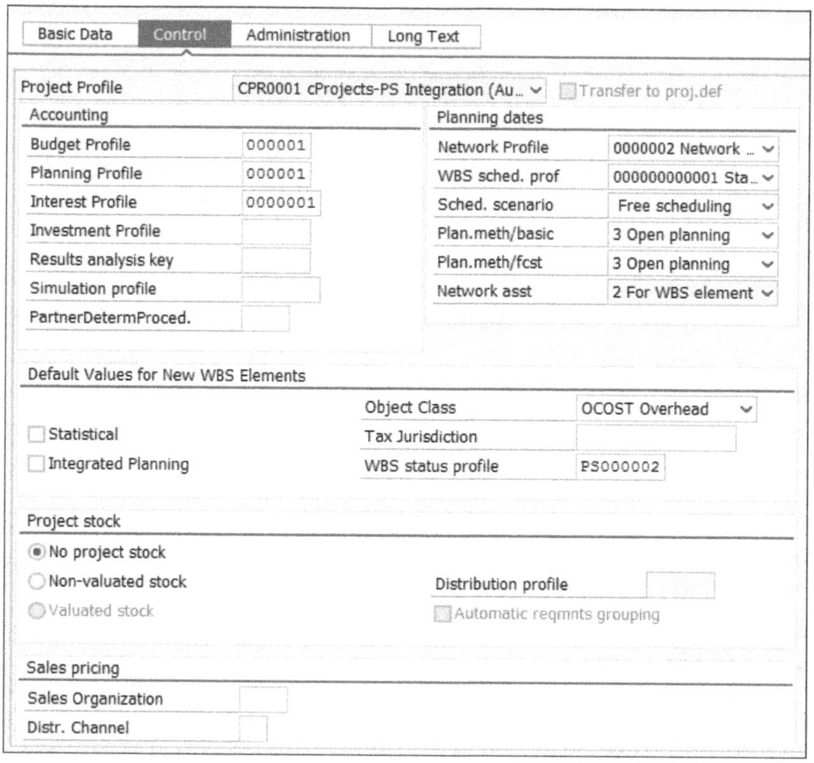

Figure 7.4 Project Control Tab

The **Accounting** section under the **Control** tab is used to define various profiles for a project such as budget profile, planning profile, interest profile, investment profile, and simulation profile. You can also configure result analysis key and partner determination procedure under this section.

The **Planning dates** section under the **Control** tab helps with things such as network and WBS schedule profile selection, planning methods, and scheduling scenarios. The values for these fields are typically maintained as standard values.

The **Project stock** section is used to define the material requirements planning (MRP) of stocks. You can also configure the distribution profile and requirements grouping from this section.

The **Administration** tab shows data such as created by, changed by, created on, last changed on, and so on. Finally, the **Long Text** tab is used to maintain any long text for a project, including project descriptions or any notes specific to the project.

After filling in the relevant fields, click the **Save** button or press Ctrl+S to finish setting up projects.

> **Note**
> For the configuration of each of these sections, it's recommended to tag team with a Project System consultant.

7.1.3 Work Breakdown Structure

The tasks that define a project are logically grouped together into structures called the WBS. A project is a group of WBSs. WBSs help break a huge project into smaller deliverables where each deliverable is denoted by a WBS. A WBS is normally represented by a hierarchy of elements called WBS elements.

To create a WBS element in SAP S/4HANA, execute Transaction CJ20N or follow SAP menu path **Logistics • Project System • Project • CJ20N – Project Builder**. From the Project Builder screen, after creating or searching your project, navigate to **Create • WBS element**. You'll arrive at the screen shown in Figure 7.5.

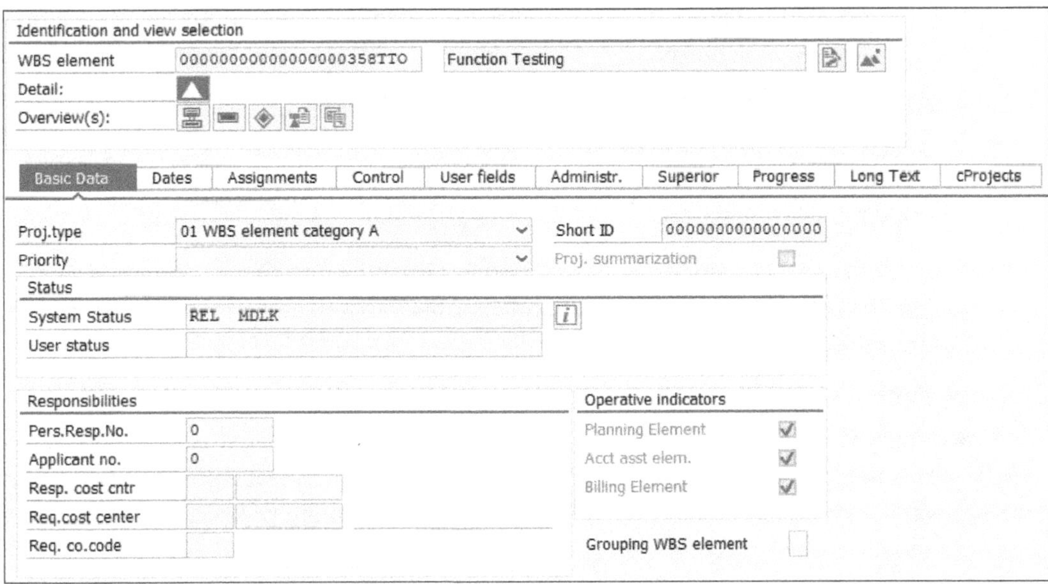

Figure 7.5 WBS Element: Basic Data Tab

As shown in Figure 7.5, the WBS element screen is divided into two sections: the **Identification and view selection** header section, and the detail section, which has tabs for **Basic Data, Dates, Assignments, Control, User fields, Administr., Superior, Progress, Long Text**, and **cProjects**.

Like projects, the WBS elements header section also has three fields:

- **WBS element**
  This field has two parts: the first part represents the unique key for a WBS element, and the second part represents the description associated with the WBS element.
- **Detail**
  This button is used to toggle between **Detail** view and **Overview** of a WBS element. By clicking on this button, you can see the **Detail** view.
- **Overview(s)**
  This button is used to toggle between **Detail** view and **Overview** sections of a WBS element. By using this button, you can switch between different overviews. There are five standard overview options available:
  - **Network Overview**: Display, change, or create multiple networks for a WBS element in one go.
  - **Activity Overview**: Display, change, or create multiple activities for a WBS element network in one go.
  - **Milestone Overview**: Display, change, or create multiple milestone usages for a WBS element in one go.
  - **PS Text Overview**: Display, change, or add multiple text types for a WBS element in one go.
  - **Document Overview**: Display, change, or add multiple document types for a WBS element in one go.

Keeping the scope of this book in mind, we'll only dive into those detail section tabs and fields that are relevant for a sales and distribution–RRB integration. Let's start with fields under the **Basic Data** tab.

As shown in Figure 7.5, the following are the fields under the **Basic Data** tab:

- **Proj.type**
  This field represents the unique ID of a project type. A project type is used to group similar projects. For example, all category A WBS element projects can be grouped under one project type.
- **Priority**
  This field is used to identify the priority for a WBS element.
- **Short ID**
  Just like projects have mask ID, WBS elements have short ID. A short ID is used to represent a WBS element with a short string. This string can be used to search a WBS element. When you view WBSs in list view, it shows the short ID instead of the actual long element name.
- **Proj. summarization**
  This checkbox is checked when you want a WBS element to qualify for project summarization.

- **System Status**
  This field represents the system status of a WBS element. Statuses on a WBS element are configured and controlled by the status profile. A Project System consultant can help you configure the status profile.
- **User status**
  This field represents the user status of a WBS element. In addition to the system status, SAP S/4HANA allows you to add user-defined statuses for a WBS element.
- **Pers.Resp.No.**
  This field represents the personal ID of the person who owns the WBS element. Typically, this person is the project manager.
- **Applicant no.**
  This field represents the personal ID of the person who applies for a WBS element. Typically, this person is the project requestor.
- **Resp. cost cntr**
  This field has two sections: responsible controlling area (the left-hand box) and responsible cost center (the right-hand box).
- **Req.cost center**
  This field has two sections: requesting cost center and responsible cost center. A requesting and responsible cost center can be the same or different. For example, say an accounting team has requested a new scanner, and the IT team is responsible for sourcing and installing the scanner. In this scenario, the requesting cost center is the accounting cost center, and the responsible cost center is the IT cost center.
- **Req. co.code**
  This field represents the requesting company code for a WBS element.
- **Planning Element**
  This checkbox is checked when you want to indicate a WBS element as a planning element. Only when a WBS is flagged as a planning element can it be used to plan costs for the supporting project.
- **Acct asst elem.**
  This checkbox is checked when you want to indicate a WBS element as an account assignment element. Only when a WBS is flagged as an account assignment element can it be used for postings on a project.
- **Billing Element**
  This checkbox is checked when you want to indicate a WBS element as a billing element. If you want a WBS to record billing, then this flag should be checked.

Note

All the three operative indicators, planning element, account assignment element, and billing element, can be checked together. Once a relevant transaction is performed on the WBS, then these indicators can't be unchecked.

- **Grouping WBS element**
  This checkbox is checked when you want a WBS element to qualify for grouping. Grouping can happen in two ways: by materials or by MRP groups.

Next, let's look at the **Assignments** tab. As shown in Figure 7.6, the **Assignments** tab has the following key fields:

- **CO area**
  This field represents the controlling area code of a WBS element.
- **Company code**
  This field represents the company code of a WBS element.
- **Bus.area**
  This field represents the business area of a WBS element.
- **Functional Area**
  This field represents the functional area of a WBS element.
- **Profit Center**
  This field represents the profit center of a WBS element.
- **Object Class**
  This field represents the object class associated with a WBS element. As a default, SAP S/4HANA provides you with four object classes: **Investment**, **Overhead**, **Earning Sales**, and **Production**.
- **Currency**
  This field represents the default currency of a WBS element. All cost- or payment-related transactions performed on a WBS element will always use this currency.
- **Tax Jur.**
  This field represents the unique tax jurisdiction code for a WBS element. Tax jurisdiction codes are used for US entities to determine tax rates.
- **Subproject**
  This field represents the unique key of a subproject to which the WBS element belongs. This field is populated when the WBS element doesn't directly fall under the parent project but belongs to a subproject instead.
- **Plant**
  This field represents the plant of a WBS element.
- **Location**
  This field represents the location of a WBS element. Location is a subentity under the main plant entity.
- **Factory Calend.**
  This field represents the factory calendar a WBS element will follow.
- **Equipment**
  This field represents the equipment ID for a WBS element. This field isn't relevant for the RRB process or sales and distribution integration. You'll see this field populated

when a WBS element is used in SAP Business Network for Asset Management, plant maintenance, production planning, or transport management processes.

- **Functional loc.**
  This field represents the unique functional location ID for a WBS element. Functional location is an organizational entity under the plant maintenance functionality.
- **Change Number**
  This field represents the unique change number ID for a change on a WBS element. This field is only populated when you enable change pointers or change numbers for the WBS configuration.
- **Ref. Elem.**
  This field represents the reference element ID for a WBS element. This reference element is for plant maintenance/Project System only and isn't required for RRB or sales and distribution–Project System integration.

Basic Data | Dates | Assignments | Control | User fields | Administr. | Superior | Progress | Long Text | cProjects

Organization

CO area	A000	Subproject	
Company code	1710	Plant	
Bus.area	0001	Location	
Functional Area	0001	Factory Calend.	01
Profit Center	YB600	Equipment	
Object Class	OCOST Overhead	Functional loc.	
Currency	USD	Change Number	
Tax Jur.		Ref. Elem.	

Figure 7.6 WBS Element: Assignments Tab

Next, we'll look at the **Control** tab. As shown in Figure 7.7, the **Control** tab has the following important fields:

- **Transfer to proj.def**
  This checkbox is checked when you want to automatically create a project for a newly created WBS element. WBS element and project share the same name and IDs.
- **Integ. Planning**
  This checkbox is checked when you want to tag a WBS element to qualify for integrated planning.

> **Note**
> Other fields under the **Accounting** section are used for standard accounting functions such as costing sheet, interest profile, result analysis, and so on, and aren't needed for RRB.

- **Network asst**
  This field is used to indicate the network assignment for a WBS element. It has three values by default: **0**, which indicates network assignment isn't enabled for a WBS element; **1**, which indicates network assignment is enabled at the project definition; and **2**, which indicates network assignment is enabled at the WBS element.
- **Plan.meth/basic**
  This field represents the planning method for basic dates for a WBS element.
- **Plan.met/fcst**
  This field represents the planning method for forecast dates for a WBS element.

The **Investment Management** section fields are populated when a WBS element is used with inventory management.

Figure 7.7 WBS Element: Control Tab

Let's look at the **Superior** tab now. This tab is important to understand the project to WBS hierarchy level in SAP S/4HANA. The example in Figure 7.8 shows a three-level hierarchy, where the parent project is at level **1**, there is a subproject at level **2**, and a WBS element at level **3**.

Basic Data | Dates | Assignments | Control | User fields | Administr. | Superior | Progress | Long Text | cProjects

Path to WBS element

Lev	WBS element	Description
1	ZK.001.AAA1	Project System
2	ZK.001.AAA3	Sub Project 2
3	ZK.001.AAA4	Project WBS Element

Figure 7.8 WBS Element: Superior Tab

The following briefly describes the rest of the WBS elements tabs:

- The **Dates** tab helps with configuration of basic dates, forecast dates, and actual dates for a WBS element. You can specify things such as duration, UoM, and actual start and end dates under this tab.
- The **User fields** tab includes fields SAP S/4HANA provides as a standard to end users to maintain any extra set of information that they can't otherwise maintain in other sections of the WBS element configuration. Think of them as the user-defined Z fields you see in sales and distribution.
- The **Administr.** tab shows data such as created by, changed by, created on, last changed on, and so on.
- The **Progress** tab is used to maintain Project System progress analysis configuration.
- The **Long Text** tab is used to maintain any long text for a project, such as project descriptions or any notes specific to the project.
- Finally, the **cProjects** tab lists the details of any collaboration project that might be linked to a WBS element.

After filling in the relevant fields, click the **Save** button or press Ctrl+S to finish setting up the WBS elements.

7.2 Dynamic Item Processing

The DIP profile, as the name suggests, helps with configuration of costs processing of dynamic items. Dynamic items are items where rate/pricing data isn't known ahead of time but is determined based on preconfigured conditions and when an underlying event occurs, for example, hours and expenses for an RRB order. These preconfigured conditions are configured within a DIP profile.

The primarily vital component to define in a DIP profile is DIP usage. For DIP usage, you configure characteristics, sources, and material determination. All three features come together to construct a DIP profile that is the core of RRB processes. The DIP profile is attached to the sales document type and item category in sales and distribution, thus forming the sales and distribution–Project System integration.

In the following sections, you'll set up a DIP profile and then add more flavor to it and make it ready for the end-to-end RRB process.

7.2.1 Dynamic Item Processing Profile

To configure a DIP profile, execute Transaction ODP1 or follow IMG menu path **Sales and Distribution • Sales • Sales Documents • Customer Service • Service Quotation/ Resource-Related Billing • Profiles for Resource-Related Billing/Quotation Creation**. Click the **New Entries** button, and you'll arrive at the screen shown in Figure 7.9.

New Entries

Dialog Structure
- Profile
  - Usage
    - Characteristics
    - Sources
      - Selection criteria
    - Material determinati
      - Criteria

Profile

DIP Profile	Description	Relevant fo...
BILLPLAN	Integration with Billing Plan	☐
PS000001	PS: SPc Reference (Add Header & Mat. Determinatn)	☐
QT	Service Quotation Profile	☐
ZC01	RRB for Customer	☐

Figure 7.9 DIP Profile

As shown in Figure 7.9, the DIP profile configuration has two sections: **Dialog Structure** and **Profile**. We'll look at different selections of the **Dialog Structure** in the sections to follow, but within the **Profile** section, you see three fields:

- **DIP Profile**
  This field represents the user-defined profile name. It can be alphanumeric.
- **Description**
  This field describes the profile name in just a few words.
- **Relevant fo...**
  This checkbox is checked if you want a DIP profile to be relevant for project services. For RRB scenarios, you don't need to check this checkbox.

Let's look at usage for one of the profiles. To do so, select profile **ZC01** (**RRB for Customer**) and then double-click on the **Usage** folder. You'll see the screen shown in Figure 7.10.

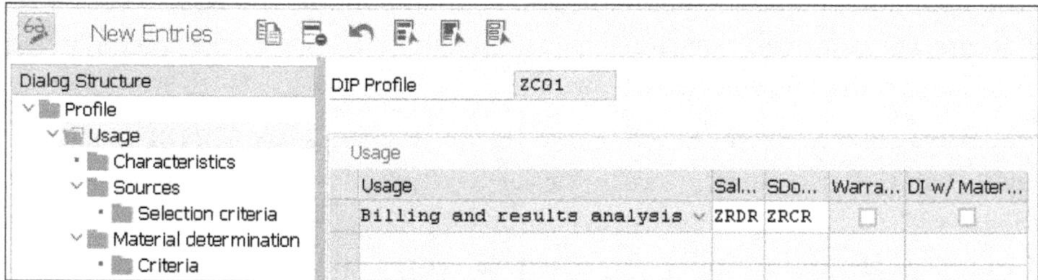

Figure 7.10 DIP Profile Usage

As shown in Figure 7.10, the DIP profile **Usage** screen has the following fields:

- **Usage**
  This field controls when the usage of a DIP profile triggers for dynamic items. By default, SAP S/4HANA provides you with two options: **Billing and results analysis** and **Quotation creation**. For RRB process, select **Billing and results analysis.**
- **Sal....**
  This field identifies the sales document type that is used to show the result of the

billing request DIP usage. For example, **ZRDR** is the document type that will display the consultant hours and expenses the consultant recorded to the project WBS. The **ZRDR** document is then reviewed and approved by the project manager.

- **SDo...**
  This field identifies the sales document type that is used to show the result of a credit memo request DIP usage. For example, **ZRCR** is the document type that will display the disputed/credited hours and expenses recorded to the WBS. The **ZRCR** document will then follow the regular credit memo request approval process. At our example client, a credit memo request must be approved by the operations and finance team before a credit memo can be issued.
- **Warra...**
  This checkbox is checked when you want system to validate the warranty for an equipment-based RRB document. In our example, because we're looking at hours and expenses (which is the sales and distribution RRB process), this checkbox isn't checked.
- **DI w/Mater...**
  This checkbox is checked if you want the system to explicitly process materials with an underlying material number. At our example client, we haven't checked this option, and we determine the material number using material determination, which is explained in Section 7.2.4. We recommend this method because then determination of material number is driven by configuration rather than a master data update.

7.2.2 Characteristics

Characteristics configuration helps you define how distinct characteristics within a DIP profile usage can contribute to a RRB business process. To get to the **Characteristics** screen from the **Usage** screen, select **Billing and results analysis** from the **Usage** field, and then double-click on the **Characteristics** folder in the **Dialog Structure**. You'll arrive at the screen shown in Figure 7.11.

Many features can be configured for individual characteristics. A few feature fields are shown in Figure 7.11, but to view other fields, you must scroll to the right. The following is an explanation for all visible and nonvisible fields within the **Charact.** configuration section:

- **Char.**
  This field represents the list of characteristics that can be configured for a DIP usage.
- **CharactRelevant**
  This checkbox is checked if you want to flag a characteristic as relevant for dynamic item creation within a DIP profile usage. For example, based on Figure 7.11, **Activity Type** will be used to process dynamic items within an RRB process.

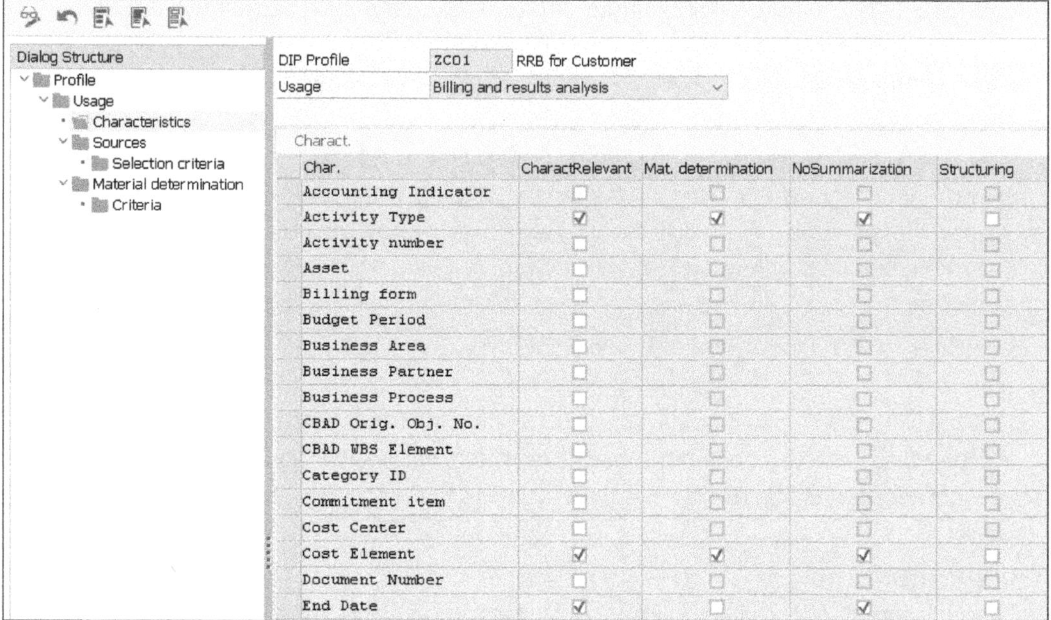

Figure 7.11 DIP Usage Characteristics

- **Mat. determination**
  This checkbox is checked if you want to flag a characteristic as relevant for material determination within a DIP profile usage. For example, based on Figure 7.11, **Cost Element** will be used for material determination within an RRB process while **End Date** won't be used for material determination.
- **NoSummarization**
  This checkbox is checked if you want to flag a characteristic as not relevant for summarization within a DIP profile usage. For example, based on Figure 7.11, no summarization of dynamic items will occur based on **Activity Type** within a RRB process. Said differently, each activity type will have its own line item in the RRB document, meaning on-site consulting will be line item 10, off-site consulting will be line item 20, and so on (where on-site and off-site are different activity types). If this checkbox wasn't checked for **Activity Type**, then all consulting hours would be summarized on line item 10 in the RRB document.
- **Structuring**
  This checkbox is checked if you want to flag a characteristic as relevant for structuring within a DIP profile usage. Structuring refers to making a characteristic available for structuring of dynamic items on the overview screen of a RRB document. Based on Figure 7.11, no structuring will happen on **Activity Type**, **Cost Element**, or **End Date**. If you decide to enable **Structuring** for a characteristic, you can add details about the structuring definition to sets that have to be appended to that characteristic.

- **Sequence**
  This field represents the sequence number for structuring. For the characteristics that have been flagged for structuring, you can assign a sequence number to them depending on how you want to show them on the processing overview screen of a RRB document. For example, let's say you flag **Activity Type** and **Cost Element** for structuring, and you add sequence number 1 for **Activity Type** and sequence number 2 for **Cost Element**. In the overview screen, you'll always see **Activity Type** listed first for the dynamic item followed by **Cost Element**.

- **Set Name**
  This field represents the unique name given to a set. Think of set as a custom Z table that can store values either as single values or a range. Sets are used to define and organize data for an underlying characteristic to which the set belongs. SAP S/4HANA provides you with four different set types:
  - **Basic sets**: These sets store only one-dimensional values. An example is expense accounts in which you store values 600001, 600002, 600003, and so on in a basic set.
  - **Single sets**: These sets are also one- dimensional sets, but within these sets, you can combine multiple sets to form a hierarchy. The only thing to keep in mind is that all the sets you combine must have the same dimensions, for example, expense accounts basic set and labor accounts basic set. You create a single set called Professional Services by combining the two basic sets Expense and Hours, which includes values 600001, 600002, 600003, and so on, and 500001, 500002, 500003, and so on, respectively.
  - **Multi sets**: These sets are like single sets with the difference that multisets can combine more than one basic and/or single set, which can be of different dimensions. For example, say you have a Professional Services single set and a Cost Center basic set. You create a multiset called Resource Billing by combining one single set Professional Services with one basic set Cost Center with values of 600001, 600002, 600003, and so on; 500001, 500002, 500003, and so on; and CC100, CC101, CC102, respectively.
  - **Key Figure sets**: These sets are like basic sets in that key figure sets can also store values that are only one-dimensional. The only difference is that these sets can store values along with a key figure. For example, billing rates key figure sets store values for hourly billing for labor offered on a project: USD 150 for off-site consulting, USD 200 for on-site consulting, and so on.
- **Set**
  This is the field where you maintain the set values.
- **Partial sets**
  This radio button is used to indicate if a row set can be expanded and broken down into partial sets.

- **Single values**
  This radio button is used to indicate to the system that a characteristic should only use single values when a row set is expanded to partial sets.
- **Upper set**
  This radio button is used if you explicitly don't want a row set to be expanded to partial sets.
- **From level**
  This field represents the from summarization level for a characteristic.
- **To level**
  This field represents the to summarization level for a characteristic.
- **Single values**
  If you have multiple structuring levels for a characteristic, then this field can help control the single value display of the set for each level. If the checkbox is checked for a characteristic, then the system will display single values of the set for that structuring level on the RRB document overview screen; if the checkbox isn't checked, then single values won't be displayed.

We'll look at an example of a set in the next section.

7.2.3 Sources

The next core component of a DIP profile usage is sources. Within this configuration step, you define source components for a DIP usage. There are two key configuration steps for sources:

- Defining actual sources along with supplementing features (mandatory)
- Configuring selection criteria for the defined source components (optional)

To get to the Sources screen from the Usage screen, select **Billing and results analysis** from the **Usage** field, and then double-click on the **Sources** folder in the **Dialog Structure**. You'll arrive at the screen shown in Figure 7.12. You can either view an existing source as shown, or you can create a new one by clicking **New Entries**.

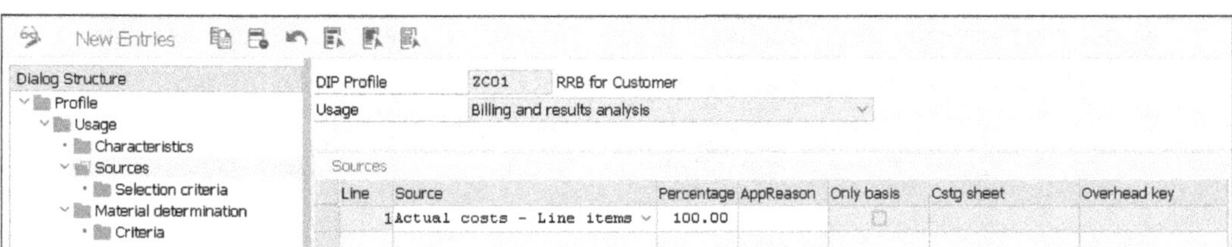

Figure 7.12 DIP Usage Sources

As shown in Figure 7.12, the **Sources** screen has the following fields:

- **Line**
  This field represents the line number of the source entry for a DIP usage.
- **Source**
  This field represents the source key that the SAP S/4HANA system will use to determine dynamic items. Following are the standard sources available in SAP S/4HANA:
  - **GMD1**
  - **Actual Costs – Line items**
  - **Actual Costs – Total records**
  - **Easy Cost Planning**
  - **Funds – Line items**
  - **Funds – Total records**
  - **Intercompany – Line items**
  - **Plan stat.ind – Total records**
  - **Planned Costs – Total records**
  - **SRM Confirmation**
  - **Statist. ind. – Total records**
  - **Statistical ind. – Line items**

  You can add more sources via table `AD01SRCTAB` using Transaction SM31. Consult a Project System consultant before adding user-defined sources.
- **Percentage**
  This field is used to set the default percentage value that is proposed on the overview screen of a RRB document. The percentage value is user editable.
- **AppReason**
  This field represents the apportionment reason code, which is tied to costs from result analysis. You don't need apportionment reason codes for the sales and distribution RRB process.
- **Only basis**
  This checkbox is checked if you want to use surcharges and not the original costs to build dynamic items. The reason this field is called **Only basis** is because in SAP lingo, they are asking if you want to build dynamic items only on the basis of surcharges. If your answer is yes, then you check the checkbox.
- **Cstg sheet**
  This field represents the unique procedure ID of the costing sheet, which is used to calculate overheard costs. In our example, we don't have the concept of overhead cost within the sales and distribution RRB process, so this field is left blank.

- **Overhead key**
  This field represents the unique overhead key ID that is used to calculate the overhead rate based on order items or materials. Again, because our example client doesn't record overhead costs within the sales and distribution RRB process, this field is left blank too.

For every source line added to a DIP usage, you can configure selection criteria. At our example client, as shown in Figure 7.12, we added a source line **Actual costs – Line items**. To add selection criteria for that line, select the line, and double-click on the **Selection criteria** folder from the **Dialog Structure** section. This takes you to the **Selection Criteria for Sources** page, as shown in Figure 7.13.

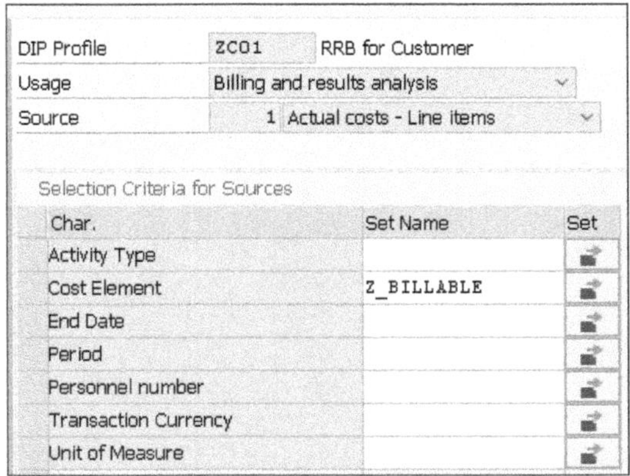

Figure 7.13 DIP Usage Source Line Selection Criteria

All characteristics that were flagged as **CharactRelevant** in the **Characteristics** configuration step show up in the selection criteria. For our RRB use case, we defined selection criteria for **Cost Element** using sets. We created a basic set called **Z_BILLABLE** and added the values to it, as shown in Figure 7.14.

To create a set, go to Transaction GS01, and the enter the set name you want to create. Next, under the **Basic data** section, based on your business requirement, enter the **Table** name, and click **Values**. Next, enter a **Field name**, and click the green check. As shown in Figure 7.14, we entered table name **AD01ATTR** and field name **KSTAR**. Once the set is created and you reach the **Create Set: Values** screen, enter values per your requirement, which we'll discuss further next, and click **Save**.

As shown in Figure 7.14, the screen for our **Z_BILLABLE** set has the following important fields:

- **Basic set**
  This field represents the set name and set description. In Figure 7.14, **Z_BILLABLE** is the set name for the basic set, and **Billable Cost Elements** is the set description.
- **Table**
  This field represents the table you want to use for your set.

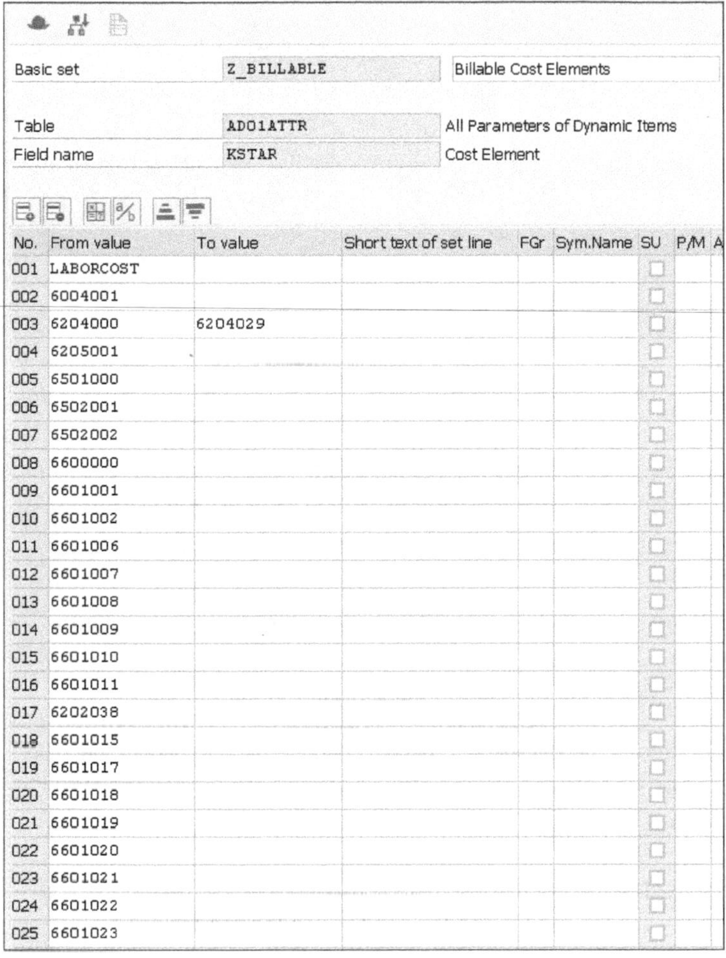

Figure 7.14 Cost Element Basic Set

- **Field name**
  This field represents the field name you want to use for your set. In Figure 7.14, because the set was created for cost elements, the underlying table and field used is **AD01ATTR-KSTAR**.
- **No.**
  This field represents the line number in a set.
- **From value**
  This field represents the from value interval of a set line. If a set line only has one value and no range, then this field will represent that one value.
- **To value**
  This field represents the to value interval of a set line.
- **Short text of set line**
  This field stores optional text associated with a set line.

- **FGr**
  This field represents the format group for a set line. Format group helps with the formatting of rows and columns of a set line within reporting.
- **Sym.Name**
  This field represents the symbolic name for a set line. Symbolic name is used in reporting.
- **SU**
  This checkbox is checked if you want to segregate or suppress the value intervals of a set line in a report writer.
- **P/M**
  This field is used to represent a plus or a minus value for a set line in a report writer. Depending on whether a value is positive or negative, it shows up differently on the report. SAP S/4HANA provides you with three default options for the **P/M** field: blank, which is for output irrespective of +/- sign; **+**, which is for output only if the value is zero or positive; and **-**, which is for output only if the value is negative.
- **AC**
  This field is used to add an additional layer of checks to records of a set line while creating a report.

The last five fields of the set configuration are used by the report writer to develop reports and don't contribute to the sales and distribution–RRB integration process. That is why for our use case, as shown in Figure 7.14, all five fields are blank.

7.2.4 Material Determination

The material determination configuration step within a DIP profile usage helps with the determination of materials within a RRB process. The actual material master configuration is still done in materials management using Transaction MM01, while this is an extension step within which you configure additional layers needed for RRB only. In other words, the core functionality of materials is still driven from Transaction MM01, but the additional features needed for RRB to work smoothly are done in this configuration.

To set up material determination and/or maintain selection criteria, you must have at least one characteristic flagged for **Mat. determination** in the **Characteristics** configuration step (see Section 7.2.2). The flagged characteristics can then be used to define criteria for material determination.

For our RRB use case, we broadly categorize materials as time-only materials and expense-only materials. Time-only materials have hours or quantity associated with them, and expense-only materials have cost associated with them. Figure 7.15 shows the materials configured at the example client site.

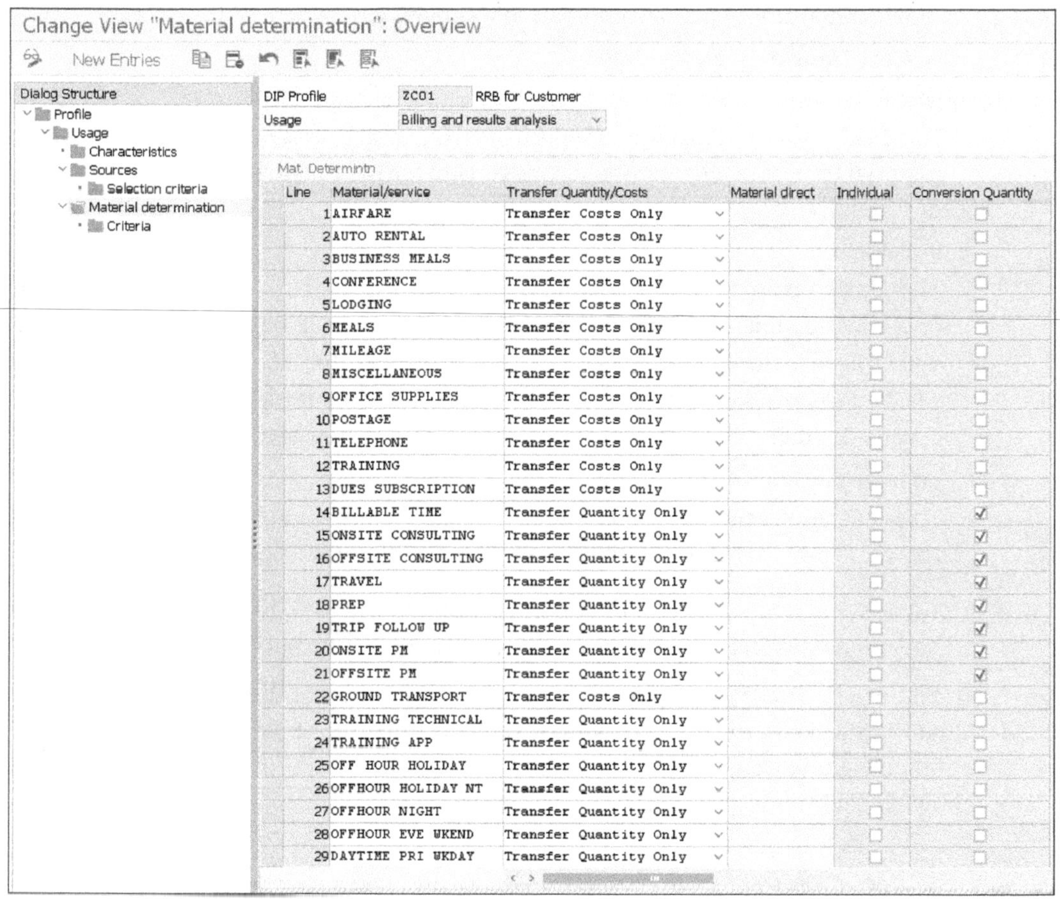

Change View "Material determination": Overview

DIP Profile: ZC01 RRB for Customer
Usage: Billing and results analysis

Mat. Determintn

Line	Material/service	Transfer Quantity/Costs	Material direct	Individual	Conversion Quantity
1	AIRFARE	Transfer Costs Only		☐	☐
2	AUTO RENTAL	Transfer Costs Only		☐	☐
3	BUSINESS MEALS	Transfer Costs Only		☐	☐
4	CONFERENCE	Transfer Costs Only		☐	☐
5	LODGING	Transfer Costs Only		☐	☐
6	MEALS	Transfer Costs Only		☐	☐
7	MILEAGE	Transfer Costs Only		☐	☐
8	MISCELLANEOUS	Transfer Costs Only		☐	☐
9	OFFICE SUPPLIES	Transfer Costs Only		☐	☐
10	POSTAGE	Transfer Costs Only		☐	☐
11	TELEPHONE	Transfer Costs Only		☐	☐
12	TRAINING	Transfer Costs Only		☐	☐
13	DUES SUBSCRIPTION	Transfer Costs Only		☐	☐
14	BILLABLE TIME	Transfer Quantity Only		☐	☑
15	ONSITE CONSULTING	Transfer Quantity Only		☐	☑
16	OFFSITE CONSULTING	Transfer Quantity Only		☐	☑
17	TRAVEL	Transfer Quantity Only		☐	☑
18	PREP	Transfer Quantity Only		☐	☑
19	TRIP FOLLOW UP	Transfer Quantity Only		☐	☑
20	ONSITE PM	Transfer Quantity Only		☐	☑
21	OFFSITE PM	Transfer Quantity Only		☐	☑
22	GROUND TRANSPORT	Transfer Costs Only		☐	☐
23	TRAINING TECHNICAL	Transfer Quantity Only		☐	☐
24	TRAINING APP	Transfer Quantity Only		☐	☐
25	OFF HOUR HOLIDAY	Transfer Quantity Only		☐	☐
26	OFFHOUR HOLIDAY NT	Transfer Quantity Only		☐	☐
27	OFFHOUR NIGHT	Transfer Quantity Only		☐	☐
28	OFFHOUR EVE WKEND	Transfer Quantity Only		☐	☐
29	DAYTIME PRI WKDAY	Transfer Quantity Only		☐	☐

Figure 7.15 DIP Usage Material Determination

As shown in Figure 7.15, the material determination screen for a DIP usage has the following fields:

- **Line**
  This field represents the line number for a material determination line.
- **Material/service**
  This field represents the dynamic item material name/number used in a RRB process.
- **Transfer Quantity/Costs**
  This field helps control how quantity and costs are determined on a sales document within a RRB process. As a default, SAP S/4HANA provides you with the following determination/transfer options:
  - Blank for **Transfer Costs Only**
  - **X** for **Transfer Cost and Quantity**
  - **A** for **Costs <> 0, Transfer Costs and Quantity**

  - **B** for **Quantity <> 0, Transfer Costs and Quantity**
  - **C** for **Transfer Quantity Only**

- **Material direct**
  This field is used to flag a material from posting, if applicable. You can either use the material to post or the material characteristic for posting depending on your business requirements.
- **Individual**
  This checkbox is checked if you don't want to summarize dynamic item materials on a sales document within a RRB process. All the materials will be displayed individually. Because summarization is necessary at our example client, this checkbox isn't selected for any of the materials. Summarization of materials occurs based on the criteria defined in the **Summarization** configuration step (see Section 7.2.2).
- **Conversion Quantity**
  This checkbox is checked if you want the system to use the sales document's UoM. If this checkbox isn't checked, the system uses the dynamic item's UoM.

To understand material determination selection criteria, we'll look at one example for a time-only material and one example for an expense-only material.

In Figure 7.15, **ONSITE CONSULTING** is a time-only material that has the **Conversion Quantity** checkbox checked. We defined the selection criteria for on-site consulting by configuring a basic set for characteristic **Activity Type** using from and to values, as shown in Figure 7.16 and Figure 7.17, respectively.

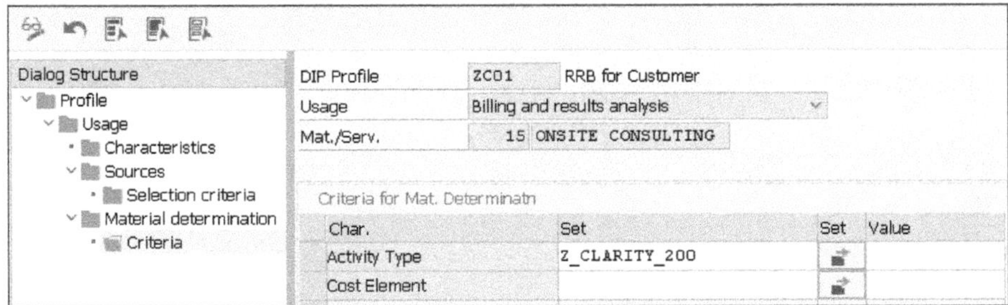

Figure 7.16 Criteria for Material Determination: On-Site Consulting

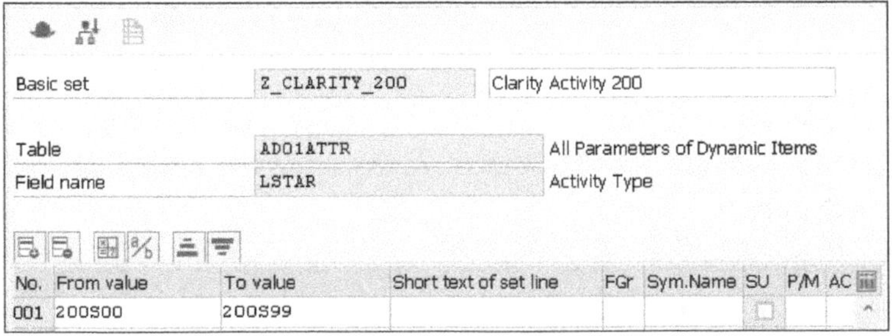

Figure 7.17 Basic Set for Material Determination: On-Site Consulting

In Figure 7.15, **AIRFARE** is an expense-only material. We defined the selection criteria for airfare by configuring a basic set for characteristic **Cost Element** using from and to values, as shown in Figure 7.18 and Figure 7.19, respectively.

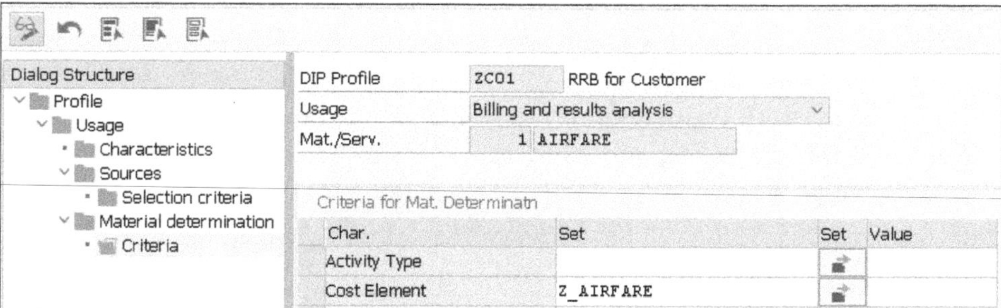

Figure 7.18 Criteria for Material Determination: Airfare

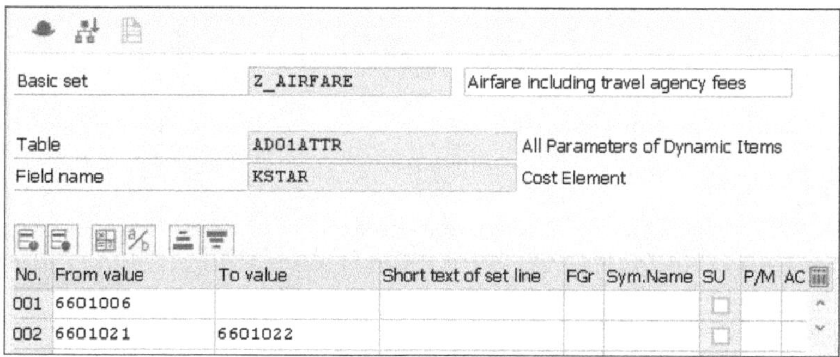

Figure 7.19 Basic Set for Material Determination: Airfare

7.2.5 End-to-End Integration

In this section, we'll look at two checkpoints—sales order types and item categories—on the sales and distribution side where you maintain RRB details for cross-referencing purposes and to complete an end-to-end sales and distribution–Project System integration.

Sales Order Type

At a minimum, you should create two sales order types, debit memo request and credit memo request, for a RRB process to function seamlessly. This can be done from Transaction VOV8, where you can either use an existing sales order type or create a new one by clicking the **New Entries** button. You should pay special attention to the following fields while creating the order type, as shown in Figure 7.20:

- **SD document categ.**
  This field represents the document category for a sales order type. For an RRB sales order type, the document category is **L**, which stands for **Debit Memo Request**.

- **Screen sequence grp.**
  This field represents the sequence group of screens for a sales order type. The screen group controls which screens show up in which order for a particular transaction. The screen sequence group for a RRB sales order type is **GA**, which stands for **Credit/ Debit Memo**.
- **Doc. pric. procedure**
  This field helps with the determination of the pricing procedure for a sales order type. The document pricing procedure value for a RRB sales order type is **F**, which stands for **DP90 W. Billing Plan**.

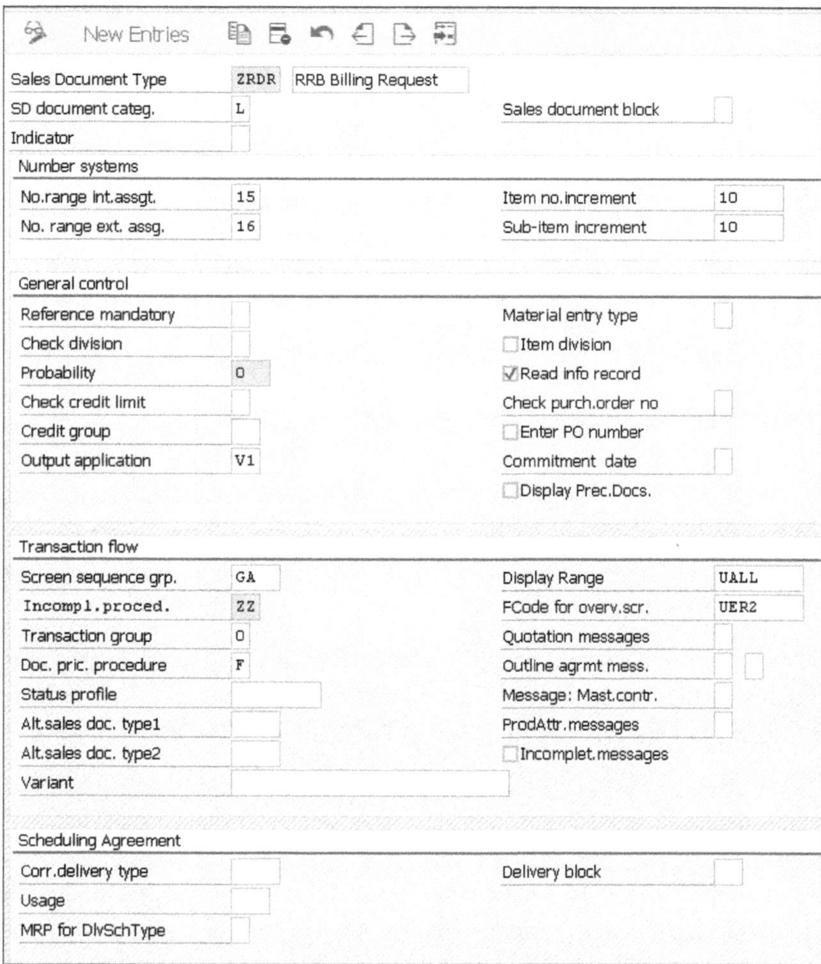

Figure 7.20 Sales Order Type for RRB Debit Memo Request

Item Category

Item category is the heart of sales and distribution and one of the primary components in the sales process. There is one configuration you must perform on the item category to tie it to RRB. To do so, go into the item category you want to use in RRB using Transaction VOV7, and scroll all the way to the bottom of the screen until you see the section for **Control of Resource-related Billing and Creation of Quotations**. Within this section, maintain the DIP profile ID in the **DIP Prof.** field, as configured in the earlier section.

At the example client, we configured DIP profile **ZC01**, which is maintained in the item category configuration of ZSTM. This ZSTM item category is used on the sales order to tag a material relevant for RRB. Figure 7.21 shows the item category configuration for ZSTM.

Control of Resource-related Billing and Creation of Quotations

Billing form		DIP Prof.	ZC01

Figure 7.21 Item Category Configuration for RRB Sales Order Type

The **Billing form** field shown in Figure 7.21 is a control field used specifically to control the display of costs versus fixed rates while running billing on a RRB sales document. At our example client, the RRB item category needs to follow the standard billing process, so we left this field blank.

7.3 Time Sheets Using Cross-Application Time Sheet

Cross-application time sheet (CATS) is a standard SAP S/4HANA solution for recording time and other tasks related to time entry. CATS has natural integrations with various functionalities such as human resources (HR), Project System, financial accounting, controlling, sales and distribution, and so on. It also connects easily with third-party time entry solutions such as Clarity, Navigator, and others. CATS is a strong, customizable tool that can be used differently with different functionalities depending on business requirements.

In this section, we'll focus on how CATS is used for RRB and sales and distribution processes only. While explaining the concepts of CATS transactions, we'll refer to a use case at the example client, which is the most common use case we've seen with most companies. It's a simple standard use case, but if your project or company has complex scenarios, you can easily configure CATS to those needs too. Once your core concepts are established after reading this section, you should be able to work on any CATS-related requirements.

Within RRB, CATS is used for recording hours, which post to a WBS and are transferred to a RRB sales order using Transaction DP91. Figure 7.22 shows how time sheet data flows through CATS within an RRB process.

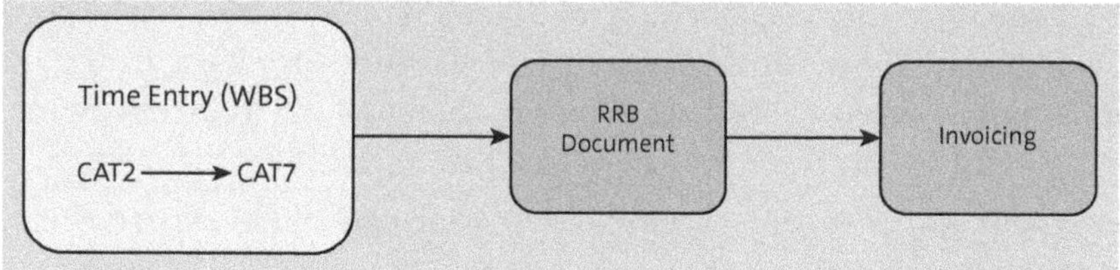

Figure 7.22 CATS within a RRB process

As shown in Figure 7.22, CATS or time entry (WBS) tile comprises two steps:

1. **Transaction CAT2**
   This transaction is used to enter time against a WBS. You can either directly entry time in CAT2 or connect it with other functionalities or third-party applications. At the example client, Clarity is used to record time, and the hours from Clarity are transferred to Transaction CAT2 using integration.
2. **Transaction CAT7**
   This transaction is used to transfer hours from Transaction CAT2 to controlling. Think of this step as the approval step to validate hours entered in CAT2. Once hours are transferred to controlling, you technically can't roll them back. You must post an adjustment in Transaction CAT2 and then send that entry to Transaction CAT7 to see the effect of the adjustment.

Once the hours flow through Transactions CAT2 and CAT7, they enter the RRB document via Transaction DP91. Transaction DP91 creates an RRB document by combining the hours on the WBS received from Transaction CAT7 and the rate from the sales order on the same WBS. The RRB document is then sent for invoicing, which completes the process. You'll learn more about this process in Section 7.5.

For now, let's deep dive into Transactions CAT2 and CAT7 to see what their roles are in the sales and distribution–RRB process.

7.3.1 Time Sheet Entry (Transaction CAT2)

Transaction CAT2 is used to enter time against a WBS. As mentioned earlier, you can either directly entry time in CAT2 or connect it to other functionalities or third-party applications. To enter time directly into CAT2, simply type in Transaction CAT2. You'll be directed to a page as shown in Figure 7.23.

There are three fields in the Transaction CAT2 initial screen:

- **Data Entry Profile**
  This field represents the data entry profile ID configured for a CATS process. **Data Entry Profile** is a core entity of CATS and controls the following:
  - Time sheet data entry method
  - Time sheet data entry screen layout

- Time sheet data entry user population: individual employees or employee groups
- Types of time sheet data allowed within Transaction CAT2
- Frequency of time sheet data entry: daily, weekly, monthly, and so on
- Approval criteria for time sheet data

You can configure multiple data entry profiles for a CATS process and authorize time sheet users to only have access to certain profiles depending on business requirements.

- **Key date**
  This field represents the date of the period for which a time sheet user plans to record time.
- **Personnel Number**
  This field represents the personnel number of a time sheet user who plans to record time using Transaction CAT2.

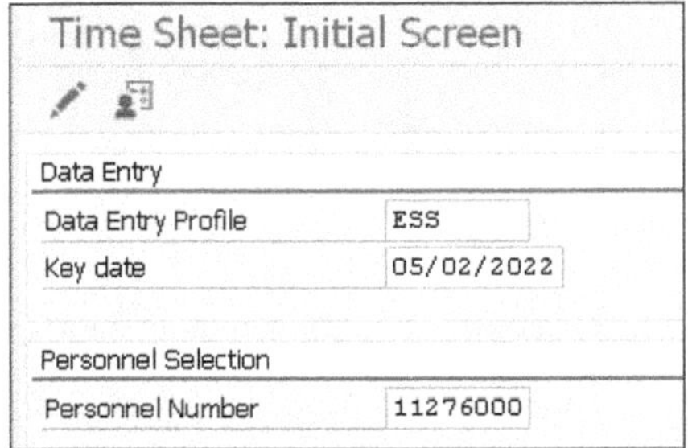

Figure 7.23 CAT2 Initial Screen

After you input **Data Entry Profile**, **Key date**, and **Personnel Number**, click on the pencil icon on the top-left area of the screen. This will take you to the **Time Sheet: Data Entry View** of Transaction CAT2, which is shown in Figure 7.24.

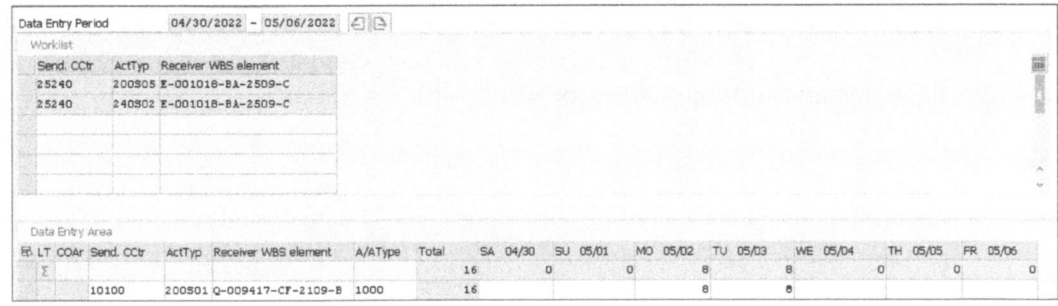

Figure 7.24 CAT2 Time Sheet: Data Entry View

The **Time Sheet: Data Entry View** has three sections: the header section, **Worklist** section, and **Data Entry Area** section. Fields within all three sections are customizable.

Using CATS configuration transactions or IMG menu path, you can easily pick and choose which fields you want to display on the data entry view.

Based on the example client's requirements, we configured the header section to only show **Data Entry Period**. Within our data entry profile, we configured the data entry period type to be weekly, which is why you see a weekly date range for **Data Entry Period**. Depending on the **Key Date** entered on the Transaction CAT2 initial screen (05/02/2022), the data entry period proposed is 04/30/2022 – 05/06/2022. You can easily move to a previous or a next period using the arrow keys of the **Data Entry Period** field.

The **Worklist** section has many fields; a few of them can be seen in Figure 7.24, while the others are hidden. Worklists can be user defined or controlled through configuration. To reach the worklist settings, execute Transaction CAC2. For the example client, the following three key fields are shown on the worklist (see Figure 7.24): **Send. CCtr**, **Act-Typ**, and **Receiver WBS element**. We'll explain these fields in detail in the next section.

The **Data Entry Area** section also has many fields. Again, based on the example client's requirements, we only enabled the fields shown in Figure 7.24, and the remaining fields were made invisible:

- **COAr**
  This field represents the controlling area for a time sheet entry. Controlling areas are set up in the controlling functionality.
- **Send. CCtr**
  This field represents the cost center tied to a time sheet entry. Generally, cost centers are department specific and are associated with an employee record of time sheet users. For example, a user belonging to the IT team will have an IT cost center, while the one belonging to the finance team will have a finance cost center.
- **ActTyp**
  This field represents the activity type ID for a time sheet entry. Depending on the activity a time sheet user performs, they can select an activity type and add hours against it. Activity types are driven by cost centers and are measured in hours (time) or quantity. You can create activity types via Transaction KL01. Examples of activity types include on-site consulting, off-site consulting, and so on.

> **Note**
>
> In Section 7.2.4, you saw that activity type is defined as a selection criteria characteristic for time-only material determination. Based on the activity type code you select in Transaction CAT2, time-only materials are determined on the RRB sales document.

- **Receiver WBS element**
  This field represents the receiver WBS element against which the time sheet user enters hours. The same WBS is present on the sales and distribution sales order and

on the expense document, which sends expense entries from the expense system to SAP and on to the RRB document. We'll discuss expenses further in Section 7.3.2.

- **A/A Type**
  This field represents the attendance or absence type code that a time sheet user chooses while entering time in CAT2. To create an absence type, you can use Transaction S_AHR_61010289 or follow IMG menu path **Time Management • Time Data Recording and Administration • Absences • Absence Catalog • Define Absence Type**.
- **Total**
  This field represents the total number of hours entered on a time sheet for a date entry period.
- **SA 04/30, SU 05/01...**
  These fields represent individual dates where a time sheet user can enter hours specific to that day. The addition of hours on all dates makes up the hours in the **Total** field.

Note

To configure different components of Transaction CAT2, such as initial screen, **Data Entry Profile**, and the **Time Sheet: Data Entry View** (including fields within **Worklist** and **Data Entry Area**), you either refer to the transactions mentioned in the previous sections or follow IMG menu path **Cross-Application Components • Time Sheet**. We suggest you work with a Project System consultant to configure Transaction CAT2 based on your business requirements.

7.3.2 Time Sheet Approval (Transaction CAT7)

Transaction CAT7 validates the hours entered in Transaction CAT2 and sends them over to controlling. This validation is strictly a technical validation to confirm things such as whether entered hours are in the correct format, the WBS element has the correct status, the operative indicators are checked properly, the period in which hours are to be posted is open, and other such technical validations. To transfer time, simply execute Transaction CAT7. You'll be directed to a page as shown in Figure 7.25.

As shown in Figure 7.25, the Transaction CAT7 initial screen has three sections: **Selection Parameters**, **Date for Entry of Activity Allocation**, and **Parameters**. First, the **Selection Parameters** section has three fields:

- **Personnel Number**
  This field represents the personnel number of the time sheet user who recorded time in Transaction CAT2.
- **Date**
  This field represents the **Data Entry Period** of the time sheet record entered by the time sheet user.

- **Document Number**
  This field represents the document number for the time sheet record entered in Transaction CAT2.

The **Date for Entry of Activity Allocation** section has one field, **Posting Date**. This field represents the date when the time sheet record was saved in Transaction CAT2. For example, if you want to transfer all Transaction CAT2 time sheets entered on 05/02/2022 to controlling, then you enter 05/02/2022 as the posting date, as seen in Figure 7.25.

Finally, the **Parameters** section has the following fields:

- **Personnel No. in CO**
  This checkbox is checked if you want the personnel number to be updated in the Transaction CAT7 controlling document during posting.
- **Ignore warnings**
  This checkbox is checked if you want to ignore warnings while running a Transaction CAT7 process. We don't recommend checking this checkbox.
- **Test Run**
  This checkbox is checked if you want to run Transaction CAT7 in test mode.
- **Application Log**
  This checkbox is checked if you want to maintain logs of errors for a Transaction CAT7 process.

CATS: Transfer to Controlling

Selection Parameters

Personnel Number	11276000	to	
Date	04/30/2022	to	05/06/2022
Document Number		to	

Date for Entry of Activity Allocation

Posting Date

Parameters

- [x] Personnel No. in CO
- [ ] Ignore warnings
- [ ] Test Run
- [ ] Application Log

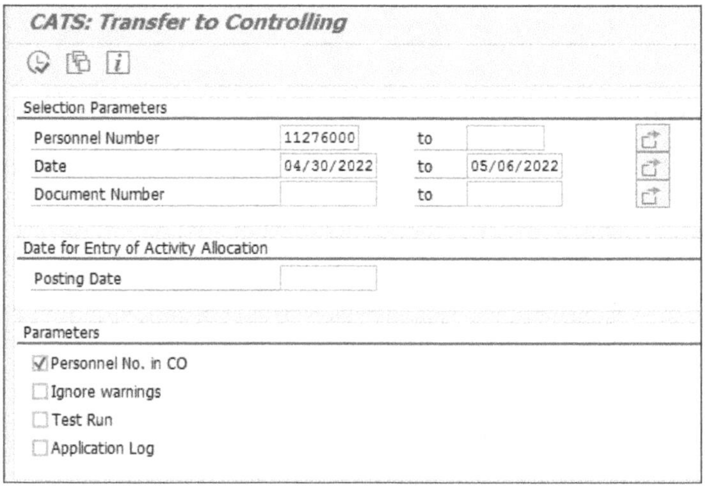

Figure 7.25 Transaction CAT7: Initial Screen

After you make selections on the Transaction CAT7 initial screen, click on the **Execute** icon on the top-left side of the screen. If all is good with the Transaction CAT2 data entry and the Transaction CAT7 selection, you'll be directed to a screen that looks something like what you see in Figure 7.26.

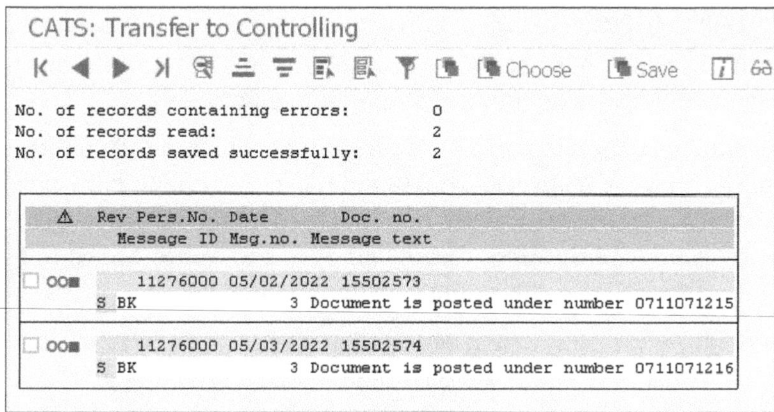

Figure 7.26 Transaction CAT7: Confirmation

As shown in Figure 7.26, the Transaction CAT7 confirmation screen has two sections: the header section and details section. The header section shows a summary of the Transaction CAT7 run, with the **No. of records containing errors**, **No. of records read**, and **No. of records saved successfully** information. In our example, everything passed successfully so errors are **0**, and records read and saved successfully show **2**.

The details section gives more context around the Transaction CAT7 run. In the left side of the table, you see a green square, which indicates that there are no exceptions, and records have processed successfully. (Other exception codes are a yellow circle, which indicates warning, and a red circle, which indicates a hard error.) Following are the rest of the columns in the table:

- **Rev**
  This column is used to indicate if a document has been reversed from controlling or transferred to controlling. A blank value in the column signifies it's transferred.
- **Pers. No.**
  This column indicates the personnel number of the time sheet user who recorded time in Transaction CAT2.
- **Date**
  This column indicates the date on which the hours are recorded by the time sheet user. In this example, because we recorded time for two days, you see two entries in the details table, one for each date.
- **Doc. no.**
  This column indicates the controlling document number that is generated because of the Transaction CAT7 run.
- **Message ID**, **Msg. no.**, and **Message text**
  These three columns are message details columns, which give you information associated with the Transaction CAT7 confirmation records.

7.3.3 Time Sheet Table CATSDB

In this section, we'll talk about a key table where CATS data is stored. Knowing details about the table is important from a reporting and support point of view.

Table CATSDB, in our opinion, is the heart of a CATS process. It's a standard SAP table that stores almost all the important data related to CATS time sheets. This table has helped us with many reporting requirements and has been our best friend when debugging and resolving a plethora of CATS issues for the various clients we've worked with. To get to table CATSDB, enter Transaction SE16N, and enter table name "CATSDB".

Figure 7.27 shows the table CATSDB selection screen. There about 100 fields on table CATSDB, using which you can run selection and get outputs based on your requirements. That is the strength and versatility of table CTASDB. To validate the example, enter **Personnel No.** and **Date** as the selection criteria and then click **Execute**.

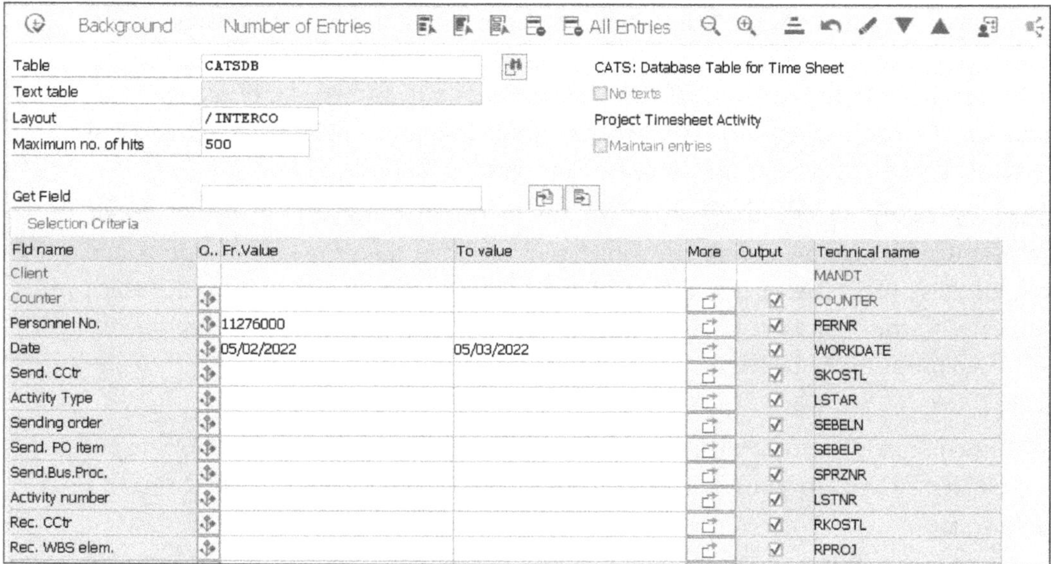

Figure 7.27 Table CATSDB: Selection

Figure 7.28 shows a snippet of the output. As you can see, you have complete visibility to all time sheet data created in Transaction CAT2 and Transaction CAT7 (keep in mind this is just a snippet of the output and you can see as many as all fields on the output depending on your needs). So, if there is a mismatch in the data you see in the RRB process versus the data you expected, this table will help you find the reason for the mismatch and potentially support you with the fix.

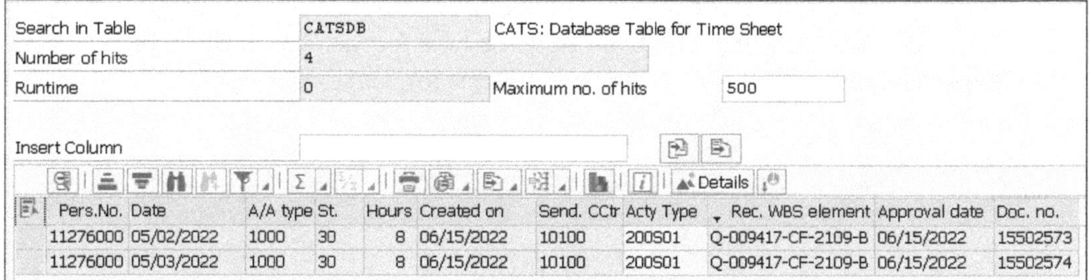

Search in Table	CATSDB	CATS: Database Table for Time Sheet
Number of hits	4	
Runtime	0	Maximum no. of hits 500
Insert Column		

Details

Pers.No.	Date	A/A type	St.	Hours	Created on	Send. CCtr	Acty Type	Rec. WBS element	Approval date	Doc. no.
11276000	05/02/2022	1000	30	8	06/15/2022	10100	200S01	Q-009417-CF-2109-B	06/15/2022	15502573
11276000	05/03/2022	1000	30	8	06/15/2022	10100	200S01	Q-009417-CF-2109-B	06/15/2022	15502574

Figure 7.28 Table CATSDB: Output

7.4 Expenses Using SAP Concur

In Section 7.2, and specifically Section 7.2.4, we talked about time-only materials and expense-only materials. Both materials form the core of an RRB process. In the previous section, we looked at time-only materials and the underlying configuration that drives them through the RRB process. In this section, we'll shift our focus to expense-only materials.

We'll use SAP Concur to explain the flow of expense data into a RRB sales document and then into invoicing. Keep in mind that expenses can be entered in SAP S/4HANA directly using an expense document type, or you can connect any third-party expense system to SAP too. At the example client, SAP Concur is used as the travel and expense solution, and that is why we're using it as a prototype for this book. But don't worry, by the end of this chapter, you'll have a good understanding of what expense types are in general, as well as how they flow into SAP S/4HANA sales and distribution via expense reports and RRB sales document or through a direct SAP accounting document (irrespective of any expense system [native or third-party]). You'll also gain knowledge about expense reports and expense users. So, let's get started!

7.4.1 Expense Reports

An *expense report* is a document an expense user uses to record expenses incurred for a project commitment. Expense reports can have project and personal expenses. Each expense incurred by an expense user, either by a credit card or cash, is attached to an expense type, which is entered directly on an expense report. Expense types are tied to general ledger accounts in SAP S/4HANA. They also have one-to-one mapping with material master records. That is how they connect with SAP S/4HANA sales and distribution and finance to complete an end-to-end expense-to-finance posting cycle.

Figure 7.29 shows an expense report from SAP Concur. To open an expense report, log in to your SAP Concur profile, and from the homepage, click on **Open Report** in the **Expenses** section. Find the report you're looking for, and then click on it.

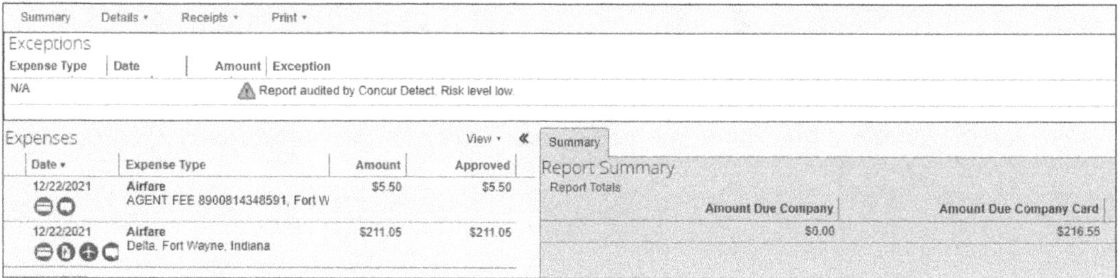

Figure 7.29 SAP Concur Expense Report

The top section of the report is the header section, which shows you information like **Summary** of the expense report, expense report **Details** (e.g., approval workflow and audit trail), **Receipts**, and **Print** options. At the center, you see the **Exceptions** section, which displays errors or warnings attached to an expense report (yellow triangle is for warnings, which can be ignored; red circles are hard errors, which must be fixed before you can submit an expense report). Next you see the **Expenses** section, which displays a list of expense types belonging to the expense report. Finally, the **Summary** section displays details behind a specific expense type (when you click on it).

7.4.2 Expense Types

Expense types are byproducts of expenses that are entered into an expense report by expense users, either directly in the SAP S/4HANA system or via an expense solution. Going back to our CATS example, let's say the consultant who had worked consulting hours on a project task had traveled on-site for the project and stayed overnight. The consultant would record hours against the WBS and would also enter airfare and lodging as expenses. When you run the RRB process (Transaction DP91) for the sales order containing the WBS, you'll see hours and expenses on the RRB sales document. We'll deep dive further into this example in Section 7.5.

Figure 7.30 shows a sample of an expense type in SAP Concur. To get to an expense type from an expense report, simply click on one expense item from the report homepage. In our example, we clicked on the **Airfare** expense item from our sample expense report in Figure 7.29.

An expense type has two main sections: **Expense** and **E-Receipt**.

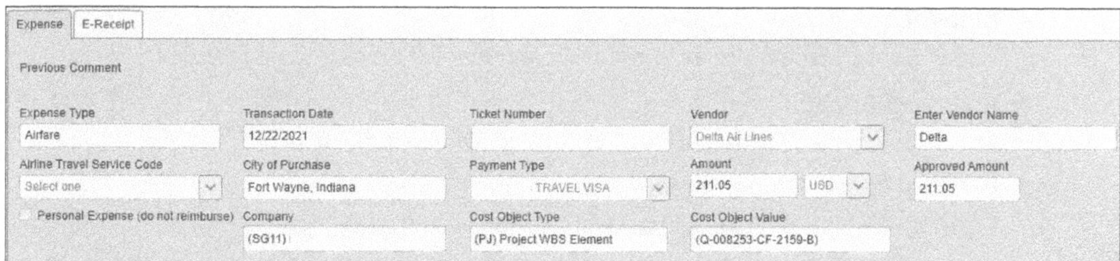

Figure 7.30 SAP Concur Expense Type

Figure 7.30 shows the different fields on the **Expense** section, which get sent over to the SAP S/4HANA system when you run the SAP Concur–SAP S/4HANA integration:

- **Expense Type**
  This field represents the expense type of the recorded expense. If a consultant has taken a flight to be on-site for a project commitment, they will record airfare as one of the expense types and tie it to the project WBS.
- **Transaction Date**
  This field represents the transaction date on which an expense was incurred. Typically, this date maps to the pricing date on the SAP S/4HANA sales and distribution RRB document.
- **Ticket Number**
  This is an optional field to record ticket number details of the airfare expense type. You won't see this field on other expense types that don't have tickets.
- **Vendor**
  This field represents the vendor's name through which an expense was made. In our example, the airfare ticket was booked with Delta Airlines, which is why you see their name as the vendor. If the expense type was for meals, then you would see the restaurant name as the vendor in this field.
- **Enter Vendor Name**
  This field supplements the **Vendor** field. If you want to allow expense users to add more details about the vendor name, then they can use this field to do so.
- **Airline Travel Service Code**
  This field represents the travel service code for an airline expense. The example client doesn't use this code.
- **City of Purchase**
  This field represents the city name where an expense is incurred. This is an important field from a tax determination standpoint.
- **Payment Type**
  This field represents the payment type for an expense. At our example client, we've configured three payment types: travel visa, personal credit, and cash.

- **Amount**
  This field represents the amount and currency for an expense type.
- **Approved Amount**
  This field represents the amount approved for an expense type.
- **Personal Expense (do not reimburse)**
  This checkbox is checked if you want to tag an expense type as a personal expense on an expense report. Personal expenses aren't reimbursed or are billed directly to the expense user.
- **Company**
  This field represents the company code to which the expense user belongs. This company code field maps to a sales organization field on the SAP S/4HANA sales and distribution RRB document.
- **Cost Object Type**
  This field represents the cost object type for an expense. At our example client, this field is mapped to WBS and cost center.
- **Cost Object Value**
  This field represents the cost object value for an expense type. In case of a WBS this field shows the WBS element ID and in case of cost center this field shows the cost center number. Both WBS and cost center are sent over to SAP S/4HANA along with other integration data.

When expense types integrate over to the SAP S/4HANA system, they create an accounting document, as shown in Figure 7.31. If you're doing expenses directly in the SAP S/4HANA system, then you create the accounting document using Transaction FB60.

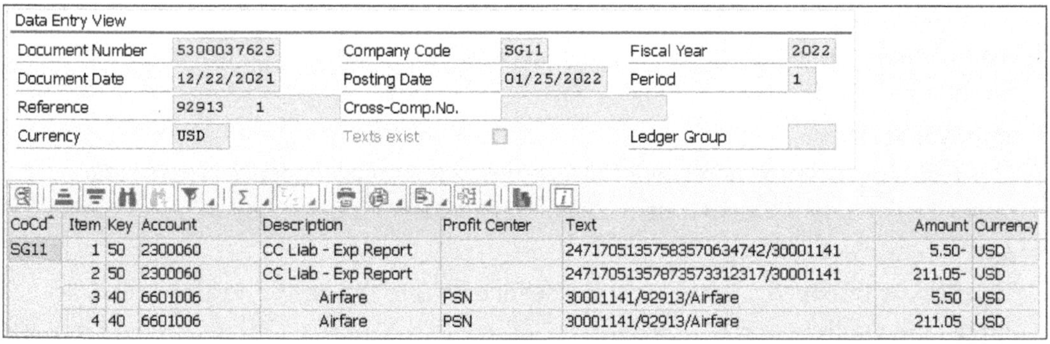

Data Entry View

Document Number	5300037625	Company Code	SG11	Fiscal Year	2022
Document Date	12/22/2021	Posting Date	01/25/2022	Period	1
Reference	92913 1	Cross-Comp.No.			
Currency	USD	Texts exist		Ledger Group	

CoCd	Item	Key	Account	Description	Profit Center	Text	Amount	Currency
SG11	1	50	2300060	CC Liab - Exp Report		24717051357583570634742/30001141	5.50-	USD
	2	50	2300060	CC Liab - Exp Report		24717051357873573312317/30001141	211.05-	USD
	3	40	6601006	Airfare	PSN	30001141/92913/Airfare	5.50	USD
	4	40	6601006	Airfare	PSN	30001141/92913/Airfare	211.05	USD

Figure 7.31 SAP S/4HANA Expense Document

Figure 7.32 shows an example of a sales and distribution RRB document in an SAP S/4HANA system, where you can see that expense type **Airfare** is mapped to **Material AIRFARE**. The two airfare expense types on the SAP Concur expense report in Figure 7.29 are combined into one airfare material on the sales and distribution RRB document.

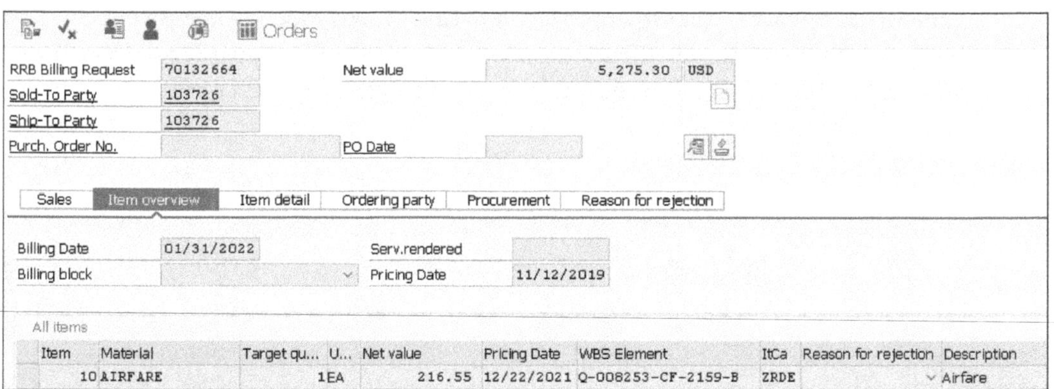

Figure 7.32 Sales and Distribution RRB Document

Figure 7.33 shows how an expense type is mapped to a general ledger account in SAP Concur. **6601006** is the general ledger code in the SAP S/4HANA system.

Figure 7.33 Expense Type General Ledger Mapping

7.4.3 Expense Users

The person who enters expense types into an expense report is called an *expense user*. In our example, the consultant who recorded hours and expenses can be referred to as an expense user in SAP Concur.

Let's say you're an expense user in SAP Concur and want to get to your user profile: simply log in to your SAP Concur profile from the homepage, and click on **Profile • Profile Settings**. Next, click on the **Expense Information** option under **Expense Settings** of your profile settings to get to your user profile. Figure 7.34 shows what an expense user profile looks like in SAP Concur.

As mentioned earlier, at the example client, we use SAP Concur for travel and expenses. That is why a user profile in SAP Concur has both settings: **Travel Settings** and **Expense Settings**. It also has the **Your Information** section, as shown in Figure 7.34, which is the general information section of the user profile where an expense user can maintain details such as **Personal Information**, **Company Information**, and so on. Within **Expense Settings**, the expense user can maintain **Expense Information**, **Expense Delegates**,

Expense Preferences, **Expense Approvers**, and **Favorite Attendees**. **Expense Information** has fields **Employee Group**, **Office Location**, **Reimbursement Currency**, **Cost Object Type**, and **Cost Object Value**. All of this information flows from the expense user profile to expense reports and then to SAP.

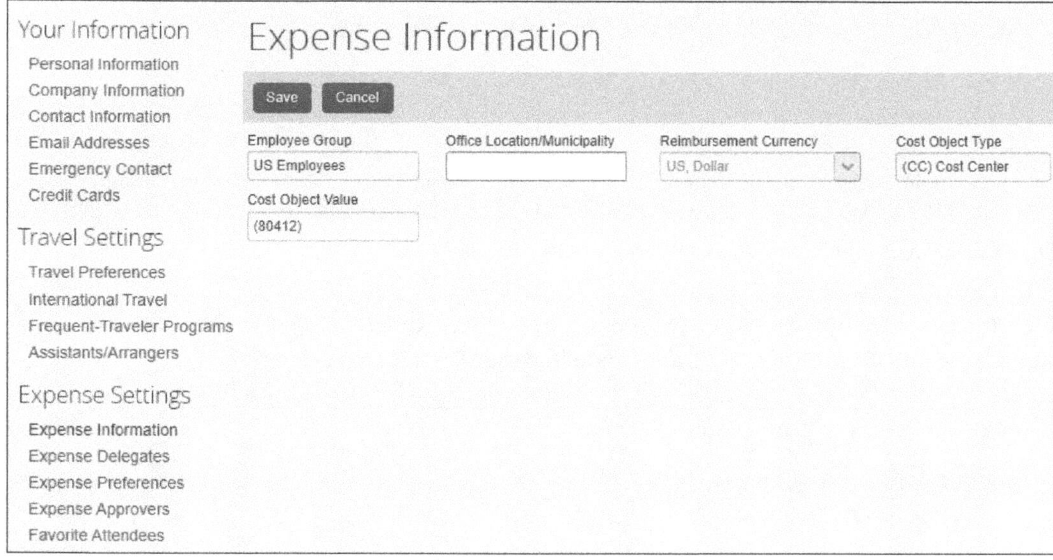

Figure 7.34 Expense User Profile

7.5 End-to-End Integration

In this section, we'll look at the steps that make up a strong sales and distribution RRB process to provide a consolidated visual representation of all you've learned in this chapter. There are a total of eight steps that contract an RRB process:

1. Create the sales order in SAP S/4HANA sales and distribution, which has a WBS element on the line item.
2. Maintain the rate for consulting hours.
3. Record consulting hours in Transaction CAT2.
4. Look at table CATSDB to validate hours posted to controlling via Transaction CAT7.
5. Create an expense report in SAP Concur.
6. Transfer the expense report to the SAP S/4HANA system and generate an expense document.
7. Run the Transaction DP91 process to generate the RRB sales document.
8. Invoice the RRB sales document.

Let's start with the creation of the sales order in SAP S/4HANA sales and distribution, which has a WBS element on the line item. Figure 7.35 shows a sales order created in SAP

S/4HANA sales and distribution. Focus your attention on line **30**, which tells you that the company has contracted 80 hours of consulting help for a client whose WBS element code is **S-106973-BA-2259-B**.

All items

Item	Material	Order Q...	Un	S	D	ItCa	HL Itm	Net price	Net value	WBS Element	Profit Center
10	102620	90	EA		...	ZSTM	0	187.00	16,830.00	S-016973-BA-2509-B	PSN
20	105670	80.0	HR		...	ZSTM	0	187.00	14,960.00	S-016973-OT-6209-B	PSN
30	104898	80	H		...	ZSTM	0	187.00	14,960.00	S-016973-BA-2259-B	PSN

Figure 7.35 Sales Document in SAP S/4HANA Sales and Distribution

Now, we'll move on to the maintaining rate for consulting hours. We created a condition type ZPRO, which is a copy of PR00, and used it to maintain the rate for consulting hours against the sales order line item, which we created in the previous step, and tied it directly to a WBS. As shown in Figure 7.36, for line item 30, an hourly rate of 187 is maintained in Transaction VK11.

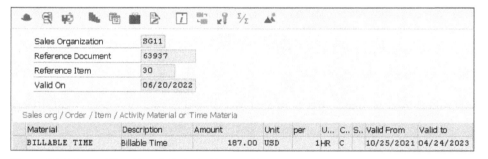

Sales Organization	SG11
Reference Document	63937
Reference Item	30
Valid On	06/20/2022

Sales org / Order / Item / Activity Material or Time Materia

Material	Description	Amount	Unit	per	U...	C..	S..	Valid From	Valid to
BILLABLE TIME	Billable Time	187.00	USD	1	HR	C		10/25/2021	04/24/2023

Figure 7.36 Consulting Hourly Rate in Transaction VK11

The next step is recording consulting hours in Transaction CAT2. In our example, consultant Mr. Johnson entered hours in Transaction CAT2 for different dates, as shown in Figure 7.37. Note that even though the hours are recorded on different days, they are still on the same WBS as the one on the sales order, which has the rate of 187.

Send. CCtr	ActTyp	Receiver WBS element	A/A...	Total	SA 02/26	SU 02/27	MO 02/28	TU 03/01	WE 03/02	TH 03/03	FR 03/04
20789	205S12	S-016973-BA-2259-B	1000	2					2		
20789	220S12	S-016973-BA-2259-B	1000	6					2	2	2
Send. CCtr	**ActTyp**	**Receiver WBS element**	**A/A...**	**Total**	**SA 03/05**	**SU 03/06**	**MO 03/07**	**TU 03/08**	**WE 03/09**	**TH 03/10**	**FR 03/11**
20789	220S12	S-016973-BA-2259-B	1000	3					2	1	
Send. CCtr	**ActTyp**	**Receiver WBS element**	**A/A...**	**Total**	**SA 03/19**	**SU 03/20**	**MO 03/21**	**TU 03/22**	**WE 03/23**	**TH 03/24**	**FR 03/25**
20789	220S12	S-016973-BA-2259-B	1000	2			2				

Figure 7.37 Consulting Hours in Transaction CAT2

The next step is looking at table CATSDB to validate hours posted to controlling via Transaction CAT7. Once hours were posted in Transaction CAT2, we ran Transaction CAT7 and moved those hours to controlling. Figure 7.38 shows a snapshot of table CATSDB, which shows hours from Transaction CAT2/Transaction CAT7.

Pers.No.	Date	A/A type	St.	ΣHours	Created on	Send. CCtr	Acty Type	Rec. WBS element	Approval date	Doc. no.
10213000	03/02/2022	1000	30	2	03/08/2022	20789	205S12	S-016973-BA-2259-B	03/08/2022	15281740
10213000		1000	30	2	03/08/2022	20789	220S12	S-016973-BA-2259-B	03/08/2022	15281741
	03/02/2022			• 4						
10213000	03/03/2022	1000	30	2	03/08/2022	20789	220S12	S-016973-BA-2259-B	03/08/2022	15281744
	03/03/2022			• 2						
10213000	03/04/2022	1000	30	2	03/08/2022	20789	220S12	S-016973-BA-2259-B	03/08/2022	15281746
	03/04/2022			• 2						
10213000	03/09/2022	1000	30	2	03/15/2022	20789	220S12	S-016973-BA-2259-B	03/15/2022	15295026
	03/09/2022			• 2						
10213000	03/10/2022	1000	30	1	03/15/2022	20789	220S12	S-016973-BA-2259-B	03/15/2022	15295029
	03/10/2022			• 1						
10213000	03/21/2022	1000	30	2	03/29/2022	20789	220S12	S-016973-BA-2259-B	03/29/2022	15328767
	03/21/2022			• 2						
				•• 13						

Figure 7.38 Hours in Table CATSDB

This brings you to creating an expense report in SAP Concur. Mr. Johnson also had expenses while he was working on the project and created an expense report in SAP Concur to record those expenses. As shown in Figure 7.39, all expenses are grouped by expense type, and, for simplicity's sake, we only expanded three expense types: **Car Rental**, **Hotel**, and **Personal Car Mileage**.

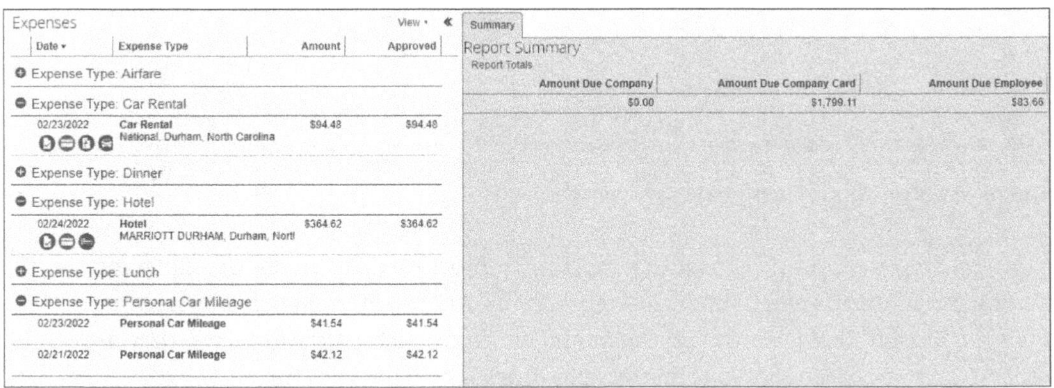

Figure 7.39 SAP Concur Expense Report

We'll continue with transferring the expense report to SAP S/4HANA and generating an expense document. Once Mr. Johnson's expense report is approved in SAP Concur, it flows into the SAP S/4HANA system through standard integrations and creates an expense document, as shown in Figure 7.40. If you're using any other expense solution or recording expenses directly in SAP S/4HANA, then Figure 7.40 will still be your landing page. You can see that the 83.66 **Mileage** expense is Mr. Johnson's personal expense and will be billed to him directly. The car rental expense type from the expense report maps to the **Autorental** cost element in the SAP expense document. The hotel expense type from the expense report maps to the **Lodging** cost element in the SAP expense document.

Data Entry View					
Document Number	5300038165	Company Code	SG11	Fiscal Year	2022
Document Date	02/24/2022	Posting Date	03/08/2022	Period	3
Reference	93069 1	Cross-Comp.No.			
Currency	USD	Texts exist		Ledger Group	

CoCd	Item	Key	Account	Description	Cost Center	Profit Center	Text	Amount	Currency
				CC Liab - Exp Report				1,799.11-	USD
				Airfare				1,231.81	USD
				Autorental				94.48	USD
				Lodging				364.62	USD
				Mileage				83.66	USD
				Johnson				83.66-	USD
				Travel, Meals				108.20	USD

Figure 7.40 Expense Document in SAP S/4HANA

The next step is running the Transaction DP91 process to generate the RRB sales document, as shown in Figure 7.41. Once hours and expenses are posted to the WBS in the SAP S/4HANA system, we run Transaction DP91 for the sales and distribution sales order. It will look at line item 30 and find the WBS on it. From the WBS, it will trace the posted hours and expenses and then populate them on the RRB document. It will get the rate of consulting hours from Transaction VK11, and multiply the rate with the hours in table CATSDB to get the end result in the RRB document. The backend configuration as to how the system knows to look at the WBS element and get all the other information about hours and expenses is what we configured in the DIP profile.

60	TRIP FOLLOW UP	2.0	HR	374.00	03/25/2022	S-016973-BA-2259-B	ZRDH	Engagement Follow Up
70	TRIP FOLLOW UP	3.0	HR	561.00	03/11/2022	S-016973-BA-2259-B	ZRDH	Engagement Follow Up
80	TRIP FOLLOW UP	6.0	HR	1,122.00	03/04/2022	S-016973-BA-2259-B	ZRDH	Engagement Follow Up
90	OFFSITE CONSULTING	2.0	HR	374.00	03/04/2022	S-016973-BA-2259-B	ZRDH	Off Site Consulting / Support
100	MILEAGE	1	EA	83.66	02/24/2022	S-016973-BA-2259-B	ZRDE	Mileage
110	LODGING	1	EA	364.62	02/24/2022	S-016973-BA-2259-B	ZRDE	Lodging
120	AUTO RENTAL	1	EA	94.48	02/24/2022	S-016973-BA-2259-B	ZRDE	Auto Rental
130	AIRFARE	1	EA	1,231.81	02/24/2022	S-016973-BA-2259-B	ZRDE	Airfare
140	MEALS	1	EA	108.20	02/24/2022	S-016973-BA-2259-B	ZRDE	Meals

Figure 7.41 RRB Document in SAP S/4HANA Sales and Distribution

The final step is invoicing the RRB sales document. At our example client, we bill hours and expenses separately on two different invoices. So, when we run Transaction VF04 for the RRB sales document, the system generates two invoices, as shown in Figure 7.42 and Figure 7.43.

60	Engagement Follow Up	2.0	HR	374.00	TRIP FOLLOW UP
70	Engagement Follow Up	3.0	HR	561.00	TRIP FOLLOW UP
80	Engagement Follow Up	6.0	HR	1,122.00	TRIP FOLLOW UP
90	Off Site Consulting / Support	2.0	HR	374.00	OFFSITE CONSULTING

Figure 7.42 RRB: Hours-Only Invoice

100	Mileage	1 EA	83.66	MILEAGE
110	Lodging	1 EA	364.62	LODGING
120	Auto Rental	1 EA	94.48	AUTO RENTAL
130	Airfare	1 EA	1,231.81	AIRFARE
140	Meals	1 EA	108.20	MEALS

Figure 7.43 RRB: Expense-Only Invoice

7.6 Summary

This brings us to the end of our coverage of RRB. Let's recap what you've learned:

- Section 7.1 talked about RRB as a process and how it's an integral part of the sales and distribution–Project System integration. We also touched on two key components of the RRB process: projects and WBS.
- Section 7.2 is the heart of this chapter where we shared our knowledge about the DIP profile and its underlying configuration. We took a deep dive into topics such as characteristics, sources, and material determination. We concluded this section with a bonus section where we highlighted the two sales and distribution checkpoints for the RRB process: sales order types and item categories.
- In Section 7.3, we turned our attention to time sheet entry using Transaction CAT2 and Transaction CAT7. We also discussed table CATSDB, which is a strong time sheet table to keep handy while debugging CATS issues.
- In Section 7.4, we pivoted our focus to expense entry using SAP Concur. We talked about expense reports and expense users. We looked at expense types closely to see how they map to the general ledger and material master. We discussed different fields of expense types that flow over to expense reports and then into the SAP S/4HANA system.
- Finally, we concluded the chapter in Section 7.5, where we walked you through an end-to-end RRB use case. It's an eight-step process starting from sales and distribution, going into RRB, and then wrapping up in finance.

In the next chapter, we'll take a look at the final integration points for sales and distribution in SAP S/4HANA in the area of production planning.

Chapter 8
Production Planning

Production planning is implemented in organizations where tangible goods are sold to end customers. The requirement from the sales document is transferred to production planning via various configuration elements. The business processes that revolve around intra-ERP integration between sales and distribution and production planning must be understood to obtain a 360-degree view from an order-to-cash to plan-to-produce business cycle.

Given the complexities of the overall business process, intra-ERP integration between the sales and distribution functionality and production planning functionality is always a very niche topic to discuss. In this chapter, we'll cover the major integration points between these functionalities in SAP S/4HANA. We'll also go over some of the key processes in the plan-to-produce business process that will be useful to the sales consultant when communicating the business requirements to the production planning consultant.

We'll begin with the material requirements planning (MRP) process. In this section, we'll look at the MRP process flow and the role of the MRP tool in the overall ERP landscape. The section will then take a deep dive into the various implementation methods for MRP in SAP S/4HANA, before concluding with a brief introduction to the scheduling process. We'll then learn how sales requirements are transferred to production planning. Then, we'll look at the key configuration elements for setting up the transfer of requirement in the system. Following that, we'll go over the variant configuration and the configuration elements that go with it. We'll also go over the make-to-order (MTO) process and planning strategies that you can leverage based on the requirement of the business. We'll wrap up this chapter with an example of an MTO process flow.

8.1 Material Requirements Planning

MRP is an inventory management system intended to increase business productivity. MRP's sole purpose is to increase a company's inventory efficiency by estimating raw material quantities and scheduling timely deliveries.

Before computer-engineered systems became common in the business world, inventory was manually recorded. With the passage of time, business users became aware of the shortcomings of manually recorded inventory, resulting in market demand and the need for a sophisticated and automated productive method. MRP was first conceptualized and implemented using computers by the aerospace industry, which was associated with General Electric and Rolls Royce, in the early 1950s. Prior to its commercialization, MRP was reinvented to work in conjunction with the existing Polaris program, which was previously used for inventory management. Stanley Black & Decker pioneered the use of MRP in 1964. More than 700 businesses had adopted MRP as their inventory management system by 1975. Since 1975, the MRP system, represented in several models, has been continuously updated to improve business efficiency. MRP is now one of the world's most popular and widely used inventory management systems.

MRP, which is primarily carried out through specialized software, aids in ensuring that the proper inventory is accessible for the production process precisely when it's required and at the lowest cost. As a result, MRP improves the efficiency, flexibility, and profitability of manufacturing operations. It has the potential to increase factory worker productivity, improve product quality, and reduce material and labor costs. MRP contributes to revenue growth by enabling manufacturers to respond to increased demand for their products more quickly and avoid production delays and inventory stock outs, which often result in lost customers. MRP is widely used by manufacturers and has unquestionably been a key enabler in the growth and widespread availability of affordable consumer goods, raising the standard of living in most countries. Individual manufacturers would not have been able to scale up operations as quickly as they have in the half-century since MRP software arrived if there had been no way to automate the complex calculations and data management of MRP processes.

With the help of the MRP process, the requirements generated from the sales are converted into procurement proposals such as planned orders and production orders. It's important to understand how different MRP procedures play a role in the overall plan-to-produce process.

In the following sections, we'll dive into the MRP process flow, along with the implementation methods for setting up the MRP procedures in the system. Finally, we'll discuss scheduling and how it's performed for external procurement and in-house production.

8.1.1 Process Flow

As mentioned earlier, MRP is the planning tool used by organizations to plan materials required for production or sales purposes. SAP has natively integrated MRP functionality in its core offering since its inception.

The prerequisite for the MRP process is the filled material master data relevant to the MRP process. We've covered the master data associated with the MRP process in

Chapter 3, Section 3.2. We recommend reviewing the important fields from that chapter before going over this section.

As shown in Figure 8.1, the process starts with forecasting data preparation. The *sales and operations planning* process is used to determine the quantities for production. Sales planning, also known as *demand planning*, addresses future needs without taking into account stocks or available capacity. The historical sales figures serve as the foundation for sales planning. The results of the sales planning process are used to plan production quantities, taking initial stocks and capacities into account.

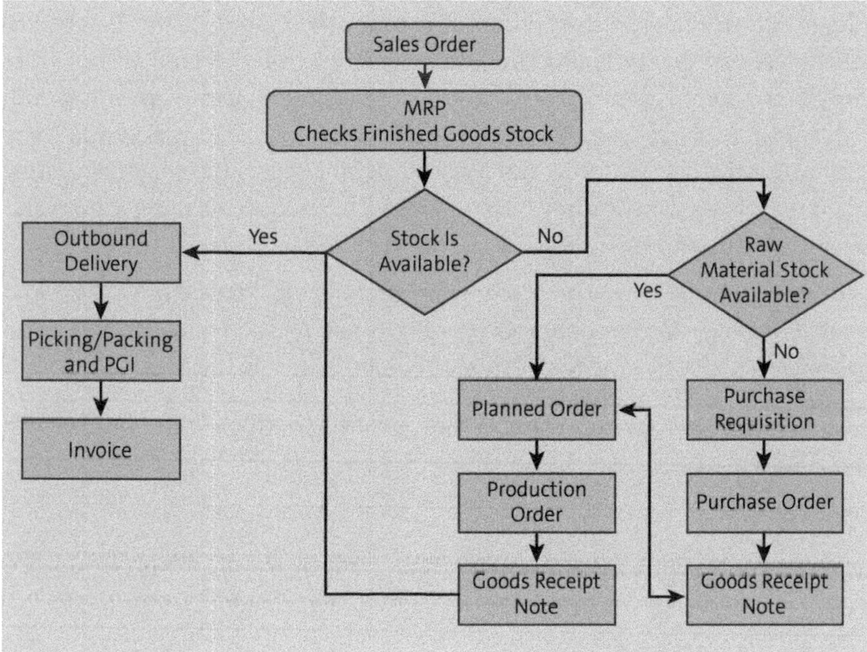

Figure 8.1 In-House Production Process

Based on the past historical sales and consumption data the required materials and quantities are forecasted. These requirements are called as *planned independent requirements*, which feed into the system with the help of demand management functionality in production planning via Transaction MD61.

The planned independent requirements are fed into the demand program. The customer requirement generated on the sales order is also fed into the program.

Based on the data provided to the demand program, the system creates the procurement proposal after running MRP via Transaction MD02. The procurement proposal consists of either the purchase requisition, which will be turned into a purchase order with a subsequent procure-to-pay cycle, or the planned order, which will be turned into a production order with a subsequent plan-to-produce cycle. Inventory management manages the quantities made available by production or by external procurement.

Note

For the material relevant for in-house production (i.e., **Procurement Type** is **In-House Production** in the **MRP 2** view), you have to maintain the **Work Center** and **Routing Data** fields in the material master as these two fields help determine production dates.

8.1.2 Implementation Methods

Organizations sell a variety of products depending on the industry in which they operate, including raw materials, finished products, semifinished products, trading goods, and so on. The product planning process differs depending on the product type that you're selling to the end customer. SAP has given you the option of implementing MRP processes based on product types. It's up to the business to decide which MRP type should be used for the material. The MRP type is maintained in the material master **MRP 1** view, as we discussed in Chapter 3, Section 3.2.6. The production planning consultant selects the MRP procedure during the MRP type configuration.

You can configure the MRP type by following menu path **Production • Material Requirements Planning • Master Data • Check MRP Types.** As shown in Figure 8.2, you can see the **MRP Type PD** has the **MRP Procedure** maintained as **D (Material Requirements Planning)**.

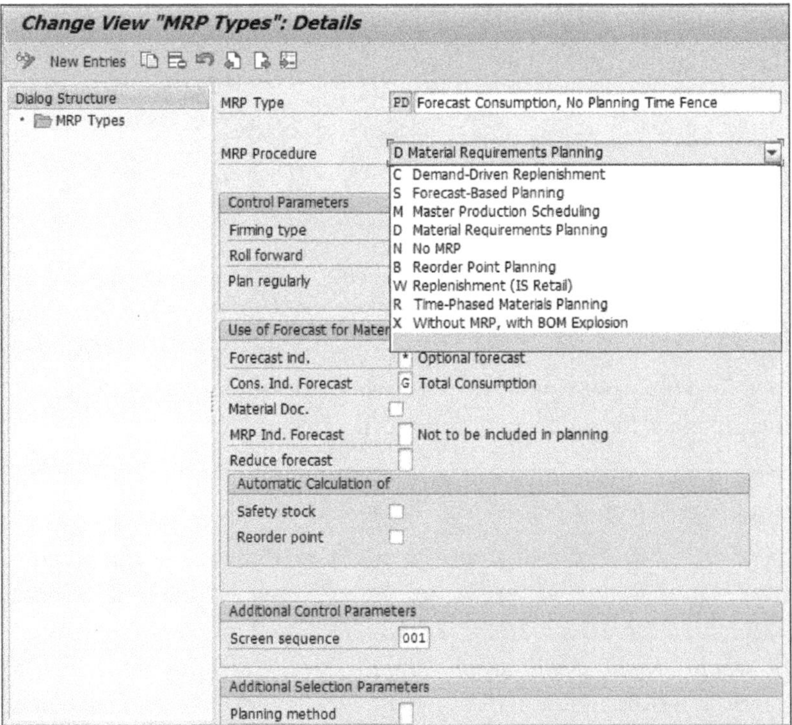

Figure 8.2 MRP Types

In this section, we won't deep dive into the MRP type configuration (which isn't necessary to walk through from a sales and distribution integration perspective); however, you'll conceptually understand the implication of commonly used MRP procedures.

As shown in Figure 8.3, MRP can be implemented in SAP with the help of the MRP procedure. MRP procedure can be further categorized into MRP and consumption-based planning (CBP). CBP is further classified into reorder point planning, forecast-based planning, and time-phased planning.

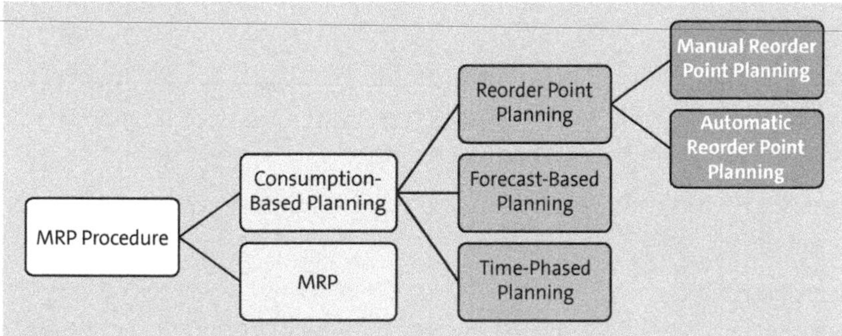

Figure 8.3 MRP Procedure

Let's explore each procedure and its implications briefly.

Material Requirements Planning: Procedure D

In the MRP procedure, sales orders, planned independent requirements, reservations, dependent requirements created by a bill of materials (BOM) explosion, and so on are all directly planned as requirements. The material's planning procedure will generate a procurement proposal only if these requirements will result in a shortage of material stocks at a specific time. There are no other circumstances that could result in a procurement proposal. MRP is especially useful for planning finished products as well as critical assemblies and components. If a material is manufactured in-house, the system also calculates the dependent requirements, or the number of components needed to produce the finished product or assembly, by exploding the BOM. If a material shortage exists, planned orders are created at each BOM level to cover requirements.

In MRP, the net requirements calculation is performed after the planning file check and at the plant level. The system determines whether it's possible to meet requirements with the existing plant stock and fixed receipts. When there is a scarcity, the system generates a procurement proposal. The net requirement calculation is different for each MRP procedure.

Calculation of available stock follows this formula:

Available stock = Quantity in hand for the plant – Safety stock + Receipt (Purchase requisition + Purchase order + Planned order) – Demand (Sales order + Delivery + Reservations + Planned independent and customer requirement)

Consumption-Based Planning

CBP is a material planning procedure that uses forecasts or other statistical procedures to determine future requirements based on past consumption values. Originally, in CBP, planned independent or dependent requirements aren't taken into account in the net requirements calculation. It's instead triggered when stock levels fall below a predefined reorder point or by forecast requirements based on past consumption values. As a result, all planned independent or dependent requirements for a specific time period should have been considered before when setting the reorder point or calculating the requirement forecast.

CBP procedures are simple materials planning procedures that can be used to meet set goals with little effort. As a result, these planning procedures are used in areas where there is no in-house production and/or manufacturing.

You can implement CBP in three ways depending on the product type. Let's explore each process in detail:

- **Reorder point planning**
  SAP S/4HANA checks whether the available stocks are below the reorder point for the material during reorder point planning. If they are below the reorder point, SAP S/4HANA generates a procurement proposal.

  Further classification of MRP types in reorder point planning is as follows:

  - MRP type VB: Manual reorder point planning
  - MRP type VM: Automatic reorder point planning

  You have to determine the reorder point manually if you're setting the MRP type as VB in the material master, or it can be calculated automatically using the material forecast using the MRP type VM.

  SAP S/4HANA checks whether the available stocks are below a certain threshold during reorder point planning.

  The reorder point should cover the average material requirement/consumption expected during the replenishment lead time, or the sum of the procurement processing time, planned delivery time, and goods receipt processing time maintained in the material master.

  Aside from average consumption, you should also consider safety stock. The safety stock exists to cover both excess material consumption within the replenishment lead time and any additional requirements that may arise as a result of delivery delays. As a result, the safety stock is included in the reorder level.

  The following values are critical for defining the safety stock:

  - Previous consumption values or future requirements
  - Timeliness for vendor/production delivery

- Service level to be achieved
- Forecast error, that is, the deviation from the expected

- **Net requirements calculation in reorder point planning**
In reorder point planning, the net requirements calculation is only carried out once the stock has fallen below the reorder level. The net requirement doesn't include the customer requirement, planned independent requirement, or reservation. The formula is as follows:
Available warehouse stock = Plant stock + Open order quantity (Purchase order, Firmed planned order, Firmed purchase requisition)

- **Forecast-based planning**
In forecast-based planning, historical data is used in the material forecast to estimate future requirements. Known as forecast requirements, they are immediately available in planning via Transaction MD04. The forecast, which calculates future requirements based on historical data, is performed at regular intervals. This has the advantage of automatically adjusting requirements to meet current consumption needs. All the parameters must be kept in the material master's forecasting view. You must also keep the consumption data in the **Additional Data** tab of the material master. You can run the forecast from Transaction MP30 or from the material master. The forecast requirement will be copied into the Transaction MD04 screen. The MRP type that you have to maintain for the forecast-based planning is VV.
The net requirements calculation for the forecast-based planning uses the following formula:
Available stock = Plant stock – Safety stock + Receipt (Purchase order, Firmed purchase order) – Requirement quantity (Forecast requirements)

- **Time-phased planning**
In time-phased planning, historical data is used in the material forecast to estimate future requirements. However, in this procedure, the planning run is only performed at predefined intervals; that is, the MRP run considers them for planning only on specific dates during the week. If a vendor consistently delivers a material on a particular day of the week, it stands to reason to schedule this material in accordance with the same cycle. To plan a material based on time phases, use Transaction MM02 to enter the **MRP type** "R1" or "R2" for time-phased planning and the planning cycle in the material master.

8.1.3 Scheduling

MRP calculates and plans procurement quantities and dates after calculating net requirements. The **Procurement Type** field in the **MRP 2** view of the material master determines whether the material is produced in-house, procured externally, or both. The procurement proposal is scheduled for materials with both procurement types;

that is, for externally procured materials, the delivery and release dates are calculated, and for in-house produced materials, the production date is calculated. The dependent requirements of the components are determined during the BOM explosion for materials manufactured in-house.

Following are the procurement proposals generated after running MRP:

- Planned orders are created for materials that are procured externally or produced in-house.
- Purchase requisitions are created for materials that are procured externally.
- Schedule lines are created for materials that are procured externally and for which a vendor source list entry and a scheduling agreement already exist in the system.

Purchase requisitions and planned orders are internal elements that can be changed, rescheduled, or deleted at any time.

Let's explore date calculation in procurement proposal scheduling:

- **In-house production**
  The system always generates planned orders in the case of in-house production. These planned orders are used to forecast production volumes. When the MRP controller is satisfied with the planning results, the planned orders are converted into production orders and sent to production.

  Basic dates such as order start date and order finish date are taken into account when scheduling planned orders.

  During each planning run, the system automatically calculates the basic dates for planned orders. The system always uses backward scheduling to determine the basic dates for planned orders; if the determined start date is in the past, the system automatically switches to forward scheduling.
- **External procurement**
  For externally procured materials, if the MRP procedure in the MRP type is **D** (**Material Requirements Planning**) or **S** (**Forecast-Based Planning**), then the system will determine the basic dates using backward scheduling. However, if the MRP procedure is **B** (**Reorder Point Planning**), then the basic dates are determined by forward scheduling.

  The order start and finish dates are calculated for planned orders. The delivery date and order release date are calculated for purchase requisitions.

Note

You can refer to Chapter 4, Section 4.1.3, to understand backward scheduling and forward scheduling.

If you define both in-house and external procurement for the material via the material type (indicator **X** in the **Procurement Type** field), you can set the procurement type as follows:

- Overwrite the indicator in the material master.
- Convert the planned order either into a production order or a purchase requisition.
- Using quota arrangements, define that a certain percentage of the material will be procured through in-house production and the remainder through external procurement.

8.2 Transfer of Requirements

The requirements are generated when a sales order is created in sales and distribution. The *requirement* is merely information about the quantity of materials needed on a given date. When a requirement is generated, it's passed to MRP to make sure that the customer receives the delivery on time.

When a sales order is created in SAP S/4HANA, the system will determine the requirement type in the sales order's **Procurement** tab, and the requirement type determines the requirement class. The requirement class governs how the sales order requirement is transferred to MRP. The configuration setup for the transfer of requirements will be discussed in the following sections.

8.2.1 Configure Requirement Class

The *requirement class* serves as a vital link between the sales and distribution functionality and the production planning functionality. It contains a variety of information related to planning strategies, availability checks, and other relevant information that is used in production planning to drive core processes such as production, scheduling, and so on. To configure the requirement classes, follow menu path **Sales and Distribution • Basic Functions • Availability Check and Transfer of Requirements • Transfer of Requirements • Configure Requirement Classes.**

You'll arrive at the screen shown in Figure 8.4, where you can create your own requirement class by clicking on the **New Entries** button. Then, you'll select the requirement class and click on the **Details** icon to arrive at the screen in Figure 8.5. We've created requirement class **Z20** for this example.

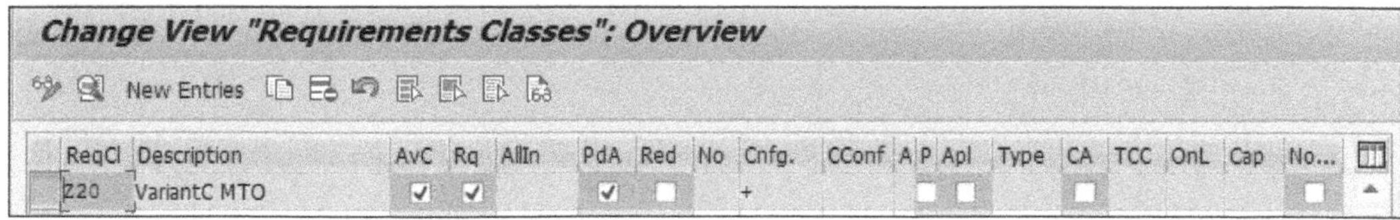

Figure 8.4 Requirement Class: Initial Screen

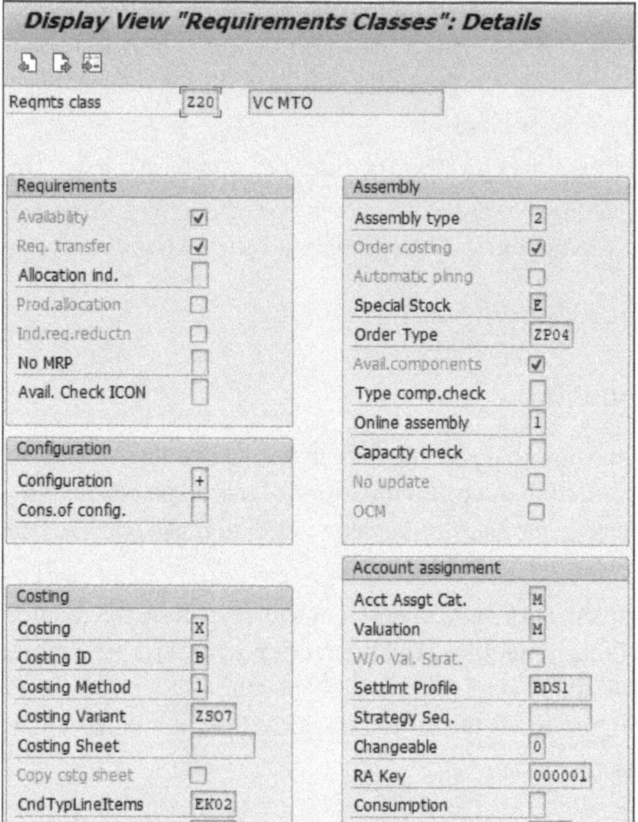

Figure 8.5 Requirement Class

Let's explore the key settings for the **Requirements** section on this screen:

- **Availability**
  You can activate the availability check at the requirement class level similar to the schedule line category level. Availability check at the requirement class takes higher precedence than the schedule line category level; that is, you can't switch off the availability check at the schedule line level if it's switched on at the requirement class level. The availability check can be switched off at the requirement class level and switched on at the schedule line category level. The availability check at the requirement class level is the global control, and the availability check at the schedule line category is the local sales and distribution-specific control.

- **Req. transfer**
  This is the prerequisite to enable the transfer of requirements to the material planning department. You can deactivate the transfer of requirements at the schedule line level. The transfer of the requirement checkbox at the requirement class takes higher precedence over the checkbox in the schedule line category level.

- **Allocation ind.**
  The allocation indicator controls customer requirements consumption with planned independent requirements; for example, if you have a planned independent requirement of 100 qty, you can see the planned independent requirement qty reduced to 50 in Transaction MD04 if you create a sales order for 50 qty after the MRP run.
- **Prod.allocation**
  You can enable the product allocation functionality associated with SAP S/4HANA for advanced ATP for the specific requirement class.
- **Ind.req.reductn.**
  If you activate the independent requirements reduction checkbox, then the goods issue posting in the delivery reduces the independent requirements from planning.
- **No MRP**
  This indicator indicates whether or not customer requirements are relevant for the planning run, that is, whether or not they are included in the net requirements calculation.

The fields in the **Assembly** section are used when you follow the assemble-to-order (ATO) process. SAP has provided the following standard planning strategies for the ATO process that you need to assign in the material master **MRP 3** view via Transaction MM02:

- **81**: Assembly processing with planned orders.
- **82**: Assembly processing with production orders.

This process includes the functions of receiving the order and planning all the order's requirements by passing the requirements to various other related functionalities. After receiving all the components, they are assembled and delivered to the customer. When a sales order is created with the planning strategy assembly processing, the system automatically creates a procurement element called the assembly order. You can choose planned order, production order, process order, and Project System element network, among other procurement elements, for the assembly order. Usually, the BOM is exploded for the assembly order for the determination of corresponding components.

Let's walk through the fields in the **Assembly** section:

- **Assembly type**
  There are two types of assembly types for the ATO business process. In static processing, you have a 1:1 relationship, that is, one procurement element for each sales order line item, and you can make the changes to the production order directly through the sales order. However, in dynamic processing, you have to make the changes directly in the production order, and there is no link between procurement

elements in a sales order, so the procurement element isn't saved in the sales order. SAP has provided the following options for the assembly type:

  - **0**: No assembly order processing
  - **1**: Planned order (static processing)
  - **2**: Production order, network, or service (static processing)
  - **3**: Production order (dynamic processing)
  - **4**: Planned order (dynamic processing)

- **Order costing**
  The field is only relevant if you choose **Assembly type 2** (production order, network, or service [static processing]). If you select this checkbox, you can create sales order costing for the sales line item, and it gets copied to the condition. If you don't select the checkbox, then the cost calculated in the production order gets sent to the sales and distribution pricing conditions, and you can't do costing at the sales order level.
- **Automatic plnng**
  This checkbox needs to be selected for the MTO scenarios where the planning immediately takes place when the order is created or changed.
- **Special Stock**
  In SAP S/4HANA, you can manage the special stocks separately. The materials procured or produced with respect to the requirement class can be managed separately to allocate the stock separately for the sales order, customer stock, or project stock. You use special stock indicator **E** for the MTO process.
- **Order Type**
  You can define the production order type for the MTO scenario in this field.
- **Avail.components**
  You can activate the availability check at the component level for the MTO scenario with respect to an assembly order. The system will check each subitem in the BOM and check whether the materials are available or not through the available-to-promise (ATP) check functionality/against the planned independent requirement.
- **Type comp.check**
  You can activate the component level checking at two levels:
  - Blank (ATP check): Availability check according to the ATP logic, which will consider the checking group assigned to the component master data or at plant level and order type.
  - **1** (Check against preliminary planning): Check against planned independent requirements with respect to each individual component, which can be achieved by the checking group defined for the component in the material master.

- **Online assembly**
  The field governs the logic of, in the event of component nonavailability, how should the system react, that is, whether to show the missing assembly part or display the missing part and then process the components. You can choose from the following options for this field:
  - Blank: No
  - **1**: Display missing parts
  - **2**: Display missing parts, then process components
  - **3**: Display and process missing parts (only in production order)
- **Capacity check**
  This checkbox indicates whether you want to consider production capacity when planning estimated production times in MTO scenarios, or whether you want to plan using lead times regardless of capacity.
- **No update**
  If you activate this checkbox, then changes to the assembly order aren't forwarded to the sales order. If you don't activate, then the changes to the assembly order are also updated in the sales order.

Controlling consultants typically configure the **Configuration**, **Costing**, and **Account assignment** fields, which deal with how value should flow into the costing functionalities.

8.2.2 Configure Requirement Types

The requirement class that you've earlier defined (**Z20**) needs to be assigned to the *requirement type*. The requirement type will be determined in the sales order, and from the requirement type, the associated requirement class will be determined in the sales order.

To configure the requirement types, follow menu path **Sales and Distribution • Basic Functions • Availability Check and Transfer of Requirements • Configure Requirement Types**. You'll arrive at the screen shown in Figure 8.6, where you have to assign the requirement class (**ReqCl**) with requirement type (**RqTy**) and click on the **Save** button (or press [Ctrl]+[S]).

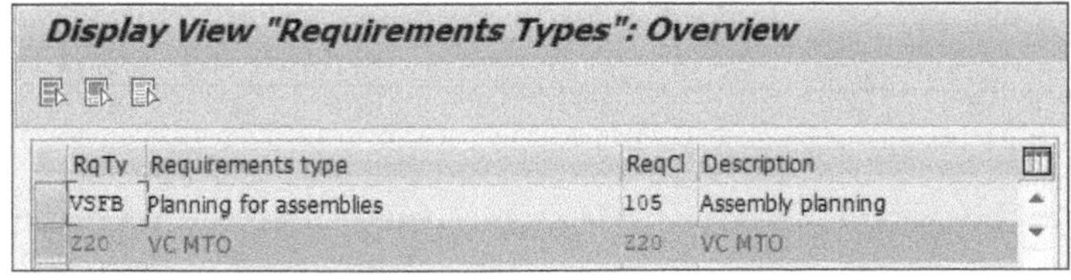

Figure 8.6 Requirement Type

As shown in Figure 8.6, we've assigned requirement type **Z20** with requirement class **Z20**.

8.2.3 Determine Requirement Types

The sales order determines the requirement type based on the item category, MRP type, and strategy group. SAP S/4HANA incorporates a search strategy to determine the type of requirement.

The material master keeps track of the strategy group. The system retrieves the strategy group from the material master and uses the strategy group's requirement type. If the strategy group isn't maintained in the material master, the requirement type is retrieved from the MRP group. If the MRP group isn't maintained in the material master, it attempts to access the requirement type from the control tables using the material type.

If the system fails to find the values using this log, then it tries to find the requirement type using the combination of MRP type and item category; if the values aren't present, it checks the value maintained only for the item category. If all of these attempts fail, the transfer of requirements doesn't apply to the sales transaction.

You can govern the determination logic in the customization menu path **Sales and Distribution • Basic Functions • Availability Check and Transfer of Requirements • Transfer of Requirements • Determine Requirement Type by Item Category and MRP Type**. You'll arrive at the screen shown in Figure 8.7.

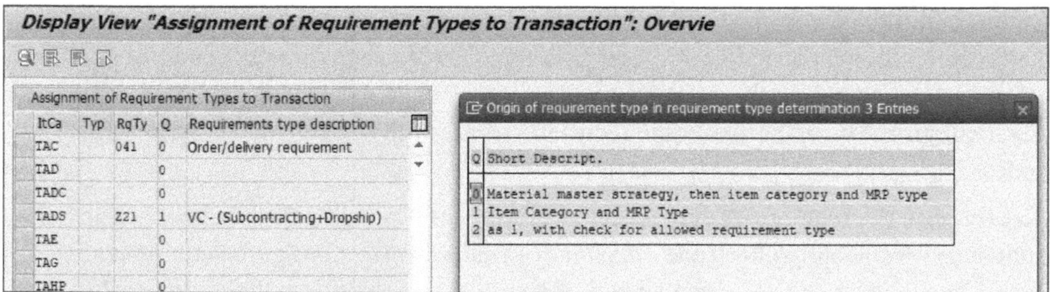

Figure 8.7 Assignment of Requirement Types to Transaction

As you can see in Figure 8.7, the requirement type (**RqTy**) is assigned against the item category (**ItCa**) and MRP type (**Typ**). You can also alter the search strategy logic by selecting the appropriate origin of the requirement (in the **Q** field). Following are the three options to choose from for the search strategy:

- **0**: If you select **0**, then the system gives the preference to the strategy group maintained in the material master. If values aren't found there, it searches the item category and MRP type.

- **1**: The system determines the requirement type with the combination of MRP type and item category.
- **2**: This is the same as **1** with an additional check for the allowed requirement type.

In our scenario, we've maintained the origin of requirement as **0** in the requirement type determination, as shown in Figure 8.7. Therefore, the system gives the priority to the strategy group maintained in the material master record for determining the requirement type in a sales order.

The strategy group **ZV** is maintained in the material master **MRP 3** view (Transaction MM03), as shown in Figure 8.8. As the system finds the strategy group in the material master, it tries to determine the associated requirement class from the strategy group configuration.

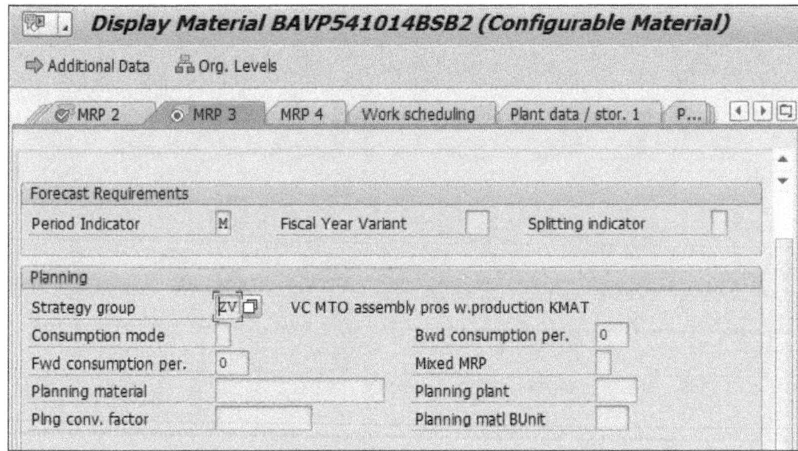

Figure 8.8 Material Master Strategy Group

With respect to this strategy group **ZV**, we've maintained the requirement type of the customer requirement as **Z20**, as shown in Figure 8.9.

Display View "Strategy": Overview

Strategy	Planning strategy description	Reqs-DM	Reqs-Cu.
ZV	VC MTO assembly pros w.production KMAT		Z20
ZY	Direct Shipment	BSF	KSL
ZZ	DS Make To Order (MTO)	BSF	KSL

Figure 8.9 Strategy Overview

Note

You can define the strategy by executing Transaction SPRO and following menu path **Production • Production Planning • Demand Management • Planned Independent**

Requirements • Planning Strategy • Define Strategy. The configuration related to strategy groups are handled by production planning consultants, so we haven't covered details of each field from the strategy group.

The detailed view of the strategy group is shown in Figure 8.10. As you can see, the **Requirements class** assigned to the strategy **ZV** is **Z20**, in this example.

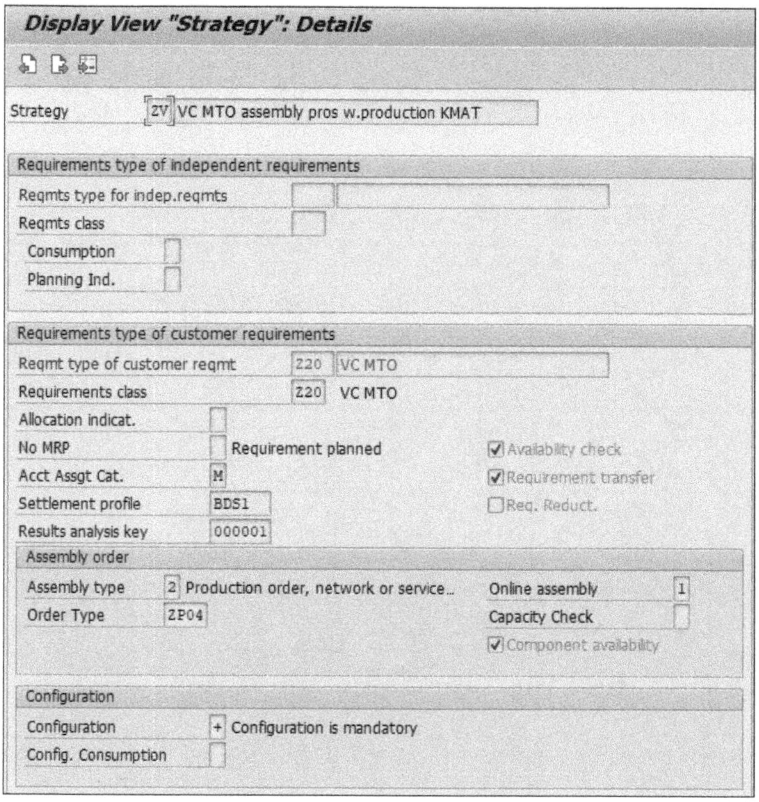

Figure 8.10 Strategy Details

8.2.4 Schedule Line Category Changes

You can enable or disable the transfer of requirements at the schedule line category level. To define the procedure for each schedule line category, follow menu path **Sales and Distribution • Basic Functions • Availability Check and Transfer of Requirements • Transfer of Requirements • Define Procedure for Each Schedule Line Category**. You'll arrive at the screen shown in Figure 8.11.

As shown in Figure 8.11, you can enable the availability check (**AvC**), transfer or requirements (**Rq**), and production allocation (**All.**) functionality at the schedule line category level by checking the corresponding boxes.

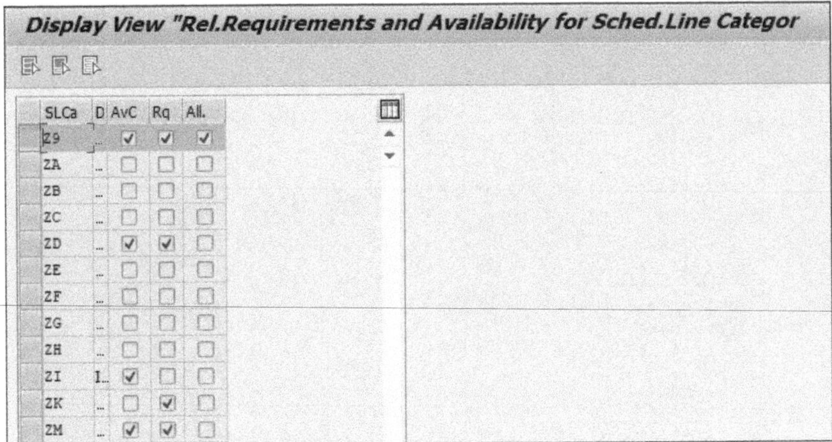

SLCa	D	AvC	Rq	All.
Z9	...	✓	✓	✓
ZA	...			
ZB	...			
ZC	...			
ZD	...	✓	✓	
ZE	...			
ZF	...			
ZG	...			
ZH	...			
ZI	1...	✓		
ZK	...		✓	
ZM	...	✓	✓	

Figure 8.11 Define Procedure for the Schedule Line Category

> **Note**
>
> The requirement class plays a global role in the availability check and transfer of requirement configuration. If the configuration isn't active at the requirement class level, then the configurations performed in the given node hold no value.

8.3 Variant Configuration

Variant configuration is used in the production of materials with varying specifications. If the customer wants to purchase such material with specific requirements, the pricing will be based on those specifications. As you'll employ attributes in the variant configuration to retain a material's specifications, you'll be able to reduce the number of material master records required for each specification. For example, consider the material Folding Knife Wooden Handle, where the length of the handle can be set by the customer when placing the order. The length parameter is used as a characteristic and assigned to the material. In brief, you can build material attributes or specifications and configure the material master to match the expectations of the customer in variant configuration. Let's take a closer look at the configuration area to set up the variant configuration in the system.

To set up the variant configuration in the SAP S/4HANA system, you must configure elements such as characteristics, classes, configuration profile, and so on. As illustrated in Figure 8.12, you must define the material's properties and values in characteristics. In addition, the class should specify where the defined characteristics will be assigned. You'll assign classes in the material configuration profile.

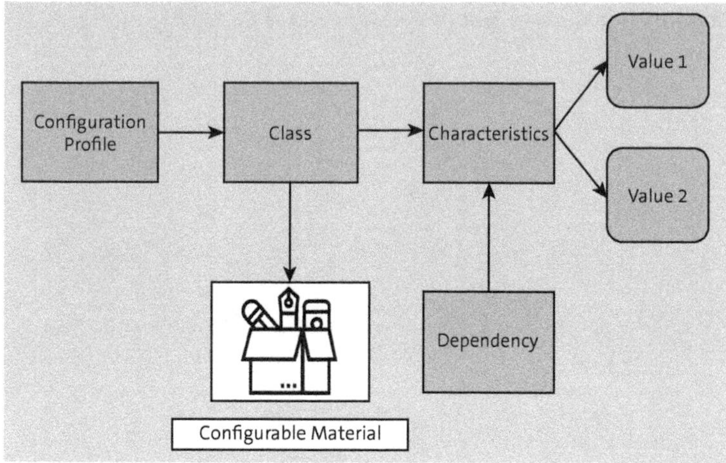

Figure 8.12 Variant Configuration

Let's go over these configurations one by one, as follows:

1. **Define the material type as configurable**
   The first step to set up the variant configuration is to define the material type as configurable. You can set up the material type by following menu path **Logistics – General • Material Master • Basic Settings • Material Types • Define Attributes of Material Types.**

   You'll arrive at the screen shown in Figure 8.13, where you select the **Material is configurable** checkbox.

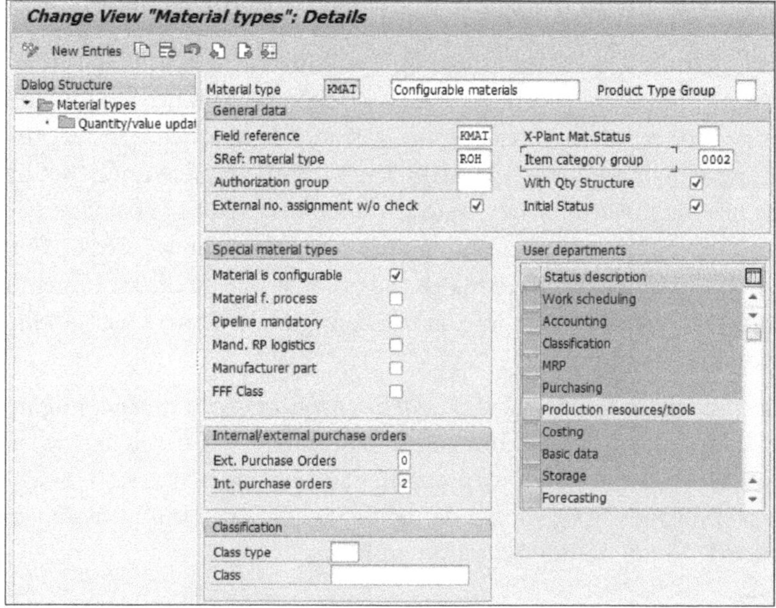

Figure 8.13 Configurable Material Type: KMAT

2. **Create the material master**
   After the material type is defined, create a material master by executing Transaction MM01, navigating to the **Basic data 2** view, and activating the **Material is configurable** checkbox in the **Client-specific configuration** section of the screen, as shown in Figure 8.14.

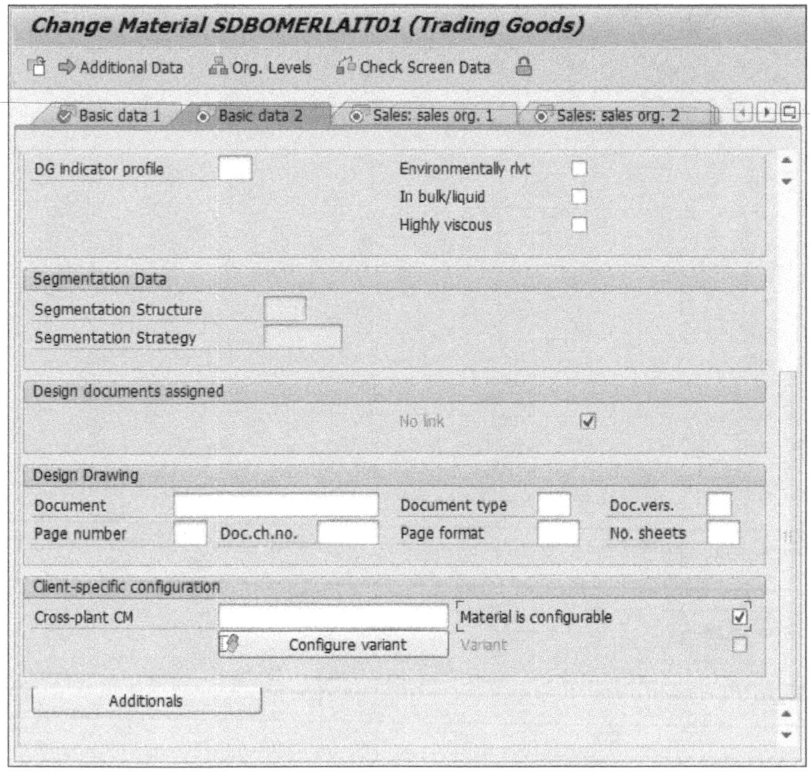

Figure 8.14 Configurable Checkbox in the Material Master

3. **Specify the characteristics for materials**
   Characteristics describe the properties of materials. You'll specify the characteristics values as numerals, characters, dates, times, and currencies.

   To create characteristics, execute Transaction CT04 to arrive at the screen shown in Figure 8.15. Enter the appropriate **Characteristic** and press [Enter]. In addition, enter a **Description**, and maintain the appropriate **Status** in the **Basic data** tab. In this example, characteristic **CH_METRIC_GUAGE** is defined with values, as shown in Figure 8.16. This characteristic represents the length of the wooden handle. Note that the characteristic **Status** should be **Released**.

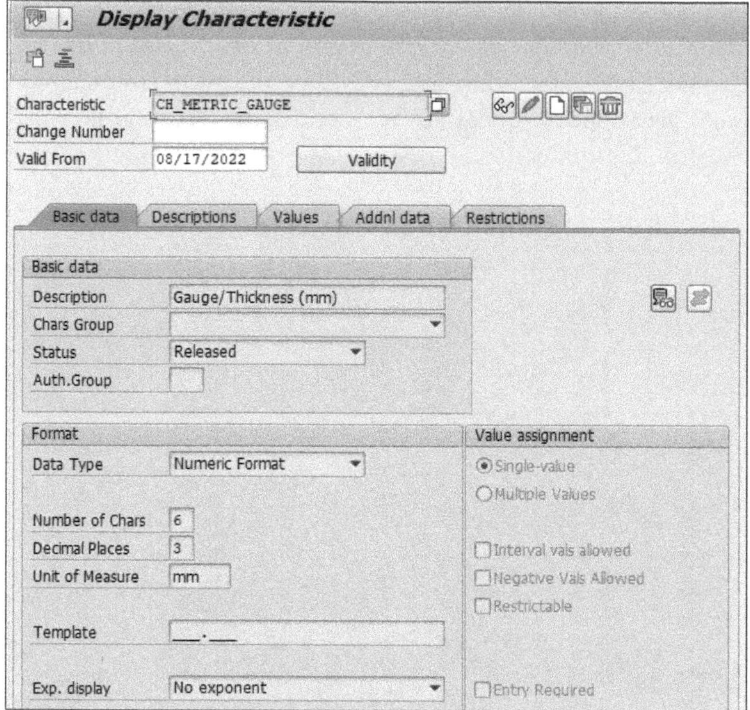

Figure 8.15 Display Characteristic

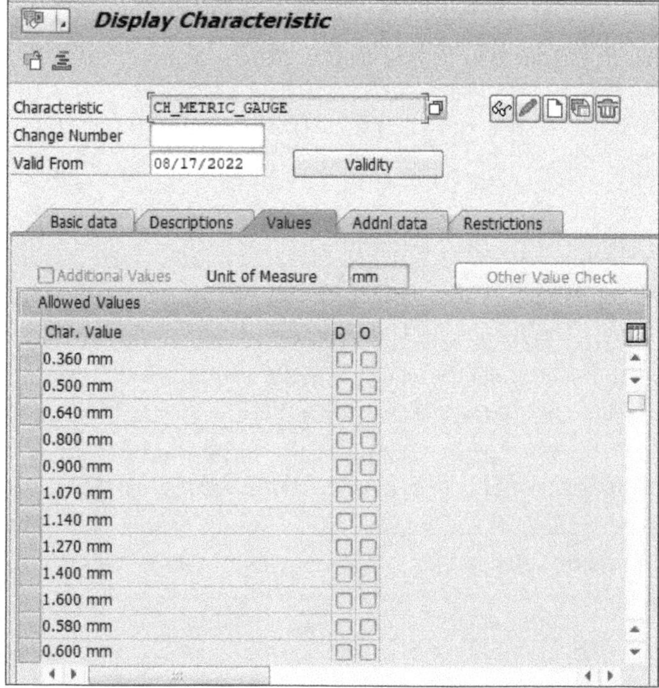

Figure 8.16 Characteristic Values

4. **Create a class for the material**
   The class will hold the characteristics you've defined in the previous step. Class types 200 or 300 are used for the variant configuration scenario. To create a new class, execute Transaction CL01. You'll arrive at the screen shown in Figure 8.17, where you enter the appropriate **Class** name and **Class type** and then press [Enter]. We've created new **Class CL_BANDSAW** in this scenario, as shown in Figure 8.17, with **Class type 300**.

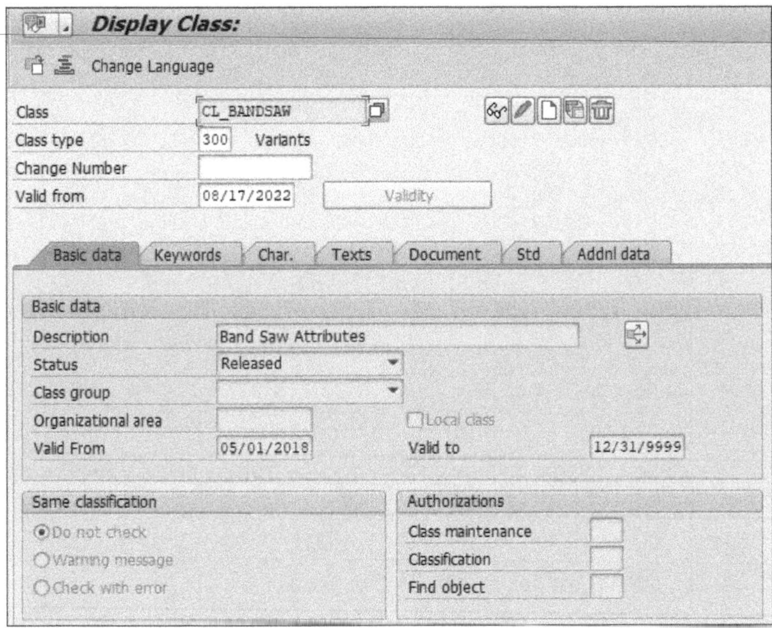

Figure 8.17 Display Class

   Next, you'll assign the characteristics values in the class you've defined. As shown in Figure 8.18, navigate to the **Char.** tab, and assign the characteristics to the class. After completing the assignment, click on the **Save** button or press [Ctrl]+[S].

5. **Assign the configuration profile to the material**
   The configuration profile is used for assigning variant classes to the material master using Transaction CU41. After executing this transaction, you'll enter the configurable material and press [Enter] to arrive at the screen in Figure 8.19, where you'll assign the configuration profile to the material. A material may have one or more configuration profiles. As shown in Figure 8.19, this configuration profile is assigned to the material with class type **(Cl...) 300**.

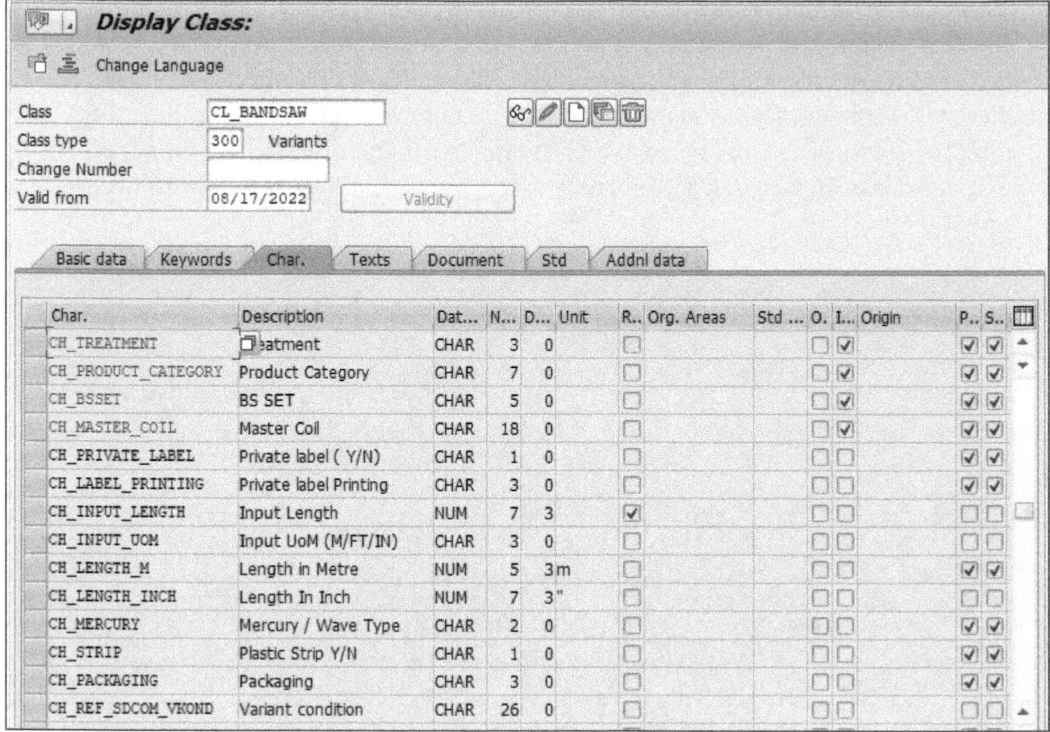

Figure 8.18 Char. Tab in the Display Class Screen

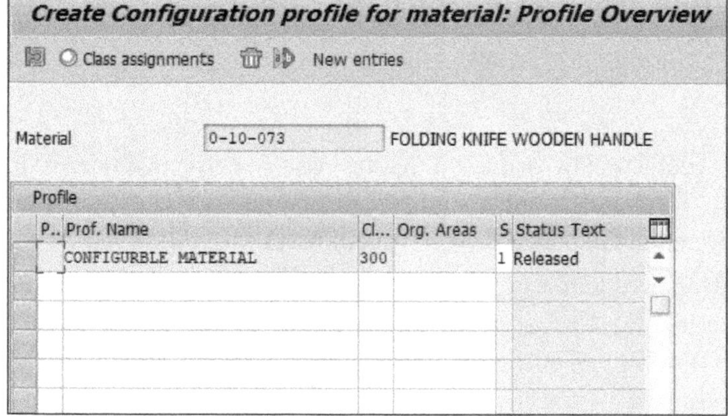

Figure 8.19 Configuration Profile

Next, you'll click on the **Class assignments** button. As shown in Figure 8.20, select the class in the **Assignments** section and press Enter. The characteristics will appear in the **General** section, where you can enter the characteristic **Value**.

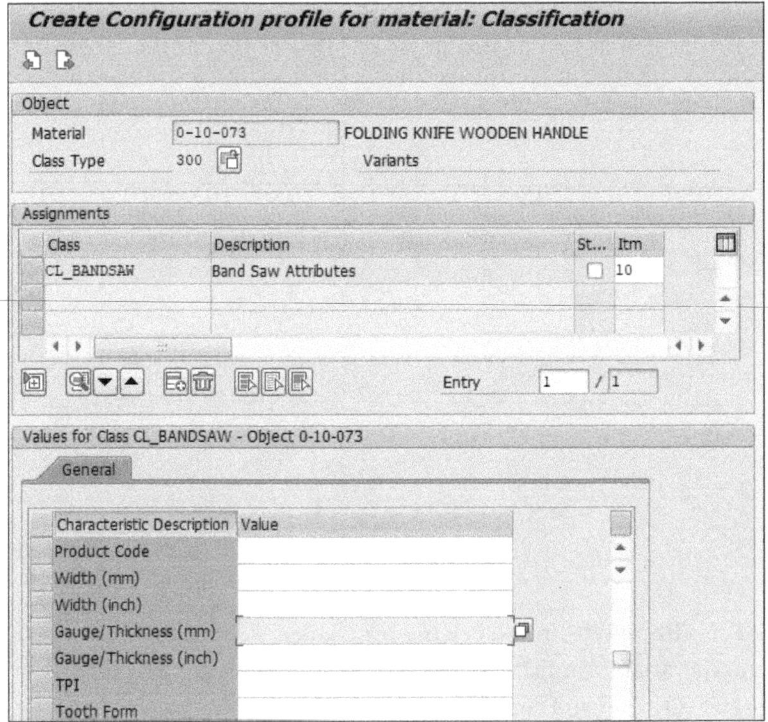

Figure 8.20 Configuration Profile

Once the configuration profile is set up and the class assignment is completed, you'll maintain the dependency where you can write pseudo code for the characteristics by executing Transaction CT04. Navigate to the **Extras** button, and select **Object Dependencies • Editor**, as shown in Figure 8.21. Figure 8.22 illustrates the resulting dependency code for the configuration profile created in previous steps.

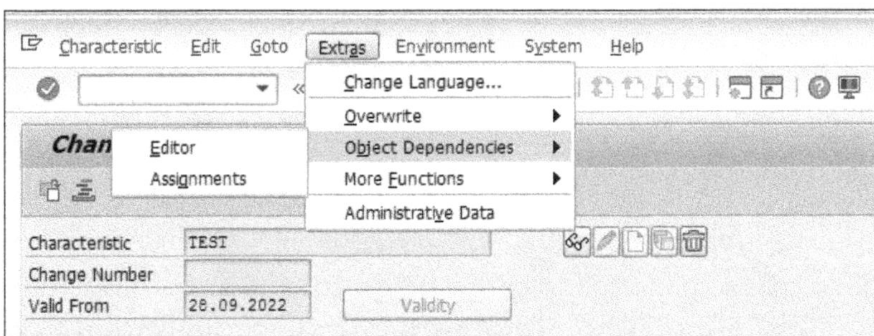

Figure 8.21 Dependencies Editor

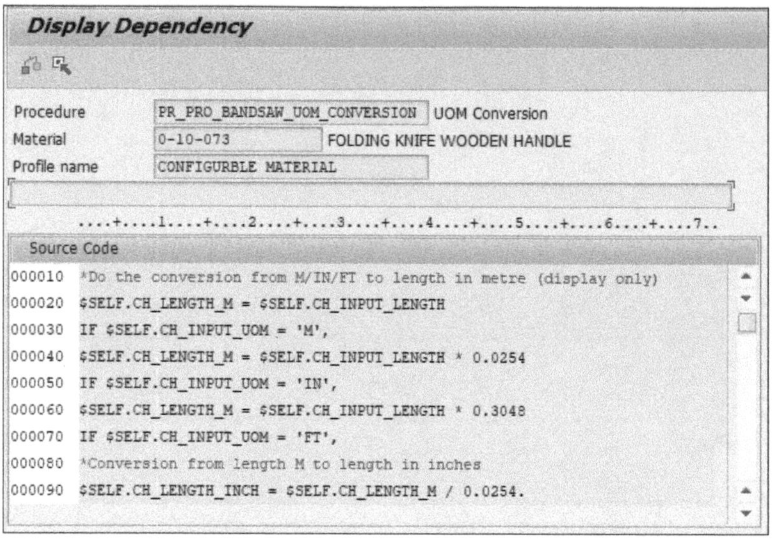

Display Dependency

Procedure PR_PRO_BANDSAW_UOM_CONVERSION UOM Conversion
Material 0-10-073 FOLDING KNIFE WOODEN HANDLE
Profile name CONFIGURBLE MATERIAL

....+....1....+....2....+....3....+....4....+....5....+....6....+....7..

Source Code

```
*Do the conversion from M/IN/FT to length in metre (display only)
$SELF.CH_LENGTH_M = $SELF.CH_INPUT_LENGTH
IF $SELF.CH_INPUT_UOM = 'M',
$SELF.CH_LENGTH_M = $SELF.CH_INPUT_LENGTH * 0.0254
IF $SELF.CH_INPUT_UOM = 'IN',
$SELF.CH_LENGTH_M = $SELF.CH_INPUT_LENGTH * 0.3048
IF $SELF.CH_INPUT_UOM = 'FT',
*Conversion from length M to length in inches
$SELF.CH_LENGTH_INCH = $SELF.CH_LENGTH_M / 0.0254.
```

Figure 8.22 Dependency

6. **Set up the variant condition type in the pricing procedure**
   You have to set up the variant condition type in the pricing procedure by executing Transaction V/08 to get the pricing of characteristics values in the sales documents. Standard variant condition type **VA00** is included in the pricing procedure, as shown in Figure 8.23.

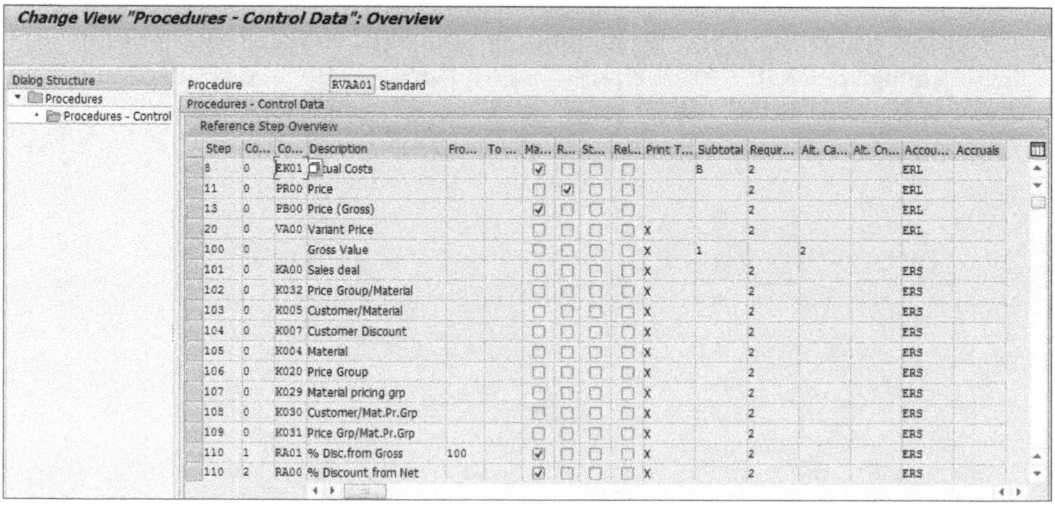

Change View "Procedures - Control Data": Overview

Dialog Structure
- Procedures
  - Procedures - Control

Procedure RVAA01 Standard

Procedures - Control Data

Reference Step Overview

Step	Co...	Co...	Description	Fro...	To ...	Ma...	R...	St...	Rel...	Print T...	Subtotal	Requir...	Alt. Ca...	Alt. Cn...	Accou...	Accruals
8	0	EK01	ctual Costs			☑	☐	☐	☐		B	2			ERL	
11	0	PR00	Price			☐	☑	☐	☐			2			ERL	
13	0	PB00	Price (Gross)			☑	☐	☐	☐			2			ERL	
20	0	VA00	Variant Price			☐	☐	☐	☐	X		2			ERL	
100	0		Gross Value			☐	☐	☐	☐	X	1		2			
101	0	KA00	Sales deal			☐	☐	☐	☐	X		2			ERS	
102	0	K032	Price Group/Material			☐	☐	☐	☐	X		2			ERS	
103	0	K005	Customer/Material			☐	☐	☐	☐	X		2			ERS	
104	0	K007	Customer Discount			☐	☐	☐	☐	X		2			ERS	
105	0	K004	Material			☐	☐	☐	☐	X		2			ERS	
106	0	K020	Price Group			☐	☐	☐	☐	X		2			ERS	
107	0	K029	Material pricing grp			☐	☐	☐	☐	X		2			ERS	
108	0	K030	Customer/Mat.Pr.Grp			☐	☐	☐	☐	X		2			ERS	
109	0	K031	Price Grp/Mat.Pr.Grp			☐	☐	☐	☐	X		2			ERS	
110	1	RA01	% Disc.from Gross	100		☑	☐	☐	☐	X		2			ERS	
110	2	RA00	% Discount from Net			☑	☐	☐	☐	X		2			ERS	

Figure 8.23 Pricing Procedure

7. **Pricing condition records**
   Once the pricing procedure is set up with the variant condition type, create condition records for condition type **VA00** by executing Transaction VK11. You'll arrive at

the screen shown in Figure 8.24, where you can maintain the condition records by setting the price in the **Amount** column for each **Variant**.

Create Variant Price Condition (VA00) : Fast Entry

Sales Organization IT01 Italian Sales Org
Distribution Channel 01 Distribtn Channel 01
Material 0-10-073 FOLDING KNIFE WOODEN HANDLE

Variants

Variant	Description	Amount	Unit	per	U...	C..	S..	Valid From	Valid to	D.	S..	S..	T..	E..	Pa...	FixValDate	A..
BASE_PRICE	Base Price x Length	100.00	EUR	1	PC	C		08/17/2022	12/31/9999								
FM	Full Merc. x Length	200.00	EUR	1	PC	C		08/17/2022	12/31/9999								
L1	Lvl 1 Wave x Length	300.00	EUR	1	PC	C		08/17/2022	12/31/9999								

Figure 8.24 Variant Price Condition Record

Now, you're ready to create sales orders for configurable materials and other relevant documents.

8.4 Make to Order

MTO production is the process of manufacturing a product specifically for a specific customer only when the order is entered into the system. The stock produced for the process is maintained with respect to the sales order. The primary benefits of this process include the ability to track the progress of the sales order and the flexibility to offer products that meet the customer's specific requirements. The other benefits include waste reduction of materials and avoidance of product overstocking. The MTO process has a lot of integration with the production planning functionality and sales and distribution functionality via requirement type and requirement class. The configuration that you've done earlier will be used to derive the configuration elements in the MTO process.

In this section, we'll first go through the overview of the different planning strategies used in SAP S/4HANA, and then we'll dive into MTO.

8.4.1 Planning Strategies

You can categorize the material based on demand patterns. The planning strategies represent the business procedures for material planning and production. The strategy is usually associated with the finished item, but it can also be associated with a planning material or an assembly material. The strategy is assigned on the material master **MRP 2** screen. SAP S/4HANA provides a diverse set of planning strategies. They define how forecasted independent requirements interact with customer independent requirements derived from sales orders and become visible to manufacturing planning and the planning run. They also specify whether or not availability check is permitted and where costs incurred during the production are ultimately settled.

The system determines the correct requirement type when creating planned independent requirements or sales orders by assigning a planning strategy to a specific material. As you saw in the previous section, the requirement type can be determined by the item category, MRP type, and strategy group assigned in the material master. The planning strategy determines which demand requirement types will be considered in the planning run for a material. It's strongly recommended that one of the SAP-provided strategies be used for each material. If a match can't be found, a new planning strategy should be created in configuration by copying an existing strategy and then making changes to the copy, rather than changing one of the as-delivered strategies.

Let's look at some of the most common material planning strategies in SAP S/4HANA:

- **Make to stock (MTS)**
  This strategy is used when materials are manufactured regardless of customer requirements. In this strategy, material production planning is dependent on independent planning derived from demand management. Individual customer requirements from sales orders have no significance in this strategy, so sales orders don't affect production. The product is stocked and then delivered to the customer as needed. This strategy is straightforward to implement and is appropriate for finished goods where the finished goods can be forecasted.

  SAP S/4HANA defines MTS production in two distinct planning strategies, 10 and 11. They differ in how they handle available stock. Planning strategy 10 will take stock into account (net requirements planning), whereas planning strategy 11 won't take stock into account (gross requirements planning), and the planned quantities are produced even though the stock is available in the warehouse.

- **Make to order (MTO)**
  In this strategy, the material production is started after the sales order requirement has been passed to the system. The production orders are directly linked to the sales orders. Forecast data or planned independent requirements aren't required in this strategy. The materials are segregated and uniquely assigned to specific sales orders. The sales order quantities are planned for production using the sales order number.

  Usually, the material involved in the MTO strategy is complex to manufacture, and an accurate forecast isn't achievable for the products. Customers are willing to wait for the lead time required to produce the material.

  The common strategies used for the MTO process are 20 and 21. The difference between the two is the cost settlement to sales order.

- **Assemble to order (ATO)**
  This falls under the purview of the MTO process. The ATO strategy aims to combine the benefits of both MTO and MTS manufacturing by getting products into customers' hands quickly while allowing the product to be adapted or altered in specific ways based on customer requests. In most cases, the time and cost of assembling the product from its components are minimal. However, the time and money required

to build the components, which are typically ordered from a supplier, can be significant. The assembly strategy has the capability to generate the production order to assemble the finished product after the sales order is created. A basic example of the ATO process is an ice cream parlor where the sales representative assembles the different flavors that the customer wants into a single cone of ice cream. The ice cream cone is assembled based on the already available flavor.

- **Configure to order (CTO)**
  The CTO concept underpins the MTO process, which means the design is chosen after the order is received. It employs customer requirements chosen from a predefined set of product features. Based on that, a specific, predefined modification or variant of a product is created using a combination of parts and assemblies. In SAP S/4HANA, you achieve the unique characteristics with the variant configuration functionality. In this way, you can configure variations of the same material based on features and options.
- **Engineer to order (ETO)**
  ETO is a type of manufacturing in which a product is designed and manufactured after an order is received. A manufacturer can meet their customers' exact specifications by using the ETO method. ETO is ideal for manufacturers of highly configurable products, which frequently necessitate close customer engagement throughout the design and manufacturing phases. You achieve the ETO business process in SAP S/4HANA with the help of Project System and the work breakdown structure (WBS), which handle complex requirements better.

8.4.2 Process Flow

Let's explore the process flow of the MTO process. In SAP S/4HANA, the MTO process has several variations, which we discussed in the previous section. We'll discuss the CTO variation in this section.

As you can see in the flow diagram in Figure 8.25, a sales order is created with the value of the required characteristic, and this initiates a demand in the production planning functionality. This is achieved via different configurations that you've completed in Section 8.2.

The second step is to run the MRP process. The procurement proposals generated after running the MRP will be determined by the procurement type in the material master's MRP view. If insufficient warehouse stock is available, then the purchase requisition will be created with the raw material required.

The procurement proposals can either be converted into the production order or process order, depending on the material for which the procurement proposal is created. For example, for a material associated with the discrete manufacturing industry, you'll have a production order, and for the company where a specific recipe is followed to create products (e.g., pharma or food products), the procurement proposal will be converted into the process order.

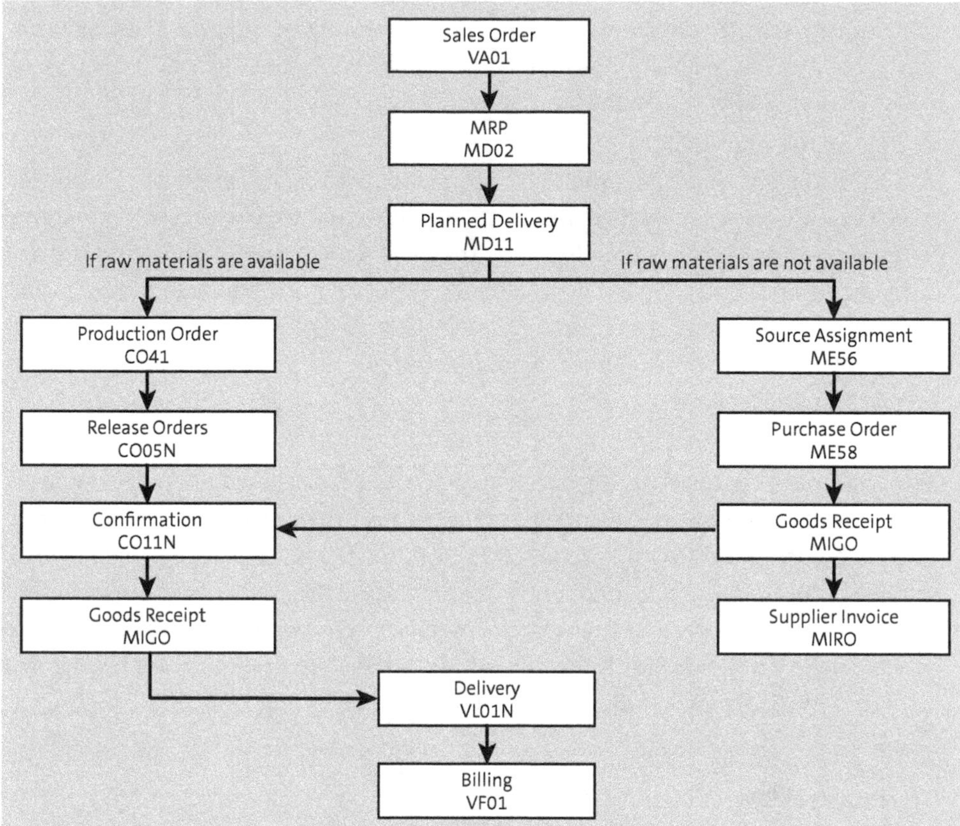

Figure 8.25 Process Flow of MTO

Then the production order or process order is released for execution to the shop floor wherein the raw materials will be consumed by the order; the finished product is manufactured and then sent to the specific location. During the production process, the cost incurred is updated on the order, which enables the users to keep track of and compare target costs and actual costs at any time.

The stock finished product is segregated based on the sales order in the stock overview. Then, the products are delivered to the end customer corresponding to the sales order. The period-end closing activities are applied to the order. This includes work-in-process (WIP) calculation and variance calculation. After this, WIP is settled to financial accounting and production variance is settled to profitability analysis with sales order as one of the characteristics.

8.4.3 Configuration Impact

In this section, we'll first explore some of the prerequisites needed to execute the MTO process. Then we'll follow an example of how the configurations you've made flow into the order-to-cash cycle.

The strategy group should be maintained for the material master. We've created a new **Strategy group ZV** to cater to your requirements, as shown in Figure 8.26. However, as standard, SAP provides strategy 20 to use for the MTO scenarios.

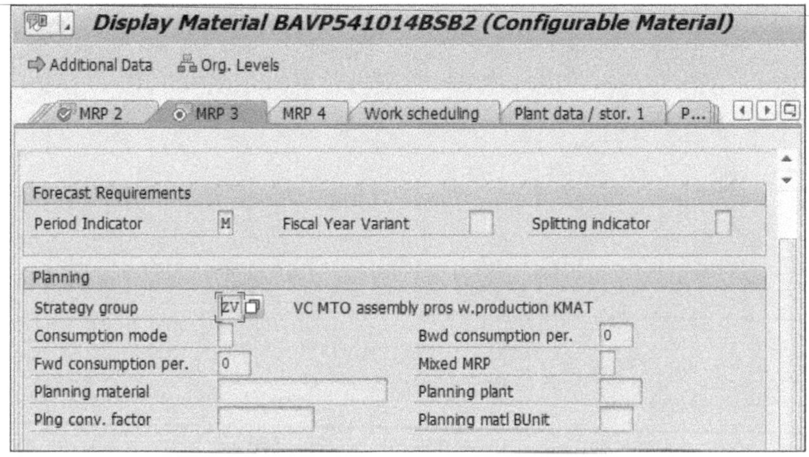

Figure 8.26 Material Master: Strategy Group

The item category associated with the MTO process should have the special stock indicator **E** (orders on hand), which will help to segregate the stock based on the sales order number. You'll also maintain the special stock indicator in the requirement class.

As soon as the sales order is created, the requirement is transferred to demand management with the help of the requirement type. As mentioned in Section 8.2, we've created a separate requirement type and assigned the requirement class. Execute Transaction VA03 to view the sales order, and navigate to the **Procurement** tab, as shown in Figure 8.27, to see the requirement type (**RqTy**).

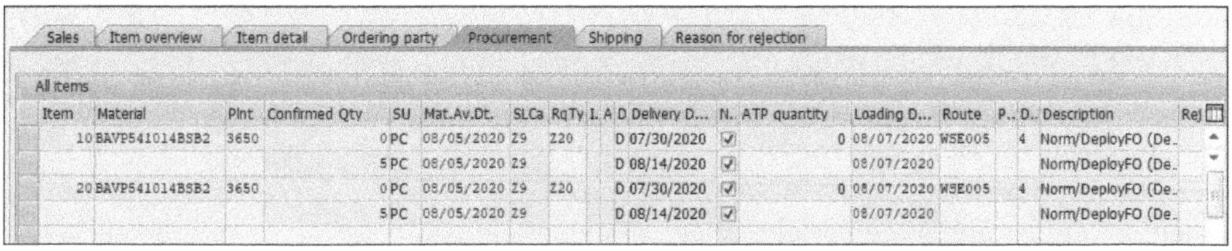

Figure 8.27 Sales Order: Procurement Tab

After running MRP, the production order is created with respect to the sales order, and you can view the production order in the schedule line **Procurement** tab, as shown in Figure 8.28, in Transaction VA03.

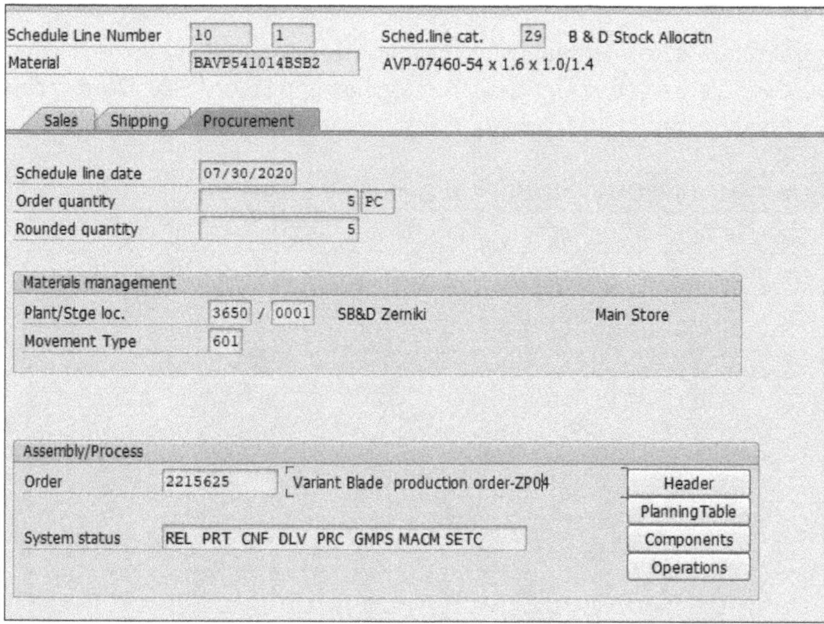

Figure 8.28 Schedule Line: Procurement Tab

You can also view the production order directly by clicking on the **Production order** button in the **Schedule lines** tab, as shown in Figure 8.29.

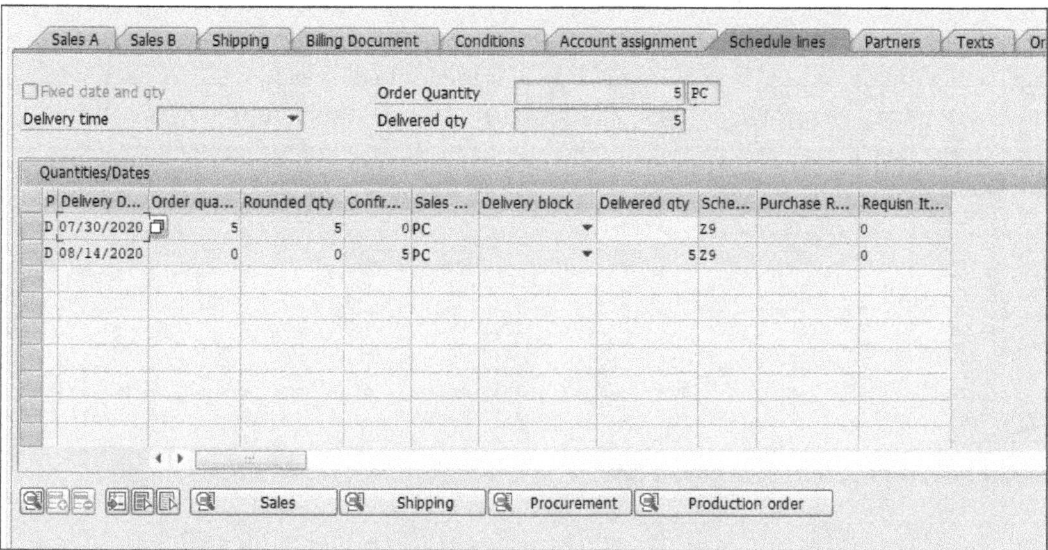

Figure 8.29 Sales Order: Schedule Lines Tab

You'll arrive at Figure 8.30, where you can see the production order is created for the material, and **Sales Order** appears in the production order; the basic dates and scheduled dates are automatically calculated based on the MRP run.

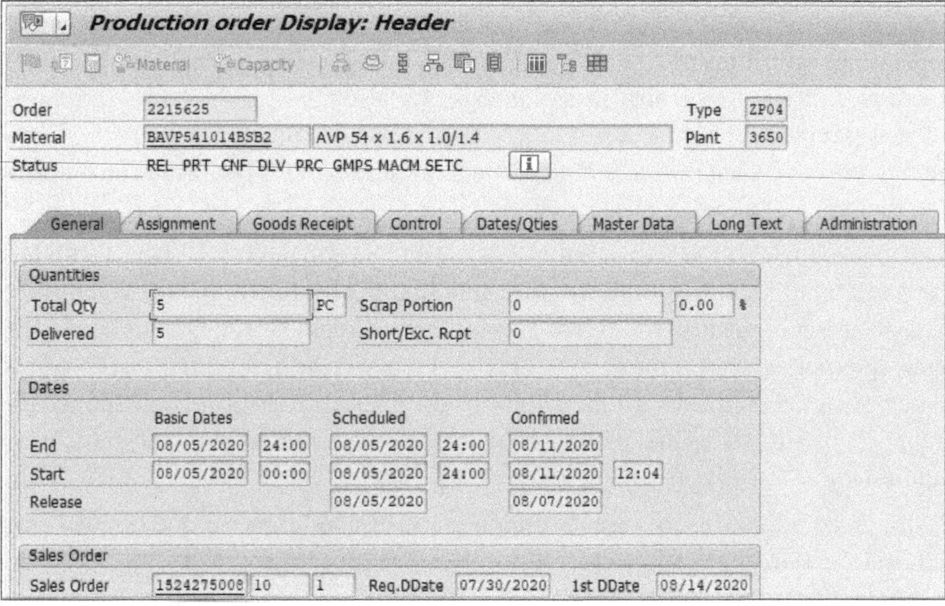

Figure 8.30 Production Order

The final order flow can be viewed as shown in Figure 8.31 by clicking on the sales order document flow in Transaction VA03.

Figure 8.31 Document Flow

Note

You can't view the production order in the document flow of the sales order. To view the production order, you have to view the schedule lines and then navigate to the associated production order.

8.5 Summary

In this chapter, we covered the integration between the sales and distribution functionality and the production planning functionality.

In Section 8.1, we introduced the concept of MRP and its implications in the SAP landscape. We briefly discussed the MRP process flow before delving into the various MRP procedures, as well as the net calculation logic. We also investigated MRP procedures, CBP, reorder point planning, forecast-based planning, and time-phased planning procedures. We concluded the section with scheduling and how it's performed on external procurement and in-house production.

Next, in Section 8.2, we looked at the crucial key integration point between the production planning functionality and the sales and distribution functionality, which is the transfer of requirements. We looked at requirement types, requirement classes, key fields, and their effects on the system. We also discussed the determination of requirement types and how the determination can be used based on the scenarios. The section wrapped up with the schedule line category fields associated with the transfer of requirements.

We discussed the concept of variant configuration, its configuration, and how it's used in the production of materials with varying specifications in Section 8.3. Regarding the pricing procedure, we briefly discussed characteristics and classes, configuration profile, and variant condition type.

In Section 8.4, we took a deep dive into the MTO process, briefly discussing MTO as a business concept and its relevance in business scenarios. We then touched on various planning strategies used in the SAP landscape, as well as the MTO process flow. Finally, we went over an example of the MTO process and how the configuration that you completed earlier came into the business process.

Appendix A
Electronic Data Interchange

Electronic Data Interchange (EDI) is a process by which systems electronically transfer data between each other. Each EDI communication, at the minimum, involves two systems: the sender system and the receiver system. The sender and receiver systems can belong to the same company or different companies. Let's consider a few examples:

- SFDC and SAP belong to company ABC where SFDC is their customer relationship management (CRM) system and SAP is the enterprise resource planning (ERP) system. Both SFDC and SAP communicate with each other via an EDI process.
- Company ABC supplies goods to company DEF, so the necessary delivery documents for the shipping to complete are transferred from ABC to DEF via EDI.

EDI integrations in SAP S/4HANA happen in a few ways; the most popular ones are using intermediate documents (IDocs), Simple Object Access Protocol (SOAP), application programming interfaces (APIs), and SAP Business Network for Procurement (previously known as Ariba Network).

In this appendix, we'll focus on EDI for sales and distribution using IDocs. We'll share our knowledge on IDoc structures and how they play an active role in the inbound and outbound EDI transactions. EDI has various benefits, which will also be highlighted in this appendix. And, finally, we'll conclude by listing key IDoc types, EDI tables, and EDI transactions you should be aware of while working on EDI projects.

To set the stage, Figure A.1 shows how a generic EDI process works between a sender and receiver system using IDoc.

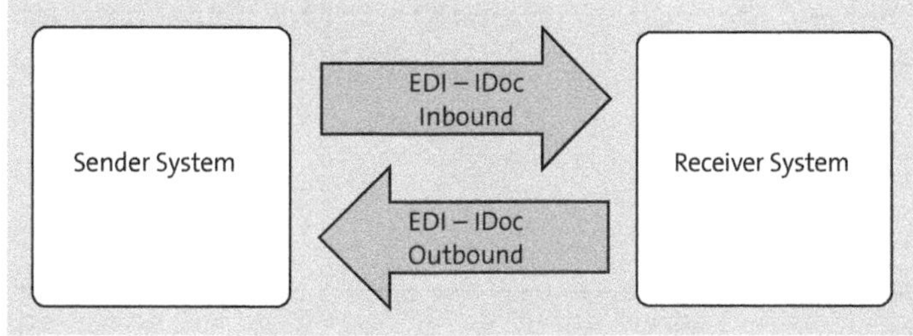

Figure A.1 EDI Using IDocs

A.1 Benefits of Electronic Data Interchange

In this section, we list key benefits of using EDI, which we experienced personally by working on multiple projects with various clients from different industries:

- Streamlined and efficient data exchange process
- Fewer user errors and manual glitches
- Cost savings
- Sustainability as the use of paper is reduced to almost zero
- Availability of electronic data for reporting
- Easy options to troubleshoot and debug data interchange issues
- Reduced timelines for data processing with quicker turnarounds and acknowledgements
- Real-time data transmission

There are many strong reasons to use EDI and IDocs. We recommend trying it on your next project—you won't be disappointed.

A.2 Electronic Data Interchange in Sales and Distribution

Traditionally, EDI in sales and distribution happened through *IDocs*. With the emergence of SAP S/4HANA, SAP launched cloud-based solutions, including SAP API Business Hub and SAP Business Network for Procurement, to support EDI transactions. But based on our experience and interviewing fellow SAP users in the industry, we realized that IDocs are still the preferred EDI option.

IDocs work smoothly with SAP S/4HANA, SAP ERP, and SAP R/3. IDocs help in translating data from one system to another. They are basically message types that can handle inbound and outbound transactions. A few examples of EDI transactions in sales and distribution are creating sales orders, sending invoices to customers, transferring post goods issue (PGI) documents, and sharing contract purchase orders. Commonly used EDI message types are listed in Table A.1.

Message Type	Description
ORDERS	For orders
ORDRSP	For order confirmation
ORDCHG	For order modification or change order

Table A.1 IDoc Message Types

Message Type	Description
GSVERF	For customer credit note
INVOIC	For customer invoice
RECADV	For receipt of shipment notification
DESADV	For shipment notification
DELFOR	For customer delivery forecast
DELJIT	For customer just-in-time delivery forecast

Table A.1 IDoc Message Types (Cont.)

In the following sections, we'll take a closer look at working with IDocs and how they're used to perform inbound and outbound transactions.

A.2.1 IDocs

IDocs are standard SAP documents used for connecting external systems to SAP or for connecting one SAP module to another. IDocs use a message interface to establish the connections between systems and modules to transmit data. They are native to SAP and can be controlled with standard transactions. Because they are customizable, you can tweak them to your business needs. IDocs are flexible to either connect directly with sender/receiver systems or to intermediate extract, transform, load (ETL) tools such as Informatica. IDocs are data storage and data transmitting mediums, with built-in logic that can be enhanced to meet your needs. Basically, they have a brain of their own that can be trained and educated. IDocs are represented by an IDoc number. IDoc number ranges are customizable in SAP. To view IDocs, you can execute Transaction WE09.

IDocs have one-to-one mapping with business objects; that is, one IDoc can contain only one business object. For example, IDoc type ORDERS01 technically could house message types QUOTES and ORDERSP, but at a given point in time, it will only contain QUOTES or ORDERSP and not both.

An IDoc structure is made of three record types: control record, data record, and status record. Figure A.2 shows a prototype of a typical IDoc structure.

A good error-proof IDoc structure has only one control record and many data records and status records. Let's look at each record type in detail to understand them better.

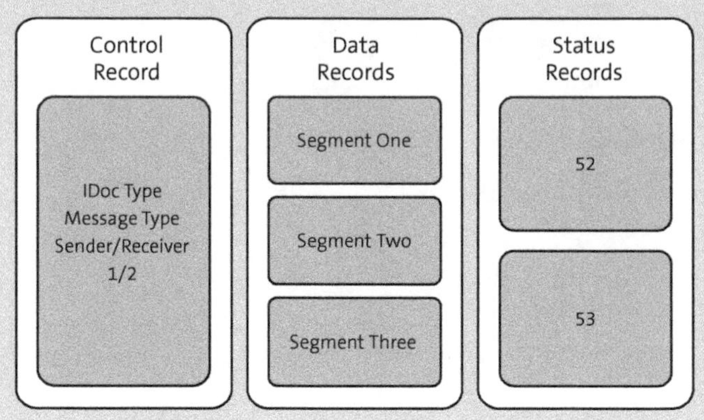

Figure A.2 IDoc Structure

Control Record

In the EDI world, the control record is also denoted as EDI_DC. A *control record* contains fields and data that control the basic functioning of an IDoc. Control records have information such as IDoc number, direction, status, sender and receiver data, partner details, technical information, address data, and additional details.

There are a few ways you can display an IDoc. The one we'll use is via Transaction WE09. Once you're in the transaction, enter the IDoc number you're looking for in the selection screen, and click **Execute**. Next, click on the IDoc number record that shows up, and then double-click on the **Control Record** entry. You'll arrive at the screen shown in Figure A.3, which is how a control record looks in SAP S/4HANA.

Display Control Record

IDoc Display

IDoc number	17021	
Direction	1	Outbound
Status	03	Data passed to port OK

Typinfo | Partner | Techn.info | Address | Details

IDoc type information

Basic type	INTERNAL_ORDER...	Replicate individual internal order (ALE)
Extension		
IDoc Type		

Logical message description

Message Type	INTERNAL_ORDER	Replicate individual internal order (ALE)
Message Variant		
Message function		
Test Flag		

Figure A.3 IDoc Control Record and the Typinfo Tab

The IDoc control record has a header section and a details section with the following tabs: **Typinfo**, **Partner**, **Techn.info**, **Address**, and **Details**.

The header section has three fields:

- **IDoc number**
  This field represents the unique number for an IDoc.
- **Direction**
  This field represents the direction of an IDoc: **2** for **Inbound** or **1** for **Outbound**.
- **Status**
  This field represents the status of an IDoc. There is a list of standard statuses SAP S/4HANA provides, but you can add custom statuses if needed. With the several clients we worked with, there was never a need to add custom statuses.

The **Typinfo** tab has the following fields:

- **Basic type**
  This field represents an IDoc type available/configured in the SAP S/4HANA system. SAP provides a list of basic types that can be used out of the box, but you can customize or copy standard basic types and create new ones too. As a best practice, we've copied standard basic types and created custom ones with additional business logic. Basic types help with the definition of an IDoc structure.
- **Extension**
  This field represents the manually created IDoc type that can be used in conjunction with the SAP standard basic IDoc type to meet business requirements. For example, the IDoc basic type may be **INTERNAL_ORDER**, which can have an **Extension** of the type **On-Premise Internal Order** and **SaaS Internal Order**.
- **IDoc Type**
  This field helps identify IDoc types for SAP release 4.0 and prior. We've seldomly seen this field being used in our experience.
- **Message Type**
  This field represents the message type of an IDoc. IDocs use messages to establish connections between sender and receiver systems, and message types are core components of the messages.
- **Message Variant**
  This field represents a unique user-defined variant for a message. If a message type is used to perform multiple subprocesses under a parent process, then the variant helps control which subprocess to run. For example, say message type `INVOIC` (variant: blank) is used for a new customer invoice, and message type `INVOIC` (variant: MOD) is used for a modified customer invoice.
- **Message function**
  This field represents a unique user-defined function code for a message. Like **Message Variant**, **Message function** also helps control subprocesses under a parent

message process. If a message variant and a message function are maintained in the partner profile of the receiving system IDoc, then the external system that is sending in the IDoc must also configure those fields for a successful inbound transmission to happen.

- **Test Flag**
  This checkbox is checked if you want to transfer IDocs to a test instance instead of a productive instance.

Next, let's look at the **Partner** tab, as shown in Figure A.4.

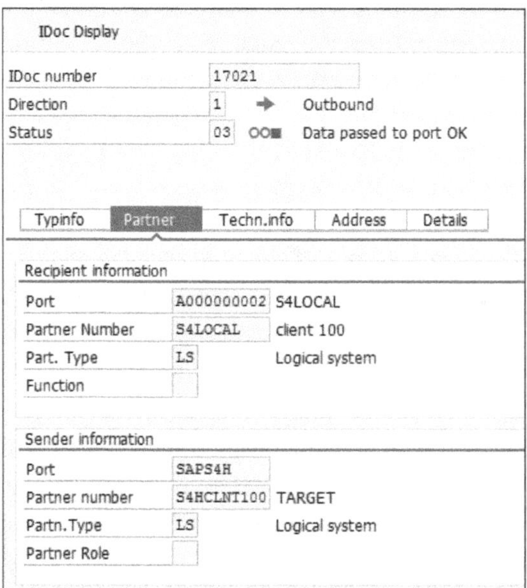

Figure A.4 IDoc Control Record Partner Tab

The **Partner** tab has two sections with four fields each:

- The **Recipient information** section includes the following fields:
  - **Port**: This field represents the port name of a recipient system.
  - **Partner Number**: This field represents the partner number of a recipient system.
  - **Part. Type**: This field represents the partner type of a recipient system. Partner types help establish the relationship between sender and receiver systems. Partner type along with partner number make a system (receiver or sender) unique.
  - **Function**: This field represents the partner function or partner role of a recipient system (e.g., sold-to party, ship-to party, etc.).
- The **Sender information** section includes the following fields:
  - **Port**: This field represents the port name of a sender system.
  - **Partner Number**: This field represents the partner number of a sender system.

- **Partn.Type**: This field represents the partner type of a sender system.
- **Partner Role**: This field represents the partner role or partner function of a sender system (e.g., sold-to party, ship-to party, etc.).

The other three tabs are described here:

- **Techn.info**
  This tab houses technical information about the IDoc, such as SAP release number, output mode, and serialization. It also has information about IDoc control record creation and update times.
- **Address**
  This tab is where you see logical addresses and standard address management information.
- **Details**
  This section has information such as interchange file, message group, reference, identification, and EDI options (standard, version, and message type).

Data Records

Also known as EDI_DD, *data records* host application data contained in an IDoc. A data record is made up of two core components: key section and segment.

The *key section* is a 55- or a 63-byte component that supports the segment component by doing the following tasks:

- Describes the structure and behavior of the segment
- Helps with the segment naming convention
- Assists in determining sequence and hierarchy of segments in an IDoc

On the other hand, *segments* within the data record store and process the wealth of data contained within a data record. Segments together with key section components are also referred to as SDATA by our ABAP counterparts. SDATA records are 1,000 bytes in length. One IDoc structure can have multiple data records, which means they can have multiple SDATA records. The hierarchy and chronology of data records is dependent on the hierarchy and chronology of segments. For each data record, the SDATA component is retriggered, which means for each record, you can technically have different SDATA structure and rules.

To modify or view data records, go to Transaction WE09. Enter the IDoc number you're looking for in the selection screen, and click **Execute**. Next, click on the IDoc number record that appears, and then click on the **Data records** folder to open it up. Figure A.5 and Figure A.6 show an example of a data record from our example client system. Figure A.5 shows the data record hierarchy you see when you click on the **Data records** folder, and Figure A.6 shows the underlying technical details of the data record if you double-click on a data record entry.

IDoc display	Additional information
IDoc 0000000000883450	
Control Record	
Data records	Total number: 000009
ZZ1APTTUS_SRVCAGRMT	Segment 000001
ZZ2APTTUS_ROLE	Segment 000002
ZZ2APTTUS_ROLE	Segment 000003
ZZ2APTTUS_ROLE	Segment 000004
ZZ2APTTUS_ROLE	Segment 000005
ZZ2APTTUS_ROLE	Segment 000006
ZZ2APTTUS_ROLE	Segment 000007
ZZ2APTTUS_SHIPTOPARTY	Segment 000008
ZZ2APTTUS_AGRMTITEM	Segment 000009

Figure A.5 IDoc Data Record Hierarchy

Short Technical Information

Direction	2	Inbox
Current Status	53	
Basic type	ZAPTTUS_ORDER1	
Extension		
Message Type	ZAPTTUS_ORDER	
Partner No.	APTTUS	
Partn.Type	LS	
Port	TRFC	

Content of Selected Segment

Fld Name	Fld Cont.
APTTUS_CONTRACT_ID	a281M000003sgKYQAY
ACCOUNT_ID	001G000000iHnpVIAS
CONTRACT_NO	00100713.0
CONTRACT_START_DATE	20200106
CONTRACT_END_DATE	20210705
CONTRACT_TYPE	Services Only
CURRENCY_CODE	USD
SIGNATURE_DATE	20200106
SERVICE_END_DATE	20210105
MAINT_END_DATE	20250630
CONTRACT_STATUS	Send to SAP

Figure A.6 IDoc Data Record Details

At our example client, we transfer data from Salesforce Apttus to SAP to create sales orders. For each data set that is transferred from Apttus, we create a separate segment record. For example, as shown in Figure A.5, for each role data, we create a separate segment, each partner data creates a separate segment, item data creates a separate segment, and so on. The data record details section, shown in Figure A.6, has two sections: **Short Technical Information** and **Content of Selected Segment**.

The **Short Technical Information** section has the following fields:

- **Direction**
  This field represents the direction of an IDoc: **1** for outbound and **2** for inbound. Ours is an example of an inbound IDoc, so the value in the **Direction** field is **2**.

- **Current Status**
  This field represents the status of an IDoc. In our example, status **53** states that the IDoc was posted successfully.
- **Basic type**
  This field represents an IDoc type available/configured in the SAP S/4HANA system. **ZAPTTUS_ORDER1** is an order IDoc type we configured in our example client's SAP S/4HANA system.
- **Extension**
  This field represents an extension IDoc type created by SAP users. Extension types are upward compatible only. At our example client, we don't use extensions, so the field is blank.
- **Message Type**
  This field represents the message type of an IDoc. We created a Z order message copying the standard ORDER message type and called it **ZAPTTUS_ORDER**, as shown earlier in Figure A.5.
- **Partner No.**
  This field represents the partner number of a sender system, **APTTUS**.
- **Partn.Type**
  This field represents the partner type of a sender system, which is a logical system is our case, so you see **LS** as the **Partn.Type** in Figure A.5 previously.
- **Port**
  This field represents the port name of a sender system (**TRFC** in our example).

The **Content of Selected Segment** section displays a list of all fields contained in the selected segment which are transferred from sender system (Apttus) to receiver system (SAP). A snippet of the field list was shown earlier in Figure A.6.

Status Records

Also known as `EDI_DS`, *status records* display a series of statuses shown during an IDoc process. An IDoc goes through many intermediary stages before it finally passes or fails for posting. Each stage is associated with a status and a status record. Examples of stages are as follows:

1. IDoc added
2. IDoc ready to be passed to application
3. Application document posted, and so on

Each of these stages have underlying status record numbers tied to them (depending on if they pass or fail), and we'll look at them in detail in this section. Status records are two characters in length, and their values range from 01 to 41 for outbound IDocs and 50 to 73 for inbound IDocs. What this means is outbound IDocs will have statuses with numbers from 01 to 41 and inbound IDocs will have statues from 50 to 73.

To modify or view a status record, go to Transaction WE09. Enter the IDoc number you're looking for in the selection screen, and click **Execute**. Next, click on the IDoc number record that appears, and then click on the **Status records** folder to open it. Figure A.7 shows the status record hierarchy.

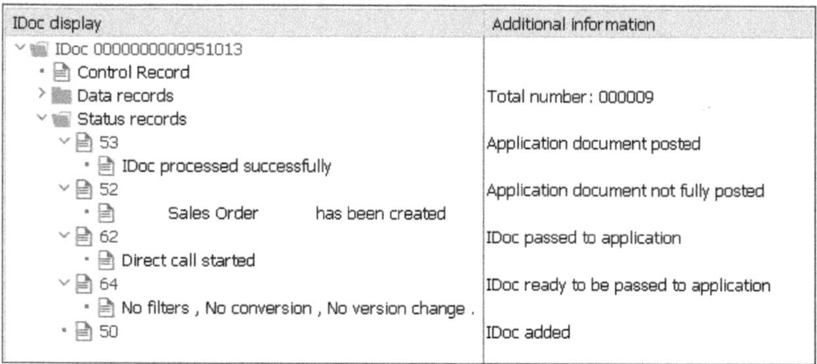

Figure A.7 IDoc Status Record Hierarchy

Figure A.7 is an example of an inbound IDoc from our example client system. As you can see, it went through four intermediate stages before it finally posted successfully within the SAP S/4HANA system. Statuses are read bottom-up. Let's walk through them now:

1. The first stage in IDoc processing is **IDoc added**, which has status number **50**. This status means the IDoc has been successfully added to the receiver system.
2. The second stage in IDoc processing is **IDoc ready to be passed to application**, which has the status number **64**. This status means the IDoc has passed initial validations and is ready to be passed to the receiver application.
3. The third stage in IDoc processing is **IDoc passed to application**, which has the status number **62**. This status means the IDoc has been passed to the receiver application.
4. The fourth stage in IDoc processing is **Application document not fully posted**, which has the status number 52. This status means the document that was expected to be created via the IDoc process has been created but not posted. In our example, the IDoc was for creation of a sales order, so the status **52** means that the sales order was created in the system but not saved or posted.
5. The fifth stage in IDoc processing is **Application document posted**, which has the status number **53**. This status means the IDoc was processed successfully, and the application document that was created in the previous stage has been posted without errors. In our example, the sales order created in the previous stage has been saved successfully in sales and distribution.

Figure A.8 shows what the details behind a status record look like in SAP S/4HANA. We double-clicked on the **52** status record to walk you through the details.

Figure A.8 IDoc Status Record Details

As shown in Figure A.8, an IDoc status record mainly has two sections: header section and details section.

The header section has the following fields:

- **IDoc number**
  This field represents the unique number of an IDoc. **951013** is the inbound IDoc number from our example client system.
- **Direction**
  This field represents the direction of an IDoc. Ours is an example of an inbound IDoc, so the value in the **Direction** field is **2**.
- **Status**
  This field represents the status of an IDoc. In our example, status **52** means that the sales order was created successfully.
- **Message**
  This field describes the **Status** field by adding more context to it. **52** is the status code for this IDoc stage, but the underlying message gives more context that sales order 65358 was created successfully within this IDoc processing stage.

The details section has three tabs:

- **Techn.Info**
  This tab displays details about time of log entry and time of database change.

- **Sts details**
  This tab has the following fields:
  - **Code**
    This field represents the system of origin from which the status messages originate. At our example client, we use messages from the standard SAP source, so this field shows **SAP** as the value in Figure A.8.
  - **Message number**
    This field represents the message number of a status record.
  - **Message type**
    This field represents the message type for a status record. SAP S/4HANA provides five standard message types: **A** (Cancel), **W** (Warning), **E** (Error), **S** (Success message), and **I** (Information).
  - **ID**
    This field represents the message class ID for a status record message. **ZFINPRJT3** is a custom message class we created at our example client, which stores status messages.
  - **Text**
    This field represents text for a status code. Text can either be extracted from table T100 of SAP or from a connecting EDI system. **&** in the **Text** field is a dynamic variable that gets values from the parameter fields. You can have up to four &s in a text message that will get their values from the **1st parameter**, **2nd parameter**, **3rd parameter**, or **4th parameter** field. By default, the first **&** will get its value from the **1st parameter**, second **&** will get its value from the **2nd parameter**, and so on.
    - **1st parameter**: This is the first parameter field used to store runtime data during an IDoc process. At our client, for a sales order IDoc, we store the phrase "Sales Order" in this parameter.
    - **2nd parameter**: This is the second parameter field used to store runtime data during an IDoc process. At our client, for a sales order IDoc, we store the newly generated sales order number in this parameter.
    - **3rd parameter**: This is the third parameter field used to store runtime data during an IDoc process. At our client, we still haven't had the need to use this parameter.
    - **4th parameter**: This is the fourth parameter field used to store runtime data during an IDoc process. At our client, we still haven't had the need to use this parameter.
- **Logging**
  This tab provides message information about the user name, program, and subroutine.

A.2.2 Inbound Transactions

Transactions that flow into a source system through EDIs, interfaces, or any other form or medium are known as *inbound transactions*. We briefly looked at a few inbound transaction examples in the previous section, which were around sales order creation. In this section, let's look closely at another good example of sales and distribution inbound transactions using IDocs: delivery creation.

Our example use case is that a consultant registers for training that is scheduled to happen next week. Training registration creates a sales order in sales and distribution in SAP S/4HANA, and the delivery on the training happens when the consultant attends the training session and completes the assessment. Figure A.9 shows a screen print of inbound transaction IDoc from our example client's SAP S/4HANA system.

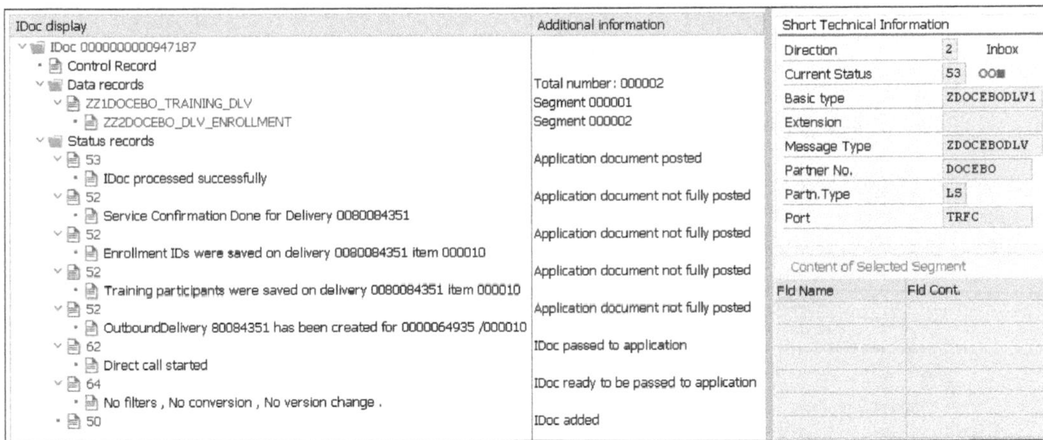

Figure A.9 Inbound IDoc for Delivery Creation

As shown in Figure A.9, inbound IDoc **947187** has one control record, two data records, and multiple status records. If you look at the right-hand side of the screen, you can confidently say this is an inbound IDoc by observing the **Direction** field and the **53** status of the IDoc, which means it's posted successfully. Data records of the IDoc have two segments that bring in the delivery-related information from the external training system to create the delivery document in SAP (information such as when was the training completed, how many participants completed the training, etc.). The IDoc goes through many stages in its processing lifecycle and therefore has multiple status records (one for each stage). The IDoc process starts with status **50**, which means the IDoc is added to the system. It then goes through status **64** and **62** to get passed to the receiver application (which is the SAP S/4HANA system). Once it reaches SAP, it finds the reference sales order line item and creates the delivery against it with status **52**, which states that **Outbound Delivery 0080084351 has been created for 0000064935/000010**. The next three **52** status records confirm the addition of training participant information and enrollment IDs to the delivery document and then finally the PGI. The final step of the IDoc process is status record **53**, which confirms the IDoc document has successfully completed all of its tasks, and the underlying application document (delivery document **0080084351**) is posted to SAP without any errors.

A.2.3 Outbound Transactions

Transactions that flow out from a source system through EDIs, interfaces, or any other form or medium are known as *outbound transactions*. A few examples of SAP sales and distribution outbound transactions are sending out shipment notifications, sending out customer invoices, sending master data to an external reporting system for budgeting and forecasting, and replicating cost element data in SAP cloud solutions.

Figure A.10 shows a screen print of an outbound IDoc from our example client system where we use IDocs to send cost center information to SAP SuccessFactors Employee Central. Cost centers are attached to employee records, so when an employee submits an expense report, their expenses get billed to their home cost center configured in SAP SuccessFactors Employee Central.

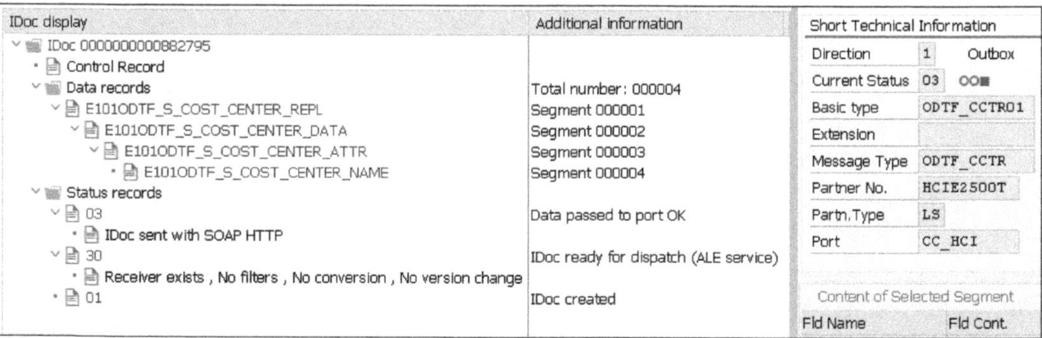

Figure A.10 Outbound IDoc for Cost Center Replication

As shown in Figure A.10, outbound IDoc **882795** has one control record, four data records, and three status records. Looking at the right-hand side of the screen, you can clearly tell this is an outbound IDoc by reading the **Direction** field, which shows the value as **1**. IDoc **882795** uses the standard IDoc type **ODTF_CCTR01** and port **CC_HCI**.

The IDoc process starts with status **01**, which is where the IDoc gets created in the sender system. The next step is status **30**, where the IDoc is ready to be sent to the receiver system via a SOAP HTTP. Finally, you see status **03**, which confirms data was passed to the receiver system without any errors. Data records indicate that the IDoc has four segments carrying cost center data such as name, number, and so on, and then transferring them over to SAP SuccessFactors Employee Central.

A.3 Types, Tables, and Transactions

In this section, we'll highlight important IDoc types, EDI tables, and EDI transactions for sales and distribution in SAP S/4HANA (see Table A.2). There are many more IDoc types, tables, and transactions, but having knowledge about just these to begin with will get the ball rolling for you.

IDoc Type	EDI Table	EDI Transaction
Inbound ▪ ORDERS01 (for sales order and inquiry) ▪ ORDERS02 (for sales order and inquiry) ▪ ORDERS03 (for sales order, delivery, and inquiry) ▪ ORDERS04 (for sales order, delivery, and inquiry) ▪ ORDERS05 (for sales order and inquiry) ▪ DELFOR01 (for delivery schedule) **Outbound** ▪ ORDERS01 (for quotation and sales order confirmation) ▪ ORDERS02 (for quotation and sales order confirmation) ▪ ORDERS03 (for quotation and sales order confirmation) ▪ ORDERS04 (for quotation and sales order confirmation) ▪ ORDERS05 (for quotation and sales order confirmation) ▪ INVOIC01 (for invoice and invoice list) ▪ INVOIC02 (for invoice and invoice list)	▪ Table EDIDS (IDoc status records) ▪ Table EDIDC (IDoc control records) ▪ Table EDID4 (IDoc data records) ▪ Table EDIDO (IDoc type values) ▪ Table TBDLS (logical system) ▪ Table EDISEGMENT (IDoc segment)	▪ Transaction WEDI (SAP menu for IDoc and EDI Basis) ▪ Transaction WE20 (partner profiles) ▪ Transaction WE21 (ports in IDoc processing) ▪ Transaction WE60 (documentation for IDoc [type, segments, record types]) ▪ Transaction WE09 (IDoc search) ▪ Transaction WE19 (IDoc testing tool) ▪ Transaction WE30 (IDoc type development) ▪ Transaction WE81 (EDI logical message types) ▪ Transaction WE82 (output types and assignment) ▪ Transaction WE47 (status maintenance) ▪ Transaction BD87 (IDoc selection and status monitor) ▪ Transaction BD67 (function module mapping for inbound ALE/EDI) ▪ Transaction IDOC (IDoc and EDI repair and check programs)

Table A.2 IDoc Types, EDI Tables, and EDI Transactions

Appendix B
The Authors

Ankita Ghodmare is a certified SAP senior consultant currently working as an SAP Billing and Revenue Innovation Management specialist at Amadeus labs. She has more than seven years of experience working on transformation projects and providing technology consulting services to clients in the manufacturing, cosmetic, and hi-tech industries. Her primary areas of SAP expertise are sales and distribution, billing and revenue innovation management, and revenue accounting and reporting. Ankita is passionate about leveraging technology to streamline and simplify business processes. Throughout her career, she has been involved in greenfield implementations, business process redesign, and continuous improvement initiatives across multiple geographies. She holds a degree in Electronics and Telecommunication Engineering from SGGSIE&T Nanded (India).

Saurabh Bobade is an SAP professional with expertise in solution architecture, presales, and business process consulting in the SAP landscape. He has more than eight years of experience in SAP S/4HANA implementations, support, and rollout projects focused on order-to-cash, revenue recognition, procure-to-pay, and subscription business processes. He is passionate about enabling customer success through technology-led business transformation. During his career, he has provided insights, system architecture, and integration strategies to global clients across multiple industries, including manufacturing, tire, hi-tech, and utilities. Saurabh has served as a trusted advisor to client executives in applying the latest SAP innovations in digital transformation initiatives and cloud adoption. He has also conducted several boot camps and training sessions on SAP solutions.

Kartik Dua is an accomplished SAP leader with extensive functional and technical experience in managing and strategizing various business processes using on-premise and cloud ERP solutions. His experience includes order-to-cash, revenue recognition, procure-to-pay, tax and treasury, financial planning and analysis, accounting, controlling, and profitability analysis. He has more than 10 years of experience, primarily in the sales and distribution and order-to-cash space. He has worked on a multitude of projects, ranging from implementation to support to cross-functional to migration, and he has collaborated with various functional and integration consultants throughout his career. Kartik is an SAP Community champion and his mantra for success is: In challenging situations, look for opportunities to thrive and not just survive. Patience, perseverance, and perspiration are the secrets to being a successful champion.

Index

C

M

N

O

P

Q

R

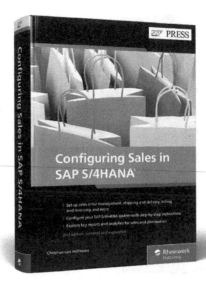

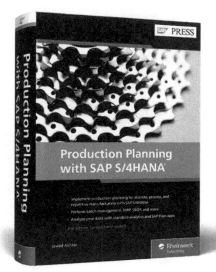

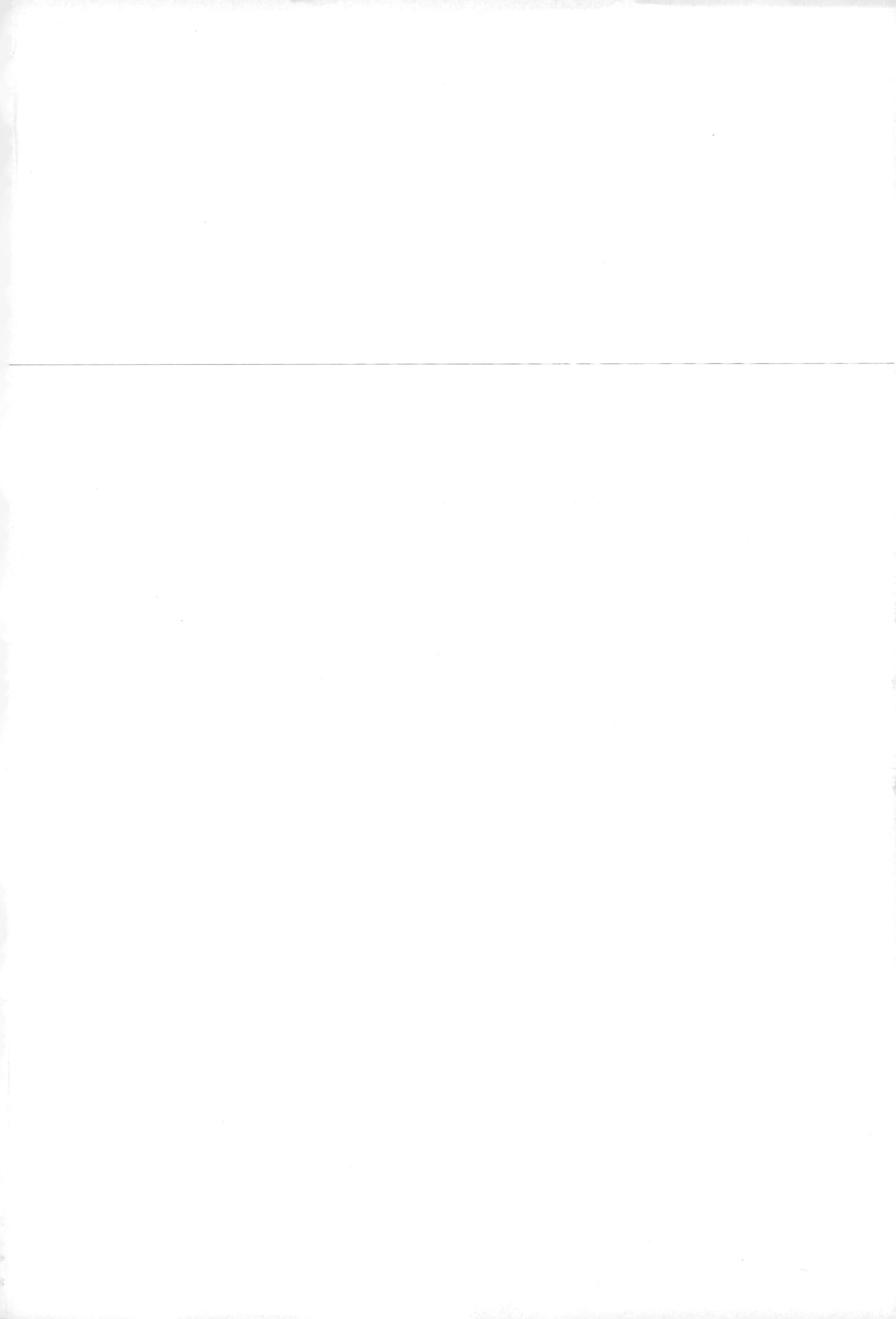